the jazz cadence
of american culture

columbia university press　　　new york

edited by robert g. o'meally

the jazz cadence

of american culture

Columbia University Press
New York

Columbia University Press
Publishers Since 1893
New York   Chichester, West Sussex
Copyright ©1998 Robert G. O'Meally

Library of Congress Cataloging-in-Publication Data

The jazz cadence of American culture / edited by Robert G. O'Meally.
　　　　p.　cm.
　　　Thirty-five essays.
　　　Includes bibliographical reference and index.
　　　Contents: Part 1. What is jazz — Part 2. One nation under a groove, or, The United
States of jazzocracy — Part 3. Jazz lines and colors : the sound I saw — Part 4. Jazz is a dance :
jazz art in motion — Part 5. Tell the story : jazz, history, memory — Part 6. Writing the blues,
writing jazz.
　　　ISBN 0-231-10448-0 (cloth : alk. paper). — ISBN 0-231-10449-9 (pbk.: alk. paper)
　　　1. Jazz — History and criticism. 2. Blues (Music) — History and criticism. 3. Afro-
Americans —Music—History and criticism.
I. O'Meally, Robert G., 1948– .
ML3508.J38 1998
781.65—DC21　　　　　　　　　　　　　　　　　　　　　　　　　　　　98–14768

Columbia University Press gratefully acknowledges permission to reprint from the following:
Merriam, Alan P. and Fradley H. Garner. "Jazz—the Word," *Ethnomusicology* 12, 13
　　　(September 1968). Used with the permission of the University of Illinois Press.
Jim and Benny Golson. "Forward Motion: An Interview with Benny Golson," *boundary 2,*
　　　23:2 (Summer 1995), pp. 53–93. Copyright © 1995, Duke University Press. Reprinted
　　　with permission.
Snead, James A. "Repetition as a Figure of Black Culture," from Gates, Henry Louis, ed.,
　　　Black Literature and Literary Theory. London: Methuen, 1984, pp. 59–79.
Wilson, Olly, "Black Music as an Art Form." Used with the permission of the Center for
　　　Black Music Research, Columbia College Chicago.
Troupe, Quincy and Ben Riley, "When the Music Was Happening Then He'd Get Up and Do
　　　His Little Dance," from "Thelonious Monk: American Composer." Courtesy Avalon
　　　Archives. Used with the permission of Quincy Troupe.

(*continued on p. 663*)

Printed in the United States of America

Designed by Linda Secondari

c 10 9 8 7 6 5 4 3 2
p 10 9 8 7 6 5

contents

PREFACE   IX

part 1:   what is jazz?

Introduction   3

CHAPTER 1   **Jazz—The Word   7**
Alan P. Merriam and Fradley H. Garner

CHAPTER 2   **Forward Motion: An Interview with
Benny Golson   32**
Benny Golson and Jim Merod

CHAPTER 3   **Repetition as a Figure of Black Culture   62**
James A. Snead

CHAPTER 4   **Black Music as an Art Form   82**
Olly Wilson

CHAPTER 5   **Remembering Thelonious Monk:
When the Music Was Happening Then He'd Get Up
and Do His Little Dance   102**
Quincy Troupe and Ben Riley

CHAPTER 6   **Improvisation and the Creative Process   111**
Albert Murray

part 2: one nation under a groove, or, the united states of jazzocracy

Introduction   117

CHAPTER 7   **What's "American" About America   123**
John A. Kouwenhoven

CHAPTER 8   **Jazz and the White Critic   137**
Amiri Baraka

CHAPTER 9   **Duke Ellington: "Music Like a Big Hot Pot of Good Gumbo"   143**
Wynton Marsalis and Robert G. O'Meally

CHAPTER 10   **Blues to Be Constitutional: A Long Look at the Wild Wherefores of Our Democratic Lives as Symbolized in the Making of Rhythm and Tune   154**
Stanley Crouch

CHAPTER 11   **The Ellington Programme   166**
Barry Ulanov

part 3   jazz lines and colors: the sound i saw

Introduction   175

CHAPTER 12   **Art History and Black Memory: Toward a "Blues Aesthetic"   182**
Richard J. Powell

CHAPTER 13   **Skyscrapers, Airplanes, and Airmindedness: "The Necessary Angel"   196**
Ann Douglas

CHAPTER 14   **Profiles: Putting Something Over Something Else   224**
Calvin Tomkins

CHAPTER 15   **Celebration   243**
Sherry Turner DeCarava

CHAPTER 16   **Black Visual Intonation   264**
Arthur Jafa

CHAPTER 17   **Improvisation in Jazz   269**
Bill Evans

VI

contents

part 4   jazz is a dance: jazz art in motion

Introduction   273

CHAPTER 18   **Jazz Music in Motion: Dancers and Big Bands**   278
Jacqui Malone

CHAPTER 19   **Characteristics of Negro Expression**   298
Zora Neale Hurston

CHAPTER 20   **African Art and Motion**   311
Robert Farris Thompson

CHAPTER 21   **Be Like Mike? Michael Jordan and the Pedagogy of Desire**   372
Michael Eric Dyson

CHAPTER 22   **"Noise" Taps a Historic Route to Joy**   381
Margo Jefferson

part 5   tell the story: jazz, history, memory

Introduction   389

CHAPTER 23   **Pulp and Circumstance: The Story of Jazz in High Places**   393
Gerald Early

CHAPTER 24   **Jazz and American Culture**   431
Lawrence W. Levine

CHAPTER 25   **The Golden Age, Time Past**   448
Ralph Ellison

CHAPTER 26   **Double V, Double-Time: Bebop's Politics of Style**   457
Eric Lott

CHAPTER 27   **It Jus Be's Dat Way Sometime: The Sexual Politics of Women's Blues**   469
Hazel V. Carby

CHAPTER 28   **Constructing the Jazz Tradition**   483
Scott DeVeaux

CHAPTER 29   **Other: From Noun to Verb**   513
Nathaniel Mackey

part 6 writing the blues, writing jazz

Introduction 535

CHAPTER 30 The Blues as Folk Poetry 540
Sterling A. Brown

CHAPTER 31 Richard Wright's Blues 552
Ralph Ellison

CHAPTER 32 Preface to "Three Plays" 563
August Wilson

CHAPTER 33 The Function of the Heroic Image 569
Albert Murray

**CHAPTER 34 The Seemingly Eclipsed Window of Form:
James Weldon Johnson's Prefaces 580**
Brent Edwards

CHAPTER 35 Sound and Sentiment, Sound and Symbol 602
Nathaniel Mackey

SOURCES 629

INDEX 633

contents

preface

At an international conference on jazz held in Paris during the spring of 1996, the Swiss scholar Fritz Gysen presented a paper arguing that although obviously there was such a thing as jazz *music*, there was no such thing as a jazz novel or a jazz aesthetic in literature. For me, this particular paper provided the conference's unexpected keynote, a jangling chord like those hit by Thelonious Monk with his forearm and elbow, an explosive splash-sound of purposeful doubt.

Clearly Professor Gysen was right. Haven't we all heard the old saw that writing about music is as meaningless as dancing about architecture? Given a certain brashness and command of lingo, anyone can shoot the breeze about the deep-set jazz nature of geological formations, Shakespeare's sonnets, or—why not?—drugstore hairnets. This crazy, scattershot impulse already appears in undergraduate papers on American literature or art: "jazz" is everywhere and serves, along with other critical clichés that rumble through the academic culture, to explain away almost any unique or complex issue in its path. Like the easiest of structuralist or deconstructionist formulas, it provides an all-purpose approach to almost every subject on the undergraduate's card: What is bowling? What is biology? What's a poem? They are not structures in a numbered series or disappearing "texts"; that was last year. Now they are *jazz*.

And yet, in spite of the curse of seeing jazz everywhere, we must not commit the matching crime of refusing to see it (to see jazz, meaning *to understand* it in profound ways as well as to visualize the music in its not strictly musical incarnations) anywhere. Interdisciplinary views of the arts are not, after all, merely a current academic fashion; at their best they offer fresh ways of perceiving new and old structures in our midst, granting "perspectives by incongruity" (to borrow a term from Kenneth Burke) as they move from discipline to discipline, art to art. Certain art forms cry out for an interdisciplinary approach. In many traditional African cultures, for example, a single word means both music and dance: "to music," so to speak, is also literally to dance; to dance is to music. A master musician is master of music's dynamic images, the music in motion through dance. Likewise, in many oral cultures, the historian is also the poet, the poet also the singer (and thus the musician and the dancer) of the words and the attitudes of a people's story and history. The artificial separation of so-called pure forms in contexts such as these represents an instance of aesthetic blindness and academic decadence.

Anthropologically oriented critics have long viewed each art as evolving from another: the gesture becomes a ritualized dance; the dance, a song; the dance-and-song, a narrative poem and a play. Thus is a group's experience recited and remembered; thus is the stage set for ancient and then modern novels (also drawing, in this boomeranging pattern of influence, on the power of gesture, dance, song, play, and history). And on it goes. In *The Commonwealth of Art*, Curt Sachs identifies a variety of vital correspondences among expressive forms:

> The artists themselves have not hesitated to profess the unity of art. Fifteen hundred years back, in the brilliant Gupta period of India (4th–6th century), painters expressly derived their art from dancing, and the dancers theirs from music. Vitruvius, the Roman, urged architects to make themselves familiar with melody and rhythm. Johann Reichardt, *Kapellmeister* to the court of Berlin around 1800, discussed the crescendo and decrescendo of the Mannheim orchestra as giving "a darker or a lighter shade to the whole coloring" and, in almost the same words, Dr. Charles Byrney, musical sightseer from England, characterized in 1773 the Mannheim achievement "as new colors—the colors in music having their shades as colors like red or blue have them in painting." And more than a hundred years later, Vincent van Gogh felt so strongly the sameness of painting and music that he eventually persuaded an old organist to teach him the elements of piano playing so he might better support his parallels.[1]

Critical language mirrors this close relation of qualities, art to art: "Melody is often said to describe a 'line' or a 'curve,' which might be 'smooth' or 'jagged'; orchestration gives 'color,' and the orchestrater has a more or less well-assorted 'palate.'" And then there are the common terms describing all the arts: "Form and structure, symmetry, rhythm, color, clearness, movement, and numberless others."[2] The jazz singer Carmen McRae once declared that anyone whose voice does not show "color" simply cannot be a singer of any kind.

The Jazz Cadence of American Culture does not posit a total collapse of artistic category; to a degree, in fact, this collection is itself organized by expressive genre, with jazz music as the constant touchstone. Nor does this book assert a direct line of artistic development from the cradle of dance or even the Word to the present extended family of art forms. Focusing mainly on U.S. expression from 1920 to 1970—from the period of cultural efflorescence associated with the 1920s through the black arts revolution of the 1960s—*Jazz Cadence* confronts two broad eras of turbulent political and artistic change during which American art forms circle and reverberate, influencing one another in unexpected ways and by unexpected means, and during which jazz music, with its sudden changes and zigzag lines, provides the key metaphor and soundtrack.

In other words, the central thesis of this collection is that in this electric process of American artistic exchange—in the intricate, shape-shifting equation that is the twentieth-century American experiment in culture—the factor of jazz music recurs over and over and over again: jazz dance, jazz poetry, jazz painting, jazz film, and more. Jazz as metaphor, jazz as model, jazz as relentlessly powerful cultural influence, jazz as cross-disciplinary beat or *cadence*.[3] Consider Muhammad Ali—boxing-dancing, spouting rhythmical rhymes, dramatically proclaiming a new world order in religion and politics.[4] Sometimes, as Brent Edwards remarked of the Ali example, the jazz effect in culture is a way either of making cultural expression political or of making political expression palpable as culture.

How, to paraphrase Ralph Ellison,[5] would modern American music (jazz's direct offsprings such as rhythm and blues as well as other twentieth-century forms) sound had there been no Louis Armstrong, no Duke Ellington, no Bessie Smith, no Charlie Parker, no John Coltrane? This book asserts that this question could be asked throughout the winding corridors of modern American culture. How, for example, would American speech sound without the impact of swing and bebop jive-talk specialists like Cab Calloway and Dizzy Gillespie (whose styles of dress, too, became national crazes)? What would our notions of personal elegance be without the example—and, in the case of commercials and movies, the background soundtrack—of the cool-beyond-cool stylings of jazz artists like Billie Holiday and Miles Davis? In the 1990s, Infiniti, Lexus, Yves St. Laurent, and Chivas Regal have all used effervescent splashes of jazz sound to evoke sophistication, romance, and nighttime opulence.

The jazz factor: this subtle set of threads seems to sparkle within virtually every aspect of modern American living. Professor Gysen is right: jazz is not *everywhere*, but it is a massive, irresistibly influential, politically charged part of our culture. The predominance of the jazz factor may make it the master trope of this American century: the definitive sound of America in our time. The sound of the American twentieth century is the jazz line.

The Jazz Cadence of American Culture is a comprehensive gathering of important essays, speeches, and interviews on the impact of jazz on the U.S. scene. Not a history of jazz, or a close reading of the music itself, or a smorgasbord of jazz writings—all of which have been attempted over and over again—this anthology takes to heart Ralph Ellison's provocative observation that much in American life is "jazz-shaped" and offers a display of eloquent statements illustrating and analyzing the jazz factor as it operates in a wide variety of expressions of U.S. life. The book works through juxtapositions sometimes smooth and seemingly inevitable, sometimes jarring and full of surprise: a literary essay beside an artist's interview beside a speech on aesthetics beside a footnoted scholarly article beside a newspaper review; Stanley Crouch next to Amiri Baraka next to Hazel Carby next to John Kowenhouven; a jam-session-style mix intended to indicate the range of responses (and counterresponses) to the music and to offer fresh perspectives through unexpected sequencings. The book is thus a teaching tool designed to open the way for a variety of new avenues in jazz studies as a growing interdisciplinary field of exploration. More an opening gambit than a finished encyclopedia, *Jazz Cadence* offers a set of preludes or vamps, setting the stage for riffs and solo-work yet to come.

Part 1 considers some problems in defining jazz, the music itself and the word as metaphor. Again the goal is not to offer final definitions but to pinpoint some of the fundamental characteristics of the music, ones that have had a substantial impact on the other arts and on U.S. culture as a whole. Where did we get this compact, evocative word? Why is it so controversial? (Max Roach's working title for his autobiography is *Jazz Is a Four-Letter Word.*) What does it tell us about American speech and the arts in America? What is *jazz*?

Part 2 continues the project of defining the music by considering the United States as the still-forming nation-state where jazz has flourished. What parallels may be drawn between this music and America's cornerstone political documents and values? Some would answer that jazz itself has become a kind of American institution, one that celebrates individual invention, resiliency, and agency—the capacity to improvise in the heat of the competitive moment—as highly as the ability to hear others and to blend creatively with them. May we say—without the blare of jingoism—that jazz offers a vital model for free democratic operation and cooperation at their highest levels? That jazz is naturally the music of our still-forming, blueprint society, that the United States is a jazz country? How so? (Stanley Crouch's article speaks brilliantly to this point.) How not?

Part 3 presents readings on the impact of jazz on the visual arts: painting, architecture, photography, film. In this arena, equations have been hinted at for years, but the specific elements of the interchanges and influences and their complexly robust, call-and-response quality are usually missed. Jazz players and composers long have celebrated Manhattan's skylines and skyscrapers, while architects in turn are touched by the jazz factor as they create structures that rise through the backbeat-steady pattern of the gridded streets to reach sololike to the top of the world. The painter Romare Bearden claimed jazz as such a potent influence that he found himself in search of visual equivalents of the harmonic intervals of Earl Hines (here he followed the advice of Stuart Davis) and the tonal colors that he heard in the piano playing and orchestrations of Duke Ellington. Bearden also commented that, for him at least, to be a painter was to "become a blues singer—only you sing on canvas. You *improvise*—you find the rhythm and catch it good and structure as you go along. Then the song is you."[6] Creating visual images of jazz musicians and jazz *music*: How is it done? What does it mean?

The fourth part of *Jazz Cadence* sees jazz as a dance. What would jazz music be were its makers not (until relatively recent years) routinely working with dancers, watching them, helping them to jump the blues? What, for that matter, would American dance (both social and in concert) look like without jazz music and the styles of body movement that fit so well with the music that they seem to be jazz music in motion? (Here, of course, it is most significant that just as tap dancers functioned as second drummers in the bands in which they appeared, many drummers—among them Buddy Rich, Jo Jones, Sid Catlett, Louis Bellson—started out as tappers, drummers of the foot and floor.)

And where, without jazz-inflected dance movement, would we get what the world knows as American styles of boxing and ball-game playing? Michael Jordan told an interviewer: "I'm always working to put surprises, something new in my game. Improvisation, spontaneity, all that stuff."[7] Slow the playback speed of a film of Jackie Robinson faking to steal home and then breaking for the plate or of Jordan or Sugar Ray Leonard in action, and these sports heroes look like they are dance-stepping and gliding on the floorboards and stomping grounds of an uptown or down-home party (or of Alvin Ailey's Dance Theater). Or think of the end-zone dances performed by football players at the ends of long dance runs around, over, and through the other teams' defensive lines. And note how often modern American choreographers like Eleo Pomare and Bill T. Jones make reference to the highly stylized, jazz-shaped movement universe of American sports. Jazz is sometimes a dance in a baseball uniform.

Jazz and history provide the next part's focus. How to express the turbulent history of an art with so many different characteristic forms (ragtime, the new uptown rag style called stride, swing, bop, "free," etc.) occurring all over the nation (and then the world), across two energized historical periods, across a century? How to tell the story of a storytelling music, one that loves to parody, lie, and signify as it probes a truth embedded deeper than fact and expressed in a language beyond words? Albert Murray certainly is right to observe that jazz singers operate first and foremost as jazz musicians whose instrument is the voice.[8] A song's words may not mean nearly as much as its melodies and other musical lines and structures. Billie Holiday sings "Back in Your Own Backyard"—where the lyrics proclaim the immediate availability of domestic joy and quietude—as a song of blues-tossed trouble. Indeed, she subverts the story's ostensible meanings to assert her own sense of how the world turns. Robert Farris Thompson might say Holiday confronts the simplistic sentiments of the song with her own sly "dances of derision."[9] Or, with Henry Louis Gates, Jr., we might say that she "signifies" on the song's words as well as its musical lines and dots.

Jazz, one is tempted to demand of the music itself, just what is your (racial, regional, national, class, gendered, signifying) story? What are the problems in its telling? How are we to confront the broad problem that jazz, by definition, is both revolutionary and traditional, many voiced and many storied; that jazz works as a frame through which multiple expressions of life can be heard, as a stage on which many stories (many versions of our history) can be projected?[10] Given all this complexity, what versions of U.S. history are sounded in this music called jazz? What national history does, say, Charles Mingus's bass have to tell?

When it comes to hearing a jazz cadence in literature (the theme of part 6), certain cases come quickly to mind: Langston Hughes, Sterling A. Brown, Vachel Lindsay, Richard Wright, Jack Kerouac, Ralph Ellison, Gloria Naylor, Michael

Harper, Toni Morrison, Albert Murray. Concerning the jazz shape of his own writing, Murray has written: "We all learn from Mann, Joyce, Hemingway, Eliot, and the rest, but I'm also trying to learn to write in terms of the tradition I grew up in, the Negro tradition of the blues, stomps, ragtime, jumps, and swing. After all, very few writers have done as much with American experience as Jelly Roll Morton, Count Basie, and Duke Ellington."[11] Ellison said that in the thirties he heard a muddy Mississippi River jazz sound—a Louis Armstrongian impulse—in T. S. Eliot's poetry, with its asymmetrical, conversational lines and its jazzlike flights of quotation and parody. How do we track this vital line of influence?

And what have jazz musicians learned from American writers? Do some of the music's young lions play and compose with the writings of Ellison, Murray, Baraka, Crouch, Morrison, Greg Tate, and others in mind? And what about literary criticism, where the influence of music is evident (see Gates on John Coltrane and the process of signifying, Hazel Carby on blues women, and Houston Baker on black literature's placement within a "blues-matrix" where blues-idiom performance before a world of trouble is for sale): have not these new terms of critical interchange had an effect on how new-scene jazz players like Geri Allen and Joshua Redman do their thing?

The what and how of jazz's meanings have been hotly debated since the beginning of the century, when this distinctive music first appeared. During the black renaissances of the twenties and sixties, these debates became something of a national dialogue, addressed in popular journals and in essays and novels such as those of James Weldon Johnson, F. Scott Fitzgerald, John Wideman, and Toni Morrison.[12] Some have argued that this music embodies something like a philosophy, a jazz-tempered attitude toward life. Throughout his work, for example, Albert Murray has made the case that jazz heralds an attitude of heroic endurance in the face of the variety of trials and woes traditionally enumerated in 12-bar blues music, where life is frankly admitted to be (in the idiom of the blues) "a downright rotten, low-down dirty shame." In Murray's view, jazz is an affirmative, progressive stance toward the "mean old world," a rough-and-ready, hopeful but unillusioned attitude toward life. In the face of the color barrier and other miseries, the jazz line, with its tremendously complex systems of creative interaction, represents the sound of joy as well as what Kenneth Burke has termed a defiant "gesture toward perfection."[13]

So, what would America be without jazz? Well, it would be duller and cornier, it would not sound like itself. And what is America, in the light of its being the homeland of this great music? *Jazz Cadence* glories in the two-way road from jazz to the other arts and back; moreover, it glories in the highways of cultural influence, with their network of exit and entrance ramps, underpasses, and bridges. Just as we want to know about jazz's impact, we wonder how in turn jazz music has been influenced by America's land- and cityscapes, by the nation's talk and by its other sounds, by its values as expressed in literature, sports, art, dance, politics, and so on. The story of these dynamic cultural mappings and exchanges is this book's main theme. Designed for specialists and nonspecialists, artists, scholars, and everyday readers, this anthology offers a critical language for talking about jazz and American life, jazz and its cousins. It is for all who would see and hear our culture more clearly; it is for all who would listen, as it were, to the songfulness of shotgun houses and skyscrapers and DeCarava photographs, hearing their stomp-blues tunes and jazz-jumping beat.

It remains to be noted that this book stems from a study group that has met at the Institute for Research in African-American Studies at Columbia University three times a year since 1994 to discuss the meaning of jazz to representatives of several fields of endeavor, academic and otherwise. Funded by the Ford Foundation to promote African-American Studies as a multidisciplinary cultural enterprise and a partnership of several institutions, ours is primarily a New York group with the following membership: Dwight Andrews, James Bartow, Michael Collins, Anthony Davis, Manthia Diawara, Ann Douglas, Gerald Early, Brent Edwards, Krin Gabbard, Paula Giddings, Farah Griffin, William J. Harris, Diedra Harris-Kelley, Travis Jackson, Margo Jefferson, Robin D. G. Kelley, Jacqui Malone, Tim Mangin, Dan Morganstern, Dawn Norfleet, Carol Oja, Robert O'Meally, Kellis Parker, Gayle Pemberton, Richard Powell, Tricia Rose, Helen Shannon, David Lionel Smith, John Szwed, Greg Tate, Jeff Taylor, Greg Thomas, Mark Tucker, Wendy Walters, Michael Washington, Peter Watrous, and André Willis.

Working from our various professional standpoints, we have held intensive sessions together on the Ellison-Baraka perspectives on U.S. music and culture, women in jazz, Thelonious Monk's musical and historical contexts, jazz's music-dance connection, jazz and painting, jazz on film, jazz and poetry, jazz and spirituality, and the avant-garde. In a sense, this book represents the group's attempt at the comprehensive interdisciplinary reader that we need: a course packet for a seminar on jazz among the disciplines. As such it makes way for the next book the group has been steadily working on, individually and collectively: our own papers, so far mainly in draft form, which have been flowing from our studies and conversations together. We hope this book encourages other cross-disciplinary conversations about this wonderful music, that it serves as a catalyst for others to dig into this rich earth for solos and ensemble works of their own.

I am delighted to thank the participants in the Jazz Study Group at Columbia University for their part in making this anthology. Thanks also to the Institute for Research in African-American Studies, Columbia University—particularly to its director, Manning Marable, and its assistant to the director, Daria Oliver—for spirited support and the use of the institute's comfortable rooms for our group's meetings. For assistance with paying for the volume and for funding our group's sessions, I am pleased to acknowledge the Ford Foundation, whose program officer, Sheila Biddle, is a beloved comrade in the struggle to establish African-American studies as a permanent part of modern higher education. For help with typing the manuscript, thanks to sunny, indefatigable Frauke Hasenclever. For assistance with editing—in the broad sense of thinking not just about making sentences but about making a book—thanks to Michael Collins and Suzanne Laizik, Sarah Wilson, and E. David Morgen. James Bartow helped immeasurably in the editing of the interview with Wynton Marsalis. Jennifer Crewe, Ron Harris, and Sarah St. Onge at Columbia University Press have been true allies in guiding this book from bulky notebook to completed volume. Brent Edwards has been the book's best friend. At every stage, his help was invaluable—in talking over the need for such a volume, suggesting entries, translating French, commenting from first to last on the book's shape, voice, and message. To him and to the group's other graduate students (several now new young profs)—Michael Collins, Travis Jackson, Tim Mangin, Dawn Norfleet, Helen Shannon, Jeff Taylor, Wendy Walters, Michael Washington, André Willis—this book is dedicated with much affection.

NOTES

1. Curt Sachs, *The Commonwealth of Art: Style in the Fine Arts—Music and the Dance* (New York: Norton, 1946), pp. 17–18.

2. Ibid., p. 18.

3. See Stephen Henderson, *Understanding the New Black Poetry* (New York: Morrow, 1973), p. 3.

4. See Genevieve Fabre and Robert O'Meally, *History and Memory in African American Culture* (New York: Oxford University Press, 1994), pp. 3–17.

5. See *The Collected Essays of Ralph Ellison* (New York: Modern Library, 1995), pp. 577–84.

6. Jonathan Bergen and Diana Dimodica Sweet, eds., *Romare Bearden* (New York: aca Gallieries, 1989), p. 50.

7. John Edgar Wideman, "Michael Jordan Leaps the Great Divide," *Esquire* 114, no. 5 (November 1990): 210.

8. See Albert Murray, *Stomping the Blues* (New York: McGraw-Hill, 1976), pp. 82 ff.

9. Robert F. Thompson, "An Aesthetic of the Cool: West African Dance," *African Forum* 2, no. 2 (fall 1966): 95–97.

10. Here I am indebted to Brent Edwards.

11. Albert Murray, "The Luzana Cholly Kick," *New World Writing*, no. 4 (October 1953): 228.

12. I have in mind Johnson's *The Autobiography of an Ex-Coloured Man*, first published anonymously in 1912 and later reissued to become a major text of the Harlem Renaissance, and Ishmael Reed's master novel, *Mumbo Jumbo* (1972).

13. Kenneth Burke, *The Rhetoric of Religion* (Berkeley: University of California Press, 1970), p. 302.

part 1

what is jazz?

introduction

"If you have to ask what it is, you will *never* know." "If you don't know what it is, well, just don't mess with it!" So many books about jazz open with such apocryphal warnings, usually ascribed to Louis Armstrong or Fats Waller, that jazz can appear to be a secret logo, the special province of the precious few. This aura of exclusivity is compounded by the music's "folk" "origins" (both loaded terms of dispute that further complicate the case) and by its definition as an improvised music, one that cannot be documented with authority by the lines and dots of conventional written systems. Perhaps most confounding is the fact that virtually all (some would say absolutely all) of jazz's indispensable pathfinders have been African-Americans. Defined as occupying the bottom of the U.S. social hierarchy and, until quite recently, outside history, blacks and their expression in art, with its own airs of exclusivity and mystery, appeared to be the dangerously unknowable (albeit at times delectably alluring) exotic, the not-Us.

And yet despite all racial romance and mystic obfuscation, jazz *is* a definable set of musical forms, transmissible not by blood transfusions or magic codes but by careful, painstaking study (at the nexus of work and play) within its particular ritual testing grounds and classrooms. It involves individual apprenticeship, no-mercy on-the-job learning, and that ancient monster of the woodshed: practice.

This part of *The Jazz Cadence of American Culture* represents an impulse to catalog the music's definitive forms—call-response exchanges, repetitions-with-a-difference, Afro-dance-beat–oriented rhythms (each beat representing, as one critic has put it, a story and a "promise"), solo breaks and other improvisations, vamp-chorus-riff-outchorus patterns, impulses to play and game, soulful changes straight out of church, and, perhaps most fundamentally, face-to-face exchanges with the blues and other musical forms. As the selections here strive toward definitions of jazz as music and toward an understanding of the cultural implications of their struggles over definitions, they take into account the continuing influence of jazz's formative sounds: blues changes, trains, city and country sounds, the croons and groans of lovers, and, crucially, the textures of the African-American voice in song and conversation. What is jazz? Jazz is the instruments talking to one another, now with intoxicating allure, now with prophesy, now with what Ralph Ellison has termed "shit, grit, and motherwit": jazz is a Harlem-inflected discussion in music. Jazz is all of the above.

This section is a first chorus among many, for in a sense every line in this book tries to define the music, aiming to outline the parts and structures of a musical form that has inspired makers of other, nonmusical forms. What is it about jazz music that has made writers want to make jazz poems and novels, choreographers jazz dances, painters jazz paintings? The writer and scholar Robert Stepto tells the story of a man in Chicago who, in the 1960s, told a haberdasher he wanted a tie that looked like Miles Davis's horn sounds! What, this section asks, did that man have in mind?

Dixieland, Traditional, Chicago Style, Hot, Swing, Kansas City Style, Bop, Progressive, Modern, Cool, West Coast, East Coast, Mainstream, Hard Bop, Funky, Third Stream, and Avant Garde are some of the terms critics have employed through the years, in communicating with the public, as labor-saving reference tags. Sometimes, too, these tags have served as rallying cries, or as slogans in calculated and systematic promotions.

To Ellington, and many other musicians, they represent divisions, ill-defined and indefensible, which tend to restrict the artist's prerogative of freedom. "If 'jazz' means anything at all, which is questionable," he has said, "it means the same thing it meant to musicians fifty years ago—freedom of expression. I used to have a definition, but I don't think I have one anymore, unless it is that it is a music with an African foundation which came out of an American environment."
—Stanley Dance

True jazz is an art of individual assertion within and against the group. Each true jazz moment (as distinct from the uninspired commercial performance) springs from a contest in which each artist challenges all the rest; each solo flight, or improvisation, represents (like the successive canvases of a painter) a definition of his identity: as individual, as member of the collectivity and as a link in the chain of tradition.

—Ralph Ellison, Shadow and Act

Jazz is a series of blues-based melodies   *—Wynton Marsalis*

Changes here meaning, as younger musicians use that word to mean "modulations," what I mean when I say image. They change very quickly. The mind, moving. . . . This music accepts repetition as an already accepted fact of life. You breathe, your heart beats, quickens with the music's pulse, and yours . . . your foot pats, these are the things we don't even think about. The point then is to move it away from what we already know, toward, into, what we only sense. Music is for the senses.
—Amiri Baraka, Black Music

Jazz me blues: what does that sound like? So and so me blues. The expression isn't dignified enough. It's not historically accurate.

Our form of music is erotic, there's no way of getting around it. But it can also be cerebral. . . . You take Miles when he's playing a beautiful thing like *Sketches of Spain* or *My Ship*. Isn't that fantastic? —Hazel Scott (in Arthur Taylor)

Swing is possible . . . only when the beat, though it seems perfectly regular, gives the impression of moving inexorably ahead (like a train that keeps moving at the same speed but is still being drawn ahead by its locomotive).

—Andre Hodeir

She sings way behind the beat and then she brings it up—hitting right on the beat. You can play behind the beat, but every once in a while you have to cut into the rhythm section on the beat and that keeps everybody together. Sinatra does it by accenting a word. A lot of singers try to sing like Billie, but just the act of playing behind the beat doesn't make it sound soulful. —Nat Hentoff

Improvisation I think is very misunderstood: people think you are simply making things up on the spot. Well, perhaps you are but in the same spirit that the old Zen painters would study a tree for years before attempting to execute a drawing of it in a single stroke. —Al Young and William J. Harris

Jazz is an extension of what Du Bois called "our spiritual strivings," our struggles for a sense of harmony in a troubling world. Rhythm understood in the broadest existential sense has helped us to survive as a people: You take what you have, whatever that is, and you drum our meaning. You hear that rhythm in church cadences; the texts themselves are musical. And you feel the same spirit and soulfulness in jazz. —Rev. Dr. James Washington (personal communication)

chapter 1

ALAN P. MERRIAM + FRADLEY H. GARNER

Jazz—The Word[*]

The history of the word "jazz" is indeed a fascinating one. Variously derived from Africa, Arabia, the Creole, French, Old English, Spanish, the Indians, the names of mythical musicians, old vaudeville practices, associations with sex and vulgarity, onomatopoeia, and other sources, its real origin has been, and may well remain, a mystery. Yet a study of the problems that have been associated with it, and a tracing of the suggestions and viewpoints that have been advanced in the literature from 1917 through 1958, provide a real journey into the background not only of the word, but of jazz itself.

A number of summary articles concerning the word have appeared in the past, but for the most part these have added nothing new to the controversy which surrounds the word. Of more importance are the original suggestions which provided the material for such summaries; thus an article by Walter Kingsley in the New York *Sun* (1917) laid down some of the basic ideas concerning African and minstrel origins of the word which have been copied, either with or without acknowledgement of the source, time and time again. A series of articles in the *Etude* in August and September, 1924, while rehashing some previous suggestions, led to one of the most extended discussions of the problem which raged through several allied journals. A third set of articles, again stressing the African origin, was set off

[*]This article was originally published as a five-part series which ran in *The Jazz Review* from March through August, 1960 (Vol. III); it was somewhat popularized and the accompanying bibliography was never published. The present version goes back to the original manuscript with some slight editorial changes. Though some further material concerning the word "jazz" has been published since 1960, it has not been incorporated here.

by an anonymous piece in the New York *Times* (1934) which led to numerous rejoinders and further suggestions. We have come to a point in the study of the word where it seems wise to review the past theories although even now it is probably impossible to decide surely which will ultimately prove to be correct.

I

Folk Adaptations: As Derived from Personal Names

Perhaps the most fascinating theory of the origin of the word "jazz" involves folk adaptations which stem from the idea of the change or corruption of personal names. Associated with this point of view are certain folktales which have been disseminated, apparently both by word of mouth and through the medium of the printed page, and which, in almost all their tellings, involve characteristics of plot and incident which are practically identical. The earliest printed appearance of one tale, so far as we have been able to discover, was in the *Music Trade Review* for June 14, 1919. The story, centering around a character named Jasbo Brown, is told as follows:

> Chicago, Ill., June 9. Roger Graham, Chicago music publisher, has his own pet theory of the origin of jazz music and firmly believes it to be the true one. Five years ago, in Sam Hare's Schiller Cafe on Thirty-first Street, "Jasbo" Brown and five other alleged musicians, members of what might have been called, with the aid of imagination, an orchestra, dispensed "melody" largely for the benefit of Sam Hare's patrons.
>
> Jasbo doubled with the piccolo and cornet. When he was sober Jasbo played orthodox music, but wrapped around three or four glasses of gin Jasbo had a way of making his piccolo produce strains of the wildest, most barbaric abandon. Strange to say, though, Mr. Hare's patrons, if they could help it, never allowed Jasbo to maintain sobriety while on the job. They liked the thrilling sensation of the piccolo's lawless strains, and when Jasbo put a tomato can on the end of his cornet it seemed as if the music with its strange, quivering pulsations came from another world.
>
> Patrons offered Jasbo more and more gin. First it was the query, "More, Jasbo?" directed at the darky's thirst; then the insistence, "More, Jasbo!" directed at the darky's music, and then just plain "more jazz!"
>
> (ANON. 1919C:32)

This story was picked up almost immediately, apparently by the New York *Telegraph* and then by *Current Opinion,* less than two months after it first appeared. In the latter journal the following was printed, and it is of interest to note that within this short span of time the story had already been changed.

> Other less erudite musical authorities are satisfied that jazz is purely of American origin. We find the New York Telegraph, Broadway's own gazet, for instance, giving the credit to Chicago.
>
> "... And Chicago presents as Exhibit A, Jasbo Brown, a negro musician,

who doubled with the cornet and piccolo. When he was sober . . . he played orthodox music, but when he imbibed freely of gin . . . he had a way of screaming above the melody with a strange barbaric abandon. One evening a young woman frequenter of the cafe where he held forth, tired of the conventional manner in which the music was played, called out, 'A little more *Jasbo* in that piece!' The cry was taken up, 'Jazz! Jazz!' and Jazz music was christened." (ANON. 1919B:97)

The next appearance of the story of Jasbo was published by no less an authority than the Lavignac *Encyclopédie de la musique et dictionnaire du conservatoire* (Singleton 1923:3327), which in 1923 translated it into French and reproduced, almost word for word, the original *Music Trade Review* version of 1919. It is undoubtedly from this source that Schneider picked up the story and, changing it a bit, reproduced it again.

C'était à Chicago, au café Schiller, tenu par un nommé Sam Hare, dans le 31e avenue. Il y avait là un négro nommé Jasbo Brown, qui avait recruté un orchestre. Jasbo jouait du piccolo (le piccolo est un instrument aigu de la famille des bugles); il jouait aussi du cornet à pistons, pour varier les plaisirs de ses auditeurs. Quand il n'avait pas bu, la musique de ses instruments était à peu près possible. Mais quand il avait absorbé quelques cocktails ou quelques verres de genièvre cela devenait de la musique exaspérée, quelque chose comme les cornets à bouquin de nos Mardi Gras d'autrefois. Et les clients du café raffolaient des sonorités désordonnées du piccolo de Jasbo. Plus c'était faux, plus ils étaient contents, et plus ils lui offraient des verres de genièvre. Et lui criaient: "Encore, Jasbo!" et, par abréviation: "Encore, Jazz!"

[It was on 31st Avenue in Chicago, in the Schiller cafe, which was run by a man named Sam Hare. There was a negro there named Jasbo Brown who had put a band together. Jasbo played the piccolo (the piccolo is a thin instrument in the bugle family); he also played the cornet, in order to vary the pleasure of his listeners. When he hadn't been drinking, he could hardly play; but when he had imbibed a few cocktails or some gin, his playing became aggravated, something like the cornets in our old Mardi Gras. And the clients in the cafe went wild for the unruly sounds of Jasbo's piccolo. The worse he played, the happier they were, and the more glasses of gin they bought him. And they yelled at him: "More, Jasbo!" and then, abbreviating it: "More, Jazz!"] (SCHNEIDER 1924:223–24)

A slightly different version, again, came a year later when Rogers shortened the story.

Then came Jasbo Brown, a reckless musician of a Negro cabaret in Chicago, who played this and other blues, blowing his own extravagant moods and risque interpretations into them, while hilarious with gin. To give further meanings to his veiled allusions, he would make the trombone "talk" by putting a derby hat and later a tin can at its mouth. The delighted patrons would shout, "More, Jasbo. More, Jaz, more." And so the name originated.

(ROGERS 1925:219)

In 1926 the story was again elaborated, this time to account for the origin of the music as well as the word, and Jasbo was credited with being the master of several instruments instead of one.

Tout le monde est maintenant d'accord outre-Atlantique; c'est à Chicago, dans la 31e Avenue, au café Schiller, qu'est né S.M. le Jazz. Le propriétaire de l'établissement, un certain Sam Have (*sic*), avait engagé en 1915 un nègre: Jasbo Brown. Celui-ci jouait tour à tour, pour distraire les clients, de plusieurs instruments: piston, flûte, clarinette, hautbois. A jeun, l'artiste exécutait des mélodies agréables, mais lorsque les cocktails faisaient leur oeuvre, il soufflait dans un instrument, en saisissait brusquement un autre et en tirait des sons cacophoniques autant qu'ahurissants. Ce nègre, comme tous ses congénères, avait un sentiment puissant du rhythme. Et ses improvisations d'homme ivre amusaient les consommateurs qui lui criaient: "Allez, Jasbo!" Il eût bientôt de nombreux imitateurs à travers l'Amérique. Ils firent comme Jasbo. D'où l'abréviation "jas," devenue "jazz."

[On both sides of the Atlantic, everyone is now in agreement that it was on 31st Avenue in Chicago, at the Schiller cafe, where Jazz was born. In 1915, the owner of this establishment, a certain Sam Have (*sic*), had hired a negro named Jasbo Brown. To amuse the clientele, Brown played a variety of instruments one after the other: cornet, flute, clarinet, oboe. When sober, the musician played pleasant melodies, but when the drinks began to do their work, he would blow in one instrument and then suddenly grab another to make sounds that were cacophonous as well as astounding. This negro, like all his kind, had a strong sense of rhythm, and his drunken improvisations amused the crowd, who yelled at him: "Go, Jasbo!" Soon there were numerous imitators across America. They acted like Jasbo. And so came the abbreviation "jas," which has become "jazz."]

(ANON. 1926:144)

The story, in relatively the same form, has since been quoted by Hart (1932), Coeuroy and Schaeffner (1926), and Goffin (1932), among others, and in almost all cases uncritically. The first and, indeed, the only flat criticism came from Schwerke (1926:679), who wrote, in connection with the Jasbo story: "Le jazz n'a pas de date, et toutes les tentatives qu'on a faites pour lui en donner une sont sans portée. . ." [Jazz cannot be dated, and all the attempts to do so are insignificant]. He further characterized it as "ridicule et fantaisiste" [ridiculous and fanciful].

But the story of Jasbo Brown was by no means confined to that particular gentleman, and its variations are quite as fascinating as the original. Thus Paul Whiteman (Whiteman and McBride 1926:122) used the same family name but changed the surname of the central character, when he wrote:

There is also a legend that a particularly jazzy darky player, named James Brown and called "Jas" from the abbreviation of his name, was the source of the peppy little word that has now gone all over the world.

A year earlier Walter Kingsley had changed the name to Jasper and the date of the story to the early part of the nineteenth century, writing:

In the twenties and thirties of the last century there was a retired planter in New Orleans whose delight it was to entertain visiting show folk. He had a dancing darky of superhuman vitality and joie de vivre who was his star exhibit whenever he threw a party. This hoofing phenomenon was named Jasper and the other slaves called him "Jazz" or "Jass" for short. Jasper could put life into a cemetery with his quaint steps, his songs, his mugging and clowning. His fame was carried far and wide by strolling troupers. Whenever a party showed up the old planter called in the sure-fire slave and shouted: "Jazz it up, Jasper."
—(KINGSLEY 1925: EDITORIAL SECTION, 3:1)

It will be seen that the story is here changed considerably, yet the element of the name and the incidents of an individual calling to a Negro performer and using his nickname remain the same; it is virtually certain that this story falls into the general Jasbo category. The Jasper version has also been cited by Osgood (1926A:17).[1]

Still another variation of the first name has been suggested by Goffin (1932:44).

Le mot jazz, doit-il son origine à un musicien noir nommé Jess qui jouait d'une certaine façon saccadée, qui se popularisa au point que l'on dit communément *To play like Jess, To play Jess* par abréviation, puis jazz par déformation, c'est là l'explication que m'en donnèrent plusieurs nègres que j'avais interrogés.

[The word jazz owes its origin to a black musician named Jess who played in a jerky, halting style, which became so popular that people began to say "to play like Jess," in shortened form "to play Jess," and then, through the deformation of that phrase, jazz. This is the explanation that I was given by many of the negroes I asked.]

This particular version has apparently never been used by other writers, although Goffin repeated the possibility in a later book (1946:62).

Although the versions relating to James, Jasper, and Jess never gained wide currency, two other variations from the original have been widely cited. In 1919 Grenville Vernon quoted an interview with James Reese Europe in the course of which Europe suggested the following:

I believe that the term "jazz" . . . originated with a band of four pieces which was found about fifteen years ago in New Orleans and which was known as "Razz's Band." . . . It consisted of a barytone horn, a trombone, a cornet, and an instrument made out of the chinaberry-tree. . . . Somehow in the passage of time Razz's Band got changed into "Jazz's Band," and from this corruption arose the term "jazz."   (VERNON 1919:5)

This version was picked up almost immediately by the *Literary Digest* (Anon. 1919a:28) and later by both Hart (1932:245) and Nelson (Goffin 1932:45) at least as a possibility, but it remained again for Schwerke to ridicule the explanation:

> Également ridicule et fantaisiste est la théorie (si toutefois elle mérite ce titre) suivant laquelle le mot jazz devrait son origine à un ensemble de quatre instruments qui se trouvait il y a quinze ans environ à la Nouvelle-Orléans, et que l'on connaissait sous le nom de "Razz's Band" (c'est-à-dire, orchestre de Razz). . . . Le "Razz's Band" passa par degrés des plus petits cafés de la Nouvelle-Orléans aux plus grands hôtels de cette ville, d'où il gagna New York. C'est là qu'au bout d'un certain temps, Razz's Band fut métamorphosé en Jazz's Band! Il ne serait pas superflu, pour compléter l'histoire, de nous dire pourquoi les habitants de New York trouvèrent la consonne "J" plus agréable à leur palais que le consonne "R." Et l'on pourrait rapporter quantité de contes aussi fantastiques que les précédents, si toutefois ceux-ci ne suffisaient pas à montrer le caractère ridicule de ce qu'on a écrit sur le jazz et le peu de prix qu'on doit y attacher.

> [Equally ridiculous and fanciful is the theory (if it even deserves that term) according to which the word jazz owes its origin to a four-instrument ensemble that played about fifteen years ago in New Orleans and that was known by the name "Razz's Band" (in other words, the orchestra of Razz). . . . "Razz's Band" gradually moved up from the tiniest cafes to the biggest hotels in New Orleans and finally left for New York. There, after a while, Razz's Band was transformed into Jazz's Band! It would not be amiss, to complete the story, to say why the inhabitants of New York find the consonant "J" more pleasing to their palate than the consonant "R." And one could report a number of tales as fantastic as the ones above, if those here did not suffice to demonstrate how ridiculous writings about jazz have been, and how little they are worth.]   (SCHWERKE 1926:679)

Osgood objected even more fully on the same linguistic grounds, remarking:

> This is a good story and as an explanation ingenious enough, though there is no hint as to what reason there could be for the changing of the rugged R of Razz into the softer J of jazz; as a rule the progression is the other way, toward strength. Incidentally, that J at the beginning of jazz is not so soft; much harder than before any other vowel except O. Say jazz and jolt out loud and compare them with jelly, jib and juice. Had we (which we haven't) a soft G before A, as before E and I (geode, gin), "gazz" would be a much more suggestive and correct spelling than jazz.   (OSGOOD 1926A:14)

The final major variation in the story of Jasbo Brown was apparently first put into print by Vincent Lopez, who changed the locale, the name, the instrument of the chief character, and the complexity of the plot.

> I have been for a long time making a study both of the word "jazz" and of the kind of music which it represents. The origin of the colloquial word jazz is shrouded in mystery. The story of its beginning that is most frequently told and most generally believed among musicians has to do with a corruption of the name "Charles." In Vicksburg, Miss., during the period when rag-time was at the height of its popularity and "blues" were gaining favor, there was a colored drummer of rather unique ability named "Chas. Washington." As is a very common custom in certain parts of the South he was called "Chaz." "Chaz" could not read music, but he had a gift for "faking" and a marvelous sense of syncopated rhythm. It was a practice to repeat the trio or chorus of popular numbers, and because of the catchiness of "Chaz's" drumming he was called on to do his best on the repeats. At the end of the first chorus the leader would say:
>
> "Now, Chaz!"
>
> From this small beginning it soon became a widespread habit to distinguish any form of exaggerated syncopation as "Chaz."
>
> (ANON. 1924D:520)

Only two years later Osgood (1926a:15) examined Lopez's theory and found it seriously wanting:

> Very pretty, indeed, though it will hardly stand examination. . . . Leaving out of consideration the chronological question as to whether the "blues" were already known when ragtime was "at the height of its popularity" (it is possible they may have been—in Vicksburg), analysis of the musical elements of the story make it improbable. Few popular ragtime numbers had "trios" to repeat, except marches (two-steps) like "The Georgia Campmeeting," and when they were repeated there was little emphasis placed upon them. . . .[2]

In 1934 Bender, who supported an African origin for the word, also discredited the Chaz origin (Anon. 1934:19:6), as did Moynahan, who three years later wrote: "I dismiss with a leer the canard once attributed—wrongly, I am sure—to Vincent Lopez, that he had heard the word 'jazz' originated as a corruption of the name of a famous drummer called 'Chas'—short for 'Charles' " (1937:15). Despite such rejections of the story, however, it was cited by Hart (1932:245) and by Nelson (Goffin 1932:45–46) without comment.

As in the more persistent Jasbo tale, the Lopez version itself gave rise to at least one variation which contains all the elements of the original story, changed and with a new name substituted.

> If we may trust a mere story, the word "jazz" comes from a band in a waterfront resort in Philadelphia, which used to have a Negro named Jack

Washington playing the drums. This Negro had developed a rhythm so fierce that the band, as a joke, used to stop playing entirely and let Jack rage on the drums alone. When the time came for Jack to play his percussion solos, the sailors would cry in delight, "Jack! Jack!"—and from this cry of theirs the odd name "jazz" is derived.   (KOOL 1925:339)

An element emphasized in some versions of this general tale type is that of the individual who arises in his excitement to shout the magic words to the performer. It will be remembered that in a 1919 version a young woman is the moving character (Anon. 1919c:97). In a version given by Moynahan the cast of characters is changed to the well-known Dixieland Jazz Band, and the individual becomes an "old fellow."

> The story usually doled out for popular consumption is the one about the Dixieland Jazz Band's job at the Booster's Club in Chicago. The band, brought from New Orleans, was still unnamed when an old fellow in the audience, stirred to high excitement by their shrill, unprecedented style of playing, jumped to his feet and shouted: "Come on, boys, jazz it up!" It makes a good story, even when the reciter goes on to explain that the word "Jazz" was an old vaudeville (!) term, meaning "to stir things up."
>
> (1937:15)

The final story of this group is perhaps the most plausible of the lot; yet it has appeared, to the best of our knowledge, but once in the literature, in 1919.

> Most people are aware of the fact that "jazz" music originated in the South, but perhaps few know just how the name itself started. The *Columbia Record* gives the following explanation: There was once a trio of dusky musicians, one a banjo player, one a singer and the third a maker of melodies by means of an empty tin can. This unusual trio came to be called the Jassacks Band, the name being the popular inversion of the jackass, the famous solo singer of the Southern States. Soon the name, according to the proverbial lore for inaccuracy, was changed to the Jassacks and by the usual method of abbreviation developed finally into just plain jazz.
>
> (ANON. 1919E:50)

A final theory which does not involve the Jasbo story, but which fits generally into the name-deformation category, was advanced by Johnson:

> The writer would like to add one more to the list of rather asinine theories on the origin of the term jazz. It is his opinion that the word was suggested by Negro preachers in their tirades on the wicked woman, Jezebel.
>
> (JOHNSON 1927:15)

It is difficult to tell whether Johnson was making a serious suggestion here, but in any case it seems hardly plausible.

The Jasbo tale type, it is clear, has had widespread dissemination both in the United States and in Europe, yet no matter what its locale, its elements indicate that it stems from a single source, probably the 1919 issue of *Music Trade Review*. Although the central character is variously named Jasbo, James, Jasper, Jess, Razz, Chas, and Jack, and although the incident occurs variously in Chicago, New Orleans, Vicksburg, and Philadelphia, it is the same story in essential development in each of its tellings. Its validity is extremely doubtful, and it may be pointed out that, by definition, a folktale is a story concerning persons, incidents, and plot which even the tellers do not believe to be true.

Folk Adaptations: As a Minstrel or Vaudeville Term

The concept of the word "jazz" as deriving from the minstrel or vaudeville show was first advanced by Kingsley in 1917. Although he felt that the ultimate source of the word was Africa, Kingsley spoke of its application to vaudeville and thus set off a series of articles which ascribed the word to that source. He wrote:

> Curiously enough the phrase "Jaz her up" is a common one to-day in vaudeville and on the circus lot. When a vaudeville act needs ginger the cry from the advisers in the wings is "put in jaz," meaning add low comedy, go to high speed and accelerate the comedy spark. "Jazbo" is a form of the word common in the varieties, meaning the same as "hokum," or low comedy verging on vulgarity. (KINGSLEY 1917: III, 3:7)

Although this origin for the term was picked up and cited by others, Kingsley was the only one to spell the word as "Jazbo." When Whiteman used the idea, he said:

> I am often asked, "What is jazz?" I know of no better definition than that given by Lieut. Comm. John Philip Sousa, U.S.N.R.F. He derives the word from "Jazzbo," the term used in the old-fashioned minstrel show when the performers "cut loose" and improvised upon or "Jazzboed" the tune.
>
> (WHITEMAN 1924:523)

Finck clearly derived his version from Kingsley's original article but used the word "jazz," saying: "Just so in vaudeville, 'jazz her up' means 'put in pep and ginger.' Not necessarily speed, for an extremely popular jazz is the slow drag" (1924:527). We have already had occasion to refer to Moynahan's explanation that "the word 'jazz' was an old vaudeville (!) term, meaning 'to stir things up'" (1937:15).

Hobson uses a still different spelling in referring to the word as a minstrel term: "Various sources for the word *jazz* have been suggested, including . . . the old minstrel-show term *jasbo*, meaning antics guaranteed to bring applause—when new numbers were flopping the backstage cry might be 'give 'em the jasbo' or 'jas it up'" (1939:94–95). Stannard uses the same spelling when he writes, "It seems likely that the word as a musical term derives from the old minstrel show backstage cry: 'Give 'em the jasbo' (meaning to introduce pep into an act)" (1941:83).

Another theory which refers indirectly, at least, to the minstrel origin was reported in *Down Beat*:

Mutual's *Answer Man* came up with what many jazz students have been waiting for: an explanation of the origin of the word jazz. . . .

. . . [I]n pre–Civil War days, Georgia Negro men competed in strutting contests for their choice of cakes, and ladies, in cake suppers. The strutting contest became known as the Cake Walk, and the winner was dubbed Mr. Jazzbo.

Further research traced the word to New Orleans during the 1830s, when *chasse beaux* was a popular French expression denoting a dandy, or a hip Gallic Don Juan.   (ANON. 1958A:10)

If the minstrel term, indeed, is to be assumed as the source of the word "jazz," we are still faced with the problem of its own origin. There seems to be no clear explanation for this unless we agree with Chapman's plausible French theory or with Kingsley as to its African origin, a problem which will be discussed below.

Translinguistic Theories

Probably the most persistent theory of the origin of the word "jazz" has been its ascription to Africa, a theory fully as widespread as—and more logical than—the series of Jasbo stories. Again, this began with Kingsley, who wrote in the New York *Sun*:

The word is African in origin. It is common on the Gold Coast of Africa and in the hinterland of Cape Coast Castle. In his studies of the creole patois and idiom in New Orleans Lafcadio Hearn reported that the word "jaz," meaning to speed things up, to make excitement, was common among the blacks of the South and had been adopted by the creoles as a term to be applied to music of a rudimentary syncopated type. In the old plantation days when the slaves were having one of their rare holidays and the fun languished some West Coast Africans would cry out, "Jaz her up," and this would be the cue for fast and furious fun. No doubt the witch doctors and medicine men on the Congo used the same term at those jungle "parties" when the tomtoms throbbed and the sturdy warriors gave their pep an added kick with rich brews of Yohimbin bark—that precious product of the Cameroons.   (KINGSLEY 1917: III, 3:6–7)

Kingsley's article was immediately picked up by the *Literary Digest*, which quoted liberally from the *Sun* article on August 25, 1917, some twenty days after its original publication (Anon. 1917:28), and a year later it was quoted fully again in *Current Opinion* (Anon. 1918:165). It was partially quoted by Finck (1924:527), discussed at some length by Osgood (1926a:11–12), reworded but ascribed to Lafcadio Hearn by Newell (1928:351), by Nelson in 1930 and Goffin in 1932 (Goffin 1932:45), by Vizetelly (1934:22:6), and by various other authors.

Leaving aside Kingsley's somewhat curious juxtaposition of the then Gold Coast, the Congo, and the Cameroons, the major problem involved in this famous quotation is the ascription of the use of the term to New Orleans creoles by

Lafcadio Hearn. A detailed reading of Hearn's collected works failed to reveal any mention of the word, and communication with Hearn scholars has been similarly unrewarding. Thus John Ball writes (1958): "After still further checking (and as I told you in Chicago, Carl Swanson, a Hearn collector from Lakewood, Ohio, has checked all his rare collection), I find no Hearn mention of 'jazz.' " It is perhaps noteworthy that Kingsley never gave the source of his reference to Hearn, nor did any of those who used the Kingsley statement from the *Sun*. Unless Kingsley had personal communication with Hearn, or unless a letter or document has gone unnoticed, this particular line of investigation seems to lead only to a dead end. This circumstance is especially regrettable since Kingsley leaned so heavily upon Hearn as the source of his information.

Kingsley, however, is not the only scholar to attribute the origin of the word to Africa. Thus the New York *Times* reported in 1934:

> Some interesting etymological discoveries in an eight-year survey conducted by Professor Harold H. Bender, head of the Department of Oriental Languages of Princeton University, and a staff of eleven associates in preparing the edition of Webster's New International Dictionary, are described. . . .
>
> It took three years to track down the origin of the word jazz, and he had to write more than 100 letters seeking information on the word. He found it to have come from the West Coast of Africa with the slaves imported to Colonial America. It became incorporated later in the Creole patois as a synonym for "hurry up."   (ANON. 1934:19:6)

A more elaborate theory includes the African origin, but traces the ultimate source to Arabia, from whence it came through Africa to the Western Hemisphere.

> I submit a few words on music and musical instruments in the Western Soudan, through whose portals Islamic culture filtered to the various West and Central African peoples, from whom America obtained not merely the word *jazz*, but much of what it stands for. . . .
>
> The term *jazz* . . . is derived from the Arabic *jaz'*, a term used in the oldest Arabic works on prosody and music, and meant "the cutting off," "the apocopation." It passed with numerous other Arabic musical terms and customs, to the peoples of the West Coast of Africa, to be handed on, in the course of time, to America.   (FARMER 1924:158)

Farmer, who wrote these words, reported that he had gathered his material during a period of research at Glasgow University during the years 1918–20. Vizetelly also held the view that the Arabic origin was the correct one:

> If one accepts the African source as correct, it may do no harm to point out that in Arabic "jaz" is vitriol; that one who allures or attracts is "jazib," and, by extension, "jazibiyah" means "charm, grace, beauty and loveliness"; also the power of attraction.
>
> It may not be amiss to cite the fact that in Hausa, an African language

that resembles Arabic, "jaiza" is used to designate "the rumbling noise of distant drums, or a murmuring as of discontented persons." In Arabic, "jaza" signifies "compensation or reward: also, complaint or lamentation." Arabic "jazb" connotes "allurement or attraction." In Hindustani, "jazba" express- es "violent desire."

Now, in view of the fact that the Arabs have always been known as great slave traders, is it not within the bounds of possibility that the term . . . ought to be labeled Arabic? (1934:22:6)

Redway proposed a compromise which would ascribe the word both to Africa and Arabia.

The peoples of the North African coast are not Negroes; they belong to the Semitic family and their language is closely allied to the Arabic tongue. Many of the words of each are almost identical. For several centuries there were migrations of North Africans into Southwestern Europe, resulting in an intermingling of the two peoples. Southwestern Europe is very dark-skinned far into the Italian peninsula and even into Central Europe.

The African migrants into Europe carried their household words with them and implanted them in the speech of the people with whom they came in contact. As an instance, the prefix "guad" found in a score of words in the Spanish peninsula is an Arabic word meaning "water." The river Guadalquiver is the Arabic "Wadi-el-Kabir." The imported African words were carried along wherever migrants from the Spanish peninsula went— in detail, into the West Indies, and they still retain their Arabic earmarks. I am inclined to believe, therefore, that both Dr. Vizetelly and Professor Bender are correct. (1934: IV, 5:2)

Finally, in this rather extensive train of derivations, there has been at least one writer who holds that the word is Creole without necessarily tracing its ultimate source to the West Indies, Africa, or the Arabic. Tamony said simply: "It is a Creole word and means, in general, to speed up" (Tamony 1939:5).

In respect to the Arabic origin of the word, the differences among the various scholars as to the meaning of the word "jaz" should be pointed out, as should the fact that some scholars insist the word is pronounced with an initial "h" sound although written as a "j" in the English orthography. The African origin of the word is perhaps more plausible, and yet inquiry from a number of Africans as well as scholars in African linguistics has failed to document its presence as a word, let alone as a word with similar meaning, on the Guinea Coast. While the necessity for further research is indicated here, the probability of finding a correlation between jazz and a like word in West Africa seems relatively dim.

One of the most plausible of the translinguistic theories derives the word "jazz" from the French "jaser," and this data was most clearly expressed by Schwerke in 1926.

Le mot jazz est d'origine française et son application à la musique est la fidèle image de son sens littéral. Il y a 250 ans, la civilisation française trouva un solide point d'appui dans les provinces (plus tard devenues États) de la Louisiane et de la Caroline du Sud. Dans les villes cultivées du Sud (la Nouvelle-Orléans et Charleston), le Français fut pour un certain temps la langue dominante, et, dans les plantations possédées par les Français, c'était la seule langue dont on usât. Les esclaves au service des Français furent obligés d'apprendre la langue de leurs maîtres, ce qu'ils apprennent, des inflexions et des modifications propres à leur race.

S'il faut en croire Larousse, le verbe français *jaser* signifie *causer, bavarder, parler beaucoup*. Dans la littérature française, *jaser* s'applique souvent à une conversation animée sur divers sujets, alors que tout le monde parle ensemble; et, souvent aussi, *jaser* traduit plus spécialement un "chuchotement badin sur de petits riens."

[The word jazz is of French origin, and its application to music is the faithful reflection of its literal meaning. Two hundred fifty years ago, French civilization had taken a firm hold in the provinces (later the States) of Louisiana and South Carolina. For some time, French was the dominant language in the cultivated cities of the South (New Orleans and Charleston), and it was the only language used in plantations with French owners. Slaves who worked for the French were obliged to learn their masters' language, and they learned it with the inflections and modifications characteristic of their race.

According to Larousse, the French verb jaser means "*to chat*," "*to chatter*," "*to prattle*," "*to talk a lot*." In French literature, *jaser* is often used to describe a conversation that touches on a variety of subjects, with everyone speaking together; and in addition, *jaser* also means more specifically "a playful whispering about little nothings."]   (1926:679)

This explanation of the word has been cited by Hart (1932:245), Hobson (1939:94), Stannard (1941:83), and Patterson (1947:53), among others, and seems to be relatively plausible. It should also be noted that the translation of jaser, "chatter," may have some vague connection with the idea held by Kingsley and others that jazbo and jazz have something to do with "speeding things up." We have previously cited the reference to the French *chasse beaux* (Anon. 1958a:10) which, as advanced by Chapman, also seems highly plausible though we have been unable to verify the reference further.

Two other translinguistic theories have been advanced: one by Charles Edward Smith, who wrote that "The word itself is not of African or French origin but is an old English word applied to Honky Tonk pianists as early as forty years ago" (1935:45), and the other reported by Vizetelly, who stated that "F. P. Vreeland traced it to the Africans, Indians and the Spaniards for the New York *Times* in 1917" (1934:22:6). We have been unable to trace the Vreeland citation even with the help of the *Times* itself.

In summary, the translinguistic theories devolve upon the origin of the term in Arabic, African, Creole, French, Old English, Indian, and Spanish vocabularies.

The latter three can probably be dismissed as having little or no relationship to fact; the Arabic and African theories, while plausible, do not seem to stand up under intense scrutiny; the Creole remains unknown. The French origin for the word seems the most plausible and may well be the original source.

Onomatopoeia

An onomatopoetic source for the word "jazz" has been suggested only by Osgood who wrote: "Is it too far-fetched to suggest that the muffled booming of the great African drum was in itself the parent of the word; that, in other words, its origin is onomatopoetic?" (1926a:11–12). Without resorting to the obvious answer to the question, it may be stated that little credence can be placed in this source.

Vulgarity and Sex

The possible association of jazz with the sex act, for which the word is used as a synonym, has been suggested by a number of writers beginning, apparently, with Clay Smith who wrote:

> If the truth were known about the origin of the word "jazz" it would never be mentioned in polite society. . . . At fifteen and sixteen I had already made tours of Western towns, including the big mining centres, when the West was really wild and wooly. Like all adolescent boys let loose on the world I naturally received information that was none too good for me and was piloted by ignorant men to dance resorts. . . . These dance resorts were known as "Honky-Tonks"—a name which in itself suggests some of the rhythms of jazz. The vulgar word "jazz" was in general currency in those dance halls thirty years or more ago. Therefore jazz to me does not seem to be of American negro origin as many suppose.
>
> The vulgar dances that accompany some of the modern jazz are sometimes far too suggestive of the ugly origin of the word.
>
> (ANON. 1924D:595)

Paul Whiteman also reported this possible source of the word, albeit somewhat regretfully. In speaking of Joseph K. Gorham he wrote:

> He did not then note down the aggregation as a jazz band, though he undoubtedly knew the word as a slang phrase of the underworld with a meaning unmentionable in polite society. . . . Sometimes I have regretted the origin of the word because I think it probably has stirred up sentiments against the music.   (WHITEMAN AND MCBRIDE 1926:18,20)

Although Smith and Whiteman had done little more than hint at the connection between the word and the sex act, Smith, especially, received a sharp rejoinder from Osgood, who commented: "This is an example of how dangerous a little knowledge may be. It is entirely true . . . that a certain obscene meaning long ago became attached to the word, but it is not the original meaning of it, nor is jazz alone in this respect" (1926a:17). Despite Osgood's vigorous denial, however, the relationship was later suggested by Tamony (1939:5), Stannard (1941:83), and Goffin (1946:63,64), among others, and was flatly defined by Johnson in 1927: "Used both as a verb and as a noun to denote the sex act, . . . 'jazz' . . . has long been a common vulgarity among Negroes in the South, and it is very likely from this usage that the term 'jazz music' was derived" (1927:14–15). It may be noted here that Weseen, in his *Dictionary of American Slang*, gives "Jazz—Sexual intercourse; to have it" (1934:22) and Berrey, in the *American Thesaurus of Slang*, gives the word *jazz* under *copulate* (1947:342).

In this connection, also, Mencken connects the music term with the American folk use of *jazz* as a verb meaning to have sexual intercourse (1948:708–09), and Mathews says, ". . . but the plain fact is that to jazz has long had the meaning in American folk-speech of to engage in sexual intercourse" (1951:709). Mathews further indicates a possible line of research in connecting the word "jazz" with "jasm" which he cites as early as 1860 from the Massachusetts author Josiah Holland (*ibid.*:899). This in turn may be connected with the American dialect word "gism" which Read (1935:453) defines as "Strength, talent, Genius, ability. Cf. spunk. In various parts of the South, *gism* has the meaning 'gravy,' or 'cream sauce.' In the North, it is commonly used to mean 'semen.' In Maine and eastern New England the word is commonly pronounced *chism*, and the writer has seen it so spelled.—Ed." Read's source was Green (1897:85), who noted, "Chism, n. *Chissum*. Seminal fluid," in 1897, although he may have traced it back as far as 1848. If the connection between "gism," "gasm," and "jazz" is real, it probably leads away from the African or American Negro, but it also leads us up a blind alley inasmuch as "gasm" and "gism" cannot themselves be traced.

Although we have no satisfactory etymology for the word "jazz" in relation to its sexual meaning, nor information concerning the earliest use of the word in this connection, there is a certain degree of logic in the assumption that the music use of the term was derived from its sexual use. Here again is a field for further research.

Spontaneous Origins

The theory of a spontaneous origin of the word has been infrequently advanced, appearing but four times in the literature. The *Outlook* in 1924 said: "Some say that it is the Negro's reminiscence of his African tomtoms. According to one story, it was an illiterate Negro in a dancehall who coined the word; for when he was asked, 'What is that you are playing?' he replied, deprecatingly, 'Oh, it's jes' jazz'" (Anon. 1924a:381). Cecil Austin simply says, " 'This band is certainly some jazz' was a fairly common expression at the time, and two dollars a night and unlimited quantities of beer always proved a strong attraction to the musicians" (1925:258), and Coeuroy and Schaeffner probe no deeper when they say, "Certains le font dériver d'une expression en usage dans les bouges de la Nouvelle-Orléans: Jazz them, boys (qui correspondrait à *Hardi, les gars*)" (1926:101). And finally, an anonymous writer quoted Joseph K. Gorham as saying, ". . . the word . . . means simply enough, and without any explanation or definition, the only thing it's possible for four such letters in such order, when pronounced, to convey—and that is just to 'mess 'em up and slap it on thick.' That's the verb 'to jazz.' The noun implies the process and the verb the action" (Anon. 1919D:47).

II

The question as to where, how, and when the word "jazz" was first used as applied to music is as much of a puzzle as its ultimate origin, with various writers holding widely different points of view.

Localities

Curiously, the earliest ascription, in 1919, of the word to a musical type, was said to have occurred in the San Francisco area; this assertion was made by Joseph K. Gorham, according to the *Literary Digest*, who said that the word was "common to the knowledge and frequent in the vocabulary of the Barbary coast" (Anon. 1919d:47). This point of view received support from Smith (Anon. 1924D:595), as previously cited, and from Tamony, who says:

Late in February, 1913, the San Francisco Seals went into training at Boyes Springs. . . . Mr. Slattery, a sports editor, had heard the word jazz in craps games around San Francisco. It is a Creole word and means, in general, to speed up. . . . Mr. Slattery, with a sports-writer's sense of the striking, began to use "jazz" as a synonym for "ginger" and "pep." In a few days the novelty was taken up by other writers and the people around the camp, and was used in all descriptions. On the field the players were full of the old jazz, and there was jazz in the effervescent waters of the springs. Everything was jazzy, including the music Art Hickman played for the entertainment of the players and visitors. . . . The music he provided was his stylization of the ragtime of the day. It was an immediate hit. James Woods, manager of the Hotel St. Francis, heard Hickman while on a visit to Boyes. After Hickman opened at the St. Francis, national use of the word was only a matter of time. (1939:5)

A different use of the word, but still in San Francisco, was reported by Osgood:

Speaking of different meanings, Ferdie Grofe . . . tells of a peculiar use of the word jazz in San Francisco, which does not seem to have obtained anywhere else. Out there in the years just preceding the War there were certain large and popular cafés which maintained orchestras and also a regular pianist, and gave cabaret performances, limited, however, to singing by young women. Each one had a solo to sing and occasionally they joined in an ensemble. They did not sing their solos from the stage where the pianist was stationed. It was part of their duties to mingle with the guests and join them at table. Whenever one of them heard the pianist begin the prelude to her number, she would rise wherever she happened to be and sing, but when the pianist decided it was time for an ensemble, he would announce,

"The next number will be jazz," and they would all troop back to the stage. There was no extra "pepping up" or rhythmic exaggeration in these choruses, and the word appears to have had no special significance as regards the music, simply meaning that it would be sung *tutti* instead of solo.

(1926A:18)

This story has been cited by a number of writers, among them Nelson and Goffin (Goffin 1932:46).

Ludwig says that the word "was first used in this country by negroes working on the docks and levees in the South" (1922:78) and is apparently referring to its music connection. More specifically, Baby Dodds says, "The word 'jazz' as a musical term, was born in New Orleans" (Anon. 1945:5), and this is echoed by Darnell Howard, "The term 'jazz' then originated in New Orleans" (*ibid.*), and by Coeuroy and Schaeffner (1926:101). The New Orleans origin is expressly denied by Stannard, who says, "New Orleans musicians themselves were not familiar with the expression" (1941:83).

Finally, both Richard M. Jones and Bud Jacobson cite New York as the location of the first use of the word in connection with music (Anon. 1945:5).

Date of First Use

The oldest reference to the word "jazz" seems to be that advanced by Chapman, who is reported to have "turned up a poster some 100 years old, with the word Jass on it" (Anon. 1958A:10). Other than this, we have Austin's statement that "the term 'jazz' in its relation to music dates from about this time [post Civil War]" (1925:258), while Clay Smith notes: " 'Jazz' was born and christened in the low dance halls of our far west of three decades ago" (Anon. 1924D:595), which would place it about 1900. Osgood, referring back to James Reese Europe, whom we have previously cited, says, "It is possible that Lieutenant Europe correctly cited the first use of jazz as an adjective, for he places it about 1900–1905, ten years at least before the term 'jazz band' came into general use . . ." (1926A:14).

Richard M. Jones is quoted as believing that

The term "jazz" originated in New Orleans during the early part of the century as a descriptive word. It wasn't until after the Original Dixieland Band added the word "jass" to its title while recording in New York during 1913 or 1914 that the word spread into other bands. It was undoubtedly a press agent's idea that first gave the word its start during the ODJB recordings. However, the word, as a musical term, was first used in New Orleans upon the return of the ODJB from New York. The word then spread to other bands in other cities.   (ANON. 1945:5)[3]

We have already had occasion to cite Tamony's date of 1913 for the word in San Francisco (Tamony 1939:5), and Darnell Howard cites the same date, saying:

I first heard the word "jazz" used musically in reference to the Original Dixieland Jass Band. This was in 1913, and the ODJB had just recorded *Livery Stable Blues*. That same year, while I was playing with the John

Wecliffe band in Milwaukee, the band's press agent erected a huge sign above the dance hall where we were playing. The large, flashy letters read: JOHN WECLIFFE'S JAZZ BAND. This caused quite a commotion, for the word "jazz" at this time was a rather shady word, used only in reference to sex. This was Milwaukee; quite a few miles north of Chicago. The ODJB was already employing the word "jazz" musically. They started their band in New Orleans. The term "jazz" then originated in New Orleans.

(ANON. 1945:5)

Baby Dodds recounts the same general story, but dates it at 1914:

The word "jazz" as a musical term, was born in New Orleans. The Original Dixieland Jazz Band, playing at the Casino in the tenderloin district of New Orleans in 1914, first employed the term. The first time I came into direct contact with the term, though, was in 1919 when I joined Fate Marable's Jazz E Sazz Band on the *Capitol Steamer* or *Steamer Sydney*. The term definitely was used first in New Orleans, before Chicago.   (ANON. 1945:5)

Still in reference to the ODJB, Jacobson was of the opinion that

Wilbur Sweatman . . . had a lot to do with originating the word "jazz." He wrote a short article for the *Chicago Daily News* in 1915 stating that he was the first person to use the term in a band. If so, the term undoubtedly started in New York. The ODJB might have picked up the term from the Sweatman Band while recording in New York, then upon returning to New Orleans, spread it around to other bands. I remember distinctly seeing the word used in Chicago in 1914; I don't believe it was any earlier. The two words, JAZZ BAND, were pasted on a high sign above the Arsonia Cafe, where Art Arseth's Band was playing at the time.   (ANON. 1945:5)

Another widely quoted description of the first use of the word appeared in *Jazzmen* in 1939, where Charles Edward Smith wrote of the Tom Brown Band:

In June, 1915, however, they could and did take a job at the Lamb's Cafe in Chicago. . . .

They didn't have union clearance on that first Chicago job. According to Tom Brown it was an attempt by union officials to low rate them that gave jazz its name. Jazz, or jass as it was then spelled, was a familiar word around 22nd Street where the red lights glowed, but it wasn't used about music. The story has it that the statement that jazz music was being played at Lamb's Cafe was a whispering campaign, the purpose of which was to smear the band. People were curious to know what "jass" music was, and they came in droves to find out. Presently the new sign out front read: "Added attraction—Brown's Dixieland Jass Band, Direct from New Orleans, Best Dance Music in Chicago."   (1939:46)

In Tom Brown's obituary in the New York *Times* in 1958, the same story is told:

Mr. Brown, a trombonist, said the term "jazz music" was first applied to his band in Chicago in 1915. It was playing at the Lambs Club there and was attracting crowds with the music that originated in New Orleans.

He related how another band at the club became jealous and complained to the union. The union issued a statement saying that "jazz music was being played at Lambs," intending to discredit the Brown band.

Instead of hurting it, Mr. Brown said, the public streamed in to see what the music was all about.   (ANON. 1958B:37:1)

The story has also been cited by a number of writers, among them Goffin (1946:64). Hart (1932:245), probably referring to the same story, says that "It was not until about 1915 that the word came into its present widespread use."

Although there are conflicting opinions expressed as to the early use of the word, it seems clear that the overwhelming support comes for a date sometime between 1913 and 1915, although earlier use may have existed in local areas.

Early Spellings

Although in fact the early spellings of the printed word are usually either "jass" or "jazz," Kingsley noted that it was "variously spelled Jas, Jass, Jaz, Jazz, Jasz and Jascz" (1917: III, 3:6–8), and Vernon said that it was sometimes spelled " 'jass' and sometimes 'jazz' " (1919: IV, 5:1–2). Nelson, in 1930, included the various spellings "jaz, jass, jaz, jazz, jasz ou jaszz" (Goffin 1932:45), and Stannard says, "The early spelling of the word was alternatively jas, jass and jaz" (1941:83). As noted above, however, very few of these alternative spellings have ever been used in the literature, and most are probably due to the inventiveness of the authors concerned.

Euphemisms and New Words for Jazz

So far as we can discover there have been three major attempts to substitute another word for jazz, as well as two other suggestions of an unorganized nature. The first of the major efforts was initiated by Vincent Lopez, who was quoted in the *Musical Courier* in 1924.

Vincent Lopez, who is doing his bit at the next meeting of the League of Composers to clarify the situation, objects to the term "jazz." Being on the inside, he feels more strongly on the subject than most of us. . . . He insists that, jazz being dead, the name ought also be dead, or, at least, ought not to be hung on to what he calls Modern Music or Modern Popular Music.

This is a point for discussion—and we must say at the outset that we agree with Mr. Lopez, that the use of the word "jazz" leads to a lot of misconception and misunderstanding, and that the progress of American music would be more rapid, that it would more readily gain universal acceptance and respect, and would take its proper place especially with the mass of our people, were the term by which it is to be called not suggestive of an unpleasant phase in our history from which we have happily escaped.

Jazz presents to the mind disorder. It is suggestive of things unpleasant, or atavistic leanings of which we are all properly ashamed, of borrowings from savages, of near-orgies that have quite properly been combatted by those who have care of the young and the morals of youth. The word has evil associations. . . .   (ANON. 1924D:36 [SIC])

Although the writer for the *Courier* agreed with Lopez as to the implications of the word and pointed out that jazz had changed a great deal since its early days, he did not agree to Lopez's term, "modern music," and suggested finally that the term jazz be kept "until it dies a natural death" (*ibid.*). Apparently nothing ever came of Lopez's suggestion, for we do not read of it again.

Shortly thereafter, in July of 1924, Meyer Davis apparently offered a prize of a hundred dollars for a new name for jazz which "must . . . be at once both dignified and comprehensively descriptive" (Anon. 1924C:28). In the only report of this prize we have been able to find, editorial comment in the *Musical Courier* said:

> . . . [P]erhaps one should say that this attempt to get a better word than jazz for the expression of American popular music in its present stage of development is laudable. It is rather difficult, however, to see what difference the name makes; and it is still more difficult to believe that any such effort will actually change the name or prevent people from talking about jazz, as long as it is jazz, in the future just as they have in the past.
>
> The thing to change is not the name but the music, and, in spite of what Mr. Davis has to say on this subject, and what others have said, jazz is still jazz. A bit better, certainly, than the weird "ad libbing" of half a dozen years ago, but a perfectly obvious development from that style.
>
> However, may someone win the hundred dollars—and here's wishing good luck to a lively and vigorous contest.   (ANON. 1924C:28)

Again the Davis contest apparently never came to a conclusion, or at least was not reported in the press, and the lucky winner and his word remain unknown.

In the meantime two unsolicited suggestions had made their way into print. The first was one from Clay Smith, in August of 1924, who said: "But why stigmatize what is good in the music by the unmentionably low word 'Jazz'? . . . Why not call it 'Ragtonia' or 'Calethumpia' or anything on earth to get away from the term 'Jazz'?" (Anon. 1924D:595). The second was proposed anonymously in the *Musical Leader* in December of 1924: the word chosen was "syncopep," which, said the writer, "represents an honest effort to provide something new within the limitations of its exponents. . . . [It is a] new way of presenting old melodies" (Anon. 1924B:568). Although the author refers to jazz influence on classical music, it appears that he envisaged syncopep as the label for modern music, serious and composed or uncomposed—whether it was to apply directly to jazz as such is unknown.

This concern over a new word for jazz apparently disappeared by the end of 1924, and it was not until 1949 that a further attempt was made to find a substitute. This occurred probably primarily as a publicity stunt for *Down Beat* magazine which headlined its contest "New Word for Jazz Worth $1000" and commented:

> For years, musicians, writers, and critics have complained there is no word to describe the music of today. The term *jazz* has lost its significance. *Swing*

just isn't swinging anymore. *Bebop* refers to one restricted school. . . . The same situation existed back in the early 30's, when the word *jazz* had been applied to the music of the Ted Lewises and the Paul Whitemans and had lost much of its virility and color. . . .

Join the fun! Help select the word to replace outworn jazz!

(ANON. 1949A:10)

In a succeeding issue S. I. Hayakawa, Marshall Stearns, John Lucas, and Stan Kenton were named as judges (Anon. 1949B:1), and on November 4, 1949, the twenty-six winners were announced:

1ST PRIZE: CREWCUT ($1000 WINNER)	14. SWIXIBOP
2ND PRIZE: AMERIMUSIC	15. X-TEMPO
3. JARB	16. RAGTIBOP
4. FREESTYLE	17. BLIP
5. MOP	18. BEATPOINT
6. NOVACLASSIC	19. IDIOISM
7. PULSEMUSIC	20. AMERITONIC
8. MESMERHYTHM	21. IMPROPHONY
9. LE HOT	22. SCHMOOSIC
10. BIX-E-BOP	23. SYNCORHYTHM
11. HIP	24. BEATFELT
12. ID	25. SYNCOPE
13. SOCK	26. REETBEAT

In an editorial in the same issue (Anon. 1949C:1), it was said:

All of the judges concurred on one thing, that none of the hundreds of words which poured in could be accepted as a suitable substitute for *jazz*. . . .

Probably now we will revert to the continued use of jazz with more satisfaction and with greater assurance. It might be nice to utilize "crewcut" once in awhile, as a change of pace and to avoid monotony. But if any word ever replaces jazz it will have to be because, like Topsy, it "just growed."

Conclusion

We have reviewed here the various suggested sources for the word "jazz" revealed in the literature of the past forty-one years, and it is clear that the evidence for one is for the most part no better than for another. It seems to the present authors that the stories of variously named musicians probably have little basis in fact, while the original use of the word as a minstrel or vaudeville term leaves us only a little closer to the original source. The African and Arabic theories remain a possibility and deserve further research, while the English, Indian, and Spanish origins are fairly clearly unfounded. The relationship to the French *jaser* remains a distinct possibility, given the French influence in the Southern

United States and in New Orleans in particular, as does the early idea that jazz as a minstrel term involved notions somewhat similar to the French translation of that word. The reference to the French, *chasse beaux*, is indeed an intriguing one which should be vigorously pursued. The onomatopoetic and spontaneous origins are highly speculative at very best, but the association of the word "jazz" in its vulgar sense remains a distinct possibility.

The earliest associations of the word with music so far as locale is concerned refer, surprisingly, to San Francisco, a possibility which remains but which does not seem logical in view of our knowledge of the beginnings of jazz as a musical form. In any event it is reasonably clear that the term came into wide usage in a relatively restricted period between 1913 and 1915. Most early spellings seem to be a figment of the imaginations of the authors who devised them, and suggestions for new words have been spectacularly unsuccessful.

We suggest the need for linguistic and philological research although we are not at all sure that the origin of jazz, the word, can ever be found.

NOTES

1. The references to Osgood in this paper are to his book, *So This Is Jazz* (1926A). Osgood's chapter dealing with the origin of the term jazz was published separately in *American Speech* (1926B); the same information is available in both places.

2. Rudi Blesh, an authority on ragtime, writes: "Early in 1897 the first instrumental number completely in ragtime and so titled rolled off the printing presses . . . 'Mississippi Rag,' by William H. Krell" (Blesh 1950:100–01). The first major ragtime success was Scott Joplin's "Maple Leaf Rag," published in 1899. From this point to the beginning of World War I the popularity of ragtime continually increased. According to Abbe Niles, "The first so-called 'blues' was *Baby Seals Blues*, which appeared in St. Louis, on August 3, 1912" (Handy 1949:13). This was followed in quick succession by other blues compositions: "*Dallas Blues* was published in Oklahoma City, on September 6, 1912. . . . Handy's *Memphis Blues*, in Memphis, on September 28, 1912 . . ." (*ibid.*). We could thus date Lopez' reference to "Chaz" in Vicksburg, Mississippi (Anon. 1924D:520), as 1913, perhaps 1914.

3. Actually, the first recording by the Original Dixieland Jazz Band was made in New York City in January of 1917.

REFERENCES CITED

Anonymous

_____ 1917 "The appeal of the primitive jazz," *Literary Digest* 55:28–29, August 25.

_____ 1918 "Why 'jazz' sends us back to the jungle," *Current Opinion* 65:165, September.

_____ 1919A "A Negro explains 'jazz,' " *Literary Digest* 61:28–29, April 26.

_____ 1919B "Delving into the genealogy of jazz," *Current Opinion* 67:97–99, August.

_____ 1919C "Jazz origin again discovered," *Music Trade Review* 68:32–33, June 14.

_____ 1919D "Stale Bread's sadness gave 'jazz' to the world," *Literary Digest* 61:47–48, April 26.

_____ 1919E "Where the word 'jazz' started," *Music Trade Review* 68:50, May 3.

_____ 1924A "Jazz." *Outlook* 136:381–82, March 5.

_____ 1924B "Jazz now syncopep," *Musical Leader* 48:568, December 11.

_____ 1924C "Jazz prize," *Musical Courier* 89:28, July 17.

_____ 1924D "Where is jazz leading America?" *Etude* 12:517–18, 520; 595–96, August; September.

_____ 1926 "D'où vient S.M. le Jazz?" *Courrier Musical* 28:144, March 1.

_____ 1934 "Origin of the word jazz traced to West Africa by Princeton men preparing new dictionary," *New York Times* 19:6, October 15.

_____ 1945 "Origin of term JAZZ," *Jazz Session* 8:4–5, July–August.

_____ 1949A "New word for jazz worth $1000," *Down Beat* 16:10, July 15.

_____ 1949B "Judges named in 'word' contest—prizes pile up," *Down Beat* 16:1,19, August 26.

_____ 1949C " 'Crewcut' contest's $1,000 word," *Down Beat* 16:1, November 4.

_____ 1958A "It comes out jazz," *Down Beat* 25:10, May 29.

_____ 1958B "Tom Brown, leader in Dixieland jazz," *New York Times* 37:1, March 26.

Austin, Cecil

_____ 1925 "Jazz," *Music and Letters* 6:256–68, July.

Ball, John

_____ 1958 Personal communication, May 2.

Berrey, Lester V.

_____ 1947 *The American thesaurus of slang*. New York: Thomas Y. Crowell.

Blesh, Rudi, and Harriet Janis

_____ 1950 *They all played ragtime*. New York: Alfred A. Knopf.

Coeuroy, André, and André Schaeffner

_____ 1926 *Le jazz*. Paris: C. Aveline.

Farmer, Henry George

_____ 1924 "The Arab influence on music in the Western Sudan, including references to modern jazz," *Musical Standard* 24:158–59, November 15.

Finck, Henry T.

_____ 1924 "Jazz—lowbrow and highbrow," *Etude* 42:527–28, August.

Goffin, Robert

_____ 1932 *Aux frontiers du jazz*. Sixth edition. Paris: Editions du Sagittaire.

_____ 1946 *Jazz from the Congo to the Metropolitan*. New York: Doubleday.

Goldberg, Isaac

_____ 1930 *Tin Pan Alley: A chronicle of the American popular music racket*. New York: John Day.

Green, B. W.

_____ 1897 *Word-book of Virginia folk-speech*. Richmond: Wm. Ellis Jones.

Handy, W. C., *ed.*

_____ 1949 *A treasury of the blues*. With a historical and critical text by Abbe Niles. New York: Charles Boni.

Hart, James D.

_____ 1932 "Jazz jargon," *American Speech* 7:241–54, April.

Hobson, Wilder

_____ 1939 *American jazz music*. New York: W. W. Norton.

Johnson, Guy B.

_____ 1927 "Double meaning in the popular Negro blues," *Journal of Abnormal and Social Psychology* 22:12–20, April–June.

Kingsley, Walter

_____ 1917 "Whence comes jass? Facts from the great authority on the subject," *New York Sun* III,3:6–8, August 5.

_____ 1925 "Jazzbo, washed up, and gravy," *New York World*, Editorial Section, 3:1, October 25.

Kool, Jaap

_____ 1925 "The triumph of the jungle," *Living Age* 324:338–43, February 7.

Ludwig, William

_____ 1922 "Jazz, the present-day live issue in the development of American music," *Metronome* 38:78–79, May.

Mathews, Mitford M.

_____ 1951 *A dictionary of Americanisms*. 2 vols. Chicago: University of Chicago Press.

Mencken, H. L.

_____ 1948 *The American language*, supplement II. New York: Alfred A. Knopf.

Moynahan, James H. S.

_____ 1937 "Ragtime to swing," *Saturday Evening Post* 209:14–15 et seq., February 13.

Nelson, Stanley R.

_____ 1930 (See Goffin 1932:44–46.)

Newell, George

_____ 1928 "George Gershwin and jazz," *Outlook* 148:342–43 et seq., February 29.

Osgood, Henry Osborne

_____ 1926A *So this is jazz*. Boston: Little, Brown.

_____ 1926B "Jazz," *American Speech* 1:513–18, July.

Patterson, Frank

_____ 1947 "Origin of jazz," *Negro Digest* 5:53, April.

Read, Allen Walker

_____ 1935 "Two New England lists of 1848," *Dialect Notes* 6(10):452–54, July.

Redway, Jacques Wardlaw

_____ 1934 "History of term 'jazz' reviewed—divergent theories of experts are thus reconciled." *New York Times* IV,5:2, October 21.

Rogers, J. A.

_____ 1925 "Jazz at home," in Alain Locke, ed., *The New Negro, an Interpretation* (New York: Albert & Charles Boni), pp. 216–24.

Schneider, Louis

_____ 1924 "La musique de plein air: de l'accordéon au jazz-band," *Conferencia* 18:215–22, August 15.

Schwerke, Irving

_____ 1926 "Le jazz est mort! Vive le jazz!" *Guide du Concert* 12:679–82, March 19.

Singleton, Esther

_____ 1923 "Etats Unis d'Amérique," in A. Lavignac, *Encyclopédie de la musique et dictionnaire du conservatoire* (Paris: Librairie Delgrave), II:3245–336.

Smith, Charles Edward

_____ 1935 "Heat wave," *Stage* 12:45–46, September.

_____ 1939 "White New Orleans," in Frederic Ramsey, Jr., and Charles Edward Smith, eds., *Jazzmen* (New York: Harcourt, Brace), pp. 39–58.

Stannard, Douglas

_____ 1941 "The Negro and Tin Pan Alley," *New Statesman and Nation* 21:82–83, January 25.

Stjernberg, Lydia Nilsson
_____ 1934 "Finding merit in jazz," *New York Times* 14:7, October 20.
Tamony, Peter
_____ 1939 "Origin of words," *San Francisco News Letter and Wasp*, No. 5, March 17.
Vernon, Grenville
_____ 1919 "That mysterious 'jazz,' " *New York Times* IV,5:1–2, March 30.
Vizetelly, Frank H.
_____ 1934 "On the trail of jazz—it appears that Arabs, Spaniards and Indians also had a word for it," *New York Times* 22:6, October 18.
Weseen, Maurice H.
_____ 1934 *A dictionary of American slang.* New York: Thomas Y. Crowell.
Whiteman, Paul
_____ 1924 "What is jazz doing to American music?" *Etude* 42:523–24, August.
Whiteman, Paul, and Mary Margaret McBride
_____ 1926 *Jazz.* New York: J. H. Sears.

chapter 2

BENNY GOLSON + JIM MEROD

Forward Motion:
An Interview with Benny Golson

jim merod: I want to talk with you today about the history of the jazz tenor saxophone. Let me start this way. I asked Mark Feldman [president of Reservoir Records] who he regards as the definitive tenor saxophonist in his lifetime. He said it was Sonny Rollins who, in the late fifties, put everything together. You and I talked about 'Trane [John Coltrane] and all kinds of cats. Talk to me about Sonny Rollins. When you listen to Sonny, what's going on?

benny golson: As I look back in retrospect, without knowing it, Sonny always had that raw, primitive kind of thing. It wasn't worked out. It was intuitive, you know? I told him this, and he laughed at me. We were talking on the phone one day. I said, "You could get up at three o'clock in the morning and play to a thousand people." He started laughing. He had that kind of talent, you know? Not that he hasn't thought things out, but the things he played came out in a natural way rather than a preconceived way. A lot of things we hear today from saxophonists sound almost computerized, like they're practicing their scales. They're practicing certain licks and everything falls into place, good planning. But it feels like Sonny is motivated by feelings at the moment . . . I'm trying to find another word . . . an animal quality, almost. You know what I mean?

jim merod: Probing, searching, prowling.

benny golson: Yeah, and, really, that's what mankind spends its life doing: probing. The animals don't, but mankind and his intellect are restless. We probe. We are always trying to answer questions, and that's what I felt Sonny had, and is still doing, with the music. I ran into him at the airport in Paris, in

October of last year. We talked about a few things while we stood there, and the subject of tenor saxophone players came up. I said, "Well, how do you feel about tenor saxophone players today?" He gave me a horizontal notation. [*laughter*] No, he said we're missing a lot of the things that jazz needs to have. He said we're losing a lot from the heart. He says, "Oh, they'll dazzle with the notes, the footwork, and the dust they kick up, but when they really get down to it, some of the heart has gone out of it." I knew exactly what he was talking about.

I spoke with Mulgrew Miller. We did this Miles Davis tribute . . . that "I Remember Miles" album I told you about. I think I sent you a copy of it.

jim merod: With Eddie Henderson on trumpet.

benny golson: Right. Well, a fellow was over from Japan. He stopped by the house and wanted to interview me to get information for some notes for the album. That same record company had done a session the week before, here in New York, which is probably gonna wind up being an import. I don't want to mention the saxophone player's name. I asked, "How do you like him?" And as the words were coming out of my mouth, his head started to go from side to side. He said, "It's the newer breed. They're all out of the same mold." There's a sameness about them. In times gone by, if you heard Ben Webster or Don Byas or Dexter Gordon, [after] two or three bars you knew who it was right away.

jim merod: Exactly.

benny golson: Today, it's hard to do that. I'm talking about tenor saxophonists. I was in Japan a couple of years ago. . . . Anyway, they were interviewing me and were going to give me a blindfold test. I told them no. I wouldn't do the blindfold test because it was all tenor saxophone players. They wanted to know why. I told them it was because I found it hard to separate who's who anymore. I'd probably miss them all, and the blindfold test would be worth nothing. They would just see me fall on my face. I told them I'd rather not do it. It's hard to tell unless you go back and play a Ben Webster. I know who that is. Or Coleman Hawkins. Or Joe Henderson—he's an individual. Or Clifford Jordan, or Prez [Lester Young].

jim merod: All of these are powerful individuals—distinct lyrical voices without equals.

benny golson: Yeah, really, these are individuals. But these young guys—they're walking through life holding hands, imitating each other.

jim merod: Why is that happening?

benny golson: Why does that happen? I'll tell you. When Charlie Parker came on the scene, he came from a different perspective, a different viewpoint, which made him epochal, as far as the alto saxophone is concerned.

jim merod: What was that word?

benny golson: Epochal.

jim merod: I got you!

benny golson: You know, a new beginning.

jim merod: I hear you, yes. I understand.

benny golson: Before him, we had Johnny Hodges. We had Pete Smith. We had

Willie Smith. I can't remember all the names. Eddie Vinson was playing.

. . . .

jim merod: Alright.

benny golson: But when Hawk came, it was completely different. John Coltrane, Ray Bryant, and I were sitting in the Academy of Music in Philadelphia in 1945. We went to hear Dizzy Gillespie, but we didn't know who this one alto player was in the double-breasted pinstripe suit that was two sizes too small with all the buttons buttoned up. When he started to play, we almost fell out of the balcony. We had never heard anything like that in our lives. So, yes, Charlie Parker had an influence on saxophone players. Not only alto players but tenor players.

Now, Don Byas was there that same night, but he wasn't so different as to be reminiscent of Charlie Parker. Charlie Parker, on the other hand, and Dizzy Gillespie were reminiscent of each other 'cause they were playing something *different*. And it was those two that caused us to recast our thinking. Later on, from Charlie Parker recordings, John Coltrane started to find himself. This was on alto saxophone. Everything that he played eventually—not in the beginning, because he was a diamond in the rough, too, let's face it, but after he found himself—the things he played were so logical that when you heard them you would say, "Why didn't *I* think of that?" He did thing after thing after thing after thing like that. Then he went beyond that. "Boy, could I ever have thought of that? I wish I could play that. I wish I could think like that." Coltrane became the beacon for a lot of tenor saxophone players, and I must confess I almost got caught up in it because it was so different. It sounded so good. I think that's what happened to a lot of tenor saxophone players.

What I hear in the ones that have this sameness . . . they're not identical. I don't mean that. But this sameness—that reminiscent quality of John Coltrane on one level or another—always goes back to things that John did. It might be permutations here or there of what he did, but the root is John Coltrane. As soon as I hear it, I know it. As *soon* as I hear it. Some are good at this, some excellent, and some are terrible. And the ones who are good and have the same kind of talent that John had . . . what a disservice to them. I hear them play, and then I wonder how they really sound—because I feel like I'm listening to somebody else.

jim merod: Right. In a way, you're not hearing their thinking or imagination at all.

benny golson: It's a tribute to, a testimony to, John Coltrane. But it's a disservice to the person doing it. I've seen a few change, and I'm not gonna name names. One fellow was dead-on John, and he wisely sought to change. He was a good saxophone player, too. He started backing away from imitation, and his own personality began to emerge. I hate to put it this way, but I hear all the time that John Coltrane really messed a lot of tenor saxophone players' minds up . . . because he played so good.

John and I were constant companions in Philadelphia. There was a time when we were together every day when we were learning to play. We went to this concert and heard Charlie Parker and Dizzy Gillespie. What did we do after the concert was over? We walked up the street with Mr. Parker, and John was saying to him, "Can I carry your horn for you, Mr. Parker?" And I was saying, "What kind of mouthpiece do you use?" Playing like that, I had to find out his secret. "What kind of reed do you use?"

jim merod: You're walking with The Man.

benny golson: "What number reed?" "What model saxophone do you play?" And he told me all this stuff. I cataloged it, and I thought, "I've got it now." Two weeks later, John called me. He asked, "Did you try that stuff Mr. Parker was talking about?" I said, "Yeah." He said, "I did, too, but nothing happened." I said, "Me, neither." [*laughter*] Idiots. I mean, we didn't know it was the talent—not the reed, not the mouthpiece, and not the horn. It was the man and his mind.

jim merod: What year was that?

benny golson: That was 1945. I'd just met John, and he was playing alto. He sounded just like Johnny Hodges. His featured number was "On the Sunny Side of the Street" (à la Johnny Hodges). We used to have jam sessions at my house, and it got to be such a drag, because my mother loved to hear him play "On the Sunny Side of the Street." We met there [to play]. Ray Bryant was on piano. My mother would holler downstairs, "Is John down there?" And he'd say, "Yes, Mrs. Golson," and we had to go into his version of "Sunny Side of the Street" before we could start the jam session. I said to her one day, "Mom, this is really kind of a drag. Every time we're gonna have a session, you holler downstairs, and John has to play 'On the Sunny Side of the Street.'" You know what she said to me? "This is my house. You play what I want you to play." [*laughter*] I said, "Okay."

jim merod: That's wonderful. That's great. I love that.

. . . .

benny golson: Oh, yeah. John was eighteen, I was sixteen, and we were neophytes—in the real sense of the word. I mean, we were just getting started. We used to have so-called rehearsals at my house, and I'd go out and buy a seventy-five-cent, fifteen-piece arrangement written by Spud Murphy that sold all over the world, I guess. It's called a stock arrangement, and it cost seventy-five cents. I bought one by Count Basie called "Rock-a-Bye Basie" and "A-Train" by Duke [by Billy Strayhorn], and we'd have a rehearsal. We'd have one tenor saxophone, one trumpet, and one alto saxophone! [*laughter*]

jim merod: For a fifteen-piece arrangement?

benny golson: For a fifteen-piece band arrangement, yes. [*laughter*] No trombone. It was terrible, but we were learning how to read.

jim merod: Was Ray in on this? Ray Bryant?

benny golson: Yeah. He was our piano player. Ray Bryant was fourteen years old.

jim merod: Charlie Persip—was he there, too?

benny golson: I didn't know Charlie then. Ray and his brother Tommy, a bass player, were in on it. Ray was fourteen, his brother was fifteen. These two guys were geniuses. Any tune that they knew, they could play in any key.

Ray Bryant got all A's in school. Nobody knows, but this guy was a genius.

I'm deviating a little, but I have to tell you this. I was in high school, he was still in junior high school. We'd go on up to his neighborhood to this little luncheonette to have a sandwich and a Coke or something. Ray and I were sitting on one side of the table, and this girl and somebody else were sitting on the other side. She had her books with her, and while we were talking, she opened up a book. She was going to do her Spanish homework. She says, "I'm having such a time with this Spanish. I don't know verbs," or something. And so Ray is sitting on the other side, and the book is upside down. He says, "What is it you don't understand?" She says so-and-so. He's looking at it upside down, and it's in Spanish. He reads it in English, right?—the way it's supposed to be. [*laughter*] When I saw that, I said, "Man, this guy is something." This guy could have been an attorney, a surgeon. He could have been anything he wanted to be, he was that bright.

jim merod: I hear you.

. . . .

benny golson: . . . I was at Ben Franklin, and Ray went to the academic high school, which was Central High. That's where all the academic students went. He went with the brains; I went down with the thugs. [*laughter*]

jim merod: That's where your thuglike nature comes from.

benny golson: It's true, it's true. But that's where I was when I learned to play. We had musicians down there. We had a jazz band there. And it was during the war years. We had what was called a canteen down on the first floor. I still have pictures of that band. I'm sitting there with my legs open. I had all my hair then, too, boy! [*laughter*] Yeah, but I watched music change, you know? And I watched us change. We had to recast our thinking. Right in the middle of trying to learn to play our instruments and another kind of music, prior to Dizzy Gillespie and Charlie Parker, we were still trying to learn something. The old, established—the traditional—thing was ours. But then we got something new put in front of us.

jim merod: You got a double challenge: swing and bebop.

benny golson: Right. Then we had to recast our thinking. We didn't understand at all what bebop was about. We knew the other stuff because we grew up hearing it all the time. But then we had to make a transition.

jim merod: Who represented the central figure in the old tradition that you were pursuing, even as Bird turned you around?

benny golson: Coleman Hawkins.

jim merod: I hear you.

benny golson: Coleman Hawkins. Later, Don Byas. Don Byas won out for me. Those two. That was it, there was nothing else for me. I didn't see how they could take it any further. I didn't see how I could go past that. Just like when I saw the 1939 Chrysler, that model where the front looked like the back— the classic streamlined model. I said, "This is it. They can't go any further. They can't go any further than this." [*laughter*] That was that art deco period, all the streamlined stuff. "They can't go beyond this," I thought. And we sailed past it, right? We passed it. Things started to happen in jazz, and we just wanted to be a part of it. We were effervescent inside. I lived to wake up in the morning to go to my music, to the saxophone. I wanted the clock to speed by so I could get up and get back to it. "What a waste of time sleeping," I would think to myself.

jim merod: Yes, exactly. I still feel that way.

benny golson: And I wished I could just stay awake. That's the way it was.

jim merod: Benny, do you think that the change in the jazz world now, where the new cats sound like they went to the same school and play with the same reed, with the same sound, and the same chops, is the function of schooling or the fact that communities have changed? You don't have the organic enclaves of young musicians now, like you and Coltrane and Ray hanging out, working year after year together. Younger cats today have to leave the neighborhood and go to a place that is essentially academicized or institutionalized.

benny golson: It's interesting that you mention that. In the beginning, jazz was so new that we had universities with no walls.

jim merod: Right in the neighborhood.

benny golson: Yes. And it was an empirical process, trial and error, bouncing off of one another. We imitated others, but that wasn't the total end. We were highly eclectic. How could there be anything else? You know, we bought the records. We listened to them. I copied solos. But we used that as a basis, intuitively. We didn't know what we were doing, but we set up our own infrastructure upon which we could build things in the future. And so, we went to teachers. I studied piano, I studied the saxophone. I did a lot of listening, and that helped me to arrive at the way I played later in life.

None of us went in the same direction. We went in diverse directions. Everybody sounded different. John [Coltrane], as did Charlie Parker and Diz, became the cause of many people going into their own beam of light when they played. Oh, we had trumpet players when Diz came on the scene who started in that direction. I remember John Berry. And Cal Massey, who was imitating Miles Davis. But sooner or later, they found their own direction. Today, it seems like younger players get caught in that tractor beam from *Star Trek*. They can't pull free of it. Whereas we did. And we admired things even after we pulled free of them because they helped us to expand our minds and our imaginations, and they taught us how to use our imaginations. All ideas are processed through the imagination.

Our playing and writing wasn't always good. Some of it was god-awful, Jim. Some of the stuff that we did was horrible. Some of us learned. Some of us didn't. Some of us are still back in the hometowns doing the local things. I just saw one of these fellows a couple of weeks ago when we did the Clifford Brown Festival. He never got out of that local situation. Maybe it's for lack of talent, or not being aggressive enough, or not being able to absorb everything that went down. I don't know. Some guys were even less than that. I watched it. They would buy new horns, they'd have the bebop glasses, the berets, everything. All the paraphernalia—"paraphernalia," I call it—that you're supposed to have. Everything except the head and the heart. They didn't have it. With all their efforts, it just never happened. I mean, I felt sorry for them.

jim merod: You've presented some powerful anecdotes to me. As you and 'Trane grew up, you headed in one direction and 'Trane headed in another direction. I remember a couple of years ago, you said to me, "I can't imagine what it would have been like if Miles had chosen me to be in that band [the Miles Davis Quintet of the late fifties] instead of 'Trane."

benny golson: Oh yeah.

jim merod: I remember that marvelous moment of self-revelation and wonderment. But here's what intrigues me: As you were developing with 'Trane, at what moment, if you can remember, did you discover 'Trane's search and your search diverging? Coleman Hawkins and Bird were both pounding on you with alternate possibilities. When did that divergence, or that break, begin to take place?

benny golson: Almost at the very beginning, when we were still amateurs.

jim merod: 1945 to 1946?

benny golson: Yes. John had that quality of hyperintensity then. He was committed. He went at things with a vengeance. I took time for other things, like the movies, a girlfriend (who eventually became my wife), relaxing, going fishing with the family. John was at that music room *all* the time.

jim merod: He was obsessed.

benny golson: We might use the word *obsessed.* I'd say totally dedicated, which is the same thing. He found time for other things, too, but not as much time was devoted to them. And he would disappear sometimes. He would go into his disappearing thing, where he would involute completely and work on whatever he was trying to do, successfully or not successfully, and then he'd emerge again. When we'd hear Charlie Parker and Dizzy Gillespie, he'd disappear for two weeks. I told you about that two-week experiment with Bird's suggestions, when he asked me if anything happened. I told him no, and he says, "Me, neither." But he was sounding different! And that was when Johnny Hodges began to wear very pale, when something else was beginning to emerge. It wasn't Charlie Parker, but it wasn't Johnny Hodges, either. Johnny Hodges had been put down somewhere along the line, and 'Trane eventually began to approach the Bird-like thing, with one major difference I noticed: John Coltrane on alto had this big sound. I mean a big, beautiful sound, too. He did a couple records, I think, on alto, but . . .

jim merod: The one with Gene Ammons and Pepper Adams, for one!

benny golson: Yeah, and there's one that they play sometimes where he was doing "Cherokee," but he was a rank amateur then. He did some things after that, I think, with Dizzy Gillespie—Dizzy's Big Band. He was playing alto. But then the tenor started to happen. And I remember how that came about. A fluke.

He was playing alto with Eddie Vinson, who was a singer and an alto saxophonist himself. Eddie Vinson had a tenor player named Louis Judge, also from Philadelphia. Vinson had come through Philadelphia and had decided to pick up a Philadelphia band to work on the East Coast, I guess, 'cause he was from Kansas City. He used Johnny Coles on trumpet and Specks Wright on drums, and Coltrane on alto, and Judge on tenor. Whoever he had on bass, I can't remember.

They were playing this gig one night somewhere, and Louis had gotten mad at Eddie Vinson about something. Right after that, they took an intermission and just left their horns laying on the chairs. When they came back after the intermission, which was usually a half hour, the band struck up, and Louis didn't return.

jim merod: But he'd left his tenor.

benny golson: He'd left his tenor there, and he was just gonna drag his feet and be a drag. You know, he was gonna come back, but he was gonna come back when he was ready. He was just gonna be late to be obstinate.

They played this tune, and in the tune was a tenor solo. It went with the spirit of the thing. Eddie knew that the tenor solo was coming up, and he looked around, but Louis wasn't there. So, he told John to pick up the tenor and play the solo on the tenor. John said, "Man, I can't. It's not my horn." Vinson says, "Play the tenor." And so, John put the alto down, picked the tenor up, and started to play. It was nothing like his alto style. He'd been listening to Dexter Gordon, admiring him. He started playing this stuff, and it sounded so good. Vinson said, "Just go ahead and play." He went chorus after chorus, and wherever Louis was, he heard it, and he came running across the stage floor. [*laughter*] Ran up on the bandstand and said, "Gimme my horn." That was the end of the tenor solo.

jim merod: And that was 'Trane's first tenor work?

benny golson: Yeah. And he liked it.

jim merod: Cleanhead Vinson makes him do the tenor!

benny golson: Yeah, and he said, "Boy, that felt kinda nice." And people were talking about it. "Man, did you hear John? He played tenor." "Boy, he sounded like Dexter Gordon." He surprised himself. So he wound up buying a tenor.

The Eddie Vinson thing was just a passing thing, though. He linked up with a fellow named Johnny Lynch, a trumpet player from Philadelphia who had been in Dizzy's band, left the band, and came back home. Lynch was a jazz trumpet player. They had a gig every week at a skating rink that had dances. Every Sunday night on Bainbridge Street and Broad Street in South Philadelphia, somewhere like that. They got some nice things together, like Bird and Diz stuff. You know, "Donna Lee" and all that. John started to bring his tenor to the gig, and, as a novelty, he might play one or two numbers on the tenor, and then put it away, because he was an alto player. But he started pulling out the tenor more—he'd play one as much as he played the other. More time went by, and the alto started to get used less and less. And finally, the alto disappeared—he was playing tenor. I said, "Isn't that weird, he's changed over to tenor."

jim merod: Do you think that was, in part, because he heard his natural voice on the tenor sax, and he was thinking of Dexter, but this change also took him a step away from Bird and allowed him to focus on Bird's material in another voice with less terror and pressure?

benny golson: I think that might be exactly what happened. I don't think he ever forgot the things that Bird did. I think he incorporated them into Dexter's stuff because he wasn't a carbon copy of Dexter.

jim merod: No, of course not.

benny golson: But he had something that was very reminiscent of Dexter, but with other elements, too.

. . . .

jim merod: I want you to say something about your relation to Don Byas.

benny golson: Don Byas, yeah. For me, it was inescapable, because I thought like him. I thought, first of all, like Coleman Hawkins, 'cause I wanted to play like him. I loved that sound so much. So I was aware of Coleman Hawkins first, with his "Body and Soul." But then I heard Don Byas. It was like somebody put more into the pot and stirred it around, you know? I mean his attack, his sound.

jim merod: Where did you first hear him?

benny golson: On a recording, of course. I think the recording might have been "Candy." If it wasn't, it's something that I can't remember, but it was around that same time. His attack, the way he grabbed those notes with such determination . . .

jim merod: Aggressively, almost.

benny golson: Yeah, yeah. Do-do-do-do-do-do-do-do-do-do. Wow, he just grabbed it! It was almost like a physical thing. As his sound was coming to meet your ear, you reached out to grab it.

jim merod: A rough-and-ready sound.

benny golson: I agree. I met him years later, at the same time that I met another person out of his school, one of my idols, Lucky Thompson. I knew Lucky a little bit. They were both around a lot at the same time that I opened in this club with Art Blakey, the first time Art and I had been to Europe, that *any* of us had been to Europe—me, [Lee] Morgan, Bobby [Timmons], and Jymie Merritt. We were playing at this club, the St. Germain.

jim merod: What year was it?

benny golson: 1958. And sitting at the bar was Don Byas and Lucky Thompson. [*laughter*] And I had to play, you know! I said, "Oh, my . . ."

jim merod: "Isn't this just my luck . . ."

benny golson: [*laughter*] Yeah, but I just did what I did.

jim merod: This was at the St. Germain?

benny golson: St. Germain. It was in the district called St. Germain. About three blocks from Notre Dame. I played, and Don heard me. And he was so impressed, he said, "Boy, it's good to hear you." And he gave me a box of reeds! On that box of reeds, he wrote, "To my man, Benny." I think I still have that box, without the reeds, of course. I had that box until I moved back here to New York this time. All those years I kept that box. [*laughter*] We became friends. Lucky and I became friends. Ben Webster and I became friends. Coleman Hawkins and I became friends.

jim merod: How about Prez [Lester Young]?

benny golson: Prez I never got to really know. Bird I never really got to know. But all the other tenor players I met from that era.

jim merod: I thought you knew Jimmy.

benny golson: Oh yeah, I knew Jimmy Forest.

jim merod: Say something about Jimmy Forrest.

benny golson: I think he's from St. Louis.

jim merod: Yeah, he was definitely from St. Louis.

benny golson: I came to know him through "Night Train."

jim merod: We all did.

benny golson: I almost got to hate him because of "Night Train," even before I met him, because, when I went down to Miami to play with a local group from Philadelphia, I must've played that song three or four times a night. I hated it. And when I met Jimmy, I found out that he didn't play just "Night Train"— he played other things. He had a big sound and everything. That was, oh, I guess, 1956.

jim merod: He had chops to burn.

benny golson: Oh yeah, he could play! That's when I was with Bullmoose Jackson.

jim merod: Who?

benny golson: Bullmoose Jackson.

jim merod: Good old Bullmoose. Who the hell is Bullmoose Jackson?

benny golson: Bullmoose Jackson was a tenor player who used to play with Lucky Millender's band. The reason they called him Bullmoose was because he looked like a bull moose. How else can I put it? [*laughter*] I mean, his appendages were long. His fingers were thick. His feet were long and thick. He could stand up and look down and see all of his heels. I mean, his heels would shoot out. And his lips were extraordinarily big. He had a big head like the angel wrestler that died. He had big shoulders and long arms like a gorilla.

jim merod: You know, *you* can say this. I can't say it. It would be politically incorrect. [*laughter*]

benny golson: [*laughter*] Well, let me tell you . . . one night, we were playing at a club in Philadelphia, and it was warm. During intermission, I was standing outside, and Bullmoose came out, too. We were dressed nice. This other guy came out, and he had had a few. He said, "Mr. Jackson, I just want to tell you . . ." Now, Bullmoose was a singer and had a beautiful voice. This guy said, "You sure can sing. Whoo," he said, "I've never heard anybody sing like you before." And Bullmoose said, "Oh, thank you." Then the guy said, "But you are one ugly M.F.!" [*laughter*] I had to pretend I didn't hear it. He had to also, as though it didn't bother him. We were very embarrassed, man!

jim merod: This guy was so drunk, he was just telling the truth.

benny golson: He was just telling the truth. He was right, but Bullmoose was as nice as he could be. A nice man.

jim merod: Isn't that wonderful.

benny golson: And in that band, Bullmoose gave me an opportunity to write jazz stuff. The piano player was Tadd Dameron.

jim merod: No kidding?

benny golson: Yep. And eventually, I got Johnny Coles, and Philly Joe [Jones], and Jymie Merritt in the band.

jim merod: What year was this?

benny golson: 1952.

jim merod: Was Tadd Dameron writing for that band?

benny golson: He only brought things in that he'd already written. Tadd wasn't doing much during that time. Bullmoose said, "Well, look, if you're not doing anything, come on out and do a few weeks with me and make some money." So Tadd said, "Okay." But it wasn't his thing. He wasn't really moved. He came out, though. He liked the way I played. I had to audition for the band. They wanted to see if I could read, and I could. They wanted to replace the trumpet player, too. They said, "You know any trumpet players?" I said, "Yeah, a very good one." I asked Johnny Coles. He said, "Oh, absolutely. No doubt about it." So, he didn't have to take a test on account of my word.

Tadd has been a big influence on my life. The very first thing I wrote was called "Shades of Dameron." We played it, and people would come up to Tadd and say, "Man, I like that arrangement of your tune 'Shades of Dameron.'" He'd say, "What a drag!" but he'd only be kidding. You'd appreciate this, knowing him. He'd come up and give me the whole act. "Man, what a drag. They come and thank me for something that you wrote." But he was really commending me, you know. He was very proud of it since it *did* sound like his composition.

jim merod: I wish we had more of Dameron's stuff.

benny golson: Definitely. I wrote a lot of other stuff that the band played. They didn't record it, but we played it live. When we played St. Louis, at the Circus Club, half of the audience were rhythm and blues fans, and half were jazz fans. Word had gotten around. Man, we'd go through our stuff, and that band was popping. It was great.

jim merod: You never had a chance to record any of this stuff?

benny golson: They didn't want to record it. The alto player was the manager. He loved it. He used to play with Jimmy Lunceford. He loved it, and Bullmoose loved it. The record company wanted the same commercial stuff.

jim merod: Don't you wish you had some of that stuff, just to hear it again?

benny golson: Oh yeah, for certain. I wrote a thing called "Mr. Mysterious" for Jymie Merritt, because he was such a mysterious kind of fellow. You never could tell what he was doing, where he was. You'd look at him and try to figure out what he was doing. You'd see him with this person, and you couldn't put two and two together. So they used to call him M.M.: Mysterious M.F. That's what it was. I just called the song "Mr. Mysterious," because we called him M.M. [*laughter*] And we played that. I don't even remember what we sounded like, but we used to play those things all the time. I don't even know where the music is. Don't remember how it went.

jim merod: I want you to probe Sonny Rollins a little further. If we push the hypothesis that Rollins, in '57 and '58, in some way summarized the history of the tenor saxophone as you were talking about before—his raw, raucous energy . . .

benny golson: Yeah. Yeah.

jim merod: . . . then we come across the point you were getting at a moment ago: the quality of the *thinking* in jazz. Many people never get to the point where they think of jazz as a thoughtful expression. It's always considered improvisatory, as if it's a spontaneous overflow of powerful feeling. But it *is* thoughtful, and it is a thinking art. With Rollins's early recordings, like *Saxophone Colossus* and *Worktime*, you hear all of this remarkable knowledge somehow coming into a lightning-quick imagination that doesn't fully know what it's up to. Yet, it produces thinking that is provocative and utterly on a different axis than Coltrane, who heads off from Rollins at a ninety-degree angle. Am I making any sense here?

benny golson: Yes, absolutely. You're absolutely right. In Rollins's playing—and I don't know if he was conscious of all this, maybe intuitively—the way he played *was* like a summation of the tenor saxophone, because he had the big sound and he played ballads. He could play ballads reminiscent of Coleman Hawkins, and yet he could do other things that were almost comedic sometimes . . .

jim merod: That's exactly right. Someone once said Rollins's humor was "sardonic."

benny golson: . . . which ordinarily would have been an aberration, but, because such humor was part of the things that were in his bag, it was acceptable. If I had done that, people would probably have thought I was strange.

jim merod: Yeah, like, "You're putting us on."

benny golson: Sure. But his humor showed up even in the type of songs that he recorded.

jim merod: "No Business Like Show Business," "The Way You Look Tonight" . . .

benny golson: Yeah, he did those. And that thing for Looney Tunes. I mean, who would ever think of doing something like that? You know what I mean?

jim merod: Yes, I do.

benny golson: That's where he was coming from—not just for the sake of being different, either. It was part of his creative process, I think, things that he saw. Some were new, some were extrapolations, permutations. Nevertheless, he had that restless quality, too, of never being satisfied, just like John Coltrane. Being satisfied is a curse, I think. You tend to slow down or come to a stop. Just like having an ego problem. That brings creativity to a halt. The ego only looks outside of itself. I don't want to name names, but players get caught up in their own abilities. Sometimes they're right—they can play. Sometimes they can't.

jim merod: You don't have to name names, and you don't even have to nod in agreement with me, but Sonny Stitt is the obvious example—a musician who gets to a certain place, derivative of Bird, obviously, and then has a hard time with the next step. In my estimation, with Stitt, we hear a magnificent talent miss its own identity.

benny golson: Someone who can't walk away from the mirror. Very competitive, he was. Oh, yeah, he chewed me up, I remember.

jim merod: He chewed everybody up if he could get a hold of them.

benny golson: In Philadelphia, before I got out of Philadelphia, they used to bring him in. I told you about that, didn't I?

jim merod: No.

benny golson: There was a place called the Blue Note in Philadelphia. They'd bring out an artist to play with the local rhythm section. Sometimes, they'd bring in a local horn, just to make it provocative. And they brought me in with him. Every night he said, "Okay, let's play so-and-so, right here, at this tempo." He wouldn't ask me if I knew it. I knew most of them, but one night he called—I'll never forget—"April in Paris," and I'd never played it. Man, I stumbled through that thing. I just didn't really know it. He danced off the walls and ceiling. The next day, I went home, and all day—from sunup till it was time to go to work—I played "April in Paris." When I went to work and he asked "What do you wanna play?" I said, " 'April in Paris.' " I knew it then.

jim merod: Yeah. But then Stitt, out of orneriness, would play something else. If he thought you were here, he'd go somewhere else.

benny golson: Yes, but then I accidentally found out that he had certain areas where he was uncomfortable. He said, "What do you wanna play?" I said, "Let's play 'A Night in Tunisia.' They want to play it." The whole band said, "Yeah, oh, yeah!" Too much pressure on him not to. He said, "Well, okay, you go ahead and play it." [*laughter*] For some strange reason, Stitt couldn't play that tune. It's just two chords. He couldn't play it! And so he went and sat down on the side. I knew I had him. I played on the ceiling, on the walls— everything. I never forgot that. Years later, after I really got to know what I was doing, we became friends, and there was no more of that.

jim merod: Maybe the opposite of the narcissism that intrudes upon musical development is the comic talent at the heart of Rollins's playing from first to last. It's really emerged over the last fifteen years. You hear a sunny, Caribbean comic broadside that he developed over time.

benny golson: I agree with that.

jim merod: It was always there as an ironic, almost philosophical, self-reflection in the earlier, straight-ahead stuff he laid down.

benny golson: Yeah, he touched the water on the Caribbean thing, on St. Thomas. Years later, he came back and really got into it. All he was playing was triads with the vibrato that they use and everything else, as though he was Caribbean and playing what they play down there. He would play those things and sound like he was from the islands. And his family *is* from the islands. Another thing: he was never afraid. I don't think he's afraid, to this day, to take chances. [Thelonious] Monk said to me once, "You play too perfect." I knew it wasn't a compliment the way he said it. I didn't know what he was talking about. He let me stew for about a minute or so, and I couldn't figure out what he was talking about. Then he said, "You got to make mistakes to discover the new stuff." And then the light went on. I was just playing. I knew that two and two was four, and five and five was ten, and that was what I was doing. After that, I began playing like a mad man. [*laughter*] Playing stuff that

I would never have tried earlier. Falling on my face, getting up. I said, "He's right!"

jim merod: Were you playing with Monk?

benny golson: No, I was playing as a sub with the band Art Blakey had at that time. He was sucking me in little by little, and the next thing I knew, I was a member of the group. I didn't want to leave New York. I wanted to establish myself there at that time as a writer.

But I loved playing with Art so much, Jim. I think I would have paid him a little bit to let me play with him. I was having so much fun, and I learned so much from it—how to project, to play louder. He'd play a drumroll, and suddenly I was pantomiming. I was playing soft and sweet and mellifluous. It didn't go with what he was playing. He'd bash hard, and I'd play flowing and pretty and mellow. He'd be buzzing along, and I was pantomiming. I didn't get the message.

One night he did something to underscore that lesson. After doing all that, he came down with a crash, BAM! BAM! he gave me another one, and then he hollered, "Get up out of that hole!" [*laughter*] "Whooee," I said. "Oh my goodness." It all hit me. I said, "I guess I *am* in a hole of a sort." He was didactic, but he didn't know it. He was always doing that. He had a penchant for it. "Play, play dynamics. Don't always play it the same. Right here, come up right here."

jim merod: That's part of what Rollins was telling you in the airport a while back when he pointed to his chest and said, "Cats aren't playing from their hearts." What Blakey was trying to instruct you to see as a young man is that the heart has its reasons. Follow it.

benny golson: Right. You play the way you talk.

jim merod: Exactly.

benny golson: Play it. Just make it musical. You know, when we talk, we don't talk in a monotone. We're up, down. We have peaks, we have valleys. We pause, and that accomplishes certain things in the music. It gives you a chance to reflect, even if for a moment, on what you just heard. It sets up anticipation for what's going to happen. You know, a good speaker does that. Musically, it works the same way, too. Good players will do that intuitively, without knowing those things. They use space. Have you ever heard players fill up every nook and cranny, and start out double-timing? Where can you go after that?

jim merod: It's monotonous.

benny golson: It gets monotonous. You have to pace yourself. Take a breath. It works. You should build if you're going to play a solo. Build up. If you start out at the top, you've got nowhere to go. If you keep doing the same thing, and then back off, it's anticlimactic. Now, Sonny knows how to use all of that. He's done many wonderful things. His style is different now than it was in the period you're talking about—in the late fifties. It's different. And he's tried the electric bass, guitars with no piano. Last time I talked to him, he told me he was not using a set of drums but the conga instead. I've never heard that. But he says, "I don't think it's working very well." [*laughter*] He had used some young drummer. He had to let him go. He's very critical about what he does, and the person he's most critical of is himself. He's unmerciful, his wife says, with himself. He tears himself apart.

jim merod: This is a tough question—you don't have to answer if it seems inappropriate—but do you think that there is a clear reason why a man of Rollins's capacities—almost infinite capacities—does not explore that really remarkable period when he was so superior? For an eighteen- or twenty-four-month period, his recorded legacy stands out like one of the brightest diamonds. Do you think one of the reasons he wouldn't go back and enter into that musical space is fear of repetition?

benny golson: I don't know. I can't answer for him. But that certainly answers it for me. It does. People say to me sometimes, "Well, you don't sound the way you used to." That's not a positive statement. I say to them, "Thank you." They're putting me down, but I say thanks because, good or bad, I feel I have to move on. As I move on, some people might not perceive it as being better. They just see it as being different.

jim merod: Perhaps they want familiarity.

benny golson: My goodness, everything else changes. We're not dressing the same way we did. The cars are not the same. Architecture is changing. Foods are changing. People change. We get older. We don't stay the same. Why must everything always be the same?

jim merod: I listened to Benny Carter about four or five nights in a row last year. We were sitting together when he wasn't playing. He sits down now between his solos. I said, "Benny, you sound very different than you did twenty, thirty, forty years ago." I said, "It's remarkable the ways in which you take ideas into that back door you've always had in improvising, and yet you've extended that approach." He turned to me and said, "Actually, Jim, not so." He said, "I'm playing exactly the way I always did." He said nothing had changed. I tried to gently argue him out of it, but could not do so.

benny golson: [*laughter*]

jim merod: Benny does not play like he used to, even if his lyrical personality remains intact.

. . . .

jim merod: I've always thought I've heard a significant element of Benny Carter in your playing.

benny golson: I've heard that before from one or two different sources. But not recently. If it's there, it's not because I tried to put it there. It's just because, during my eclectic period, it was still in the jazz reservoir somewhere as a residue.

jim merod: Can you imagine what I hear that is the echo or the influence of Benny Carter on your approach?

benny golson: Sure I can. Sometimes I find myself—in fact, that happened to me yesterday when I was practicing . . . I got into a thing, and I said, "Oops. I don't want to go back to that." I felt myself slipping back. I was doing something, and I said, "I don't want to do that." I did it another way. Jim, I don't want to go back.

jim merod: Do you mind if I push this into a technical area? I don't know how to tell you what the similarity is between Benny Carter's improvisational logic and your own, but I hear it nowhere else except in Carter and Golson. It is what I called earlier this "backdoor" quality. There's a way that you move through the changes, invert the expected logic in some way. Carter inverts it, too. You both move into side corridors. I don't even know how to say this adequately.

benny golson: Oh, our oblique approaches!

jim merod: Yes. Absolutely different from other players, something that nobody else even begins to imagine. What is the technical quality of this nameless obliquity?

benny golson: What can I tell you other than it *is* oblique and that it happens at the moment? It's nothing that we work out. I don't think it's anything that can be worked out. I was talking to a fellow recently. I had him over to the house a couple of weeks ago and he was talking about diminished chords. I find a lot of fellows are going home and practicing certain things to fit certain situations, and I feel that it's cheating. It's not really ad-libbing. You go home, and you practice this thing. You memorize it, and you go on the job, and you play it. That man was talking about how he had worked out some things on a diminished chord, and he was trying to explain it to me. He asked, "Well, what do *you* work out?" I said, "I don't work out anything." He asked, "What do you do?" I said, "I learn the chord thoroughly, inside and out, and I find that I have many more possibilities than patterns would afford me. It's limitless as to what I can do then, once I really understand it."

jim merod: Great response.

benny golson: "I do things that I don't even know I'm going to do." He asked, "Well, like what?" So I said, "Well, I'll play a straight diminished chord." I then went through something based on the chord, and he said, "Whoo, gee. What was that?" I said, "I don't know, but I knew it was based on the chord." So, don't tie yourself down to patterns, learning patterns. Don't cheat yourself. You know that's like coming into this big building and just living in one room. You can go into any room when you want to, any time you want. When you learn the chord thoroughly, you can do all kinds of things. You can put in nonharmonic tones and notes that don't have anything to do with the chord. Then you're using something called tonal magnetism. The basic chord is going to influence you only if you are caught in the throes of that chord. No matter what you play, it's going to be within the boundaries of that chord. If you learn the chord, and you hear that chord, you'll hear the chord ringing like a bell when you're playing. Then you can do all sorts of things, and you know it's going to fit with the chord. That's what I was trying to convince him of. He's a very good student. Three saxophone players come by to visit from time to time. Two tenor players and one alto player. One of them is extraordinary.

jim merod: I think you've talked to me about him.

benny golson: Ron Blake. Yeah, that guy's something. He comes around and says,

"Show me something." He's with Roy Hargrove. This guy can play. He came down to my table one night, and I invited him to come back on a Sunday night and play. I'd like to give him a chance. Because *that's* where music's going, with the younger players.

jim merod: Well, it happened for you.

benny golson: Yeah, but I didn't tell you about that. We got put down by the traditionalists. When we were coming up, trying to recast our thinking. . . .

jim merod: You and 'Trane?

benny golson: Yeah. We played in the same bands together. But we were the aberrations, man. Ray Bryant was there to hear Dizzy Gillespie with us. All three of us were in one of these big bands, local bands, at the same time. Some piano players were playing stride. We'd play, and they'd say, "What are you playing? You play like you got a mouthful of hot rice." Bop drummers were trying to play. People would say, "Where's the bass drum?" And we'd play, and they'd say, "Where's the melody?" I mean, we got put down something awful. But I didn't care. The desire to play that new music was overwhelming. So, when I hear youngsters, and they're doing things different, my mind is wide open. Why does everything have to be the same? Some are better than others. When they come to me and ask, "What about this?" or "What about that?" I'm going to tell them. I have no secrets. I'll tell them all they want to know, and if they decide they want to use it, fine. If they don't, okay.

Same fellow as before—Ron Blake—was talking to me. "What can I do?" he asked. He can play a good sax. He plays classical saxophone. He did a thing with the Chicago Symphony on alto that's legit. You'd never think that he knew anything about jazz when you hear that recording. I mean, legit. He says, "What can I do?" I said, "Well, your sound sounds a little thin." We got to talking about that. I was showing him how to get more sound out of the horn. I told him that the sound of the sax is much like walking. Walking does not begin with the feet. It begins here, and the sound begins here in the head, also. You have to hear it here—in the skull—and all you're trying to do, then, is to realize what you're hearing. And when you do, the body is strange. It sometimes unconsciously does all sorts of things to compensate, to bring to life what's missing. Just as a blind man is more acute of hearing, or, if one leg is shorter than the other, you'll do certain things with your body to make up for that. If a guy's too tall, you're gonna see him stooping, you know. Your mouth—I wrote about this in my book—will sometimes intuitively, and involuntarily, if you are hearing all this and want it to come out of your horn, change shape in the cavity. The tongue might go to the back a little bit. You open your throat up. Different things happen intuitively, because you're trying to get at this sound whatever way you can aside from changing the reed and the mouthpiece. And the bite that you take on the mouthpiece, the size of your tongue and your lips—all these things come into play.

jim merod: I asked Jimmy Rowles one time how it was that Ben Webster got that incredible massive sound. He said that one of the things at work was the fact that Webster used the biggest, thickest reed he could get. When other saxophone players tried to play that reed, they couldn't make a single sound. They could not get it to vibrate.

benny golson: That's what happens with mine. Matter of fact, reed manufacturers give me reeds. They make a special reed for me, Jim.

jim merod: Rico?

benny golson: Well, it's a Rico factory, but they make Rico, La Voz, and several different brands. A lot of people don't know that they make this special reed for me. I went through many boxes of reeds—box after box of reeds. I was having problems because I wasn't getting my sound. One smart fellow there gave me the hardest reed they have, a #5 Rico. Not very many play on that one or the hard La Voz. This man came up with an idea. He made a box of reeds specially for me that are harder than what they normally make. When I was out in Los Angeles on one of my business trips, I took my horn to the factory. He took me to a room. He said, "Try one of these." I put it on, and that was it. But the only thing about it is, if your chops are not up to par when you go down to the lower register, you're gonna get a thump. Everything stops, because it takes more air to make the reed vibrate. So, you've got to have it together.

jim merod: In the diaphragm.

benny golson: You've *got* to have it there. Otherwise, if your chops are a little weak, it'll dominate you. You can play fine up in the high registers. But if you decide to go down low, you might hear a thump where the reed stops vibrating shut, and then nothing comes out. That can happen. You have to be careful. If you're not up to par, you'll have to play short phrases, because the air is expended more rapidly. When you play, you've got to make that reed vibrate. I find that I have more control with that kind of resistance. Give me a soft reed and my whole style changes—I'll play nothing that night. My whole style will change with a soft reed that's easy to blow.

jim merod: Why is that? Do you need to feel that resistance in order to think?

benny golson: Yeah, I need the resistance. Without it—now this is a strange thing—without that resistance, it's like giving a speech or a lecture on a fine PA system, where you enjoy the sound of your voice because it sounds so good. I play strange, and I play horrible, when the reed is soft. I can tell when somebody else is playing a soft reed. I can hear it. For example, when the reed is soft, you can almost put it up to your nose and blow it.

jim merod: Maybe this is true of many saxophonists, but it sounds as if you are always in some kind of a dialogue with yourself. The sound coming back at you, that you produce, continues to generate the sound, as if there are two voices.

benny golson: Oh, definitely. Absolutely. When that sound is bad, even if the reed is good, the sound is demoralizing to me. It's like somebody sticking a needle in and drawing something out, instead of putting something in, when you're playing. If you're listening to somebody play, and the sound is not good, you leave. We can turn off the record player. But when it's you, it's horrible. No matter what you do, it's you. No matter where you go to play that horn— whether it's in the men's room, down the hall, on the stage—it sounds terrible. That, to me, can be very demoralizing. And yet, there are people who can overcome that. Charlie Parker. It didn't make any difference to him. He could play anybody's horn and never lose a beat.

jim merod: And he *played* everybody's horn.

benny golson: Played them, he did.

jim merod: Had to.

benny golson: Right. And he always sounded great. And he always had *his* sound. I'm not one of those kind of people. Boy, if the horn is a little recalcitrant when the reed doesn't sound right, I'll still play, but I don't feel it. I'm not as inspired. When everything is laying right, and the group sounds good, I become inspired. It's a thing that comes every now and then. Not every night, not every night. I've had some good nights in San Diego.

jim merod: Well, you sure have.

benny golson: But that doesn't come every night. You can't say, "Well, tonight I'm going to do this. I'm gonna really be on it." To be inspired, you can't push buttons. And when it does arrive, you accept it, boy, with open arms!

jim merod: And you don't stop, either.

benny golson: No. You might be long-winded, and everything you set out to do—no matter how arbitrary it is, how removed it is, how far afield it is—comes out right. Man, you're sailing. You're sailing. You're in solitary, unoccupied, airspace above the earth.

jim merod: Whooeee!

benny golson: That's where you are. I can't put it any better than that.

jim merod: That's pretty good, Benny.

benny golson: That's where you are, then. Man, let me tell you, that's something to experience. And if you could just record it all—see what's happening not only in the mind but what's happening to your body functions, what's happening in the heart, when everything's epitomized . . . man, you're definitely in an altered state. In truth, we're usually in an altered state when we play, anyway. You see the things we do when we play—closing our eyes, raising our hands, and raising one leg off the floor. In a social conversation, you never think of doing anything like that. It's like digging in your nose. You know? I'll bend way down. Freddie Hubbard will turn around, spin, and take the horn out of his mouth, definitely in an altered state. I've talked to a psychologist about that. He asked me about the altered state. I thought about it, and then I wrote about it. I've seen people in an altered state play pretty bad, yet they were in an altered state. They were playing nothing. So being in an altered state doesn't mean it's consequential. It just means it's an altered state.

jim merod: When you're talking about the inner life of jazz improvisation, you also have that other phenomenon—a chord resonating in your mind. When you're really on, it's ringing. When you're not on, the chord is not so visible or sonically available to you, I would imagine.

benny golson: Chords are always available, but what you can do with them . . .

jim merod: . . . changes if they're not significant to you.

benny golson: Right, right. Right, that *is* the difference. People talk about music.

"Music is ethnic," they say. Music in and of itself is *not* ethnic. Notes are merely servants. They only do what we tell them to do. If we know how to write something that's ethnic, then it becomes ethnic. Music in and of itself is not ethnic. Notes are only tonal documentations of pitch, that's all. But what we do with them, now, that's something else. That's where the real heroes are. I've heard melodies that are awful. And I've heard some brilliant stuff, too. Some of Monk's tunes . . . I hate ditties. This guy, Monk, has written some of the most profound ditties you ever want to hear in life! I hate ditties, but I love his.

jim merod: By "ditty," you have in mind which of his songs? That's an interesting way to put Monk's cheerfulness.

benny golson: Any of his tunes. That's why they're recorded so much. They're ditties. Ditties are almost like little throwaways. Just something to pacify you while you're in the bathroom, you know. But what marvelous ditties Monk's are!

jim merod: "Trinkle-tinkle"?

benny golson: Yes, "Trinkle-tinkle."

jim merod: I thought that would be one that you're calling a ditty.

benny golson: What ditties this guy has written. The most profound ditties you ever want to hear.

jim merod: Maybe, more accurately, we could call them fragments.

benny golson: No, they're complete. Because . . . well, I'll tell you what it might be: Monk's songs might be fragments that are developed.

jim merod: That may be exactly what they are.

benny golson: Fragments that are developed. You could say that. But, in the end, they are whole things. Nevertheless, you might say they're fragments. Absolutely. Yeah.

jim merod: Well, Monk's compositions get into your own writing, and yet, you don't write in fragments. You don't like ditties.

benny golson: Not consciously.

jim merod: I'm wondering what pressure the powerful part of Monk's achievement—his vision and bizarre humor—adds to your work.

benny golson: What comes into my mind? I don't think it's Monk. I don't think "Monk" when I write. And I don't think of playing when I write. The saxophone player does not exist then. Benny Golson the saxophone player is not on this earth. He doesn't exist, because I don't think like that as a writer. I don't think anything about the saxophone. Conversely, when I play the saxophone, I don't have anything to do with Benny Golson the writer. I'm a saxophone player. When I come to the drawing board to write, usually the thing that dominates my writing is a melody. Something that's melodic. No matter what tempo it is, it has to have some melodic direction and content that I hope would be memorable. Something that's melodic. The other thing is rhythm. Melody and rhythm. Those two things I need in order to go to the drawing board when I'm gonna write something. I've got to have some find of melodic flow that's logical, but not so logical that it's predictable. But logical so that, when you hear it, it sounds like it could not have been anything else, even though it might be unpredictable. When I first wrote "Along Came Betty" . . . certainly that wasn't predictable. Nobody could tell where it was going when they first heard it.

jim merod: It has a waltzlike feeling.

benny golson: No, not to me.

jim merod: It has a skating, flowing, languorous movement.

benny golson: It might, by extension, maybe. But when I played in Japan years ago, and John Lewis was my piano player, he said to me, "It's so logical. So logical." And yet, it was different: the first eight bars in one key, the second eight bars in another key. Then it goes to a bridge. It finishes up and comes back to the same key again. With "Stablemates" [another Golson song], the structure on that thing is so different, you know. It doesn't have the usual number of bars. Miles [Davis] delighted in that thing when he recorded it. He said, "Man, that was really something. How did you think of that?" "That's just where my mind went," I told him. The song, even though it was a jazz tune, was melodic. It is highly melodic. It has a melody, rather than things that sound like documentations of pitch and are different than any melody.

jim merod: You said something earlier that was provocative. You were talking about ethnic music.

benny golson: "Music in and of itself is not ethnic."

jim merod: Correct. One could write ethnic music, however, but that becomes a caricature. I thought you were suggesting that.

. . . .

benny golson: Musically, it's Esperanto, a universal language, that theoretical universal language that we're talking about. I liken music to being a literal, universal language already, intuitively. I cannot say any more. I remember saying that Monk's " 'Round Midnight" played in New York and " 'Round Midnight" played in Italy will have the same effect on jazz fans. They don't have to try to translate anything. They hear the same things. No translation necessary. They understand the twelve tones that are being used to produce it. It's interesting.

jim merod: Now you open the corridor specifically to your theme. What is it, almost impossible for us to describe, that is so engaging about a song like "Along Came Betty" or " 'Round Midnight"? Both are jazz classics, but what is the magic at work?

benny golson: I love those songs.

jim merod: What is it, Benny, that provides such a hook in a song like " 'Round Midnight"?

benny golson: Simple. And people don't realize this. The magic is the basic thing that comprises a melody. Melodies are formed, first of all, by the choice of notes. Second, by the intervals between one note and others. And third, by whatever syncopation you use as a composer. So it's note choice, intervals, syncopation. The person who writes a good melody will know that if you go downward, you can't keep going downward. You have to make a leap up. And if you go up, you'll eventually have to make a leap down. You must have climaxes in your melody. And climax can come at the end of the tune, obviously, but you can have miniclimaxes. M-I-N-I. They can occur within the song. You can have gradual climaxes, say 25 percent—I'm just giving you a number so you understand—or 50 percent or 75 percent and end with 100 percent. There are all kinds of things that, when you understand them, will give you unusual melodies.

I think about all those things when I write my tunes. Every one of them. The notes, first of all. When I wrote "I Remember Clifford," I agonized over each note. And when I left one note, where was it going to the next note? That's the interval. A minor third has a sound to it, and when you go up a sixth, it has another sound. But yet, you can't arbitrarily put a sixth in here or a minor in there. It has to go along in the scheme of things. By the same token, you understand the term *tough love*—where something in and of itself might be valid, but it has no place in the scheme of things—so you forsake it in and of itself. You might have a great lick, but it doesn't work in the situation you have. "Let's not abuse it," you think. "Let's not push it. Let's save it for something else. Walk away from it." That is the kind of thing I'm talking about. Sometimes jazz songwriters don't understand that. They don't understand tough love. That term sounds right, so I'm going to use it.

jim merod: The notion of tough love seems to be a trope for aesthetic and compositional judgment.

benny golson: Absolutely, absolutely. Sound judgment. Sound judgment. Absolutely. Now, I'm gonna see if I can find something for you here on my computer.

jim merod: While you're finding it, talk about that Saturday night three years ago when you and Kenny Barron were playing together in La Jolla. You guys had played three nights in a row, and you included that incredible pair of Barron songs, "Voyage" and "Phantoms."

benny golson: You know, I was just learning "Voyage" then. The first time we played it, I made some mistakes on the melody.

jim merod: By the time you guys got to Saturday . . .

benny golson: I knew it by then.

jim merod: Wednesday, Thursday, Friday, you guys worked it out. On Saturday night, you played "Voyage" in the first set and you played "Phantoms" in the second set. If you remember—I certainly will never forget—you both took "Phantoms" out of the room, into the stratosphere. It went so far out it was almost beyond the audience's ability to respond, except with hilarity.

benny golson: [*laughter*] Yeah, I don't remember which night it was, but I remember being there and playing it.

jim merod: How the hell does that happen? What is it that gets into a band to make that kind of energy—dynamics—that build so completely, so perfectly?

benny golson: I'll print a hard copy of my recent written piece on that. I have it under the heading of "Performance." I explain that.

jim merod: Serious, serious madness. That stuff was serious that night.

benny golson: Okay, here it is: "Laws of Creativity." I really went through a lot of pain to get these statements down. Usually, people talk about the things that you do. I'm talking about things you don't normally do. A lull in one's execution, for example, because that's a part of creativity, too. I'm trying to give a viewpoint on the whole thing, the entire performing activity. Not just the meat, but the personalities, situations, and things like that. So, I'm talking about a lot of diverse things. I'm talking about ego, and I'm talking about punctuality. I'm talking about drugs, writing legibly so as to retrieve things, how important that is. And lulls—to know that they come about. That's a natural thing, and a writer shouldn't think, "So this is how it ends."

jim merod: [*laughter*]

benny golson: Which I've done sometimes, early in my career. You write to make a deadline, then you cut the whole piece. About eight o'clock, people in the studios are telling you, "Look, we've got to have it by so-and-so. Sit down and finish it." A half hour later you're still sitting there. [*laughter*]

jim merod: Recently, I was listening to Bird with the Tommy Potter, Duke Jordan, Miles Davis band that used to play the Three Deuces. They were recorded in 1947, and even in those awful reproductions of that group, what you hear is exactly what you were saying about Bird. He doesn't need to be in dialogue with himself. He doesn't have to have a certain quality of sound at work for him. The man was just always able to produce something. What you hear there has an almost Mozartean quality of joyful, sublime height.

benny golson: That's a good word for Bird's performing gift.

jim merod: Why is it so difficult for artists of all kinds—whether they're painters or poets or musicians—to enter into that quick, happy, elevated production of art?

benny golson: Because you get into artistic areas where you can't fully insinuate yourself into the immediate situation. You can't project yourself completely. You can't create situations that you'd like to be in. You just can't. It's like you can't say, "I'm gonna make that woman love me even though she's madly in love with someone else." You might pull it off, but you can't depend on it. I mean, you just can't. Certain things just have to be right. Sometimes you don't have control over what those elements are. Some elements might be present, and yet the situation is still bereft of elements that might be keys to your own creativity. Perhaps one little thing is not happening, and you don't know what that is. But for things to happen at a high level, circumstances have to fall into place. *Then* it happens. Other than that, it's not gonna happen. Some guys want to play, the rhythm section is cooking, and they've got a new instrument. But they don't have the talent, or maybe they don't know the tune. Maybe they feel uncomfortable because they're used to playing with somebody else. They can't get this elevator thing going. They can't get off. They can't get enough speed to get off the landing field. Sometimes that happens. I heard Phil Woods use a phrase. He said, "I couldn't get up tonight." It's like taking off. He couldn't, so then he's just going around the field. He couldn't get up. He said, "I couldn't get up tonight."

jim merod: Certainly a telling phrase, a double entendre.

benny golson: You can't control it.

jim merod: Well, all this has something to do with self-confidence.

benny golson: That's a part of it.

jim merod: Also, group dynamics and the chemistry of human relationships.

benny golson: That's what I'm thinking, too.

jim merod: And it has to do with talent.

benny golson: Yeah, exactly what's at risk in the act of creativity.

jim merod: So you get all those things . . .

benny golson: All those things in the same pot brewing. That's when personality is involved. Definitely. I speak about that in my piece on performance, too. Certain personal things. You feel a certain way, therefore certain things are, or are not, going to happen.

. . . .

jim merod: How do you see the future of jazz in a world in which there are very few neighborhood communities of the kind that you and John Coltrane grew up in, the kind in which the generation (or almost a generation) ahead of you— Red Rodney, Buddy de Franco, and Joe Wilder in Philadelphia—also grew up with stable support structures. Many cats in New York once had that experience, too. And there was once a San Francisco scene for young musicians to work and learn together. But that world's not out there anymore. The young players have to get the Jamie Ambersoll tapes, or go to North Texas State University, or to the Berklee School [College] of Music. How does jazz stay fresh and dynamic? Perhaps, during the Vietnam War, everything in our society changed. The economics of culture changed, and jazz retreated and then became commercialized. Some young musicians are getting benefits that older musicians never received, because record companies are looking to exploit a "youth market." They sign young kids but forget legendary players who are still very much alive. That creates an imbalance not only for jazz as a whole but for these young musicians who are given unearned opportunities to perform at levels they're not up to.

benny golson: I understand. I understand all of that. You're right.

jim merod: I'd like to hear your thoughts about this crisis of "the jazz scene."

benny golson: I think I understand all of this. The brain is an organ, part of a central nervous system that you can see, look at. You can touch it, you can smell it. The mind, on the other hand, you can do none of those things with, and yet it's a product of the brain. The mind is capacious. It's capable of holding incalculable amounts of information. It's much more functional than the best computer we have now. It can reason. And yet, unfortunately, some of the musicians of this era whom you're talking about use only a small portion of their minds. I think that's where the problem is.

First of all, I have to say that, overall, musicians have to recast their thinking about what they're doing. Those who tend to sound the same are focusing only on a small area of music. You've got to get back to basics. Some of the younger ones are doing that. What I mean is that, even after they have developed, they become eclectic in their listening. I went on a trip, took all young musicians with me, and what music did they take? They had Louis Armstrong. They had Louis Jordan. And I said, "Now, what's happened?" This young trumpeter, Terrence Blanchard, was one of them. He was listening to Louis Jordan and some people that you would think are not jazz musicians. Earl Bostic, for instance. This is what I'm talking about. They're trying to broaden their range of interests, I guess.

jim merod: I wonder what a kid can get out of Earl Bostic.

benny golson: Technique.

jim merod: I suppose.

benny golson: Technique, I mean—not style. Certainly not style, but some technique. John Coltrane used to talk about Bostic all the time. But many younger players are painting themselves into a very small area. Music—not necessarily jazz, but music itself—has no boundaries. Some of these fellows are putting boundaries all around themselves because of immaturity, because of limited taste, because of what's expedient financially, because of being used and not knowing that they're being used. There are people out there who use them. Exploitation begins the minute young musicians are acclaimed as icons. They are not really icons, of course, but, potentially, they might be. Potential means that which exists in possibility. And one of the things that helps them now— I use that word *help* advisedly—is that the people who promote this thing called jazz see that they're young and that they've got talent. So, how do the promoters palm them off to the listening audience, some of whom are informed, some of whom are not, and some of whom don't care? Imagine this. Here's a man who's new on the scene. He's eighteen years old, and he's the newest thing since Santa Claus, and you've got to hear him. He's fantastic. And they might get a little . . . what do you call that . . . testimonial. "So-and-so says he's great." Like they did Ornette Coleman when he came on in the late fifties. "John Lewis says he's great." "Gunther Schuller says this man," et cetera. "Leonard Bernstein says he's this and that."

jim merod: He *must* be great, then, right?

benny golson: Sure, if he's got his own album, he's only eighteen, and Ron Carter's playing bass with him. Ron told me about that. He said, "No, I won't record with this guy. You're not gonna make use of my name helping to promote him." Jim, they came to me, too, a while back, to help . . . who's the trumpet player being plugged right now, the one who is playing with Ron Blake?

jim merod: Roy Hargrove.

benny golson: Yeah. They wanted me to do an album with him six years ago. I told them no. No, no, no, no. The idea was to give him credibility. I said, "No. No, I don't think so." Some of these guys can play. But they're not there—wherever that is—yet. They're not where John Coltrane was at their age. I don't care how bright the star is. They're not where Sonny Rollins was, or Coleman Hawkins, or Don Byas. That takes time, man. It's a disservice to the youngsters who get caught up in this, because they, like the audience, start to believe the hype. And when you start believing that you're there, you don't have to try so hard anymore.

jim merod: The death of the spirit.

benny golson: Yeah. I saw Elvin Jones the other night, and we were talking about a young tenor player, I heard him, and I said, "He sounds good." When I say he sounds good, I don't mean he sounds like John Coltrane or Sonny Rollins, but, relatively speaking, he sounds good. But I'm always thinking of potential. Jim, how well are you going to play when you're eighteen or nineteen years old? What will you have to draw upon? What kind of experience would you have had?

jim merod: Not much.

benny golson: That's exactly what Elvin says about this young tenor player. He says, "Yeah, I've been trying to talk to him because he's playing okay, but he's playing lots of licks, things that you've heard before, you know." That is not taking the thing that we love so much about jazz, not really taking it forward. This imitativeness causes jazz to spin around in place rather than move on. And that disturbs me, because I would like to see it be the way it used to be, when you'd hear a couple of notes and you'd know who it was. Today, I can't, especially with the tenor players. It's hard for me to tell who's who anymore. It seems like they have the same attack, the same phrasing, the same patterns. They're not carbon copies of each other, but there's such a similarity, it sounds like they all went to the same school, had the same teacher, and studied out of the same book. And listened to the same records. You know what I mean?

jim merod: Because that's basically true.

benny golson: In many instances, I don't think I'm hearing the person that I'm listening to. I'm hearing somebody else, or a composite person, out there. That's what I feel. Particularly with saxophonists. It shouldn't be like that, and maybe it will turn around. Maybe it'll turn around. But in order for it to turn around, the young players are going to have to recast their thinking. They're going to have to listen all over again, and not just listen to one or two people. You have no idea the people I've listened to. It's ridiculous the people I've listened to, and the kinds of music I now listen to. I listen to some of the old rock 'n' roll, and I listen to some of the new stuff. The rap stuff I can't listen to much, but I'll listen to it to see what they're doing rhythmically. I listen to country and western, and I listen to the classics. I also listen to opera because of my wife, Bobbie. I listen to big bands. I listen to artists of the day and from the past, and I find that refreshing. As Elvin said, and I quote him in my book, "You can't lock into any one thing; you have to be flexible, because music is always changing." Like Sonny Rollins, if I can remember his quote. He said, "No musician is ever satisfied from one day to the next, because he always feels it can be better." And a truly great person feels like that. If you stand there rubbing and petting and deifying that thing you have written, the whole world and time itself is moving on. Then you automatically are behind the times. We have to make time our confederate. And that's a good thing, because time moves in one indefatigable direction, and that's always forward. Time has never been known to move backward, not in this world. We're always going to come up with new things, permute some of the old things, extrapolate, but give them some kind of luster they didn't have before. I think that's what creativity's about. It always has what I call forward motion. We always want to be moving forward. I don't know any really consequential creative people who are standing still. Samuel Beckett wrote once, "I heard a voice say, 'Imagine.'" That stays in my mind. "Imagine." And I say, "Yes, I hear that same voice." Creative people I know hear that same voice. "Imagine. What if?" Man, that's the fuel that propels us forward. What if? Boy, that's something to get involved in. What an adventure that is. That's exciting.

jim merod: A few weeks ago, you said something that kind of startled me.

benny golson: What's that?

jim merod: You spoke right to an awareness that I'd been holding for many weeks before that. When we talked you went right to it. I don't know how we got there, but you said, "Jim, probably the best tenor saxophonist of the Coltrane school playing right now is Pharoah Sanders."

benny golson: People don't realize that.

jim merod: Exactly.

benny golson: Even other tenor players. I mean, he's right out of the John Coltrane school.

jim merod: Oh, absolutely.

benny golson: Other tenor players will tear you up with all those notes, but Pharoah's going in another direction. John Coltrane could play one note and lay you out. I don't hear other saxophone players doing that. They're all over the horn, but they don't give you the one note. And it's the slow tempo—it's the ballad—that is the acid test. When you're playing a fast tempo, you can hide. There are lots of hiding places. You can skim by. But when you slow it down, you're stripped of all your clothing. You're totally exposed. Nowhere to hide. And whatever's there in your art, that's what's gonna come out. And if it's not there, people will see it's not there on the ballad. But Pharoah has that great sound. I said, "Pharoah, if I had your sound or your soul!" He doesn't walk around with a big chest, though.

jim merod: He's very humble.

benny golson: Right, a very humble man.

jim merod: But he's spirited, and he does all the things you're pointing to. Dexter [Gordon] used to say the litmus test for the tenor saxophone player is "Body and Soul." What are some ballads that, for you, divide the real thing from the fraud?

benny golson: You know what? Any ballad. Just take the tempo down. I don't care what it is. Then the player is totally exposed. No double-timing or triple-timing. Play it right, but play a ballad as a ballad. That's the litmus test, right there.

jim merod: Almost nobody talks about Bird in terms of his ballad playing, the way he used to play "Laura." And yet, the way he played "Laura" was astonishing.

benny golson: He sang into his horn. Not literally, but it sounded like he was singing to his horn. Talking about that, Sonny Rollins is one of those players who used something from the old school when he played ballads. And you know what that was? He learned the words to the song as he learned the melody.

jim merod: That was Dexter's trick, you know.

benny golson: They learned the words. That tells you something.

jim merod: Play it like you're speaking the words.

benny golson: Yeah. That places a musician inside the song rather than beside it, or on top of it, or under it.

jim merod: Which is why I like singers who give lyrics room to gather light. When a singer like Mary Stallings sings, you hear the words afresh. And you hear the melody set off. You hear a human being present herself, and you feel your own relations to the world redefined.

benny golson: That's true for a horn player, too, you know. If the words are going through your mind, it gives you certain feelings, because the words tell a story, and you just happen to be along for the ride with your instrument. As the story is being told, essentially you're telling the story, too—the story that you've heard and are hearing again. You're telling that story.

jim merod: You know another storyteller, a great saxophonist of monumental proportions—Cannonball [Adderley].

benny golson: Oh yeah. "Stars Fell on Alabama." He used to play that tune, and that was from the old school. I used to say, "Why would a modern saxophone player who played so hip be playing 'Stars Fell on Alabama'?" He played it because he liked it. Why shouldn't he? Who's to say who should not do something? If somebody says, "I play trumpet, but I want to tap-dance while I play the trumpet," who's to say he shouldn't do it? Perhaps I want to record with a piccolo and a herd of elephants. Well, if you can get the herd of elephants, and the place is strong enough to hold them, why not do it?

jim merod: For example, you find Pharoah Sanders doing that African juju stuff when he puts bells on his ankles. He does a whole lot of dancing then, right in the middle of, say, his first set.

benny golson: Oh really? I didn't know that.

jim merod: Absolutely. I mean, he'll lay you out with a ballad. He'll rip it up with something that is very fast. And then he'll go over to that juju stuff. Truly infectious energy there.

benny golson: That's alright. Why shouldn't he? People say to me, "Oh, you don't sound the way you used to. Why don't you play that way?" I will not permit anybody to micromanage my life. I resist it. I resist it. Yet, I'm not unreasonable, because I'll always listen. I always listen first to make sure that I'm in tune and that I'm not doing something that's crazy or unreasonable.

jim merod: Given what you're saying about the jazz culture today, part of the problem—at least with the relative absence of big bands—can be put in a very specific and eccentric form. Duke Ellington, over the course of fifty years, not only wrote for individual members of a band for which he had a unique professional admiration but also set up in his writing and in his orchestras a context of intimacy—an ensemble, in fact, in which the saxophone always emerged. In the Ellington Orchestra, whether it was Harry Carney or Johnny Hodges or Ben Webster or Paul Gonsalves, the saxophone sound carried a special kind of majesty. Young players today don't have many bands to play in that would allow them to step forward, and they seldom ever hear such beautiful and majestic sound.

benny golson: No, they don't have that. Musicians will never again get the benefit of that kind of experience unless music changes somehow. But that's passé now, the things that Duke did. It doesn't mean that his work is not valid. It's just from another era. There's room for all of us if we make room for the newer things. But that doesn't mean that older things are not worthy of our love. They're not defunct. The musical book just gets thicker. The things that Duke did are highly consequential, even though there might not ever be another orchestra like Duke Ellington's. Jazz musicians come together and do things in honor of him, but there's no ongoing moneymaking thing from day to day. That might not happen again.

jim merod: The economics of travel would prevent it, no doubt, Frank Foster's success in keeping a version of Count Basie's band going notwithstanding.

benny golson: Right. But the big band is a thing we keep going back to. We keep going back to it because it has been so valid and consequential for so long. It has been kitchen-tested.

jim merod: Let's end on a note that looks ahead with that sense of the movement forward you were talking about earlier.

benny golson: Of forward motion?

jim merod: Yes. Do you see a way to bring the jazz heritage into the school curriculum, or into greater educational awareness, without a revolutionary change in the school system?

benny golson: [*laughter*] Well, you might have said part of it for me, because I wrote an article a while ago for the music educators' magazine. You know, they have a thing every year—what do they call it? It's like a seminar . . .

jim merod: Is it NAJE [National Association of Jazz Educators]?

benny golson: Yeah, that's it. I was asked to write something, and I know I made some enemies when I wrote my article, because I stated in it that students are getting shortchanged. Not totally, but in certain areas, because we find, in place after place, teachers who didn't, or couldn't, make it in the mainstream of things, in the workplace, playing at clubs and recording. They couldn't make it there, so they became teachers.

jim merod: That's the old joke, of course—if you can't do anything else, become a teacher.

benny golson: I base this observation on a lot of experience.

jim merod: Old jokes sometimes have their truths.

. . . .

benny golson: Students who are forming concepts, trying to get their musical infrastructure into place, should be given every advantage. *Every* advantage. Don't walk them up the narrow corridor when the boulevard is there. Give them the benefit of everything. Everything that you can possibly do. If economics is a problem, then maybe certain things can't be done in the schools. But let students know about it all. Later, on their own, they can get this recording and listen to it, or hear that arrangement.

I met a little kid the other day. Since he's learning how to play classical guitar, I gave him two CDs by Andrés Segovia. He called to thank me. I asked him what he thought about Andrés Segovia. He said, "Oh, it's unbelievable." I said, "Well, you already knew about him, didn't you?" He said "No, I've never heard of him." So, we got to talking about jazz, and I mentioned Dizzy Gillespie. He said, "Who?" Some of the teachers are going to have to get themselves out of teaching. That's obvious. Not in every case. I'm talking about certain instances. They have to get themselves out of the way. It's not about them, or their personalities. It's about helping the student to realize his goals, to become what he wants to become, a professional musician who's capable of performing and/or writing and making a living. It's not about the teacher and his ego.

jim merod: I think, in many fields, that is what the professor wants the student to be: a disciple.

benny golson: Right. Right. And it's not about that. It's not about that at all. I feel that is happening many times in the world of jazz education. But it's not about the teacher. It's about the student. It's about the student.

chapter 3

JAMES A. SNEAD

Repetition as a Figure of Black Culture

The Scope of Repetition in Culture

The world, as force, may not be thought of as unlimited, for it *cannot* be so thought of; we forbid ourselves the concept of an infinite force as incompatible with the concept "force." Thus—the world also lacks the capacity for eternal novelty.   (NIETZSCHE, *The Will to Power*)

After all, people have by now had to make peace with the idea that the world is not inexhaustible in its combinations, nor life in its various guises. How we have come to terms with the discrepancy between our personal growth—the very model of linear development—and the physical plane upon which life unfolds, characterized by general recursiveness and repetition: this must be the concern of culture. "Coming-to-terms" may mean denial or acceptance, repression or highlighting, but in any case *transformation* is culture's response to its own apprehension of repetition.

Apart from revealing or secreting the repetitions of material existence, a third response is possible: to own that repetition has occurred, but that, given a "quality of difference" compared to what has gone before, it has become not a "repetition" but rather a "progression," if positive, or a "regression," if negative. This third response implies that one finds a scale of tendencies from culture to culture. In any case, let us remember that, whenever we encounter repetition in cultural forms, we are indeed not viewing "the same thing" but its transformation, not just a formal ploy but often the willed grafting onto culture of an essentially philosophical insight about the shape of time and history. But, even if not in intentional emulation of natural or material cyclicality, repetition would need to manifest itself. Culture as a reservoir of inexhaustible novelty is unthinkable. Therefore, repetition, first of all, would inevitably have to creep into the dimension of culture just as into that of language and signification because of the finite supply of elementary units and the need for recognizability. One may readily classify cultural forms according to whether they tend to admit or cover up the repeating constituents within them.

The important thing about culture is that it should not be dead. Or, if dead, then its transformations must continue to live on in the present. Culture must be both immanent and historical: something *there* and something to be studied in its present form and in its etiology. Our modern notion of "culture" only arises early in this century, after a 500-year period of English usage as a noun of process rather than identification, referring rather to the tending of animals or crops than to types of music, literature, art and temperament by which a group of people is aware of and defines itself for others and for itself.[1] But this initial connotation may still be preserved. "Culture" in its present usage always also means the *culture* of culture: a certain continuance in the nurture of those concepts and experiences that have helped or are helping to lend self-consciousness and awareness to a given group. Culture must not only be immanent now but also give the promise of being *continuously* so. So the second way in which repetition enters the dimension of culture is in the necessity for every culture to maintain a sense of continuity about itself: internal changes notwithstanding, a basic self-identity must not be altered. Strangely enough, however, what recent Western or European culture repeats continuously is precisely the belief that there is *no* repetition in culture but only a difference, defined as progress and growth.

It was Swift who said that "happiness . . . is a perpetual Possession of being well deceived."[2] We are not far here from a proper definition of culture. At least a type of "happiness" accrues through a perpetual repetition of apparent consensus and convention that provide a sense of security, identification and "rightness." Yet, however fervently culture nurtures this belief, such a sense of security is also a kind of "coverage," both in the comforting sense of "insurance" against accidental and sudden rupturing of a complicated and precious fabric, and in Swift's less favorable sense of a "cover-up," or a hiding of otherwise unpleasant facts from the senses.[3] Like all insurance, this type of *coverage* does not prevent accidents but promises to be able to provide the means to outlive them. Furthermore, this insurance takes full actuarial account of the *most* and *least* likely points of intrusion or corruption to the self-image of the culture, and covers them accordingly.

For example, most cultures seem quite willing to tolerate and often assimilate certain foreign *games*—such as chess, imported to Europe from the Middle East as early as the First or Second Crusade in the twelfth century, or lawn tennis, developed and patented in England in 1874 from an earlier form of tennis. The fate of foreign *words* in language, however, has been frequently less happy, as witnessed in the *coverage* that European national languages institute against diluting "invasions of foreign words" exemplified in England by the sixteenth-century "Cambridge

School" (Ascham, Cheke and Wilson), in seventeenth-century France by the purism of Boileau and the Académie Française (a linguistic xenophobia which has by no means yet run its course) and by the recurrent attempts to expel foreignisms from the German language beginning with Leibniz in the seventeenth and Herder in the eighteenth century (most recently seen in the less innocuous censorship of the National Socialists in the current century).[4]

Finally, as in all insurance, you pay a regular premium for *coverage*: culture has a price. Might Swift's phrase "Flaws and Imperfections of Nature" not also include the daunting knowledge that the apparently linear, upward-striving course of human endeavor exists within nature's ineluctable circularity, and that birth and life end up in death and decay?[5]

Cultures, then, are virtually all varieties of "long-term" coverage, against both external and internal threats—self-dissolution, loss of identity; or repression, assimilation, attachment (in the sense of legal "seizure"); or attack from neighboring or foreign cultures—with all the positive and negative connotations of the "cover-ups" thus produced. Black culture is no exception. Cultures differ among one another primarily in the tenacity with which the "cover-up" is maintained and the spacing and regularity of the intervals at which they cease to cover up, granting leeway to those ruptures in the illusion of growth which most often occur in the *déjà-vus* of exact repetition.

In certain cases, culture, in projecting an image *for others*, claims a radical difference *from others*, often further defined qualitatively as *superiority*. Already in this insistence on uniqueness and "higher" development we sense a linear, anthropomorphic drive. For centuries (and especially within the last three) Europe has found itself in hot contest internally over this very issue. Culture has been territorialized—and, with it, groups of its diverse adherents. Cultural wars have become territorial wars have become cultural wars again, and indeed into this maelstrom have been sucked concepts of "race," "virtue" and "nation," never to re-emerge.[6] What startles is not so much the content of these cross-cultural feuds as the vehemence and aggression with which groups of people wrangle over where one *coverage* ends and another begins. The incipient desire to define "race" and "culture" in the same breath as "identity" and "nationality" finally coincides with the great upheavals of the seventeenth and eighteenth centuries in Europe— among them, the overturning of the feudal monarchies of central Europe and the discovery and subjugation of black and brown masses across the seas. The word "culture" now gains two fateful senses: "that with which one whole group aggressively defines its superiority 'vis-à-vis' another"; and a finer one, "that held at a level above the group or mass, for the benefit of the culture as a whole, by the conscious few (i.e., the distinction between *haute* and *basse culture*)."[7] At the same time as Europeans were defining themselves over against other European nations and even some of them against members of their own nations, they were also busy defining "European culture" as separate from "African culture," the ultimate otherness, the final *mass*. Only having now reached this stage can we make any sense whatever of the notion of "black culture" and what it might oppose.[8]

"Black culture" is a concept first created by Europeans and defined in opposition to "European culture." Hegel, for example, saw "black culture" as the lowest stage of that laudable self-reflection and development shown by European culture, whose natural outcome must be the state or nationhood. In his by no means untypical nineteenth-century view, Hegel said that black culture simply *did not exist* in the same sense as European culture did. Black culture (as one of several non-Western cultures) had no self-expression (i.e., no writing); there was no black *Volksgeist*, as in Europe, and not even particular tribes or groupings of Africans seemed in the least concerned to define themselves on the basis of any particular *Volksgeist*. Hegel (like most of Europe) was confused by the African: where did blacks fit into "the course of *world history?*":[9]

> In this main portion of Africa there can really be no history. There is a succession of *accidents and surprises*.
>
> There is *no goal*, no state there that one can follow, no subjectivity, but only a series of subjects who destroy each other. There has as yet been little comment upon *how strange a form of self-consciousness* this represents.

These remarks give a rather fascinating definition of European culture (at least as Hegel introduces his countrymen in his "we") by inversion:

> We must forget all categories that lay at the bottom of our spiritual life and its subsumption under these forms; the difficulty [in such forgetting when examining Africa] lies in the fact that we repeatedly must bring along that which we have already imagined.

Because Hegel gives the first and still most penetratingly systematic definition by a European of the "African character" (and, consequently, of black culture), albeit in a severely negative tone, it is worth quoting him at length:

> In general it must be said that [African] consciousness has not yet reached the contemplation of a fixed objective, an objectivity. The fixed objectivity is called God, the Eternal, Justice, Nature, natural things. . . . The Africans, however, have *not yet* reached this *recognition of the General*. . . . What we name Religion, the State, that which exists *in and for itself*—in other words, all that is *valid*—all this is not yet at hand. . . . Thus we find nothing other than man in his immediacy: that is man in Africa. As soon as Man as Man appears, he stands in opposition to Nature; only in this way does he become Man. . . . The Negro represents the Natural Man in all his *wildness and indocility*: if we wish to grasp him, then we must drop all European conceptions.
>
> What we actually understand by "Africa" is that which is without history and resolution, which is *still* fully caught up in the natural spirit, and which here must be mentioned as being on the threshold of world history.

Hegel's African has an absolute alterity to the European. This fact conveniently enables us to re-read Hegel's criticism as an insightful classification and taxonomy of the dominant tendencies of both cultures. The written text of Hegel is a century and a half old, but its truth still prevails, with regard to the tendencies, in the present-day forms to be discussed later, of the cultures that Hegel describes.

What are the main characteristics that Hegel finds to distinguish black culture from European culture? Interestingly, Hegel begins by implying that black culture is resilient because reticent, or by nature of its very backwardness untouchable: it is totally *other* and incomprehensible to the European, whereas other cultures, such as the native American, have combated the European and have lost:

> the subjection of the land has meant its downfall. . . . as far as tribes of men are concerned, there are few of the descendants of the first Americans left, since close to seven million men have been wiped out . . . the entire [native] American world has gone under and been suppressed by the Europeans. . . . They are perishing, so that one sees that they do not have the strength to merge with the North Americans in the Free States. *Such peoples of weak culture lose themselves more and more in contact with peoples of higher culture and more intensive cultural training.*[10]

Noteworthy here is the persistent connection of physical and territorial suppression, attachment and extermination with cultural inadequacy.

Hegel's definition of black culture is simply negative: ever-developing European culture is the prototype for the fulfillment of culture in the future; black culture is the antitype, ever on the threshold. Black culture, caught in "history-lessness" (*Geschichtslosigkeit*), is none the less shielded from attack or assimilation precisely by its aboriginal intangibility (though particular blacks themselves may not be so protected). According to Hegel, the African, radical in his effect upon the European, is a "strange form of self-consciousness" unfixed in orientation towards transcendent goals and terrifyingly close to the cycles and rhythms of nature. The African, first, overturns all European categories of logic. Second, he has no idea of history or progress, but instead allows "accidents and surprises" to take hold of his fate. He is also not aware of being at a lower stage of development and perhaps even has no idea of what development is. Finally, he is "immediate" and intimately tied to nature with all its cyclical, non-progressive data. Having no self-consciousness, he is "immediate"—i.e., *always there*—in any given moment. Here we can see that, being there, the African is also *always already there*, or perhaps *always there before*, whereas the European is *headed there* or, better, *not yet there*.

Hegel was almost entirely correct in his reading of black culture, but what he could not have guessed was that in his very criticism of it he had almost perfectly described the "there" to which European culture was "headed." Like all models that insist on discrete otherness, Hegel's definition implicitly constituted elements of black culture that have only in this century become manifest. Only after Freud, Nietzsche, comparative and structural anthropology and the study of comparative religions could the frantic but ultimately futile coverings of repetition by European culture be seen as dispensable, albeit in limited instances of "uncovering." Moreover, the very aspects of black culture which had seemed to define its nonexistence for the phenomenologist Hegel may now be valued as positive terms, given a revised metaphysics of rupture and opening.[11]

The Types of Repetition: Their Cultural Manifestations

They are after themselves. They call it destiny. Progress. We call it Haints. Haints of their victims rising from the soil of Africa, South America, Asia . . .

(ISHMAEL REED, *Mumbo Jumbo*)

Hegel as a prophet of historical development was notorious but not unique. We may accept that his assumptions have long been and still are shared, particularly the view that culture in history occurs only when a group arrives at a state of self-consciousness sufficient to propel it to "their destination of becoming a state":

> formal culture on every level of intellectual development can and must emerge, prosper and arrive at a point of high flowering when it forms itself into a state and in this basic form of civilization proceeds to abstract universal reflection and necessarily to universal laws and forms.[12]

The word "state" (*Staat*) is to be defined not as a strict political entity but as any coherent group whose culture progresses from the level of immediacy to self-awareness.

How, then, do European culture and black culture differ in their treatment of the inevitability of repetition, either in annual cycles or in artistic forms? The truly self-conscious culture resists all non-progressive views; it *develops*. Hegel admits the category of change, and even the fact of cyclical repetition in nature, but prefers not to look at it or, if at all, then not from a negative "oriental" but from a positive "occidental" standpoint. In such a view, Hegel states:

67

> Whatever development [*Bildung*] takes place becomes material upon which the Spirit elevates itself to a new level of development, proclaiming its powers in all the directions of its plenitude.[13]

Hence emerges the yet prevailing "third option" mentioned above as a response to repetition: the notion of progress within cycle, "differentiation" within repetition.

So the first category where European culture separates itself from "oriental" and "African" cultures is in its treatment of physical and natural cycles. This separation into "occidental" and "*oriental*" must seem amusing to anyone familiar with—among other Western texts—Book IV of Ovid's *Metamorphoses*, where the "pessimistic" and "oriental" viewpoint appears in the lips of an "occidental" predecessor of Hegel, Pythagoras:

> Nothing is constant in the whole world. Everything is in a state of flux, and comes into being as a transient appearance . . . don't you see the year passing through a succession of four seasons? . . . In the same way our own bodies are always ceaselessly changing. . . . Time, the devourer, and all the jealous years that pass, destroy all things, and, nibbling them away, consume them gradually in a lingering death. . . . Nor does anything retain its appearance permanently. Ever-inventive nature continually produces one shape from another. . . . Though this thing may pass into that, and that into this, yet the sum of things remains unchanged.[14]

The truth is that cyclical views of history are not "oriental," but were widespread in Europe well before the inception of historicism, which began not with Hegel but long prior to the nineteenth century (and here one might mention as Hegel's precursors Bacon or Descartes in the Enlightenment, the progressive *consummatio* in the eschatology of Joachim of Floris, the Thomist orientation towards teleology, or even go back to the "final" triumph of the Heavenly City of St Augustine of Hippo). The debate in Western culture over the question of the shape of history, for most of its course, has been pretty evenly waged, with the advantage perhaps initially even somewhat on the side of the cyclical view. Only with the coming of scientific progressivism (as predicted and formulated by Bacon in *The Advancement of Learning* in 1605) was the linear model able to attain pre-eminence, and then not for some 200 years.[15] The now suppressed (but still to be found) recognition of cycles in European culture has always resembled the beliefs that underlie the religious conceptions of black culture, observing periodic regeneration of biological and agricultural systems.[16]

Black culture highlights the observance of such repetition, often in homage to an original generative instance or act. Cosmogony, the origins and stability of things, hence prevails because it recurs, not because the world continues to develop from the archetypal moment. Periodic ceremonies are ways in which black culture comes to terms with its perception of repetition, precisely by highlighting that perception. Dance often accompanies those ritualistic occasions when a seasonal return is celebrated and the "rounds" of the dance (as of the "Ring Shout" or "Circle Dance") recapitulate the "roundings" of natural time: Christmas, New Year, funerals, harvest-time.[17] Weddings especially are a reenactment of the initial act of coupling that created mankind and are therefore particularly well suited as recognitions of recurrence. Conscious cultural observance of natural repetition no longer characterizes European culture. The German wedding festival, for example, the *Hochzeit*, is today fully divested of its original ties to the repeating New Year's festival *Hochgezît*, and the sense of an individual marriage as a small-scale image of a larger renewal and repetition is now gone.[18] Outside of the seasonal markings of farmers' almanacs, the sort of precise celebration of time's passage and return that we see in Spenser's *Shepheards Calendar* or in the cyclical mystery plays has been out of general favor in recent times (or simply consigned to the realm of the demonic as in the Mephistophelean "I've already buried heaps of them!/And always new blood, fresh blood, circulates again./So it goes on . . ."[19]).

Yet the year does still go around: how does European culture deal with perceived cycles? Recurrent national and sacred holidays are still marked, but with every sense of a progression having taken place between them. The "New Year's Resolution" and its frequent unfulfillment precisely recalls the attempt and failure to impose a character of progression and improvement onto an often non-progressing temporal movement. Successive public Christmas celebrations and ornamental display vie to show increase in size, splendor or brightness from previous ones (although, significantly, the realm of sacred ritual, while immediately coexisting with the commercial culture, still works to bar any inexact repetition of religious liturgy, such as in the Nativity service). Other contemporary cycles, such as the four-year intervals of the Olympic Games and presidential elections, fervently need to justify their obvious recurrence by some standard of material improvement or progress: a new or larger Olympic site or new Olympic records; a new or better political party or personality.

In European culture, financial and production cycles have largely supplanted the conscious sort of natural return in black culture. The financial year is the perfect example of this Hegelian subsumption of development within stasis. For repetition must be exact in all financial accounting, given that, globally, capital ultimately circulates within closed tautological systems (i.e., decrease in an asset is either an increase in another asset or a decrease in a liability, both within a corporate firm and in its relations with other firms). The "annual report" of a business concern, appearing cyclically in yearly or interim rhythm (always on the same "balance-sheet date"), contains ever the same kinds of symbols about the concern's health or decrepitude. It is only the properties of *difference* between $year_2$ and $year_1$ (as quantified by numerical changes in the symbols—say, in the cashflow matrix) which determine how the essentially exact repetitions are to be evaluated and translated into a vocabulary of growth and development. Capital hence will not only necessarily *circulate* but must consequently also *accumulate or diminish*, depending on the state of the firm. Economics and business, in their term "cyclicality," admit the existence and even the necessity of repetition of decline but continually overlay this rupture in the illusion of continuous growth with a rhetoric of "incremental" or "staged" development, which asserts that the repetition of decline in a cycle may occur, but occurs only within an overall upward or spiral tendency.[20]

The discourse of capital in European economic parlance reveals a more general insight about how this culture differs from black culture in its handling of repetition. In black culture, repetition means that the thing *circulates* (exactly in the manner of any flow, including capital flows) there in an equilibrium. In European culture, repetition must be seen to be not just circulation and flow but accumulation and growth. In black culture, the thing (the ritual, the dance, the beat) is "there for you to pick it up when you come back to get it." If there is a goal (*Zweck*) in such a culture, it is always deferred; it continually "cuts" back to the start, in the musical meaning of "cut" as an abrupt, seemingly unmotivated break (an accidental *da capo*) with a series already in progress and a willed return to a prior series.[21]

A culture based on the idea of the "cut" will always suffer in a society whose dominant idea is material progress—but "cuts" possess their charm! In European culture, the "goal" is always clear: that which always is being worked towards. The goal is thus that which is reached only when culture "plays out" its history. Such a culture is never "immediate" but "mediated" and separated from the present tense by its own future-orientation. Moreover, European culture does not allow "a succession of accidents and surprises" but instead maintains the illusions of progression and control at all costs. Black culture, in the "cut," builds "accidents" into its *coverage*, almost as if to control their unpredictability. Itself a kind of cultural *coverage*, this magic of the "cut" attempts to confront accident and rupture not by covering them over but by making room for them inside the system itself.[22]

In one unexpected sphere of European consciousness, however, such an orientation towards the "cut" has survived: on the level of that psychological phenomenon which Freud fully details as the eruption of seemingly unwilled repetitions of the past into the individual's present life—*Wiederholungszwang* or *repetition compulsion*. On the individual psychic level, cultural prohibitions lose their validity. Hence in repetition compulsion, as Freud describes it, repetition—an idiosyncratic and immediate action—has replaced memory, the "normal" access to the past. Instead of a dialogue about a history already past, one has a restaging of the past. Instead of relating what happened in his or her history (Hegel's category of objectivity), the patient re-enacts it with all the precision of ritual.[23] This obsessive acting-out of the repressed past conflict brings the patient back to the original scene of drama. Repetition compulsion is an example of a "cut" or "seemingly fortuitous" (but actually motivated) repetition that appears in explicit contradiction to societal constraints and standards of behavior. Society would censure the act of unwilled repetition as much as or even more than the original trespass: both are against custom (*Sitte*), or un-moral (*unsittlich*), but the lack of will in repetition compulsion makes it also uncanny (*unheimlich*). Jacques Lacan's fruitful idea of the *tuché*—the kind of repetition "that occurs *as if by chance*"—seems to complete the identification here of repetition as one further aspect of non-progressive culture to have been identified within the limits of the European individual consciousness.[24] By virtue of its accidence (or of its accidental way of showing through) the cycle of desire and repression that underlines repetition compulsion belongs together with the notion of the "cut."

Repetition in black culture finds its most characteristic shape in performance: rhythm in music, dance and language.[25] Whether or not one upholds the poet-politician-philosopher Léopold Senghor's attempts to fix the nature of black culture in a concept of *négritude*, it is true that he has well described the role that rhythm plays in it: "It is the most perceptible and least material thing."[26] Where material is absent, dialectics is groundless. Repetitive words and rhythms have long been recognized as a focal constituent of African music and its American descendants—slave-songs, blues, spirituals and jazz.[27] African music normally emphasizes dynamic rhythm, organizing melody within juxtaposed lines of beats grouped into differing meters. The fact that repetition in some senses is the principle of organization shows the desire to rely upon "the thing that is there to pick up." Progress in the sense of "avoidance of repetition" would at once sabotage such an effort. Without an organizing principle of repetition, true improvisation would be impossible, since an improviser relies upon the ongoing recurrence of the beat.

Not only improvisation but also the characteristic "call and response" element in black culture (which already, in eliciting the general participation of the group at random, spontaneous "cuts," disallows any possibility of an *haute culture*) requires an assurance of repetition:

> While certain rhythms may establish a background beat, in almost all
> African music there is a dominant point of repetition developed from a

dominant conversation with a clearly defined alternation, a swinging back and forth from solo to chorus or from solo to an emphatic instrumental reply.[28]

That the beat is there to pick up does not mean that it must have been metronomic, but merely that it must have been at one point begun and that it must be at any point "social"—i.e., amenable to restarting, interruption or entry by a second or third player or to response by an additional musician. The typical polymetry of black music means that there are at least two, and usually more, rhythms going on alongside the listener's own beat. The listener's beat is a kind of *Erwartungshorizont* (to use a term taken from a quite different area), or "horizon of expectations," whereby he or she knows where the constant beat must fall in order properly to make sense of the gaps that the other interacting drummers have let fall.[29] Because one rhythm always defines another in black music, and beat is an entity of relation, any "self-consciousness" or "achievement" in the sense of an individual participant working towards his or her own rhythmic or tonal climax "above the mass" would have disastrous results.

While repetition in black music is almost proverbial, what has not often been recognized in black music is the prominence of the "cut." The "cut" overtly insists on the repetitive nature of the music, by abruptly skipping it back to another beginning which we have already heard. Moreover, the greater the insistence on the pure beauty and value of repetition, the greater the awareness must also be that repetition takes place not on a level of music development or progression, but on the purest tonal and timbric level.

James Brown is an example of a brilliant American practitioner of the "cut" whose skill is readily admired by African as well as American musicians.[30] The format of the Brown "cut" and repetition is similar to that of African drumming after the band has been "cookin' " in a given key and tempo, a cue, either verbal ("Get down" or "Mayfield"—the sax player's name—or "Watch it now") or musical (a brief series of rapid, percussive drum and horn accents), then directs the music to a new level, where it stays with more "cookin' " or perhaps a solo—until a repetition of cues then "cuts" back to the primary tempo. The essential pattern, then, in the typical Brown sequence is recurrent: "ABA" or "ABCBA" or "ABC(B)A," with each new pattern set off (i.e., introduced and interrupted) by the random, brief hiatus of the "cut."[31] The ensuing rupture does not cause dissolution of the rhythm; quite to the contrary, it strengthens it, given that it is already incorporated into the format of the rhythm.

In jazz improvisation, the "cut"—besides uses similar to Brown's—is the unexpectedness with which the soloist will depart from the "head" or theme and from its normal harmonic sequence or the drummer from the tune's accepted and familiar primary beat. One of the most perfect exemplars of this kind of improvisation is John Coltrane, whose mastery of melody and rhythm was so complete that he and Elvin Jones, his drummer, often traded roles, Coltrane making rhythmic as well as melodic statements and "cutting" away from the initial mode of the playing.[32]

Black music sets up expectations and disturbs them at irregular intervals: that it will do this, however, is itself an expectation. This peculiarity of black music—that it draws attention to its own repetitions—extends to the way it does not hide the fact that these repetitions take place on the level of sound only. The extension of "free jazz," starting in the 1960s, into the technical practice of using the "material" qualities of sound—on the horns, for instance, using overtones, harmonics and subtones—became almost mandatory for the serious jazz musician and paralleled a similar movement on the part of European musicians branching out of the classical tradition. But black music has always tended to imitate the human voice, and the tendency to "stretch" the limits of the instrument may have been already there since the wail of the first blues guitar, whisper of the first muted jazz trumpet or the growl of the first jazz trombonist.

The black church must be placed at the center of the manifestations of repetition in black culture, at the junction of music and language. Various rhetorics come into play here: the spoken black sermon employs a wide variety of strategies, such as particularly *epanalepsis* ("because His power brings you power, and your Lord is still the Lord") or *epistrophe* ("give your life to the Lord; give your faith to the Lord; raise your hands to the Lord"). Emphatic repetition most often takes the form of *anaphora*, where the repetition comes at the beginning of the clause (instead of at the beginning and at the end in the first example above, or at the end in the second case). Such a usage of repetition is not limited to the black church, however, and may even be derived in part from the uses of repetition in the key church text, the Bible, as in the following anaphora from Psalms: "The Lord remaineth a King forever. The Lord shall give strength unto his people. The Lord shall give his people the blessing of peace" (29:10–11).

Both preacher and congregation employ the "cut." The preacher "cuts" his own speaking by interrupting himself with a phrase such as "praise God" (whose weight here cannot be at all termed denotative or imperative but purely sensual and rhythmic—an underlying "social" beat provided for the congregation). The listeners, in responding to the preacher's calls at random intervals, produce each time it "cuts" a slight shift in the texture of the performance. At various intervals a musical instrument such as the organ and often spontaneous dancing accompany the speaker's repetition of the "cut." When the stage of highest intensity comes, gravel-voiced "speaking in tongues" or the "testifying," usually delivered at a single pitch, gives credence to the hypothesis, that, all along, the very texture of the sound and nature of the rhythm—but not the explicit meaning—in the spoken words have been at issue.

Repetition in black literature is too large a subject to be covered here, but one may say briefly that it has learned from these "musical" prototypes in the sense that repetition of words and phrases, rather than being overlooked, is exploited as a structural and rhythmic principle. The sermon on the "Blackness of Blackness" which occurs early in Ralph Ellison's *Invisible Man* lifts the sermonic and musical repetitions (Ellison says he modeled this sequence on his knowledge of repetition in jazz music) directly into view in a literary text—and not just in the repetitions of its title.[33] The *ad hoc* nature of much black folklore and poetry, as well as its ultimate destination in song, tends to encourage the repeating refrain, as in this paean to the fighter Jack Johnson:

Jack Johnson, he de champion of de worl'
Jack Johnson, he de champion of de worl'
Jack Johnson, he de champion
Jack Johnson, he de champion
Jack Johnson, he de champion
Jack Johnson, he de champion of de worl'[34]

The "AABBA" repetitive format of so much black folklore and folk-lyric often finds its way into the black novel (as it does into the blues) in unaltered form. In Jean Toomer's *Cane*, the mixture of "fiction, songs, and poetry," presented against the theme of black culture in transition, provides a fine opportunity to view some typical (and not so typical) uses of repetition in the black novel. From the poem "Song of the Son" to the very last page, the repetitive forms of black language and rhetoric are prominent until one notices that gradually the entire plot of the novel itself has all along been tending towards the shape of returning the circle:

O land and soil, red soil and sweet-gum tree,
So scant of grass, so profligate of pines
Now just before an epoch's sun declines
Thy son, in time, I have returned to thee,
Thy son, I have in time returned to thee.[35]

Toni Morrison continues this use of repetition, particularly in *Song of Solomon*, with Sugarman's song and the final song of "Jake the Only Son of Solomon." In the latter song, where Morrison describes "the children, inexhaustible in their willingness to repeat a rhythmic, rhyming action game," and the will of black language to "perform the round over and over again," she puts into words the essential component of her own written tradition. Leon Forrest (most notably in *There is a Tree more Ancient than Eden*) and Ishmael Reed are able to tap a long series of predecessors when they include folk-poems and folklore in their narratives, whose non-progressive form they need not feel constrained to justify.

But particularly in the work of Reed (mainly *Mumbo Jumbo*, but also quite noticeably in *The Free-Lane Pallbearers* and *Flight to Canada*) the kinds of repetition we have seen to have been derived from spoken discourse become only an emblem for much wider strategies of circulation and "cutting" in black writing and a model, or supplemental meter, for their future employment. The explicitly parodistic thrust of the title *Mumbo Jumbo* first of all rejects the need of making a definitive statement about the "black situation in America" and already implies, as all parody does, a comparison with, as well as regeneration of, what has come before and the return of a pre-logical past where, instead of words denoting sense, there was "mumbo jumbo." Jes Grew, the main "force" in the novel, besides being disembodied rhythm ("this bongo drumming called Jes Grew") or Senghor's "la chose la plus sensible et la moins matérielle," is ironically the essence of anti-growth, the avatar of a time "before this century is out" when, Reed predicts:

men will turn once more to mystery, to wonderment; they will explore the vast reaches of space within instead of more measuring more "progress" more of this and more of that.[36]

Jes Grew epidemics appear and reappear *as if by accident:* "So Jes Grew is seeking its words. Its text. For what good is a liturgy without a text?"[37] But there is no text to be found (besides Jes Grew's "rhythmic vocabulary larger than French or English or Spanish"), for the "text" is in fact the compulsion of Jes Grew to recur again and again—the "trace" of one such appearance is *Mumbo Jumbo*, the novel, but at the end of it we are left again with the text of the quest, which is the repetition of the seeking.

Reed elides the "cut" of black culture with the "cutting" used in cinema. Self-consciously filmable, *Mumbo Jumbo* ends with a "freeze frame" not only underscoring its filmic nature, but also itself an example of a common cueing device for cinematic "cuts." Reed, also, in the manner of the jazz soloist, "cuts" frequently between the various subtexts in his novel (headlines, photographs, handwritten letters, italicized writing, advertisements) and the text of his main narrative. The linear narrative of the detective story and the feature film (*opening scenes, title credits, story,* final *freeze frame*) also structures *Mumbo Jumbo*, but there is no progressive enterprise going on here, despite such evidence to the contrary. The central point remains clear right to Reed's very last words: "the 20s were back again. . . . Time is a pendulum. Not a river. More akin to what goes around comes around."[38] The film is in a loop.

The Return of Repetition

Repetition is reality and it is the seriousness of life. He who wills repetition is matured in seriousness. . . . Repetition is the new category which has to be brought to light.   (KIERKEGAARD, *Repetition*)

In almost conscious opposition to Hegel's idea of "progressive" culture, European music and literature, perhaps realizing the limitations of innovation, have recently learned to "foreground" their already present repetitions, "cuts" and cyclical insights. As European music uses rhythm mainly as an aid in the construction of a sense of progression to a harmonic cadence, the repetition has been suppressed in favor of the fulfillment of the goal of harmonic resolution.[39] Despite the clear presence of consistent beat or rhythm in the common classical forms of the ostinato or the figured bass or any other continuo instrument, rhythm was scarcely a goal in itself and repetition seldom pleasurable or beautiful by itself.

Although the key role of "recapitulation" in the "ABA" or "AABBAA" sonata form (often within a movement itself, as in the so frequently ignored "second repeats" in Beethoven's major works) is undisputed in theory, in live performance these repetitions often are left out to avoid the undesirability of having "to be told the same thing twice." Repeating the exposition, as important as it no doubt is for the "classical style," is subsumed within and fulfilled by the general category called "development." By the time the music does return to the home tonic, in the final recapitulation, the sense is clearly one of repetition with a difference. The momentum has elevated the initial material to a new level rather than merely re-presenting it unchanged.[40] Even though the works of Wagner and his followers represent a break from this traditional formal model of development derived from the sonata form, the Wagnerian leitmotiv, for instance, is anything but a celebration of repetition in music. In the *Ring*, Wagner's consummate vehicle for the leit-motivic style of composition, the recurrent musical phrases are in fact a Hegelian progression or extended accumulation and accretion to an ultimate goal or expression that begins somewhat during the early part of the *Götterdämmerung*, or even starting late in *Siegfried*; the leitmotivs are invested in installments throughout *Das Rheingold* and *Die Walküre* and are then repaid with interest by the end of the *Götterdämmerung*.

In the pre-serial era, only Stravinsky took the already present expectations of concealed repetition in the classical tradition and uncovered them by highlight-ing them. In *Petrushka* (1911) and *Le Sacre du printemps* (1913) particularly, the use of the "cut" and the unconcealed repetition is striking. In the First Tableau of *Petrushka*, an abbreviated fanfare and tattoo from snare drum and tambourine set off the first section (rehearsal numbers 1–29)—itself in ABACABA form—from the magic trick (30–2), which is the new, much slower tempo after the "cut." The magic trick concludes with a harp glissando and a brief unaccompanied piccolo figure—the next "cut"—leading to the famous "Danse russe" (33–46), overtly repetitive in its ABABA form, which then ends in a snare-drum "cut" (here, in 47, as well as elsewhere—at 62, 69 and 82). In *Le Sacre du printemps* exact repeti-tion within and across sections exceeds anything that had come before it. Moreover, Stravinsky has developed his use of the "cut," varying the cue-giving instrument.[41] Interestingly, both Stravinsky compositions resemble black musical forms not just in their relentless "foregrounding" or rhythmic elements and their use of the "cut" but also in being primarily designed for use in conjunction with dancers.[42]

In European literature, the recovery of repetition in this century is even more striking. Blatant repetitions of the folkloric, traditional or mnemonic sort that had characterized European oral poetry, medieval sagas and other forms of narrative right into the late sixteenth-century baroque literature began to be transformed into the pretense of an external reality being depicted, culminating in *literary real-ism* in the late nineteeth century. The picaresque "cuts" found in the segmented narratives of *Lazarillo de Tormes* (1554) or even *Don Quixote* (1605)—where a quite literal "cut" breaks off the manuscript before chapter 9—were soon becom-ing a thing of the past, aside from the rare extravagance of Sterne, whose *Tristram Shandy* (1760–7) was an outstanding exception. In a sense, all representational conventions such as literary realism suppress repetition and verbal rhythm in the telling in favor of the illusion of narrative verisimilitude. Thus they would portray an outside world, exhaustible in its manifestations, by the supposedly inex-haustible and ever-renewable resource of writing—hence evading the need for "repeated descriptions" of that world.

Until recently—particularly before the Dadaists, and their "cutting" practices; or the cinema-inspired "montagists," Joyce, Faulkner, Woolf, Yeats and Eliot—this practice had been dominant. Now its dominance has begun to ebb somewhat. With Joyce, most of all, we have realized that the incessant repetition of particular words (such as "pin" or "hat" in the early Bloom chapters of *Ulysses*) are not descriptions of objects seen repeatedly in the external environment and then described, but intentional repetitions of words scattered here and there in a text by its author as if by accident.

Narrative repetition tends to defuse the belief that any other meaning resides in a repeated signifier than the fact that it is being repeated.[43] Among European or American dramatists, Tom Stoppard, in *Travesties*, comes closest to understanding this insight. This play (in which Joyce plays a major role, along with Tristan Tzara and Lenin) not only refuses to cover up its repetitions but makes clear that there must be a definite "cut" between them. The "cut" is explained in the stage directions as a manifestation of the unreliable memory of the main character, Henry Carr:

> One result is that the story (like a toy train perhaps) occasionally jumps the rails and has to be restarted at the point where it goes wild. . . . This scene has several of these "time slips," indicated by the repetitions of the exchange between BENNETT and CARR about the "newspapers and telegrams." . . . It may be desirable to mark these moments more heavily by using an extraneous sound or a light effect, or both. The sound of a cuckoo-clock, artificially amplified, would be appropriate since it alludes to time and to Switzerland.[44]

Underlying this notion of "time" is not just Freud's idea that repetition is a remedy for the failure of memory, but the related and necessary acceptance of rupture: in the smooth forward progress of the play; in the insistently forward motion of "time" on those occasions when history "jumps the rails and has to be restarted at the point where it goes wild."

The cuckoo-clock in *Travesties* (borrowed from the "Nausicaa" chapter of *Ulysses*, where it has a slightly different function) is the perfect signal for "cuts," as it is itself an emblem of time. When in Act I Tzara repeats the word "DADA" thirty-four times in response to Carr's homily "It is the duty of the artist to beautify existence," one begins to think that the word's meaning in the contexts, or even its etymology (interesting as it might be for "DADA"), are beside the point. A previous "cut" has made the point more clearly. Tzara (well known in real life for his "cut-ups," or poems stuck together at random), while trying to seduce Gwendolen, cuts up and tosses the words of Shakespeare's eighteenth sonnet (which she has been reciting) into a hat, shakes them up, and pulls the words one by one out of the hat. Instead of the expected random version of the original, a quite lewd poem, using the same words as the former sonnet, emerges:

> Darling, shake thou thy gold buds
> the untrimmed but short fair shade

shines—
see, this lovely hot possessions growest
so long
by nature's course—
so . . . long—heaven!
and declines,
summer changing, more temperature complexion. . . .[45]

What is the point of Stoppard's "travesty" of Shakespeare? The cutting of the sonnet should have produced only "mumbo jumbo," or at best "clever nonsense," as Carr had called Tzara's prior recitation of the word "DADA." But the emergence of the "new" poem is the emergence of the real: instead of poetry, lechery is Tzara's concern. The true message of the sonnet is not transcendent (about beauty) but immediate, in that it consists of words on paper that can be cut, but which signify only in the context of speaking, not by virtue of being masterfully arranged. Language—even Shakespeare's—here is shown to be, on the most obvious level, exactly what is there, not what is elsewhere: it is of desire, not of meaning.

The outstanding fact of late twentieth-century European culture is its ongoing reconciliation with black culture. The mystery may be that it took so long to discern the elements of black culture already there in latent form, and to realize that the separation between the cultures was perhaps all along not one of nature, but one of force.

NOTES

1. Raymond Williams, who calls the word "culture" "one of the two or three most complicated words in the English language," gives a thorough survey of the usage of the word in *Keywords* (London and Glasgow: Fontana, 1976), pp. 76–82.

2. Jonathan Swift, *A Tale of a Tub, and Other Satires* (1704; London: Dent, 1975), p. 108.

3. Throughout *A Tale of a Tub*, Swift (like Carlyle after him) employs images of undress and disrobing to denote death and pathology, while equating dress with the power of culture and language.

4. For the English examples, see Simeon Potter, *Our Language* (Harmondsworth: Penguin, 1976), pp. 59–61, 117–21. For the German attempts to expel foreign—especially French—words, see Robert Reinhold Ergang, *Herder and the Foundations of German Nationalism* (New York: Columbia University Press, 1931; repr. Octagon, 1966), pp. 131–2, 142–3, 163.

5. Contrast the Lenten admonition for the administering of ashes on Ash Wednesday, a statement of life as inevitable decay—"Memento, o homo, quod cines es, et in cinerem rivertaris" ("Remember, O man, that dust thou art and to dust though shalt return")—with Pascal's use (in *Fragment d'un traité du vide*) of metaphors of human growth when speaking of the development of culture: "not only each man advances in the sciences day by day, but . . . all men, together make continual progress in them as the universe grows older." Quoted in *The Encyclopedia of Philosophy* (New York: Macmillan, 1967), p. 484.

6. Ergang, op. cit., p. 7. See also Leo Weinstein, *Hippolyte Taine* (New York: Twayne, 1972), pp. 81–2.

7. That this separation between "culture" and "mass" is a "central concept of German fascist ideology" and directly leads to the identification of the "élite" army with the forces of national culture (and, conversely, the transformation of culture into a weapon) is most convincingly shown in Klaus Theweleit, *Männerphantasien 2: Männerkörper—zur Psychoanalyse des weissen Terrors* (Hamburg: Rowohlt, 1980), pp. 47–64, in the chapter "Masse und Kultur—Der 'hochstehende Einzelne,' " and pp. 64–74, "Kultur und Heer." Goering is quoted as saying during the Nuremberg trials: "The Americans simply are not cultured enough to understand the German point of view," in ibid., p. 47.

8. I have chosen for the purposes of this essay to discuss "European culture" in contrast to "black culture," meaning the culture of both Africans and Afro-Americans, as the only usefully identifiable entities. I have refrained from any mention of "American culture," agreeing on the whole with Ralph Ellison when he states, "I recognize no American culture which is not the partial creation of black people," and confident in the assertion that the terms "European" and "black" effectively exhaust the major manifestations of culture in contemporary America. See John Hersey (ed.), *Ralph Ellison: A Collection of Critical Essays* (Englewood Cliffs, NJ: Prentice-Hall, 1974), p. 44.

9. Hegel's quote and those below it are from G. W. F. Hegel, *Die Vernunft in der Geschichte*, 5th rev. ed. (Hamburg: Felix Meiner, 1955), pp. 216–18; translation and italics are mine.

10. Ibid., pp. 200–1; translation and italics are mine.

11. I use the word "revised" advisedly here, since the proponents of the "new openness" never cease to point to historical benefactors going as far back as Plato. My tendency is to pick out Nietzsche as the principal "revisionist," but the key role of "rupture" in Freud, Heidegger and Husserl compels their mention here. For Jacques Derrida's views on Nietzsche, for instance, see *Spurs: Nietzsche's Styles*, trans. Barbara Hariow (Chicago: University of Chicago Press, 1979); French title *Éperons: Les styles de Nietzsche* (Venice: Corbo e Fiori, 1976). For the idea of "opening," see Derrida, *Of Grammatology*, trans. Gayatri Chakravorty Spivak (Baltimore, Md: Johns Hopkins University Press, 1977), "The Hinge" ("La Brisure"), pp. 65–73; French title *De la grammatologie* (Paris: Minuit, 1967). See also Spivak's preface, pp. xxi–xxxviii, for a good introductory summary of the Derridian-Nietzschean critique of "the metaphysics of presence." See also Geoffrey Hartman's well-known essay "The Voice of the Shuttle: Language from the Point of View of Literature," in *Beyond Formalism* (New Haven, Conn.: Yale University Press, 1970), pp. 337–55, and his more recent *Saving the Text: Literature, Derrida, Philosophy* (Baltimore: Johns Hopkins University Press, 1981).

12. Hegel, op. cit., pp. 163, 173; translation is mine.

13. Ibid., pp. 35–6.

14. Ovid, *The Metamorphoses*, trans. Mary M. Innes (Harmondsworth: Penguin, 1970), pp. 339–41, ll. 148–271. Pythagorean ideas on recurrence derive both from a belief in metempsychosis (transmigration of souls—see Plato's *Phaedrus*, 248E–249D) and from Pythagoras' likely belief in a periodic historical cycle (Great Year) of 9000 years or more, which involved an exact repetition in each phase. See J. A. Philip, *Pythagoras and Early Pythagoreanism* (Toronto: University of Toronto Press, 1966), p. 75.

15. The area of philosophy dealing with such issues—the philosophy of history—has been recently (approximately since Croce and Toynbee) rather neglected. The view of Hegel or Augustine on one side, being roughly opposed in their historical concept

to Nietzsche or Vico on the other, may be said approximately to delimit the poles of Western discourse on the subject, although the opposition is more fluid than a simple counterposition. For fuller discussion of this broad and highly complex issue, consult: on Bacon, Benjamin Farrington, *Francis Bacon: Philosopher of Industrial Science* (London: Macmillan, 1973); on the general topic of the philosophy of history, Sir Isaiah Berlin, *Vico and Herder: Two Studies in the History of Ideas* (London: Hogarth Press, 1976), Manfred Buhr, *Zur Geschichte der klassischen bürgerlichen Philosophie: Bacon, Kant, Fichte, Schelling, Hegel* (Leipzig: Phillip Reclam, 1972), Kenneth Burke, *Permanence and Change: An Anatomy of Purpose*, 2nd rev. ed., Library of Liberal Arts (Indianapolis: Bobbs-Merrill, 1965), Karl Löwith, *Meaning in History* (Chicago: University of Chicago Press, 1949), and G. A. Wells, *Herder and After: A Study in the Development of Sociology* ('S-Gravenhage: Mouton, 1959). For a recent attempt, see Peter Munz, *The Shapes of Time: A New Look at the Philosophy of History* (Middletown, Conn.: Wesleyan University Press, 1977). See also Sacvan Bercovitch, *Puritan Origins of the American Self* (New Haven, Conn.: Yale University Press, 1975), on the idea of progress and growth in English and American thought in the seventeenth century.

16. See Mircea Eliade, *The Myth of the Eternal Return, or, Cosmos and History*, trans. Willard R. Trask (Princeton, NJ: Princeton University Press, 1974), in the chapters "Archetypes and Repetition" and "The Regeneration of Time," pp. 3–92; French title, *Le Mythe de l'éternel retour: archétypes et répétition* (Paris: Gallimard, 1949). See also Eliade, *Patterns in Comparative Religion*, trans. Rosemary Sheed (Cleveland, Ohio: World, Meridian Books, 1963); French title, *Traité d'histoire des religions* (Paris: Gallimard, 1949). Indeed, it may be that black culture in its initial stages is rarely found outside such ritualistic employment, and that "African Art in Motion" (to use Robert F. Thompson's phrase) is closely linked to those cyclical events that speak of the return and reproduction of a previous event, in which there can be no question of "progress."

17. Robert F. Thompson, in "An Aesthetic of the Cool," *African Forum*, 2.2 (Fall 1966), p. 85, refers to African religions as "danced faiths." See also Eileen Southern (ed.), *Readings in Black American Music* (New York: Norton, 1971), pp. 41–7, for James Eight's description of the yearly "Pinckster" slave celebrations that originated in the Middle Colonies of early America, and pp. 50–1 for Latrobe's description of festival dances of African origin in New Orleans. For a precise listing of particular dances used in conjunction with particular annual festivals, see Leonore Emery, *Black Dance in the United States, from 1619 to 1970*, University of Southern California, Ph. D. (Ann Arbor, Mich.: University Microfilms, 1971), the section "Special Occasion Dances," pp. 50–102.

18. Eliade, *The Myth of the Eternal Return*, p. 26. Keith Thomas, *Religion and the Decline of Magic* (New York: Scribner, 1971), explains the transition in perhaps more unconventional terms.

19. Johann Wolfgang von Goethe, *Faust, Part One*, trans. Louis MacNeice (Oxford: Oxford University Press, 1952), p. 49; Goethe, *Faust*, kommentiert von Erich Trunz (München: Beck, 1972), p. 48, ll. 1371–3: "Wie viele hab' ich schon begraben!/Und immer zirkuliert ein neues, frisches Blut./So geht es fort . . ."

20. See Paul M. Sweezy, *The Theory of Capitalist Development* (Oxford: Oxford University Press, 1942), for a fuller—and for Marx's—analysis of this need for upward growth. Max Weber, *The Protestant Ethic and the Spirit of Capitalism* (New York: Scribner, 1958), chs. 2 and 5, illustrates the psychological ramifications of this need for growth.

21. The "cut" is most often signaled by a master drummer, as in the description of the Dagomba "Atwimewu" drum in John Miller Chernoff, *African Rhythm and African Sensibility: Aesthetics and Social Action in African Musical Idioms* (Chicago: University of Chicago Press, 1979), pp. 43–67. See also the cinematic definition of *"cutting, editing, or montage,* which changes the picture all at once from one view to another," in Ralph Stephenson and J. R. Debrix, *The Cinema as Art* (Harmondsworth: Penguin, 1965), p. 238.

22. Examples of such systematization of accident are found in all cultures where oracles play a strong role. Two examples are the *sortes Virgilianae* in early European history, or the randomized systematology of the *I Ching,* or "Book of Changes," in China, which uses random entry into a fixed, stable system.

23. Sigmund Freud, "Erinnern, Wiederholen, und Durcharbeiten" (1914), in *Studienausgabe,* ed. A. Mitscherlich, A. Richards, J. Strachey, 11 vols (Frankfurt a.M.: S. Fischer, 1969–), *Ergänzungsband: Schriften zur Behandlungstechnik,* pp. 210–11. The definitive statement on *Wiederholungszwang,* insofar as Freud was capable of making such statements, is to be found in "Jenseits des Lustprinzips" (1920), *Studienausgabe,* vol. 3, pp. 228–9. For the interesting and related phenomenon of *déjà raconté,* see Freud, "Über fausse reconnaissance [déjà raconté] während der psychoanalytischen Arbeit" (1914), *Studienausgabe, Ergänzungsband,* pp. 233–8.

24. Jacques Lacan, *The Four Fundamental Concepts of Psychoanalysis,* trans. Alan Sheridan (London: Hogarth, 1977), p. 54; French title, *Les Quatre Concepts fondamenteaux de la psychanalyse: Le Seminaire, Livre XI* (Paris: Seuil, 1973).

25. Chernoff, op. cit., p. 55: "In African music, the chorus or response is a rhythmic phrase which recurs regularly; the rhythms of a lead singer or musician vary and are cast against the steady repetition of the response. . . . We [in the West] are not yet prepared to understand how people can find beauty in repetition." Chernoff puts it well in another passage: "The most important issues of improvisation, in most African musical idioms, are matters of repetition and change" (p. 111).

26. Quoted in ibid., p. 23: "Cette force ordinatrice qui fait le style nègre est le rythme. C'est la chose la plus sensible et la moins matérielle."

27. See ibid., p. 29, on the continuity of African rhythmic forms in America. Also see Ruth Finnegan, *Oral Literature in Africa* (Oxford: Clarendon, 1976), and Southern (ed.), op. cit., *passim.* Also of interest in this regard is Janheinz Jahn, *A History of Neo-African Literature: Writing in Two Continents,* trans. Oliver Coburn and Ursula Lehrburger (London: Faber, 1968); German title, *Geschichte der neoafrikanishchen Literatur* (Düsseldorf and Cologne: Eugen Diederichs Verlag, 1966).

28. Chernoff, op. cit., p. 55. Although the beat need not have been begun and kept from a conductor's initial count (because it may have in the interim "cut" or changed to another meter), it must be there at every point to "pick up" or to "follow."

29. The term as I use it derives from the work of H. R. Jauss, as in the article "Literatur als Provokation der Literatur-Wissenschaft," contained in the collection *Literaturgeschichte als Provokation* (Frankfurt a.M.: Suhrkamp, 1970).

30. Chernoff, op. cit., p. 55.

31. Thompson, in his *African Art in Motion: Icon and Act in the Collection of Katherine Coryton White* (Los Angeles: University of California Press, 1974), pp. 10–13, takes Hegel's term *Aufheben,* meaning "a simultaneous suspension and preservation," and uses it of the African "cut" in the concept of "Afrikanische [sic] Aufheben." Thompson's term must be mentioned here as a good approximation of the nature of

the "cut," in which every previous pattern that had first been "cut" away from still exists in suspended form until it is "cut" back to.

32. See Bill Cole, *John Coltrane* (New York: Macmillan, 1976), pp. 72–3 and *passim*.

33. See Ellison's interview with John Hersey in Hersey (ed.), op. cit., pp. 2–3, 11.

34. Lawrence W. Levin, *Black Culture and Black Consciousness: Afro-American Folk Thought from Slavery to Freedom* (New York: Oxford University Press, 1977), p. 432.

35. Jean Toomer, *Cane* (New York: Boni & Liveright, 1923), p. 21. For the circular form of the novel, see Brian J. Benson and Mabel M. Dillard, *Jean Toomer* (New York: Twayne, 1980), pp. 82–6. See also Addison Gayle, *The Way of the New World: The Black Novel in America* (Garden City, NY: Doubleday, 1975), p. 98.

36. Ishmael Reed, *Mumbo Jumbo* (New York: Bantam, 1972), pp. 247, 28.

37. Ibid., prologue, p. 5.

38. Ibid., p. 249.

39. Schenker's analyses present the extreme pole of the view that linear, descending cadential resolution is the aim of every tonal work. For discussion of this idea, see Maury Yeston (ed.), *Readings in Schenker Analysis and Other Approaches* (New Haven, Conn.: Yale University Press, 1977).

40. For two splendid analyses of the role and consequence of repetition in the sonata, see Donald F. Tovey, *Essays in Musical Analysis*, vol. 1: *Symphonies* (London: Oxford University Press, 1978), pp. 10–14; Charles Rosen, *The Classical Style: Haydn, Mozart, Beethoven* (London: Faber, 1977), pp. 30–4. Also see W. H. Hadow, *Sonata Form* (London: Novello, n.d.).

41. A fairly complete catalog of "cuts" in *Sacre* follows, with the instruments involved and practice numbers in brackets: violin (12); timpani and brass drum (37); clarinet and piccolo (48); piccolo and flute (54); viola, cello, double bass, tuba, trumpet (57); bass drum (72); clarinet and violin (93); cornet and viola (100), addition of tuba, bassoons, timpani and bass drum (103–18); bass clarinet (141); piccolo, flute and timpani (201).

42. Chernoff, op. cit., pp. 65–7, speaks very well on the essential inseparability of drumming and the dance. He quotes one African drummer (p. 101) as saying "every drumming has got its dance."

43. For a brief and fascinating philosophical speculation on one kind of narrative repetition, see Jacques Derrida, "Ellipsis," in *Writing and Difference*, trans. Alan Bass (Chicago: University of Chicago Press, 1978), pp. 294–300; French title, *L'Écriture et la différence* (Paris: Seuil, 1967). See also Daniel Giovannangeli, *Écriture et répétition: approche de Derrida* (Paris: Union Générale d'Éditions, 1979), for the effects upon the signifier/signified relationship of repetition.

44. Tom Stoppard, *Travesties* (New York: Grove, 1975), p. 27, Act I.

45. Ibid., pp. 53–4.

chapter 4

OLLY WILSON

Black Music as an Art Form*

the title "Black Music as an Art Form" is a particularly intriguing and problematic one. Intriguing because it implies, first, that black music exists in some context other than art, and second, that its existence as art is, in some way, peculiar and distinct; and problematic because it raises the old question of what is really meant by the term "black music." Moreover, the title raises the complicated issue of what is meant by the term "art."

Given this plethora of unresolved issues, my first reaction to being asked to discuss this topic was simply to declare the task impossible and request that I write on a subject which contained fewer ambiguities. Upon reflection, however, I realized that it would be of importance to attempt to come to terms with these ambiguities. I became aware that my own understanding of Afro-American music would be considerably enhanced if I could clarify, at least for myself and perhaps for others as well, some of the issues raised by the title. I therefore withdrew my reservations and agreed to consider the topic, in full awareness that such an undertaking would be fraught with precipitous intellectual pitfalls.

The first step in the clarification of issues posed is a consideration of the meaning of the term "black music." This question has been addressed by a number of different forums since the inception of its popular usage in the sixties. Among the early attempts to define "black music" was that of a panel of the Symposium in

*This paper was read at the National Conference on Black Music Research at Fisk University, Nashville, Tennessee, in March 1982. I want to thank Joan Stiles, a student in my doctoral seminar in 1980, for allowing me to work with and modify her transcriptions of Davis's solos. The part of the transcription of the 1964 solo in brackets is from Fr. Kerschbaumer, *Miles Davis* (Graz, 1978), here transposed to concert pitch.

Black Music held at Indiana University in 1967. The proceedings of that symposium were subsequently edited by Dominique-René de Lerma and published as *Black Music in Our Culture* (1970). Black music was defined in many ways during that conference, from the facetious "black lines and dots on a white page" to the all-inclusive "any music produced by Black people." It was ultimately defined, however, by the consensus of that assembly as music which is, in whole or significant degree, part of the musical tradition of peoples of African descent (de Lerma, 1970). While this definition certainly is accurate in general terms, it is also circular and, hence, inadequate as an operational definition; that is, a definition which focuses on those qualities which exclusively denote the term being defined. Black music is, of course, music which comprises the musical tradition of peoples of African descent. However, in order for it to be perceived as a distinct tradition, it must have specific qualities which are discernible and demonstrable. A successful operational definition would be one in which these qualities were made reasonably explicit. Unfortunately, these qualities are somewhat elusive, especially if they are approached in a quantitative manner. In addition, any attempt to define black music, particularly as it exists within the United States, is made more difficult by the fact that the music of black Americans, like that of all ethnic groups within the United States, is influenced by other cultures. Although, historically, American social and political forces have worked to denigrate and exclude African-American cultural patterns from the broader society, these attempts have always failed, and cultural interaction more than cultural isolation has characterized the American experience. Thus, black American music has both influenced and been influenced in important ways by several non-black musical traditions, thereby making it more difficult to pinpoint precisely the essential aspects of the music which make it a part of a larger African or black music tradition. Nevertheless, the empirical evidence overwhelmingly supports the notion that there is indeed a distinct set of musical qualities which are an expression of the collective cultural values of peoples of African descent. This musical tradition has many branches which reflect variations in basic cultural patterns over time, as well as diversity within a specific time frame. However, all of these branches share, to a greater or lesser extent, a group of qualities which, taken together, comprise the essence of the black musical tradition. The branches of this tradition, though influenced in different ways and degrees by other musical traditions, share a "critical mass" of these common qualities. It is the common sharing of qualities which makes up and defines the musical tradition.

Most people who have considered the question recognize this commonality. The problem comes in determining the nature of that "critical mass" of qualities. One frequently hears an individual claim simultaneously that while black music clearly exists, it is impossible to define. I suggest that the problem with definition is that the approach to that definition has been faulty. Most approaches have been quantitative. Investigators have attempted to define the music by specifying the degree to which a particular musical characteristic was present. While this approach is valuable as far as it goes, it inevitably results in confusion about the nature of the music. In an article entitled "The Significance of the Relationship of African to Afro-American Music" published in *The Black Perspective in Music*, I proposed a different approach to the problem (Wilson, 1974). The substance of that approach is that the essence of the black music tradition consists of "the common sharing of a core of conceptual approaches to the process of music making and, hence, is not basically quantitative but qualitative. The particular forms of black music which evolved in America are specific realizations of this shared conceptual framework which reflects the peculiarities of the American black experience. As such, the essence of their Africaness is not a static body of something which can be depleted, but rather a conceptual approach, the manifestations of which are infinite. The common core of this Africaness consists of the way of doing something, not simply something that is done" (Wilson, 1974, p. 20).

A thorough discussion of all of the African and, by extension, Afro-American, conceptual approaches to the process of making music is out of the purview of this paper; but a brief consideration of a few such concepts should be instructive. Among these are predilections for conceiving music in such a way that the following occur (Wilson, 1981):

1. The approach to the organization of rhythm is based on the principle of rhythmic and implied metrical contrast. There is a tendency to create musical structures in which rhythmic clash or disagreement of accents is the ideal; cross-rhythm and metrical ambiguity are the accepted and expected norm.
2. There is a tendency to approach singing or the playing of any instrument in a percussive manner; a manner in which qualitative stress accents are frequently used.
3. There is a tendency to create musical forms in which antiphonal or call-and-response musical structures abound. These antiphonal structures frequently exist simultaneously on a number of different architectonic levels.
4. There is a tendency to create a high density of musical events within a relatively short musical time frame—a tendency to fill up all of the musical space.
5. There is a common approach to music making in which a kaleidoscopic range of dramatically contrasting qualities of sound (timbre) in both vocal and instrumental music is sought after. This explains the common usage of a broad continuum of vocal sounds from speech to song. I refer to this tendency as "the heterogeneous sound ideal tendency."
6. There is a tendency to incorporate physical body motion as an integral part of the music-making process.

An analysis of any genre of black music will reveal the existence of demonstrable musical characteristics which consistently reflect the presence of these underlying conceptual approaches (as well as others I have not mentioned). It is precisely the pervasive existence of these qualities which gives the music its distinctive character. Black music, then, may be defined as music which is, in whole or significant degree, part of a musical tradition of peoples of African descent in which a common core of the above-mentioned conceptual approaches to music making are made manifest.

The question of what constitutes "art" is an equally vexing one. Western philosophers have been discussing this issue for centuries; the present article is not an appropriate forum for the reconsideration of the substance of that discussion. It becomes necessary, however, to review, if only in a general manner, the basic Western understanding of the meaning of the word "art" if we are to address the question of black music as "art."

Plato in *The Republic* defines art or fine art as the imitation of nature. Art, in this sense, is a man-made copy of something which preexists in nature. The painting, drama, or musical sound which is mistaken for its realistic natural model, is held to be the highest form of art. "The theory of *The Republic* assumes that the aim of art really is to promulgate scientific and philosophical truths and that the artist, possessing neither, tries by emotionalized imitation to give the impression that he possesses both" (Gotschalk, 1962, p. 35). Most philosophers disagree with Plato's theory, because there are countless examples of what is conventionally understood to be art which do not seek to imitate nature, but rather to reinterpret that which exists in nature or to create something which *never* existed in nature.

More recent Western theories of fine art may be characterized as belonging to one of two schools: the expressionist and the formalist. Among the most important of the expressionists have been Leo Tolstoy and most nineteenth-century writers on the subject, and John Dewey in the twentieth century. Fundamentally, the expressionists hold that fine art is the expression of feelings, "the objectification of pleasure," and/or "the expression of a vital insight into reality" (Gotschalk, 1962, p. 39). This definition seems partially true, but appears to leave out much of what is important in an artistic experience—that which cannot be adequately explained as a form of expression. The history of Western aesthetics contains the work of many who argue that art is not simply the expression of emotions (Eduard Hanslick, 1854; Clive Bell, 1914; Susanne K. Langer, 1974; and Leonard Meyer, 1956). Several of these writers point out that the most basic expressions of feelings (i.e., a cry of pain or anguish, a shriek of terror, a spontaneous utterance of joyous laughter) are not considered to be of artistic importance. Moreover, much of what is considered important in an outstanding painting, play, or musical composition defies characterization as an expression of either a specific or general set of emotions. Specifically, those aspects of art such as form, structure, and logical continuity are not adequately covered by expressionist theories of art. What makes something have the quality of art, thus, clearly involves factors which go beyond the expression of feeling or the objectification of pleasure.

The formalists define fine art as "the construction of significant form," "the delineation of characteristic form," or "the achievement of organic form" (Gotschalk, 1962, p. 39). Among the major exponents of this idea were Clive Bell (Bell, 1914) and Roger Fry (Fry, 1925). Again, as was the case with the expressionist theory, this definition seems to be weakened by its exclusiveness. It does not adequately explain the relationship between human expression of emotions and art.

In addition to the formalists' and expressionists' views of art, Freudian psychologists developed another theory of art. "Artistic activity, according to the psychoanalysts, is an expression of primitive dynamisms, of unconscious wishes, and uses the objects and scenes represented to embody the secret fantasies of the artist" (Langer, 1974, p. 176). This theory may tell us something about the origin of artistic impulses but is inadequate as a definition of art because it does not deal with the substance of that which is recognized as art, nor does it suggest a criterion by which we make qualitative judgments about art.

Perhaps the most adequate definition of art as currently understood by the Western world is that given by D. W. Gotschalk in his book *Art and the Social Order*. Gotschalk develops what he calls a "relational theory" of fine art (Gotschalk, 1962, p. 39). He defines fine art as "the shaping of a four-dimensional object—material and form, expression and function—in the direction of intrinsic perceptual interest. . . . This relational theory accepts the de facto truth of the form and expression theories," and "can also interrelate these truths as diverse fragments of a more comprehensive theory" (Gotschalk, 1962, p. 40). The most convincing aspect of Gotschalk's definition is his recognition of the fact that, in contemporary Western thought, art or fine art is viewed as those products of man which are "intrinsically interesting to perceive." In this view, any object so skillfully produced that it invokes perceptual interest has the quality of fineness of art. However, that which distinguishes fine art proper from other man-made objects, which may also elicit perceptual interest to some degree (for example, artifacts), is the centrality and eminence of intrinsic perceptual appeal to their reason for existing. Put simply, products which are considered "art" are those that exist primarily for reasons of their own appeal; this idea is embodied most explicitly in the popular phrase "art for Art's sake." While a brilliantly decorated door, chair, or hand-made grain basket may be said to have artistic appeal, such objects are not considered fine art in the same way that a novel, symphony, or abstract painting is. This is because the former products exist primarily for utilitarian purposes, while the latter products exist only as objects of concentrated perceptual interest. The latter products were made by a creative individual as a means of expressing something of that person's experience. The artwork is thus a symbolic expression of experience consciously transformed.

In this view of art, the test of whether a man-made product is art or not is whether it exists primarily as an object of perceptual interest. This view also allows for products of man to have relative degrees of fineness of art. The utilitarian objects which are unusually exquisite from a perceptual point of view are considered art to the degree that this aspect of their function is important. Hence, in the field of architecture, those buildings which are aesthetically and intellectually stimulating are considered works of art, while those that are perfectly functional as buildings but contain little of intrinsic perceptual interest are not. The Taj Mahal, St. Peter's Basilica, and the Capitol building in Washington, D.C., are works of art in addition to being functional buildings, but the local Sears, Roebuck and telephone company buildings are not. This means, of course, that it is quite possible for society's view of a product's "fineness of art" to alter with time. Something that was considered to be of modest artistic interest at one age may be viewed primarily as an object of fine art at another. Witness, for example, the ancient Egyptian, Greek, or Chinese vases that adorn the exhibitions in contemporary Western museums. These are man-made products which were designed for utilitarian purposes; yet, in the context of contemporary Western society, their function is exclusively as objects of perceptual interest, i.e., objects of fine art. As a matter of fact, much of the music, drama, sculpture, and painting that was created strictly for religious or secular functional purposes in past civilizations exists in twentieth-century Western societies solely as products of fine art.

There is another aspect of the notion of art in the Western sense which we must consider before attempting to discuss black music as art. There are many products of man which exist primarily to engage our perceptual faculties but which are not normally regarded as art. Television situation comedies, newspaper cartoons, much popular music, athletic contests as spectacles, circus shows, etc., all exist to stimulate us perceptually, but are generally considered entertainment rather than art. Though the concepts of entertainment and art are not necessarily mutually exclusive—that is, something which is entertaining may be art, and something that is art may also be entertaining—they do imply different things. The verb "to entertain," taken from the French word "entretenir," literally means to hold (*tenir*) between (*entre*). It connotes in traditional usage "to divert," "to amuse," or "to hold one's attention." The nature of entertainment is to engage our perceptual faculties temporarily; to fascinate us and, thereby, provide immediate satisfaction; in a word, to provide amusement and diversion.

On the other hand art implies something different. The encounter with art makes a more lasting impression. It is an experience which not only fascinates us fleetingly, but continues to engage our intellect as well as our aesthetic sensibilities for some time to come. The work of art requires that we become involved with it in profound ways. The act of experiencing an outstanding work of art, whether it be music, painting, literature, or drama, requires that we actively interact with it as symbolic expression. Art requires concentrated active participation. One can return again and again to a work of art because it is rich in detail and engages our awareness in different ways at each encounter.

To summarize, the distinction between entertainment and art is that entertainment, while engaging our aesthetic sensibilities, is immediately gratifying, less concentrated in content, and tends not to make a lasting impact on us. Art, on the other hand, requires our active involvement, is highly charged with content, and profoundly influences our sense of ourselves and the world for years to come.

Up to this point I have discussed the nature of art in Western societies. This view of art, however, is a view that is not universally shared. It is also a view which was not always held in the West. It is, rather, the result of specific cultural developments that have occurred within the history of Western civilization.

Within the West African cultural context, the concept of art as defined in the West does not exist. Art is not viewed as an activity or product of man whose sole purpose is "intrinsic perceptual interest." On the contrary, within the African context the aesthetic ideal is integrated with the utilitarian ideal. That is, art is not separate and distinct from utilitarian function, but the quality of "intrinsic perceptual interest" is seen as an integral aspect of the utilitarian function. Thus, while there are no museums, theaters, or concert halls in traditional African societies, there is an abundance of functional products of human creativity which involves painting, sculpture, drama, and music. The creative dimension of the product or activity is viewed as an inseparable aspect of that product's nature, and is impossible to detach from its functional reason for existence. Accordingly, Western scholars sometimes refer to works of artistic interest that occur within African (as well as most non-Western) societies as functional art because the works are always produced for some utilitarian purpose.

The recognition of an African concept of functional art is of significance in understanding black music as art within the United States. This is so because, like other aspects of culture which exist at the conceptual stage, it tended to persist and to affect the nature of Afro-American art in the United States. As a consequence, creative activities of the first generations of Afro-Americans were based on African conceptions modified by the peculiar circumstances of slave existence in the New World. Hence, seventeenth- and eighteenth-century Afro-American creative products and activities were functional in the African sense. This is borne out in the abundance of early Afro-American utilitarian products and performance practices (e.g., music and dance) in which the aesthetic and utilitarian ideals were viewed as shared aspects of that product or activity. In early Afro-American music this is seen most vividly in the association of music with work or religion. Religious songs (either African or Afro-American Christian) and work songs comprised the bulk of early Afro-American music not only because they were the most acceptable forms of music making within the debilitating institution of slavery, but also because these functional contexts were consistent with African concepts of creative activity.

The question of this music as art, therefore, has to be approached from the perspective of African (and African diasporal) concepts of creative activity. One important consideration of a work's artistic worth is the measure of its functional efficacy. However, the principal consideration is the criterion mentioned earlier as that which distinguishes art from entertainment. Specifically, Afro-American music was art when it required active aesthetic involvement, was highly charged in symbolic content, and profoundly influenced its listeners. This was the case even though it did not exist solely as a product of "perceptual interest." The degree to which a specific work of music embodied traditional African conceptual approaches to the process of music making in a unique and powerful synthesis determined the degree to which that individual work invoked those qualities cited above, and, hence, the degree to which it was a successful work of art. It is vitally important to remember this criterion as the only valid measure of artistic quality of early Afro-American music. Functional efficacy must not be separated from consideration of artistic merit.

The consideration of Afro-American music produced after 1800 as art raises another issue because, by this time, there were Afro-American cultural patterns which were distinct from African cultural patterns. That issue is related to a larger question of the fundamental nature of Afro-American culture. Perhaps the most brilliant exposition of this issue is found in the writing of W. E. B. Du Bois.

In his classic book *The Souls of Black Folk*, written in 1903, Du Bois described in penetrating poetic terms what can be called the duality of Afro-American culture.

> After the Egyptian and Indian, the Greek and Roman, the Teuton and Mongolian, the Negro is a sort of seventh son, born with a veil, and gifted with second sight in this American world,—a world which yields him no true self-consciousness, but only lets him see himself through the revelation of the other world. It is a peculiar sensation, this double-consciousness, this sense of always looking at one's self through the eyes of others, of measuring one's soul by the tape of a world that looks on in amused contempt and pity. One ever feels his twoness—an American, a Negro; two souls, two thoughts, two unreconciled strivings; two warring ideals in one dark body, whose dogged strength alone keeps it from being torn asunder.

> The history of the American Negro is the history of this strife—this longing to attain self-conscious manhood, to merge his double self into a better and truer self. In this merging he wishes neither of the older selves to be lost. He would not Africanize America, for America has too much to teach the world and Africa. He would not bleach his Negro soul in a flood of white Americanism, for he knows that Negro blood has a message for the world. He simply wishes to make it possible for a man to be both a Negro and an American, without being cursed and spit upon by his fellows, without having the doors of Opportunity closed roughly in his face.   (16–17)

Black music in the United States reflects the duality of Afro-American culture of which Du Bois speaks—"the two souls, two thoughts, two ideals." On one hand, there exists what might be described as the basic or folk African-American musical tradition. This tradition evolved directly from the West African musical tradition and shares most concepts and values of that tradition while simultaneously selectively incorporating important aspects of Western musical practice. It is the musical tradition of the majority of black Americans, the people to whom Du Bois refers as "Black Folk," or to whom Leroi Jones refers as the "autonomous Blues People" (Jones, 1963). It most clearly expresses the collective aesthetic values of the majority of black Americans and proceeds along a line of development which, while influenced by factors outside of Afro-American culture, is more profoundly affected by values within the culture. It is clearly music within Du Bois's veil. Hollers, cries and moans, early spirituals, rural work and play songs, rural blues, gospel music, urban blues, and soul music are the principal expressions of this tradition.

On the other hand, there exists a tradition in Afro-American music which dates from at least 1800. This tradition is characterized by a greater interaction and interpenetration of African and Euro-American elements, although the fundamental qualities which make it unique are rooted in African conceptual approaches to music making. Culturally, this tradition is a closer reflection of the second ideal to which Du Bois refers; that is, the American ideal as white America envisions. It is, rather, a reinterpretation of that American ideal as viewed through the prism of black American experience; it involves a unique reinterpretation of the broader American experience from a black vantage point.

This second Afro-American music tradition finds its initial expression in the popular music of the late eighteenth and early nineteenth century. Beginning with the colonial practice of allowing black musicians to perform Euro-American religious, dance, and military music, it ultimately resulted in a black tradition of reshaping the Euro-American qualities of the music to African-American norms. This process of cultural transformation became the salient characteristic of this tradition. The musical forms most often associated with this tradition were preexisting Euro-American forms, but the significant features of their presentation are Afro-American. Necessarily, this tradition requires an awareness of the Euro-American tradition as well as the Afro-American and therefore finds its greatest exponents in those sectors of Afro-American society that are most conversant with Euro-American musical practices.

Eileen Southern in her seminal work *The Music of Black Americans* has cited numerous examples of late eighteenth- and early nineteenth-century musicians whose peculiar performance of European music was in effect a transformation of that music (Southern, 1971). It was precisely that transformation which made the music unique and, as a consequence, highly desired by whites. The numerous colonial black military fifers and drummers and the black fiddlers for white balls are examples of those in the vanguard of this tradition. The brass bands of Frank Johnson, A. J. Connor, and others in the middle of the nineteenth century cited by James Monroe Trotter (1878), Maud Cuney-Hare (1936), and Samuel Floyd (1978) continue this tradition. Finally, the post–Civil War black minstrel tradition, the black marching and circus band tradition, the ragtime tradition, the arranged spiritual tradition, the black musical comedy tradition, and much of the entire jazz tradition are all expressions of this second tradition.

It is important to cite the dual nature of Afro-American music in order to come to grips with the question of black music as art. This is so because while both traditions share, in different ways, the basic African approaches to music making, the criteria by which one judges their content as art vary. In the first tradition, the artistic quality has to be approached in the manner associated with the African tradition; that is, the work must be judged by the capacity of its aesthetic content to achieve its functional purpose. One is concerned here not with music as an abstract object of art, but as an agent which causes something to happen. The function of the early Afro-American religious song was not simply to bring aesthetic pleasure to the listener, but to create a spiritual liaison between man and his God. The function of the music was to create a communion of participants who interact with each other and their concept of God for the collective good. Each religious song must be judged on the basis of how well its particular statement of musical content achieves this end. This functional view of art remains of importance in each of the musical genres of this tradition. One sees it reflected in one of the continuing debates within the contemporary gospel music community, a debate which centers around whether the music should be performed solely for religious purposes rather than for entertainment or artistic purposes. Those performers who have internalized basic African concepts insist that the music should serve an exclusively religious functional purpose.

In addition, within this first tradition, the basic criteria of value and merit are those qualities indigenous to the Afro-American music tradition. They provide the principal focal point of value judgment. The two reasons given above explain why, historically, the forms of music in the first tradition are less understood and appreciated as art by the broader American society.

The second tradition, which involves cultural transformation, is more compatible with western values. Within this tradition, music clearly exists as objects of "perceptual interest," either as entertainment or art. The fundamental criteria for artistic measure here, however, are still primarily based on African conceptual approaches to music making. These criteria are augmented by shared values of the broader culture, and, hence, genres of this tradition are more readily understood and accepted by the broader American society. Indeed, it is within this second tradition that most cross-cultural interaction between Euro-American music and Afro-American music has taken place.

I wish to consider briefly two examples of Afro-American music as art: one from what I have referred to above as the first, or basic, Afro-American tradition, and the other from the second Afro-American music tradition. The first example is a work song entitled "Katie Left Memphis." This particular version was sung by a prisoner in Parchman Penitentiary known as Tangle Eye and recorded as part of New World Records *Roots of The Blues* album (N.W. 252, 1977). The song's title refers to a steamboat called "Katie Belle" which at one time was very popular in the Yazoo delta region of the Mississippi river, the region between Memphis and Natchez, Mississippi. The text contains references to the steamboat spinning around in a sandbar before skimming out to a deep channel, and a warning to young men to buy a return ticket on the train called the "Yellow Dog" before going out for a night of carousing in the bawdy houses of Memphis.

The function of this song is to facilitate the task of chopping wood. As is typical of African and Afro-American work songs, in this song the process of chopping the wood becomes an intrinsic part of the music. The sound produced by the ax creates a component of the music which is essential to the structure of the song. The music, then, is not simply accompanying the work, but the work becomes the music, and the music becomes the work.

A brief analysis of the song will reveal how the utilitarian and artistic functions of the song are interrelated. The song is based on a poetic structure in which the last word of every two lines, each of which is repeated, forms a rhyme. These four lines become a verse. Following the statement of the first verse, the chorus—"Oh, Rosie, Oh gal, Oh Rosie, O Lord gal"—appears. The chorus is followed by two additional verses and the piece concludes with a return of the chorus. Following is the text:

VERSE ONE   Little George said fo the Katie was *made*

Arkansas City gonna a'be her *trade*

CHORUS Oh Rosie, oh gal

Oh Rosie and a' Oh Lord, Gal

VERSE TWO The boats in the bayou turning well around an *round*

The drive wheel knockin' Ala-well-a-bama *bound*

VERSE THREE You go to Memphis, don't you well you act no *hog*

Buy a ticket and catch the well the Yellow *Dog*

(CHORUS AGAIN)

The general structure of the text is reinforced musically by the usage of the

EXAMPLE 1

same rhythmic pattern for the verses and a slightly different rhythmic pattern for the chorus (see Ex. 1). The pattern associated with the verses consists of eighth notes (or subdivisions of eighth notes) on the first three beats of the measure followed by the sound of the ax on the fourth beat. The second measure consistently uses two eighth notes followed by a quarter note, a quarter rest or a vocal grunt or hum on the third beat, and a single-beat value on the fourth beat sounded by the ax. The rhythmic pattern in the chorus uses ornamented quarter notes for the first three beats of the measure followed by the sound of the ax on the third beat; the second measure has two eighths and a quarter note, respectively, on beats one and two, a rest on the third beat, and the ax stroke on the fourth beat. In both verse and chorus the ax sound is consistently heard on the fourth beat of each measure.

The modal melody is based almost entirely on an elaborate ornamentation of two essential notes a minor third apart. The technique of rocking back and forth between notes a minor third apart is a common melodic device used in African and Afro-American music and is sometimes referred to as a "pendular third." This third relationship is also used as a means of establishing an antecedent-consequent

EXAMPLE 1 *(continued)*

or call-and-response relationship between the first statement of a line of text and its subsequent repetition. Such a relationship is accomplished by invariably terminating the first line of each verse with the upper pitch, A, of this interval and ending the repetition of that text with the lower pitch—F#. Since F# is the tonal center, the first phrase has an open-ended or antecedent feeling, and the second phrase has a closed or consequent feeling.

I have notated the song in $\frac{4}{4}$ meter because the setting of the text seems to be best subsumed under that meter. The fact that the frequently used two ♪♪ ♩ pattern begins exactly four beats apart at important words (*Little George—Katie was*) accounts for much of its metrical importance as a downbeat. Within this metrical scheme, however, two things occur which weaken the $\frac{4}{4}$ meter. First, the fourth beat (normally unstressed) is consistently accented by the occurrence of the ax sound. Because these accents persistently occur on this beat and are at equidistant time intervals from one another, they establish a counter-rhythm whose principal accents clash with the implied accents of the meter in the voice. In a simple way, the ax sounds are used to imply a subtle counter-rhythm, which relationship is emphasized by the contrast in timbre between the ax sound and the voice. In addition, the accents in the ax are complemented by the melodic accents which occur in the voice part; the vocal line is organized so that an accent occurs on alternate beats. Note, for example, the melodic and stress accents on the second beat (normally weak) of the first two measures. These weak-beat accents used in conjunction with the strong ax-sound accents of the fourth beat tend to reinforce the implied clash of accents and create the resultant counter-rhythm feeling. Finally, on still another level, a call-and-response relationship is established between the voice and the sound of the ax. The voice sounds on the first three beats of the first measure and the first two beats of the second measure of every line. This call is answered by the ax on the fourth beat of each measure. "Katie Left Memphis" is also rich in other aspects of the Afro-American musical tradition. A wide range of vocal nuances, frequent usage of implied subdivisions even when the text does not call for them, and anticipation and delay of accents immediately before or after a major beat are all used here in a fresh manner.

The utilitarian function of this song was to facilitate the process of chopping wood. The activity of chopping was carried on in the context of an aesthetic circumstance. In considering this simple song from the point of view of art, one has to assess the degree to which this song successfully combines its utilitarian task with the creation of something which is of aesthetic significance. My response to this particular song is that it does this eminently well. As a listener, I want to participate in this music-making process even to the point of chopping wood, because the song is high in musical content and reinforces Afro-American musical values in a unique and convincing manner.

The second example I wish to consider is Miles Davis's classic recording of "On Green Dolphin Street" (*Jazz Track*, Columbia Records). My approach to this work as art is, in many respects, the same as my approach to any work of musical art in Western culture. It is a work whose artistry is its main reason for existence. My approach to the music of Miles Davis differs from my approach to a work written within the Euro-American tradition, however, because the parameters of aesthetic significance in the music of Davis are all consistent with African-American conceptual approaches to music making. However, the Davis music may also include aspects of Euro-American tradition which complement those parameters in ingenious ways. An analysis of the Miles Davis solo improvisation may be instructive in this regard.

"On Green Dolphin Street" is a popular song adapted from the theme song of a 1947 movie entitled *Green Dolphin Street*. It was written by Ned Washington and Bronislau Kaper and, while a charming enough melody, was usually performed in a somewhat saccharine manner by popular singers of the late forties and fifties. The Miles Davis Quintet's recording of this tune transforms it completely and places it squarely within the modern jazz tradition.

The original melody is based on a thirty-two bar phrase structure form. It consists of four eight-measure phrases, each of which is subdivided into sub-units of four measures each. The last of these phrases contains a four-measure extension. The entire structure may be diagrammed as follows:

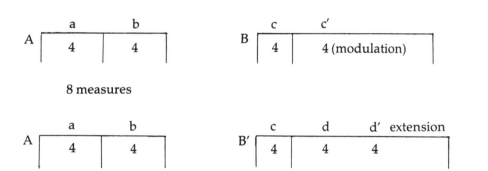

The Miles Davis Quintet's version of this song alters the original in certain important ways. The original harmonic structure of the first eight-bar phrase is altered by the double bass playing a tonic-pedal ostinato in which the second, third, and the last half of the fourth beat are emphasized (see Ex. 2). In addition to creating a mild degree of metrical clash between the meter in the melody and the bass line, the tonic pedal creates a sense of harmonic stasis throughout the entire eight measures. The static feeling is released in the second eight measures by having the rhythm section move to a different kind of accompaniment pattern (bass and bass drum occur on the first beat of the measure, piano plays more syncopated and percussively articulated chords) in which the harmonic rhythm moves much faster. At measure sixteen, there is a return to the harmonically static texture for eight more measures. The last phrase then returns to the faster harmonic movement and propulsively driving rhythm. The effect of this change is important. It creates, on a larger level, an alternation between contrasting textures in such a way that the second eight-measure phrase becomes an answer or response to the first phrase. In other words, an antiphonal or call-and-response relationship exists between the two units. This subtle change has added a new dimension to the original phrase structure, a dimension which occurs as a consequence of the application of Afro-American musical approaches to this song and thus transforms the original song.

EXAMPLE 2

The solo improvisation exploits this antiphonal relationship between the two phrases. Notice, for example, that Davis consistently uses long sustained tones in projecting a directed lyrical melodic line against the harmonically static but counter-rhythmic pedal point (m. 1–8 and 17–24 in both choruses and especially m. 30–32 in the first chorus). He also highlights the timbral distinctions between the rhythm section and his instrument by leaving relatively long spaces of silence between his entrances (first chorus, m. 7–8, 18–19, 27–28; second chorus, m. 10).

EXAMPLE 2 (*continued*)

The sections of long, held notes contrast with rapidly ascending scalar lines which he tends to play during the rhythmically driving phrases (first chorus, m. 10–12, 16, 25–27). He occasionally unites the two kinds of contrasting musical gestures by using the ascending scalar lines to introduce the long sustained notes, thereby creating a synthesis of the contrasting material (second chorus, m. 3–4, 15–16 and 25–27). This is all done in a rhythmic manner which makes his solo line seem to float above the rhythm section; this feeling is achieved by Davis's use of a myriad of techniques that cause the most important accents of his line to occur in places that contrast with those of the rhythm section. He consistently plays slightly ahead, behind, or between the primary pulse or its sub-division. He also changes the degree of rhythmic drive in his phrases to achieve this feeling. It is this latter quality to which jazz musicians refer when they speak in glowing terms of Miles Davis's "sense of time."

EXAMPLE 2 *(continued)*

Another quality of Miles Davis's improvisation in this piece is his astute sense of motivic development. He demonstrates that astuteness by the prominent treatment of a motive which occurs originally at the end of the first half of the song's fourth phrase and becomes the motivic basis of the four-measure extension (Ex. 2, m. 28). The most important feature of this motive is the descending interval of a third or, sometimes a fourth, which originally ended on the dominant of the key (Ex. 2, mm. 28–31). Davis does not begin to use this motive until measure seventeen of the first chorus. At this point we hear an interval expansion of the motive followed by a series of rhythmic and melodic variants of the idea, each of which occurs at a different place in the metric scheme. The motive returns in measure five of the second chorus and is again focused upon in several transposed and rhythmically altered versions. At measure twenty-five of the second chorus, the characteristic scalar line prepares for the beginning of a final series of statements of this motive, each of which involves a subtle shift of rhythm.

A unique aspect of Miles Davis's improvisational technique is his shaping of phrase structure so that the end of a phrase sounds like a new beginning. Note, for example, the extension (or tag) at the end of the statement of the melody in which the downbeat of the first measure becomes the end of his line rather than the beginning (Ex. 2, m. 36 of melody to m. 1 of first chorus; see also m. 29–32 of first chorus and m. 1–2 of second chorus).

Davis uses a variety of techniques to create this extraordinary solo. Subtle timbral changes, percussive attacks and releases, antiphonal substructures, multiple cross rhythms, etc. are all here. The success of this solo results from Davis's particular employment of these factors to create a meaningful musical statement. That statement is based on an imaginative usage of the values associated with Afro-American music, and it is a work of art.

In summary, black music may be defined as a musical tradition of peoples of Sub-Saharan African descent, which consists of a shared core of conceptual approaches to the process of music making. These concepts reflect deeply-rooted values of this culture and, in essence, consist of fundamental ways of approaching the musical experience. An analysis of any genre of black music will reveal the existence of demonstrable musical characteristics which consistently reflect the presence of these underlying conceptual approaches, and it is precisely the pervasive existence of these qualities which gives the music its distinctive character.

Black music as art may exist, at least within the United States, on two different levels. On one level, it exists as part of the "basic" or folk African-American musical tradition, a tradition which derives most of its concepts and values from West African musical traditions although it incorporates some important aspects of western musical practice. In this tradition, the artistic aspect of the music is inextricably associated with its functional role. Hence, its role as art cannot be separated from its utilitarian function. Therefore, any evaluation of this music must be cognizant of its multifaceted nature and consider its efficacy in achieving its function.

On another level, black music may exist as part of a second musical tradition in which Euro-American musical forms are characteristically transformed to become consistent with Afro-American cultural practices. Within the tradition, the music exists clearly as an object of "intrinsic perceptual interest" and thus is compatible with Western concepts of art. The questions that one raises in evaluating this music as art are the questions one raises when considering any activity or object as art in a Western sense; that is, does it require active aesthetic and/or intellectual involvement? is it highly charged in content? does it profoundly influence one's sensibilities? and does it yield new insight on repeated exposure? Obviously, those questions cannot be answered without an awareness of the unique cultural values, artistic techniques, and sensitivities of those who created the particular work in question, for all works of art reflect the cultural biases of its creators.

Ultimately, the basic criterion used to determine if a work of music is art, in either the traditional African sense of "functional art," or the Western sense of "pure art," is the same. That criterion is the degree to which that music, either as part of a more complex utilitarian experience or existing alone, significantly informs and enriches our lives.

REFERENCES

Armstrong, Robert P. *The affecting presence.* Urbana: University of Illinois, 1971.

Bell, Clive. *Art.* New York: Stokes, 1914.

Cuney-Hare, Maud. *Negro musicians and their music.* Washington D.C.: Associated Publishers, Inc. 1936.

Danquah, J. B. *The Akan doctrine of God.* London: Cass, 1946.

de Lerma, Dominique-René. *Black music in our culture.* Kent, Ohio: Kent State University Press, 1970.

Du Bois, W. E. B. *The souls of black folk.* 1903. New York: Fawcett Publications, 1961.

Floyd, Samuel A., Jr. J. W. Postelwaite of St. Louis. *The Black Perspective in Music,* 1978, 6, 151–167.

Fry, Roger. *Vision and design.* New York: Coward-McCann, 1925.

Gotschalk, D. W. *Art and the social order.* New York: Dover Publications, 1962.

Hanslick, Eduard. *Vom Musikalisch-Schönen.* Leipzig: R. Weigel, 1854.

Jahn, Janheinz. *Muntu.* New York: Grove, 1961.

Jones, Leroi. *Blues people.* New York: Morrow, 1963.

Langer, Susanne K. *Philosophy in a new key.* 1942. Cambridge, Massachusetts: Harvard University Press, 1974.

Meyer, Leonard. *Emotion and meaning in music.* Chicago: University of Chicago Press, 1956.

Southern, Eileen. *The music of black Americans: A history.* New York: W. W. Norton & Co., Inc., 1971.

Trotter, James Monroe. *Music and some highly musical people.* New York: Boston, Lee and Shepard, 1878.

Wilson, Olly. The significance of the relationship between Afro-American music and West African music. *The Black Perspective in Music,* 1974, 2, 3–22.

Wilson, Olly. The association of movement and music as a manifestation of a black conceptual approach to music making. In *International Musicological Society Report of the Twelfth Congress.* Daniel Heartz and Bonnie Wade, editors. Basel: Bärenreiter Kassel, 1981, 98–105.

what is jazz?

DISCOGRAPHY

Jazz Track. Columbia Records CO-61165. Miles Davis, Cannonball Adderley, John
    Coltrane, Bill Evans, Paul Chambers, Billy Cobb.
Roots of the Blues. New World Records, NW 252, 1977.

chapter 5

QUINCY TROUPE + BEN RILEY

Remembering Thelonious Monk: When the Music Was Happening Then He'd Get Up and Do His Little Dance

quincy troupe: Mr. Riley, the first question I want to ask you is when you first heard Monk.

ben riley: Okay. When I first heard Thelonious, it was an album, "Carolina Moon," and I brought it home, and I was playing it one morning on my way to school, and my mother said, "Now that's music." So I said, "Well, she's listening to this, and I'm trying to get into it, and something must be happening with it." So that's my real first moment, first acknowledgment of Thelonious, that record.

quincy troupe: And when's the first time you saw him?

ben riley: First time I saw Thelonious was at the old Five Spot. The date I can't recall at the moment. But it's easy to find. It was the band with John Coltrane, Shadow Wilson, and Wilbur Ware. And I guess this was the most awesome quartet that I'd heard in my life, going there from nine to four every night that they worked. I was sitting in there or standing outside listening to four great musicians. Really fantastic for me. That was the first time I heard them, and that just really blew my mind, listening to that quartet.

quincy troupe: Why? What was it about that quartet?

ben riley: It's just the uniqueness of the sound that they had; they had no one else's sound. And the musicianship that they exhibited was so fantastic. Nobody was overly energetic, as far as looking physically moved, but you could just take yourself anywhere you wanted to because they had control of the ship and you had control of where you wanted to go, you know, mentally.

quincy troupe: And you were telling me in the room that you saw Monk on a regular basis?

ben riley: Oh yes, now. . . . The new Five Spot on Eighth Street is the first chance I got an opportunity to be around him every night, when for six weeks I worked opposite him with his quartet. And I was with three different trios. I started with Bobby Timmons and then with Junior Mance and then I worked with Walter Bishop, Jr.

quincy troupe: When was this?

ben riley: This was about sixty-four. So Thelonious came in the room after the sixth week we were there, the last week, and he looked up at the stage, and I was still there, working. And he walked over to me and said, "Who the hell are you, the house drummer?" And kept going. And those were the first words he had spoken to me for six weeks. "Who the hell are you? Are you the house drummer?" And he kept going!

So that Monday, we closed on Sunday, and that Monday I had a phone call about eight in the morning saying, "We'd like you to come down to Columbia because Mr. Monk is recording, and we'd like you to come down," And I hung up. Because I have a friend of mine who used to do things like that, call me up and say, "Miles is looking for you and come down and we're gonna do so and so." So I hung up thinking it was a joke.

So the phone rang again, and somebody said, "This is no joke. We're down here at Columbia studio waiting for you." So I went down, and there they were. So we did this date, and he never said nothing to me *again*. I walked in, he never said good morning, he said nothing. I put the drums up, and after I got everything set and he saw that I was ready, he started playing. He still hasn't said a word to me. So we finish this whole half of an album, and while we're listening to the playback he walks over to me, and he says, "Would you like some money?" And I said, "No, I'll wait for the check." And he said, "I don't want anybody in my band being broke." [*laughter*] And so I said, "In your band?" He said, "Yes, do you have your passport ready?" I said, "No." He said, "Well, we're leaving Friday." And that was it; I was in the band.

quincy troupe: Is that the way he always did things?

ben riley: That's the way he did it with me. He just never . . . And then while we were on the plane, he said, "You didn't think I was listening to you." And I asked him, I said, "You know, I'd like to have a rehearsal." He said, "I know you can play, that's why I hired you." He said, "If we rehearse, you're gonna learn how to cheat." So he said, "You just do what you've been doing, and everything is gonna work out all right."

quincy troupe: What was this album? What was the album you all recorded?

ben riley: I think it was "It's Monk's Time." I think that was the album, "It's Monk's Time."

quincy troupe: Can you remember some of the tunes on it?

ben riley: Now that you mention it, no. I can't, I can't. It's strange. But I can't remember any of it. Actually, a lot of tunes, I never knew the titles. Because I knew the melodies when I heard them, and then the way he introduced each of his songs without speaking, I always knew what he was gonna do because he introduced them, then he stated the tempo, so I never had to worry about what the tune was. But I never could think of all the titles except for some of the tunes that I knew anyway, you know?

quincy troupe: Can you describe what it was like that first time playing with him in Columbia studios? I mean, what were your feelings, I mean, to play with him?

ben riley: Oh, *shit*. I said, "This is awesome," you know. I mean, here's a person that I had admired for the few years that I really knew who he was. And now to get up here and play with him was just awesome. And then the second thing is the music that I thought I knew. Well, listening to him all the time is a different thing from when you're sitting up there and you actually have to play this music. 'Cause you're not used to the tempos, you're not used to the feeling of each other, so now you have to get yourself in tune about how the other guys play and how they phrase and how they feel; and it was just an awesome feeling for me. So I said, "Well, he wouldn't have called for me if he didn't appreciate some of the things I had done, so let me give it my best shot. And then hope that's gonna be good enough."

quincy troupe: Did he ever say anything about what it was that he liked about what you did, I mean, why he picked you?

ben riley: No, through the course of the years, he and I spent a lot of time together. And he would talk to me more, I guess, than he did a lot of people. But he would always say things in little rhymes or he'd point out little things in situations that I was supposed to keep my eyes and ears open for, you know.

Like he would say, "Just because you're the drummer doesn't mean you have the best beat, you know?" And then he wouldn't say anything for a while. He'd let that sink in. And then he says, "You know, most musicians can only play in three tempos. Slow, medium, and fast." And so now he's letting me know that all these different reasons why he's playing all these things in these different tempos is to make me become aware that there's more than three ways to play. You gotta play in between all of these three things. So he got me to, really. He just never told me anything unless he thought I was ready to make another move. Then he'd say some other things to help prepare me, and I didn't realize all this until later on. Because he never came directly out and said anything. He wanted you to feel that you discovered all these things yourself, you know. Yeah, that was like going to the university. I mean, you had one of the highest points of your musical career working with him.

quincy troupe: What was he like, personally speaking?

ben riley: He was a very witty and very sensitive person. And in a way, I believe that's why a lot of times he gave you these different airs and these different little gestures that he would do. He didn't want you to get too close because he was a very sensitive person. He was a very sensitive person. And he had one hell of a sense of humor.

quincy troupe: Could you give me an example?

ben riley: We were in Finland at a classical concert, and the room was full of reporters, and they kept asking him, "How do you feel about classics and jazz?" You know? And everyone wanted him to answer, give them some type of definition between classical and jazz musicians. So he says, "Two is one." And that stopped the whole room. No one else said anything else. He said, "Two is one." And that stopped the whole thing, you know, he just stopped it. Caused silence. He really had some funny stuff.

quincy troupe: Was his music difficult to play?

ben riley: Well, one reason is because of the simplicity of it. It was so beautifully put together that it was really simple, but most people would try to put what wasn't really needed or what shouldn't have been there. When all you had to do was let the music play itself.

So that really made it difficult. Because the more I got involved with him and the longer I was around listening to him, the more I found out what *not* to play; that was the beauty of it, you know. And I'd say, now, "What could I leave out to let this thing just open up by itself," you know? 'Cause he used to tell me all the time; "Don't solo through everybody's choruses while they're playing," he said, " 'cause you'll get a chance to play."

Because I used to play like Max, and I used to play like Roy Haynes a lot when I was younger. And he said, "Now you don't have to do that. Just learn how to swing and make everybody move to certain places, and then the rest of it will take care of itself."

So I kind of learned spaces with him and I learned how to utilize silence. He was a master at using space and silence. He would leave you, and you would think he wouldn't know where he was at, but then bang.

quincy troupe: Tell me one funny thing that happened to the band.

ben riley: Oslo, I think it was, 1965—a big concert. We were playing, I forget what it was, one of the tunes, and I think we must have played like twenty minutes, and Larry Gales was with us then.

So, oh boy, we thought we were swinging, and we just, we were having a grand time. And we had no knowledge that we were playing on the wrong beat. And Thelonious had been sitting there, and I happened to notice, see, he hasn't moved, you know. Generally when we were having a good time, he shows some kind of emotion or some movement or something. He hasn't moved for this whole time we're playing.

And then all of a sudden, he finally got fed up with us playing on a wrong tempo, wrong time, and he said, "One." And he took his finger, and he said, "One." [*laughter*] I say, now that's . . . how much humor can you look for in a guy who can sit there that long and say, "Well, you don't know where you are, but I'm gonna let you play, hoping that you find out where you are." And we never found that one, until finally he said, "One." That was amazing for him to even do that, you know, but it was something that we all needed. Because now it brought us back in, and we started thinking again. That's the kind of person he was. He'd let you work things out, and if he saw that you weren't going to make it, or couldn't make it, then he'd guide you back in.

quincy troupe: What was the most difficult Monk tune?

ben riley: I'd say the most difficult tune for me was "Blue Monk."

quincy troupe: Why?

ben riley: Because he would never play it where I could fit my little things that I had set up for it, and he kind of sensed that I didn't do this song that well, so he would never play it at a tempo that I could utilize the things I liked to do best. He'd make me find another way to approach this song, which was beautiful for me, 'cause then it made me play the song. But I hated it. 'Cause it's just, it flowed so, and it had so much space that I couldn't find anything to do with it, you know. But he kept playing it until I did. But he kept doing it in a way that he made me kind of feel my way through. So I really appreciated that from him.

quincy troupe: The whole thing between the drums and Monk's piano, the space: can you describe that relationship, I mean, with you and him?

ben riley: I think playing with Thelonious for a drummer was like playing with a tap dancer. You see, the tap dancer would set up a certain rhythm, and then you'd have a chance to either correspond or play that rhythm again. And to me, that's the kind of situation that I had with Thelonious, it's like we were dancing with each other, you know? And he left space for me to do my little thing, and then I waited so he'd do his thing, and then he left another space for me to do my thing. 'Cause one of those things he used to say was, "When I play my solo, my little song, you let me play my little song, and I'll let you play your little songs." And that meant, "Don't play all over my stuff; you'll have a chance to play your stuff." So I guess that's where we get that utilization of space. And I think that's, for a drummer, one of the greatest things you would have.

quincy troupe: What was the dancing, the dancing that he would do?

ben riley: The dancing, yes. The dancing was funny. Because I have a funny story about Philly Joe Jones. One day after I had been with Thelonious for a while, Philly Joe came at me, and he said, "Damn. Uh." Philly said, "Damn," he said, "you know you're all right." And I said, "Why?" And he said, "Because I had to play five times with Monk before he danced."

You see, Monk, if the music wasn't going the way Monk really wanted it, then he wouldn't dance. That goes back to the Oslo story. We weren't doing it right, so he wasn't dancing, you see. But when his music was happening, then he'd get up and do his little dance. 'Cause he was feeling good, and he knew you knew where you were and the music was swinging, and that's what he wanted. So he said, "Well, I don't have to play now. You're making it happen."

quincy troupe: Somebody said to me that he'd send signals with his dances. Miles told me that the whole thing with his back to the audience was to tell people what to do. Did he do that?

ben riley: Well, for me, I had the feeling that when he got up and danced, it kind of raised me up some more to put more effort and more energy into the music. I felt that him dancing meant that the music was happening. 'Cause he used to say, "I want you to swing hard, swing very hard, and then swing as hard as you can swing." See? So, every time he danced, man, that just meant that something was happening with us and that we needed to just give it some more energy, some more energy.

quincy troupe: So with something like that, the timing has to be . . .

ben riley: Oh, right on it. Yeah, *right on it.*

quincy troupe: Can you talk about that? A little bit about the timing, if you can?

ben riley: Well, we go back to the, to speaking of the three different principles of slow, fast, and medium. You know that it's very easy to play things fast, 'cause if there's a mistake, it goes by so fast that you don't really have to worry about it until the next time it comes around. Medium, you have more time to think about it, so you try to be correct. And if you're playing slow, you got all day to try and make it right. So, when he plays in between all of these things, now you can't rely on any one of these three principles. You definitely have to be in sync with what's going on. And so the time becomes really important to make each phrase or each combination of notes come out correct.

quincy troupe: And off the bandstand, you and he would talk.

ben riley: We had many times that we would just walk. He was very worldly, knowledgeable. He kept up with all the world. It didn't look like he knew what was going on in the world, but he could sit down and he could tell you about everything that happened internationally and everywhere else. He was on it, but he just never would say anything. Unless he was in a certain setting. Then he would say something.

We were also drinking buddies, so we would always wind up in somebody's pub or some other bar or something.

He was a very sensitive person, a very knowledgeable person. And I think a lot of things happened to him that he took, that he held within. He never would release them. And I think in the end it finally caught up with him, you know.

quincy troupe: Why do you think he stopped playing?

ben riley: As I say, I think a lot of things that happened finally just made him shut himself out. Well, you know, like I told you before, I stopped playing. 'Cause after a while all these things that I saw going on and all the things that I felt that he saw going on, they just got to where they weighed too heavy on him. And for me, I just had to quit for a while. I couldn't take it any longer. And I think some of the things may have weighed very heavy on his mind.

quincy troupe: Was it . . . was it . . . was it the club, racism?

ben riley: Well, it's a . . . a whole coterie of things, you know. Being in America like for, especially a jazz musician, no matter what color he is but just being black, too, is a heavy, heavy load you'd have to carry on your shoulders.

quincy troupe: Why did the group you all had stay together so long? Could you name the people who were in that band?

ben riley: Yeah. It was Charlie Rouse, Larry Gales, and myself. We were together longer than any of the other bands that he had. Plus we had a lot of work, and there was a great camaraderie. All four of us were friends. So it really helped a lot. And at that time, there was no problem of him not feeling like he wanted to work. He relished the idea of going to work every night. And then we were traveling quite a bit, and we went on two world tours. And things were really, really looking good.

quincy troupe: How many albums did y'all make?

ben riley: I don't know whether it's five or six with that particular group. I'm not sure now.

quincy troupe: Do you know which one . . . did he have a favorite or did you have a favorite?

ben riley: No, I never listened to too many of them. I still don't listen to too many things I'm on. Maybe it takes a year before I'll even listen to something that I played on, you know. I always have an idea of what I did and always have an idea of what I wanted to do and couldn't reach. So I said, "I'm not going to listen to this right now. Let me see if I can go over here and improve what I think that I didn't do on this last one." And then when I go back sometimes I'm surprised at some of the things that I've done. Said, "Boy, I didn't know that I made it, you know." It's harder for me to listen to myself. It's easier for me to hear someone else and enjoy what I'm doing but I can't listen to myself too well. I criticize myself a little too much.

quincy troupe: Since you all played together and were a road band and a recording band, what were some of the differences? I mean, what were some of the differences, say, like playing in the clubs and then you have to go in the studio?

ben riley: Musicwise, when the thing was happening right, you could feel the audience. Recording inside of a studio, you have to manufacture something with the people that are in there with you, and hopefully you can get that feeling again. But in a club the audience helps motivate you. I was recording just recently, and with all of these different glass walls and all of these booths that they put everybody in, the separation now is so vast that you very rarely feel the person next to you, you know.

quincy troupe: Yeah. I mean was Monk . . . was he any different in the club . . .

ben riley: No.

quincy troupe: . . . than in the recording studio?

ben riley: And that's the key. He told me, "Never change the way you're playing. Whether you're here or there. Always try to maintain that one level." I think that's what happens to all of the great artists. They don't think of being in one room or another. They carry what they feel from this room to the next room. So that's why when you hear them play on records they always sound great because they haven't separated themselves because they went into another situation. Dizzy did that to me one summer. Boy, we were having so much trouble on this stage with the sound crew and everything. And everybody was complaining and going crazy. Dizzy came up right after us and hit like *that*, and the band was swinging, right away. And they had the same sound. So it's a matter of you taking here and putting it over there. Don't ever let it change. Just take what you have and go with it.

quincy troupe: We were talking about playing with Monk being almost like a religious thing. Can you talk about that a little bit?

ben riley: Yeah, with Monk you really knew that you were involved in something that was going to be part of history. You could kind of feel that, that you were involved with a person that was on another plane than your peers that you grew up with and most of the guys around you. You knew that there were very few guys that stood head and shoulders above all the other guys. And when you worked with him or Miles or Dizzy and Trane and Sonny Rollins, you knew these guys were on a plane above what was happening. So you spiritually became in tune with them, and the music became so spiritual, you know? Like you weren't thinking of time. You weren't thinking of how great you were gonna be or how great they were. You were just thinking about putting your whole self into what was going on at that particular moment.

quincy troupe: Did being on the cover of *Time* magazine have any effect on him?

ben riley: In 1964 when the *Time* article came out, Thelonious felt very good about himself because I think finally he understood that there were a number of people very interested in what he was playing and what he was doing.

quincy troupe: It didn't change him or anything, him being on the front cover?

ben riley: No, actually I think it made him play more because now he knew people were listening to him. He had a great enthusiasm when we went out to work because now he knew that he could see people standing in line waiting to come in to hear him play. That made him really feel good, and he attacked the music with great enthusiasm.

quincy troupe: If he could see all of this interest in his music by a lot of people now and films and all kind of things, I wonder how that would affect him.

ben riley: Well, today, with the attention that he's getting, it's a good question. I would go back to the fact that the group called Sphere that I was involved with recorded our first album in dedication to Thelonious. The music that we wanted to play was his music, and we decided that maybe if this album was good enough it would encourage him to return to playing again. But the day that we went to record, he passed away that morning while we were in the studio, so he never had a chance to hear the music.

quincy troupe: He was, you know, one of the founders of modern jazz here at Minton's. He was called the prince of bebop. And then some people say that he didn't really play bebop. What would you say to that?

ben riley: The word "bebop" is kind of hard for me to just get along with, I guess, because they had to label it something. I just looked at it as new, fantastic music that was exciting. I just found it very, very moving music and very uplifting music. And I just can't label it.

quincy troupe: And how did Monk's music tie in?

ben riley: I guess because he was one of the first composers. So he wrote a lot of the first things that were played. And Dizzy's first big band: he was the pianist in it, and some of his music was played by Dizzy's band.

quincy troupe: Did you have much experience with his family, his family life?

ben riley: Yes, we had a . . . a fairly close-knit quartet. And his children during the summer would be with my children. And we had like a family style. We would go on certain trips with the band, and we would all take our families with us. So if we went to Princeton or Yale or Baltimore or short trips like that on one-nighters, we would take our family because it was usually afternoon concerts at the colleges. So we would all take our families with us. So we became like a close-knit little group.

quincy troupe: Did he rely a great deal on Nell?

ben riley: Well, Nellie was the background for him, yes. Nellie, he never went anywhere without Nellie. The whole time I was with him, every trip we made, Nellie was there. She was, you know, she was his heart.

chapter 6

ALBERT MURRAY

Improvisation and the Creative Process*

In a sense, my topic, which is improvisation and the creative process, adds up to what the conference should add up to. The conference has not come up with blueprints or prescriptions. It has come up with ideas. I am going to talk about the nature of the creative process; about improvisation, which has to do with how you do what you have to do—how to hang loose and get the maximum. And in order to do that you have to know everything that has to do with what in jazz is called "the break"; and that is what improvisation has to do with.

First, a note or so toward a basic definition, or in any case a notion which serves as a basic guideline for my own procedure as an apprentice to the aesthetic image in general and to literature in particular. Art is the ultimate extension, elaboration, and refinement of the rituals that reenact the primary survival technology; and hence it conveys basic attitudes toward experience of a given people in a given time, place, circumstance, and predicament. It is, I submit, the process of extension, elaboration, and refinement that creates the work of art. It is precisely play that is indispensable to the creative process. I am so glad that we say, "You are going to *play* music." You don't *engineer* it or *work* at it. The word "play" has lost its true meaning. As I am using it here, I want it to be the full meaning of the word "play," as it resides at the very center of all culture, and certainly therefore at the center of art. Play in the sense of competition or contest; play in the sense of chance-taking or gambling; play in the sense of make-believe; play also in the sense of vertigo, or getting high, or inducing exhilaration; play also in the direc-

*Delivered at the conference sponsored by the Dallas Institute of Humanities and Culture in 1983, entitled "What Makes a City: The Economics of Taste."

tion of simple amusement or entertainment—as in children's games; and play in the direction of gratuitous difficulty—as in increasing the number of jacks one catches or the height or distance one jumps, or decreasing the time one runs a given course; gratuitous difficulty also in the sense of wordplay; or play in the sense of sound—as in a Bach fugue. I submit that such play or playing around is precisely what is involved in the process André Malraux is referring to when he suggests that art is the means by which forms of raw experiences are transformed or rendered into style.

This brings us to stylization. To stylize is to conventionalize. It is to create a pattern which becomes a way of seeing things and doing things. Convention can function both as the container and the thing contained. It provides the structure as well as the content of human consciousness. It is the quality of human consciousness that is the most profound concern of art. What art provides is the most fundamental human equipment for existence. It provides images, representative anecdotes, emblems that condition us to confront what we must confront, and it disposes us to do what we must do, not only to fulfill ourselves but also to survive as human beings in a given place, time, circumstance, and predicament. . . .

So play becomes convention and convention is a pattern of procedure. The convention of playful option-taking is what I call "the blues idiom" and jazz music. I define the jazz musician as one who approaches or creates or plays all music as if improvising the "break" on the traditional twelve-bar blues tune. Which brings me not only to improvisation and the creative process but also to blues idiom procedure and the "jam session" as the representative anecdote for life in the United States. By improvisation, of course, I most definitely do not mean "winging it" or making things up out of thin air. The jazz musician improvises within a very specific context and in terms of very specific idiomatic devices of composition. I want to mention several of these devices.

First, there is the "vamp," which is an improvised introduction. This is not unique to the blues idiom statement, but it is used in a special idiomatic way by the jazz musician. The jazz composition is also made up of a series of "choruses" which function like stanzas in a poem. . . . Another device for blues idiom statement is the "break," which is a disruption of the normal cadence of a piece of music. The "break" is a device which is used quite often and always has to do with the framework in which improvisation takes place. . . . The break is an extremely important device both from the structural point of view and from its implications. It is precisely this disjuncture which is the moment of truth. It is on the break that you "do your thing." The moment of greatest jeopardy is your moment of greatest opportunity. This is the heroic moment. . . . It is when you establish your identity; it is when you write your signature on the epidermis of actuality. That is how you come to terms with the void. . . .

This kind of improvisation is applicable to educational methods, to scientific method, to inventions. Your knowledge of chordal structure and progression is your knowledge of the experience data of mankind; it is all the wisdom and mistakes of the ages. That is what you "riff" on or improvise on. . . .

The most inventive, the most innovative jazz musician is also one with a very rich apperceptive mass or base, a very rich storehouse of tunes, phrases, ditties which he uses as a painter uses his awareness of other paintings, as a writer employs his literary background to give his statements richer resonances. As a matter of fact, the musician is always engaged in a dialogue or a conversation or even argument—not only, as in a jam session, with his peers—but also with all other music and musicians in the world at large. Indeed, his is an ongoing dialogue with the form itself. He achieves his individuality by saying "yes and also" to that with which he agrees, and by saying "no," or in any case, "on the other hand" to that with which he disagrees. . . . Yes, all of this is as applicable to science and engineering and political procedure as it is to music and literature and all of the other arts.

There is also the very fundamental matter of the "railroad onomatopoeia" that was established by the folk blues guitar and harmonica players—such as Leadbelly, or Robert Johnson. . . .

There is also that matter of the African-derived "talking drum." The blues is percussive statement. It is the talking drum that has become the old, down-home American locomotive with its chugging pistons, its ambiguous and ambivalent bell, and its signifying, insinuating, tall tale–telling whistle. The definitive characteristic of Afro-U.S. life style is its tendency to refine all movement, indeed all human activity, in the direction of dance beat elegance.

Such is the special nature of the musical convention that I call the blues idiom. This is fine art. The fact that all this is done not in the simple matter of producing music which is simply programmatic, but is consummate skill at producing instantaneous response to life and a matter of improvising, or making up your life or of being perpetually creative as you live your life, is what makes this important in thinking about the city.

Improvisation, as it functions in the blues idiom, is something that not only conditions people to cope with disjuncture and change but also provides them with a basic survival technique that is commensurate with and suitable to the rootlessness and the discontinuity so characteristic of human existence in the contemporary world. . . . However such improvisation proceeds, when it succeeds it puts you on good terms with life. It generates an atmosphere of well-being and celebration. It is music to have a good time with.

part 2

one nation under a groove,
or, the united states
of jazzocracy

introduction

When it comes to issues of culture, the very idea of *nation* is a contested space. What makes a "national culture" cohere as one entity? This thorny problem becomes a whole briarpatch in the United States, with its rush and clash of peoples, its cool mesclun and hot gumbo mix of voices, values, and ways. Edward Said's assertion that the story told in art *is* the nation is quite compelling here. What is the United States? It is *The Narrative of the Life of an American Slave*, it is *Howl*, it is *The Woman Warrior*. It is the American story told in the country's poetry, in its dramas and dances, in the visual arts. And—quite significantly for our purposes—it is the story performed in that art form where telling the story is one of the definitive requirements and invocations: "Tell the story, baby! Tell the story." The United States is the story told in the eloquent art of jazz.

This equation of jazz and America is easy enough to figure: Jazz is freedom music, the play of sounds that prizes individual assertion and group coordination, voices soloing and then (at their best) swinging together, the one-and-many *e pluribus unum* with a laid-back beat. Jazz is based on both the spirituals and the blues, where the notes of hope are edged by doubt and near despair: "I don't know what my mother wants to stay here for," one spiritual says. "This world ain't been no friend to her." And the blues: "I been down so long, down don't worry me." Jazz is comedy, American-style: comedy darkened by tragic experience in our land. And it is jazz (along with spirituals and blues) that sets the stage for such newer musics as rhythm and blues, rap, and so forth, to which the nation's youth move every Saturday night. For all its supposed abstruseness, jazz is an insistently democratic music, one that aims to sound like citizens in a barbershop or grocery line, talking stuff, trading remarks. Jazz is a music makable by anyone with the chops to get with it. (*Chops* meaning here neither sheer technical nor natural ability but other highly cultivated jazz assets, perhaps most notably the achievement of a personalized jazz voice. Recall that jazz's greatest singers, Louis Armstrong and Billie Holiday, never had great range or vocal gymnastic abilities; they had little—in Billie's case, no—conventional music training as such. They had a certain grainy, meditative truthfulness, they had swing, they had musicality to spare, they had soul. No acrobatic vocal technique, but they had everything else.)

According to this jazz/democracy perspective, in the growing blueprint society that is the United States we are all improvisers, making it up as we go along and depending on flexibility and resiliency—both hallmarks of the music—to make our way together. In a nation requiring, in the words of Constance Rourke, "resiliency as a prime trait,"[1] jazz is the canonical sound track, suggesting not just shiftiness in a new land but the grace under pressure associated with, say, Lester Young's cool sideways horn telling it like it is, whispering, chuckling, rhapsodizing the sweet thunder of rough-smooth melodies that bespeak a national modus operandi: a U.S. culture. It's a music that evokes America at least as much as a Sousa march in a Fourth of July parade or even the fife and drums of "Yankee Doodle Dandy." There's something about Lionel Hampton's "Flying Home," or Ella Fitzgerald's "Lady Be Good," or Sarah Vaughan's "Lullaby of Birdland" that outflagwaves them all. Or try Basie's "Good Morning Blues" or his "One O'Clock Jump." Try Bird's "Parker's Mood."

Paradoxically, while some hear in jazz these broad American themes, others hear in it the essence of black particularity, mystery, and memory: blackness traced in rhythm and tune back to the Old World of Africa. Some hear in jazz the sound of black fire and fury and revolution. (See Clay's speech in Baraka's *The Dutchman* and Henry Dumas's "Will the Circle Be Unbroken?"). According to this formula, if jazz is a national music, then it is the beautiful noise of the *black* nation, with sister and cousin musics sounding off elsewhere in the black diaspora. But even here we are confronted with an American paradox, not a hopeless racial contradiction. For, ironically enough, it is precisely by pulling back from the nation's canonized European traditions and insisting on their own "dirty" tones and "unorthodox" fingerings, "dark" timbres, "Chinese" intervals, instruments, voicings, etc., precisely by thumbing their noses at the thou-shalt-nots of the academy, that jazz makers created something that was not only new and black but robustly, definitively *American*.

This paradox is not so hard to fathom. Just as Joyce's fiction is rich with the vernacular blarney of Dublin, the Brer Rabbit tales started out as trickster stories that rang with the secret, rebellious in-group truth of what it meant to be black in America and then were translated all over the world. Likewise, Count Basie's music reflects the breakfast dances, shoe-shine parlor jams, and stage shows of black Oklahoma City and Kansas City, where his band and its antecedents first flourished; at the same time, though, again like Joyce's *Dubliners*, it reflects broader values, national and international. "The Negro," as Richard Wright said, "is America's metaphor."[2] And again, jazz is America's music, so much so that despite the cruelty of black unfreedom at home, it made perfect sense for Louis Armstrong to serve the U.S. government as Ambassador Satch and for antidemocratic nations routinely to ban from their airwaves that subversive free sound of America, jazz.

By the way, beware anyone who tells you what a jazz composition or solo means as if it were a handbook or a slogan scratched on a chalkboard. "Music is always suspect," as the expression goes, with its interpreters always seeing what they want to see there. But as we read this section, can we not agree on this much: Somehow jazz is black music, with the voices and values of U.S. Negro life and times (even when nonblacks are playing it, for, as literary historian Gina Dent has asserted, you don't have to be black to be a carrier of black culture). In the same breath, it is the music of the country that its creators (often with little affection) call home. Call it freedom music with a tragicomic black arc. Perhaps it is not sheer projection to hear in it—along with the bodacious song of exuberant freedom and triumphant elegance—the troubled blue sound of a dream-deferred people, still hotly at war. In a place of political freedom, says Cornel West, what we had was rhythmic freedom. Maybe the rhythmic freedom in jazz has helped provide the sound from which other freedoms, political and otherwise, eventually (slowly) have flowed.

NOTES

1. Constance Rourke, *American Humour* (New York: Harcourt, Brace, Jovanovich, 1931), p. 86.

2. Richard Wright, *White Man, Listen!* (New York: Doubleday, 1957), p. 109.

I wanted a song that would touch me, touch my life and theirs. . . . A Portuguese song, but not a Portuguese song. A new world song. A song branded with the New World.

—Gayl Jones

I believe that Hemingway, in depicting the attitudes of athletes, expatriates, bullfighters, traumatized soldiers, and impotent idealists, told us quite a lot about what was happening to that most representative group of Negro Americans, the jazz musicians—who also lived by an extreme code of withdrawal, technical and artistic excellence, rejection of the values of respectable society. They replaced the abstract and much-betrayed ideals of that society with the more physical values of eating, drinking, copulating, loyalty to friends, and dedication to the discipline and values of their art.

—Ralph Ellison, *Going to the Territory*

In all its styles, jazz involves some degree of collective ensemble improvisation, and in this it differs from Western music even at those times in its history when improvisation was required. The high degree of individuality, together with the mutual respect and co-operation required in a jazz ensemble carry with them philosophical implications that are so exciting and far-reaching that one almost hesitates to contemplate them. It is as if jazz were saying to us that not only is far greater individuality possible to man than he has so far allowed himself, but that such individuality, far from being a threat to a co-operative social structure, can actually enhance society. —Martin Williams

I'm looking at it like this: if you have a group, the group is like a painting, a masterpiece. Each one of the instruments represents a specific color and the diversity of the colors makes it beautiful. You've got five pieces and none of them sound alike, but they must have unity. So you take red, orange, blue, green or purple: each color in its diversity is supposed to be beautiful. Each one has a role, and when one of the colors overlaps onto another, you have chaos. Therefore, each one should be thinking in terms of the whole, in terms of the beautification of the diversity of the instruments. Paintings don't clash, like a purple going over into another color. They stay what they are but it's the whole picture that makes for the togetherness. Unity.

—Dizzy Gillespie (in Arthur Taylor)

But none of this can be totally separated from Music. Because that was the great definer and link, the extension cord of blackness in me. And so everything (else) had a music to it. A shimmer of sound you heard as you saw it, or you saw as you heard it. The blues hugged me close to the streets and the people. That was what we breathed and Saturdays was when we breathed (full out). And its blackness was the constant.

The people, the life, the rules, the mores, the on-the-street definitions of what was beautiful or hip. The constant background of our breathing, the blues, was always everywhere. And Saturdays raised up like a great space mural (blues as) companionship of thought and feeling; it was feeling. The real good-looking girls and tough dudes, who you wanted to make laugh and impress, the style you had to perfect was black—black and blue.   —Amiri Baraka, *The Autobiography of LeRoi Jones*

To battle the embittering forces of prison life, [Edward] Ryder learned to play the trumpet and embraced the tradition of improvisation handed down by Louis Armstrong, who also learned the trumpet while incarcerated, in a New Orleans reform school.

And Ryder drew strength from the words of cultural critic Albert Murray, for whom the jazz artist is a heroic American archetype who relies on the idea of "the break"—whether it be a shift in rhythm, a social injustice or other adversity for inspiration.

"The Nation [of Islam] did not have flexibility," Ryder says. "That's the thing about improvisation, you have to be willing to bend."   —Hugh Bronstein

"It all sounds like pure nonsense syllables to me."

"Nonsense, nothing!" cried Simple. "Bop makes plenty of sense."

"What kind of sense?"

"You must not know where Bop comes from," said Simple. astonished at my ignorance.

"I do not know," I said. "Where?"

"From the police," said Simple.

"What do you mean, from the police?"

"From the police beating Negroes' heads," said Simple. "Every time a cop hits a Negro with his billy club, that old club says, 'BOP! BOP! . . .BE-BOP! . . . MOP! . . . BOP!'

"That Negro hollers, "Ooool-ya-koo! Ou-o-o!'

"Old Cop just keeps on, 'MOP! MOP! . . . BE-BOP! . . .MOP!' That's where Be-bop came from, beaten right out of some Negro's head into them horns and saxophones and piano keys that plays it. Do you call that nonsense?"   —Langston Hughes art taylor: Have you ever felt any kind of protest in your music?

don byas: I'm protesting now. If you listen you will notice I'm always trying to make my sound stronger and more brutal than ever. I shake the walls in the joints I play in. I'm always trying to sound brutal without losing the beauty, in order to impress people and wake them up. That's protest, of course it is. I've always felt like that. . . . My form of protest is to play as hard and strong as I can. In other words you did this and you did that so now take this!   —Arthur Taylor

I could just see that big, dark, smiling, sweating, strong-looking crinkly-haired Joe Williams at DeLisa's singing that song. Holding the mike in one hand, and walking with that head way, way up in the air, carrying the mike with him as he walked, chest way out, shoulders way back, singing "Every Day"! And everybody would be screaming and throwing money up there on the stage and he wouldn't even look at the money. Step over it, singing and swinging, preaching a natural gospel of power—that fin-ger-popping, hip-swinging, bust-you-in-the-mouth-if-you-mess-with-me kind of power!

And I walked and sang, "Well, it ain't nobody worried . . . and it ain't nobody cryin'!"

—Frank London Brown, Trumbull Park (Chicago: Regnery, 1959)

The art—the blues, the spirituals, the jazz, the dance was what we had in place of freedom.   —Ralph Ellison, Shadow and Act

chapter 7

JOHN A. KOUWENHOVEN

What's "American" About America*

The discovery of America has never been a more popular pastime than it is today. Scarcely a week goes by without someone's publishing a new book of travels in the bright continent. Magazines here and abroad provide a steady flow of articles by journalists, historians, sociologists, and philosophers who want to explain the United States to themselves, or to itself, or to others.

The discoverers of America have, of course, been describing their experiences ever since Captain John Smith wrote his first book about America almost three hundred and fifty years ago. But as Smith himself noted, not everyone "who hath bin at Virginia, understandeth or knows what Virginia is." Indeed, just a few years ago the Carnegie Corporation, which supports a number of college programs in American Studies, entitled its quarterly report "Who Knows America?" and went on to imply that nobody does, not even "our lawmakers, journalists, civic leaders, diplomats, teachers, and others."

There is, of course, the possibility that some of the writers who have explored, vicariously or in person, this country's past and present may have come to understand or know what America really is. But how is the lay inquirer to judge which accounts to trust? Especially since most of the explorers seem to have found not one but two or more antipodal and irreconcilable Americas. The Americans, we are convincingly told, are the most materialistic of peoples, and, on the other

*The first version of this essay was given as a lecture at the University of Colorado, August 3, 1954, and published in the *Colorado Quarterly*, Winter 1955. Later versions were read at Smith College and at the Columbia University Seminar on American Civilization. The present version is revised from one published in *Harper's* magazine, July 1956.

hand, they are the most idealistic; the most revolutionary, and, conversely, the most conservative; the most rampantly individualistic, and, simultaneously, the most gregarious and herdlike; the most irreverent toward their elders, and, contrariwise, the most abject worshipers of "Mom." They have an unbridled admiration of everything big, from bulldozers to bosoms; and they are in love with everything diminutive, from the "small hotel" in the song to the "little woman" in the kitchen.

Maybe, as Henry James thought when he wrote *The American Scene*, it is simply that the country is "too large for any human convenience," too diverse in geography and in blood strains to make sense as any sort of unit. Whatever the reason, the conflicting evidence turns up wherever you look, and the observer has to content himself with some sort of pluralistic conception. The philosopher Santayana's way out was to say that the American mind was split in half, one half symbolized by the skyscraper, the other by neat reproductions of Colonial mansions (with surreptitious modern conveniences). "The American will," he concluded, "inhabits the skyscraper; the American intellect inherits the Colonial mansion." Mark Twain also defined the split in architectural terms, but more succinctly: American houses, he said, had Queen Anne fronts and Mary Ann behinds.

And yet, for all the contrarieties, there remains something which I think we all feel to be distinctively American, some quality or characteristic underlying the polarities which—as Henry James himself went on to say—makes the American way of doing things differ more from any other nation's way than the ways of any two other Western nations differ from each other.

I am aware of the risks in generalizing. And yet it would be silly, I am convinced, to assert that there are not certain things which are more American than others. Take the New York City skyline, for example—that ragged man-made Sierra at the eastern edge of the continent. Clearly, in the minds of immigrants and returning travelers, in the iconography of the admen who use it as a backdrop for the bourbon and airplane luggage they are selling, in the eyes of poets and of military strategists, it is one of the prime American symbols.

Let me start, then, with the Manhattan skyline and list a few things which occur to me as distinctively American. Then, when we have the list, let us see what, if anything, these things have in common. Here are a dozen items to consider:

1. The Manhattan skyline
2. The gridiron town plan
3. The skyscraper
4. The Model-T Ford
5. Jazz
6. The Constitution
7. Mark Twain's writing
8. Whitman's *Leaves of Grass*
9. Comic strips
10. Soap operas

11. Assembly-line production
12. Chewing gum

Here we have a round dozen artifacts which are, it seems to me, recognizably American, not likely to have been produced elsewhere. Granted that some of us take more pleasure in some of them than in others—that many people prefer soap opera to *Leaves of Grass* while others think Mark Twain's storytelling is less offensive than chewing gum—all twelve items are, I believe, widely held to be indigenous to our culture. The fact that many people in other lands like them too, and that some of them are nearly as acceptable overseas as they are here at home, does not in any way detract from their obviously American character. It merely serves to remind us that to be American does not mean to be inhuman—a fact which, in certain moods of self-criticism, we are inclined to forget.

What, then, is the "American" quality which these dozen items share? And what can that quality tell us about the character of our culture, about the nature of our civilization?

Skylines and Skyscrapers

Those engaged in discovering America often begin by discovering the Manhattan skyline, and here as well as elsewhere they discover apparently irreconcilable opposites. They notice at once that it doesn't make any sense, in human or aesthetic terms. It is the product of insane politics, greed, competitive ostentation, megalomania, the worship of false gods. Its by-products, in turn, are traffic jams, bad ventilation, noise, and all the other ills that metropolitan flesh is heir to. And the net result is, illogically enough, one of the most exaltedly beautiful things man has ever made.

Perhaps this paradoxical result will be less bewildering if we look for a moment at the formal and structural principles involved in the skyline. It may be helpful to consider the skyline as we might consider a lyric poem, or a novel, if we were trying to analyze its aesthetic quality.

Looked at in this way, it is clear that the total effect which we call "the Manhattan skyline" is made up of almost innumerable buildings, each in competition (for height, or glamour, or efficiency, or respectability) with all of the others. Each goes its own way, as it were, in a carnival of rugged architectural individualism. And yet—as witness the universal feeling of exaltation and aspiration which the skyline as a whole evokes—out of this irrational, unplanned, and often infuriating chaos, an unforeseen unity has evolved. No building ever built in New York was placed where it was, or shaped as it was, because it would contribute to the aesthetic effect of the skyline—lifting it here, giving it mass there, or lending a needed emphasis. Each was built, all those now under construction are being built, with no thought for their subordination to any overall effect.

What, then, makes possible the fluid and ever-changing unity which does, in fact, exist? Quite simply, there are two things, both simple in themselves, which do the job. If they were not simple, they would not work; but they are, and they do.

One is the gridiron pattern of the city's streets—the same basic pattern which accounts for Denver, Houston, Little Rock, Birmingham, and almost any American town you can name, and the same pattern which, in the form of square townships, sections, and quarter sections, was imposed by the Ordinance of 1785 on an almost continental scale as what Wolfgang Langewiesche has called "a diagram of the idea of the Social Contract," a blueprint for a future society in which men would live each in his own domain, free and equal, each man's domain. clearly divided from his neighbor's.

Whatever its shortcomings when compared with the "discontinuous patterns" of modern planned communities, this artificial geometric grid—imposed upon the land without regard to contours or any preconceived pattern of social zoning—had at least the quality of rational simplicity. The section lines, along which roads and fences run due north-south and due east-west, and which are so clearly visible from a plane over most of the U.S.A., make most of the nation exactly what an airplane pilot wants country to be: graph paper. As Langewiesche, the pilot, has said: "You can time your [plane's] shadow with a stop-watch across two lines, and get your exact speed. You can head the airplane down a section line and check your compass. But you hardly need a compass. You simply draw your course on the map and see what angle it makes. Then you cross the sections at the same angle. You can't miss. If you want to go exactly west, you get on a fence and follow it." And this simple gridiron pattern, mimicked in the city's streets, horizontally controls the spacing and arrangement of the isolated rectangular shafts which go to make up the skyline.

The other thing which holds the skyline's diversity together is the structural principle of the skyscraper. When we think of individual buildings, we tend to think of details of texture, color, and form, of surface ornamentation or the lack of it. But as elements in Manhattan's skyline, these things are of little consequence. What matters there is the vertical thrust, the motion upward; and that is the product of cage, or skeleton, construction in steel—a system of construction which is, in effect, merely a three-dimensional variant of the gridiron street plan, extending vertically instead of horizontally.

The aesthetics of cage, or skeleton, construction have never been fully analyzed, nor am I equipped to analyze them. But as a lay observer, I am struck by fundamental differences between the effect created by height in the RCA building at Rockefeller Center, for example, and the effect created by height in Chartres cathedral or in Giotto's campanile. In both the latter (as in all the great architecture of the past) proportion and symmetry, the relation of height to width, are constituent to the effect. One can say of a Gothic cathedral, this tower is too high; of a Romanesque dome, this is top-heavy. But there is nothing inherent in cage construction to invite such judgments. A true skyscraper like the RCA building could be eighteen or twenty stories taller, or ten or a dozen stories shorter, without changing its essential aesthetic effect. Once steel cage construction has passed a certain height, the effect of transactive upward motion has been established; from there on, the point at which you cut it off is arbitrary and makes no difference.

Those who are familiar with the history of the skyscraper will remember how slowly this fact was realized. Even Louis Sullivan—greatest of the early skyscraper architects—thought in terms of having to close off and climax the upward motion of the tall building with an "attic" or cornice which should be, in its outward expression, "specific and conclusive." His lesser contemporaries worked for years on the blind assumption that the proportion and symmetry of masonry architecture must be preserved in the new technique. If with the steel cage one could go higher than with load-bearing masonry walls, the old aesthetic effects could be counterfeited by dressing the façade as if one or more buildings had been piled on top of another—each retaining the illusion of being complete in itself. You can still see such buildings in New York: the first five stories perhaps a Greco-Roman temple, the next ten a neuter warehouse, and the final five or six an Aztec pyramid. That Aztec pyramid is simply a cheap and thoughtless equivalent of the more subtle Sullivan cornice. Both structures attempt to close and climax the upward thrust, to provide an effect similar to that of the *Katharsis* of Greek tragedy.

But the logic of cage construction requires no such climax. It has less to do with the inner logic of masonry forms than with that of the old Globe-Wernicke sectional bookcases, whose interchangeable units (with glass-flap fronts) anticipated by fifty years the modular unit systems of so-called modern furniture. Those bookcases were advertised in the nineties as "always complete but never finished"—a phrase which could with equal propriety have been applied to the Model-T Ford. Many of us remember with affection that admirably simple mechanism, forever susceptible to added gadgets or improved parts, each of which was interchangeable with what you already had.

Here, then, are the two things which serve to tie together the otherwise irrelevant components of the Manhattan skyline: the gridiron ground plan and the three-dimensional vertical grid of steel cage construction. And both of these are closely related to one another. Both are composed of simple and infinitely repeatable units.

The Structure of Jazz

It was the French architect, Le Corbusier, who described New York's skyline as "hot jazz in stone and steel." At first glance this may sound as if it were merely a slick updating of Schelling's "Architecture . . . is frozen music," but it is more than that if one thinks in terms of the structural principles we have been discussing and the structural principles of jazz.

Let me begin by making clear that I am using the term jazz in its broadest significant application. There are circumstances in which it is important to define the term with considerable precision, as when you are involved in discussion with a disciple of one of the many cults, orthodox or progressive, which devote themselves to some particular subspecies of jazz. But in our present context we need to focus upon what all the subspecies (Dixieland, Swing, Bop, or Progressive Jazz) have in common; in other words, we must neglect the by no means uninteresting qualities differentiating one from another, since it is what they have in common which can tell us most about the civilization which produced them.

There is no definition of jazz, academic or otherwise, which does not acknowledge that its essential ingredient is a particular kind of rhythm. Improvisation is also frequently mentioned as an essential; but even if it were true that jazz always involves improvisation, that would not distinguish it from a good deal of Western European music of the past. It is the distinctive rhythm which differentiates all types of jazz from all other music and which gives to all of its types a basic family resemblance.

It is not easy to define that distinctive rhythm. Winthrop Sargeant has described it as the product of two superimposed devices: syncopation and polyrhythm, both of which have the effect of constantly upsetting rhythmical expectations. Andre Hodeir, in his analytical study, *Jazz: Its Evolution and Essence*, speaks of "an alternation of syncopations and notes played on the beat," which "gives rise to a kind of expectation that is one of jazz's subtlest effects."

As you can readily hear, if you listen to any jazz performance (whether of the Louis Armstrong, Benny Goodman, or Dave Brubeck variety), the rhythmical effect depends upon there being a clearly defined basic rhythmic pattern to enforce the expectations which are to be upset. That basic pattern is the 4/4 or 2/4 beat underlying all jazz. Hence the importance of the percussive instruments in jazz: the drums, the guitar or banjo, the bull fiddle, the piano. Hence too the insistent thump, thump, thump, thump which is so boring when you only half-hear jazz—either because you are too far away, across the lake or in the next room, or simply because you will not listen attentively. But hence also the delight, the subtle effects good jazz provides as the melodic phrases evade, anticipate, and return to, and then again evade the steady basic four-beat pulse which persists, implicitly or explicitly, throughout the performance.

In other words, the structure of a jazz performance is, like that of the New York skyline, a tension of cross-purposes. In jazz at its characteristic best, each player seems to be—and has the sense of being—on his own. Each goes his own way, inventing rhythmic and melodic patterns which, superficially, seem to have as little relevance to one another as the United Nations building does to the Empire State. And yet the outcome is a dazzlingly precise creative unity.

In jazz that unity of effect is, of course, the result of the very thing each of the players is flouting: namely, the basic 4/4 beat—that simple rhythmic gridiron of identical and infinitely extendible units which holds the performance together. As Louis Armstrong once wrote, you would expect that if every man in a band "had his own way and could play as he wanted, all you would get would be a lot of jumbled-up, crazy noise." But, as he goes on to say, that does not happen, because the players know "by ear and sheer musical instinct" just when to leave the underlying pattern and when to get back on it.

What it adds up to, as I have argued elsewhere, is that jazz is the first art form to give full expression to Emerson's ideal of a union which is perfect only "when all the uniters are isolated." That Emerson's ideal is deeply rooted in our national experience need not be argued. Frederick Jackson Turner quotes a letter written by a frontier settler to friends back East, which in simple, unself-conscious words expresses the same reconciling of opposites. "It is a universal rule here," the frontiersman wrote, "to help one another, each one keeping an eye single to his own business."

One need only remember that the Constitution itself, by providing for a federation of separate units, became the infinitely extendible framework for the process of reconciling liberty and unity over vast areas and conflicting interests. Its seven brief articles, providing for checks and balances between interests, classes, and branches of the government, establish, in effect, the underlying beat which gives momentum and direction to a political process Richard Hofstadter has called "a harmonious system of mutual frustration"—a description that fits a jazz performance as well as it fits our politics.

The aesthetic effects of jazz, as Winthrop Sargeant long ago suggested, have as little to do with symmetry and proportion as have those of a skyscraper. Like the skyscraper, the total jazz performance does not build to an organically required climax; it can simply cease. The "piece" which the musicians are playing may, and often does, have a rudimentary Aristotelian pattern of beginning, middle, and end, but the jazz performance need not. In traditional Western European music, themes are developed. In jazz they are toyed with and dismantled. There is no inherent reason why the jazz performance should not continue for another 12 or 16 or 24 or 32 measures (for these are the rhythmic cages in jazz corresponding to the cages of a steel skeleton in architecture). As in the skyscraper, the aesthetic effect is one of motion, in this case horizontal rather than vertical.

Jazz rhythms create what can only be called momentum. When the rhythm of one voice (say the trumpet, off on a rhythmic and melodic excursion) lags behind the underlying beat, its four-beat measure carries over beyond the end of the underlying beat's measure into the succeeding one, which has already begun. Conversely, when the trumpet anticipates the beat, it starts a new measure before the steady underlying beat has ended one. And the result is an exhilarating forward motion which the jazz trumpeter Wingy Manone once described as "feeling an increase in tempo though you're still playing at the same tempo." Hence the importance in jazz of timing, and hence the delight and amusement of the so-called "break," in which the basic 4/4 beat ceases and a soloist goes off on a flight of fancy which nevertheless comes back surprisingly and unerringly to encounter the beat precisely where it would have been if it had kept going.

Once the momentum is established, it can continue until—after an interval dictated by some such external factor as the conventional length of phonograph records or the endurance of dancers—it stops. ("No stopping," as the signs on the thruways and parkways have it, "except for repairs.") And as if to guard against any Aristotelian misconceptions about an end, it is likely to stop on an unresolved chord, so that harmonically, as well as rhythmically, everything is left up in the air. Even the various coda-like devices employed by jazz performers at dances, such as the corny old "without a shirt" phrase of blessed memory, are often harmonically unresolved. They are merely conventional ways of saying "we quit," not, like Beethoven's insistent codas, ways of saying, "There now; that ties off all the loose ends; I'm going to stop now; done; finished; concluded; signed, sealed, delivered."

We think of jazz as a twentieth-century phenomenon, and it is true that it did not emerge as a national music until after the First World War. But there are close (and unexplored) analogies between jazz and other forms of popular arts which have deep roots in our national life. One is the nineteenth-century minstrel show. Constance Rourke gives a vivid description of it in her classic work on *American Humor*:

> Endmen and interlocutors spun out their talk with an air of improvisation. . . . In the dancing a strong individualism appeared, and the single dancer might perform his feats on a peck measure, and dancers might be matched against each other with high careerings which belonged to each one alone; but these excursions were caught within the broad effect. Beneath them all ran the deep insurgence of the Negro choruses . . . and the choral dancing of the walk-around made a resonant primitive groundwork.

Here we have several analogies with the structure of jazz—especially the improvisatory manner and the individual flights of fancy and fantasy held together by a rhythmic groundwork (the 4/4 beat of the walk-around). And there are other ways in which jazz is related to the minstrel show. The minstrel characters—Jim Crow, Zip Coon, Dan Tucker—were blackface creations, and many jazz musicians, both white and Negro, perpetuate the atmosphere of burnt-cork masquerade.

Related to these analogies are those between the form of jazz and the form of the humorous monologue, the dominant form in the tradition of American humor, from Seba Smith's Major Jack Downing to Mark Twain and Mr. Dooley and on down to the TV and night-club entertainers of our own time. In these humorous monologues the apparent "subject" is of as little importance as is the tune from which a jazz performance takes off. It is the "talking around" the subject without hitting it, the digressing and ramifying, which matters.

Twain and Whitman

Since Mark Twain is the acknowledged master of the humorous monologue in our literature, let us look at an example of his work. His writing was, of course, very largely the product of oral influences. He was a born storyteller, and he always insisted that the oral form of the humorous story was high art. Its essential tool (or weapon), he said, is the pause—which is to say, timing. "If the pause is too long the impressive point is passed," he wrote, "and the audience have had time to divine that a surprise is intended—and then you can't surprise them, of course." In other words, he saw the pause as a device for upsetting expectations, like the jazz "break."

Mark, as you know, was by no means a formal perfectionist. In fact he took delight in being irreverent about literary form. Take, for example, his account of the way *Pudd'nhead Wilson* came into being. It started out to be a story called "Those Extraordinary Twins," about a youthful freak consisting, he said, of "a combination consisting of two heads and four arms joined to a single body and a single pair of legs—and I thought I would write an extravagantly fantastic little story with this freak of nature for hero—or heroes—a silly young Miss [named Rowena] for heroine, and two old ladies and two boys for the minor parts."

But as he got writing the tale, it kept spreading along and other people began intruding themselves—among them Pudd'nhead, and a woman named Roxana, and a young fellow named Tom Driscoll, who before the book was half finished had taken things almost entirely into their own hands and were "working the whole tale as a private venture of their own."

From this point, I want to quote Mark directly, because in the process of making fun of fiction's formal conventions he employs a technique which is the verbal equivalent of the jazz "break"—a technique of which he was a master.

When the book was finished and I came to look round to see what had become of the team I had originally started out with—Aunt Patsy Cooper, Aunt Betsy Hale, the two boys, and Rowena the light-weight heroine— they were nowhere to be seen; they had disappeared from the story some time or other. I hunted about and found them—found them stranded, idle, forgotten, and permanently useless. It was very awkward. It was awkward all around, but more particularly in the case of Rowena, because there was a love match on, between her and one of the twins that constituted the freak, and I had worked it up to a blistering heat and thrown in a quite dramatic love quarrel, [now watch Mark take off like a jazz trumpeter flying off on his own in a fantastic break] wherein Rowena scathingly denounced her betrothed for getting drunk, and scoffed at his explanation of how it had happened, and wouldn't listen to it, and had driven him from her in the usual "forever" way; and now here she sat crying and broken-hearted; for she had found that he had spoken only the truth; that it was not he, but the other half of the freak that had drunk the liquor that made him drunk; that her half was a prohibitionist and had never drunk a drop in his life, and although tight as a brick three days in the week, was wholly innocent of blame; and indeed, when sober, was constantly doing all he could to reform his brother, the other half, who never got any satisfaction out of drinking, anyway, because liquor never affected him. [Now he's going to get back on the basic beat again.] Yes, here she was, stranded with that deep injustice of hers torturing her poor torn heart.

Mark didn't know what to do with her. He couldn't just leave her there, of course, after making such a to-do over her; he'd have to account to the reader for her somehow. So he finally decided that all he could do was "give her the grand bounce." It grieved him, because he'd come to like her after a fashion, "notwithstanding she was such an ass and said such stupid, irritating things and was so nauseatingly sentimental"; but it had to be done. So he started Chapter Seventeen with: "Rowena went out in the back yard after supper to see the fireworks and fell down the well and got drowned."

It seemed abrupt [Mark went on], but I thought maybe the reader wouldn't notice it, because I changed the subject right away to something else.

Anyway it loosened up Rowena from where she was stuck and got her out of the way, and that was the main thing. It seemed a prompt good way of weeding out people that had got stalled, and a plenty good enough way for those others; so I hunted up the two boys and said "they went out back one night to stone the cat and fell down the well and got drowned." Next I searched around and found old Aunt Patsy Cooper and Aunt Betsy Hale where they were aground, and said "they went out back one night to visit the sick and fell down the well and got drowned." I was going to drown some of the others, but I gave up the idea, partly because I believed that if I kept that up it would arouse attention, . . . and partly because it was not a large well and would not hold any more anyway.

That was a long excursion—but it makes the point: that Mark didn't have much reverence for conventional story structure. Even his greatest book, which is perhaps also the greatest book written on this continent—*Huckleberry Finn*—is troublesome. One can scarcely find a criticism of the book which does not object, for instance, to the final episodes, in which Tom rejoins Huck and they go through that burlesque business of "freeing" the old Negro Jim—who is, it turns out, already free. But, as T. S. Eliot was, I think, the first to observe, the real structure of *Huck Finn* has nothing to do with the traditional form of the novel—with exposition, climax, and resolution. Its structure is like that of the great river itself—without beginning and without end. Its structural units, or "cages," are the episodes of which it is composed. Its momentum is that of the tension between the river's steady flow and the eccentric superimposed rhythms of Huck's flights from, and near recapture by, the restricting forces of routine and convention.

It is not a novel of escape; if it were, it would be Jim's novel, not Huck's. Huck is free at the start, and still free at the end. Looked at in this way, it is clear that *Huckleberry Finn* has as little need of a "conclusion" as has a skyscraper or a jazz performance. Questions of proportion and symmetry are as irrelevant to its structure as they are to the total effect of the New York skyline.

There is not room here for more than brief reference to the other "literary" items on our list: Whitman's *Leaves of Grass*, comic strips, and soap opera. Perhaps it is enough to remind you that *Leaves of Grass* has discomfited many a critic by its lack of symmetry and proportion, and that Whitman himself insisted: "I round and finish little, if anything; and could not, consistently with my scheme." As for the words of true poems, Whitman said in the "Song of the Answerer"—

> They bring none to his or her terminus or to be content and full,
> Whom they take they take into space to behold the birth of stars, to
>   learn one of the meanings,
> To launch off with absolute faith, to sweep through the ceaseless rings
>   and never be quiet again.

Although this is not the place for a detailed analysis of Whitman's verse techniques, it is worth noting in passing how the rhythm of these lines reinforces their logical meaning. The basic rhythmical unit, throughout, is a three-beat phrase of which there are two in the first line (accents falling on *none, his,* and *term . . . be, tent,* and *full*), three in the second (*take, take,* and *space . . . hold, birth, stars . . . learn, one, mean*), and three in the third (*launch, ab, faith . . . sweep, cease, rings . . . nev, qui, gain*).

Superimposed upon the basic three-beat measure there is a flexible, non-metrical rhythm of colloquial phrasing. That rhythm is controlled in part by the visual effect of the arrangement in long lines, to each of which the reader tends to give equal duration, and in part by the punctuation within the lines. For example, the comma pause after the second three-beat measure in line two (after *stars*) tends, since the first line consisted of two such measures, to establish an expectation of rest which is upset by the line's continuing for another measure. Then, in the final line, the placement of the comma pause reverses the pattern, requiring a rest after the first measure and doubling up the remaining two.

It is the tension between the flexible, superimposed rhythm of the rhetorical patterns and the basic three-beat measure of the underlying framework which unites with the imagery and the logical meaning of the words to give the passage its restless, sweeping movement. It is this tension and other analogous aspects of the structure of *Leaves of Grass* which give to the book that "vista" Whitman himself claimed for it.

If I may apply to it T. S. Eliot's idea about *Huckleberry Finn,* the structure of the *Leaves* is open at the end. Its key poem may well be the "Song of the Open Road," as D. H. Lawrence believed. "Toward no goal," Lawrence wrote. "Always the open road. Having no direction even. . . . This was Whitman. And the true rhythm of the American continent speaking out in him."

As for the comics and soap opera, they too—on their own frequently humdrum level—have devised structures which provide for no ultimate climax, which come to no end demanded by symmetry or proportion. In them both there is a shift in interest away from the "How does it come out?" of traditional storytelling to "How are things going?" In a typical installment of Harold Gray's *Little Orphan Annie,* the final panel shows Annie walking purposefully down a path with her dog, Sandy, saying: "But if we're goin', why horse around? It's a fine night for walkin' . . . C'mon, Sandy . . . Let's go . . ." (It doesn't even end with a period, or full stop, but with the conventional three dots or suspension points, to indicate incompletion.) So too, in the soap operas, *Portia Faces Life,* in one form or another, day after day, over and over again. And the operative word is the verb "faces." It is the process of facing that matters.

America Is Process

Here, I think, we are approaching the central quality which all the diverse items on our list have in common. That quality I would define as a concern with process rather than product—or, to re-use Mark Twain's words, a concern with the manner of handling experience or materials rather than with the experience or materials themselves. Emerson, a century ago, was fascinated by the way "becoming somewhat else is the perpetual game of nature." The universe, he said, "exists only in transit," and man is great "not in his goals but in his transitions."

This preoccupation with process is, of course, basic to modern science. "Matter" itself is no longer to be thought of as something fixed, but fluid and ever-changing. The modern sciences, as Veblen observed forty years ago, cluster about the "notion of process," the notion of "a sequence, or complex, of consecutive change." Similarly, modern economic theory has abandoned the "static equilibrium" analysis of the neo-classic economists, and in philosophy John Dewey's instrumentalism abandoned the classic philosophical interest in final causes for a scientific interest in the "mechanism of occurrences"—that is, process.

It is obvious, I think, that the American system of industrial mass production reflects this same focus of interest in its concern with production rather than products. And it is the mass-production system, *not* machinery, which has been America's contribution to industry.

In that system there is an emphasis different from that characteristic of handicraft production or even of machine manufacture. In both of these there was an almost total disregard of the means of production. The aristocratic ideal inevitably relegated interest in the means exclusively to anonymous peasants and slaves; what mattered to those who controlled and administered production was, quite simply, the finished product. In a mass-production system, on the other hand, it is the process of production itself which becomes the center of interest rather than the product.

If we are aware of this fact, we usually regard it as a misfortune. We hear a lot, for instance, of the notion that our system "dehumanizes" the worker, turning him into a machine and depriving him of the satisfactions of finishing anything, since he performs only some repetitive operation. It is true that the unit of work in mass production is not a product but an operation. But the development of the system, in contrast with Charlie Chaplin's wonderful but wild fantasy of the assembly line, has shown the intermediacy of the stage in which the worker is doomed to frustrating boredom. Merely repetitive work, in the logic of mass production, can and must be done by machine. It is unskilled work which is doomed by it, not the worker. More and more skilled workers are needed to design products, analyze jobs, cut patterns, attend complicated machines, and coordinate the processes which comprise the productive system.

The skills required for these jobs are different, of course, from those required to make handmade boots or to carve stone ornament, but they are not in themselves less interesting or less human. Operating a crane in a steel mill, or a turret lathe, is an infinitely more varied and stimulating job than shaping boots day after day by hand. A recent study of a group of workers on an automobile assembly line makes it clear that many of the men object, for a variety of reasons, to those monotonous, repetitive jobs which (as we have already noted) should be—but in many cases are not yet—done by machine; but those who *like* such jobs like them because they enjoy the process. As one of them said: "Repeating the same thing you can catch up and keep ahead of yourself . . . you can get in the swing of it." The report of members of a team of British workers who visited twenty American steel foundries in 1949 includes this description of the technique of "snatching" a steel casting with a magnet, maneuvered by a gantry crane running on overhead rails:

> In its operation, the crane approaches a pile of castings at high speed with the magnet hanging fairly near floor level. The crane comes to a stop some-where short of the castings, while the magnet swings forward over the pile, is dropped on to it, current switched on, and the hoist begun, at the same moment as the crane starts on its return journey. [And then, in words which might equally be applied to a jazz musician, the report adds:] The whole operation requires timing of a high order, and the impression gained is that the crane drivers derive a good deal of satisfaction from the swinging rhythm of the process.

This fascination with process has possessed Americans ever since Oliver Evans in 1785 created the first wholly automatic factory: a flour mill in Delaware in which mechanical conveyors—belt conveyors, bucket conveyors, screw convey-ors—are interlinked with machines in a continuous process of production. But even if there were no other visible sign of the national preoccupation with process, it would be enough to point out that it was an American who invented chewing gum (in 1869) and that it is the Americans who have spread it—in all senses of the verb—throughout the world. A non-consumable confection, its sole appeal is the process of chewing it.

The apprehensions which many people feel about a civilization absorbed with process—about its mobility and wastefulness as well as about the "dehumanizing" effects of its jobs—derive, I suppose, from old habit and the persistence of values and tastes which were indigenous to a very different social and economic system. Whitman pointed out in *Democratic Vistas* ninety years ago that America was a stranger in her own house, that many of our social institutions, like our theories of literature and art, had been taken over almost without change from a culture which was not, as ours is, the product of political democracy and the machine. Those institutions and theories, and the values implicit in them, are still around, though some (like collegiate gothic, of both the architectural and intellectual variety) are less widely admired than formerly.

Change, or the process of consecutive occurrences, is, we tend to feel, a bewil-dering and confusing and lonely thing. All of us, in some moods, feel the "prefer-ence for the stable over the precarious and uncompleted" which, as John Dewey recognized, tempts philosophers to posit their absolutes. We talk fondly of the need for roots—as if man were a vegetable, not an animal with legs whose dis-tinction it is that he can move and "get on with it." We would do well to make ourselves more familiar with the idea that the process of development is universal, that it is "the form and order of nature." As Lancelot Law Whyte has said, in *The Next Development in Man*:

> Man shares the special form of the universal formative process which is common to all organisms, and herein lies the root of his unity with the rest of organic nature. While life is maintained, the component processes in

man never attain the relative isolation and static perfection of inorganic processes. . . . The individual may seek, or believe that he seeks, independence, permanence, or perfection, but that is only through his failure to recognize and accept his actual situation.

As an "organic system" man cannot, of course, expect to achieve stability or permanent harmony though he can create (and in the great arts of the past, has created) the illusion of them. What he can achieve is a continuing development in response to his environment. The factor which gives vitality to all the component processes in the individual and in society is "not permanence but development."

To say this is not to deny the past. It is simply to recognize that for a variety of reasons people living in America have, on the whole, been better able to relish process than those who have lived under the imposing shadow of the arts and institutions which Western man created in his tragic search for permanence and perfection—for a "closed system." They find it easy to understand what that very American philosopher William James meant when he told his sister that his house in Chocorua, New Hampshire, was "the most delightful house you ever saw; it has fourteen doors, all opening outwards." They are used to living in grid-patterned cities and towns whose streets, as Jean-Paul Sartre observed, are not, like those of European cities, "closed at both ends." As Sartre says in his essay on New York, the long straight streets and avenues of a gridiron city do not permit the buildings to "cluster like sheep" and protect one against the sense of space. "They are not sober little wads closed in between houses, but national highways. The moment you set foot on one of them, you understand that it has to go on to Boston or Chicago."

So, too, the past of those who live in the United States, like their future, is open-ended. It does not, like the past of most other people, extend downward into the soil out of which their immediate community or neighborhood has grown. It extends laterally backward across the plains, the mountains, or the sea to somewhere else, just as their future may at any moment lead them down the open road, the endless-vistaed street.

Our history is the process of motion into and out of cities; of westering and the counter-process of return; of motion up and down the social ladder—a long, complex, and sometimes terrifyingly rapid sequence of consecutive change. And it is this sequence, and the attitudes and habits and forms which it has bred, to which the term "America" really refers.

"America" is not a synonym for the United States. It is not an artifact. It is not a fixed and immutable ideal toward which citizens of this nation strive. It has not order or proportion, but neither is it chaos except as that is chaotic whose components no single mind can comprehend or control. America is process. And in so far as Americans have been "American"—as distinguished from being (as most of us, in at least some of our activities, have been) mere carriers of transplanted cultural traditions—the concern with process has been reflected in the work of their heads and hearts and hands.

chapter 8

AMIRI BARAKA

Jazz and the White Critic

Most jazz critics have been white Americans, but most important jazz musicians have not been. This might seem a simple enough reality to most people, or at least a reality which can be readily explained in terms of the social and cultural history of American society. And it is obvious why there are only two or three fingers' worth of Negro critics or writers on jazz, say, if one understands that until relatively recently those Negroes who *could* become critics, who would largely have to come from the black middle class, have simply not been interested in the music. Or at least jazz, for the black middle class, has only comparatively recently lost some of its stigma (though by no means is it yet as popular among them as any vapid musical product that comes sanctioned by the taste of the white majority). Jazz was collected among the numerous skeletons the middle-class black man kept locked in the closet of his psyche, along with watermelons and gin, and whose rattling caused him no end of misery and self-hatred. As one Howard University philosophy professor said to me when I was an undergraduate, "It's fantastic how much bad taste the blues contain!" But it is just this "bad taste" that this Uncle spoke of that has been the one factor that has kept the best of Negro music from slipping sterilely into the echo chambers of middle-brow American culture. And to a great extent such "bad taste" was kept extant in the music, blues or jazz, because the Negroes who were responsible for the best of the music were always aware of their identities as black Americans and really did not, themselves, desire to become vague, featureless, Americans as is usually the case with the Negro middle class. (This is certainly not to say that there have not been very important Negro musicians from the middle class. Since the Henderson era, their number has increased enormously in jazz.)

Negroes played jazz as they had sung blues or, even earlier, as they had shouted and hollered in those anonymous fields, because it was one of the few areas of human expression available to them. Negroes who felt the blues, later jazz, impulse, as a specific means of expression, went naturally into the music itself. There were fewer social or extra-expressive considerations that could possibly disqualify any prospective Negro jazz musician than existed, say, for a Negro who thought he might like to become a writer (or even an elevator operator, for that matter). Any Negro who had some ambition towards literature, in the earlier part of this century, was likely to have developed so powerful an allegiance to the sacraments of middle-class American culture that he would be horrified by the very idea of writing about jazz.

There were few "jazz critics" in America at all until the '30s and then they were influenced to a large extent by what Richard Hadlock has called "the carefully documented gee-whiz attitude" of the first serious European jazz critics. They were also, as a matter of course, influenced more deeply by the social and cultural mores of their own society. And it is only natural that their criticism, whatever its intention, should be a product of that society, or should reflect at least some of the attitudes and thinking of that society, even if not directly related to the subject they were writing about, Negro music.

Jazz, as a Negro music, existed, up until the time of the big bands, on the same socio-cultural level as the sub-culture from which it was issued. The music and its sources were *secret* as far as the rest of America was concerned, in much the same sense that the actual life of the black man in America was secret to the white American. The first white critics were men who sought, whether consciously or not, to understand this secret, just as the first serious white jazz musicians (Original Dixieland Jazz Band, Bix, etc.) sought not only to understand the phenomenon of Negro music but to appropriate it as a means of expression which they themselves might utilize. The success of this "appropriation" signaled the existence of an American music, where before there was a Negro music. But the white jazz musician had an advantage the white critic seldom had. The white musician's commitment to jazz, the *ultimate concern*, proposed that the sub-cultural attitudes that produced the music as a profound expression of human feelings, could be *learned* and need not be passed on as a secret blood rite. And Negro music is essentially the expression of an attitude, or a collection of attitudes, about the world, and only secondarily an attitude about the way music is made. The white jazz musician came to understand this attitude as a way of making music, and the intensity of his understanding produced the "great" white jazz musicians, and is producing them now.

Usually the critic's commitment was first to his *appreciation* of the music rather than to his understanding of the attitude which produced it. This difference meant that the potential critic of jazz had only to appreciate the music, or what he thought was the music, and that he did not need to understand or even be concerned with the attitudes that produced it, except perhaps as a purely sociological consideration. This last idea is certainly what produced the reverse patronization that is known as Crow Jim. The disparaging "all you folks got rhythm" is no less a stereotype, simply because it is proposed as a positive trait. But this Crow Jim attitude has not been as menacing or as evident a flaw in critical writing about jazz as has another manifestation of the white critic's failure to concentrate on the blues and jazz attitude rather than his conditioned appreciation of the music. The major flaw in this approach to Negro music is that it strips the music too ingenuously of its social and cultural intent. It seeks to define jazz as an art (or a folk art) that has come out of no intelligent body of socio-cultural philosophy.

We take for granted the social and cultural milieu and philosophy that produced Mozart. As Western people, the socio-cultural thinking of eighteenth-century Europe comes to us as a legacy that is a continuous and organic part of the twentieth-century West. The socio-cultural philosophy of the Negro in America (as a continuous historical phenomenon) is no less specific and no less important for any intelligent critical speculation about the music that came out of it. And again, this is not a plea for narrow sociological analysis of jazz, but rather that this music cannot be completely understood (in critical terms) without some attention to the attitudes which produced it. It is the philosophy of Negro music that is most important, and this philosophy is only partially the result of the sociological disposition of Negroes in America. There is, of course, much more to it than that.

Strict musicological analysis of jazz, which has come into favor recently, is also as limited as a means of jazz criticism as a strict sociological approach. The notator of any jazz solo, or blues, has no chance of capturing what in effect are the most important elements of the music. (Most transcriptions of blues lyrics are just as frustrating.) A printed musical example of an Armstrong solo, or of a Thelonious Monk solo, tells us almost nothing except the futility of formal musicology when dealing with jazz. Not only are the various jazz effects almost impossible to notate, but each note *means something* quite in adjunct to musical notation. The notes of a jazz solo exist in a notation strictly for musical reasons. The notes of a jazz solo, as they are coming into existence, exist as they do for reasons that are only concomitantly musical. Coltrane's cries are not "musical," but they *are* music and quite moving music. Ornette Coleman's screams and rants are only musical once one understands the music his emotional attitude seeks to create. This attitude is real, and perhaps the most singularly important aspect of his music. Mississippi Joe Williams, Snooks Eaglin, Lightnin' Hopkins have different emotional attitudes than Ornette Coleman, but all of these attitudes are continuous parts of the historical and cultural biography of the Negro as it has existed and developed since there was a Negro in America, and a music that could be associated with him that did not exist anywhere else in the world. The notes *mean something*; and the something is, regardless of its stylistic considerations, part of the black psyche as it dictates the various forms of Negro culture.

Another hopeless flaw in a great deal of the writing about jazz that has been done over the years is that in most cases the writers, the jazz critics, have been anything but intellectuals (in the most complete sense of that word). Most jazz critics began as hobbyists or boyishly brash members of the American petite bourgeoisie, whose only claim to any understanding about the music was that they knew it was *different*; or else they had once been brave enough to make a trip into a Negro slum to hear their favorite instrumentalist defame Western musical tradition. Most jazz critics were (and are) not only white middle-class Americans, but middle-brows as well. The irony here is that because the majority of jazz critics are white middle-brows, most jazz criticism tends to enforce white middle-brow standards of excellence as criteria for performance of a music that in its most profound manifestations is completely antithetical to such standards; in fact, quite often is in direct reaction against them. (As an analogy, suppose the great majority of the critics of Western formal music were poor, "uneducated" Negroes?) A man can speak of the "heresy of bebop" for instance, only if he is completely unaware of the psychological catalysts that made that music the exact registration of the social and cultural thinking of a whole generation of black Americans. The blues and jazz aesthetic, to be fully understood, must be seen in as nearly its complete human context as possible. People made bebop. The question the critic must ask is: *why*? But it is just this *why* of Negro music that has been consistently ignored or misunderstood; and it is a question that cannot be adequately answered without first understanding the necessity of asking it. Contemporary jazz during the last few years has begun to take on again some of the anarchy and excitement of the bebop years. The cool and hard bop/funk movements since the '40s seem pitifully tame, even decadent, when compared to the music men like Ornette Coleman, Sonny Rollins, John Coltrane, Cecil Taylor and some others have been making recently. And of the bop pioneers, only Thelonious Monk has managed to maintain without question the vicious creativity with which he first entered the jazz scene back in the '40s. The music has changed again, for many of the same basic reasons it changed twenty years ago. Bop was, at a certain level of consideration, a reaction by young musicians against the sterility and formality of Swing as it moved to become a formal part of the mainstream American culture. The New Thing, as recent jazz has been called, is, to a large degree, a reaction to the hard bop-funk-groove-soul camp, which itself seemed to come into being in protest against the squelching of most of the blues elements in cool and progressive jazz. Funk (groove, soul) has become as formal and clichéd as cool or swing, and opportunities for imaginative expression within that form have dwindled almost to nothing.

The attitudes and emotional philosophy contained in "the new music" must be isolated and understood by critics before any consideration of the *worth* of the music can be legitimately broached. Later on, of course, it becomes relatively easy to characterize the emotional penchants that informed earlier aesthetic statements. After the fact, is a much simpler way to work and think. For example, a writer who wrote liner notes for a John Coltrane record mentioned how difficult it had been for him to appreciate Coltrane earlier, just as it had been difficult for him to appreciate Charlie Parker when he first appeared. To quote: "I wish I were one of those sages who can say, 'Man, I dug Bird the first time I heard him.' I didn't. The first time I heard Charlie Parker, I thought he was ridiculous. . . ." Well, that's a noble confession and all, but the responsibility is still the writer's and in no way involves Charlie Parker or what he was trying to do. When that writer first heard Parker he simply did not understand *why* Bird should play the way he did, nor could it have been very important to him. But now, of course, it becomes almost a form of reverse snobbery to say that one did not think Parker's music was worth much at first hearing, etc., etc. The point is, it seems to me, that if the music is worth something now, it must have been worth something then. Critics are supposed to be people in a position to tell what is of value and what is not, and, hopefully, at the time it first appears. If they are consistently mistaken, what is their value?

Jazz criticism, certainly as it has existed in the United States, has served in a great many instances merely to obfuscate what has actually been happening with the music itself—the pitiful harangues that raged during the '40s between two "schools" of critics as to which was the "real jazz," the new or the traditional, provide some very ugly examples. A critic who praises Bunk Johnson at Dizzy Gillespie's expense is no critic at all; but then neither is a man who turns it around and knocks Bunk to swell Dizzy. If such critics would (or could) reorganize their thinking so that they begin their concern for these musicians by trying to understand why each played the way he did, and in terms of the constantly evolving and redefined philosophy which has informed the most profound examples of Negro music throughout its history, then such thinking would be impossible.

It has never ceased to amaze and infuriate me that in the '40s a European critic could be arrogant and unthinking enough to inform serious young American musicians that what they were feeling (a consideration that exists before, and without, the music) was false. What had happened was that even though the white middle-brow critic had known about Negro music for only about three decades, he was already trying to formalize and finally institutionalize it. It is a hideous idea. The music was already in danger of being forced into that junk pile of admirable objects and data the West knows as *culture*.

Recently, the same attitudes have become more apparent in the face of a fresh redefinition of the form and content of Negro music. Such phrases as "anti-jazz" have been used to describe musicians who are making the most exciting music produced in this country. But as critic A. B. Spellman asked, "What does anti-jazz mean and who are these ofays who've appointed themselves guardians of last year's blues?" It is that simple, really. What does anti-jazz mean? And who coined the phrase? What is the definition of jazz? And who was authorized to make one?

Reading a great deal of old jazz criticism is usually like boning up on the social and cultural malaise that characterizes and delineates the bourgeois philistine in America. Even rereading someone as intelligent as Roger Pryor Dodge in the old *Record Changer* ("Jazz: its rise and decline," 1955) usually makes me either very angry or very near hysterical. Here is a sample: ". . . let us say flatly that there is no future in preparation for jazz through Bop . . . ," or, "The Boppists, Cools, and Progressives are surely stimulating a dissolution within the vagaries of a non-jazz world. The Revivalists, on the other hand have made a start in the right direction." It sounds almost like political theory. Here is Don C. Haynes in the April 22, 1946 issue of *Down Beat*, reviewing Charlie Parker's *Billie's Bounce* and *Now's the Time*: "These two sides are bad taste and ill-advised fanaticism. . . ." and, "This is the sort of stuff that has thrown innumerable impressionable young musicians out of stride, that has harmed many of them irreparably. This can be as harmful to jazz as Sammy Kaye." It makes you blush.

Of course there have been a few very fine writers on jazz, even as there are today. Most of them have been historians. But the majority of popular jazz criticism has been on about the same level as the quoted examples. Nostalgia, lack of understanding, or failure to see the validity of redefined emotional statements which reflect the changing psyche of the Negro in opposition to what the critic might think the Negro ought to feel; all these unfortunate failures have been built many times into a kind of critical stance or aesthetic. An aesthetic whose standards and measure are connected irrevocably to the continuous gloss most white Americans have always made over Negro life in America. Failure to understand, for instance, that Paul Desmond and John Coltrane represent not only two very divergent ways of thinking about music, but more importantly, two very different ways of viewing the world, is at the seat of most of the established misconceptions that are daily palmed off as intelligent commentary on jazz or jazz criticism. The catalysts and necessity of Coltrane's music must be understood as they exist even before they are expressed as music. The music is the result of the attitude, the stance. Just as Negroes made blues and other people did not because of the Negro's peculiar way of looking at the world. Once this attitude is delineated as a continuous though constantly evolving social philosophy directly attributable to the way the Negro responds to the psychological landscape that is his Western environment, criticism of Negro music will move closer to developing as consistent and valid an aesthetic as criticism in other fields of Western art.

There have been so far only two American playwrights, Eugene O'Neill and Tennessee Williams, who are as profound or as important to the history of ideas as Louis Armstrong, Bessie Smith, Duke Ellington, Charlie Parker or Ornette Coleman, yet there is a more valid and consistent body of dramatic criticism written in America than there is a body of criticism about Negro music. And this is simply because there is an intelligent tradition and body of dramatic criticism, though it has largely come from Europe, that any intelligent American drama critic can draw on. In jazz criticism, no reliance on European tradition or theory will help at all. Negro music, like the Negro himself, is strictly an American phenomenon, and we have got to set up standards of judgment and aesthetic excellence that depend on our native knowledge and understanding of the underlying philosophies and local cultural references that produced blues and jazz in order to produce valid critical writing or commentary about it. It might be that there is still time to start.

chapter 9

WYNTON MARSALIS + ROBERT G. O'MEALLY

Duke Ellington:
"Music Like a Big Hot Pot of Good Gumbo"*

robert o'meally: The other night you started the lecture ["Jazz for Young People," held at Lincoln Center in 1992] with "It Don't Mean a Thing If It Ain't Got That Swing." There's something definitive about that statement, and there's something definitive about Duke's sense of swing. If you were going to tell somebody about the rhythm in Duke Ellington, what would you say?

wynton marsalis: If we are going to talk about Duke Ellington's rhythm, I think we have to talk about many rhythms, because swinging is about coordination. It's about attaining an equilibrium of forces that many times don't go together. Someone who loves to swing is a great facilitator, and Duke Ellington is the very greatest of the great facilitators, because he played every style of rhythm that we know. He played with Coltrane's rhythm section; he had his rhythm section with Sam Woodyard on the drums and Jimmy Woode on the bass and the rhythm section with Sonny Greer on the drums and Jimmy Blanton playing the bass. And they don't swing in one style. They had the shuffle swing; they had slow, slow, deep-in-the-pocket groove swing; church grooves; the Afro-Cuban pieces; ballads with the brushes; exotic grooves on an album like *Afro-Bossa*.

When you talk about rhythm in Duke Ellington, you're talking about so many things. He could play in the bebop style, too. I don't think there's any aspect of Afro-American music and American music that was closed to Duke Ellington. He could go through any door and do something hipper than who-

*This interview was conducted in 1992 for a short film made as part of a Smithsonian Institution exhibit on Duke Ellington called "Beyond Category," which opened in Washington, D.C., in April 1993.

ever was in that door before him. I've seen a lot of pictures of him where he's at concerts, and he just has a look in his eyes that says, "I'm gonna figure out what this is very shortly."

robert o'meally: Somebody might say, "Oh, Ellington, he was just a dance player, he just played for dances." That's not quite true, or even quite fair to what it means to be a dance player, is it?

wynton marsalis: Well, I think playing for dances is much more fun than playing for concerts, and it fulfills more of the role of jazz music. A lot of times there is a tendency to compare jazz music to European classical music or to American classical music. We have to understand that jazz music has a totally different history, it has different objectives, and anyone who says, "That's just for dances" has never played a dance. You have to have the right tempo, and above all you have to be swinging, because you want the people to get off their butts and get on to the dance floor and shake those butts. Dance bands in jazz have an unmistakable joy in their swing.

Also, the jazz musician gets inspiration from dancers. I can remember when I was growing up in New Orleans playing the street parades. When I would play them, you could look at the dancers and you'd see rhythms to play on your horn. And Duke Ellington realized more than any other musician the value of dance rhythms and the value of the combination of jazz and dance. That's why he puts out albums as late as the 1950's and 1960's, albums like "Live at the Bal Masque," where you get a bunch of people together and dance. It's a great album. He understood the importance of romance in body movement—the romantic aspect of body movement—to jazz music.

robert o'meally: As a young jazz player, you were drawn to people like Coltrane and Miles and small group jazz. And big bands were stiff and corny to you. What was it about Duke that struck you as different?

wynton marsalis: Well, when I was growing up I never listened to big band music because I thought that was like some old people who would drink a little Geritol or something and then they'd go in the ballroom and dance to some old "In a Mellow Tone" or something. And whenever I heard some of Duke's music, I wouldn't really listen to it. I'd say: "Oh Duke, yeah, he was an old man." I didn't know anything about Duke Ellington.

When I was nineteen or twenty, Stanley Crouch, who is a writer in New York and a good friend of mine, would come by my house and leave these Duke Ellington albums. And I remember that's the first Duke Ellington I ever really started listening to (actually it's a collection, *The Smithsonian Collection of Classic Jazz*, that Martin Williams annotated and wrote notes for). I realized that it was much more sophisticated than what I had been hearing. First, the songs were in all different keys; there were arrangements, and they had a sophistication that I previously thought only existed in European music in terms of compositional sophistication. Songs like "Bragging in Brass"—I would listen to that over and over again. And "Koko" and "Daybreak Express." The things that Duke did with form. . . . And then songs like "Diminuendo and Crescendo in Blue." And then I'd say, "These guys were doing this in the nineteen *thirties*!" We have a long way to go in terms of trying to address the actual sophistication of jazz music. Duke Ellington's music is not only sophisticated as music on a technical level, but it also works from an emotional and spiritual standpoint. It is highly accurate; he actually knows how to describe American life in tone. "Daybreak Express" sounds like a train and then like some people on a train. Listening to "Moon over Cuba," you think you are *there*. He knows how to transport you to another place.

robert o'meally: Let's think of our high school teacher coming to the exhibit, and he or she teaches music and never thought of *teaching* Duke Ellington but thinks of him as a "tune writer." Can you tell that person something about Duke's compositional sophistication that might clear things up on this score?

wynton marsalis: The point I always try to impress on educators about the music of Duke Ellington is that it's music that is significant to teaching students about living in this country and in this time.

Duke Ellington's music is based on a skyscraper and on conceptions that come out of the American experience. It's based on the blues; his system of harmony comes out of the blues. It's not a simple form of harmony; it's only simple if you don't examine it. Indeed, his form of harmony is just as complex as any that's ever existed.

When I say the music is like a skyscraper, what I mean is that jazz is organized in choruses, so each chorus will represent something like a floor of a skyscraper. It has the same structure, but something very different goes on in each floor. So if you try to say, "Well, let's compare Duke Ellington's music to a Beethoven symphony," you can't do that because Beethoven's music comes from agrarian culture, addressing a monarchy, that type of a political situation, and Duke Ellington's music deals with democracy and a technological culture.

So we have failed in the educational system to assess American culture properly. This is why our kids across the board—rich, poor, black, white, Mexican, whatever they are—really lack a fundamental understanding of American culture. This is also why we have so many problems getting it together in this country. Everybody wants to fight from their vantage point. We don't understand that there are common threads that run through all of us. Duke Ellington's music is an important key to understanding that, because he is the central figure in the central achievement of American culture, which is jazz music. And the fact that I can go in the United States of America and hear all these high school bands and college bands and never hear a Duke Ellington arrangement, never hear young musicians come into contact with the work of the greatest master of American composition, lets me know that we have a lot of work to do.

robert o'meally: David Berger told me the other night that fifty percent of Ellington's music is played in unison. He said, though, that then Ellington will surprise you: then there will be this gospel voicing coming up against the blues, or there will be a "wrong note," he'll call it, or a dissonance. Can you talk a bit about the kind of sound of surprise in the music?

wynton marsalis: He uses the different elements of the orchestra in very imaginative ways and to create surprise by setting up expectations and then doing something else. To work on a piece of music is like a big crossword puzzle: the more elements you have to deal with, the more complex the puzzle. You're dealing with the form, which is like a skyscraper. You're dealing with the various personalities of the musicians, which can be used to illuminate different aspects of the very same melody. You're dealing with the harmony, which can change over and over again. You're dealing with the melody, which can be embellished. You're dealing with the rhythm, which can be anything—it can also be changed. And you're dealing with sixteen or seventeen instruments that you can combine in any way. Plus you have the mutes that he used. He has all different kinds of mutes—and not only would he use mutes, he used whatever the band members could do: slapping instruments, honking effects, half-valve effects with Rex Stewart. He had imagination and great humor.

With Duke Ellington, it's like a big pot of gumbo. You can make it more shrimp, more okra, more beef, more chicken—one spoonful might be all shrimp: "Damn, there's a lot of shrimp in this gumbo." The next one might be some sausage and the next one might be okra. So the next one might just be some rice and some gravy and some of that good gumbo juice. So when you're dealing with Duke, he's somebody whose music is like a big hot pot of good gumbo and every spoon that you pick up is gonna have a great proportion to it and it will surprise you pleasantly. You'll say, "Oh, okay, I didn't know you could do that."

robert o'meally: Before he became a musician professionally, he was a painter and considered a professional career as such. Many people have pointed out—Albert Murray points out somewhere—that he was a *colorer*; he remained an image maker and colorist. Does that strike you as true?

wynton marsalis: Well, I think that the thing about Duke Ellington that's most interesting is that he's not just a musician. He would've been great in any art form. Some musicians have a specific musical ability, a technical ability. They can hear well, they're prodigious on their instruments, they can catch on to music very quickly. Other musicians have more of an overall conception of form in art. They understand the purpose of art, which is to take stuff that goes on in everyday life and transform it into something that you can enjoy checking out—organize it. Now Duke used to be a painter, and that means that he was dealing with the organization of light and darkness on canvas. So we find the same type of attitude that we might find in a painter like Matisse: somebody who is a great colorist, who could just put a little splotch of something over there, and then you look at it all, and there's the sun over there, and there's some trees, and then there's something you don't know what it is, but it looks good against that other thing, and that's how Duke is in music. When he has the orchestra playing, he can go from blue to red to green.

A lot of Duke Ellington's titles are colors. "Mood Indigo," let alone all of the blue—everything *in blue*; *green*, as in envy; and many, many colors come into our music. And Duke is the supreme colorist in jazz. He knew how to combine those visual tones and make colors vibrate when they're set against each other. They have a certain vibration that they set up; so do musical tones.

robert o'meally: One of the things that's unique about Ellington is that early on he was writing longer pieces just as you said, having a bigger conception, trying to get a bigger slice of American life. Can you talk about Ellington as a experimenter with form?

wynton marsalis: Well, the thing you have to realize about Duke Ellington's conception of form is that it is *the* conception of form to have in American music. He wrote in forms that have not been addressed. The AABA song form, the twelve-bar blues form, these were just devices that Duke Ellington used at will. Some of his sections have seven bars, some have fifteen. He wrote in a concerto form that he invented. He wrote in blues forms that he came up with. He came up with blue mood forms. His long forms, extended forms, they haven't been analyzed properly. He has forms where he'll present a small part, like the "Tattooed Bride"; he'll start off with a melody, and then that melody will become the basis of the harmony, and then he'll take the melody notes and turn them into the bass notes and put another melody on top of it. . . . I could go on; the variations in his forms are endless because he understood the function of form, which is to organize whatever you want into something cohesive. He wasn't bound by conventional forms.

robert o'meally: Ellington played the piano brilliantly, but people often used to say that his real instrument was the orchestra. There's something unique about the fact that he was a great composer who had these men who had been with him forever. Can you talk about Ellington the man who played the orchestra?

wynton marsalis: Well, I think that one of the greatest achievements in the history of art is the Duke Ellington orchestra. Ellington stayed on the road; he wrote this enormous body of music; and he hired these musicians who were the greatest musicians on their instruments, who I'm sure many times gave him tremendous problems. He went through fifty years of everybody's personal lives and them being on the road missing their families and him missing his family, but that love for the music and their love for the music kept them out here playing.

By the time that band got to 1959 or 1960, that's a sound that will never be heard again. I only regret that I wasn't alive to really hear that band because you have people who had been in the band twenty-five years. Think of the power of that saxophone section playing together that long! On albums like *Anatomy of a Murder*, you can kind of get a feeling for it, but an album in no way captures the sound of an orchestra. I know that that was a sound of such magnificence and maturity. All of these musicians have such a confidence in Duke Ellington and a love for him as a man. You have to have that to play somebody's music the way they played his music. He was willing to sacrifice whatever he had to sacrifice for the sake of his music, and that's what his music sounds like. It's the ultimate dedication and the ultimate gift that Duke Ellington is giving us through his music. He wasn't a materialistic man. "Let everybody else have the money, let me have the kicks." That's what he would always say. "I get all the kicks." He got to stand up every night and hear Johnny Hodges play, plus Lawrence Brown, Ray Nance, Rex Stewart, Cootie Williams, Paul Gonsalves, Harry Carney.

Harry Carney, that's an example of the type of men that played with Duke forever. Harry Carney—fifty years, the ultimate professional every night with his horn, every record date driving Duke to gigs. Think of the type of emotion that had to be passing forth in that band. These men went from young manhood to being old men playing his music. When Harry Carney set up with his baritone to play "Mood Indigo" or to play "It Don't Mean a Thing If It Ain't Got That Swing" in 1967, now what was he thinking about? Something they had played since 1929 or 1930! What that orchestra represents as a musical organization is that type of longevity, that kind of intimacy and power.

robert o'meally: Somebody at the Manhattan School of Music told me recently that every great composer has always had a great composer that inspired him or her. David Berger was there and said, "What about Duke?" and the guy said, "Well in his case it was the band." His band really inspired him to write for them; it was a mutual inspiration society.

wynton marsalis: He got tremendous inspiration from the band, but, you know, it wouldn't be what you would think. It's not that they sat around talking about music; I'm sure they did, but when you get a crew of musicians together, they're always hamboning or playing some little phrase or talking about something. Not about music, they'll talk about their family life. Maybe somebody grew up in the church, and they'll do mock church services. All this kind of stuff is what goes into the music. One guy's personality would be a certain way, and they'll give him a nickname based on that. He would have a certain phrase that he'll say all the time, that would become a tune. Another one might be bald-headed so they would tease him, call him "Shiny" or something, and he might respond in his music.

With a band of sixteen, seventeen people, crazy musicians, on the road, you have inspiration for composition because they're from all different parts of the country, they live totally different lives, they know whole different groups of people. As a part of the band, you interface with everything they know. You go to dinner at their aunt's house, or Auntie So-and-So who's from here. You sit down in the living room, and they're talking about when old Jeb-from-Whatsis came over there and did this. And the cats in the band are teasing the guy whose aunt's house it is and saying, "Man, we didn't know you were this country. They got the toilet out in the back!" You go to somebody else's house—they might have been a son of a doctor or something—sitting up in their house, everybody trying to be straight, and somebody in the band is drunk and falling all over the people's stuff. In a band all these kinds of things go on. You're always with somebody getting teased or somebody's mad at somebody, and you're making light of it. Or somebody's farting in the trumpet section, and everybody is else like, "Man, you know, if you do that again I'm gonna knock you out."

This is the kind of stuff you made music out of. It's not like everybody was saying, "Yes, this is great music we're gonna play tonight." Somebody slapped somebody in the head, or somebody wants to reach and pull a knife out and cut somebody: that's the music. What Duke would do is, he'd see one guy go for his knife and want to cut another one in a big argument; now see, that night they're gonna play some fours against each other. Like he would always put Ray Nance and Cootie Williams together; they would solo right after each other a lot, because Ray Nance took Cootie Williams's place when he left Duke's band. Duke had that kind of mind. He said, "Oh, okay, Ray Nance took your place, he left me to go to play with Benny Goodman, now you and him have to solo back to back." Cat Anderson, they say he was a belligerent type of cat. I mean, all those things work, and it's not anything that's publicized. Somebody might think Johnny Hodges is a certain way, but you'd have to be in the band to know. You really have to be in the band to know how these guys are, and that's what Duke was a master of: he was a master of perception. He was very perceptive. He knew how different people fed off of each other, and he also knew what was important about what was going on.

The music is not a dissertation, it's just an everyday life thing. Somebody has a hotel room on the second floor, and he doesn't like being on the second floor: he's superstitious; he has to be on the seventh. So he comes down to the front lobby with his robe on, because he's just realized he's on the second floor. He was too tired when he checked into the hotel. But now he's downstairs with his robe and some slippers on, talking about, "Man, I have to get another room," and the hotel is sold out. You know what I mean? Okay, that's a tune.

robert o'meally: Often, I think, the analogy is made between Ellington and Shakespeare writing for particular actors or other dramatic groups serving a stock company that can do Shakespeare in the morning and comedy in the afternoon. Is there an analogy to be made between a dramatic group and Ellington's band, with all these players?

wynton marsalis: Well there's an analogy to be made between the situation that Ellington had and the type of situation that Shakespeare had, with a set group of people to do his material because whenever you get a certain group of people together who come from different places, they create a type of group dialogue, and it's this dialogue that you play off of in your work. Like, you know one person is a certain way; so okay, I'll do this for them.

If it's a diverse enough group—and that's what you really are looking for, if you are organizing an ensemble of people—then you will have in this microcosm an example of all the different types of people in the world. Duke Ellington's orchestra had the intellectual, like Harry Carney. Then he had somebody who would just knock somebody out, like Cat Anderson or Cootie Williams. Then he had somebody with a real ecumenical conception, like Lawrence Brown. And then he'd have somebody who was really funny, like Tricky Sam Nanton, or somebody who was really a sweetheart, like Ray Nance. Or somebody with high intellectual and technical capabilities, who also can swing, like Jimmy Hamilton. So when he wants some lace, he'd deal with Jimmy Hamilton; when he wants some grit, Cootie Williams; when he wants something pristine, Lawrence Brown. When he wants something that is just sheer beauty and romantic essence, Johnny Hodges. When he wants something that's just stank and greasy, Sam Woodyard. Duke knew how to get these qualities.

That's how the world is, you just think about how you are with your family: You have one uncle who is the craziest of everybody, he'll come over to the party, to the Thanksgiving dinner, and everybody is going to laugh. Then there's somebody else who is real sullen, who's not going to say that much, but everybody likes them. And then there's somebody who is always going to tell you what the problem with the world is. Then there's somebody else who's just cool, and they're just gonna be cool with everybody. Using all these personalities and situations, this is what you try to do in art, in your art form, and this is what Duke Ellington was the supreme master of doing.

robert o'meally: People underestimated Ellington's powers as a pianist. I remember one TV show where Mingus was talking about playing the bass, looking over, and not knowing what chord Ellington might play or how he might voice it. Can you talk a bit about Ellington the pianist?

wynton marsalis: The first thing about Duke on piano is that he could swing the band. I mean he had a tremendously huge sound. If you have a big sound on any instrument it means you can play. It's very hard to have a big sound and be sad, because the sound is generally the last thing that really develops. I'm not talking about a loud sound but a big sound; he could play softly, and it still had that same power. A lot of times I tell kids if you want to develop your sound, play softly. If you want to develop that, you play with intensity and power; do the exact opposite of what you think you would have to do to do that. Real intensity means you can play soft, and it's still powerful. Well, Duke could do this. He understood the role of the piano. The piano is the most complex instrument in the band because it's a rhythm section instrument, it's a solo instrument, it's a percussion instrument, it's a string instrument, it can sound like a brass instrument. Duke Ellington would wait, and at just the right time he would play three notes. And you'd say, "That's just exactly how that had to be."

robert o'meally: He built his band in a sense using ideas of the traditional New Orleans band, and he would sometimes play music in a New Orleans style. Of course he wrote the "New Orleans Suite." Can you say another word about Duke Ellington, man of New Orleans?

wynton marsalis: Well, the reason I call Duke Ellington a New Orleans musician is that he realized more successfully than anybody what New Orleans music afforded the world of music. First, he knew how to write that New Orleans counterpoint, and that was the greatest achievement, because then you could have that real sophistication and complicated musical texture. You could have that type of joyous rhythmic lift that counterpoint gives you, but in the style of jazz, not from Bach or Beethoven, not from European music. Then, he understood the form and structure of the New Orleans music, the significance of the different characteristics of New Orleans music: the meaning of that beat and the fourth beat. He understood the romance of New Orleans music, and he understood the romance of a lot of people from different places getting together unified in one cause. This is what we hear in his music. It is really, truly New Orleans music, from the whorehouse to the parade to the picnic to the church. Duke could deal with it all. He developed it, so when you hear him in his late life, he's still dealing the New Orleans music.

robert o'meally: You said earlier that it's important that he was an *American* composer. In what sense is Ellington, in Albert Murray's phrase, the quintessential American musician?

wynton marsalis: Duke Ellington is the quintessential American musician because throughout his development we can see how a progression should go in our country. First, his music is about American themes: it's about people, places, things; it's not about monarchy, it's not about an agricultural environment. It's about cities, technology, telephones, trains, airplanes. Even more, it's about interpersonal relationships, which, except in opera, is something that European music very seldom is about. Nobody else is gonna write music about what Cootie Williams thought about Ray Nance.

Duke Ellington started off saying that he played Negro music, hyphenated American, Afro-American music. We find that as he grew older, he dropped that. So when people would ask him, "Tell us about your people," he'd say, "My people are *the* people." So we see a progression. Somebody who is first dealing with a race conception, which is in the past, tied to tribalism; whether it's a source of pride or whatever else, it's a tribalistic conception. To progress further, he says: Look, I'm out here representing people, the human race. This music represents the United States of America, American life. That means that if you are a Mexican, it represents you.

First, his music might just be about Harlem. Then he'd write music about Shakespearean plays or music based on *The Nutcracker Suite* or some paintings of Degas. He may do anything. He'd write for a television show, he'd write for movies; he'd write about all types of relationships, different types of cities, the way somebody's pie tasted in Iowa—and it wasn't just a Negro person's pie, it could be anybody's. He was trying to really truly deal with the conception of the United States of America, and we see through this fifty-year development that that is what he was doing.

He outdistanced a lot of people because while he was going forward, we're still going backward. "What about pride in the race?" people would ask him. "What do you mean, race, man?" he would say. "A race is physiological; I'm dealing with someone else. I was into that in the 1920s and 1930s; you all are thirty years late." I saw once in an interview, he was asked, "Why are you not dealing with the Civil Rights protest?" and he said, "Man, I dealt with that. I dealt with that in the 1930s and 1940s. More power to that, but I'm trying to deal with something else." A lot of battles he had fought already. Now maybe the nation wasn't up to the battle at that time. But in his own personal life, I could see how he wouldn't want to go backward. He was constantly trying to move forward in terms of his understanding of the world and his place in the world as a man of extreme importance and significance.

robert o'meally: One thing one hears in his music from the first to the last is his play with trains, the sound of the train or wheels and the kind of whistle. I heard you talking the other night about growing up in New Orleans, growing up with a train sound yourself. Can you talk about Ellington and the train thing?

wynton marsalis: Well, Ellington loved trains. Trains represent a certain type of freedom: they represent communication, and they represent the ability to get from one place to another with a group of people to see some other people. And also a train represents incantation and percussion; so you hear whoo-whoo, whoo-whoo, chug-a-chug-a, chug-a-chug-a, ca-junk, ca-junk, ca-junk.

. . .

When I was a boy growing up in Canton, Louisiana, we lived right down the street from the railroad tracks, and all night I could hear the trains. The trains have a romantic sound: you hear them in the darkness, and they're coming from somewhere and going to somewhere else, bringing something. You don't know what it is. But there's just something about the sound of it; it's just percussive, it sounds like a machine, it sounds like something human, it has a voice in it. It sounds like a lot of things; it sounds like one thing. You hear a train, and you think of a whole bunch of things, but it's still one thing.

You would always be disappointed if you saw a train that just had one car on it. You know, damn, what kind of train is this? Where is the caboose? You always look at the train a certain way. You want a variety of cars, too. You don't want to look at a train and all of them be box cars. You want to see that little flat car, that little round one with the tank, you want to see it all—and this is how Duke's music was, shuffling. You have trombones down there playing and the bass, the clarinets. You start with that sound, then something else comes in on top; that's your voice, commenting: "Okay, that's how I feel looking at that."

robert o'meally: Ellington ended up his career playing sacred music, and once again you hear dissonant harmonies and these funny notes, all kinds of play with the voice. What's the significance of the sacred concerts?

wynton marsalis: I think that in the sacred concerts, Duke was just trying to go back to the beginning. At the end, one of Beethoven's last string quartets is an F-major quartet, done almost in the style of Haydn. After all that complex music he had written, he said "Okay, boom: here it is, just something profoundly beautiful and simple that addresses something fundamental. This is why I was attracted to music." This is what I guess Beethoven would be saying. And I think this is what Duke Ellington was saying: ultimately it's a spiritual, to the glory of God, because everything is created by God. This whole crazy thing that we live in, this thing of such magnificence, so much joy and pain: it's all homage to God. And that's to go back to the beginning. That's the beginning of the blues, the spiritual music, the beginning of jazz, spiritual music. The beginning of soul is the spiritual proposition, the conception of spiritual improvement.

robert o'meally: How would you summarize the experience of Duke Ellington's music?

wynton marsalis: Coming into contact with Duke Ellington's music is like the first time you came into contact with anything that was profound and made you feel good. It's like the first time you ate some ice cream, and you said, "Damn, what is this?" When you come into contact with Duke Ellington, you're interfacing with the very substance and essence of what American life is about. It takes a while to really understand what it is, but it's worth that; it's worth that extra effort that it takes. Because once you understand it, it transforms your life, and it opens you up to a world of beauty that perhaps you didn't know existed. It's as though you were eating at McDonald's, and I brought you to my house, and my mama fixed you some of that gumbo. You'd say, "Oh, I didn't know that this is what eating was about!" Then, every time you eat, you think something different from what you thought before. And that's how Duke's music is. Not just every time you listen to music, but when you walk out of your door in the morning: you say, "Hmmm," you walk with a swing, and that's important.

chapter 10

STANLEY CROUCH

Blues to Be Constitutional: A Long Look at the Wild Wherefores of Our Democratic Lives as Symbolized in the Making of Rhythm and Tune*

Part I: Blue Rebellion Breakdown

I stand here not as a scholar of the Constitution but as a student of the human soul, which is what any writer with the ambition to capture the whys and wherefores of our lives must be. Before I have finished this talk, I hope to have examined the metaphor of the Constitution as it applies to a number of things in our society, and I hope also to have looked at a few of the elements that threaten not so much the democratic institutions of this country as much as they tend to lessen the morale necessary to work at the heroic expansion of this democracy into the unlit back streets and thickets of our civilization. I have chosen to be that ambitious. And in the process of expressing my ambition, I might kick off another version of a good number of the pitched intellectual battles I have had with people whom we continue to mistakenly describe by their color, since no one has ever seen anyone who is actually white or black, red or yellow, however close a few here or there might be. That level of imprecise identification in such a technologically advanced society is one of the ironies of our time and our place in the history of America and of the world.

As a writer, I find it ironic that I began working on these ideas in public at Harvard University in 1992, when I spoke on the thirty-seventh anniversary of the death of Charlie Parker, whose consciousness was swallowed by the grim reaper in Manhattan's Fifth Avenue Stanhope Hotel on March 12, 1955. It was

*Delivered on April 7, 1995, at Michigan State University, for The Symposium on Science, Reason, and Modern Democracy.

nearly ten years after the performance of *Koko*—a harmonic skullcracker built on the chords of *Cherokee*—had announced Parker's ability to extend our expectations of jazz improvisation. Legend lays it down that the virtuoso Kansas City alto saxophonist died while laughing at an act on a television variety show, an electronic update of the minstrel and vaudeville tradition Parker had so poorly fought against throughout his career. A statistic of his own excesses, the innovative genius had been nursed round the clock by not a Jewish princess but a Jewish baroness, one who had driven North African ambulances during World War II yet survived to so scandalize her Rothschild family that, so continues the legend, she was paid off to badly drive her Bentley and enthusiastically host her Negro jam sessions out of sight and out of earshot.

Parker is a man I have come to know quite well since I began working on his biography in 1982. But Parker is most important to what I have to say today because he represents both the achievement and the myth of jazz as well as the trouble we Americans have deciding whether we will aspire to the heroic individuality symbolized by Abraham Lincoln and Martin Luther King, Jr., or sink down into the anarchic individuality represented by Billy the Kid and the various bad boys our society has had crushes on for over a century. However great his talent surely was, Parker was celebrated as much in the half light and the darkness of the night world for his antics, his irresponsible behavior, his ability to embody what Rimbaud called "the love of sacrilege." He was a giant of a bluesman and a jazz improviser of astounding gifts, but his position in the world and in the overview this address seeks has much to do with praise he received for being an outlaw, a sort of praise that speaks directly to a number of our dilemmas.

Since our actual preparation for becoming a democratic society was outside the law, dumping tea in Boston Harbor while disguised as Indians and fomenting rebellion, since our moral assaults on the limitations of our democracy were expressed in the illegal actions of the abolitionists who worked the Underground Railroad and predicted the sorts of activities that people of conscience would later replicate when spiriting Jews beyond the death camp clutches of the Nazis, it is not hard to understand why we have such a high position in our pantheon for the bad boy. We love riotous outsiders as much as we once loved the sort of eloquence we no longer hear from our politicians. And in our straining against the constraints of modern civilization, we, like Baudelaire and Rimbaud, have a love of symbolic violence.

That symbolic violence has two sides, one rooted in a democratic assertion, an expression of the culture's vitality, a breaking away from European convention in pursuit of a social vision that eventually allowed for recognition and success beyond the limitations of family line and class. The other is a set of appetites focused on the exotic, bedeviled by a nostalgia for the mud, given to a love of sensationalism that completely hollows out a pretentious vulgarity. From the moment Americans joyously dumped that tea into Boston Harbor, we were in the process of rebelling against what was then a traditional denial of the colonized underdog's access to dialogue. But that Indian disguise also exhibited perhaps the first burst of what would evolve into the love of the ethnic mask as witnessed in burnt cork stage presentations and the cinematic symbol of Al Jolson's jazz singer moving from eastern European provincialism into the Negro rhythmic bustle of American popular art.

Since the rise of American nationalism that took off at an express tempo following the War of 1812, our art has as frequently reflected disdain as celebration. We love to make fun of the rules and prick those who think themselves superior for all the wrong reasons, especially since our democracy tells us that the little David of the common man can knock down the Goliath of wealth, unfairness, privilege. We believe the smart money can always be wrong. In the first third of the nineteenth century, the Yankee Brother Jonathan and the backwoodsman Davey Crockett often outwitted the stuffed shirt, as would the burnt cork minstrel show figures who stood in for the rural whites endangered by the con men of the big city. Our art tends to pull for the underestimated and the outsider, perhaps because so many of us originate in groups and classes that were once outside the grand shindig of American civilization, noses pressed against the ballroom's huge windows. We have great faith in the possibility of the upset. There is no American who doesn't understand well the statement "They said it couldn't be done, but we did it."

That dictum is basic to our national character and underlies the virtues of our society as much as it does the vulgar volleys against convention we presently find so worrisome in popular art. What we are now witnessing is a distorted version of our own understanding of the battle between the old and the new that is basic to an improvisational society such as ours, where policy is invented to redress previous shortcomings or to express attitudinal shifts. It is central to being an American that one doesn't necessarily believe that limitations will last very long, primarily because we have seen so many changes take place in everything from technology to the ongoing adjustments of policy. It is part of our history, from Eli Whitney, Thomas Edison, Henry Ford, and the Wright brothers in the machinery of modern life to Abraham Lincoln, Martin Luther King, and Sandra Day O'Connor in political influence and high national office.

But what we see as tendencies in our contemporary popular art is what has happened to the extension of identification with the outsider to a love of the scandalizing bad boy. This is a love that has evolved in our century from the silver screen gangster to MTV gangster rap, introducing a few other kinds of bad boys along the way. We have moved swiftly from the cardboard goody-goody to Cagney, to Bogart, to Edgar G. Robinson, motorcyled forward to Brando and James Dean, hopped the racial fence to play out sadomasochistic rituals with Miles Davis, Malcolm X, and now Spike Lee, not leaving out all of the adolescent rock-and-roll intoxication our society guzzles to the point of hangovers left now by Prince or Madonna or Public Enemy. As Gregory Peck says, "The audience loves the bad guy because he will come up with a surprise."

Those surprises were first seen in our century in slapstick, with the many variations on the pie in the face of the society man and matron. That harmless disdain for smugness and pretension made us laugh when the superficially bad boy and comic figure, from Chaplin's Afro-balletic tramp to Eddie Murphy's *Beverly Hills Cop*, unleashed chaos at the pompous gathering. But Peck's observation says much about the dark glamour that surrounds the worst of rock and the lowest of rap, where the canonization of antisocial posturing and the obnoxious appropriation of the racial stereotype has been basic to rock criticism at least since the elevation of the Rolling Stones and Jimi Hendrix. As rock critic Gregory Sandow says, "It's all about the love of the outlaw. The outlaw is going against everything you want to fight in the society, he's doing all the things you would like to do and being the way you would like to be. He's beyond the pale of convention, and if he's black, it's even better."

Sandow's observation is corroborated when one reads the bulk of rock writers on the subject of rap, they who were so quick to shout down racists or fume about Jesse Helms and the 2 Live Crew obscenity trial, but are almost always willing to indulge their own appetites for contemporary coon shows, for the brute glamour of this racial replay—and affirmation—of "the love of sacrilege," of the extensions of Jolson's statement, "You ain't heard nothing yet." For these writers, and perhaps for the bulk of white rap fans, the surliest rap recordings and videos function as experiences somewhere between viewing the natives boiling the middle class in a pot of profanity and the thrill of gawking at a killer shark in an audio aquarium. For Negro rap fans we see another version of the love of the noble savage, the woolly-headed person from the street who can't be assimilated, who is safe from our American version of the temptation of the West.

All of those tendencies clearly express our young people's dissatisfaction with the shortcomings of our culture, but it is a dissatisfaction had on the cheap. In the world of the prematurely cynical, the bad boy reigns, for he represents retreat into pouting anarchy. Of course, our kind of capitalism doggedly allows for almost any kind of successful career, even one that earns millions or television time or tenure selling defeatist visions, playing on or cultivating appetites for ersatz savagery, trumpeting segregation and substandard levels of scholarship on the campuses of our best universities. At the lowest and highest levels, say from Louis Farrakhan or from some professor of "victim studies," we hear all of the carping about the meaninglessness of American democracy, of the tainted moral character of the men who attended the Constitutional Convention and whipped the tragically optimistic fundamentals of our social contract into championship form.

Behind that carping, when what we discover is not merely opportunistic, we learn something quite distinct about the maudlin as it relates to the cynical. We come to understand that unearned cynicism, much more frequently than not, is no more than a brittle version of sentimentality. It is a failure of morale, a cowardly flight from the engagement that comes of understanding the elemental shortcomings of human existence as well as the founding fathers of this country did. Those given to no more than carping are unprepared to address the tragic optimism at the center of the metaphor that is the Constitution. They know nothing of heroic engagement, the engagement that would not allow one to misunderstand the singing of "We Shall Overcome" in the town square of Prague as Dubček stood on a balcony looking into the faces he had been exiled from seeing in the flesh by the Communist party. It is an engagement that would not allow one to miss the meaning of the Red Chinese troops having to destroy a crudely built Statue of Liberty with even cruder means when the night was filled with the familiar violence of totalitarianism in Tiananmen Square. That engagement would recognize that the very success of our struggle to extend democracy has inspired the world, and much of that extending has been the result of the efforts of people at war with the social limitations that were so severely imposed upon Negro Americans.

One cannot speak of Negro culture in this country without speaking of the blues. The blues, which I shall soon talk about in detail, have much to do with the vision of the Constitution, primarily because you play the blues to rid yourself of the blues, just as the nature of our democracy allows us to remove the blues of government by using the government. The blues is a music about human will and human frailty, just as the brilliance of the Constitution is that it recognizes grand human possibility with the same clarity that it does human frailty, which is why I say it has a tragic base. Just as the blues assumes that any man or any woman can be unfaithful, the Constitution assumes that nothing is innately good, that nothing is lasting—nothing, that is, other than the perpetual danger of abused power. One might even say that the document looks upon power as essentially a dangerous thing that must never be allowed to go the way it would were it handled by the worst among us, many of whom remain unrecognized until given the chance to push their ideas on the world. The very idea of the amendment brings into government the process of social redemption through policy. By redemption I mean that the Constitution recognizes that there may be times in the future when what we now think of as hard fact might be no more than a nationally accepted prejudice, one strong enough to influence and infect policy. So you use the government to rid yourself of the blues of government.

The Constitution is also a blues document because it takes a hard swinging position against the sentimentality residing in the idea of a divine right of kings. Sentimentality is excess and so is any conception of an inheritance connected to a sense of the chosen people. The Constitution moves against that overstatement with the same sort of definition Jesus had when his striking down the idea of a chosen people prefigured what we now think of as democracy, an open forum for entry that has nothing to do with any aspect of one's identity other than his or her humanity. I must make clear that I am not talking so much about religion here as I am about the idea that the availability of universal salvation is a precursor of the idea of universal access to fairness that underlies our democratic contract. Universal salvation means that no one's identity is static, that one need only repent and be born anew. That is what I meant earlier about social redemption: every policy structured to correct previous shortcomings in the national sensibility that have led to prejudicial doctrines or unfair treatment is a form of governmental repentance. Once again, using the government to rid the blues of government.

Yet the Constitution, like the blues singer willing to publicly take apart his own shortcomings, perceives human beings as neither demons nor angels but some mysterious combination of both. That is why the revelations of scandal and abuse that rise and fall throughout our history, including our deeply human susceptibility to hypocrisy and corruption, prove out the accuracy of the Constitution. Every time we learn of something unfair that has happened to a so-called minority group, or even a majority group like American women, we perceive anew how well the framers prepared us to face the tar and feathers our ideals are periodically dipped in—even if those framers might have been willing to tar brush some ideals themselves! Every time there is any sort of scandal or we learn another terrible thing about some president or some hanky-panky in governmental contracts, we see more clearly how important freedom of the press is and how important it is for public figures to have to account for their actions. Ask Boss Tweed, ask Richard Nixon; both were felled by the press. The framers of this blues document could see it all and they knew that for a society to sustain any kind of vitality it had to be able to arrive at decisions through discourse that could stand up to the present or lighten the burdens wrought by the lowest aspects of the past.

In essence, then, the Constitution is a document that functions like the blues-based music of jazz: it values improvisation, the freedom to constantly reinterpret the meanings of our documents. It casts a cold eye on human beings and on the laws they make; it assumes that evil will not forever be allowed to pass by. And the fact that a good number of young Negro musicians are leading the movement that is revitalizing jazz suggests a strong future for this country. I find this true because of what it takes for young Negroes to break free of all the trends that overtake them perhaps even more comprehensively than they do the rest of American youth. I find this true because Afro-American culture is essentially oral, and any oral culture is in danger of being dictated to by whoever has command of the microphone.

There is a large dream in the world of jazz, and that dream is much richer than anything one will encounter in the ethnic sentimentality of Afrocentric propaganda. What those young jazz musicians symbolize is a freedom from the taste-making of mass media and an embracing of a vision that has much more to do with aesthetic satisfaction than the gold rush culture of popular entertainment, where one takes the clichés of adolescent narcissism into the side of the mountain rather than a pickaxe, some pans, and a burro. These are young Americans who have not been suckers for the identity achieved through unearned cynical rebellion; they seek individuality through affirmation, which puts them at war with the silly attire and hairdos that descend directly from the rebel-without-a-cause vision of youth that Hollywood began selling adolescent Americans nearly forty years ago, when the anti-hero started to emerge. Less in awe of youth than of quality, those who would be jazz musicians would also *be* adults, not just shriek for adult privileges, then cry foul when the responsibilities are passed out. They have a healthy respect for the men and women who laid an astonishing tradition down. In their wit, their good grooming, their disdain for drugs, and their command of the down-home and the ambitious, they suggest that though America may presently be down on one knee, the champ is about to rise and begin taking names.

But in order to get you to truly appreciate the direction these young musicians are taking, I should conclude this talk with a longish discussion of what the blues and jazz traditions offer us in the way of democratic metaphors, aesthetic actions closely related to the way in which our very society is organized.

Part II: Blues to Be There

Transition Riff on the Big Feeling

I am quite sure that jazz is the highest American musical form because it is the most comprehensive, possessing an epic frame of emotional and intellectual reference, sensual clarity, and spiritual radiance. But if it wasn't for the blues, there would be no jazz as we know it, for blues first broke most clearly with the light and maudlin nature of popular music. Blues came up from this land around the turn of the century. We all know that blues seeped out of the Negro, but we should be aware of the fact that it also called backward into the central units of the national experience with such accuracy that it came to form the emotional basis of the most indelible secular American music. That is why it had such importance—not because it took wing on the breath, voice, and fingers of an embattled ethnic group, but because the feelings of the form came to magnetize everything from slavery to war to exploration to Indian fighting to natural disaster, from the woes of the soul lost in unhappy love to the mysteries, terrors, and celebrations of the life that stretched north from the backwoods to the steel and concrete monuments of the big city. It became, therefore, the aesthetic hymn of the culture, the twentieth-century music that spoke of and to modern experience in a way that no music of European or Third World origin ever has.

In a number of ways, the blues singer became the sound and the repository of the nation's myth and the nation's sense of tragic recognition. It was probably the sense of tragic recognition, given its pulsation by the dance rhythms of the music, that provided blues with the charisma that influenced so many other styles, from jazz to Tin Pan Alley to rock. In the music of the blues the listener was rescued from the sentimentality that so often threatens the soul of this culture, either overdoing the trivial or coating the significant with a hardening and disfiguring syrup. Surely, the Negroes who first came to hear the blues weren't at all looking for anything sentimental, since the heritage of the work song and the spiritual had already brought them cheek to jowl with the burdens of experience, expectation, and fantasy. In the sweat- and ache-laden work song, the demanding duties of hard labor were met with rhythm, and that rhythm, which never failed to flex its pulse in the church, was the underlying factor that brought together the listeners, that allowed for physical responses in the dance halls and the juke joints where blues emerged as the music of folk professionals. Blues all night in guitar keys, the development of a common source of images, a midnight-hour atmosphere of everyday people out to rhythmically s*cratch their own—and somebody else's—itching, sensual essences*.

Yet there was always, as with any art given to the lyrical, a spiritual essence that referred as much to the desire for transcendence as it did to any particular tale of love and loss or love and celebration. In both cases, what was sometimes rightfully considered lewd could also constitute a sense of romantic completeness that was expressed with equal authority by men and women, that fact itself a motion toward women's liberation and the recognition of libidinous lore that transcended gender conventions. In fact, the first popular blues singers who rose to professional status were women such as Bessie Smith. And with the evolution of the blues singer into the jazz musician, an art came forward that was based in the rocky ground and the swamp mud of elemental experience while rising toward the stars with the intellectual determination of a sequoia. It was also symbolic, as had been the erotic wholeness basic to blues, of American democracy.

Part III: The Democratic Swing of American Life

In 1938, the great German novelist Thomas Mann, who had fled Nazism in his homeland, delivered a lecture from one end of America to another that was published as a small volume under the title *The Coming Victory of Democracy*. It is only sixty-five pages in length, and there are a few aspects of it that are now outdated, but the overall sense of the world and the observations Mann provides about democracy connect very strongly to the processes and the implications of jazz, which brings a fresh confluence of directness and nuance not only to the making of music but to the body of critical thought its very existence has challenged in vital ways that are peculiarly American.

The vision of jazz performance and the most fundamental aspects of its aesthetic are quite close to Mann's description of democratic thought. "We must define democracy as that form of government and of society which is inspired above every other with the feeling and consciousness of the dignity of man." The demands on and the respect for the individual in the jazz band put democracy into aesthetic action. Each performer must bring technical skill, imagination, and the ability to create coherent statements through improvised interplay with the rest of the musicians. That interplay takes its direction from the melodic, harmonic, rhythmic, and timbral elements of the piece being performed, and each player must have a remarkably strong sense of what constitutes the *making* of music as opposed to the *rendering* of music, which is what performers of European concert music do. The improvising jazz musician must work right in the heat and the pressure of the moment, giving form and order in a mobile environment, where choices must be constantly assessed and reacted to in one way or another. The success of jazz is a victory for democracy, and a symbol of the aesthetic dignity, which is finally spiritual, that performers can achieve and express as they go about inventing music and meeting the challenge of the moment.

Those challenges are so substantial that their literal and symbolic meanings are many, saying extraordinary things about our collective past as well as the dangers and the potential of the present. In fact, improvisational skill is such an imposing gift that the marvelously original Albert Murray has written in *The Hero and the Blues*, "Improvisation is the ultimate human (i.e., heroic) endowment." The very history of America's development bears this out, as does much of the history that preceded it. But perhaps no society so significant has emerged over the last five centuries that has made improvisation so basic to its sensibility. Even the conflict between Cortés and the Aztecs, for all its horrific dimensions, pivoted on the element of improvisation. As the French writer and critic Tzvetan Todorov observes in his startling *The Conquest of America*, "It is remarkable to see Cortés not only constantly practicing the art of adaption and improvisation, but also being aware of it and claiming it as the very principle of conduct: 'I shall always take care to add whatever seems to me most fitting, for the great size and diversity of the lands which are being discovered each day and the many new secrets which we have learned from the discoveries make it necessary that for new circumstances there be new considerations and decisions; should it appear in anything I now say or might say to your Majesty that I contradict what I have said in the past, Your Highness may be assured that it is because a new fact elicits a new opinion.' "

That quote sounds more than a little like an attitude foreshadowing the constitutional vision of amendments spoken of earlier, and it is also similar in tone and content to the way jazz musicians have explained how different nights, different moods, and different fellow musicians can bring about drastically dissimilar versions of the same songs. Part of the emotion of jazz results from the excitement and the satisfaction of making the most of the present, or what the technocrats now call "real time." Todorov follows that quote with an idea that is basic to the conception of improvising jazz: "Concern for coherence has yielded to concern for the truth of each particular action."

In jazz, however, *comprehension* of each particular action, the artistic truth of it, will bring from the better and more inspired players reactions resulting in overall coherence. And it is the achievement of coherence in the present that is the great performing contribution jazz has made to the art of this century.

I

Just as American democracy, however periodically flawed in intent and realization, is a political, cultural, economic, and social rejection of the automated limitations of class and caste, jazz is an art in which improvisation declares an aesthetic rejection of the preconceptions that stifle individual and collective invention. But the very history of Afro-Americans has always been dominated by a symbolic war against the social and artistic assembly line, especially since stereotypes are actually forms of intellectual and emotional automation. In fact, slavery was a forerunner of the nation's social compartmentalization, especially the sort upheld by the pieties of stereotypes. Those stereotypes maintained that certain people came off an assembly line in nature and one needn't assume them capable of the endless possibilities of human revelation. They had a natural place, which was inferior, and they were sometimes to be pitied and guided, sometimes feared and controlled, but were never to be considered more than predictable primitives who functioned best in subservient positions.

The aesthetic revelation in the present that is so central to jazz improvisation repudiated such attitudes and rejected what Charlie Parker called "stereotyped changes." But long before the emergence of Parker, the level of virtuoso craftsmanship that evolved in the improvising world of jazz redefined both instrumental sound and technique in an ensemble where this idiomatic American music met all the criteria demanded of musical artistry. Even virtuosity took on a new meaning, a meaning steeped in unprecedented liberation. And it was no coincidence that this frontier of artistry came from Afro-Americans and eventually spoke to and for all. As this writer pointed out in an essay called "Body and Soul," "Given the attempts to depersonalize human beings on the plantation, or reduce them to the simplicity of animals, it is understandable that a belief in the dignity of the Negro and the joyous importance of the individual resulted in what is probably the century's most radical assault on Western musical convention. Jazzmen supplied a new perspective on time, a sense of how freedom and discipline could coexist within the demands of ensemble improvisation, where the moment was bull-dogged, tied, and given shape. As with the Italian artists of the Renaissance, their art was collective and focused by a common body of themes, but for jazzmen, the human imagination in motion was the measure of all things."

The degree of freedom introduced into Western music by black Americans has touched some of the few truly good jazz writers deeply and has inspired in them ideas of substantial significance in twentieth-century aesthetics. Getting beyond the noble savage school that shapes the thinking of too many jazz critics of whatever hue or background, Martin Williams points out in his largely superb *The Jazz Tradition* that there has never been a music in the Western world that allowed for so much improvisation on the parts of so many, which raises telling issues. Williams articulates the depth and meaning of this improvisational freedom quite clearly when he writes, "In all its styles, jazz involves some degree of collective ensemble improvisation, and in this it differs from Western music even at those times in its history when improvisation was required. The high degree of individuality, together with the mutual respect and co-operation required in a jazz ensemble carry with them philosophical implications that are so exciting and far-reaching that one almost hesitates to contemplate them. It is as if jazz were saying to us that not only is far greater individuality possible to man than he has so far allowed himself, but that such individuality, far from being a threat to a co-operative social structure, can actually enhance society."

Williams also makes an observation that helps clarify the human *wholeness* jazz proposes through its bold performance conventions: "The Greeks, as José Ortega y Gasset has pointed out, made the mistake of assuming that since man is the unique thinking animal (or so they concluded him to be), his thinking function is his superior function. Man is at his best when he thinks. And traditionally, Western man has accepted this view of himself. But to a jazz musician, thought and feeling, reflection and emotion, come together uniquely, and resolve in the act of doing." This artistically extends Mann's phrase "a new and modern relationship between mind and life" from *The Coming Victory of Democracy*. That new relationship in this context demands a cooperation between the brain and the body that is perhaps fresh to Western art, since the levels of perception, conception, and execution take place at such express velocities that they go far beyond what even the most sophisticated information about the consciousness is presently capable of assessing. These musicians hear what is played by their fellow performers, are inspired to inventions of their own, hold their places in the forms of the songs, and send tasks to their muscles that must be executed so swiftly that all functions of mind and body come together with intimidating speed. In the process, a bold and unprecedented radiance is brought to the performing ensemble. The music of jazz uniquely proves out Mann's dictum that "to come close to art means to come close to life, and if an appreciation of the dignity of man is the moral definition of democracy, then its psychological definition arises out of its determination to reconcile and combine knowledge and art, mind and life, thought and deed."

2

Though the skills that make for jazz are the result of a musical evolution that probably began the moment African slaves started reordering music they heard from and were taught by the slave masters, this writer would again say that it is a dangerous simplification to hear jazz primarily as a music protesting the social conditions of Afro-Americans, even if its seminal inventors were often subjected to social limitations based on race. That reduces the monumental human achievement of a sustained artistic vision that allows for the expression of every passion, from delicate affection to snarling rage at the very demons of life at large, those tragic elements that no amount of money, power, or social inclusion will hold at bay. If social problems in and of themselves were the only things that provoke the creation of great art, a century as bloody as ours would have inspired far more original and profound aesthetic achievement than it has. No, the miracle of this improvisational art is the fact that the techniques Africans arrived with evolved into *aesthetic conceptions* that reinvented every kind of American music they came in contact with, from folk to religious music to dance tunes, and finally achieved the order that is jazz, where all those aspects of American musical expression were brought together for a fresh synthesis.

That fresh synthesis was the product of a down-home aristocracy of men and women whose origins cut across class and caste, who might or might not be able to read music, might or might not have used conventional technique, but who all had in common the ability *to make musical* sense during the act of playing. In no way did their rising to artistic prominence from the bottom, middle, or top of the social strata on the steam of their own individual talents and wills conflict with the collective concerns of the music. By doing so, they actually enhanced our understanding of the music's democratic richness, proving through their work what Mann meant when he said, "Real democracy, as we understand it, can never dispense with aristocratic attributes—if the word 'aristocratic' is used, not in the sense of birth or any sort of privilege, but in a spiritual sense." A jazz musician would probably say *soul*, knowing that those who possess the deepest spiritual connection to the music can come from anywhere and *have* often enough to affirm the merit system of aesthetic expression. It is actually the whole point of democracy itself: a society is best off and most in touch with the vital when it eliminates all irrational restrictions on talent, dedication, and skill.

No matter what class or sex or religion or race or shape or height, if you can cut the mustard, you should be up there playing or singing or having your compositions performed. You should, in fact, after all the practice and the discipline necessary to push your art into the air as a professional, be taking on the ultimate democratic challenge, which means bringing into the aesthetic arena the fundamentals of Constitutional discourse, checks and balances, policy, and the amendments in which you symbolically use government to rid yourself of the blues of government. When that challenge is met, children, we hear the lucidity rising into the air that is the bittersweet truth of the blues to be there—what Hernando Cortés predicted, what the framers put together, and what we, and our descendants, as all-American children of the Constitution, will continue to reinterpret until the end of our time in the quicksand of history.

chapter 11

BARRY ULANOV

The Ellington Programme

For years, when Duke Ellington was questioned about his next work, the answer was always the same: "My *African Suite*. It will be in five parts, starting in Africa and ending with the history of the American Negro." Occasionally little African sketches were performed by the band, as *Old King Dooji* and *Ko-Ko*. Every once in a while Duke would recast the score in his mind as an opera, fit it out with a libretto at once melodramatic and ironic and dream his way through an act or two. He even had a name for it for a while, *Boola*—not to be confused with the Yale University song of the same name.

After a decade of such answers, such sketches, and such dreaming, Duke produced *Black, Brown, and Beige* at his 1943 Carnegie Hall concert. He not only produced it, he explained it: "It is a tone parallel to the history of the American Negro." The programme was fixed, firm, and clear. It started with Negroes working in the fields, working on the railroads, working on the levees, working and singing, but not because "it is the nature of the Negro to sing at his work." As Duke insisted in the first part of a series he wrote for me in *Swing* magazine in 1940, this is "a myth which must be exploded. . . . It was at the commands of their overseers that the Negroes created their work songs. Fearful of the silence of these groups of blacks, their masters commanded them to raise their voices in song, so that all opportunity for discontented reflections or plans for retaliation and salvation would be eliminated."

The whole structure of *Black, Brown, and Beige* can be followed in Duke's *Swing* series. *Come Sunday*: "Their religious music developed into the sole source of hope and solace for the enslaved coloured peoples throughout the entire South." The

Civil War theme: "Into the music of the Negro there crept a new note. Then was born the strain of the blues. . . . Throughout the length and breadth of America, humanity suffered and the plaintive Negro blues answered the cries . . . the first adoption and acceptance of Negro music by a majority of the white peoples." Emancipation: "Upon the heels of the act of liberation came the singing joyous anticipation of freedom. Two camps formed among the Negroes. There were the older people who sternly adhered to the spiritualistic music, shunning change, bewildered and fearful of the new order of things, and there was the new generation, joyful and inspired by their new-found freedom, and proud that their bonds had been overthrown."

And so it goes, theme by theme, bridge by bridge, through the migrations from the West Indies, the influences that helped construct the Negro community in the United States, the Spanish-American War, the removal of the Negro to the big city. It ends with the blues, the "low, ugly, mean blues," the blues that "ain't nothin' but a cold gray day and all night long it stays that way," the blues with which the second movement, *Brown*, and the whole work change colour and focus.

The last section of Ellington's three Bs, *Beige*, is about the composer's life. The first trips to New York: "We went out every evening regardless of whether we had money or not, and we met all the hip guys. I got a big thrill when I strolled into the Capitol Club at 140th and Lenox, down in the basement, and found the Lion working there. We went the rounds every night, looking for the piano players. We didn't have any gold, but then Sonny Greer was good at that sort of thing. He would stride in, big as life, and tell the man . . ." The Ellington establishment: "Our band changed its character when Bubber Miley came in. He used to growl all night long, playing gut-bucket on his horn. That was when we decided to forget all about the sweet music." The first trip to Europe: "These gentlemen introduced me to Lady somebody and told me she was really the McCoy and she raved about my band and I felt really set up . . . and then Windsor was standing out in the middle of the floor there and giving me this big long eulogy. And after that, that's when he came over and he says, 'Won't you have a drink with me at the bar?' He said what are you drinking? So I said gin. So he said he would have the same. Up to that time I always thought gin was sort of a low drink, but since that time I always feel rather grand when I drink gin."

There is more to *Black, Brown, and Beige*, ornamental furbelows that add tints and shades and textures to Duke's colour wheel. But the substance is anthropology, sociology, and personal history as indicated. It has always been thus. That is the Ellington programme.

From the first, Duke's large-scale programmatic works have been much criticized. Starting in 1935 with *Reminiscing in Tempo*, his earliest attempt to spin ten-inch 78 r.p.m. sides into larger structures than the three-minute record form usually permitted, each ambitious new work has found its answering contempt. The "concertos"—*Clarinet Lament* and *Echoes of Harlem*—and the two-sided *Crescendo and Diminuendo in Blue: Black, Brown, and Beige, Blue Belles of Harlem*; and *The Perfume Suite: New World A-Comin'*; and the *Liberian Suite, A Tone Parallel to Harlem, A Drum Is a Woman*, and *Such Sweet Thunder*—each has been called "pretentious" or "arty," "inflated" or "fumbling." "Such a form of composition is entirely out of Ellington's ken" was one reviewer's dismissal of *Black, Brown, and Beige*. But is it? How different, really, are the long sagas and suites and "parallels" from the early little works, *Black and Tan Fantasy, East St. Louis Toodle-Oo, The Mooche,* and *Creole Love Call*, of which everybody approves, even the admirers of "the real jazz"?

Duke has always been a teller of tales, three-minute or thirty. He has always been concerned about his race, sometimes to the point of agony. He has never failed to take compass points, wherever he has been, in a new city, a new country, a redecorated nightclub; to make his own observations and to translate these, like his reflections about the place of the Negro in a white society, into fanciful musical narratives. What, after all, is *Black and Tan Fantasy*, with its shrewd juxtaposition of plunger solos by Bubber Miley and Tricky Sam, the Chopin funeral march, and Barney Bigard's crescendo in scooped pitch, but a wry comment on life among the coloured? What is the wail that Adelaide Hall contributes to *Creole Love Call* or the growl Baby Cox gargles in *The Mooche* but an attenuated version of the blues section of *Black, Brown, and Beige*?

There are like comments, similar wails and growls, in almost all of Ellington's records, early and late; and always set in the midst of melodrama, pocket-sized or operatic. The titles give the stories away: *Mood Indigo, Black Beauty, Awful Sad, Rent Party Blues.* In the stories, the blues appear again and again, but with a difference, with a degree of pretentiousness, if you like; they appear as "indigo," a blue light, a blue ramble, a blue feeling, a blue tune, a bundle of blues—anything to avoid the literary or musical cliché. The blues appear by name, by implication, by inference: *Black Beauty* is not the name of a horse, but the equine overtones of the title suggest the intended irony.

Harlem, too, has long been an obsession with Duke. Starting in 1927 with *Harlem River Quiver*, the Negro quarter of New York has made its way, street by street, atmosphere by atmosphere, through his music. There is *Harlem Twist* and *Harlem Flat Blues, Jungle Nights in Harlem* and *Blue Harlem, Drop Me Off at Harlem* and *Harlem Speaks, Echoes of Harlem* and *It Was a Sad Night in Harlem, Uptown Downbeat* and *Harmony in Harlem, I'm Slappin' Seventh Avenue* and *Harlem Air-Shaft*, the Sugar Hill section of *Black, Brown, and Beige* and *A Tone Parallel to Harlem*. These are not simply a songwriter's grab bag of titles, felicitous or not as the case may be. They are names for moods and customs, people and places and events in Duke's life and his musicians'. This is what it meant to come north from Washington in 1923, to move not many miles but social leagues, to establish oneself on the Hill, to earn the title of royalty in a small inbred kingdom where the palace is never anything more than a white man's relinquished apartment house in a faded neighbourhood in which the air-shafts carry a little air, more sound, and the distant odour of tenement life, even into the palace.

Duke is Harlem's poet; Harlem, about which so many of the short pieces of the twenties boast and so many of the long ones of the forties and fifties reminisce. This is not a subtle poetry. Ellington ballads of Harlem are sentimental. Some of them simper. They have about them an air of the exaggerated. This is the part of the world where Duke became a leader, where he and his Washingtonians were the only organized band: "We were only five, but we had arrangements on everything, and it was what we've now named conversation music, kind of soft and gutbucket." This is where the band substituted at the Cotton Club for King Oliver, who did not think the money was good enough, and expanded to twelve men and became famous. This is where all the African associations were first made, by nightclub producers and record companies and band bookers; by all the many layers of people who took their two or ten or twenty per cent and were entitled to call themselves "management"; by all the people who journeyed uptown for a night of primitive entertainment, of belly bouncers and snake-hips dancers and jungle music. It was, as they said, life in the raw, like the liquor: "We called it 'ninety-nine per cent.' One more degree either way would bust your top, we said."

Not only management and the audiences it enticed uptown accepted the African nonsense. So did Duke. One of the half-dozen or more *noms de disque* he used when he recorded away from home, which then was Victor, was "The Jungle Band." Under the name of "The Harlem Footwarmers," the band recorded *Jungle Jamboree* and *Snake Hip Dance*. As "The Ten Blackberries," it did a *Jungle Blues*; under its own name, *Jungle Nights in Harlem* and *Echoes of the Jungle*. The Africa of Duke's music has always echoed more of the Cotton Club jungle, of The Jungle Band, The Harlem Footwarmers, and The Ten Blackberries, than the true African jungle. What makes the story line of *A Drum is a Woman* so embarrassing, especially when it is made visible by actors and dancers, is this *papier-mâché* and pasteboard version of primitive life. The setting of the long work is ostensibly a Caribbean island. Actually it is the Cotton Club, *circa* 1928. One suspects that the *Liberian Suite* and the other bits and snatches of Africana in the Ellington library spring from the same source. All of Duke's jungle nights have been spent in Harlem.

Duke is not, then, meticulous about his sources. He is something less than a scholar. His *métier* is the theatre, the theatre of personal emotions, the theatre of exquisite extravagances, the theatre of perfect timing, the theatre of the great Negro actors, musicians, singers, and dancers whose portraits he has drawn. They make up a very small gallery of men and women Duke admires, artists who, like Duke, broke down the barriers, personalities like Duke, characters, artists. Bert Williams was one, the gentlest of comedians; Rex Stewart and Tricky Sam between them translated his affable accents into half-valve cornet bleats and trombone grunts. "Bojangles," the dancer Bill Robinson, was another; Ben Webster made the memory of the master of taps warm with his warmest of tenor sounds. Willie "The Lion" Smith was Duke's own portrait, a very personal tribute to the man with whom he used to stroll the town and share the rent parties and "think piano." Florence Mills's grandeur was turned over to Harold Baker's trumpet, but Harold never had to do very much because it was a made-over magnificence and not so much Florence Mills's as Bubber Miley's; her portrait was Bubber's *Black Beauty* just barely re-scored.

Some of Bubber is in all of Duke's portraits, in each of his dramas. For when Bubber entered Duke's life in 1924 the pattern was set by which Duke has been cutting his music ever since. Bubber was the first of Duke's voices, actually many voices in one: basso buffo and romantic tenor lead, crackling coloratura and sobbing contralto. He would go wherever the trumpet registers would permit him. When the normal apparatus of his instrument forced a stop, his imagination could always carry on, adding, for example, the rubber cup of a plumber's plunger to a mute to produce his great growls or little scolding rumblings. Bubber translated slogans on signboards and church hymns into jazz figures. Everything he saw or heard had a place on his horn.

After Bubber, the Ellington troupe filled out quickly and easily. Every man had a part to play: Barney Bigard, simple, sober, and swinging; Tricky Sam, comic, pseudo-philosophical; Posey Jenkins, bumptious; Lawrence Brown, tender, romantic, but never quite maudlin; Harry Carney, gruffly sentimental; Johnny Hodges, insinuating. Even those whose solos were less frequent were called upon to produce the same identifying sounds each time up: Toby Hardwicke, a plaintive melody; Juan Tizol, a more brusque statement of the same sort of tune.

Those who succeeded the originators of the Ellington rôles had to be allowed a few of their own idiosyncrasies. For Cootie Williams's growling was never quite so witty as Bubber's, never so carefree, never so serious. Rex Stewart had a little of Freddy Jenkins's kind of humour but much more of his own. And nobody ever really replaced Tricky Sam Nanton; he was too tricky; his magic died with him.

In recent years the original sounds have been reduced to echoes twice and thrice removed. Ray Nance, for all his theatrical brilliance, has never equalled the blowzy good humour of Cootie or the meditative wit of Bubber. Harold Baker and Clark Terry make some pleasant sounds, but sounds quite lacking in the ironies or the gusto of Cootie and Rex. Jimmy Hamilton has achieved a round classical clarinet effect, but nothing like Barney's beat. The saxophone innuendo has been preserved by Carney and Hodges, but without the acrid brass comments it has sometimes slipped into sleaziness or insipidity. The Cotton Club jungle has worn down to the spirit gum.

There was a moment in the early forties when a mixture of casts—some left over from the original company, some new to the organization—produced a fine fresh new repertoire. After years of trying to get a true bass spokesman, even to the point of employing two bassists, Duke had found his man in Jimmy Blanton. A like search for a tenorman came to an end with Ben Webster. Billy Strayhorn, in the first excitement at finding himself playing John Fletcher to Duke's Shakespeare, contributed a small library of bracing scores. But Blanton died and Ben departed and somewhere along the line the difference between the composers asserted itself forcefully. The major resource of the Ellington Theatre proved itself once again the Ellington imagination.

Lacking a full roster of voices, and with the splendour of the forties dissipated, Duke turned again to the Negro theme, to anthropology, sociology and personal history. But everything now was on a bigger scale. Now he was a regular performer at Carnegie Hall and its opposite numbers in Philadelphia, Boston, Chicago, and points west. Now he was, finally, a composer with a band. Now he was no longer the "*petit maître*" Constant Lambert had found him in 1934, only a little master, but at that "considerably more than many people thought either jazz or the coloured race would produce." Now he produced what at least the record companies could call "major works," *i.e.* works that occupy at least one side of a twelve-inch long-playing record.

The themes remain more or less the same: the people of colour; high life in Harlem and, sometimes, elsewhere; the Ellington environment. Provision is made for the newer if not exactly the brighter Ellington voices, for Baker and Terry, Paul Gonsalves, Britt Woodman, and Quentin Jackson. On stage Duke introduces each "major work" with a vagabond syntax that makes one wonder why he bothers. But if one listens carefully, both to the words and the music, one discovers why. One finds, for example, that in titling a piece about *Othello* with a quotation from *A Midsummer Night's Dream* ("I never heard so musical a discord, such sweet thunder"), he has gone right to the root of Othello's problem. His blunt and jazzy explanation is probably closer to the substance of the play than the long and involuted commentaries of most Shakespearean scholars. He is concerned, he tells us, with "the sweet and swinging, very convincing story Othello told Desdemona. It must have been the most, because when her father complained and tried to have the marriage annulled, the Duke of Venice said that if Othello had said this to his daughter, she would have gone for it too." The music is satisfactory too, at least as fair a pass at Shakespeare as Mendelssohn and Berlioz and Tchaikovsky made; and for our time anyway a good deal less hackneyed.

Major work? Who knows? But certainly it is the same sort Duke has been writing for the last thirty-five years, a tale well told, full of fanfare and flourish, swinging, with some embarrassing extravagances and many more endearing ones. Others may find more complicated patterns in Duke Ellington's career, more stages in his development. I find mostly one stage, and on it essentially one programme. As we all know, every theatre must have a programme. This is Duke's.

part 3
jazz lines and colors:
the sound i saw

introduction

ralph Ellison, the novelist who had first aspired to compose music (and whose own trumpet sound, friends recall, had a beautifully clear, singing quality), has the main character in *Invisible Man* observe that musicians not only can hear and feel the music, they can *see* it, too. A cursory look at jazz-tune titles suggests some of what players see when they look at the music: "Multicolored Blue," "Kind of Blue," "Transblusency," "Honky Tonk Train," "Moanin'," "Pretty Woman," "Stolen Sweets," "Catfish Sam'mich," "Country Preacher." Max Roach says that when he was recording "Money Jungle" with Duke Ellington and Charles Mingus, Duke turned out the studio lights and asked the musicians as they played to hold in their minds the picture he wished the music to evoke: a thick forest where a vivid green snake slid in dark branches, the slithering cash beast in the jungle of commercial greed.

On the other hand, any music—and certainly jazz, with its complex systems of story line and counter story line, conversational gaminess, antic wit, quotation, understatement, parody and pastiche—says more than song titles can convey. In this music, where a song's lyrics may be undermined or scatted to the four winds by a vocalist (or an instrumentalist singing the lyrics to him/herself with tongue in cheek), a song's words are also quite unreliable guides to the music's imagery and true significance. The truth is that seeing this music means listening intently to the music itself, listening until you get the picture. Certain aural images do recur in jazz: trains, sex, talk, dances, marches, revelry, foods, cityscapes, heroic praise songs, churches, country roads, roadhouses. Sometimes the visions are political, like Ellington's snake in the garden. Or consider the multicolored blue voice of Abby Lincoln on the album, *We Insist!* where Abby croons, bops, and screams for justice in the American scene.

As jazz musicians react to the sights around them and project color, texture, image, line, and story line into their music (and sometimes onto canvases, viz. Ellington, Miles Davis, Paul Gonsalves—all Sunday painters), visual artists, in turn, respond to the achievement of the makers of jazz. Some of this reaction is unmistakable, though nearly impossible to track: In what sense is Manhattan's "jazzy skyline" influenced by the music of the thirties (as the music was affected by the Empire State Building, launched, as the swing era took flight, in just over one year's time)? In what sense do both skyline and jazz spring from a culture that wants to swing and soar and solo? (See Ann Douglas's essay on this airborne quality in Jazz Age culture.)

At times, the influence of the music on artists *can* be reliably traced: Mondrian, Matisse, Stuart Davis, Jackson Pollock, Aaron Douglas, Romare Bearden, Bob Thompson, Norman Lewis, and Roy DeCarava are among those who explicitly learned from the techniques and structures of jazz. For these artists, the challenge has been not merely to offer documentary representations of specific jazz players but to play jazz, as it were, with their cameras, canvases, papers, hammers, chisels, and paints: to communicate what Steven Tracy has called "a brush with the blues." The painter-sculptor Alfred J. Smith actually assembled bands of protégé artists to work/play together on pieces he had conceived/composed as visualizations of the music. And he insisted that his sculptors pay special attention to the sounds of themselves, and the band of artists as a whole, while they were creating.

Of course a visual artist is not literally drumming or blowing and blocking chords, and the techniques and traditions of painting spring from previous paintings, above all, not from music. Again, let's not make the mistake of seeing jazz everywhere: jazz on Keats's Grecian urn, jazz on a dinosaur's tooth. But let's take note of the jazz influence on many, many visual artists. When Bearden divides his canvas into three sections on one side and two on the other and says it's his version of 3/4 time working with and against 2/4 time, as in jazz, we'd better pay attention. (Wynton Marsalis has this particular painting hung prominently in his Manhattan apartment and recalls Bearden's explication of its multimetered musical meanings.) When Stuart Davis says he learned a great deal about space and interval from the left hand of virtuoso jazz pianist Earl Hines, a secret to Davis's art is unlocked.

And there are other secrets sounding here: the artist's complex percussive play with form and texture, the improvisations, the patterns of "call-and-recall" (Bearden's wonderful phrase), the games of color and space, the purposive silences. Stanley Crouch said that once when he turned on the radio he first heard a "silence," but somehow he sensed it was an energized, anticipatory good-humored *Monk* silence; sure enough, at the end of the "silent" break, in came Thelonious, dancing at the keyboard. How do these Monk silences translate into visual terms? How do Mingus's tone poems affect the kaleidoscopic colors of Norman Lewis? How does Bird's way of playing affect Pollock's bent-knee dance style of painting? "Do you photograph jazz?" someone asked Roy DeCarava at the

Museum of Modern Art in New York, where his 1995 show had just opened. "No," he answered, evidently tired of the question. "But I do photograph jazz *players*. And jazz rooms are so dark, there's never enough light to shoot, supposedly. So I have to *improvise*. I'm doing what the jazzmen are doing, see? I'm operating in the moment. I've gotten some good pictures that way." The title of a DeCarava show of portraits of jazz players: "The Sound I Saw."

In the area of moving pictures, the African-American dance-beat orientation that helps define jazz music also has had a mighty impact. Those making films about jazz figures acknowledge having tried to capture jazz values on screen and even having tried to operate as teams or combos whose collaborations have the antagonistic cooperation (i.e., the with-and-against playing style of jazz) and the swinging coordination of jazz music makers themselves. Some speak of efforts to give each film its own voice in the jazz sense of full-throated individuality of expression as opposed to easy imitations or technical trickbags. But there's more going on here than any commentator has spelled out: What is the effect on modern filmmakers— those quick, improvising cut-and-paste artists—of such jazz virtuosos as Bud Powell or John Coltrane? Of such cut-out minimalists as Thelonious Monk or Count Basie? What does it mean when a young filmmaker says she wants to learn to edit film the way Aretha Franklin sings?

When you're scatting you can almost see the notes. You can see your half-tones and you know how they're supposed to sound because you see the keyboard in your head.   —Betty Carter (in Taylor)

Bird said, "Hear with your eyes and see with your ears." I never forgot that.
                                                              —Art Blakey (in Taylor)

Sometimes I imagine I paint, with watercolors or oils, a crystal-clear lake in the sky reflecting the shadows of invisible trees upside down beneath sunkissed, cotton-candy snow.   —Duke Ellington

My approach to rhythms . . . is the use of space, of silence. It's not that there's necessarily *nothing* going on. There's always a pulse there. But there are times when there's nothing *but* the pulse. We used to discuss this up on 52nd Street with Charlie Parker and Miles Davis: the whole [question] of time. His basic quarter note, his *time* was there: that's why Miles was so profound, because he *worked* at that. It didn't take a lot; the rhythm was there even though you didn't have a rhythm section. Some of the horns, like Lester [Young] and Bird [Charlie Parker], had a built-in rhythm section. They didn't need a drum or a bass player. When they played, you felt the pulse. So that allowed the drummer to do colors. It *freed* us. With these people, it was always there: the silence, the meter. The pulse was there, in the silence. Bearden's paintings are like that.   —Max Roach (in Schwartzman)

Clearly Max's words had inspired him, but Bearden had also been listening to the music for a long while. He explained that recently, at Robert Blackburn's Printmaking Workshop, a recording made by Max and Clifford Brown had come over the radio: "And I just took a brush and painted the sounds, the color rhythms, and the silences on a big sheet of plastic using a volatile benzine medium which dries within four or five minutes. Then I pressed the paper over it and made this oil-on-paper." Bearden called it A Portrait of Max: in Sounds, Rhythms, Colors and Silences *and made Max a gift of the work.*   —*Myron Schwartzman*

Stuart Davis's work has often been compared with jazz, the form of music he spent much of his time assimilating. He once remarked that jazz was the first native expression of modernism and likened the excitement he had felt at seeing Matisse paintings in the Armory Show to that he received when listening to piano players in the Negro saloons he frequented as a Henri student. In speaking of his mural for Studio B, WNYC, Davis had asserted that "the tonal intervals of music have their counterpart in painting in intervals of tone, color, contrast, size and direction." Carrying his analogy to the dynamics of music even further, Davis described his Hot Still Scape for Six Colors (1940) as ". . . 'Hot' because of its dynamic mood, as opposed to a serene or pastoral mood. Six colors, white, yellow, blue, orange, red, and black were used as the materials of expression. They are used as the instruments in a musical composition might be, where the tone-color variety results from the simultaneous juxtaposition of different instrument groups."   —Diane Kelder and Stuart Davis

When Albert [was] on that piano it was like a mirror anyway. Not cause he went round with his silk handkerchief and flicked off every spot of dust before he'd sit down to play, not because he polished the keys and the gleaming wood like McKinley used to do his glasses. It wasn't him fussing and worrying the wood and ivory and brass of the piano like he was a janitor or something. It was after he got it just like he wanted it and the music started coming out that you could find yourself, find your face grinning back at you like in a mirror.

—John Wideman

Technic is the result of a need—
new needs demand new technics—
total control—denial of
the accident—
State of Order—
organic intensity—
energy and motion
made visible—
memories arrested in space,
human needs and motives—
acceptance—   —Jackson Pollock (in Walker)

Numerous subsequent writers on Pollock have noted the close visual approximation of his technique in these photos to the extemporaneous aspects of jazz. As early as 1945, in fact, one prescient critic had compared the "flare, spatter and fury" of Pollock's paintings to modern music, citing both as the result of inspired improvisation. As already noted, Pollock loved jazz, and he played his records constantly, "rocking and rolling" for days on end to Dizzy Gillespie, Bird, Dixieland, and bebop. What undoubtedly attracted him to this type of sound was not just its rhythm and tempo, but its naked presentation of honest and deeply felt emotion. By the late forties, with his confidence momentarily increased, Pollock could tell his wife that jazz was "the only other creative thing happening in this country." On those occasions when she was invited out to the barn, Krasner could experience the analogy on her own. Now, when her husband started painting, she saw that he would "take off, so to speak," working in a similar mode of impromptu freedom. —Ellen Landau

This series, "The Black Forest," based on the musical concepts of Cecil Taylor, attempts to relate the discipline of musical expression to visual expression. Music is composed in units of time in the same way art is composed in units of space.

One thing that I have always admired about musicians is their ability to communicate with one another through the use of pure sound. In addition, they perform their art in communion with one another, thus experiencing a force which fuses their individual expressions into one harmonious whole, moving in time. As we border on the threshold of sound and sight, we compose through the use of geomonic (geometric-harmonic) shapes as a form of visual orchestration, moving in space.

In support of this concept, a Howard University faculty research grant has enabled me to assemble "The Geomonic Band," an apprentice workshop whose members are: Ronald Beverly, design major; Andy Jacob, painting major; Stella McCalister, design major; Terry York, art education major; and myself as the arranger, composer, and conductor of the band. As an alternative teaching instrument, I can, through this workshop, teach and experience the technical, conceptual, and spiritual values of being an artist.

—Alfred J. Smith (in Howard University Gallery of Art)

DeCarava believes that the black person has an affinity with photography just as he has with jazz. He contends that the person whose life is devoted to the elemental task of surviving is forced by circumstances to be more realistic and more truthful than the person who isn't. The black man, in this instance, has to "read" the white man accurately and swiftly. If he doesn't, his chances of surviving the latter's tyranny are considerably diminished. Because he deals with the immediacy of his life's irregular pattern by meeting unorthodox demands with improvised answers, the black man finds jazz and photography suited to his instincts.

Jazz, in its most exciting form, is an art of musical improvisation. It is an immediate creation. Photography is likewise immediate. The photographer must be there with his camera, and his subject must be there. And when the three meet in harmony at precisely the right instant, the photographer's art is conceived. Gestation and birth take place later in the darkroom.

But the ultimate element linking jazz, photography, and the black creator is the element of reality. Jazz music emanates from the reality of the musician's life experiences. In photography there is the undeniable reality of the thing from which the lens and the film take their image. Those realities eagerly welcome the embrace of the ungilded reality of the black man's experience in a hostile racist environment. That sums up a significant DeCarava belief.   —Elton Fax

In more than a few ways, the techniques of jazz represent the kind of mediation that [filmmaker] John Ford saw between literal policy and the practical policy that was improvised. As Peter Stowell observes in John Ford, *"In film after film Ford demonstrated that the march of civilization is epitomized by tensions engendered in the spirit versus the letter of the law. Mediators are needed to bring the two into harmony." Jazz musicians are such mediators. Their art allows the letter of the law that is composition made in the past to meet the spirit that is improvisation made in the present. They bring into harmony the past and the present, the known and the unknown, the familiar and the unexpected, the exotic flowers of the swamp and the universal crown of the stars.*

—Stanley Crouch, "Bull Feeney Plays the Blues"

chapter 12

RICHARD J. POWELL

Art History and Black Memory: Toward a "Blues Aesthetic"

Although many African-American artists have been the subjects of general art histories and art biographies, the actual works themselves have more or less been relegated to a position of illustrating that history rather than being central to it. Questions regarding the existence of a unique school or style of "African-American art" and the recognizable traits and relationships of such to African and Western art traditions are frequently addressed, yet to a great extent they are still left unanswered.[1]

Contemporary efforts by scholars and critics to define an "African-American," or "black" aesthetic have resulted in no clear consensus of meaning or value. Many have completely rejected the notion of an African-American aesthetic, and argue that it is impossible to distinguish common characteristics among the works of African-American artists.[2] On the other hand, when preconceived notions about the art of African Americans are shattered by artists working in widely employed modes of Western modernism and postmodernism, confusion among the critical rank and file sets in.[3] Among the many false assumptions implicit in these arguments concerning "African-American" art are the misconceptions that: (1) so-called Western modes of modern and contemporary art making are essentially European in origin, and (2) the term "African-American" art presupposes that all black artists would be creating in that mode. Tripped by these fallacies, those purporting to define "African-American" art offer an empty term; its use as a tool of visual segregation attests to its hollowness.[4]

Not surprisingly, others suggest that the term "African-American" art is largely a by-product of the political climate of the late 1960s and early 1970s, and that it has very little to do with aesthetic issues.[5] Certainly, the countless printed arguments addressing group shows by black artists underscore this point of view. Nevertheless, in the midst of critical impasses, accusations, and counteraccusations, the ultimate question which comes to the surface is the applicability of so-called white European aesthetic standards and alleged "established values" to African-American art. But because of the aroused passions surrounding the notion of the all-black show and the absence of a comprehensive and practical definition for "black" art, one is left with an almost totally ineffectual body of art commentary, deficient in the kind of scholarly depth and analytic breadth that is endemic to the critical genre.[6]

Even when scholars have acknowledged the presence of an "African-American" aesthetic, it is almost always seen as synonymous with a social realist style, or with what is described by some as nationalistic and didactic art.[7] Although this emphasis on an object's "content" and sociopolitical import—seen in the works of both black and white artists—is now receiving a much warmer reception than it did a decade ago, focusing on it alone often obscures the formal issues which concern so many African-American artists. Furthermore, when one sees the "African-American" aesthetic as limited to realistic works which rely strongly upon social and political messages for their appreciation, other works which stretch one's capacity to "read" a meaning are somehow placed outside of this "African-American" sphere, regardless of the attitudes underlying them.[8]

One of the first scholars to grapple with this notion of a racial idiom in art was Alain Locke. In writings as early as 1924, this Rhodes scholar and Howard University professor of philosophy expressed his hopes for an African-American art that would seek visual nourishment from its legacy—both remembered and recollected—of African ancestral arts. Along with the visual impetus from Africa, it was Locke's expectation that "a new technique, enlightening and interpretative revelations of . . . feeling" and a "lessening of that timid imitativeness" would enter into the African-American artist's repertoire, triggering "fresher and bolder forms of artistic expression."[9] These ideas, which seem fundamental to the formulation of an African-American aesthetic, reverberated throughout the remainder of the twentieth century, all the while laying down additional groundwork for future discussions.

In the 1980 exhibition catalogue *Romare Bearden, 1970–1980* published for the Mint Museum in Charlotte, North Carolina, one encounters several critical essays that fulfill Locke's 1924 prescription for fresher, more empathetic inquiries into an African-American cultural psyche.[10] In that catalogue, Albert Murray and Dore Ashton explore Bearden's art in its aesthetic totality, paying particular attention to Bearden's place in modern art history and to his collaged glorification of childhood memories, human rituals, and the African-American landscape. In their descriptions, Murray and Ashton adjust their critical antennae not just to the obvious parallels with Western European art but to the equally apparent, but rarely articulated, connections with black culture. It is in their careful appropriation of a language (which is normally used to describe a fashionably dressed citizen of Harlem, a stirring jazz performance, or a twelve-bar blues composition) that their critical faculties emerge as a possible gauge for subsequent critiques of selected African-American artworks. One finds especially in Albert Murray's essay a plausible and pliant equation in his discussion of Romare Bearden's style and the aesthetic pull of black music. That "blues timbres, downhome onomatopoeia, urban dissonance, and cacophony"[11] can be seen as musical counterparts to the high-affect colors, improvisational patterning, and perspectival distortions of Bearden's art suggests ways of seeing other works of art, and may even have the potential of defining the contours of a larger aesthetic. In Bearden's work, in other words, black music functions as a powerful inspiration and *lieu de mémoire*.

The early career of African-American painter Aaron Douglas (1899–1979) illustrates this black art/black music connection. Douglas's aesthetic values consciously shifted from a Western European and academic mode to what he described in the mid-1920s as a mode negotiating the spaces between African-American music, memory, and visual art.[12] After completing his studies at the Universities of Nebraska and Kansas, and after several years of teaching art in an all-black high school in Kansas City, Douglas moved to New York City. Upon his arrival in 1925, Douglas worked for a brief period in the stockrooms of the NAACP's official magazine, *The Crisis*. From 1925 through 1927, Douglas took art lessons from Winold Reiss, a German painter and graphic designer, who himself was a student of American Indian art and Old and New World "racial types."[13] It was primarily through Reiss's encouragement that Douglas embarked on an African-American–influenced painting style that was destined to become his signature style in murals and book designs.

In later years Douglas discussed his initial doubts about Winold Reiss's insistence that in order to explore that "inner thing of blackness," he would have to visit the museums and galleries that had African art on display:

> I clearly recall his [Reiss's] impatience as he sought to urge me beyond my doubts and fears that seemed to loom so large in the presence of the terrifying spectres moving beneath the surface of every African masque and fetish. At last, I began little by little to get the point and to take a few halting, timorous steps towards the unknown. I shall not attempt to describe my feelings as I first tried to objectify with paint and brush what I thought to be the visual emanations or expressions that came into view with the sounds produced by the old black song makers of antebellum days when they first began to put together snatches and bits from Protestant hymns, along with half remembered tribal chants, lullabies and work songs. . . .[14]

As evidenced in this recollection of Douglas's, his search for a particular "style," though initially starting with African sculpture, soon gave way to a reassessment of and a new appreciation for African-American musical arts. The African sculptures that he saw in the downtown museums and galleries became the formal backdrops for the cabaret blues and storefront spirituals that he experienced uptown. Obviously, Douglas realized that if he wanted his art to speak to the masses of black people, then it would have to have the same vitality, spirit, and ability to transfigure as did African-American music.

Douglas's artistic presence was definitely felt during his first five years in New York City. In easel paintings, murals, and book illustrations, Aaron Douglas developed a geometric style that was in sync both with African-American rhythms and with concurrent Art Deco design tenets. The flat and generalized delineation of figures, with an emphasis on precisionistlike color changes was described by Douglas as "suggestive of the uniqueness found in the gestures and bodily movements of Negro dance and [in] the sounds and vocal patterns . . . of Negro song."[15]

Aaron Douglas's *Crucifixion*, a 1927 illustration from James Weldon Johnson's *God's Trombones*, is a good example of how one formal quality of African-

Aaron Douglas, *Crucifixion*, 1927.
Oil on board, 48"×36". Private Collection of Drs. Camille and William Cosby.

American musical expression—a tendency toward polyphonies and polymetrics—is visually achieved.[16] Douglas's depictions of Jesus Christ, the Roman soldiers, and the cross are reduced to a succession of silhouetted shades of purple and lavender, and illusionistically overlaid with diagonal and concentric bands of lighter tones. This composition, with the overlaid circles and diagonal band of contrasting values, creates a complex work in spite of the simplicity of the silhouetted forms. Along with Douglas's intentional fragmenting of this biblical scene, an aural quality is evoked by his use of tonal gradations. From the sunlike core containing Christ to the surrounding fragments of "light" which get gradually darker and darker as they emanate from the haloed figure, the multivalenced facets of *Crucifixion* recall the layers of sound in traditional black church services. A turn-of-the-century visitor to "Little St. Johns" in South Carolina gives his musical impressions from a black revival service and, in doing so, expresses some of the same characteristics that Aaron Douglas's *Crucifixion* displays:

> The blending was close, the effect rich and full, the passionate, dramatic melody (with gradations of tone which sharps and flats are inadequate to express . . .) now and then rising in a rush of sound into the harmony of some strange, chromatic, accidental chord. Individual voices were distinguished . . . all feeling, as if without knowledge or intent, for that vibrating sense which attests perfect harmony, or for that unjarring flow of perfect unison; . . . some were singing antiphonally, . . . using indifferently and irrelevantly harmonies of the 3rd, 5th, or 6th, producing odd accidental concords of sound, strange chromatic groups of semitones, and irregular intervals. . . .[17]

This language mixes musical terminology with visual allusions, thus suggesting, at least in the mind of this visiting commentator, a kind of sensory "glide" in the music's effect. The preacher's sermon, the deacon's response, the congregation's vocal acknowledgment, and the simultaneous singing, calling out, screaming, crying, moaning, clapping, and foot patting from various church members are akin to the visual faceting and layering of compositional elements of *Crucifixion* and, as suggested in a survey of other twentieth-century African-American–inspired creations, the works of many other artists as well.[18]

Another painting by Douglas that also takes its cues from a multisensorial, rhythmic, and recollected impulse is *Song of the Towers*. One of the four panel paintings—collectively called *Aspects of Negro Life*—that Douglas created in 1934 for the 135th Street Branch of the New York Public Library, *Song of the Towers* was described by the artist in the following manner:

> A great migration, away from the clutching hand of serfdom in the South to the urban industrialized life in America, began during the First World War. And with it there was born the creative self-expression which quickly grew into the New Negro Movement of the twenties. At its peak, the Depression brought confusion, dejection, and frustration.[19]

Perhaps more than previous works by Douglas, *Song of the Towers* represents a major departure from his more orchestrated, romantic depictions of modern black life.[20] Here, a gigantic cogwheel, skyscrapers, and the burning smokestacks of urban industrialization are shown off-kilter, pulling his figural elements and one's perceptions of this scene into a kind of spatial ambiguity. Although Douglas's architectural and human silhouettes in *Song of the Towers* are similar to previous examples, the multiple themes in this latter work—migration, escapism, urban industrialization, creative self-expression, confusion, and dejection—along with the slanting and swaying scenery, bring it into a category entirely unto itself.

Without question, the three core images in Douglas's *Song of the Towers*—a silhouette of a man (on the far right) shown ragged, running on a cogwheel, and carrying a suitcase; another man (in the center) shown standing at the top of the cogwheel and holding up a saxophone; and a third man (in the lower left corner)

Aaron Douglas, *Aspects of Negro Life: Song of the Towers*, 1934.
Oil on canvas, 9'× 9'.
Schomburg Center for Research in Black Culture, Art & Artifacts Division, The New York Public Library, Astor, Lenox and Tilden Foundations (Photo: Manu Sassoonian). Reprinted by permission.

shown in repose and dazed—are visual representations of the black music and culture of that era. This "pack my bags and make my getaway" theme, although based on the actual black migration experience, can be found as well in 1930s black music (W. C. Handy's "St. Louis Blues," and Robert Johnson's "Dust My Broom"), and in depression-era black literature (Sterling Brown's "Long Track Blues" and Richard Wright's "Big Boy Leaves Home").

The section of the painting that best visualizes Douglas's notion of "creative self-expression" is the silhouette of the man holding a saxophone. As art historian Robert Farris Thompson has pointed out in his study of Kongo-influenced cultures in the black Americas, the ecstatic, arm-raised gesture is an answer "to the challenge of the crossroads, to the presence of death, to the proximity of God."[21] Fusing the metaphysical import of this gesture with the creative connotations of the saxophone, Douglas conveys a shared message here about musical and spiritual upliftment.

The concentric circles in Song of the Towers, like those in Crucifixion and other works by Douglas, act as a kind of zoom lens, taking the viewer into the center of painted matters, so to speak. From a core which includes the man, his saxophone, and the Statue of Liberty (shown in the implied far distance), one could conclude that one of the painting's primary themes is the musical and cultural contributions of blacks to America.

The "confusion, dejection, and frustration" that Douglas referred to in his written description of Song of the Towers is no doubt represented by the figure in the lower left corner of the canvas. Appearing disoriented and somewhat oblivious to all that surrounds him, this figure is a kind of painted incarnation of the Depression, as well as a figural evocation of the lowly blues, that component of the music and culture which is about failure and tragedy. Above his head is a skeletal hand which, like the Dance of Death cycles in sixteenth-century European art, is a convoy to the other side of Douglas's cogwheel of life and death.

On a more formal level, Song of the Towers can be seen as a blues idiom artwork in terms of Aaron Douglas's overall stylistic approach. The layering of a pure abstraction over a representational scene is not unlike a similar phenomenon in black music, where an improvised solo rides over a fixed melodic composition.[22] In both cases, the artist must be aware of the standard version in order to make nonstandard changes or additions. The key difference, of course, is that in the performed context, several musicians contribute to a final product, whereas in Douglas's painting, he is the rhythm section, the chorus, the soloist, the composer, and the conductor. The collection of creative ingredients that constitute the bands of Fletcher Henderson, Duke Ellington, and Count Basie is transposed here to the world of painting through what art historian David C. Driskell has referred to in Douglas's murals as "an intriguing blend of abstract construction with objective perception."[23]

The formal complexities of classic African-American painting and in the sounds flowing from African-American music are also expressed in the multilayered sensibilities of the black folk aesthetic. Writing in the early 1930s, novelist and folklorist Zora Neale Hurston described this design attitude in African-

American homes during the early years of the Depression:

> On the walls of the homes of the average Negro one always finds a glut of
> gaudy calendars, wall pockets and advertising lithography. . . . I saw in
> Mobile, Alabama a room in which the walls were gaily papered with

Alison Saar, *Blue Boy*, 1986.
Tin, copper, and linoleum, 34″×18″. Collection of Richard and Jan Baum, Los Angeles, CA.

Sunday supplements of the *Mobile Register*. There were seven calendars and three wall pockets. One of them was decorated with a lace doily. The mantle-shelf was covered with a scarf of deep, homemade lace, looped up with a huge bow of pink crepe paper. Over the door was a huge lithograph showing the Treaty of Versailles being signed with a Waterman fountain pen.

It was grotesque, yes. But it indicated the desire for beauty. And decorating a decoration, as in the case of the doily on the gaudy wall pocket, did not seem out of place to the hostess. The feeling [in] back of such an act is that there can never be enough beauty, let alone too much. . . .[24]

Hurston's description of this African-American "will to adorn," through a kind of *collage sensibility*, bears a striking resemblance to the layered images of Douglas and to a whole world of African-American mixed-media, assemblage, and collage artists. From the assembly of objects found on graves—black and white—in the African-American–influenced southern United States to the newspaper-lined walls in the homes of poor, rural black folk, this persistently rhythmic and unabashedly folkloric impulse cuts across time and through the minds and imaginations of innumerable people who identify with the African-American tradition.[25]

It was this engagement with cultural memory—via the innovations of artists like Aaron Douglas and Hurston's anonymous, Mobile, Alabama, assemblagist—that propelled an artist like Romare Bearden (1914–88) to embrace a style in the early sixties that Albert Murray described as being "conditioned by the blues-idiom in general and jazz musicianship in particular."[26] In a 1964 interview, Bearden spoke about his transition from being a nonfigurative, abstract painter to being a culturally grounded and rhythmically oriented collagist: "I felt that the Negro was becoming too much of an abstraction, rather than the reality that art can give a subject. . . . What I've attempted to do is establish a world in which the validity of my Negro experience could live and make its own logic."[27]

For Romare Bearden this excavating of the "Negro experience" necessitated a departure from the nonfigural and noncontextual constructs of his paintings of the fifties and a movement instead toward an art of pieced and patched realities.[28] With an approach that (1) combined cut and torn photographs from illustrated magazines; (2) presented Aaron Douglas's silhouette within a new, vigorous context; and (3) rearranged these odd scraps of colored paper, bits and pieces of human parts, sculptural segments, and slices of nature into a loosely structured narrative, Bearden invested black imagery with a sense of newness and energy which really hadn't been transmitted in American art since the late forties. Appropriately, the public's response to these new, fusion works by Bearden was one which recognized both the dreamy, fictive qualities in his imagery and the real, documentary aspect of his work. Dore Ashton made note of this peculiar dichotomy in perception in 1964:

> Although Bearden's stress is insistently on art, it is in the artlessness of the "real" that the power of these photomontages lies. The times and places he depicts are unmistakable, no matter how much regulated by his plastic manipulations. In this sense, Bearden's photomontages may be compared

with the best film documentaries which, through their uncompromising severity, their strict adherence to visual fact, transcend reportage and become art. Depth of feeling and discipline are the keys.[29]

One might add to Ashton's assessment that in works like *Carolina Shout* (from the 1974 *Of the Blues* series), Bearden recognized the artistic potential and validating power of African-American life and music. By donning the mantle of a cultural *rememberer* or, in the parlance of African peoples of the western Sudan, a *griot*, Bearden, like Eldzier Cortor's folk interior in the 1947 painting *Americana*, turned old gazettes and newspapers into something timeless, expressive, and real.

Bearden's career-long search for an African-American reality through art is in

Romare Bearden, *A Walk in Paradise Gardens*, 1955.
Oil on canvas, 27" × 23 ⅓".
Museum of African-American Art, Tampa, Florida. © Romare Bearden Foundation/Licensed by VAGA, New York, NY.

some ways echoed in a statement made by artist Aaron Douglas over sixty years ago. Writing to the poet Langston Hughes, Douglas set forth the following strategy for creating an authentic "Negro" art:

> Your problem Langston, my problem, no our problem is to conceive, develop, establish an art era. Not white art painted black. . . . No, let's bare our arms and plunge them deep through laughter, through pain, through sorrow, through hope, through disappointment, into the very depths of the souls of our people and drag forth material crude, rough, neglected. Then let's sing it, dance it, write it, paint it. Let's do the impossible. Let's create something transcendentally material, mystically objective. Earthy. Spiritually earthy. Dynamic.[30]

Though couched in the romantically imagistic language of a young artist, Douglas's strategy for establishing his very own "art era" was predicated, like Bearden's aesthetic experiments of forty years later, on a thorough excavation of African-American history and memory. What Douglas sought to tap was a reality that was often raw, unpolished, and marginalized. A reality that was variegated and multifaceted in character. A reality that could be both spiritual and material. A reality that, if we had to come up with a metaphor for all of the above, would be embodied in cultural expression like "the blues." Surely, in an effort to define

Romare Bearden, *Carolina (Shout of the Blues)*, 1974.
Collage with acrylic and lacquer on board. 37 ¹/₂" × 51".
Mint Museum of Art, Charlotte, North Carolina. Museum Purchase: National Endowment for the Arts Matching Fund and the Charlotte Debutante Club Fund. (Photo: David Ramsey.) © Romare Bearden Foundation/Licensed by VAGA, New York, NY.

African-American art and/or culture, scholars should acknowledge this thematic and expressive vein within the production of selected twentieth-century works which, by virtue of their respective artists, have a predetermined, *conscious* basis in a "mystically objective" African-American reality such as in "the blues."

The riffs in art and time that are created by generation after generation of African-American artists bring to mind the declaration of Amiri Baraka that "all styles are epochs. They come again and again. What is was, and so forth."[31] One might also add to this statement that because styles are cyclical like the seasons,

Eldzier Cortor, *Room No. 6*, c. 1946–49.
Oil on gesso on board, 31¹/₂" × 42".
Private Collection, New York. Courtesy of the Kenkeleba Gallery, New York.

they are ultimately revolutionary and redemptive. The blues, as the delta of twentieth-century African-American culture, spawns inlets of style that color a vast and gray ocean of tradition. From the anonymous songsters of the late nineteenth century who sang about hard labor and unattainable love, to contemporary rappers blasting the airwaves with percussive and danceable testimonies, the blues is an affecting, memory-induced presence that endures in every artistic overture made toward African-American peoples.

NOTES

1. Three recent publications have attempted to answer this question and, in doing so, have offered up several intriguing approaches to the concept of "African-American" art: Richard Powell, ed., *The Blues Aesthetic: Black Culture and Modernism* (Washington, D.C.: Washington Project for the Arts, 1989); Alvia Wardlaw, ed., *Black Art/Ancestral Legacy: The African Impulse in African American Art* (Dallas, Tx.: Dallas Museum of Art, 1990), and *New Generation: Southern Black Aesthetic* (Winston-Salem, N.C.: Southeastern Center for Contemporary Art, 1990).

2. Barbara Rose, "Black Art in America," *Art in America* 58 (September/October 1970), p. 55; and Hilton Kramer, "Black Art or Merely Social History," *New York Times*, June 26, 1977, p. D25.

3. "Daubings Protest Geneva Show of Paintings by Afro-Americans," *New York Times*, June 12, 1971, p. 25, recounts what happened when Swiss youth protested against an exhibition of eight black American artists. In the eyes of the protesters, the exhibition (which included works by Romare Bearden, Sam Gilliam, and Richard Hunt, among others) was not genuinely "Afro-American," nor did it give an "adequate representation" of the black protest movement in the United States. About eighteen years later, the vandalizing of artist David Hammons's sixteen-foot-high billboard/painting of a blond and blue-eyed Jesse Jackson (*How Ya Like Me Now*, 1989) by disgruntled black youth in Washington, D.C., is yet another example of censuring the works of African-American artists because of dashed expectations.

4. Elsa Honig Fine, *The Afro-American Artists* (New York: Holt, Rinehart and Winston, 1973), p. 281. Recently art historian and cultural critic Kobena Mercer discussed the inherent problems with the current terminology for artists of the African diaspora in a lecture entitled "Transcultural Icons and Aesthetics in African Diaspora Media Arts," delivered at the College Art Association, on February 21, 1991, in Washington, D.C.

5. Rose, "Black Art," p. 54

6. Ibid.

7. Edmund B. Gaither, "Introduction," in *Afro-American Artists: New York and Boston* (Boston: National Center of Afro-American Artists, 1970), n.p., and Hilton Kramer, "Trying to Define 'Black Art': Must We Go Back to Social Realism?" *New York Times*, May 31, 1970, p. D17.

8. See Ann Gibson, "Two Worlds: African-American Abstraction in New York at Mid-Century," *The Search for Freedom: African-American Abstract Painting, 1945–1975* (New York: Kenkeleba Gallery, 1991).

9. Alain Locke, "A Note on African Art," *Opportunity* 2 (May 1924), pp. 134–38.

10. *Romare Bearden, 1970–1980* (Charlotte, N.C.: Mint Museum, 1980).

11. Albert Murray, "The Visual Equivalent of the Blues," in *Romare Bearden, 1970–1980*, p. 18.

12. For information on Aaron Douglas see: Mary Schmidt Campbell, *Harlem Renaissance: Art of Black America* (New York: Harry N. Abrams, for the Studio Museum in Harlem, 1987).

13. For information on Winold Reiss see: Jeffrey C. Stewart, *To Color America: Portraits by Winold Reiss* (Washington, D.C.: Smithsonian Institution Press, for the National Portrait Gallery, 1989).

14. Aaron Douglas, "The Harlem Renaissance," unpublished manuscript dated March 18, 1973, Special Collections, Fisk University, Nashville, Tennessee.

15. Aaron Douglas, untitled, unpublished manuscript, n.d. (ca. 1966), Special Collections, Fisk University, Nashville, Tennessee.

16. James Weldon Johnson, *God's Trombones* (New York: Viking, 1927).

17. John Bennett, "A Revival Sermon at Little St. Johns," *Atlantic Monthly* 98 (August 1906), p. 257.

18. For a discussion of how African-American culture informs artists across racial and ethnic lines see: Richard Powell, ed., *The Blues Aesthetic: Black Culture and Modernism* (Washington, D.C.: Washington Project for the Arts, 1989).

19. Aaron Douglas, printed handout on *The Aspects of Negro Life* panels, October 27, 1949, Manuscripts Division, Schomburg Center for Research in Black Culture, New York Public Library, New York, New York.

20. Douglas's decided shift to a more political stance in *The Aspects of Negro Life* murals was noticed by at least one critic of his day: T. R. Poston, "Murals and Marx: Aaron Douglas Moves to the Left with PWA Decorations," *New York Amsterdam News*, November 24, 1934, p. 1.

21. Robert Farris Thompson, *Four Moments of the Sun: Kongo Art of Two Worlds* (Washington, D.C.: National Gallery of Art, 1981), pp. 176–77.

22. Albert Murray's description of Kansas City jazz "stylizations" in *Stomping the Blues* (New York: McGraw-Hill, 1976), p. 170, bears a striking resemblance to Douglas's improvisational approach to layering and patterning one set of designs on top of another image.

23. David C. Driskell, *Two Centuries of Black American Art* (Los Angeles: Los Angeles County Museum of Art, in cooperation with Alfred A. Knopf, 1976), p. 68.

24. Zora Neale Hurston, "Characteristics of Negro Folk Expression," in *Negro Anthology*, ed. Nancy Cunard (London: Wishart, 1934), p. 40.

25. Kongo-influenced grave decorations in Afro-America are discussed in Robert Farris Thompson, *Flash of the Spirit: African and Afro-American Art and Philosophy* (New York: Random House, 1983), pp. 132–42.

26. Albert Murray, "The Visual Equivalent of the Blues," in *Romare Bearden, 1970–1980*, p. 18.

27. Romare Bearden, as quoted in Charles Childs, "Bearden: Identification and Identity," *Artnews* 63 (October 1964), p. 62.

28. Lowery Sims, "The Unknown Romare Bearden," *Artnews* 85 (October 1986), pp. 117–20.

29. Dore Ashton, "Romare Bearden—Projections," *Quandrum* 17 (1964), p. 110.

30. Aaron Douglas, letter to Langston Hughes, December 21, 1925, Langston Hughes papers, James Weldon Johnson Memorial Collection of Negro Arts and Letters, Beinecke Rare Book and Manuscript Library, Yale University, New Haven, Connecticut.

31. Imamu Amiri Baraka, *In Our Terribleness* (Indianapolis, Ind.: Bobbs-Merrill, 1970), n.p.

chapter 13

ANN DOUGLAS

Skyscrapers, Airplanes, and Airmindedness: "The Necessary Angel"

Manhattan Rising

If the blues were the roots of America's modern religious sensibility, jazz was its oxygen; if the blues were buried treasure under the ocean's floor, jazz was the deep-sea diver bursting back up into the air. The generation that invented jazz was the first "to get our feet off of the ground!," as the expatriate poet Harry Crosby put it, the first to defy gravity and colonize space. It coined the word "airmindedness" and advertised its day as "the Aerial Age." Radio shows were "on the air," planes toured the heavens, and buildings competed with clouds. Everywhere people were netting the sky and finding in the air what seemed an androgynous free-for-all of spiritual energy.

Netting the sky was part of the imperial ambition of the time, of the invisible but all-powerful American empire taking over the world via its machinery, its media, and its near-monopoly on modernization, means far more effective than the old-style method of territorial conquest. William James's perception of "the air [as] itself an object" was translated in the 1920s into the commodification of the air as a marketable product, as radio frequencies, airplanes, and skyscrapers. But the religious focus James brought to his studies of the meaning of space in a world "whanging with light" was not altogether lost. Pilots like Eddie Rickenbacker, a hero of the Great War, sometimes saw themselves as "chosen pawns of the creator," and proponents of airmindedness used forbidden religious terms and phrases like "miracle," the "Holy of Holies," "saint," "evangelist," and "apostle" to describe the new creatures and events of the aerial age. Some predicted "aerial therapists" and "aerial sanitariums" where patients could have the benefit of the "therapeutic heavens" and become emblems of "the risen soul."

Scott Fitzgerald, whose first spoken word as a baby was "up," took "toploftiness" as his aesthetic, and Zelda, a famous high diver in her youth, aspired to be a "falcon ace." Living at the Plaza, the Fitzgeralds' favorite hotel, in the mad and glorious days of the early 1920s, she used her belt to lash the elevator to the floor they were staying on. The Plaza, designed by the architect Henry Janeway Hardenbergh in 1907, was itself in height (though not otherwise) an early example of the skyscraper impulse; and without elevators (new in the 1880s) shuffling between ground and sky, the skyscraper age would have been impossible. Elevators were somehow meant for the Fitzgeralds. They belonged to them, like a title.

Fitzgerald wrote an unforgettable vignette of elevator travel in a story entitled "May Day" (1920). Two intoxicated revelers, who call each other "Mr. In" and "Mr. Out," are getting into an elevator at the Biltmore Hotel (another high building, dating from 1913):

> *"What floor, please?" said the elevator man.*
> *"Any floor," said Mr. In.*
> *"Top floor," said Mr. Out.*
> *"This is the top floor," said the elevator man.*
> *"Have another floor put on," said Mr. Out.*
> *"Higher," said Mr. In.*
> *"Heaven," said Mr. Out.*

Scott's best material lay in the Believe It or Not zone, the place where fable has become truth; drunk and foolish as they are, Mr. In and Mr. Out, demanding to go "higher," to "heaven," were prompted by fact, not fancy.

The skyscraper was the offspring of the steel frames introduced in Chicago after the Great Fire of 1871; the first steel-skeleton building in New York was the Tower Building at 80 Broadway, built in 1889. Steel frames meant that, for the first time in history, a tall building did not need to emulate a pyramid, did not need to be heavier at its base to support its vertical thrust, however high, but could, rather, spring straight from the earth with no visible dependence on it. New York's skyline began to rise in the 1890s, and it gained 100 feet in the years between 1920 and 1926. During this time the skyscraper's basic design did not alter. As Hugh Ferriss, the city's most talented and influential architectural delineator, wrote in *The Metropolis of Tomorrow* (1929), "Buildings . . . have simply grown higher and higher." The verb "grow" suggested a process both natural and magical, high stories "built with a wish," as Nick Carraway says of the skyline in *The Great Gatsby*. What was to stop the Biltmore from inching "higher" on request or of its own volition? "Heaven" might not be an unreasonable goal. A number of skyscrapers boasted "Cloud Club" restaurants at their summit, and the Chrysler Building had, one story above its Cloud Club, an "Observation Deck" whose ceiling was covered with stars and whose hanging lamps looked like planets.

New York and Chicago were competitors in this race for the air. (Boston, increasingly a noncontender in the megalopolis category, showed little interest in skyscrapers.) Chicago boasted America's most innovative architects—John

Wellborn Root, Louis Sullivan, and Frank Lloyd Wright; absorbing the influence of Darwin, Herbert Spencer, Walt Whitman, and Thoreau, they subscribed to a consciously "American" architectural look devoid of what Root called "purely decorative structures," a live image of "freedom," "newness," "harshness and crudity." But New York soon took the lead. The motto of New York State was and is "Excelsior!"—which is just a high-toned version of Mr. In's "Higher!" By 1929, America boasted 377 urban buildings that had more than twenty stories, fifteen of which were more than 500 feet high; 188 of them were in New York.

The race for the air was conducted within New York as well. The architectural historian Wayne Attoe distinguishes between a "democratic" skyline, in which buildings complement one another, and a "star" skyline, in which buildings compete with each other; in Manhattan, buildings challenged each other directly. In 1908, a 700-foot tower made the Metropolitan Life Insurance Company Building the world's tallest; in 1913, the title went to Cass Gilbert's Woolworth Building at 233 Broadway, at 800 feet; in 1930, the Chrysler Building, designed by William Van Alen, claimed the championship. The Chrysler Building had a competitor in the Bank of the Manhattan Company, under construction at the same time and designed by H. Craig Severance, Van Alen's ex-partner (there was a personal side to this architectural rivalry), but right after the bank's official opening, Van Alen hoisted a secret 185-foot spire into place on top of the Chrysler Building and surpassed his competitor. "No old stuff for me!" he exclaimed. "Me, I'm new! Avanti!" In 1931, the Empire State Building established its supremacy.

The erection of the Empire State Building was the stuff of instant legend, an example of "automatic architecture," in the phrase of Rem Koolhaas, the fulfillment of New York's promise to James in 1907 that "there was nothing that was not easy." Thanks to assembly-line production, buildings could be put up five times faster than they had been only a decade before, and the Empire State Building rose at the rate of close to a floor a day, without a break, until it reached its height of 102 stories or 1,250 feet, a satisfying 277 feet higher than the Eiffel Tower. A temporary restaurant was installed on the site to cut the laborers' lunch break to a minimum; every recent contribution to construction and labor efficiency—bulldozers, cranes, scaffolding, chutes, paint sprayers—was in full use. In 1930, as the actual construction was just beginning, its designer, Richmond Shreve, made clear the nature of the feat: materials from all over the United States and the world "must come together and fit together with accuracy of measurement and precision of time." "Six months ago the working drawings . . . had not been begun; one year from now it will have been completed . . . fifty million dollars . . . twenty thousand tenants . . . two million square feet . . . fifty thousand tons of steel . . . rising nearly a quarter mile."

Buildings, sometimes fine ones integral to the city's heritage, were torn down in the haste to put up bigger, newer ones. The old Madison Square Garden was razed to make way for the New York Life Insurance Building; the old Waldorf-Astoria's site became that of the Empire State Building. The Waldorf Astoria's elevators were salvaged, but the rest of the building was dumped into the sea five miles off Sandy Hook. "The destruction of the Waldorf [was] planned," Koolhaas writes, "as part of the construction [of the Empire State Building]." It's once again the streamlined American symbiosis of destruction and production, the emphasis not on the product but on accelerated production, on productivity itself.

Most New Yorkers thought (mistakenly, as it turned out) that the skyscrapers would be as transient as the buildings that had been demolished to make way for them. In *The North American Review* of November 1929, the sculptor Gutzon Borglum lamented that "our greatest buildings are ephemeral," and a *New York Times* editorial of October 26, 1926, remarked: "As for building for eternity, the need does not exist. Thirty years from now they will be tearing up the city once more." Hugh Ferriss, drawing the "Imaginary Metropolis" of tomorrow, a city he thought of as in the near-future, envisaged entirely new buildings; not a single building of the 1920s is to be seen on these pages. If Chrysler produced a new model every year, why shouldn't architects do the same? The skyscrapers were not only technology, soon to be junked as obsolete, but pop and mass art, and whatever else it may be, mass art is transient, disposable, replaceable. Even allowing for advertising value, the skyscrapers yielded little or no profit, because office rents did not always cover the steep cost of the necessary elevator and maintenance service. Critics commented on their wastefulness, but the architect Claude Bragdon, writing in *The American Mercury* in March 1931, explained that the motive behind them was not in any case financial but "psychological." The nation's need for self-expression, not its economic imperatives, had produced the new skyline.

Manhattan was engaged in revolutionizing its architectural identity, and shifts in architecture always spell shifts in the psyche of the people who build it. We all know the shock that comes when a new and different building goes up amid the old familiar structures of a neighborhood. It's as if we were committed, without warning, willy-nilly, simply by the new building's obtrusiveness, its "sticking out," to sponsoring and incorporating it into our corporeal and psychic image or idea of ourselves. We instinctively know that buildings have designs on us; they insist on speaking for us, on being extensions of those who build and behold them. In the "Epilogue" of *The Metropolis of Tomorrow*, Ferriss explained that "architecture influences the lives of human beings"; "specific consequences," "subconscious" effects, will turn up in our "thoughts, feelings and actions." Buildings, in other words, affect our unconscious and quite possibly emanate from it. Koolhaas says that the skyscrapers were Manhattan's Rosetta Stone, the hieroglyphics of the modern American nation; skyscraper Manhattan offered the spectator the biggest sculpture, the largest-scale self-portrait yet seen in the world, a case study, one might say, set in stone.

It is important to note that skyscrapers did not become the dominant form of modern urban architecture in England or Europe. Visiting foreigners might be awestruck in America by what the Englishwoman Mary Borden called "the scaffolding of the world of the future," but on their home turf they were unwilling, as the art historian Robert Hughes has pointed out in *The Shock of the New* (1981), to consign the amount of space a skyscraper required to a building that would serve only one purpose—a commercial one—instead of answering to the many domestic, trade, and civic uses that buildings in Paris or London were designed and accustomed to accommodate. Raymond Hood, New York's leading skyscraper designer, finished the flamboyant black-and-gold American Radiator Building at 40 West Fortieth Street (just behind the New York Public Library) in 1924. A few years later, the National Radiator Company in London asked him to design a building for them, in collaboration with the English architect J. Gordon Reeves. The London firm also wanted a black-and-gold decor, but their building was to be only eight floors high, in contrast to the New York model's twenty-two floors, itself a very modest height in New York at the time.

Europeans and Englishmen have always liked to feel at home in their cities; the out-of-scale skyscrapers might, to their mind, dwarf the city inhabitant and his concerns. There were reservations at home as well. A sketch of 1921 by Edward Hopper entitled *Night Shadows* shows a man seen from above, from, one deduces, a very tall building. A huge lamppost casts a foreboding diagonal shadow before the tiny figure; he looks lost. Frank Lloyd Wright, the pioneer in low-lying organic architectural design, acknowledged the skyline's nighttime beauty—"a shimmering verticality, a gossamer veil, a festive scene-drop hanging against the black sky to dazzle, entertain and amaze"—but he could not forget, he wrote in *The Disappearing City* (1932), that the skyscrapers were "volcanic crater[s] of blind, confused human forces . . . forcing anxiety upon all life." "The skyscraper," Wright said, is "no longer sane." Wright's negative take was, however, largely an anomaly in America.

James, who took pleasure in New York's "heaven-scaling audacity . . . and the lightness withal," saw the beginnings of the skyscraper age. Returning by train in the late 1890s from a dispiriting stay amid the overcheerful Chautauqua lecture crowd, he found the revitalization he needed, he told the listeners of his lecture "What Makes a Life Significant?" (1899), in the sight, near Buffalo, of "a workman doing something on the dizzy edge of a skyscaling iron construction"; this was human nature "in extremis." His image was literalized three decades later in Lewis Hine's *Sky Boy* photograph, the most famous of the ones he took during the construction of the Empire State Building: a young man is going to work on the building, ascending a cable; in the background we see, not, as we might expect, the city spread below, but a distant Hudson River and sheer air.

There were links between the skyscrapers and the new media; they hosted radio (and later television) wiring and served as advertisements for the industries that financed them. The self-promoted "frankly spectacular" RCA Victor Building culminated in a series of clustered Victrola-needle-like points. The Chrysler Building sported hubcaps amid its decoration, and the Radiator Building was lit at night to glow softly in the dark like an immense incandescent radiator. Marshall McLuhan has argued that the media offer to human senses and powers, not unbeatable competition, but extensions and accelerators, and by this reading, the skyscrapers were central to the first full-fledged media age; their upward thrust was meant to spur in their viewers, not comparison, but identification, even self-glorification. Admirers as well as detractors emphasized their prodigious, defiant quality: "a freak," "a stunt," "a great feat," a "tour de force" were titles bestowed on the Chrysler Building. The skyscraper was an energy-mad era's supreme self-valorization. With its steel frame and dizzying climb upward, it was a literal demonstration of Ronald Fieve's "grandiosity with a basis in fact," of James's "will to believe" or, as he later thought he should have titled it, "the *right* to believe," the *American* right to believe.

Wallace Stevens, born in 1879, was a Harvard man; although he did not study with James, he became a self-conscious subscriber to his "Will to Believe." Stevens began to write in something like his mature manner—sensual yet abstract, pampered, at moments rococo, but austere—when he was living in Manhattan, the "electric town," as he called it, in the first decade and a half of the century. Despite his attachment to his hometown, Reading, Pennsylvania, despite the intermittent unemployment and loneliness he experienced, Stevens stayed on in New York because there, he knew, he could become the poet he wanted to be. An advocate of "supreme fiction," he was never a proponent of "terrible honesty," and in New York, he wrote, "I can polish myself with dreams [and] live in a fine false way." Although he left for Hartford, Connecticut, in the spring of 1916 to please his new wife and pursue a career in the insurance business, he regretted the move. "I miss New York abominably," he wrote one friend, but it lived on in his poetry, if not as subject, as aesthetic principle and ideal. Like Fitzgerald, Stevens favored verbs like "bloom," "gust," "flash," "glitter," "enlarge," "flock," "buoy," "blow," and "flutter"—all suggesting matter effacing its boundaries, extending its promise, rearranging its relationship with gravity, matter in a state of translation. It is no accident that his poetic awakening occurred in New York at the start of the skyscraper era; buildings attract muses and poets, too.

Describing his poetic as the "visible announced," as the "object" extended through "the proliferation of resemblances," an aesthetic based, in other words, on the changes affected in matter when it is extended outward and upward into air, when space, not time, is its predominant element, Stevens could be describing the effects sought by the architects of the skyscrapers; indeed, his language is almost identical to that used by their early promoters. The Woolworth Building, finished while Stevens was still in the city, was a solid cream-colored mass studded with windows, an extraordinary five thousand of them, elaborated with Mozartian delicacy. It rose to a Gothic tower, "gradually," in the words of Cass Gilbert, its architect, "gaining in spirituality the higher it mounts," and it was "acknowledged as premier," a 1916 promotional pamphlet claimed, "by all those who aspire toward perfection and . . . use visible means to obtain it." Material excess has triggered spiritual self-realization. The Woolworth Building, too, proceeded by a "proliferation of resemblances," by self-perpetuation with variations, to an annunciation of the visible; it, too, "celebrate[d] the marriage / Of earth and air," in the words of an early Stevens poem, "Life Is Motion."

To convince the skeptics of their claims, Spiritualists had tried to photograph the invisible world unveiled in séances. Although the fairies, spirits, and other supernatural phenomena captured by their cameras proved upon investigation to be doctored superimpositions—it seemed fair, many of them felt, to falsify evidence to gain adherents to truth—the phenomenon was still imaginatively resonant; it was another form of the "marriage / Of earth and air," another way of using "visible means" to capture "spiritual perfection." The skyscrapers made the affinities between the old Spiritualist medium and the new media explicit. Like the Spiritualist photographers, their architects aimed to achieve the look of "a soul . . . photographed in heaven," in the phrase of the critic Elizabeth Kendall; they, too, produced the ineffable without sacrificing the delights of the concrete, an act of resurrection that honored the body as well as the soul.

The promotional pamphlet about the Woolworth Building elaborated at length its varied perspectives and services and conveniences, the multitudes of office holders and employees it held; everything one could ever want or need was apparently contained within it or sighted from it. As if to advertise the plenitude and plurality of its resources, the Chrysler Building's elevators were made of dozens of different kinds of inlaid wood, including Japanese ash, English gray hardwood, Oriental walnut, American walnut, and Cuban plum-pudding wood; no two elevators were the same. The more severe Empire State Building struck its own note of intoxicating self-sufficiency. At the center of the spare but magnificent lobby was a huge gleaming aluminum bas-relief of itself; at the heart of the building, "fine and false," in Stevens's phrase, to the core, lay its own proud self-image. Modern taboos against open displays of narcissism did not hold here. When a reviewer of Ferriss's *Metropolis of Tomorrow* wrote that the book was a "gorgeous feast," he was acknowledging the affinities between the new urban architecture and the older matriarchal values of oral gratification, self-love, and spiritual aspiration; the skyscrapers were very much, to recur to James's words, a "solid meal" and not a "printed bill of fare."

Ferriss himself offered evidence of the ties between the new architecture and older matriarchal ideals and practices. Arriving in New York from his native St. Louis as a young man in 1912, he worked with Gilbert on the Woolworth Building, and in the next two decades his drawings figured in the construction and publicity of many of the city's most notable skyscrapers, including the Radiator Building, the Chanin Building, and the Chrysler Building. But the city Ferriss drew in *The Metropolis of Tomorrow* seems less modernistic than mystic, less a futuristic city than an experiment in psychic research. Details are vague, suns are in eclipse; buildings are shafts of bodied and varying light, looming out of the shadows like spirits summoned at a séance. In fact, Ferriss dabbled in Spiritualism, Theosophy, and Gurdjieff study groups—he and Jean Toomer were in the same Gurdjieff class in 1925—and he tells us that the skyscraper, the emblem of the "subconscious," "possesses an individual existence, varying—now dynamic, now serene—but vital as is all else in the universe." By "vital" he meant something like the *élan vital* of William James's friend Henri Bergson, the French philosopher; James sometimes used the same phrase to describe his version of the subconscious, though he usually called it, as did many Spiritualist and Mind-cure practitioners, the "subliminal self." Catching the matriarchal and Mind-cure reverberations of Ferriss's aesthetic, Rem Koolhaas describes his world of primal shadows as "the . . . womb of Manhattanism."

The feminine parallel might at first puzzle the student of New York's skyscrapers. No women were involved in designing and building them; if the decade was engaged in "reading the phallus," Manhattan might supply the text. Storming the sky, the skyscrapers were, whatever else they advertised themselves to be, an announcement of modern man's role as the belligerent pugilist-prophet of Krutch's "No-God": "There is no God and I am his prophet." Yet, as if to substantiate Freud's worst fears about a fatherless world, delirious New York also paid paradoxical homage to a feminine principle that "blurred the issue of paternity," as Koolhaas puts it. Mass art in extremis, Manhattan's new architecture expressed and proved the relation between modern popular art and old-style Victorian matriarchy.

The skyscraper phenomenon, a historical hybrid, began in the prewar decades, the heyday of the Titaness, and peaked in the boom years dominated by her matricidal offspring; some of its finest manifestations, though planned in the flush years of the boom, actually went up or were completed after the Crash, amid the mood reversals instigated by the Depression. A historical mongrel, the skyscraper offered a cultural crux, a nexus of apparently contradictory ideas, a powerfully utopian and fully realized coalition of modern masculine technology and phallic style with old-fashioned subliminal and matriarchal impulses. The moderns purported to despise the Titaness in all her guises, but the skyscraper nonetheless represented her influence via the return of the repressed; the repressed matriarchal culture had come back, less as Fury and Demon—that came in full force, I've suggested, a bit later—than as a form of toploftiness, an unrecognized yet "Necessary Angel" (the term was Stevens's) at the apex of 1920s Manhattan. The model is Jamesian rather than Freudian; James had his own ideas about the return of the repressed.

According to James, the unconscious or "subliminal self" was the diffuse and permeable "fringe" part of the psyche, the part that extends the self and diffuses it into the outer world, physical and spiritual, an instance of psychic matter revealing its secret identity as light. It represents another form of awareness which operates outside conscious control, replenishing and expanding the limited, knowable self; the subliminal self tells us, in James's words in a letter of 1906, that "the world our 'normal' consciousness makes use of is only a fraction of the whole world in which we have our being." Unlike the Freudian unconscious, James's subliminal self was not a traitor ambushing the unwary conscious self but a potential resource, even a friend, less a trap than an enlargement and an enkindling, offering a bigger, freer space for the activities of the self than the self unaided can command. One must consider the contrast between Freud at work in his dark, private, book-and-object-crammed study, and James, thinking aloud as he lectured, liking to stop in the classroom and look out the window. Freud's unconscious was an indoor affair, a powerful generator below basement level; for James, the man who loved the "acrobatic" American climate "whanging with light," the unconscious was a kind of outdoors, full of the wonders and terrors of the world we acknowledge to be beyond our control. In his version of the unconscious, the air has been not shut out but let in; the subliminal self is the outdoors that is, so to speak, indoors, our own access to the weather of the universe.

Freud's unconscious works on a hydraulic model drawn from physics; in a world of limited space, energy, and motion, one thing automatically dislodges or imperils another. Given this dynamic, the conscious part of Freud's psyche must try to displace or repress the unconscious part, which in turn must struggle to regain its place; this struggle on the part of the unconscious for expression and dominance is what Freud meant by the return of the repressed. James honored the hydraulic principle as he did all theories with a basis in fact (he nicknamed it, after a student misnomer that amused him, the "hydraulic goat"), but his notion of the unconscious nonetheless expressed a tenacious reservation about it; he believed that there might be modes of placing that meant, not conflict for territory, but rather new ways of making room, forms of expansion and contraction difficult to conceptualize but nonetheless real. A surgeon operating on the human brain, James pointed out, is on one level simply dealing with finite matter in a portion of the cranium, a circumscribed small space; on another level, however, he's dealing with an organ that itself creates and peoples a world, though one invisible and unheard in the operating room. The many do fit into the one; the infinitely multiple can be contained in the discrete.

In James's more elastic scheme, the return of the repressed involved, not conflict between conscious and unconscious selves, though he knew that such conflict might well be present, but fresh forms of collaboration between them; something like coexistence, even cooperation, between conscious and unconscious is possible. It's not so much the return of the repressed as the survival of the unacknowledged, the re-emergence or expansion of the subliminal self. The matriarchal element of the all-male-designed skyscraper was the return of the repressed in a Jamesian guise, a happier guise than the one Freud described: the denied unconscious element continues to serve body and mind as nourishment though not as conscious idea, much less as aim or ideology.

It's important to stress that James's view of the unconscious included, even as it de-emphasized, Freud's idea of the unconscious, but the reverse was decidedly not the case; whatever his limitations, James knew more about conflict than Freud did about peace. Freud gave scant attention to what later psychoanalysts dubbed the "conflict-free ego sphere," the place where the self learns and adapts and changes, not only because it must, but because it wants and needs to for its own full self-expression. He always cast the return of the repressed as struggle and punishment. In his schema, collaboration between conscious and unconscious might occur in rare and elated moments of creative breakthrough (moments that usually prove costly), but hardly as an everyday reality or opportunity. James's pragmatic stress on experience and results is very different; most of us know that what we forget or deny returns to us in several ways, by several routes—sometimes as unexpected Freudian vengeance, sometimes as Jamesian surprise reinforcement, even deliverance. America's moment of self-discovery spelled both the exhilaratingly dark return of Freud's "primaeval man within us" and an infusion of atmospheric optimism, an access of Jamesian weather, "a tremendous muchness," as James put it, "suddenly revealed" as if through "an open window."

Harry Houdini, a New York magician, illustrates my point about how the Jamesian return of the repressed operates. His career spanned the Victorian and the modern eras, and it was a paradigm of the tensions between them. Houdini liked to close his show with the line "Will wonders never cease?" and he, too, netted the sky. Born Ehrich Weisz in Budapest in 1874 to a Jewish family (his father was a cantor) and raised in Wisconsin, before he was ten he was working the circus and carnival circuit billed as the "Prince of the Air." His later feats included jumping from one airplane to another while both planes were in the air and getting out of a straitjacket while suspended from a skyscraper. He had matriarchal interests as well. He had practiced as a Spiritualist medium, and when his adored mother died in the 1910s, he tried repeatedly and vainly to reach her through séances and telepathy. Embittered by his failure, he embarked on his career as an exposer of mediumistic fraud. In other words, Houdini had learned the tricks of the trade which he devoted his last years to attacking as a would-be believer—"I was *willing* to believe, even *wanted* to believe," he wrote in his autobiography—and many of his fans and enemies alike insisted that he had not altogether shed these beliefs, that he himself proved the existence of the magical powers he derided.

In his autobiography, *A Magician among the Spirits* (1924), Houdini recounts a striking exchange with Freud's muse, Sarah Bernhardt, for whom he gave a special show in Paris right after the Great War. Bernhardt, who had acted almost as often in America as in Europe, was an admirer of the skyscrapers; on a visit to the States she talked about designing one herself. She had written a book titled *Dans les nuages* (*In the Clouds*) about her adventures as a balloon aviatrix in the late 1870s, and she created a "flying costume" for women during the Great War. Although she, too, was credited with magical powers, they seemed to be failing her by the time she and Houdini met. A leg had been amputated in 1915, and she was no longer young. Gallant to the last, she'd gone on performing on one leg, on rare but electric occasions propped up by a staff bearing the French flag.

Bernhardt was enthralled by Houdini's show. When it was over, she said, "in that wonderful speaking voice with which she . . . has thrilled thousands of auditors": " 'Houdini, you do such marvellous things. Couldn't you—could you bring back my leg for me?'" Houdini was shocked. "You know my powers are limited," he told her, "and you are actually asking me to do the impossible." "But," she insisted, "you do the impossible." Bernhardt believed in the effects she created; she was only asking him to do the same. (Though he did not restore her leg, they parted friends.) Houdini's wife also believed he could do the impossible. He died on Halloween in 1926, the victim of a demented fan who, taking Houdini's magical powers of invulnerability at face value, directed a series of unexpected and lethal blows to his abdomen; his wife spent the next decade in séances, trying to establish contact with him.

The title of Houdini's autobiography, *A Magician among the Spirits*, hardly advertised the incredulity the text itself was meant to document, and his signature line, "Will wonders never cease?," if intended as irony, was also an invitation. His shows during the 1920s involved re-creating all the effects the mediums achieved—tappings, voices, apparitions—then demonstrating the "trickery," the purely human means that produced them. But while his interest lay in the moment of exposure, in the demonstration of fraud, in "terrible honesty" as entertainment, his viewers' most eager attention went to the pretense not the fact, the impostor not the critic. In their eyes, he gained his force in part through possession of the powers he had repudiated but assimilated; he suggested to others his own denied source of sustenance. What he repressed did not fight him as much as it fed him. A similar logic was evident in the skyscrapers.

Inside Raymond Hood's tall, clean-featured Daily News Building (1929), at 150 East Forty-second Street, was a surprise in the form of a stunningly farfetched lobby which featured a moving ten-foot inset globe with a mirror beneath it and a black glass-faceted ceiling above; it was one of the womb structures Koolhaas finds everywhere on the all-masculine architectural scene. What had seemed suppressed had been but submerged, and it had resurfaced to complete rather than challenge the dominant design. If the moderns' tactic of appropriation, an activity brought to a peak in Manhattan's new skyscrapers, was the matricidal one of ripping the babe betimes from the womb, killing the mother to save the child, one must remember that the child snatched from the mother's womb is still part of the mother; the mother destroyed to save the child nonetheless lives on in the child. The best of the matriarchal culture which the skyscraper era officially repudiated was less essentialist than all-inclusive, vitally concerned with inmost corporeal and spiritual truths, and it was this culture on which Stein and James built their modernist art; it was carried, intact, in the womb of the skyscrapers.

This male-female presence, the realized alliance of masculine and feminine impulses, was crucial to the special euphoria of top promises fulfilled, the sense of heaven here on earth that the skyscrapers inspired in those who designed and viewed them. Only when the masculine and feminine elements are present in equal strength, only when the genders collaborate rather than compete, only when they come fully abreast or flush of each other, can the artifact or culture involved be, by a process of simultaneous gender reinforcement and gender cancellation, both gender-doubled and beyond gender and so satisfy the deepest needs of the human heart, mind, and psyche. Houdini remarked that "if the wish is father to the thought, it is mother to the hallucination." The New York skyline, "built with a wish," was that thought and that hallucination.

Marianne Moore believed that, to be "exact," one must be "reckless," and she chose a like-minded passage from William James when she wrote a preface to a later compilation of her work in *The Marianne Moore Reader* (1960): "Man's chief difference from the brutes lies in the exuberant excess of his subjective propensities. Prune his extravagance, sober him, and you undo him." Skyscraper Manhattan embodied James's "exuberant excess of . . . subjective propensities," the modern American psyche boldly, irrepressibly proliferating in symbols, symptoms, and self-advertisements, a pandemonium of the pleasure principle, at once the city that Ford Madox Ford celebrated in 1926 as "the city of the good time" and the apotheosis of the "world elsewhere" envisaged by classic American literature and improvised, in a different guise, by the new jazz music "riding free on the air," in J. A. Rogers's words; it was materialist pragmatism converted into what Spiritualists and psychic researchers would have called its "astral body" as sheer poetry.

American Masquerade

The Manhattan skyline, "star" architecture in the full theatrical sense of the word, suggested not just the immensity and aspiration of James's "subliminal self" and its "will to believe" but the diverse drama of his "will to personate." Fittingly, Forty-second Street, memorialized in song by Al Dubin and Harry Warren in 1933 as the heart of New York's theater district, boasted more than its share of skyscrapers. The Chanin Building at 122 East Forty-second Street was designed by Sloan and Robertson in 1929 to stand high and gorgeous opposite the site of what was to be the Chrysler Building; with its terra-cotta–clad tower lit by floodlights at night, its promoters advertised it as the "mise-en-scène of the romantic drama of American business." The Chrysler Building's lobby featured doorways designed to look like draperies parted before a deep embrasure; "Curtain's up," as they said nightly at theaters on West Forty-second Street. William Van Alen, its architect, was dubbed "the Ziegfeld of his profession."

Hugh Ferriss summed up the impact of Hood's controversial Radiator Building in *The Metropolis of Tomorrow*: "It stops people daily in their tracks; they exclaim how much they like or dislike its emphatic form and radical color scheme." Agreeing with Louis Sullivan that "form follows function," that, in a building, "utility" comes before conventional notions of beauty, Ferriss nonetheless added a characteristically Manhattan proviso: "Effect follows form." Ferriss had participated in amateur theatricals at the Theatre Guild in his early days in the Village with his wife, Dorothy Lapham, an illustrator and editor at *Vogue*, and he knew that conventional beauty might be forsworn but drama was a necessity.

On one occasion in 1931, a group of skyscraper architects came to a costume ball at the Astor Hotel dressed as their buildings. Van Alen wore a cardboard facsimile of the Chrysler Building façade; a cut-out effigy of its tower was his party hat. Duke Ellington believed that New Yorkers were by definition "performers," and so were their newest buildings. There's a wonderful story about a very tall Texas college student named Jack Earle who liked to visit the touring circuses and their sideshows in the 1920s; at seven foot seven he welcomed the companionship of other freaks and monstrosities. On one such occasion, Clyde Ingalls, a Ringling Brothers entrepreneur, sized him up and asked: "How would you like to be a giant?" Earle was already gigantic, but Ingalls was offering him something different and better: the chance to turn a physiological attribute, or disability, into a persona, a role, and a profit. (Earle accepted the offer.) So, too, with Manhattan's new buildings. They weren't just gigantic; in an immense act of impersonation and appropriation, they played at being "giants," giants from a range of cultures as diverse as those represented in the Ringling Brothers' sideshows.

When I argued that the skyscraper drew on the repudiated older matriarchal culture as sustenance rather than idea or ideology, I meant that the moderns could use matriarchal forms and impulses in order to express and champion a worldview, a set of cultural values, that was antithetical to those held by the Titaness at her most repressive. James's thinking had lent itself to matriarchal gifts and needs while it criticized matriarchal claims, and similarly, Houdini used what seemed magical powers to disprove their existence; this paradoxical utilization of old energy with new for the modern task was the era's supreme act of appropriation. Nowhere was the urban moderns' espousal of America's cultural pluralism (so distasteful to the Titaness) clearer than in their most characteristic architecture, suffused though it might be with echoes of the older matriarchal ethos.

If the skyscraper represented, as some said, Babel, the implications weren't all bad. Babel was a cacophony of different languages; so were the skyscrapers. As New York's theaters became important for the world's dramas—with pioneering productions of Ibsen, Shaw, Synge, and Strindberg, as well as of plays and musical revues by a host of American talents, many of them of immigrant or Negro stock—its new architecture made itself the host for motifs and styles from widely diverse cultures, present and past. Zigzag designs from American Indian culture and angular geometric patterns from ancient Babylon and Assyria and Africa contradicted and supplemented Gothic towers, gargoyles, and Art Deco ornamentation. Writing about *The Skyscraper* in 1981, Paul Goldberger calls it "the art of grafting . . . historical forms onto modern frames."

Gilbert Seldes had explicated this grafting tactic three decades earlier in *The Great Audience* (1950). Protesting the standardization imposed by the new mass media, he made an eloquent and sustained plea for heterogeneity and diversity. Drawing explicitly on James, particularly *The Varieties of Religious Experience* and *A Pluralistic Universe*, he argued that America, with its vast geographical spread, was in its very nature a land of "pluralities"; unlike the more homogeneous and cramped Europeans, Americans "lead plural lives in a diversity of climates." The nation was founded on the revolutionary principle that anyone can become an American by a simple act of will; in Seldes's words, "He not only can make something of himself, he can make himself over." Seldes was eliding the unequal difficulties of Americanization faced by different racial and ethnic groups to focus on what he took to be the essential dynamic of American citizenship. There are no Americans, he believed, in the sense that there are British, Italian, French, German, or African people. Whoever chooses to be an American is choosing, whether he knows it or not, to belong to a country that is part German, part Italian, part English, part African, and so on *ad infinitum*, and thus anyone who elects to be an American automatically partakes of all these nationalities and races himself.

A male colleague of Ruth St. Denis, the histrionic modern dance pioneer, once remarked: "She acted all the time; she couldn't get away from it." Yet he found her "a genuinely natural person . . . at all times," because "her natural self was an actor." As Seldes understood him, the "natural self" of the American was an actor, too. Citizenship in America was an almost infinitely multiple act of impersonation; the essence of the stable American identity was to have no stable identity at all. The "plurality of lives" we "crave" but cannot, Freud had insisted in

"Thoughts for the Times on War and Death," have, was, to Seldes's mind as to James's, the American reality. "Variety" is Seldes's central word and concept here, and he drew it in part, he tells us, from James, and in part, I believe, though he doesn't say so, from the New York theatrical sheet he was fond of quoting, *Variety*, begun by the journalist Sime Silverman in 1905. Specializing in factual reportage and an abbreviated show-biz idiom, the trade paper took its name from the famous theatrical tradition; it was the word that best conveyed the racial and immigrant plurality of the American polis and the diverse, mixed entertainment that Seldes considered its most characteristic and valuable self-expression. It's an ideal the new architecture honored, too; the Manhattan skyscraper was a creature much like Seldes's American citizen, a loose coalition of multiple selves whose purpose was "to offer attractively more kinds of experience" by extending, almost indefinitely, "the range of choice."

Interest in variety was not a modern monopoly. Late-Victorian culture had been fascinated by foreign and imported Orientalism; Ruth St. Denis's most celebrated early dances, *Rahda* (1906) and *Egypta* (1910), paid homage to the mysterious East. The eclectic Manhattan skyscraper on one level simply continued this fascination; among the events and influences that the art historian Eva Weber cites as important for the Art Deco style, seen at a peak in the Chrysler Building, are the opening of King Tutankhamen's tomb in 1922 and the flood of interest in Egyptian, Assyrian, and Minoan art it released. But unlike the Oriental motifs in St. Denis's dances, many of the foreign elements represented by the modern skyscraper were from America's own buried cultures. Just as Martha Graham, St. Denis's successor, turned to American Indian and black dance for many elements in her choreography and pioneered in having people of color in her dance troupe, the skyscrapers of the 1920s drew ideas and sustenance from local as well as foreign sources. Native American art, increasingly on view in the city's art galleries; *Primitive Art* (1928), the pioneering study by Zora Neale Hurston's mentor Franz Boas; Negro music; and the anthropological, historical, and literary researches into African and African-American culture undertaken by members of the Harlem Renaissance and their allies—all played a part in the skyscraper aesthetic.

The "sky-scaling iron construction" that James saw near Buffalo satisfied his need for "something primordial and savage"; later observers and practitioners of the new urban architecture had similar thoughts. One design submitted for the Chicago Tribune Building of 1923—Raymond Hood won the contest—was by the German architect Heinrich Mossdorf; it culminated in the massive head of an Indian wielding a tomahawk. Mossdorf was half-spoofing, but he, too, like D. H. Lawrence in *Studies in Classic American Literature*, published the same year, was reminding America of its primitive peoples, its role as King Kong in the modern world. Hood's Radiator Building, with its Gothic-primitive fancifulness and innovative black-brick and gold-leaf coloration, made one viewer think of "jazz," of "tom-toms and gleaming spear points," of the "Ku Klux [Klan]" and prizefighter "Jack Johnson's Golden Smile." (The 1920s mindset was not, as I've repeatedly remarked, a civil-rights mentality—note how casually this reviewer elides discordant elements.)

Texas-born Jack Johnson, more than six feet tall and one of the greatest of all heavyweights, had held the world championship from 1908 to 1915, the first Negro ever to do so, to the horror of most white fans and the delight of all black ones. Johnson combined a terrific wallop with an extraordinary lightness and speed of motion; he could redirect his left punch in what seemed mid-air. A fascinated and unhappy Jack London reported that watching him defeat the white heavyweight champion Tommy Burns in 1908 was like watching "a grown man cuffing a naughty child." Heavy shells in the Great War were nicknamed "Jack Johnsons."

Johnson was a complex, good-natured, and intelligent man fond of reading Herbert Spencer and Gibbon, but confronted with a solid wall of prejudice, he reacted with brutal in-the-ring sniping, drunken escapades, and a series of white mistresses and wives. Still, he had a partial refuge. "Thank God for the theatre," Essie Robeson remarked after a particularly ugly racial incident; Johnson could play a decent bass and sing ragtime, and as soon as he won the championship, he set off on a three-month vaudeville tour. After he'd lost the title in 1915, he continued his vaudeville career, appearing on the same bill with Ethel Waters in Philadelphia in November 1921 on a tour she did with Fletcher Henderson. Johnson also organized his own jazz orchestra and fronted the Harlem establishment that became, in other hands, the Cotton Club; he staged exhibition fights and starred in two all-black-cast boxing films, *As the World Turns* and *For His Mother's Sake*.

By the time the Radiator Building was finished, Johnson had become something of a national hero; America was more eager to welcome its black talent than it had been a decade earlier. His story hit Broadway in 1926 as *Black Boy*, a play written by Jim Tully and Frank Dazey and produced by Horace Liveright, with Paul Robeson in the lead. Everyone knew about "Jack Johnson's golden smile," golden because he had been wont to flash it at hostile white crowds just as he prepared to finish off some forlorn "white hope" in the ring and collect another huge purse, golden because even his enemies conceded the magnetism of that magnificent cheek-to-cheek grin, one of those "rare smiles" Fitzgerald described in *The Great Gatsby* that seem to concentrate and project the amplitude and excitement of a world, not a person. Like the Radiator Building, Johnson was a hieroglyphic in black and gold, part of what the critic Peter Brooks has called (in a different context) the "aesthetic of astonishment."

The new serial comic strips of the day were part of that aesthetic, too; Popeye and Krazy Kat and others were transforming the already combustible American language into a series of linguistic explosions. John Held, Jr., the most famous illustrator of the Jazz Age, did a cover for the February 3, 1927, issue of *Life* called "Comic Strip Number," full of his trademark angular forms here uttering strange ballooned words: "Wauf!" "Pow!" "Wham!" "Socko!" "Glug!" "Zowie!" and "Bam!" (after the "Bambino," as Italian-American fans called Babe Ruth). Like the language of the comic strips, like Babe Ruth's swing and Johnson's punch, the Radiator Building was an explosive force, part of the "frightfully expensive scenery built to knock the beholder's eye out," in the words of *The New York Times* on

November 3, summing up two decades of architectural history.

In *Beer Can by the Highway* (1961), John Kouwenhoven, trying to explain jazz, used an urban metaphor: the city's grid is comparable to jazz's basic 4/4 or 2/4 beat, and the skyscrapers are its solo improvisations. New York in the 1920s became a mecca for jazz musicians: Louis Armstrong, Sidney Bechet, Jelly Roll Morton, and many others left Chicago for short or long periods of time to gig with New York bands and artists. What better acoustic chamber could they have had than a city built *of* solid stone and *on* solid stone? (Chicago rests on mud, not stone; its skyscrapers were made possible by caissons invented in the bridge-building orgy of the 1870s and 1880s.) Those who built skyscrapers had much in common with their jazz musician peers; the Jamesian ethos of improvisational pluralism serves to explicate both the new music and the new architecture. Sounding much like Bix Beiderbecke, Raymond Hood pledged not "to build the same building twice," and he never did. As an admiring interviewer noted in a *New Yorker* profile of him on April 11, 1931, the only quality common to his buildings was their "dramatic" look.

After the quasi-Gothic Radiator Building of 1924 came Hood's Daily News Building of 1929 at 150 East Forty-second Street. Despite its spectacular lobby, it had a blunt top (no Gothic tower here) and a flat façade broken by radical set-backs and horizontal stripes. When Royal Cortissoz, the *Herald Tribune*'s art critic, said that the building wasn't architecture, Hood, who seemed to talk in sharp explosive bursts, replied: "So much the better!" The Daily News Building, at least on the outside, prefigured the starker look of his next big venture, the McGraw-Hill Building at 330 West Forty-second Street, built in 1931. Although its startling blue-green color was a tribute to its Art Deco antecedents, many architectural historians consider it the start of the International style in America, a style antithetical to the Gothic eclecticism that had characterized Hood's early career. His designs for Rockefeller Center (begun in 1929 and finished in 1940), the first skyscraper group in New York's—or indeed any city's—history, were another new idea, one whose widespread application the Depression postponed more or less indefinitely.

Hood may have encountered James's writings in his college days at Brown University at the turn of the century, but in any case he was a kindred spirit. Born in Rhode Island in 1881 to well-to-do Baptist parents of old New England stock, he studied at the Ecole des Beaux Arts in Paris in the 1900s and later moved to Greenwich Village. There the bon vivant Hood patronized Placido Mori's restaurant, where Mori trustingly fed him on credit—"He must be a genius," Mori decided; "he eats so much"—and occupied himself by decorating the waiting room to his unvisited office with gilt paper. Lack of funds stopped the project, but his friends called the anteroom "Hood's Gold Room"; it was a partial anticipation, it seems, of the Radiator Building's color scheme. Hood was over forty when he got the all-important commission for the Chicago Tribune Building in 1923, and during his long and obscure apprenticeship, his only "method," in his words, was "to do everything that comes up as thoroughly and as hard as possible—not to miss an opportunity—to work blindly but hard," to "work without thinking"; New York induced "a sort of coffee-existence—you live on your nerves." Koolhaas sums up the Hood ethos as "Manhattan: no time for consciousness."

Many in his day were talking in dire terms about the growing congestion of urban life, a state of affairs worsened by skyscrapers, but Hood declared: "Congestion is good." In his designs for Rockefeller Center, with its fountains, skating rink, terraces, and restaurants, its different heights and shapes and widths, he created large-scale conviviality, an outdoor cabaret alive with intimate impersonality. Frederick Lewis Allen described it as a "shipboard scene full of animation and sunlight and the sense of holiday," a place, like the Harlem jazz clubs Hood sometimes visited on a spree, where congestion was turned into fun. Hood found the activity of crowds suggested the improvisatory collaboration of neighbors. He agreed with his colleague Harvey Wiley Corbett that "people swarm to the city *because* they like congestion," and he saw New York as "the first place in the world where a man can work within a ten minute walk of a quarter of a million people. . . . Think how it expands the field from which we can choose our friends, our co-workers and contacts, how easy it is to develop a constant interchange of thought!" Congestion was just instant gratification as a way of life.

Hood built differently each time, he said, because he built according to the needs of the people who used the building, not according to the tastes of those who looked at it. As the ebullient young Hemingway had remarked, "Fuck literature!" Hood insisted, "This beauty stuff is all bunk!" Speaking of literature, Hood was not a reader; he told the *New Yorker* interviewer that in four years "nobody will read." Like Vachel Lindsay's motion pictures, like Hurston's "Negro Expression," like Duke Ellington expressing in his music a picture he saw in his mind's eye, Hood, too, was a creature of body literacy, of hieroglyphics. His own fancy played a part in his creations, too. If he had been "under the spell of . . . Chinese pagodas" when he built the Radiator Building, he said, it would have looked like a Chinese pagoda. Why not? "A man should have as many horizontal or vertical lines as [he] wants." As *The New Yorker* put it, "Hood builds what Hood feels"; it's the jazz ethos. Indeed, in their work methods, his large office staff resembled a jazz band more than a bureaucracy; work was done in a ferment of creative chaos. Hood hired an efficiency expert, but he promptly fired him when he caught the man checking up (as it was presumably his job to do) on the draftsmen's time cards.

The New Yorker saluted Hood as the "brilliant bad boy" of American architecture, and he welcomed the absence of tradition manifest in the skyscrapers; traditions, in his opinion, were merely "hurdles which must be jumped." He saw New York—its people and buildings crowded every which way on an irregular non-grid-like grid, constantly shoved into instant close-ups and surprising long-shot vistas—as an unending exercise in shifting perspectives as stimulation. To his mind, it compelled innovation, and he counted himself lucky to face "the problems of a new and modern city, the problems which architects and city planners have dreamed [of] for years. Can there, then, be a better time and place for an architect?" Once again the absence of tradition allowed the artist to be "free as the breeze," "free as the devil," free to find a "freedom of the spirit" and embody it in stone and glass and steel. Pressed to define his style, he responded: "I am as much in the air about style as I am about everything else." Hood wore his hair cropped; it looked, in the words of *The New Yorker*, like "a shock of amazing gray-black bristles sticking straight up in the air." He built and flew endless kites and he loved to set off firecrackers and watch their aerial pyrotechnics. "In the air," in the American air, was just the place Raymond Hood wanted to be.

The Rising Generation

There were people going farther and faster into the sky's "inmost day" (a phrase from Crane's "Voyages") than the skyscraper architects: the new breed of stuntsters called pilots. In 1927, Charles Lindbergh made the first successful non-stop transatlantic solo flight. The twenty-five-year-old Lindbergh departed from New York's Roosevelt Field at 7:52 a.m. on May 20 and landed at 10:22 p.m. on May 21 at Paris's Le Bourget airport; he had covered roughly three thousand miles in thirty-three and a half hours, averaging about 100 miles per hour. On arriving in France, his first words to the assembled crowd, excited to frenzy long before his appearance, were strikingly modest "I am Charles A. Lindbergh," he said, and offered the French officials his letter of identification. But all the world knew who Lindbergh was; everyone within reach of a radio or a newspaper had been following his flight.

Three pairs of pilots, six in all, had tried to cross the Atlantic in 1926. All lost their lives, but experts agreed that the team approach was the safer one. Yet Lindbergh chose to go it alone, without a partner, without even a radio or life raft. He had no interest in daredevil acts; he flew without co-pilot, radio, or raft because he knew that the lighter his plane, the safer he would be and the greater his chance of success. Lindbergh, the "Galahad of the Air," had disarmed before the air, and his calm, his self-confidence, his aura of reserves yet to be tapped— arriving at Le Bourget, he said he was "tired but not exhausted"—seemed bestowed by the air itself as reward.

Like Fitzgerald, an ardent fan, Lindbergh hailed from Minnesota, and Fitzgerald fancied affinities between them. He hoped Lindbergh's flight might offer a "way out" of the growing desperation and violence of the Jazz Age: "Maybe our restless blood could find frontiers in the illimitable air." In Paris, Janet Flanner reported for *The New Yorker* the response of Anne, Comtesse de Noailles: "More generous than Christopher Columbus, he has delivered to us the continent of the sky." Harry Crosby thought Lindy might be "the new Christ"; even Hemingway called him an "angel." Hart Crane admitted in a letter home to being "a little jealous of Lindy!" and began to think of *The Bridge* as a parallel aerial feat, a modern "myth" of "Time and Space." He subsequently researched and wrote a section for *The Bridge* on pilots and the "alcohol of space" entitled "Cape Hatteras."

No other parade of this parade-crazy era, including the huge parades celebrating the close of the Great War and the return of its troops, attracted as much attention as the one in honor of Lindbergh's victorious return to the States. In New York on June 13, 1927, a crowd of New Yorkers and visitors estimated at 4.5

million turned out; 1,800 tons of confetti and ticker tape stormed down on his entourage. *The New York Times* devoted fifteen pages to the occasion, the *Herald Tribune* nine, the *American* ten, the *World* eight, the *Mirror* twenty-three, and the *Daily News* sixteen. George M. Cohan wrote a popular song about "Lindy"; a new dance was christened the "Lindy Hop," and a Pennsylvania railroad car sported his name. Lindbergh's flight provided free advertising for the new aeronautic interests (after his flight, he worked with Trans World Airlines), but like Madison Avenue advertising, like the skyscrapers, it finally publicized excitation itself. Excitation, one must add, distasteful to the proper and straitlaced young man who kicked it off.

Lindbergh quickly came to hate the flood of publicity his flight unleashed, but before he could duck from view, photographers had snapped him repeatedly in what became his trademark look: young ("My heart," Damon Runyon wrote, "how young he seemed!"), clean-cut, blond, Nordic—Hitler was an early admirer of Lindbergh's; unfortunately, the attraction proved mutual—hatless, tousled. One year later, Amelia Earhart became the first woman to cross the Atlantic by air—as a passenger, not as a pilot—but in 1932 she flew her own craft over the Atlantic. Fair-haired and blue-eyed, she was promoted as "Lady Lindbergh," and she emulated Lindy's hatless, windblown look. Harry Crosby threw away his hats, still *de rigueur* for men as for women, and urged his contemporaries to "stand bare-headed on the top of the hill with the thunderbolt of the sun in our heads." Most Americans went on wearing hats, but hats did not stop their hopes from rising higher than planes could climb.

Men and women had been rising into the air in lighter-than-air balloons filled first with hot air, later with hydrogen gas, balloons that rose by the law of gravity, since the late eighteenth century, but sustained flight in heavier-than-air craft, flight that defied or repealed gravity's law as the skyscrapers did, had been first successfully ventured by the Wright Brothers, Orville and Wilbur, in Kitty Hawk, North Carolina, on December 17, 1903. The Wrights' plane traveled 120 feet in twelve seconds before it came down; those seconds changed history. Their achievement went almost unpublicized, however, for five years. There had been few eyewitnesses at Kitty Hawk, and as Orville Wright later wrote, "Scarcely anyone [could] believe in it until he actually saw it with his own eyes." Recognition did not come for another five or six years, after further demonstrations by the Wrights in America and Europe.

Leading the pack as usual when it came to publicizing the spankingly modern, the *World* assigned a full-time reporter to the aerial beat as early as 1910. But it was, of course, the Great War, the first war in history to be fought in the air as well as on land and sea, that forced the fledgling American aviation industry into overnight maturity. The industry had not existed in 1909, but by 1914 its profits totaled $1 million; by 1919 they stood at $14 million. Government airmail service was inaugurated in 1918, and the first scheduled passenger flight took place in 1914. The first nonstop cross-country flight came in 1923; it took twenty-seven hours. In the last six months of 1928 alone, $1 billion worth of aviation securities were traded on the New York Stock Exchange; new aviation facilities in the

United States included 61 passenger lines, 47 mail lines, and 32 express lines serving trade areas that contained 90 million people. Technological progress was so fast that planes built from 1927 through the mid-1930s were outmoded, obsolete, within six months. Extensive advertising began only in the mid-1920s, but by April 1928, the aviation interests were boasting in print and on the air of sponsoring "well over a million miles of useful commercial flying"; the "astounding miracle of man's conquest of the sky [has] become an accepted fact of everyday life." A miracle is the ultimate in magic, and Hollywood, the nation's chief manufacturer of magic, began filming and fictionalizing America's colonization of the sky. The movies bore exuberantly airminded titles like *Air Circus*, *Cloud Riders*, *Flight*, *Sky Skidder*, *Won on the Clouds*, *Phantom Flyer*, and *Wings*.

Like the skyscraper craze, the infatuation with "airmindedness" was in good part an American phenomenon. Although European intellectuals and artists, most notably the Futurists of Italy led by Filippo Tommaso Marinetti, were wildly excited by aviation, and the response to Lindbergh's flight was as intense in Paris as it was in New York, the unalloyed enthusiasm of Americans for aviation long outlasted that of their European and English peers. As Joseph J. Corn, the historian of the aviation cult, points out in *The Winged Gospel* (1983), numerous anti-aviation articles with titles like "The Aerial Peril" and "The Airship Menace" were appearing in the English press even before the war, and the war, in which planes damaged and wrecked civilian areas in unprecedented aerial warfare, left most of England and Europe with what we today would consider a realistic assessment of aviation's potentially lethal role in world affairs; this had no real echo in America until the 1930s and the rise of Fascism's openly worldwide ambitions. America's size and isolation, its exemption from the Great War, its ongoing freedom from fears of invasion and attack, and its long tradition of tying utopian hopes to technological advancement kept its enthusiasm for aviation white-hot. Only in America could you get mass-produced piggy banks, purses, fans, clocks, lamps, and (a rarer item) coffins shaped like airplanes.

Predictably, city dwellers used airplanes more extensively than rural citizens did; by 1919, 48 percent of airline business was concentrated in seven urban areas, with New York in the lead. The Great War's ace pilots found the metropolis highly receptive to their skills and stunts. Jack Savage, a reckless and charming Englishman, aviator, and veteran, attracted Madison Avenue's eye when he skywrote HELLO USA above the city; it was he who piloted the plane used in Edward Bernays's Lucky Strike skywriting campaign of 1928. Hubert Fauntleroy Julian, the West Indies–born black pilot who emigrated to Harlem in 1921 and was dubbed the "Black Eagle" by the New York *Telegram*, didn't fly in the Great War—no Negroes were allowed in the air corps—but he was the first Negro to obtain a pilot's license, and he, too, contributed to New Yorkers' entertainment.

As a Negro, Julian never got the backing the all-Anglo-Saxon Lindbergh effortlessly attracted. Indeed, he experienced obstacles and reverses that would have stopped a lesser spirit. There was the plane meddled with, or "crooked," in his word, by rival white French pilots in Ethiopia, where he served briefly in 1930 as Haile Selassie's personal pilot. His planned journey to Africa, set to begin in the summer of 1924 on (of course) July 4, was delayed because Clarence Chamberlain, his white patron, wouldn't let him take off until the money due him had been raised from the gathered crowd. The plane Julian planned to use was cheap and ramshackle, all he could afford, and it crashed in Flushing Bay five minutes after takeoff. Fights between Julian's West Indian friends and rival American Negroes also on occasion disrupted his plans; a gang of American blacks trashed a plane he had put on exhibition in a vacant Harlem lot to convince the "doubting Thomases" and attract donations for his next flight.

White journalists loved Julian for the colorful copy he provided, but they invariably cast even his most heroic exploits in terms of updated minstrel comedy, presenting him as a boastful and too stylish Zip Coon figure. Dignified reminders from Julian, "No monkey business with this story. It's very serious," were of no avail. Like many West Indian and American blacks, Julian used two forms of English; he called it being "ambidextrous." In addition to various European and African tongues, he spoke both Standard English and a mixture of West Indies and Black English; journalists liked to parody what they saw as his linguistic confusion. But Julian, an ebullient man and a positive thinker, refused to be discouraged. On his first flight as a young pilot training in Canada, he had "discovered the air, a new medium unlike any other," he tells us in his autobiography, *The Black Eagle* (1964): "This, I felt, was my real element," and he never left it for long. When last seen, he was a world-renowned arms dealer who did most of his work in Africa and Cuba. He'd become a freedom fighter of sorts, one with his eye on the profits as well as the ideals at stake. (Julian's final days are uncharted, and perhaps not yet over; he dropped out of sight sometime in the 1970s, but we have no hard evidence of his death. The customary biographical entry on him today reads "Julian, Hubert Fauntleroy [1897–?].")

Julian was early dubbed the "Lindbergh of His Race," and despite his lack of financial backing, expert firsthand witnesses agreed that he was Lindbergh's equal as a pilot; he was certainly his superior in terms of political intelligence and sympathies. Unlike the "Lone Eagle" (or the "Lone Ostrich," as a disillusioned reporter later redubbed Lindbergh) the "Black Eagle" detested Fascism of all kinds. In the late 1930s, he attempted to assassinate Mussolini, or so he said, and on another occasion, he challenged Hitler's minister Hermann Göring to a duel in the air; he resented the attack on blacks as "apes" in Hitler's *Mein Kampf*. (Göring did not accept the challenge.) Julian tried in vain to convince F.D.R. that Pan-Africanism and Third World development might one day end America's world supremacy if its racism continued unchecked. Unlike the suspiciously modest Lindbergh, Julian had few peers as a showman, even in the Jazz Age; one of his mottos was "Make headlines and always leave calling cards."

Julian once told the press that a doctor had pronounced him "phenomenally perfect"; tall, athletic, light-skinned, with aristocratic features, and impeccably dressed on all occasions, he was a glamorous and charismatic man, a sheik-type, black America's more sophisticated version of Rudolph Valentino. (Unfortunately, though he'd help produce and publicize a film by black director Oscar Micheaux, *The Notorious Elinor Lee*, in 1940, he never made a movie himself.) A follower of Marcus Garvey in the 1920s and pilot to Father Divine, the Harlem guru and conman, in the 1930s, Julian neither smoked nor drank, but he did believe that "tak[ing] a maiden a day" was good for a man's health. Essie, his boyhood sweetheart and devoted wife, didn't seem to mind; it was she who thought up Julian's kisses-for-sale fund-raising act in the mid-1920s. The kisses went for a steep $5, but his customers got, he tells us, their money's worth. He lost Haile Selassie's favor temporarily when he crashed the Emperor's costly plane (this was the plane the French aviators had "crooked") on a surprise exhibition flight in Ethiopia. When reporters asked him on his return to New York why he had taken the plane up, he explained: "I wanted to give the Emperor a thrill. After all, even an emperor needs a thrill, now and then."

Harlem got its share of thrills, too. In April 1923, there were signs everywhere reading: WATCH THE CLOUDS—JULIAN IS ARRIVING FROM THE SKY. He parachuted on this occasion from a plane down onto Seventh Avenue and 140th Street dressed in a skin-tight scarlet outfit and bearing a sign for Hoenig Optical (the Harlem eyeglasses concern that funded the leap). Six months later, he descended on Harlem once more, this time wearing a devil's costume, complete with horns and tail, and playing a saxophone. He was trying, he told reporters, "to make the world a more fundamental place to live." Again, one can't trust the accuracy of the reportage where Julian is concerned, but the sentiment of "a more fundamental place" sounds right. Julian lectured at Negro colleges, telling students to learn from his example that "you can do anything you please," and barnstormed across America with the Negro aerial performers Marie Dickinson and William Powell. Fittingly, Tom Moore, his New York mentor and agent, was a musician; Julian loved Harlem's jazz clubs and revues, and he lifted members of the various "Blackbirds" casts, literally speaking, to new heights.

Julian never camouflaged his hunger for publicity or his *amour propre*—telling the New York press what Haile Selassie looked like, he said, "The Emperor elect is a fine man with a beard, who looks something like I do"—but there was a larger purpose to his self-display. He named the plane he tried to fly to Africa *Abyssinia*, and the legend on its side read: DEDICATED TO THE ADVANCEMENT OF THE NEGRO RACE. All his exploits, he tells us, had one "basic cause . . . and that is that I am a Negro." Facing the racism of 1920s America, he had determined to show that "Negroes really are as other men are," capable of the most difficult and daring feats modern man can attempt. As (in the *Evening Graphic*'s words) "this only black bird ever to cleave the azure on man-made wings," Julian represented "white man's magic," in the words of his biographer, John Peer Nugent, "in a black man's hands."

Before air traffic was regulated, Julian liked to swoop his plane daringly close to Harlem's buildings, as if making a raid or preparing to land; hopes of landing amid the city's crowded streets were not deemed fantastic. Operation of the new heavier-than-air planes of the 1910s and 1920s, with their built-in need of long takeoff runways, clearly required non-urban spaces, but Americans of the 1920s didn't want to think so; they expected and even planned inner-city airports in New York and elsewhere whose foundations would rest on a series of skyscrapers.

The ceiling murals in the Chrysler Building's lobby included a picture of airplanes; a projected (never built) "150-story Super-Skyscraper," to go up on Broadway and Church Street, expected to use its rooftop acreage as a landing field. How could an Aerial Age, airminded to an extreme, not expect skyscrapers and airplanes to make sense of each other? Planes were seen as the answer to the urban congestion Hood loved and others protested; the limitless sky would accommodate and alleviate the traffic that was overtaxing the earth. It was some compensation for this lost dream of inner-city airports when a swank Art Deco–fronted Airlines Terminal, not an airport but a PR symbol and a clearinghouse for various commercial airlines and their passengers, opened at 42 Park Avenue opposite Grand Central Station in 1938.

Some speculated that the aviation age might breed an "aerial person," a kind of superhuman American creature who would live in the newly habitable altitudes. Couples got married in airplanes, and a few expectant mothers, hoping to elevate if not improve the species, jumped into planes (piloted, of course, by others) when their labor pains began and delivered in space members of what *The New York Times* saluted as "the Rising Generation." Young Jack Chapman was a member of this generation; though not born in the air, he took to it early as a pilot. By the age of eleven, he had become a national hero, but he found himself mandatorily if prematurely retired in 1927 by a law that specified people must be sixteen or older to have a flying license. Many people believed that Americans would soon own their own planes and operate them as easily as they did their cars. Henry Ford, who had taken Emerson's injunction "Hitch your wagon to a star" as his motto, was doing a steady business in a large "trimotor" and a small "flying flyver" by the late 1920s. On August 7, 1926, a New York *Sun* columnist was inspired to print this ditty:

> *I dreamed I was an angel*
> *And with the angels soared,*
> *But I was simply touring*
> *The heavens in a Ford.*

In his autobiography, Julian tells of one early flight in which his plane failed him and he was forced to land by parachute in a farmyard. An irate farmer soon appeared, shotgun in hand, to get this "thief" who had set his chickens "squawking away in a panic." "Hold on, hold on," Julian shouted as he disentangled himself from the parachute; "it's a messenger from heaven come to call on you." Amazed, if only by the sight of a black angel, the farmer put up his gun and Julian made his escape. In his memoir, *We* (1927), Lindbergh records a similar incident that occurred in his early days as a stunt pilot at local fairs and exhibitions. His plane had grounded near Maben, Mississippi, and to pay for the new propeller he'd been obliged to purchase, he offered to take six citizens of Maben up in his plane. One old Negro woman came up to ask him: "Boss! How much you all charge toah take me up to Hebben and leave me dah?" Like Bernhardt asking Houdini to restore her leg, like Fitzgerald's Mr. In and Mr. Out demanding to go to heaven, this woman had simply surveyed the scene and assumed the best. As Julian was reported to have said when serving as master of ceremonies at the Harlem premiere of *The Notorious Elinor Lee*, "On with the show. Let joy be unconfirmed." For a brief, wonderful moment, the realities of the Aerial Age seemed to prove that, in Stevens's words in *The Necessary Angel* (1951), "absolute fact includes everything that imagination concludes."

BIBLIOGRAPHICAL ESSAY

Robert A. M. Stern, Gregor Gilmartin, Thomas Mellins, *New York 1930: Architecture and Urbanism between the Two World Wars*, a masterpiece of scholarship and prose, is the definitive work on New York's architecture in the 1920s, exhaustive, filled with precise information, making imaginative connections between the buildings and the larger metropolitan culture at every turn. Its predecessor, *New York 1900: Metropolitan Architecture and Urbanism 1890–1915* (New York: Rizzoli, 1983), by the same authors, is of equal scope and value. Christopher Tunnard and Henry Hope Reed, *American Skyline: The Growth and Forms of Our Cities and Towns* (Boston, Mass.: Houghton Mifflin, 1953) compares the various architectural schools; John Burchard and Albert Bush-Brown, *The Architecture of America: A Social and Cultural History* (Boston. Mass.: Little Brown, 1961) is an indispensable over-all history which criticizes the failure to deal with vertical space by the skyscraper architects, favors the Chicago school, and describes the erection of the Empire State Building in detail; see also Jonathan Goldman, *The Empire State Building Book* (New York: St. Martin's Press, 1980). William R. Taylor's *In Pursuit of Gotham* has an excellent chapter on the skyscraper city as "visual text"; John A. Kouwenhoven, *The Columbia Historical Portrait of the New York* (1985; rpt., New York: Harper & Row, 1972) discusses the origin of the word "skyline." Peter Conrad, *The Art of the City* (New York: Oxford University Press, 1984) makes Fitzgerald's story "May Day" central to its discussion of skyscrapers; the story is in F. Scott Fitzgerald, *Babylon Revisited and Other Stories* (New York: Scribner's Sons, 1960).

Skyscrapers have inspired some of the best writing to date about New York; in a class by itself is Rem Koolhaas, *Delirious New York: A Retroactive Manifesto for Manhattan*, which is, as its title suggests, a kind of updated Futurist manifesto about New York's power of intoxication, written with the ferocity of hindsight and filled with breathtaking insights, extraordinary writing, and a passionate, hallucinated love of its subject; it's the starting point and ending place for any consideration of the New York skyscraper, and it led me to spend hours and days walking and looking around New York's buildings—the Chrysler, Empire State, Daily News, and McGraw-Hill buildings in particular became charged, irreplaceable love objects. Paul Goldberger, *The Skyscraper* (New York: Alfred A. Knopf, 1989), also superb, focuses on the heterogeneity and abundance of the Manhattan style. Extremely useful and perceptive are Charles Jencks, *Skyscrapers—Skycities* (New York: Rizzoli, 1980) and Wayne Attoe, *Skylines: Understanding and Molding Urban Silhouettes* (New York: John Wiley, 1981), which speaks of "netting the sky." Robert Hughes, *The Shock of the New* (New York: Alfred A. Knopf, 1981) is an excellent, comparative study of modernist culture. Cervin Robinson and Rosemary Haag Bletter, *Skyscraper Style: Art Deco New York* (New York: Oxford University Press, 1975) and Eva Weber, *American Art Deco* (Greenwich, Conn.: Dorset Press, 1985) are first-rate studies of the Art Deco style that dominated many of New York's skyscrapers, particularly the Chrysler Building. Nathan Silver, *Lost New York*

(New York: American Legacy Press, 1967) documents (and laments) the buildings razed to make way for other buildings, *Yesterday's Tomorrows: Past Visions of the American Future*, ed. Joseph J. Corn and Brian Horrigan (New York: Summit Books, 1984) includes pictures of projected plans and designs for the coming urban utopia.

The Woolworth Building is described and eulogized in *The Cathedral of Commerce* (New York: Woolworth Building, 1916). Hugh Ferriss, *The Metropolis of Tomorrow* (1929; rpt., Princeton, N.J.: Princeton Architectural Press, 1986) includes a fine essay by Carol Willis about Ferriss's career and aesthetic. On **Raymond Hood**, see "Man Against the Sky," a profile in *The New Yorker* (April 11, 1931), 24–27; Walter H. Kilham, Jr., *Raymond Hood, Architect: Form Through Function in the American Skyscraper* (New York: Architectural Book Publishing, 1973); and Robert A. M. Stern, *Raymond Hood* (New York: Rizzoli, 1985). On William Van Alen, see Kenneth Murchison, "The Chrysler Building As I See It," *American Architect* 138 (1930), 24–30, an interview. Edward Hopper's *Night Shadows* is reproduced in *Art of the Twenties*, ed. William S. Lieberman (New York: Museum of Modern Art, 1979). Orrick Johns made the comparison between the Radiator Building and **Jack Johnson**; he said the building "broke through the color line" (cited in *New York 1930*, 576). Jack Johnson's career is ably detailed in Denzel Batchelor, *Jack Johnson & His Times* (1956; rpt., London: Weidenfeld & Nicholson, 1990); Al-Tony Gilmore, *Bad Nigger! The National Impact of Jack Johnson* (Port Washington, N.Y.: Kennikat Press, 1975); and Randy Johnson, *Papa Jack: Jack Johnson and the Era of White Hopes* (New York: The Free Press, 1983); Lawrence Levine discusses Johnson's status as a black folk hero in *Black Culture and Black Consciousness*. Jack London called for a white champion to "remove the golden smile from Jack Johnson's face" (cited in Al-Tony Gilmore, *Bad Nigger!*, 35).

For **Wallace Stevens**'s years in the city, see the intelligent, fair-minded biography by Milton J. Bates, *Wallace Stevens: A Mythology of Self* (Berkeley: University of California Press, 1985). Critical studies that have helped me in understanding Stevens's aesthetic include the superb Helen Hennessy Vendler, *On Extended Wings: Wallace Stevens' Longer Poems* (Cambridge, Mass.: Harvard University Press, 1969), which stresses Stevens as a poet of "eddyings"; Harold Bloom's brilliant *Wallace Stevens: The Poems of Our Climate* (Ithaca, N.Y.: Cornell University Press, 1976), which sees Stevens as peculiarly Emerson's heir, a poet of "surprise and wonder"; and Elisa New, *The Regenerate Lyric* (Cambridge, England: Cambridge University Press, 1983); New first brought "Life Is Motion" to my attention. See also Wallace Stevens, *The Necessary Angel: Essays on Reality and the Imagination* (1951; rpt., New York: Vintage, n.d.) for his own statement of his aesthetic. Wallace Stevens, *The Palm at the End of the Mind*, ed. Holly Stevens (1971; rpt., New York: Vintage, 1972) and *The Collected Poems of Wallace Stevens* (1959; rpt., New York: Vintage, 1982) are the standard collections of the poetry; not all the poems are reprinted in both collections. William James's essay "What Makes a Life Significant?" is included in William James, *Essays on Faith and Morals* (New York Meridian Books, 1967).

For **Houdini**, see Christopher Milbourne, *Houdini: The Untold Story* (New York: Thomas Y. Crowell, 1969) and Harry Houdini, *A Magician Among the Spirits* (New York: Harper Bros., 1924). Edmund Wilson was fascinated by Houdini, whom he saw as the embodiment of secular skepticism, of what one might call the will to *dis*believe; Houdini is determined, in Wilson's words, "never [to be] duped," and this gives him "a certain nervous excitement, as of a man engaged in a critical fight." See "Houdini" and "A Great Magician" in Edmund Wilson, *The Shores of Light* (1952; rpt., New York: Farrar, Straus & Giroux, 1974).

On **Ruth St. Denis**, see the excellent Suzanne Shelton, *Divine Dancer: A Biography of Ruth St. Denis* (Garden City, N.Y.: Doubleday, 1981), which pays special attention to her use of Oriental motifs; on Orientalism and its place in late-Victorian American culture, see T. J. Jackson Lears, *No Place of Grace* (New York: Pantheon, 1981). Elizabeth Kendall, *Where She Danced*, a classic work of American Studies written in a prose so buoyant, open, charged, and evocative as to deserve comparison with the work of Scott Fitzgerald, is itself a profound, moving exposition of American light and air, brilliant on St. Denis and the other pioneers of modern dance. Modern dance was largely an American invention, and Kendall downplays the darker side of her figures—St. Denis made a devastatingly bad choice of a partner/husband in the opportunistic, even untalented Ted Shawn, and the mistake shadowed and diminished her career; Isadora succumbed to open alcoholism and a series of affairs with men bent, it seemed, on destroying her; Martha Graham, also an alcoholic, was early as famous for her histrionics of sadistic willpower as for her indisputable genius as a dancer/choreographer—to emphasize modern dance as part of women's rediscovery and assertion of their untrammeled, uncorseted bodies at the turn of the century, involving a "rhapsodic" release of "a primal spirit of animal delight" and a new awareness of the open spaces in which the freed body moves and choreographs its way. In Kendall's words, by putting "a solo human figure in space" (xiv), St. Denis, Duncan, and Graham sought "the means to look at the other world, to colonize it" (213). Isadora "incorporated a new upper body space, and along with it, the air above the stage" (68); Martha Graham's avant-garde costume, made of yards of synthetic jersey, twisting in motion, in *Lamentation* (1930) "recalled . . . a skyscraper reeling" (208).

It can be no accident that dancers left the concert hall for out-of-door movement in the 1900s and 1910s, heading toward California and the promise of Hollywood (where St. Denis established her famous school in 1915), just as buildings were rising in height, planes were first coming into use, and the media were being invented; the air had become an irresistible invitation to the extended play of the human body and imagination. Marshall McLuhan is trailblazing on the media as human wishes come true (a utopian fantasy he at moments shares) in *Understanding Media: The Extensions of Man* (New York: McGraw-Hill, 1964). Jack Earle's story is told in Robert Bogdan, *Freak Show: Presenting Human Oddities for Amusement and Profit* (Chicago, Ill.: University of Chicago Press, 1988).

Roger E. Bilstein, *Flight in America: From the Wrights to the Astronauts* (Baltimore, Md.: Johns Hopkins University, 1984) is a definitive account of **the development of aviation**. Joseph J. Corn, *The Winged Gospel: America's Romance with Aviation 1900–1950* (New York: Oxford University Press, 1983) is a detailed, imaginative study of the "airmindedness" cult, full of fascinating Americana. On the pioneers of aviation, see Tom Crouch, *The Bishop's Boys: A Life of Wilbur and Orville Wright* (New York: W. W. Norton, 1989). The two best biographical treatments of Lindbergh are Leonard Mosley, *Lindbergh: A Biography* (Garden City, N.Y.: Doubleday, 1976), which takes a critical view, and Joyce Milton, *Loss of Eden: A Biography of Charles and Anne Morrow Lindbergh* (New York: HarperCollins, 1993), an important, favorable account which details the young Lindbergh's belief in airmindedness, his conviction that aviation would usher in a peaceful utopia, and his subsequent disillusion. Milton rightly sees airmindedness as an extension of something like the Mind-cure ethos, and proves her point by documenting the Lindberghs' late interest in New Age thinking, a resurgence of Mind-cure in the 1950s and 1960s; Anne's *Gift from the Sea*, a best-seller of 1955, was itself an important source of revamped Mind-cure attitudes.

Mary S. Lovell, *The Sound of Wings: The Life of Amelia Earhart* (New York: St. Martin's Press, 1989) is an impartial and compelling account. **Amelia Earhart**, born in 1897 in Kansas, tried social work and medical school before becoming a pilot; she was a tomboy as a child and a 1920s-style feminist as an adult who denied, of course, that she was a feminist, at least in the older, Victorian sense of the word—her views were simply "modern thinking," she said. She wanted women to emulate men ("Women must try to do things as men have tried" [13]) by choosing lives of hard work, adventurousness, freethinking on manners and morals (she was reluctant to marry, insisting on a contract for marital freedom with her husband, George Putnam) and technological expertise: women should learn "the art of flying by instruments only" (124), she believed, an art that, so far, only men had mastered. Although she was not a natural as a pilot and never became a first-rate one, by 1935 a poll established that she and Eleanor Roosevelt were the best-known women among Americans (Hitler and F.D.R. were the best-known men); she had shrewd commercial instincts, publishing a book after each major flight, one audaciously titled *The Fun of It* (New York: G. P. Putnam, 1932), and a charmingly nonchalant style; turning to her husband over breakfast one morning in 1930, she asked casually, "Would you mind if I flew the Atlantic?" (179). George Putnam, the entrepreneurial head of the famous publishing firm, didn't mind; he published Lindbergh's *We* (1927) and all his wife's books, and pioneered in promotion, once arranging to be kidnapped to publicize a book. As one observer put it: "George would have stopped on the middle of a rotten plank over a chasm a hundred feet deep to broadcast his reaction to a waiting world" (84). Putnam was an appropriate mate for an airminded stuntster; a "conjuror" whose "instinct for the spectacular was almost occult" (79), in the words of a friend, he seemed at moments to have magical powers himself.

On **Hubert Julian**, see John Peer Nugent, *The Black Eagle* (New York: Stein and Day, 1971) and his own high-spirited memoir, with John Bullock, *Black Eagle* (London: The Adventurers Club, 1964).

See **Constance Rourke**, *American Humor*, for her dazzling interpretation of the **American hybrid identity** that Gilbert Seldes explicated in *The Great Audience* (New York: The Viking Press, 1950). Rourke, a graduate of Vassar, was a professor there from 1910 to 1915, and a frequent visitor to New York. Although she moved back home to Grand Rapids, Michigan, in 1915, where she lived with the strong-minded, tyrannical mother she adored until her death in 1941 at the age of fifty-six, she continued to spend weeks and months every year in New York; a reserved, cool, and enigmatic creature, she nonetheless frequented Harlem clubs and Broadway shows, loved the movies (she sold *Davy Crockett* to Hollywood in 1934, but the movie was never made), jazz, and later swing. Like the skyscrapers, like *The Great Audience*, *American Humor* is a celebration of the polyglot national character.

Paul Poiret, seeking redress against the American clothing business for pirating his designs, rebuked Americans for their habit of imitating others and themselves—they lack, he wrote in *En Habillant l'Epoque* (1930), any sense of "property" and "propriety"; "don't you know," he indignantly demanded, that "to copy is to steal?"—but Rourke saw that the fun, excitement, and risk are greatest when one steals one's style. With no indigenous traditions save what it can export, steal, or fabricate, America has sustained a "grotesque" (the word is not pejorative for Rourke) performance in "mimicry" specializing in borrowings from dazzlingly diverse sources—the British, the Europeans, its own Indians and Negroes; her heroes in *American Humor* are itinerant Yankee peddlers, the shrewd middlemen who passed on the stories and ways of one geographic or ethnic group to others, making American culture an endless chain letter forever being added to, forwarded, and never arriving at a final destination. Like Seldes, Rourke sees American culture as ethnic, racial vaudeville—her first important published piece, which appeared in *The New Republic* on August 7, 1919, was titled "Vaudeville"—as appropriation, transformation, and assimilation, defined as much by its methods of transmission and reproduction as by the content of what is transmitted. In this view, what is most original in American culture is, paradoxical as it may sound, its gift for fast-and-loose imitation, role-playing, and replication, even mass production and media reproduction, the apparently infinite process of change as exchange, the endless reproduction of similar objects, images, and sounds.

Commenting on the new mass-produced fashions cut from cheap fabrics—what Coco Chanel popularized as "the poor look"—that allowed everyone a daily change of attire in class-blind clothes, a businessman in Muncie, Indiana, told the Lynds: "I used to be able to tell something about the [class] background of a girl applying for a job by her clothes, but today I have to wait till she speaks, shows a gold tooth or otherwise gives me a . . . clue" (*Middletown*, 101). The "final decision," as *The New Yorker* put it on November 28, 1925, "as to whether artificial jewelry can ever be considered permanently smart," a question "on which depends the future peace of the world," was answered in the affirmative; wealthy girls who could afford diamonds delighted in glass beads, and working-class girls could now buy that long drop of single-strand pearl necklace *de rigueur* for the flapper's fancier moments. James's "will to personate" was literalized in the 1920s, opening the door to the vast charade in which Rourke locates the promise of American life. Karl Marx's collaborator, Friedrich Engels, strangely enough, made a similar point. Outliving Marx by over a decade (Engels died in 1895), he came to fear that America would disprove their prophecy of a revolution by an ever more impoverished proletariat against its capitalist masters, thus resisting the reality principle, a law of diminishing returns that Marx championed as sternly as Freud did. In a letter of December 2, 1893, Engels said that "American conditions involve very great and peculiar difficulties" for the spread of Marxist ideas among the working classes. Chief among these difficulties are the diversity of the American people—"Irish . . . German . . . Czechs, Poles, Italians, Scandinavians, etc. And then the Negroes"—and the nation's "prosperity, no trace of which has been seen here in Europe for years now," which allows working-class people to fancy themselves, even to become, middle-class (Karl Marx and Friedrich Engels, *Basic Writings on Politics and Philosophy*, ed. Lewis S. Feuer [Garden City, N.Y.: Anchor, 1959], 458).

chapter 14

CALVIN TOMKINS

Profiles:
Putting Something Over Something Else

For the opening of a memorable Romare Bearden show at the Cordier & Ekstrom gallery in February, 1975, Arne Ekstrom engaged Danny Moore's five-man jazz group and a fine blues singer, Denise Rogers, whose resonant, earthy voice delighted the predominantly but by no means exclusively black opening-night crowd. The show was called "Of the Blues," and the pictures all sang in tune: "Carolina Shout," "Storyville," "New Orleans Farewell," "At the Savoy," "Kansas City 4/4," and fifteen other collage paintings, richer in color than any of Bearden's previous work, more luminous, more complex. The series did not illustrate the blues or chart the history of the blues or anything like that; each painting had come out of Bearden's memory and experience. Growing up in Harlem in the twenties, Bearden lived and breathed the music and came to know most of the great performers. Duke Ellington, Fats Waller, Billie Holiday, Louis Armstrong, and Jelly Roll Morton were his early masters (to be joined later on by Duccio, Vermeer, Delacroix, and Mondrian). Ekstrom had urged him to paint the blues series, and the two men agreed that it had been a fine idea. During a break between sets by the musicians, Bearden answered a friend's question about the paintings. "One of the things I did was listen to a lot of music," he explained. "I'd take a sheet of paper and just make lines while I listened to records—a kind of shorthand to pick up the rhythm and the intervals." When Bearden was starting to paint seriously, in the thirties, he got a lot of help and encouragement from Stuart Davis. Bearden would go downtown to see Davis, who lived in Greenwich Village, and would usually find him listening to Earl Hines records. Once, he asked Davis why he liked Hines so much, and Davis said, "For his wonderful sense of intervals." Hines made the pauses between notes into something important; the silences were as expressive as the sounds. In Bearden's painting, the separations between colors, or between different values of a color, are expressive in this way. Like Hines, Bearden is a virtuoso of the interval.

A heavyset man of sixty-three, with features that look more Russian than anything else, Romare (he pronounces it "Rome-ery") Bearden has the unusual ability to appear at all times both perfectly composed and entirely spontaneous. He is so light-skinned that most people meeting him for the first time assume he is white. At this particular juncture, we seem to be stuck with the term "black," however, and Bearden is generally referred to as America's leading black painter. His work is in the Museum of Modern Art, the Metropolitan, the Whitney, and other museums. The Modern gave him a retrospective exhibition in 1971; the show subsequently went on tour, and ended up in the Studio Museum in Harlem, around the corner from Bearden's old West 125th Street studio. He has been elected to the American Academy and Institute of Arts and Letters—the hallmark of acceptance by the cultural establishment—and he is a member of the board of the New York State Council on the Arts. His work is much in demand these days—a recent series of brilliant collage paintings on the theme of Homer's Odyssey, which he showed at Cordier & Ekstrom last spring, was so successful, aesthetically and otherwise, that he has already redone the series in watercolor—and while he and his wife, Nanette, continue to live very simply, in a fourth-floor walk-up apartment on Canal Street, they have built a vacation house and studio on some property owned by Nanette's family on the Caribbean island of Saint Martin.

Most of Bearden's friends agree that he is painting better than ever. "His work has a kind of warmth and satisfaction that's new," according to Harry Henderson, a writer and editor with whom Bearden collaborated on "Six Black Masters of American Art," a book for young readers. "His new paintings lack the harshness of some of the earlier ones; they seem to glow. It's something that's come out of Romie—his proud feeling about what black people have achieved."

Pittsburgh

Three boys, aged ten to twelve, are shooting marbles in the back yard of a boarding house in Pittsburgh, in the neighborhood known as Lawrenceville, one day in 1926. A strange kid with braces on both legs appears out of nowhere and stands watching them. "What the hell you looking at?" says Bearden's friend Dennis. Dennis is a pretty rough kid. The newcomer doesn't reply, just stands there, and after a while Dennis gets up and belts him one. Then Dennis and Bearden's cousin Charlie and Bearden all start beating on the stranger—who still doesn't say anything, or even cry—until Bearden's grandmother happens to look out the window and comes out wielding a broom. She picks up the strange kid and carries him into the house. His name is Eugene. "And then he got to be our friend," Bearden says, telling the story many years later. "He'd had infantile paralysis, and he couldn't run with us—he couldn't even eat very fast—but he was always around the house."

Although Bearden was born in Charlotte, North Carolina, where his father's family came from, his parents lived in Harlem, and Harlem is where he grew up. He used to visit his Charlotte relatives in the summer, and later he began spending summers in Pittsburgh, with his mother's mother. She lived near the steel mills and took in boarders, as many as twenty at a time. This was the period of the first great black migration from the rural South to the Northern industrial cities. Bearden remembers his grandmother's rubbing new boarders at night with cocoa butter. "They didn't realize, when they first started, the terrific heat from those furnaces," he says. "They'd strip to the waist, and when the furnace doors opened, the flames would lick out like evil tongues and scorch them. But they were making forty or fifty dollars a week, which was a tremendous wage in comparison with what they'd been getting. I loved it there. I found it fascinating looking at the mills. For a while, I spent my summers in Pittsburgh, and then, after my first year of high school, in Manhattan, I decided I preferred living in Pittsburgh, so I went to school there."

Bearden was twelve the summer he met Eugene. Nobody knew anything about Eugene at first—where he lived or who his parents were. One day, he showed Bearden some drawings he had done, on sheets of brown paper. Bearden was enthralled. "He'd done one drawing of a house of prostitution not far from where we lived, run by a woman named Sadie. We always liked to go there and try to sell newspapers, because the music was so interesting—that kind of rolling piano. Eugene had drawn Sadie's house with the façade cut off, so you could see in all the rooms. And somebody had shot off a pistol, and the bullet was going all through the house. Women were on top of men, and the bullet was going through them, into the next room and the next, until it came down through the ceiling into the front parlor, and Sadie had her pocketbook open, and the bullet had turned into coins and was dropping into her pocketbook. I said to Eugene, 'You did this? Can you teach me to do it?' He said, 'Sure.' So I started taking drawing lessons from Eugene.

"My grandmother set up a table in my room, and Eugene and I would go and draw every day. All his drawings were about what happened in Sadie's house, and I was just trying religiously to copy what he did. After a week or so, my grandmother came around wanting to see what we had done. She took one look, and she grabbed all those drawings and threw them into the furnace. She said, 'Eugene, where did you ever see anything like that?' Eugene said, 'My mother is a whore. She works over at Sadie's place.' My grandmother told him, 'Eugene, don't you go home tonight.' My grandmother finished making dinner for everybody, and then she got a big suitcase and all three of us went to Sadie's, and she knocked on the door. The music was going, and Sadie came to the door, and as soon as she saw my grandmother she knew what had happened. 'I didn't want this boy here,' she said. My grandmother said, 'I'm not coming in, but you let Eugene go up and get his clothes, because I'm taking him home to live with me.' So Eugene and I went up to where he lived, which was way up on the top floor; you could look down through the cracks in the floor into the room below. We brought Eugene back to live with us. His mother would come every Sunday to visit him. They'd sit in the front room, where there was an old German clock that had written on it 'Every Hour Wounds. The Last One Kills.' How I hated to look at that! Eugene never did any more drawings after he left Sadie's house. He died about a year later, and we went to his funeral. But I always thought that with his drawings he could have been another Lautrec. That was the first time I ever thought about drawing—and then for years I forgot about it."

Harlem

Bessye J. Bearden did not approve of her son's wanting to become an artist. This was the Depression, and people were starving. Bessye J. was an activist, a tremendously energetic and public-spirited woman—New York editor of the *Chicago Defender*, the widely read Negro weekly; chairman of her local school board (after having been the first woman appointed to a school board in New York City); national treasurer of the Council of Negro Women; a member of the executive board of the New York Urban League. She had dealt in real estate, and in 1935 she was appointed Deputy Collector for the Third New York Internal Revenue District. She was a political force in Harlem, having been the manager of several congressional campaigns, an organizer of the National Council of Negro Women, and the founder and first president of the Negro Women's Democratic Association—someone you came to when you wanted to cut through red tape and get action. Everyone in Harlem knew Bessye J., and Bessye J. knew everyone: Eleanor Roosevelt and Mary Bethune, councilmen and judges, editors and mayors, not to mention all the musicians and singers and actors who played at Connie's Inn or the Lafayette Theatre, half a block from the Bearden's apartment, which was on the third floor at 154 West 131st Street. (From a front window you could see the Tree of Hope, the famous old elm at the corner of Seventh Avenue and 131st Street, where out-of-work actors used to gather and talk.) Duke Ellington was a friend of the family, and bought an oil from Bearden's first formal exhibition. Fats Waller and his lyricist, Andy Razaf, and Razaf's wife, the singer Minta Cato, used to drop in regularly. Bearden remembers his mother as someone who was constantly in movement and among people. "Once, I came into the house and found her crying," he recalls. "I asked if she was sick. She said, 'No, I'm just by myself.' She had to be with people all the time." His father, Howard Bearden, worked for the New York City Department of Health as a sanitation inspector. He was an intelligent, sensitive man, and a drinker; he was very much in Bessye J.'s shadow.

Bessye Bearden had helped any number of young people get started in their careers—the actor Canada Lee, for one—and she and Howard felt that Romare, their only child, should stick to his original plan, which had been to become a doctor. After two years at Boston University, he transferred to New York University, where he majored in mathematics, with the idea of going on to medical school, but while he was at N.Y.U. he started drawing for the college humor magazine. He met E. Simms Campbell, the highly successful black cartoonist, who gave him advice and encouragement; he began contributing a weekly political cartoon to the nationally circulated *Afro-American*. Bearden was also being urged at this period to become a professional baseball player. He had been Boston University's star varsity pitcher, and for two summers while he was in college there he pitched for the Boston Tigers, a Negro team that often played exhibition games with semi-pro clubs. Bearden was told that if he wanted to "pass" he could easily play in the majors (this was before Jackie Robinson broke the color line), but he had no inclination to do that. His inclination, more and more, was to continue drawing.

It was the Depression, curiously, that gave many Negroes the chance to be artists. In 1935, Bearden went to a meeting of Harlem artists at the Y.M.C.A. on 135th Street. He was amazed to find forty or fifty there—he had been told that there were very few Negro artists. This was the beginning of the Harlem Artists Guild, headed first by the painter and muralist Aaron Douglas and then by the sculptor Augusta Savage. Bearden himself was ineligible for the Works Progress Administration art program, because of his family's income, but the knowledge that other Negroes were devoting themselves seriously to painting and sculpture made a strong impression on him. "I found that the W.P.A., even at the worst time of the Depression, gave artists a salary and materials to work with," Bearden says. "It gave minority artists what they could never have afforded otherwise." In 1936, a year after he graduated from N.Y.U. with a bachelor's degree in science, he enrolled in the Art Students League, to study with the German expatriate George Grosz. Grosz's corrosive line drawings and watercolors of German society "made me realize the artistic possibilities of American Negro subject matter," Bearden once wrote. At first, he was still thinking mainly in terms of political cartooning, but Grosz changed his mind about that. It was Grosz, he said, who "led me to study composition, through the analysis of Brueghel and the great Dutch masters, and who in the process of refining my draftsmanship initiated me into the magic world of Ingres, Dürer, Holbein, and Poussin."

A year and a half at the League constituted Bearden's only formal training in art. In 1938, he took a job with the New York City Department of Welfare as a caseworker. He continued to live with his parents, but as soon as he could manage it he rented a studio at 33 West 125th Street, which was then on the edge of Harlem; across Fifth Avenue, the neighborhood was all white. Jacob Lawrence, another young painter, had the studio on the floor beneath, and soon afterward the poet Claude McKay moved into the building. "Things were still very lively in Harlem then," Bearden recalls. "So much of the life in those days was lived out in the open, on the street. People were still coming in from the South, and you still had the house-rent parties—somebody would need to raise money to pay the rent, so they'd throw a party, pass out little cards on the street, and you'd come and pay a quarter for admission, and there would be plenty to eat and drink and usually some good music, and that way you got to meet all sorts of people."

The Harlem artists were a close-knit group in the late thirties. They met regularly at "306"—306 West 141st Street, where Charles Alston and the sculptor Henry Bannarn lived, sharing a big studio that for a short time also doubled as a W.P.A.-sponsored art school. Alston, an accomplished painter, who was related to Bearden by marriage, kept open house for all the creative talents of the day.

"There was always a hot discussion going on at 306," according to Alston. "Langston Hughes would drop by, and Claude McKay, and sometimes William Saroyan or Bill Steig or Carl Van Vechten, from downtown. Musicians, too—Andy Razaf, and Sammy Stewart, and John Hammond, the jazz musicologist, and lots of others." When Bannarn moved out, Alston shared the place for a while with Ad Bates, who was a dancer with the Doris Humphrey/Charles Weidman troupe, and who also worked as an artists' model at the Art Students League. Bates organized several art exhibitions at 306, including Bearden's first one-man show in 1940 (mostly student work); later, he introduced Bearden to a number of white artists downtown, including Stuart Davis and Walter Quirt.

"There was a great interchange of people coming up to Harlem from all over," Bearden recalls. "You got to know all kinds of people—actors, musicians, under-world characters, intellectuals, society types. I met García Lorca once at a party. There was always a lot of movement from place to place, and it was so easy to know people." In those days, the center of Harlem was Seventh Avenue and 135th Street. Negroes had started to move to 135th Street about 1902. W. E. B. Du Bois, James Weldon Johnson, Augusta Savage, and other prominent people lived on 135th, although the really fashionable blocks were 138th and 139th between Seventh and Eighth, streets of handsome town houses, several of which were designed about the turn of the century by Stanford White for wealthy clients, and inhabited since the twenties by well-to-do black doctors, lawyers, and entertainers; they were known locally as Strivers' Row. The famous night clubs were all within a few blocks of 135th and Seventh. Negro customers were not allowed in the Cotton Club or Connie's Inn (once a year, the Cotton Club revue would play at the Lafayette, so the Harlemites could see it), but Charles Buchanan, the manager of the Savoy Ballroom, used to let the Harlem artists in free to dance there, and Bearden and his friends went several times a week.

Bearden, Alston, Bannarn, Bates, Norman Lewis, Ernest Crichlow, Francisco Lord, Vertis Hayes, Jacob Lawrence, and the other artists had their own special gathering places. They would usually drop in every night at a place called Joe's, on Seventh Avenue at 137th Street, and later in the evening would go on to Mom Young's, on 132nd between Seventh and Lenox, where for a quarter you could get a coffee can full of beer and a steaming bowl of gumbo or chili or whatever Mom was making that day. "Of course, it wasn't all good times and laughter," Bearden points out. "This was still the Depression."

Bearden worked for the city from nine to five and painted for several hours in the evening. For a long time after his studies with Grosz, he had not been able to get started on his own. The same piece of brown paper, unmarked, had remained on his easel for weeks at a time. One evening, leaving the studio with Claude McKay, he heard the familiar sound of keys jangling—prostitutes jangled keys to attract business—and, turning around, saw what he describes as the smallest and homeliest woman he had ever seen. "She said, 'Two dollars, boys.' Then she said, 'A dollar?' Then, 'Fifty cents?' Then, 'A quarter?' Finally, she said, 'For God's sake, just take me.' She was so pathetic I told my mother about her, said she was in the wrong business, and my mother got a job for this woman—Ida. After that, Ida came every Saturday to clean my studio. And in the studio was my easel, with the piece of brown paper on it. When you're young, you have a lot of ideas and a lot of dreams, but you don't have the ability to realize them; I think that as you mature you don't have the same kind of ideas and dreams, because you let the work make its own fantasy. Anyway, Ida would come once a week to clean, and the brown paper was there on the easel, and one day she asked if it was the same piece of paper, and I told her that it was—that I didn't have my ideas together. She said, 'Why don't you paint me?' Well, the way I must have looked at her she could see what was going through my mind. 'I know what I look like,' she said. 'But when you can look and find what's beautiful in me, then you're going to be able to do something on that paper of yours.' That always sort of stuck with me, what she said."

When Bearden did find his way, it was with a series of paintings based on his childhood memories of the rural South. Painted in tempera on brown paper, they are characterized by strong, bright colors and stylized, highly formal composition. Most of the Harlem artists then were working in the predominating vein of social realism, influenced by Thomas Hart Benton and by the Mexican muralists. From the start, Bearden's paintings were more lyrical, and were concerned more with plastic values than with social themes. "Romie was never a poor kid," Charles Alston once said. "He was straight out of the middle class, and the urban middle class at that. Jake Lawrence grew up in the middle of real Harlem poverty, and there's always been something very simple and direct about his approach, but Romie's approach to art is more intellectual. He's read a great deal all his life, and he's been intensely curious about many different kinds of art."

Alston introduced Bearden to African sculpture, and Claude McKay took him to meet Charles Christopher Seifert, an elderly gentleman who had filled his comfortable Harlem home with books on African and Afro-American history. In 1935 Seifert took Bearden and a number of other young artists to see the first exhibition of African Negro art put on by the Museum of Modern Art. What Bearden got from this experience was not racial pride so much as a sense of the tremendous formal power and majesty of African art. Twenty years later, he used fragments of Benin heads and Dan masks in his own collage paintings.

The artist's life in Harlem had its bizarre aspects. Once, Bearden was commissioned to paint a portrait of an underworld figure's two children. Working from a photograph, he struggled nervously with the compositional problems, trying to make it look like a Degas. Then a friend of his came in and said he was going about it all wrong. Acting on his friend's advice (the promised completion date was fast approaching), he took the photograph downtown and had it blown up on photosensitized canvas; then he got a professional retoucher to put in the color until, he says, "the two kids looked as if they were made up for Forest Lawn." When the father came, with his bodyguard, to claim the picture, he was so moved that he broke into tears and insisted on paying fifty dollars more than the agreed-on price. "Eramor," he said (Bearden had signed it with his first name spelled backward)— "Eramor, you're one hell of a painter." Another time, Bearden invited an exotic dancer to spend the night in his studio. Unknown to Bearden, her luggage contained an eight-foot python (her working costume), which got loose during the night and entwined itself around his easel. "Some people have looked at my work and said it was Surrealism," he said recently. "But these things were all around me all the time. The things I saw every day—the people, the music, the dancing. My models were as great as Lautrec's."

"I think the artist has to be something like a whale," Bearden has said, "swimming with his mouth wide open, absorbing everything until he has what he really needs. When he finds that, he can start to make limitations. And then he really begins to grow."

Paris

Bearden lived in Paris for six months in 1950, and did not paint a single picture. He studied philosophy at the Sorbonne, under the G.I. Bill of Rights. He lived at 5 Rue des Feuillantines, near the Luxembourg Gardens, and spent a good part of his time just wandering around the city. Paris in the early fifties, he says, was very much like Harlem in the twenties. "There was that sense of something happening, and of life being lived out in the open, on the streets. Paris has never been a city for somebody who wants to find himself. It's too seductive. Of course, I thought I'd go right to the Louvre, but it got to be like something in Kafka's 'Castle.' I could never bring myself to go there. There was too much to see and do just walking the length and breadth of Paris."

By the time Bearden got to Paris, in early February of 1950, he was a fairly well-established artist, with half a dozen one-man shows to his credit. Caresse Crosby had seen his work in 1943, when she was trying to organize a group show of Negro artists, and decided on the spot to give him a solo show in her G Place Gallery, in Washington, D.C. Bearden was in the Army then; he served for three years with the 372nd Infantry, a Negro regiment, doing Stateside duty in a number of different posts before his discharge, in 1945, with the rank of sergeant. Soon after a show of Bearden's "Ten Hierographic Paintings" in Washington, Caresse Crosby introduced him to the New York dealer Samuel Kootz, who represented Adolph Gottlieb, William Baziotes, Robert Motherwell, Carl Holty, and several other first-generation Abstract Expressionists. Kootz gave Bearden three one-man shows between 1945 and 1947, and during this period his work also appeared in a number of important group shows and museum exhibitions. His paintings of the forties are rather austere in color and are figurative, usually being related to literary or Biblical themes. He painted a series called "The Passion of Christ," and other works were inspired by the Iliad, "Gargantua and Pantagruel," and García Lorca's "Lament for Ignacio Sánchez Mejías." Close friends of Bearden's say that his mother's death, in 1943—she was in the hospital, recovering from an operation when she contracted pneumonia and died—was a profound shock to him, and that the change is evident in the sombre, stained-glass quality of his "Passion of Christ" series. For Bearden, the Biblical allusion was not religious but humanistic—an attempt to reach beyond personal experience to universal archetypes that would be communicable to others. Bearden's first show at Kootz—the "Passion of Christ" series—sold out, and a number of important collectors, among them Sam Lewisohn, became regular purchasers of his work.

Still, the art market in the forties was not what it became in the late fifties and sixties, and Bearden could not make a living from his picture sales. He went back to work for the Department of Welfare in 1946, and again painted in his spare time. His new studio was in the Apollo building, at 243 West 125th Street, between Seventh and Eighth Avenues. The Apollo Theatre, next door, had succeeded the Lafayette as the leading Harlem showplace for big bands and headliners, and 125th Street, with the Theresa Hotel and the Harlem Opera House and the Apollo, had become the center of a rather different Harlem from the one in which Bearden grew up. There had been a race riot in Harlem in 1943, and during the war years the area was declared off limits to white servicemen. The atmosphere was less ebullient in the postwar years than it had been in the thirties. The Harlem Artists Guild was no longer active. Many of the artists had moved away, and Bearden's friendships with Baziotes, Holty, and others who showed at Kootz did not completely offset a feeling of loneliness and isolation. He had no particular interest in emulating the gestural Abstract Expressionist work of Jackson Pollock and Willem de Kooning, whose influence on New York artists was already immense; at the same time, he had not really found his own aesthetic alternative. He had heard a lot about Paris, of course, from Claude McKay and others, and late in 1949 he took a leave of absence from his job with the city and in 1950 went over to see it for himself.

Americans in Paris on the G.I. Bill used to congregate at the big cafés on the Boulevard du Montparnasse—the Coupole and the Sélect—or else at the ones around Saint-Germain-des-Prés. Albert Murray, a young black writer, who became one of Bearden's close friends, remembers meeting Bearden for the first time at the Coupole: "Romie was with Myron O'Higgins, the poet. I couldn't tell if he was a Russian or what—people used to say about Romie over there that, seeing him first, you thought it must be either Khrushchev or Jean Genet. But then he put his head back and laughed, and I thought, Nobody but a Negro man is going to laugh like that. Romie already knew everybody, it seemed. He was going to all the galleries, looking in all the shops, being part of Paris."

James Baldwin and Richard Wright were both in Paris then, and Baldwin read part of his first novel, "Go Tell It on the Mountain," to Bearden and a few others one night in Bearden's room on the Rue des Feuillantines. Bearden also knew a number of French artists and intellectuals, many of whom he had met in the atelier of the painter Jean Hélion. Kootz had given Bearden letters of introduction to Picasso, Braque, and Brancusi. Picasso was on the Côte d'Azur, and anyway, Bearden said, meeting him would have been like shaking hands with the Eiffel Tower. He did call on Braque, who was polite but formal, and on Brancusi, who became a friend. "I went to see him often in his studio, in the Impasse Ronsin," he said. "He wasn't working anymore. I used to go shopping for groceries with him. In the markets, at noon and again in the late afternoon, they would ring a bell five minutes before closing time. The prices would drop a little after the bell, and Brancusi would always wait until the last minute to shop. He had that quality of a real peasant."

Although Bearden never met Matisse, he and his friends used to see him from time to time. "Once, I was sitting at the Dôme when Matisse walked by with a friend," Bearden said."There was a rustle of excitement in the café, and all the waiters came out to see him, and as he passed they applauded. Matisse didn't notice at first, until his friend called his attention to it; then he turned and came back and shook hands with all the waiters, one by one. Oh, Paris was just wonderful for me. I liked everything about it. If you were an American, there was a way to get whiskey very cheap then and give parties for almost nothing. One night, a bunch of us were eating in a restaurant in Montparnasse, and we'd met some Russian musicians and asked them to come along to a party and play. On our way to the party, I heard jazz coming from an apartment, and it seemed to me that it didn't sound like French musicians playing, so I went up and knocked on the door, and there inside the room were Sidney Bechet and Roy Eldridge and Minta Cato, the singer who had been married to Andy Razaf, and a few others. I knew them! They were just having some fun by themselves. So I had them come along to the party. And it was a terrific party. Finally, at about three in the morning, they made us leave, and we ended up continuing the party out on the street—the music and the dancing.

"Another time, I was having dinner with Sam Menashe, the poet, and another poet named Sam Allen, a guy I'd known in the Army, at a little working-class restaurant called Signe de la Bonne Étoile. It was a misty March night, and after dinner Menashe said we should go and look at Notre Dame; it was a perfect night to see it. When we got to the *quai* on the Left Bank opposite the Ile de la Cité, Menashe took us down the steps to the cobblestone walk along the river, and we looked up at the cathedral from there. It was spotlighted, but in the mist the uppermost sections were barely visible, and the spires seemed to move endlessly up into the sky. For the first time, I really had a feeling of the Gothic cathedral as the hand of God, with a finger pointing to Heaven. I'd never had such a feeling of extension and height. A few days later, I was in a place called Chez Inez, run by Inez Cavanaugh, an American jazz singer, who was married to the jazz impresario Timme Rosenkrantz. I met a Chinese guy there who offered me one of his cigarettes, and I didn't realize it was hashish. I smoked French Gauloises then, and this didn't taste much different. Anyway, I smoked two of his hashish cigarettes, and I was thinking about Notre Dame, about going there again. I don't know how I got there—it seemed like right after I had the thought I was down there by the water looking at Notre Dame. And I thought I saw an angel walking across the Seine. It was late at night, and there was nobody around to talk to but a woman, a prostitute. I told her I'd just seen something amazing, an angel walking across the river. She said, 'Men are all alike.' I asked her what she meant. She said. 'Look up at Notre Dame. Don't you see all those angels holding up the whole goddam cathedral? Don't you think they get tired? And you're worried about one of them taking a little walk at night.' She said, 'Don't you want to come home with me?' I said no, I was going to go and paint a picture of that angel walking across the river. But, of course, I didn't do it. I couldn't *ever* do a painting in Paris."

Bearden went home in August of 1950. He had applied for a Fulbright grant, and had been told he must return to the United States in order to collect it. He expected the Fulbright to send him back to Paris right away; even so, it wasn't easy to leave. Albert Murray, who was staying another month before returning to a teaching job at Tuskegee, was with him the day before he left. "Romie spent the whole day buying paper," he recalls. "All kinds of drawing papers—rice papers, special sizes and surfaces, different colors. His eyes got more and more moist the later it got. 'This goddam Paris,' he kept saying."

New York

Bearden did not get the Fulbright, and it was many years before he returned to Paris. He tried to get started painting again, with little success. Painting seemed enormously difficult. In his studio in the Apollo building, surrounded by musicians and rehearsal studios, he began to think that maybe the thing to do was to write a popular song that would make a lot of money and get back to Paris that way. Although he knew next to nothing about the technical aspects of music (he had taken violin lessons very briefly as a child, and hated them), Bearden had a lot of friends in the music business. Fred Norman and Larry Douglas, professional arrangers, helped him get started, and over the next couple of years Bearden, who seems to be one of those people who can do almost anything they set their minds to, achieved some success as a songwriter. About twenty of his songs were record-ed, one of which, "Seabreeze," became a substantial hit. By the midfifties, Billy Eckstine, Oscar Pettiford, and others had recorded it, and Seagram Distillers had used the song to promote a mixed drink.

"I just turned away from painting," Bearden has said of this period. "And mean-while the years were going by. One day, I went to see Hannah Arendt and her hus-band, the philosopher Heinrich Blücher, who were friends of mine. He said, 'You're wasting your life. In the first place, you don't even believe in what you're doing. Do you think Irving Berlin and Cole Porter could do what they do if they didn't believe in it?' Hannah said I was just going to wreck myself as a painter. I thought about that. But, you know, when you're serious about something, you don't really like doing it. Painting is so difficult; the canvas was always saying no to me. And all the time I was getting more and more nervous. One night, I thought I was going to die. I called my father and said I thought I must have can-cer of the stomach. But when I went to the doctor he examined me and said noth-ing was wrong. A couple of weeks later, I felt sure I was going to have a heart attack. Then, one day, walking on the street, I suddenly felt I couldn't walk a step farther. The next thing I knew, I was in the hospital. I asked the nurse, 'Where am I?' She said I was in the psychiatric ward at Bellevue. A doctor came by, and I asked him what had happened to me. 'You blew a fuse,' he said. Just what Arendt and others had said was going to happen to me had happened."

Gradually his life came back together. "I just had to be a painter; that was it," he concluded. "Some people are like that. I've always thought Delacroix could easily have been a great writer, while a man like Courbet could only have been a painter." Bearden feels that his marriage, in 1954, was what really gave him the strength to return to painting. He met Nanette Rohan at a benefit party in Harlem to help the survivors of a West Indies hurricane; she herself had grown up on Staten Island, but her parents came from Saint Martin. She and Bearden were married soon afterward. "I was on Miltown then," he recalls. "Nanette said if I was going to be a painter I couldn't be on pills, and she threw them all out. I never had any more nervousness after that."

One of the problems that Bearden felt most acutely was the meagerness of his formal art training. Reading in Delacroix's "Journal" that Delacroix had spent a lot of time copying the work of Old Masters, he decided that this would be a way he could learn more about painting. He was reluctant to go to a museum and copy there, in public, but he found that he could take a reproduction of a painting to a photography studio and have it blown up in black and white and then copy that, substituting his own color scheme for the original. "I did that with Giotto, Duccio, Veronese, Rembrandt—right on up to Monet," he said. "I spent three years copying. The one I had the most trouble with was Rembrandt. It was that picture in the Metropolitan, 'Pilate Washing His Hands.' There were so many subtle rhythms and carefully planned relationships that I finally had to give up on it."

Another problem was color. Bearden found that color as he had been using it in the past tended to break apart the forms that he was dealing with—to weaken the overall structure. He became interested in exploring color for its own sake, and this led him increasingly into abstraction. At about this time, in the late fifties, he met a Mr. Wu, a scholar in the fields of Chinese art and calligraphy. Bearden arranged to study with him informally. What he learned about Chinese landscape painting had to do mainly with pictorial space: the open corner, which allows the viewer's eye to enter the painting, and the areas left unfinished, so that the onlooker may complete them in his imagination; the contrast of masses and voids; the Chinese perspective, in which distant mountains bulk much larger than the shapes in the foreground. He began painting on rice paper (the paper he had bought in Paris), gluing it to the canvas and then tearing away sections, tearing them upward and across the picture plane until some motif engaged him, then adding more paper and painting in additional areas. By the late fifties, Bearden was painting in a totally nonrepresentational style, but one that had little in common with the work of Pollock or de Kooning. Some of his paintings of these years have the ancient, eroded look of rock faces or weathered walls. Others suggest the architectural solidity of Cézanne.

Occasional commissions and sales were not enough to let Bearden paint full time. In 1952, he had gone back to work for the Welfare Department and had been assigned to keep track of the city's fluctuating population of gypsies. "I wasn't enthusiastic about the idea at first, but eventually I hated to leave them," he has said. "I began to know so many families. They were truly a culture within a culture. They had such a strong sense of identity—anyone who wasn't a gypsy they used to call *gagco*. They came from India originally, and migrated into Persia and Europe. There seem to have always been gypsy tribes—Rumanian gypsies, Hungarian gypsies, Spanish gypsies—each with its own separate identity. They did certain kinds of traditional work. Relining copper pots and kettles was one of their specialties, and, of course, fortune-telling. We used to have an immigrant population coming in that believed in gypsy fortune-tellers, and a lot of gypsies lived down on the lower East Side, around Orchard Street and the Bowery. But that faded out, and they moved to Queens and Coney Island. Their way of life was disintegrating. You don't have any longer the hundreds of small circuses and carnivals that they followed, and their old trades are no longer needed. Young people were marrying nongypsies, which had never happened before. The children were being forced to go to school."

Bearden's job was to keep an eye on the gypsies—their movements in and out of the city, their problems and needs. Few of them could read, and they had little interest in the laws of the *gagco*. When a gypsy got into a fight, or was arrested for stealing or for a con job, Bearden would go to Police Headquarters and do whatever he could. The gypsies had their own system of justice, he found. "They had trials, and they abided by the judgments. For example, a bridegroom found on his wedding night that his bride had been badly burned from her neck to her ankles as a child, so he took her back to her family and demanded his money back. It was an arranged marriage, and money had been paid. He lost the case, because sexually she was fine."

Not all the gypsies Bearden encountered were poor. "Once, I had to go and see a man in Brooklyn, a guy named Mike. He lived in a storefront, and his wife and children lived in another storefront nearby. He was a huge man, who must have weighed over three hundred pounds. He wore a white suit, like Mark Twain. And I made the mistake of asking him something about his job. He hit the ceiling. 'Look at my hands!' he yelled. 'I've never worked a day in my life!' His sons did repair work on milk-pasteurizing machines, and they supported him in style. He just sat there all day listening to music on his hi-fi, and every hour or so one of his daughters would come in with food—either Chinese food or barbecued spareribs. After he'd finished, he'd throw the ribs in the back room, where there were some of the biggest rats I've ever seen. He also had a rackful of guns, and now and then he'd take down a rifle and start shooting at the rats. Not at *them*, exactly; he'd wait until a rat got up on a piece of china—a cup or a plate—and then he'd try to shoot it out from under him."

Bearden worked with the gypsies off and on for fourteen years. Then, in 1966, his income from painting enabled him to leave the Welfare Department for good. The experience had always been interesting, but in the end it was rather saddening and it helped to strengthen Bearden's own feeling that the path of separatism within a culture is basically self-defeating. Like his friend Ralph Ellison, the writer, Bearden has tried to make art out of the totality of his experience as an American. "Al Murray says that when a person comes to America from some other country, he becomes four things," Bearden said not long ago. "Even though his ancestry may be Greek or French, if he becomes an American he becomes part Anglo-Saxon, part Indian, part frontiersman, and part black. Those are the main cultural roots that make the American character. You see the evidence all the time. Athletes slapping each other's hands instead of shaking them—that started with blacks. And jazz music. I don't think any critic has ever gone into it, but Abstract Expressionism is very close to the aesthetics of jazz. That's the feeling you get from it—involvement, personality, improvisation, rhythm, color. In the twenties, Benny Goodman used to come up to Harlem a lot. He was teaching himself about jazz the only way he could, and he had to become a little black to learn it. By the same token, when I started copying and learning from those pictures by Vermeer and Delacroix and the rest, in a sense I was joining the white world. It's all a little more complicated than some people try to make out."

Canal Street

For the first two years of their married life, the Beardens lived on West 114th Street, in an apartment they shared with Bearden's father. They needed more space, and when a friend told them in 1956 of an artist's loft that was being vacated on Canal Street, they took it. The move to lower Manhattan in no way weakened Bearden's ties with the black community. In fact, it was in the Canal Street loft that the Spiral Group of black artists was formed, in 1963. The civil-rights movement was in full swing then, and the original purpose of the meeting at Bearden's loft was to discuss going down as a group to that summer's March on Washington. They decided at that time to work together on the common problems of black artists. With the exceptions of Bearden and Jacob Lawrence (who was out of town at the time, and did not join the Spiral Group), very few black artists had been able to show at any of the rapidly proliferating New York galleries. Many competent black artists had difficulty exhibiting their work in New York, and the opportunities for younger artists seemed almost nonexistent. The Spiral Group—the name, contributed by Hale Woodruff, was intended to suggest a movement up and out—included Bearden, Alston, Woodruff, Calvin Douglass, Norman Lewis, Merton Simpson, Emma Amos, Perry Ferguson, Richard Mayhew, James Yeargans, Earl Miller, William Majors, Reginald Gammon, Al Hollingsworth, and Felrath Hines. They rented a small room on Christopher Street, in the Village, where they met once a week and eventually put on exhibitions of work by the members.

At one of the early Spiral meetings, the idea of a collaborative effort came up—a painting on which several artists could work together. Bearden thought about this afterward, wondering how it could be done. The solution that occurred to him was collage. He cut a lot of pictures out of the magazines that Nanette liked to read—*Life, Vogue, Harper's Bazaar, McCall's, Ebony*—and took them to the next meeting, but nobody responded to his idea. Bearden, however, was sufficiently interested to try a few experiments on his own. He made half a dozen small collages, pasting his cutouts to sheets of typewriter paper and filling in with drawing and watercolor. He chose pictures that suggested to him something out of his own experience—jazz musicians, landscapes, street scenes, African sculpture, urban black faces. Reginald Gammon saw them and suggested taking them to a photo shop to be photographed and blown up (as Bearden had done earlier with reproductions of the Old Masters). Bearden did this, but at first the results did not particularly interest him. The large photomontages were rolled up in a corner of the Canal Street loft when Arne Ekstrom came there early in 1964 to discuss

Bearden's next exhibition, scheduled for the fall. Ekstrom had shown Bearden's abstract paintings in 1961, at what was then the Cordier & Warren Gallery, on Madison Avenue. He looked at some new abstract canvases that Bearden showed him. "I felt a lack of movement, a sort of lost momentum," Ekstrom recalls. "I had just moved into a new gallery, in the French & Company Building, and I was worried that the paintings wouldn't hold up in the large space there." Then he noticed the rolled-up photomontages in the corner, asked to see them, and said immediately, "That's your next show."

Bearden's "projections," as he and Ekstrom agreed to call them, were the basis for everything he has done since 1964. When they were shown at the Cordier & Ekstrom gallery that fall, Bearden's old friend and fellow-artist Ernest Crichlow said, "Romie, it looks like you've come home," and most of the others at the opening felt the same way. "It was not only an aesthetic but an emotional breakthrough for Romie," Crichlow said later. "There was something entirely fresh about them, about that vision." It was as though Bearden had reinvented collage, which became in his hands the ideal medium for the transmission of all he had learned as an artist and as a man.

The "projections," of course, were really prints. Each was issued in an edition of six, and sales were very encouraging. But Bearden wanted to find a more direct way of working in collage. He tried gluing his cutout photographs to canvas, but the glue made the canvas warp. It occurred to him that many of the Old Master paintings he had copied in the fifties had been on wood panels, so he did some research at the Metropolitan Museum, where a friend in the restoring room let him examine the backs of some of the old panel paintings, and afterward he went to John Schindler, a commercial designer who was a former classmate at N.Y.U., and Schindler helped him devise a Masonite panel with a special wood backing that would not warp. Then he was free to develop and deepen his new method, and also to work with color. All of Bearden's former discoveries seemed to come together in the new collage paintings: the shallow space of Byzantine mosaics, the strong forms of African sculpture, the spatial harmonies of Chinese landscapes, and, most significant of all, the carefully planned structure of Vermeer and the little Dutch masters. "Because many of the paintings I was doing were of interiors," he has said, "I began to look again at Vermeer and Pieter de Hooch and Jan Steen. I found that, especially with Vermeer and Steen, a lot of the work was controlled, like Mondrian's, by the use of rectangles over rectangles. I really think the art of painting is the art of putting something over something else, and in a way these new pictures of mine, while they used representational images, were more abstract than the work I'd been doing before. I would work with rectangular shapes that were in proportion to the overall rectangle of the whole painting. Delacroix said of the Dutch that in their purity and nobility of form they rival the Greeks. That was the quality I was trying to get. I wanted to make my formal language strict and classical, in the manner of the great Benin heads. But I also thought that by using photographs that way, almost cinematically, I could convey a sense of 'You are there'—a documentary feeling that would have something to do with the speed-fractured tempo of contemporary urban life."

The images that Bearden worked with were predominantly those of Negro life, but the way he fragmented and combined these images gave them another character and another dimension. Bearden felt that he did not have the right to use someone's photograph intact without permission. Superimposing the features of a Benin bronze on a contemporary black face, however, or giving someone grass for hair and corn for teeth, or combining three or more photographs into a composite face whose features were jarringly out of scale changed more than the individual likeness. In Bearden's paintings, the Southern sharecropper's cabin and the Harlem street take on mythic overtones. This is quite deliberate on Bearden's part. A number of the paintings clearly echo major themes in Western art: the Annunciation, La Primavera, Susannah at the Bath. (Bearden's Susannah bathes alone in a cabin in the woods, watched only by a bird.) His "Woman in a Harlem Courtyard" alludes specifically to Pieter de Hooch's "The Spinner and the Housemaid." The prevalence of ritual (as Albert Murray has phrased it) in American Negro life became the dominant theme of Bearden's mature work.

Certain images recur throughout his paintings of the sixties. Trains, for example, and birds—"journeying things," Bearden has called them. "Trains are so much a part of Negro life," he explains. "Negroes lived near the tracks, worked on the railroads, and trains carried them North during the migration." The "conjur woman," another recurring image, was a strong presence in the rural South of Bearden's boyhood, and a link to the ancient mysteries remembered from Africa; even in Pittsburgh, living in the house in back of his grandmother's, there was an old woman much feared for her power to put spells on people, and in Harlem as late as the thirties there were people like Black Hermann, a performing magician who also sold roots and strange potions in his drugstore on Lenox Avenue.

The blind guitarist of many Bearden paintings is a memory of a certain old Mr. Johnson, of Lutherville, Maryland. When Bearden was a boy, he sometimes visited his paternal grandmother, who after his grandfather's death had married a Methodist minister named Charles Cummings and moved from Charlotte to his parish in Maryland. A parishioner had a special cake she used to make, in several iron pans that had come down from the time of slavery; the cake looked like a watermelon, and had chocolate seeds, which she cut out and inserted by hand in the red batter. She would make a batch of watermelon cakes and get Romare to deliver them around town in a wagon he pulled. "Mr. Johnson, her husband, would always come along when I delivered those cakes," Bearden recalls. "He was blind, and he played the guitar. Whenever he heard somebody on the road, he'd ask who it was, and then he'd say, 'Get him over here. I had a dream about him last night, and he was laid out in his coffin so plain . . .' Of course, everybody made tracks as soon as they saw us coming." Mr. Johnson is also Tiresias, the blind prophet of Greek drama, the man with inner sight.

Inevitably, perhaps, in the emotional climate of the sixties, critics read social content into these powerful and evocative paintings. They saw "tormented faces," "vision of beauty and horror," and the travail and anguish of the Negro's existence; the work, as the *Times* noted, was "propagandist in the best sense." Bearden has made it plain that this was not part of his intention. "A lot of people see pain and anguish and tragedy in my work," he conceded a while ago. "It's not that I want to back away from this, or to say that those things are not there. Naturally, I had strong feelings about the civil-rights movement, and about what was happening in the sixties. But you saw that on television every night, you saw the actuality of it, and something was needed, I thought, other than to keep repeating it in art. I thought there were other means that would convey it better than painting."

Bearden believed, moreover, that the Negro was becoming something of an abstraction in the sixties, a sort of caricature of protest and injustice. For his own part, he wanted as he said in 1964, to "establish a world through art in which the validity of my Negro experience could live and make its own logic." Bearden was concerned with art, not propaganda. "I have not created protest images," he said "The world within the collage, if it is authentic, retains the right to speak for itself."

Standing on the terrace of Albert Murray's apartment, on West 132nd Street, one day in 1971, looking across at the rows of four-story buildings that make up the block on Lenox Avenue between 132nd and 133rd, Bearden conceived the idea for his largest painting. "The Block" is actually six pictures joined together, making an eighteen-foot work. When it was shown at the Museum of Modern Art, in Bearden's 1971 retrospective exhibition there, it was supplemented by an audio collage of street sounds that had been tape-recorded, but Bearden now feels that this was not a good idea. The painting needs no accompaniment. It shows not only the street and the houses but also (shades of Eugene) the rooms behind the façades, where people are eating, bathing, making love, attending church (the block has two churches), getting their hair cut—just going about the ordinary business of life. The feeling conveyed is one of celebration.

When the Metropolitan Museum was planning its ill-fated "Harlem on My Mind" show, in 1968, Bearden was asked to be a consultant. He agreed at first, but when he saw how the plans were developing he withdrew. "They were giving it a sort of light, sensational treatment," he has explained. "I thought it deserved something more in-depth than that. I was so mad I never even went to see the exhibition."

Bearden has done as much as anyone to celebrate the achievements of black artists, both living and dead. In 1966, he organized a show called "Art of the American Negro" in a transformed basement on 125th Street—the first time since the nineteen-thirties that an exhibition of Negro artists of such scope had been seen in Harlem. The following year, Bearden and Carroll Greene, a collector of nineteenth-century black American paintings, put together a huge exhibition called "The Evolution of Afro-American Artists: 1800–1950" in the Great Hall of City College, with a hundred and fifty works by fifty-five artists. This was something of an eye-opener to a large number of people, blacks as well as whites, who had never before seen paintings by Joshua Johnston, Robert S. Duncanson, Henry Ossawa Tanner (the first black artist to win a prize at the Salon des Artistes Français), and other nearly forgotten talents. A great deal of research had gone into organizing the show, and Bearden became something of a scholar in the field. With Harry Henderson, he has recently completed a book on the history of Afro-

American art, to be published by Doubleday in 1978.

An increasing number of young blacks are studying art in school and college these days, and more and more have been deciding to make careers as artists. Although the odds are heavily against success for anyone in this line, it still seems harder for a young black than for a young white artist to find a gallery willing to show his work, and with this in mind Bearden, Ernest Crichlow, and Norman Lewis started the Cinque Gallery in 1969. The Cinque (named for the African prince who led a successful revolt aboard the slave ship *Amistad* in 1839) operates under a grant from the New York State Council on the Arts, which pays all its administrative costs; it is now at 2 Astor Place, around the corner from Joseph Papp's Public Theatre, in space donated rent-free by Papp, and the artists who show there receive a hundred per cent of the proceeds of anything they sell. In its first years, the Cinque showed only young unknowns, but lately it has broadened its scope to exhibit older black and other minority artists who have been overlooked by the commercial galleries. Marcia DuVall, the administrative director, is besieged by artists who want to show there. Most of the younger artists who come in want to meet Bearden, she says. "I think Romie's success is maybe more of an influence than his work," says Chris Shelton, the Cinque's first administrative director. "They see one black man who's made it, and that makes them think they have a chance, too. Romie sees them all. When he gets home from his own studio at night, his phone never stops ringing. He spends most of his free time now helping other artists."

Sitting in Albert Murray's apartment not long ago, Bearden said he would feel better about the current crop of young artists if they showed more of an interest in aesthetic problems. "Most of the questions I hear now are about making it," he said. "I get very few who seem to have a real historical interest in the craft. Of course, this is a difficult time for artists. Valéry said that the invention of the machine destroyed man's patience. To sit down today and paint like van Eyck is impossible, or to do something like the Unicorn Tapestries, where, I'm told, there are more than a hundred different kinds of flowers and plants portrayed. Talent can even get in the way of an artist now, because every artist coming up must make a whole new tradition for himself. In the Renaissance, when there was such an explosion of skill, it was possible for men who were not great painters to paint great pictures just by leaning on the achievements of a Leonardo or a Raphael. That's not possible now. Only a great artist can make a great painting today. What's essential is that you make some statement, that you offer some vision of life. For example, Persia—Iran—seems to be largely a desert country. But in Persian miniatures I've never seen any desert. There's always the garden, which is in daylight, but at the top the stars are out. It's the vision of the oasis. Cézanne wasn't particularly talented, nor was van Gogh. It was only late in life that Cézanne got all he needed to do what he wanted to do, and when he confronted that mountain of Sainte-Victoire he had the means, he had his vision of the world. Now we seem to be at the end of an era, the romantic era. Even Mondrian was a kind of romantic with his idea that the world could be transformed through art. The notion that everyone is creative is all romanticism, and that seems to be ending, but it's not clear what will take its place. There is a kind of interregnum now."

Murray put an Earl Hines record on the record-player, and the two men listened to it intently. In addition to novels, Murray has written extensively about jazz—his magnum opus in this field, "Stomping the Blues," came out last year. When the Hines record was over, he played some Fats Waller, and then some James P. Johnson, king of the old Harlem stride pianists. After that, he put on a very early side of Louis Armstrong, with a great, ringing Armstrong solo.

"One time, I was in Spain," Bearden said. "In Málaga. It was in 1950. For some reason, I went to a funeral. There was all that mournful music, and then, after the burial, somebody began to blow on a trumpet, another kind of sound entirely, and an Englishman who was standing next to me turned and said, 'You see, now life has taken over again.' I think that's what art is—it celebrates a victory. A blues singer up at the old Lafayette, she sings about waking up one morning, there's a letter from my man, he done left me, I'm going down to the river and God knows what I'll do—but then here comes Freddy Jenkins on the trumpet, playing with a mute in, and he does a funny kind of riff that turns what might have been tragic into something else, into farce, so you don't feel like going out and committing suicide after all. Life is going to triumph somehow."

242

chapter 15

SHERRY TURNER DECARAVA

Celebration

Life sounds through the photographs of Roy DeCarava in singing tones. Beginning with the world, his pictures reshape and renew those things that we know but cannot bring ourselves to say. They are unflinching, yet feeling before the human condition as they carry us with them on a meditative journey through an imagery of relationships. The central spaces of DeCarava's photographs portray people and light, people and time, people and space, people and people. We can see these things, but other relationships are sensed in the photographs that are invisible, mysterious and deeply affecting. Something exists here between flesh and soul. There is no dispassion, no objective documentation. These are intense, perceptive images that recall the artist as one who renders a state of consciousness; drawing on the social, the historical and the aesthetic, forming a visual altar place for our lost memories, bringing present, past and future into one unified moment. The images emerge as quiet discoveries of subtle observation and elegant understatement, revealing themselves and their subjects in a poetry of vision.

The pictures capture a moment of life that slowly unfolds its intimacy with the world—the strong, youthful beauty of a Mississippi freedom marcher, the nature of trees near numbered tombstones, the shimmering mirror beneath a mother's feet as she walks with her children in morning light. Rendered through a translucency of surface with detail recorded in the darkest areas, these pictures express a strength of imagery that reads beyond the sharpness of the focus. It is the concept of beauty within the photographs that embraces them and us. DeCarava express-

This essay was originally published as the monograph text of *Roy DeCarava: Photographs* (Carmel, Calif.: Friends of Photography, 1981).

es this quality through an ever-changing balance between rational order and intuitive process. Spatial clarity, formal coherence and structural definition are dynamically integrated with chiaroscuro, mystery and an imprecision of form. There is also a moral aesthetic in the work, a sense that truth is beauty. These concerns are central to the manner and place in which we meet the pictures. In the broadest of terms they express a fusion of classicism and spiritualism, a joining of the human-centered and the nonmaterial aspects of life.

If we discard a useless soda can, Roy DeCarava finds echoes of beauty in its glistening surfaces. If we deem certain architecture devoid of human imprint and ugly, in *Four arrows and towel* he presents it as a Greek chorus in a modern tragedy. If we throw away a human life by our uncaring and deem it untouchable, he presents Christ as a man in *Louise*. There is a fundamental paradox in our lives that the artist understands and uses to express his values. Life and all the things that are necessary for its survival—among them love, companionship, feelings—are the expressions DeCarava acknowledges in his subjects. He often depicts couples, for example, as an embodiment of the dual nature of love and the intensification of life forces. DeCarava understands that life is also fraught with other kinds of duality, however. There are relationships he sees and chooses to photograph that may not seem as positive, but are, nonetheless, very real. Some of these images, like that of the face in *Ex-fighter*, are difficult to encounter. There are also other energies that go counter to positive life process, as in *Cab 173*, where a man in broad daylight becomes a creature of the dark. Such forces in DeCarava's pictures are both visible and invisible; they may manifest themselves as a psychological valent of terror or fear, as a social valent of abandonment or as an ambiguous human form. Yet there is no *nature morte* in the images. The pictures display a life-energy as both positive and negative elements coalesce and an interpenetration and exchange of such forces occurs on many levels. In the midst of these illusions, however, the photographs express not struggle but a sense of utter stillness.

Roy DeCarava began his career in art as a painter. His early childhood in New York City devoted to sidewalk chalk-art was followed by classes at Textile High School that opened up the possibilities of pursuing what he decided at the age of 9 would be his life's goal—to be an artist. Early in his career he consciously set high standards for his work, even to the point of tediously mixing all his colors from dry pigment, oil and varnish. This was more expensive than buying ready-made paint, but he insisted on doing such things though he could not afford the time or money. He had a self-described sense of mission, a strong sense of purpose.

His formal training began in 1938 at The Cooper Union, where he completed two years of studies and learned the fundamentals of painting. After leaving Cooper Union he went directly to the Harlem Arts Center, a WPA organization offering a range of art courses to Harlem-area residents. In 1944 he enrolled for a year in the George Washington Carver Art School in Harlem. It was here that he first met and studied with painter Charles White, whose attitude toward art was directly inspirational to him for its social responsiveness.

As a young painter working during the day as a commercial artist, DeCarava began to use a camera to make quick sketches for his paintings. He explored the medium gradually for several years before deciding, in 1947, to use photography rather than painting as his mode of artistic expression. "It was the directness of the medium that attracted me. Through the camera I was able to make contact with the world and express my feelings about it more immediately." Continuing the imagery of his paintings in the new medium, he knew precisely what he wanted to do in photography.

There is no sense of groping toward expression in his early photographs from the late 1940s, just as (with consistent experience in artwork from the time he was five years old) there was no searching for the purpose of his life once he had decided to become an artist. The work from his late teenage years into his twenties exhibits powers of emotional observation combined with succinctness of design; the limited technical training of his hand had been balanced by the tutoring of his eye. Through his high school courses, exposure to books and the work of other painters, he had begun the process of immersing himself in art history. That wider visual history, prominently including the work of Van Gogh and American John Sloan as well as the Mexican muralists David Siequeros, Rivera and Orozco, seems almost to have burst upon his consciousness at the age of seventeen, and defined a time when he was able to reach for a more sophisticated involvement with the drawing and painting he had done since childhood. Later, during the 1950s, every spare moment was devoted to his self-development as he turned to photography, although the demands of supporting a family while working and being active in the area of black arts left him little opportunity to engage the wider professional community.

Edward Steichen, then Director of photography at the Museum of Modern Art, became aware of DeCarava's work at this time through the efforts of Homer Page, a professional photographer who had helped DeCarava mount his first show at Mark Perper's 44th Street Gallery in 1951. Steichen encouraged him to apply for a Guggenheim Fellowship as a means of supporting himself while pursuing an intensive period of work and, in 1952, he became the ninth photographer to receive the award.

Some of the work produced during this period was published through the efforts of Langston Hughes, who co-authored with DeCarava in 1955 the slim volume *The Sweet Flypaper of Life*. The book received much critical acclaim, including awards for the best book of the year from both the *New York Times* and the *Herald Tribune*.

In 1958 DeCarava extended this personal work by entering the commercial art field as a freelance photographer. The jobs initially came sporadically, but in 1965 he was with *Sports Illustrated*, which cushioned his marginal livelihood. In 1975 he left the magazine in order to teach photography at Hunter College in New York City, where he is currently Distinguished Professor of Art.

To understand the sentience of DeCarava's photographs one can approach them through their shapes. Each picture seems as distinct as the human beings they often depict or the forms they decipher, yet they do form visual patterns. The subjects of many of these pictures compel their own order, for this work offers one of the most sensitive portrayals of contemporary urban life and culture. Clearly, this specific subject matter does not represent the totality of DeCarava's vision, yet it is an essential aspect of his oeuvre, and his life experience is fundamental to the production of his art.

DeCarava expresses his personal vision through structures of space that form a signature of his art. This characteristic of his work is clearly evident in his exploration and development of the idea of the scale of urban space in relation to people and the impact of perspective as visual play and social revelation. These organizing spatial principles marshal physical relationships which undergo transformations of form, substance and meaning that assume, through time, the shape of an intricate improvisatory music.

A wall is a construction made by human hands, with bricks arranged until their horizontal layering produces an imposing verticality. Its surfaces can suggest to an eye attuned to the unique tonal capabilities of black and white photography, seemingly infinite values of gray. A wall can be an enigmatic visual cipher, the urban monolith which paradoxically stands as a uniquely human achievement or a destructive mark upon the living environment, as it is difficult to separate the idea of a wall from its social imperatives. Each brick carries the weight of time, effort and human energy, expressing both the reality and the aesthetic of density, of intensity of labor and of the social processes of human connection and disassociation.

Walls that can only occur in cities, that seem to vault endlessly outward in all directions often suggest in DeCarava's work a metaphor for our social existence in this environment. Fundamental to their depiction is the concept of relative scale, presented as a multivalent relationship between people and the enveloping tonal expanse which provides complexities for those who can see them, an inherent richness of form and meaning.

It is hard to imagine a greater disparity than that presented in *Two boys, vacant lot*. The children appear inconsequential compared to the geometric wall that soars not only in two directions but three as its horizontal expanse rides a strong oblique dimension. Evenly toned printing controls the power of this receding plane and holds its incidental brick patterns in restraint. The vacant, rubble-strewn lot extends the wall forward and serves as a visually disordered counterbalance, yet transforms it. The entire picture, including the wall, becomes a vacant lot. Our sense of the desolation extends and deepens. Children play here: they have taken on the vocabulary of the environment and become abstract ciphers themselves.

There is sheer beauty in this desolation, however, in the subtle tonalities, the incidental flecked highlights of rubble swept ashore to the wall, in the wall itself breaking at the edge of the picture as geometric design gives way to an impressionist suggestion of sky. In the context of this beauty there is a communication, for here on the wall floats a "C," the ever present urban graffiti scrawl, underlined for emphasis yet still mysterious. In spite of their small size, the children dominate this landscape, and the wall, in its vertical ascension, replays their vital presence. It is the gesture of extension, depicted in the edge of light on an open, up-swung arm, that provokes the picture's assay of the power of spirit, though anguish evident in the child's face might venture elsewhere.

The relationship between people and walls is reformulated and given a different connotation in *Woman walking, above*. Here the wall becomes a sidewalk and street, upending our expectations by creating a sense of vertigo as its vertical dimension extends horizontally instead. The social meaning of the disparity in human scale is muted by the visual expression of the grace in human motion as the laws governing our perception of the "wall" are manifest as a cadence of discrete parts. However massive and intimidating the urban concrete expanse, the artist establishes the human value of this space; he constructs it as an expanse necessary for living, breathing, walking. While the street purports to define the appropriate spatial boundaries in this picture, it is the woman who generates tempo as her gait measures a distance that will repeat itself, suggesting a kinetic progression through the picture that infuses the image with another rhythm and transcends implied and limiting boundaries. Even though she walks away from us, we have a sense of her interiority, and thus she comes close as her pedestrian motion captures a more elusive emotional life. The surrounding expanse mirrors this quiet beauty. The street and sidewalk are an understated, neutral expanse upon which her dark, erect figure is a strong accent. Subtle tones flicker like lights along her pathway. Litter interrupts like accidentals on a sheet of music, while the tree branches hold notes the length of her hemline. An implied arc above echoes and frames her grace. The restrained reading of rhythm and space merge into a lilting, gently swinging, up-tempo vision, as her ability to cadence the environment into the nonmaterial realm of music materializes.

Within these shifting contexts for the imaginative dimensions of size and space, other meanings evolve. *Man on elevated* asks in subtle tonalities, how small a space can confine a man and his spirit, his humanity, so large by implication? With *Child in window, clothesline*, we see a small black child, jailed in the most immense of spaces, as "Anna Heil" recalls another Anne of history. It is daring to render such vast spatial contradictions, but the formal content is sobered by the prints' social connotations. This is a real man, a real child; and neither are elevated into icons beyond our grasp of their personal humanity. Although we are separated from one by great distance and our perception of the other is diminished by the imperviousness of an elevated train's design, one can feel the people intensely and personally. It is the beauty that impels us to come close in spite of the space: it is also some unspeakable element, perhaps fear, perhaps empathy. These walls are both jails and not jails; they confine and destroy, but they can also liberate by what they reveal. They provoke a serious engagement of the psyche, for we want to see but we don't. If such distinctions require a separation of spirit, it is possible that the integration of formal beauty and photographic reality is nuanced and finessed here to render such "otherness" blind. Assaying the great magnitude and the human dimension of these urban spaces, the photographs invite us instead to experience discrete sensibilities, and the images induce sight.

In other photographs there are grand tableaux of people and walls, definitive through their delineation of human endeavor: ancient walls, as in *117th Street*, against which are open to us the ebb and flow of communal activity, and they suggest a proscenium for the summation of an appreciation of life. There is in *Home for the aged, yard*, a wall that looks backward to *Two boys, vacant lot*, photographed fifteen years earlier. The recent picture carries a more sophisticated configuration of light that the experience of printing implied by the interim would suggest, and equally the symbolism of the vacant lot that was previously dominant finds even more palpable echoes here. This wall shelters birds and weeps at the human scene before it. Held in tonal restraint, it is nonetheless a wall of great emotion.

DeCarava's *tour de force* is perhaps the elucidation of such metaphors from dematerialized *Sun and shade*. The symbolic construction is a play upon three superimposed walls in the print: the sidewalk, the boundary between light and dark across which two children intensely interrelate and a wall of fusion that encompasses the expanse of sun and shade. The sidewalk gives physical substance to the other two and helps to define with its texture their aesthetic values. Light is an activating principle in this image, a delineator of action. It has the capacity, like the artist himself, of transforming reality, of creating its own shapely silhouette of one child and enlivening the figure's fluid dynamism. In this most ultimate of situations, where two children with toy guns are involved in a play that appears as a foil to the struggle of life and death, the obvious metaphor of stark contrast in black and white was avoided, for the darkness is not quite black but has its own rich range of tonalities. It also has an emotional equivalent: in its obscurity and its lack of readability is a feeling of the mysterious. We can penetrate the darkness, however; there is air in it, light and a child's life. These things of value draw us in; once inside, we experience the photographer's vision of the dark.

248

This shadow has an infinite space within it. If the sun side is a sidewalk, the shade side is the firmament with billions of stars and galaxies, with mysterious black holes and spreading clouds. If light is a formal, descriptive quality, crisp and linear, that provides a clarity of definition, then darkness is the intuitive process that delineates mystery in spatial indistinction.

There is complexity inherent in these concepts of light and dark. We are presented with diametrically opposed values of sun and shade that the artist renders as minimal tonal equivalents while preserving their peculiar aesthetic personalities. The shadow might have been printed totally black, or could have been opened up to render more clarity. In the face of these possibilities, the choice DeCarava made in the early 1960s can be appreciated as an evolving expression of his aesthetic that eschews easy formulations and achieves an elegant poise by negotiating the improvisation of a contentious balance.

I like the image very much because it is an excellent metaphor—light and shade, black and white, life and death. It took me a long time to print it properly—over ten years. I tried all sorts of things to make it work, to have this shadow dark and yet show the boy in the shadow; and to have the light part, the sunlit part, light with detail even though it was very bright. I didn't want to sacrifice one element for the other. I tried all sorts of things but nothing worked. One day I said, well, I'm just going to try to print it very soft and see what happens, and that's what really worked. I printed it on the softest paper I could find and pushed it as far as possible on the dark end, and it came out perfectly. [1]

This and the following passages quoted in italics are taken from an extended series of interviews with Roy DeCarava conducted by the author from 1969 to 1980.

It is the children who focus our interest in this print, who express the human drama and, with the ethics of their social interaction, are assured an important role. Yet, ten years of tonal modulation of the image is expressed through the richness of thought that contradiction implies:

Who cares about two kids in sun and shade? I showed them in the symbolic visual context of the struggle of their life. They're in conflict with where they are, with each other, with two sides of a question—one black, one white. Many of my pictures represent deliberate, calculated choices. They may seem outlandish but it is because I try to force things to work based upon my determination that they are right, true. I don't look for pat things, I look for what I know, for what I feel is positive. Everything in my work is purposeful, even the accidents.

The visualization of the harmonics between people and their environment is a poetic matrix in which DeCarava's human imagery is often rooted. The wall may function as a screen upon which the personal, often solitary figure projects larger than any given physical reality. While this construct engages a play of a wide range of formal qualities, its ultimate function is to evoke and provoke, to extend the act of seeing into a wider state of enlightenment.

I guess you might say that Louise *is about art and nature. It's about architecture and empty benches and derelict chairs. And a man asleep in the face of art and nature. And it's about graffiti. And it's about the presence of unseen things and seen things in terms of the artwork on the architecture. It's a strange combination of forms. The tree, if it did not have the trunk embedded in the reality of the grass and the sidewalk, could be part of the image painted on the wall. The juxtaposition of a live human figure and the painted figure of the dead Christ is no coincidence. The little black windows function as a counterpoint to other things, like the doorway where the bereaved figures cluster and the shape of the man lying down. It's similar to* Two men leaning on posts *except that in this case one is an image and the other is real. Then the word* love . . .

DeCarava explores other means of evoking content from the presence of human figures in urban spaces, particularly through his treatment of perspective. Searching ways of engaging literal perspective in order to see with more complexity and more deeply in the confines of the frame, DeCarava's images often and simply use this given of environmental design as a way of getting one down a street; yet it is rarely a place of departure connected to a destination. Rather, it begins nowhere in particular and ends nowhere at all, and in so doing it sets up a space for flow. It extends the two dimensional nature of the wall and becomes more than an important spatial armature; for it subsumes the role of a grand trope, with its disappearing and expanding focus implying a figurative order of experience. There is a breadth of vision in many of these pictures, a grasp of the intricate and dynamic relations of life as they are braced and focused through its amplification of time and space.

It is of no small significance that images of New York City streets in 1952, such as *Stickball*, present clear testimony that the city streets were not only clean, with few potholes, but they were also inviting. Yet the picture obliquely reminds us that no safer place of play exists for these children of the city. The cars are parked at the curb while people move about and children assume places in the foreground. Further in the distance, people cluster to the sidewalk perimeters, and cars command a place in the street. For the moment of this picture, however, the children can play stickball. The square bases are drawn in chalk around the manholes, the game pauses momentarily to let a truck and car pass. A boy on the left, a strange expressive figure, walks alone, the entire stretch of block his own. Shade hides others as it extends from the building on the right. A child strides across the distant, sunlit intersection, dominating its space. These people are insignificant in the vast scale defined by the city's grid network. They are also so vital and expressive they can each project their unique individuality across even this great expanse. Their life-force dominates just as the small child draws us to and makes meaning out of a distant intersection. As though to underscore the point, the camera's exposure occurs at a moment when all trucks and cars appear not only stopped, but utterly motionless. Is it that the vehicles know, too, and express their deference, or are they just being, for the moment, less threatening?

This clear, spacious and stately street, this place for flow is defined in great detail and breadth. The building facade is a dense buttress of harsh forms, flanking the receding and emerging line of perspective and providing rich visual contrast to it. These elements form an insistent cacophony, cushioned by the trees framing the picture's foreground and held at bay by sheets of sunlight. The fluid motion in these inhospitable public spaces reveals a personal time in which individuals closer than possible bring to us both their solitude and their communal longing.

DeCarava uses perspective in simple settings as well: in *Catsup bottles, table and coat*, he presents an interior scene of the ordinary as both objects and as a moment of experience. A reviewer, writing of the beauty and perfection of this photograph, once exclaimed how artfully the scene had been arranged; but it was not arranged, like all of DeCarava's pictures, it was photographed as found, for discovery is one of the signal, compelling aspects of his creative work.

The metaphoric levels in this image suggest a rich setting in the midst of its empty plates. The photograph presents the paraphernalia and the time of taking dinner. Neither the items on the table nor, we imagine, the restaurant is fancy; the coat is timeworn. Yet light, shadow and darkness envelope these common objects and project the human life they represent with a quiet luminosity. Empty of material value yet full of spiritual value, the scene is an altar place of beauty, humanity and loneliness. There are numbers here, two catsup bottles and one coat. People who are alone, and often eat alone, live the meaning of such numbers.

There is a sense of quiet and ironic humor in viewing a table where the meal has already been completed and where we were not invited to eat. There is also a pun, serious but perhaps unintentional, on the bountiful table scenes of romantic still-life paintings, rendered here in its modern manifestation as an almost bare table stacked with used dishes. Yet none of these ideas approaches the heart of the image. The picture really exists as an invitation; the receding and converging perspective lines of the table's edge quietly marshal us toward the back, where we are invited to enter into darkness.

The photographer expresses himself through this mystery and seeks to resolve the natural unease people experience with darkness, with the unknown. For

DeCarava this space is nor fearsome, it is a lively obscurity, penetrated by an element of light and an implied sense of order and reason. It also connects us to vital life processes that depend upon intuitive, intense feeling, for when one experiences darkness, one experiences an intense awareness of self. Thus, *Catsup bottles* presents two portraits, although both subjects, not being physically present, are only implied. The woman at the table and the viewer in the darkness are close to one another. There is a circuit of shared intimacy in this picture that is carried by the diminished light; perspective creates an entranceway through the corridors of which we imperceptibly slip into the coordinates of a space greater than the physical, a space of intimate confines.

My concern is always in how I use the light, process my highlights, modulate my grays. The emphasis is really not on the black tones. Most of my images that seem black are not black at all, they are a very dark gray. I only use black when there is a black object, when it's solid, when it's a black wall. But space is not black unless there is no light, and since there is always a little bit of light, such space is always dark gray.

Light has its own particular qualities. Sometimes it can be declarative, as in *Graduation*. Other times it leaves trackings that are purely mysterious, as in *Embroidered blouse*. But in *Catsup bottles* it is a soft, tender reminder of the edge of things. It renders visible the substance of a woman in the folds of her worn coat. Light is a cloth upon the table for our eyes to experience. The feast here, whether apparent or in the dark, is the manifestation of translucent light.

I often use a commonplace object as a symbol. I find it incongruous that a coat hanger should play such an important part in an image [Coat hanger, 1963], but it does. It defines the quality of the image, the maximum light of the image, because everything is dark. In a way it defines the content and importance of the photograph because it's part of a human's belongings. It's a coat hanger and what does it do? It hangs coats and coats hang on people. While there are other things in the image that suggest human activity, it is the coat hanger that has a personal, individual quality to it. It is true that it has probably seen many coats in its day, but it is still more unique, more personal than anything else because of the strength of its light and because of its position in the rectangle. This is a picture about nothing; an empty store, a restaurant—not even that. It's a lunch counter with tables! There is this elegant light on this plebeian coat hanger. It's just gorgeous. The blackness in this photograph has to be modulated and printed in such a way that it is not a flat wall but becomes space that you can go into and emerge out of; not a black mass but a black opening. The key lights hold the print in a physical way, they hold the black by defining the print so that you can go dark. If they weren't there, it would be a dark pit, a dark print. This same effect occurs in most of my work. In Coltrane and Elvin the highlights on the horn define the parameter of the print. As long as I maintain them it is possible to do almost anything in the image. They give the print a sense of reality, and by defining the reality of it they keep it on anchor so it doesn't go away or sink.

There are a lot of things in my pictures that have deep meaning, not just in the intent, but in their coming into being, their making. But before they can be made you have to understand what is being made. It's almost like you are redefining a situation, saying that this is more than what it is. It's not a lunch counter with a coat hanger; it's more than that.

DeCarava's ability to convincingly marshal pictorial space to the visual requirements of his emotional poetry gives architectural rigor to the images and also serves as armature for a nonspecified field of meaning. It evolves in his work as a way of addressing the creative demands that are his own and that photography especially imposes in the process of locating artistic authenticity. In *Subway stairs, two men*, a play on perspective strategically displayed in bilateral symmetry brings many meanings forward.

I was conscious of everything, the banisters, the ceiling lines, these two figures on either side; and then, the man at the telephone, standing there like a period at the end of a sentence.

Descent along this staircase is impelled by the logic of our position, carried by the arms of the downward flow of perspective. Logic itself is not enough, however, to beckon the viewer to enter the picture as we are further enticed with glimmering pieces of paper scattered near the two columnar figures who stand like Greek statuary, marking the entrance to their underworld. In these lower depths, two men, one black, one white, are intensely unaware of each other. A third half-figure stands before a tool of communication that gleams incongruously. The intersecting, multiple perspective lines emphasize the isolation of the figures who have come here by coincidence on their way to somewhere else. They appear by their stances to be willfully unaware of each other; yet their studied avoidance only serves to emphasize the relationship to which they seem averse.

The central portion of this image contains only empty floor space. It has no content beyond its function as a visual void, a vacancy, and becomes a place for the mind and eye to wander, to contemplate a quiet and extraordinary pathos in the midst of a commonplace scene in the New York subway system.

The tone and tempo of *Dancers* suggests a totally different sense of perspective. Rather than no action, there is jazz dance action. The dramatic presentation of social events in this great funnel-like space is both visceral and elegantly distilled.

This photograph was taken at a dance of a social club at the 110th St. Manor at Fifth Avenue. It is about the intermission where they had entertainment, and the entertainment was two dancers who danced to jazz music. That's what this image is all about; it's about these two dancers who represent a terrible torment for me in that I feel a great ambiguity about the image because of them. It's because they are in some ways distorted characters. What they actually are is two black male dancers who dance in the manner of an older generation of black vaudeville performers. The problem comes because their figures remind me so much of the real life experience of blacks in their need to put themselves in an awkward position before the man, for the man; to demean themselves in order to survive, to get along. In a way these figures seem to epitomize that reality. And yet there is something in the figures not about that; something in the figures that is very creative, that is very real and very black in the finest sense of the word.

So there is this duality, this ambiguity in the photograph that I find very hard to live with. I always have to make a decision in a case like this—is it good or is it bad? I have to say that even though it jars some of my sensibilities and it reminds me of things that I would rather not be reminded of, it is still a good picture. In fact, it is good just because of those things and in spite of those things.

The figures bespeak a sophistication and a hipness. They have a quality of life that's free, that's abundant; that dares to mock itself and that dares to be "whatever they am and don't give a damn." There's that quality to it, a rebellion against what they should be and an acceptance of what they are and what they want to be. Whether HE likes it or not, whether he thinks it's for him—when it's really not for him at all, it's for US. So there's that quality too, which ameliorates the other aspect of it, which is really within me as much as it is within them, the dancers. There's a personal involvement with what's going on here in an entirely different way than there is in other pictures. Here there's a resistance on my part, but it's all to the good because it's about feeling, what you know, what you want and don't want.

The importance of the occasion expands even further this duality of the performers, for there are not only dancers present, there is also an audience that confers upon the dancers their right to be there: a waiter who walks his own specialized protocol and pursues a responsibility that he has; and the photographer who has done what he must. They validate each other and create a consensus. A ritual is taking place, a communion, as they participate in the social process of culture and partake in the spirit of community.

DeCarava sees people in other ceremonies that protect and nourish, yet perplexing insights can arise from the interpenetration of the visual and social contexts. Ritualized behavior reflects the performance of tasks undertaken in the service of societal or group goals and finds expression in images such as *7th Avenue Express*, where the construct of perspective spatially interprets the singular, endless direction of such activity. The goal and circumstances of the picture are so ordinary that one might momentarily question their existence. This is the time of going to work and getting home: the ritual of sitting, holding one's own hands, wearing the felt fedora and the black wool coat. In this glimpse of white-collar life, however, the ritual is not unduly emphasized, but is a background against which we sense the personal expression of each man. It serves as a framework through which DeCarava elicits a quality of life from certain moments socially constructed to be devoid of expressly human individuality. There is a tender poignant feeling to these men; a sense of their solitude even in their uniformity. Then there is the common, ordinary inconsequence of the moment, of whether or not to disturb your neighbor with a comment or a remembrance, which could humanize the question of why people agree to barter their personal identities. The formality of the perspective heightens the perception of personal time in the subway train by constraining the rhythm and repetition of the men through space while leaving open the larger question of human destination.

The strong design of many of DeCarava's pictures serves as a foil for the observations and their understated, quiet expression; and this dichotomy is essential to the poetry of his social landscapes. Pictures of great intensity and proportion can result when these concepts are layered, as in *Gittel*, creating a montage effect that provides a dense visual and philosophical field. On the left side, closely packed signs, textures and odds and ends of the real world project a coherent, if tension-filled, flat surface. On the other side illusions of light, reflections in a store window, have a dreamy, delicate effect and produce a sense of endless depth and time.

These two aspects of the montage—one hard-edged, insistent and communicative in its reality, the other impressionistic and ambiguous in meaning—are more tangibly concrete than the content of the image itself.

The meaning of *Gittel* is not expressed so much by the perspective or scale, although echoes of both are present. The woman—a motionless apparition—and the mirrored window reflections serve as focal points, creating a dual time zone, while the figure of the child, moving *contra obligato*, along the corridors of perspective, suggests contradiction. Through them a tension and balance evolves that intimates many meanings. This is one of the earliest of images to present the subject as a mysterious metaphor, expressing a complex psychological reality in a moment of stillness. As these spatial visualizations compound they create a dense visual and interpretive matrix while their surface holds a sense of stillness that resonates like an audible tone. A simply constructed image such as *Hallway* presents a set of interactions between illusion and reality that evoke a similar visual-auditory nexus.

If ever I wanted to be marooned with one photograph, I think I would want to be marooned with Hallway *simply because it was one of my first photographs to break through a kind of literalness. It didn't break through, actually, because the literalness is still there, but I found something else that is very strong, and I linked it up with a certain psychological aspect of my own. It's something that I experienced and is, in a way, personal, autobiographical. It's about a hallway that I know I must have experienced as a child. Not just one hallway; it was all the hallways that I grew up in. They were poor, poor tenements, badly lit, narrow and confining; hallways that had something to do with the economics of building for poor people. When I saw this particular hallway I went home on the subway and got my camera and my tripod, which I rarely use. The ambiance, the light in this hallway was so personal, so individual that any other kind of light would not have worked. It just brought back all those things that I had experienced as a child in these hallways. It was frightening, it was scary, it was spooky, as we would say when we were kids. And it was depressing. And yet, here I am an adult, years and years and ages and ages later, looking at the same hallway and finding it beautiful.*

I can never understand that. I mean, here was something that was ugly and brutalizing, and it turns into a beautiful photograph. Maybe it's because it is the past. It's behind me and I can see things in it that have nothing to do with my personal well-being. I can look at the textures of it and the light of it and the space of it and think of it in a larger sense. I still would not like to live in a hallway like that, but the important thing is what it evokes in me in terms of my past and my present. I can now see things of beauty within the body of its ugliness. For those reasons this photograph is a very powerful image. Both because of and in spite of its contradictions, its origins and what they mean, it is still a beautiful image. It's part of the seduction that's involved in art, I think, when you start with reality and make something else of it. The least you can do is to make something three-dimensional into something two-dimensional, but hopefully you go much beyond that. You can profit from a negative and make a positive. As beautiful as the photograph is, the subject is not beautiful in the sense of living in it. But its beauty is in being alive—strange that I should use that word living! But it is alive.

As light transforms this structure, a strange ambiance pervades the picture. *Hallway* projects a state of being that is not supported by its objective reality; the walls seem to swoon and there is perhaps a feeling of malaise. It has a dream-like quality, provoking sensations that are at once physical and visceral, with a sense of floating, a loss of physicality. Opposed to this is the relentless progression of perspective into a somber, darkened portal towards a rear light that gives off no light. This is an image, like many others, that was not found but recalled. It recalls the footsteps of a human presence to this darkened hallway as it breathes on the bare edge of the real.

While interior landscapes of the mind were explored throughout the 1950s, DeCarava's vision often returned to the outside, as well, where his photographs sought to contend with the larger and more labyrinthine aspects of the emergent modern and urban environment. During this period he continued the search for a way to express both the complexity and simplicity of city life opening new perceptions and discoveries for himself. He developed a mode of kaleidoscopic vision much more dynamic in its spatial configuration than his earlier studies and built upon oblique, intersecting lines and angular forms that charge intangibles such as air and atmosphere with meaning. This concept accomplishes more than a convincing formulation of reality; it often develops into a dramatic organization of space during the 1960s that can carry sharp and pointed undertones of danger, as in *Between cars* or *Four arrows and towel*, while it explores the aesthetic qualities that come from the variable geometric faceting of light. Within the translucent pattern that results, meaning flickers across the surface of these prints as wedges of light bring imagery in and out of focus. Kaleidoscopic vision does not essentially present a relationship of human scale to the environment, as do the images that reflect modes of wall and perspective, but it serves as a reconstructed, variable, multiple lens, a formal metaphor of vision which can directly explore psychological relationships. It often articulates the sense of the fragmentation of modern life, a disruption of the flow of time and space: yet these tangible physical aspects give way before the imprecise, interior interpretation of that experience.

The density of content that emerges in these photographs is often conveyed through metaphor, as in *Graduation*, a quiet image of a young lady depicted in a moment that represents a culminating *rite de passage*, her high school graduation. She is prepared for the day. Her carefully adorned body expresses the fulfillment of her obligations, the tutoring of her mind and heart, for she is an integrated whole, and is presented as beauty itself.

Juxtaposed to her figure is her environment. All around is desolation—a vacant lot, a street whose mysteries are garbage and decay and news of war in South Korea. She seems unaware, except for a slight turn of her head toward the lot, that she also participates in another *rite de passage*, one with symbolic overtones that are vast, provocative and personal. We don't believe she'll ever be touched by the encroaching shadows, though her forward movement is inevitable. The lot threatens her, the slices of shadow cut across her path and dare her as images on the wall vainly chorus her tragedy. Still, we perceive her as not moving.

She stands as a sentinel for all our hopes; for purity, for innocence, for positive life value. In this sense she is a classic figure, not only in the purely visual terms that define her drapery and her quintessentially feminine stance, but in philosophical terms as well. Yet we wonder what the future of this young woman will be. An artistic *tour de force* is forged out of these disparate and oppositional elements; our belief in her survival is mandated by our perception of her beauty and *vice versa*.

In the midst of this suggestive imagery a singular black hole absurdly sits in the center of the composition. The object itself, the artist tells us, is an overturned bus stop sign—a fallen soldier, a victim of urban chaos. It is also a void that emanates signals as a conscious controlled form in a context of disorder. *Graduation* has changed from reality to metaphor to metaphysics.

During the late 1950s DeCarava first began to photograph music and musicians, particularly jazz. Over the years this involvement led to hundreds of pictures of artistic and historical importance. He initially worked at festivals and late-night clubs in New York, and later in other cities as well, photographing musicians of this time. A key photograph from the period [*Haynes, Jones and Benjamin*] fuses his kaleidoscopic vision to the discourse of jazz, creating an image that pulsates with the interplay of shape, light, plane and movement; with sound and sense.

Embodying rhythm and grace, this picture presents jazz as the classical American music. Jazz exists as a moment to moment expressive interchange between musical voices, not unlike the play of individual pictorial voices of light, shape, shadow and plane in the print. Rhythm, echoing its ancestral African drums, distills a taut but multilayered polysyllabic aesthetic. The composition of *Haynes, Jones and Benjamin* has a vital, architectonic feel in the upbeat tempo, the heel lifted from the floor and the slight tilt to the stage. From floor to ceiling the formalities swing. The intense density of *Graduation* here becomes open, crystalline space modulated by a delicate range of tonal values across which the viewer's eyes are free to peruse and explore. The figures, with their succinct, dynamic shapes, staccato like quarter notes across these tonal reflections of space. This could only be a photographic image and it could only be about jazz.

It is also not about jazz. With a subtle but important shift of emphasis it is about workers, albeit the musician as worker. While musicians physically carry their instruments on stage and street, they carry the music mentally as well, and although the labor involved is a labor of love, their attitudes necessarily reflect discipline, tautness and control. The two converging figures, Roy Haynes and Jimmy Jones, talk business; Joe Benjamin coolly carries his bass in a barely struggling, easy ballet-like step of balance. Indeed, *Haynes, Jones and Benjamin* is not about physicality as much as it is about the personal aesthetics of dignity in the work of improvisatory movement, a thematic defined as dance whose development can be traced through *Graduation; Woman walking, above, Dancers, 117th Street* and *Stickball* among others. This sense of dignity in human vitality is expressed through space, flow through time and confluence through improvisation. The picture moves with these daily rhythms of a working life until its patterns crystallize this timeless music to locate its temporal qualities in individual creativity.

There are muted elements of contrast in these images between the figures and their surrounding space that reiterate the importance of contradiction and opposition as pictorial elements in DeCarava's work. Other photographs, however, depend on the aesthetic impact of contradiction as an organizing principle such that other visual aspects become secondary to it. This visual disparity is found in a richly diverse group of pictures including *Window and stove*, *Man leaning on post, truck* and *Subway ceiling*. The earliest of these, *Window*, contrasts the physicality of an old stove and its pots with the translucent montage of an adjoining window, rendering the polarities of existence and feeling in seen forms that reach their synthesis in an unseen person. *Out of order* presents an organization of the wildly disparate, with pictorial and literary iconography explicitly stating contradictions and implicitly expressing a society's attitudes toward its female population.

Two women, manikin's hand, on the other hand, implies psychological disparity without stating it. In this picture DeCarava establishes a vehicle for the projection of his own psyche as it mingles with reality, and in the process he transgresses a surreal American landscape. Two passersby stand before a display window, each one isolated and different. In the center the white hand of a manikin seems to reach out toward them, threatening ominously from the draped shadows of this barricaded window. The artist has called it "the ghost hand," and as an archetypal element it appears under different guises in a number of pictures, such as *Broken railing*, *Force* and *Boy in print shirt*. There is an hypnotic silence created in *Two women* as our attention swings between the women and the hand. An absurd padlock sits in the sun and marks time. The woman on the left is defined by her scarf, beautiful in the congruence of its texture and tone, volume and design. Her face reflects a condensation and concentration of form suggesting an interior state of being. The hard, linear, savvy face of the other woman balances the bare edge of beauty's visage. Their identities slip imperceptibly back and forth from anonymous pedestrians to priestesses of beauty and wisdom.

Many other things contribute to the singular impact of this photograph. Made in 1950, it is one of DeCarava's first close, personal views of people on the street. Being close and having that physical proximity express more than just distance cannot be taken for granted in photography, either in its mechanics or in the photographer's development of a requisite attitude. One first has to consciously choose this engagement, then devise ways of doing so unobtrusively. It is a perplexing question about the psychological order of space that DeCarava represents in *Two women*. An intensely communicative image, powerfully rooted in but removed from its immediate subject, we search for some explanation that will bring us from its representation of a precipice of fear to a more rational world. In one moment it all could have changed, for these women had merely stopped to admire clothes in a store window. Yet by feeling the shifts and discontinuities of time and pictorial space, the photographer locates a moment where everything is happening while nothing appears to happen.

The complexity of human response to danger is the subject of this picture, danger in the streets, in our lives: imaginary or real dangers that spill out from places as we pass. Yet there is an unknown element: Is the ghost hand seeking to cauterize a victim or is it trying vainly to touch, to feel? That the image portrays a social dichotomy between black and white reflects some objective reality. The visual statement here is hardly polemical; indeed, it is richly ambiguous.

What is difficult in this picture is not objective reality, then, but its psychic projections; for the violence is not finite, it only threatens. The perverse truth is that were the extended hand directly threatening, we might more readily accept it. Such acts accomplish an end, and there is no enduring reminder of the event as bodies disappear. The act depicted here, however, has no end; its terror is infinite, always hovering, waiting. There is an insanity here, a reality that Kafka knew was inexorably linked with the struggle for compassion. Light strokes an eyelid; harsh, glinty light makes metallic curls shine; *Two women* presents a dialectic of the sensuous and the surreal.

One always returns to the closeness of these photographs, to how deeply they sense and elicit a subtle understanding from the interior nature of the subject. Perhaps this is why the personal studies and portrayals most directly express the artist's perceptions of human life, uncovering what is deeply important to the artist, the viewer and the individual depicted. There is no intervening formal device here, no single visual conception that arranges the picture. It has all been reduced to a minimum in order to address the question of proximity through the window of shared senses and convictions. Although the physical distance varies, the achievement of intimacy extracts poetic visual terms from the artist's own attunement. This is a difficult proposition whose heritage reaches back to shamanic traditions that unmask fear, courage and beauty in the healing task of artistic performance.

There are discoveries in these images. The photographic presence of the subjects and the heightened sense of their physical surface seems to diffuse outward, carrying an intangible, eternal presence. They are recalled images that, like *Hallway*, imply a dream-like state. The images seem to wait as we slip into their presence, outside of time. We discover the eyes of a haunted house in *Ex-fighter* and ethereal unions in *Milt Jackson*, yet we sense parallel movement in their differing prologues and ends.

There is a dance ritual in Haynes, Jones and Benjamin. *It is a dance of being, a dance of leaving, a dance of beginning and of playing. It is a movement that is not about walking but about movement.* Milt Jackson *moves from that ritual to religion, because if ever there was a moment of religiosity, this is the moment that I felt. There was an out-of-this-world concentration of the musician, and there was a sense of reverence in his posture, in his attention and his concentration, just in the way he held himself—the thrust of his neck, the hands almost clasped in prayer. That's why I like this image: there's nobility about his standing. In a way it reminds me of* Woman in sandals *and* Tombstones and trees. *There's that straightness about it, that uprightness, that rooted quality; it has a regal quality.*

There is something joyous about people being totally committed to what they're doing. It's part of the excitement in seeing musicians work. You can almost see them play; not hear them, but see them play. They are so totally committed, so involved and so with the sound that even if you don't understand the particular music, it is still a joy to behold.

This is what I found attractive, and it applies to anything that people do. It is a healthy, a human and a very beautiful capacity. I think everything in the picture works toward that. The out of focus figures, even my little dots come across; everything down to his beautiful striped suit, which is ever so subtle and ever so beautiful. The image speaks of a true religion, if you will. It is religion of commitment, the religion of work and the religion of selflessness; of giving oneself to what one does completely.

This photograph of a famous music figure portrays him in a moment of anonymity. There are portraits of other anonymous people here that do not portray them in a conventional sense. A portrait of a man need not be of his face; in the worker's hands of *Man with two shovels* we find an image that recalls Van Gogh's *Potato-eaters*. Similarly, the car in *White car and dots* is the object of a close, personal encounter and expresses many mysteries. In *Cab 173* a hand has its own dangerous persona in the darkened dominion of a numbered cab. Shadow and architecture in *Apartment for rent* assume a human aura as they talk to each other. The central figure in *Man with clasped hands* is flanked in his portrait by anonymous pedestrians who pursue their unrelated lives, yet the younger man is necessary to the older and something in the young woman is attendant like an angel. In *David* a small child stands in the streets of a slum with the name of a biblical warrior and a face of African aesthetic perfection, veiled in the expression of another time. A set of photographs—*Night feeding* and *Sherry and Susan* —elucidates the responsibility of life.

These studies are wide-ranging in their content and vision, yet they share a mastery of visual essences that allows the physical substance of one's work to exist simultaneously with spiritual aura. In *Elvin Jones*, an image of the jazz drummer, such formal qualities achieve a finely tempered expression. There is almost no light illuminating the subject, yet we have a picture that explains a man. The things of his mind, what he has thought and where he has been, are visible on his face. There is an ambiguity in his face, an intense inwardness, a feeling pain, anger, even meanness; yet it is not offensive, but beautiful. Jazz musicians express great intensity, and as sweat delineates the movement of Jones' face, it glistens like thorns. Flesh is dematerialized before our eyes by more than light, by more than what we can just see. The moment becomes the beatitude of a man.

Photographs where a fully developed montage structures the image and emerges as the subject itself appear at first to contradict the direct visual expression of these personal studies. Instead of presenting singular subjects, the reflected light in pictures such as *Hotel* and *Couples* creates multiple images and layers of illusory depth. In *Pepsi*, a densely packed, tension-filled surface projects from the closely packed juxtaposition of chaotic form and texture visually interprets the numbing brutality of urban blue-collar work. The meaning of montages such as *Hotel*, on the other hand, comes from their expression of implied mystery.

I don't know what I'm photographing except that I know I'm photographing a duplicity of the image, one which is real and one which is the reflection.

Each mystery evokes a meaning which in its turn evokes the unknown. In *Couples*, images float through the amorphous, dream-like space while a walking couple ambiguously interprets the expression of another relationship. The finite forms and the infinite nature of feelings, the definitions of line and the gradations of tones, the terminal of surface and the endless reflected space, intermingle in an expression of loss and love.

DeCarava's exploration of multiple levels of content led in the 1960s to his development of a mode that fused his perspective and close personal studies, creating a succinct poetic form. These pictures would seem to instruct us to see in two ways, to see in and out of focus simultaneously. Such vision enables the bridging of spatial and temporal zones that separate figures; it requires that we make connections to unify and synthesize distinct imagery, bringing everything close. The closeness depends sometimes on our grasp of religious themes within a context of other meanings, as in *Subway station, Canal Street,* where the human relationships depicted mingle associations of western spiritual imagery with psychological projections of the artist. In other prints, such as *Coltrane and Elvin,* we observe a relationship already in existence which is nevertheless open to a wide range of interpretation.

In these images, the recognizable presence of one of the two figures is reduced by blurred focus. This figure assumes the nature of a sign as its tangible physical body diffuses into a imprecision of being. In its very ambiguity and its proximity to the other clearly depicted person, the unfocused figure serves as visible evidence suggesting the existence of something implied in the photograph but not seen—the intimate and mysterious nature of a human relationship. Through their bivalent mode these photographs represent an enduring sign of human relatedness.

The aspect of diminished physicality reaches its zenith when images are radically cropped, and reduced to near abstract forms. Emphasizing bold quality of design and rhythmic harmony, the resulting pictures—*Force, Woman in sandals, Bill and son* and *This site,* for example—achieve a strength of beauty and meaning that carry within their signs an emblematic quality. Extreme cropping also isolates the subject from its original context and often makes recognition difficult. It disrupts our normal visual vocabulary and compels us to see things in unconventional ways. Images such as *Force* are dazzling in design, puzzling and provocative in form and content.

I wanted to express something that always seems to happen to people, black people in this particular case. They are removing this woman from a demonstration, and it is a display of force. Force is short for force and violence. I wanted people to look at this as an abstraction, then to discover what it was. This image is just a very small part of a negative. No matter how abstract it is, it's still what it is and you really can't escape it. It could have been made very dramatic, very forceful with all the gory details, but I don't think that's necessary. There are areas in which force manifests itself in pervasive ways and in quiet ways. Force, violence isn't always spectacular and monumental and epic. Sometimes it is very quiet and insidious, almost imperceptible. In a way that's the approach I took in this photograph. It's the force of running water wearing down the rock as opposed to a volcanic force.

I think the action of water wearing the rock is stronger and more pervasive than the volcano. The trouble when this kind of force is applied to people is that the people don't know that the water is running, that the force is being used against them. They just know that things aren't right, but they don't know why. If it was volcanic, they could understand what it was and could defend themselves because they would know what to expect, where it was coming from. The kind of force I have depicted, on the other hand, is very subtle, but it works both ways. The same kind can be applied by either side; the force of the resistance. There is also another aspect to it—force as the desire and will by the majority of people in the world to reach sunlight. A drive for life, for fulfillment, is also force. It is stronger than those being used against these people, except that the forces being used against them are concerted and conscious, whereas the will to life is still in its unconscious, intuitive stages.

In DeCarava's early work, the movement of singular figures through the environment captured the essence of human vitality in its many guises—a girl walking, musicians struggling, pedestrians in dance-like motion. There is a sense of flow in these images, as well as stasis, periodically stopping the visual narrative or impeding its progress to emphasize an internal pulsation of figures who command our attention. Rhythm and flow emerge as distinct spatial engines in the developing dialogue between movement and stillness in DeCarava's work. As a repeating moment *versus* many moments in fleeting transition, rhythm and flow have potentially conflicting roles. Yet DeCarava exploits them equally to transform physical substance into the shape of motion and time. In the 1960s, rhythmic vision emerged as a major means of pictorial construction. *Three men with hand trucks* emphasizes the specialized steps developed by garment workers to pull their loads against a tonally flat background. Such work breaks men's faces, bends and twists human bodies; the dimensions of the photograph rest in balance between this reality and its tonal dance.

Bent heads also generate rhythmic impulses in *Four men*, as a group of strong, steady, centered individuals contemplates something known and something seen. Rich, sumptuous skin tonalities resonate with these impulses; the inner direction of the men emerges outward as the crown of a head is bowed. Eleven years later, in *Asphalt workers*, figures again emit rhythmic signals in a picture about many kinds of work. The heroic central figure carries the composition in the lift of his shovel. Surging downward and upward simultaneously across a range of tonal patterns, the dynamic power of his stance contributes to the impact of this statement about the labor of black men. The figure becomes a pivotal image through which the photograph achieves a state of suspended motion and time.

My pictures are immediate, and yet at the same time, they're forever. They present a moment so profoundly a moment that it becomes an eternity. It's almost like physics; there's an arc of being. There's a beginning, then the peak is reached and then there's the end. It's like the pole vaulter who begins his run, shoots up, then comes down. At the peak there is no movement. He's neither going up nor going down. It is that moment I wait for, when he comes into an equilibrium with all the other life forces—gravity, wind, motion, obstacles. Pushing up, he's stronger; coming down, he's weaker. The moment when all the forces fuse, when all is in equilibrium, that's the eternal . . . and that's jazz . . . and that's life. That's when I believe life reaches its zenith, when the artist can anticipate that, can feel that, can absorb and use it. This applies not only to motion but to all things before the camera. For example, an expression can be in transit, and there are points when that expression is meaningless because it's so transitory. But, there are moments when that expression reaches a zenith, when it is so real it becomes universal, it finds its stillness. If you don't capture it at that moment, all you get is a transitory particular. When you find it at the right moment, it is not only particular, it is universal. The only way to do this is to be in tune, to have the same sense of time that the subject has. This means you have to give yourself to the subject, accept their sense of time.

In recent years the concepts of rhythm and flow have changed in DeCarava's photographs. Rhythm has become muted and flow has shifted from element to subject. Along with this change came a redefinition and a reappraisal of its character. Flow has become anything of this world that moves—people, objects, even intangibles of the real world like light and atmosphere—anything with the energy to issue forth in all directions at once as in *Fourth of July, Prospect Park*. It is the people who flow up and down, back and forth with light and shadow in *Public school entrance*. It is both the material and the immaterial that flow on a street in *Regal*. In these photographs the confinement of perspective is circumvented, and life is expressed in a manner consonant with space and time.

In this newest work DeCarava has reshaped one of the basic formal principles that organizes his vision and the world he photographs. Although still classically composed, people no longer struggle against space but are held in it, embracing the dual processes of vitality that carry all moments. This concept is not unknown in black culture; Langston Hughes suggested something of it in his poem *The Negro Speaks of Rivers*. It is a philosophy that implies self-confidence in the openness and willingness to accept life in all its manifold forms and occurrences. It carries pictorial and philosophical complexity in the flow. There is a loss of individuality implied, the muting of individuality in a consideration of the consonance of things. We wonder, however, on seeing *Fourth of July*, what will become of the little boy, the one who holds the transparent plastic tube. Telescoping this question back through the many images in DeCarava's *oeuvre*, we find it implied, in one form or another, in almost every picture. Concern and respect for the individual human life is central to this work.

DeCarava expresses the relationship of people to a totality of experience through his moment of ordering environmental space. Utilizing known and invented designs to order a changing and variable world, he creates an image that couples his artistic intent with the immediate photographic given and creates a space that reveals through radiant structure. His pictures achieve a sense of the now and forever, a tangible reality and the sign of many realities. Lacking the palette he had used as a young painter, he created, through such visual constructs as montage and wall, canvases upon which to render comparable expression.

When Roy DeCarava photographs people, he encodes his knowledge, his love, his understanding. In the face of stereotypic images about black people, he has sought to depict them as they really are. He understands their capacity for compassion, for strength and for the positive values of life in the context of a long and difficult history, for his intelligence has been nurtured in these communities. While the photographs penetrate the values and ethos of American culture, however, the meaning of the work does not fundamentally rest with its portrayal of a particular community. Rather, DeCarava offers thought-provoking images that radiate the nature and potential of human sensibility, a personal responsibility to formulate human life through the context of the visual and the social imagination.

These images are intended to bring us close. Through sensuous texture and resonant tone, with a sense of stillness, quietness and waiting, they focus upon one loved, upon the possibility of love, even when it is not returned or is not yet acknowledged by another. The visual expression begins with a love of light and structure and depends upon a creative conduit between his intimacy with the pictorial process and the social world. These spheres are mediators and transporters of comprehension as they carry his brief moment in an eternal vision. Each of Roy DeCarava's photographs—sensate and loving yet profoundly social and visual—reveals ineluctable beauty and celebrates life.

chapter 16

Black Visual Intonation

When I was thinking about what I wanted to do at this conference, the first thing I thought about was giving my talk with my back to the audience as a sort of allusion to Miles Davis, you know, postural semantics and all. But then I had this dream, which I'm going to tell you about.

I was in Clarksdale, Mississippi, where I grew up. I was in my bedroom, the room I remember growing up in, sitting and listening to music—the kind of music my mom used to call psychological music. You know, jazz, rock, reggae, anything that was strange (to her). And I was sitting in the room with The Alien—I don't know how many of you saw the movie *The Alien*—and we were just chilling, you know, just grooving, like me and my friends did when we were growing up. And my mom pops her head in the room occasionally like she did when I was with my friends and smiles and sort of steps back out. And my father creeps in without saying anything and turns down the volume on the music. Eventually, my friend The Alien gets up and splits. And then my father comes in and says, "Who was that big-headed nigger you were in here with?"

I don't want to be a big-headed nigger, so I'm not going to do this with my back to the audience. But, I am going to use digressions like Marlon Riggs did in his talk. One thing that's been interesting for me to see so far in this conference is the anxiety around what I would call the performative. The very first night Stuart Hall stood up and gave his talk, and I felt a little bit like that guy in the Memorex commercial. I thought, damn, he's relentless. I mean, I turned to the people next to me and said it was like listening to John Coltrane—it just didn't stop. And then after that Cornel West came out and did his thing, you know, "Give me an Amen!" He doesn't say it, but you know what he wants. Then bell hooks came on, and she did her thing, and Marlon did his incredible thing. And then there was Hazel Carby. She was interesting. She was the only person who got the "oooh" effect. She got this effect when she was pointing out the relationship between certain male academics and Zora Neale Hurston.

My primary interest is in Black film. When I first got into film at Howard University, the people who were there—Haile Gerima, Alonzo Crawford, Abiyi Ford—were very much concerned with questions around Black cinema and with defining what it was. At that time, they would have probably defined Black film as something like "We're against Hollywood," which is interesting because that definition allows you to get to certain kinds of places, and it's clear. But eventually I started to ask myself, well, is that enough? It seems they had put us in this binary opposition with Hollywood that can be kind of limited. I thought we had to ask more sophisticated questions about what Black cinema was and, in fact, could be.

One of the first things I asked was, well, if this work is supposed to be Black film, why does it use what is essentially strictly classical Hollywood spatial continuity? You know, was it significant that you respected all of the 180-, 360-degree rules around spatial organization? Was that arbitrary?

They would show the work of Oscar Micheaux, whom anyone who's interested in Black cinema, or American cinema, for that matter, should be familiar with. (I find it incredible that Black filmmakers don't know Oscar Micheaux. That's kind of like being a jazzman and not knowing Louis Armstrong.) And they would always present Oscar Micheaux's work as an example of what not to do. I got this a lot: it was incompetently realized; its class and color politics were all messed up. But I felt like they never really looked deeply into his work and saw what was worth studying.

David Bordwell and Kristin Thompson did a very interesting analysis of Ozu, the master Japanese filmmaker. They demonstrated that the spatial paradigm Ozu employed wasn't a deficient control of a Hollywood spatial paradigm, but that, in fact, it was an alternative paradigm—which oftentimes ran parallel to the Hollywood one, but just as often would transgress it.[1] Donald Ritchie, who is considered an early expert on Ozu, would say, "This is a guy who's considered one of the most controlled formal filmmakers in the world, but he got sloppy at those moments." Right.

But what was interesting about Bordwell's and Thompson's analysis was that it provided an entrée into analyzing Black film. And I started to look at Micheaux's work and said, wow, this is not an accident; this is consistent over the course of his career (and I think he made more than thirty-eight feature films). It just got badder and badder and badder.

I'm going to do a little jump right here.

I had read the anti-essentialist position in that last cinema issue of *Screen*,[2] and I said, wow, I really don't agree with some of the things that the anti-essentialists are saying. I mean, I had a hard time understanding (and perhaps it was my misunderstanding) what they were trying to say. So I said, well, I must be an essentialist. And then I read what the essentialists were saying, what they were supposed to be saying, and I said, well, maybe I'm just an "anti-anti-essentialist." What I've come to now is what a friend told me when I asked how she would describe me. She called me a "materialist retentionist" (something like that).

What that means is that I have a belief in certain levels of cultural retention. People carry culture on various levels, down to the deepest level, which I would call a kind of core stability. Nam Jun Paik, the godfather of video art, has this great quote: "The culture that's going to survive in the future is the culture that you can carry around in your head." The middle passage is such a clear example of this, because you see Black American culture particularly developed around those areas we could carry around in our heads—our oratorical prowess, dance, music, those kinds of things. There are other things not so easy to carry. Architecture, for example. When we got here, we didn't have an opportunity to make many buildings. Not right off, at least. So I have this notion of core stability and how that informs what we do, of cultural sophistication and how we apply that to the task of constructing Black cinema.

I like to think about films and the kinds of things that are possible. For example, I want to do Martin Luther King's life in the style of *In the Realm of the Senses* (Nagisa Oshima's amazing hard-core feature). I want to do Malcolm X's life as a series of moments—Malcolm arriving home at two o'clock in the morning and looking in at his little girls asleep. I like the stories that Bruce Perry tells in his biography of Malcolm X—like when he says that Malcolm X was, in fact, in love with another Betty. And in his anxiety about whether Betty was actually going to accept his proposal of marriage, he asked Betty Shabazz to marry him instead. A few weeks later, he ran into the first Betty's brother, and was being congratulated by him, you know, "Congratulations on your marriage, brother Malcolm. But why didn't you ever call our sister back? She's been waiting for you. She wanted to accept the proposal." And Malcolm X broke down and started crying.[3] That's the Malcolm X I want to see. And I would like to know what kind of version of Little Richard's life Andrei Tarkovsky would do.

I think understanding culture and having a sophisticated understanding of applying culture to the construction of Black cinema means we have to understand how culture gets played out in various arenas. And we have to be able to look at these arenas to see how Black people have intervened to transform them into spaces where we can most express our desires. A classic example, of course, is basketball. Like the question that went around for a long time (before Michael Jordan made it irrelevant) about who was the best basketball player, Magic Johnson or Larry Bird. That depends on what you mean by best, obviously. If you use a rational Western evaluation of what's best, then you come up with the statistical, which means who can put the most balls in the hoop, right? And by that definition, certainly Larry Bird can be measured with the best there's ever been. Bird can put the ball in the hoop. Anybody that tells you he can't has got a serious racial anxiety thing happening. But then you have to ask yourself, if Black people enter into this game, which was invented by Dr. Hans Nasmith (and we know he certainly didn't create it with Black folks in mind), how has it been transformed? And how many levels does that play itself out on? I mean, is it just that we function as players, or have we affected other aspects of the game? And if you ask yourself these kinds of questions, then the question of who's the best basketball player becomes irrelevant. What you're going to end up with is Larry Bird coming down the floor, going up for a shot. Two points. He comes down again. Two points. Then maybe he'll shoot one of those long ones he's good for. Three points, you know. But then Michael Jordan will come down, spinning acrobatically in apparent defiance of all known laws of gravity. Ten points.

Black pleasure (not joy)—what are its parameters, what are its primal sites, how does Black popular culture or Black culture in general address Black pleasure? How does it generate Black pleasure? How do those strategies in Black music play out the rupture and repair of African-American life on the structural level? How do they play out the sense of the lost and the found? How are Black people preoccupied with polyventiality (a term of mine)? "Polyventiality" just means multiple tones, multiple rhythms, multiple perspectives, multiple meanings, multiplicity. Why do we find these particular things pleasurable? How do African retentions coalesce with the experiential sites in the New World, with new modes of cultural stability? What does Wesley Brown's "tragic magic" mean when he says, "I played in a Bar Mitzvah band. And it was a great job until I got hit by that tragic magic, and I start playing a little bit before the beat, a little bit behind the beat. I couldn't help myself. I lost the job." This whole question of addressing Black pleasure is a critical thing.

I've heard people talk about issues of representation and the content of culture. But I'm trying to figure out how to make Black films that have the power to allow the enunciative desires of people of African descent to manifest themselves. What kinds of things do we do? How can we interrogate the medium to find a way Black movement in itself could carry, for example, the weight of sheer tonality in Black song? And I'm not talking about the lyrics that Aretha Franklin sang. I'm talking about *how she sang them.* How do we make Black music or Black images vibrate in accordance with certain frequential values that exist in Black music? How can we analyze the tone, not the sequence of notes that Coltrane hit, *but the tone itself,* and synchronize Black visual movement with that? I mean, is this just a theoretical possibility, or is this actually something we can do?

I'm developing an idea that I call Black visual intonation (BVI). What it consists of is the use of irregular, nontempered (nonmetronomic) camera rates and frame replication to prompt filmic movement to function in a manner that approximates Black vocal intonation. See, the inherent power of cinematic movement is largely dependent on subtle or gross disjunctions between the rate and regularity at which a scene is recorded and the rate and regularity at which it is played back. Nonmetronomic camera rates, such as those employed by silent filmmakers, are transfixing precisely because they are irregular. The hand-cranked camera, for example, is a more appropriate instrument with which to create movement that replicates the tendency in Black music to "worry the note"—to treat notes as indeterminate, inherently unstable sonic frequencies rather than the standard Western treatment of notes as fixed phenomena. Utilizing what I term alignment patterns, which are simply a series of fixed frame replication patterns (and I have 372 at this point), the visual equivalencies of vibrato, rhythmic patterns, slurred or bent notes, and other musical effects are possible in film. You could do samba beats, reggae beats, all kinds of things. This is just a beginning for trying to talk about certain possibilities in Black cinema.

NOTES

1. David Bordwell and Kristin Thompson, "Space and Narrative in the Films of Ozu," *Screen* 17, no. 2 (Summer 1976), 41–73.
2. *Screen* 29, no. 4 (Fall 1988).
3. Bruce Perry, *Malcolm: The Life of a Man Who Changed Black America* (Barrytown, N.Y.: Station Hill Press, 1991). Distributed by The Talman Co.

jazz lines and colors

chapter 17

BILL EVANS

Improvisation in Jazz

There is a Japanese visual art in which the artist is forced to be spontaneous. He must paint on a thin stretched parchment with a special brush and black water paint in such a way that an unnatural or interrupted stroke will destroy the line or break through the parchment. Erasures or changes are impossible. These artists must practice a particular discipline, that of allowing the idea to express itself in communication with their hands in such a direct way that deliberation cannot interfere.

The resulting pictures lack the complex composition and textures of ordinary painting, but it is said that those who see well find something captured that escapes explanation.

This conviction that direct deed is the most meaningful reflection, I believe, has prompted the evolution of the extremely severe and unique disciplines of the jazz or improvising musician.

Group improvisation is a further challenge. Aside from the weighty technical problem of collective coherent thinking, there is the very human, even social need for sympathy from all members to bend for the common result. This most difficult problem, I think, is beautifully met and solved on this recording.[*]

As the painter needs his framework of parchment, the improvising musical group needs its framework in time. Miles Davis presents here frameworks which are exquisite in their simplicity and yet contain all that is necessary to stimulate performance with a sure reference to the primary conception.

[*]Editor's note: Evans is referring to the Miles Davis record *Kind of Blue*, for which this essay serves as liner notes.

Miles conceived these settings only hours before the recording dates and arrived with sketches which indicated to the group what was to be played. Therefore, you will hear something close to pure spontaneity in these performances. The group had never played these pieces prior to the recordings and I think without exception the first complete performance of each was a "take."

Although it is not uncommon for a jazz musician to be expected to improvise on new material at a recording session, the character of these pieces represents a particular challenge.

Briefly, the formal character of the five settings is:

"So What" is a simple figure based on 16 measures on one scale, 8 of another and 8 more of the first, following a piano and bass introduction in free rhythmic style. "Freddie Freeloader" is a 12-measure blues form given new personality by effective melodic and rhythmic simplicity. "Blue in Green" is a 10-measure circular form following a 4-measure introduction, and played by soloists in various augmentations and diminutions of time values. "Flamenco Sketches" is a 6/8 12-measure blues form that produces its mood through only a few modal changes and Miles Davis' free melodic conception. "All Blues" is a series of five scales, each to be played as long as the soloist wishes until he has completed the series.

part 4

**jazz is a dance:
jazz art in motion**

introduction

In *Steppin' on the Blues: The Visible Rhythms of African American Dance*, Jacqui Malone highlights the interconnectedness of black dance, instrumental music, and song. In the dynamically vibrant circle of the public jazz dance, dancer swings singer swings band swings dancer. Whether or not it is true, as many aestheticians contend, that dance is the parent of all art, it is certainly the case that the dancer is a reigning potentate within this U.S. black cultural triumvirate of singer-instrumentalist-dancer. Many jazz players declare the absolute indispensability of dance to what they do as musicians: New Orleans and Mobile marching band players, for example, have always drawn rhythms, melodic phrases, and other musical ideas from their dance-marching fellows, especially from the more creative dancers beyond the band's own ranks, the "second liners." Musicians have studied and responded to the moves of dancers in a multitude of settings where they played together: players have learned from chorus-line dancers, floor-show steppers, partying jitterbuggers bumping and jumping with the music, and especially tap dance performers, the best of whom could provide complex foot-drum rhythms and take choruses as if they were members of the jazz bands with which they performed. The tap dancer Honi Coles always insisted, for instance, that it was tap dancers who first "dropped the heel" in a way that created the bomb-drop rhythmic syncopations later characteristic of bebop. If he's right, perhaps dancers were the first great percussionists in the movement that defines the modern in jazz, the first of the boppers. Which makes way for the fascinating question of the influence of the feet of the bebop tappers on the feet of the poetry of the Beats, so strongly influenced by the sideways horns and zigzag lines of bop music.

Without making any false separation of jazz music from jazz dance—not only is the influence from one to the other very strong and immediate, but in many cases the dancer *is* the musician (as with tap kings Bill Bojangles Robinson, Baby Laurence, and John Bubbles), and the musician is an excellent dancer (Cab Calloway, Ella Fitzgerald, Jimmy Rushing)—this section of *Jazz Cadence* presents a set of meditations and taxonomies of jazz qualities in dance and music. In the spirit of the Robert Farris Thompson article, *Jazz Cadence* takes for granted the African connection to jazz music/dance. What would U.S. jazz be without its ongoing infusion of African ingredients? And what would so-called modern dance be without its Africanist and specifically jazz dimensions?

This section also takes for granted that U.S. sports at their finest become elegantly stylized jazz dances. Is it any surprise that Miles Davis was a credible boxer (as some of his associates learned the hard way) or that the boxer Sugar Ray Robinson was an excellent dancer who liked to work out to the sound of jazz? Or that in the twenties and thirties the basketball team called the Harlem Renaissance was featured as part of the floor show at the Renaissance Ballroom in Harlem?

Finally, this section delights in the richness of the mystery that at its center (or, better, at its off-center) jazz music is about the human body grooving with the beat, swaying with a partner, reveling in good-time houses, "steppin' on the blues."

I still say that the best sculpture in the United States was created by Negroes in Harlem's Savoy Ballroom, where they were doing variations on the wonderful dance called the Lindy Hop. The angles and shapes—they were unbelievable.　　—Romare Bearden (conversation with editor, April 1980)

Dancing the cakewalk was very popular just before the turn of the century and afterward. It had evolved from slavery, when blacks mimicked the formal dances of the whites, sometimes, evidently, to the delight of the slave owners. Clearly, the blacks were doing some subtle things unseen by the whites, who doubtless were amused by these "inferior" blacks attempting their dances. The cakewalk had resilience, however, and toward the end of the century fashionable whites were doing it. So here was a black dance parodying white dance danced by trendy whites. Finally, black dancers, responding to the new popularity of the dance, displayed it, improvised on it, and ended up dancing a black dance parodying white dance danced by whites now danced by blacks. Singing a song in black skin in blackface is part of the same structure; the black dancers are doing something else in their cakewalk, and so is the black singer.　　—Gayle Pemberton

In those days, down in our small corner of South Carolina, proficiency in dance was a form of storytelling. A boy could say, "I traveled here and there, saw this and fought that, conquered him and made love to her, lied to them, told a few others the truth, just so I could come back here and let you know what things out there are really like." He could communicate all this with smooth, graceful jiggles of his round bottom, synchronized with intricately coordinated sweeps of his arms and small, unexcited movements of his legs. Little girls could communicate much more.　　—James A. McPherson

[Balanchine] was a ballet choreographer who worked in the ballet medium and subscribed to a ballet aesthetic. Throughout his career, he introduced to the ballet canon Africanist aesthetic principles as well as Africanist-based steps from the social, modern, and so-called jazz dance vocabularies. He brought these innovations to ballet while maintaining his grounding in the ballet aesthetic. The result was still ballet, but with a new accent.

—Brenda Dixon Gottschild

There comes a point where musicians, being limited by man-made instruments, can't bend to a certain thing you want to express. The dancers have to bend, so they can express music the band can't. The dancers become a note by the way they stand or move, and the people can feel it.

—Verta Mae Grosvenor, former dancer with the Sun Ra Archestra

art taylor: Do you think boxing is comparable to music?

max roach: I think it is a definitive skill and that it's been raised to the level of an art form by black fighters. It's not just beating somebody but is as highly-developed as fencing or tennis. Rhythm has something to do with timing.

Where, when and how to slip punches is all rhythmic. Setting up somebody is done rhythmically. I know quite a few boxers who make a point of having something to do with a percussion instrument. Sugar Ray Robinson and Johnny Bratton both played the drums. Quite a few fighters got involved in music so they could develop the kind of coordination that was required. Dancing has a lot to do with good boxing too because it's very rhythmic. The same is true of baseball, and you could see it in Jim Brown's running when he was playing football. The way he could slip tacklers came from a keen rhythmic sense, as did the knowledge of when to take a breath and when to make a phrase, so to speak.

—Arthur Taylor

I was jiggling my shoulders as I shadowboxed, trying to get that rhythm flowing through my arms and legs. . . . In the minutes before I would box, I was searching for that rhythm. In some of the bootleg shows there had been a band playing between the bouts, and that music would be blaring as I came into the ring. I always wished they had continued to play while I was boxing. I think I would've boxed better.

Rhythm is everything in boxing. Every move you make starts with your heart, and that's in rhythm or you're in trouble.

Your rhythm should set the pace of the fight. If it does, then you penetrate your opponent's rhythm. You make him fight your fight, and that's what boxing is all about. In the dressing room that night I could feel my rhythm beginning to move through me, and it assured me that everything would be all right.

—Sugar Ray Robinson

"You got a hard kind of voice," he said now. "You know, like callused hands. Strong and hard but gentle underneath. Strong but gentle too. The kind of voice that can hurt you. I can't explain it. Hurt you and make you still want to listen."

—Gayl Jones

Ted Williams is a very close friend of mine. He heard one of my records, Up in Erroll's Room, took it to the ball park and put it on the loud-speaker. He told a newspaperman that three of his men started power hitting, started getting the swing of the bat. He said, "Listen to that tempo," and they ended up hitting way above their average and it worked for them. It was a pleasure to read that.

—Errol Garner (in Arthur Taylor)

Pollock enveloped himself in a heady atmosphere of his own creation while working on Autumn Rhythm. *In order to produce this picture, he is seen to have quickly and expertly flipped, flung, twirled, thrust, and splattered his pigment, manipulating mundane hardware-store materials with a masterful combination of abandon and grace. Namuth's superb shots of Pollock painting* Autumn Rhythm *disclose a man totally immersed in his work, alternately hunching over, leaning sideways, leaping in the air, shifting one foot forward, then the other, crossing his legs, stepping back from and stepping into the canvas.*

—Ellen G. Landau

Improvisation is the ultimate human (i.e., heroic) endowment. It is, indeed; and even as flexibility or the ability to swing (or to perform with grace under pressure) is the key to that unique competence which generates the self-reliance and thus the charisma of the hero, and even as infinite alertness-become-dexterity is the functional source of the magic of all master craftsmen, so may skill in the art of improvisation be that which both will enable contemporary man to be at home with his sometimes tolerable but never quite certain condition of not being at home in the world and will also dispose him to regard his obstacles and frustrations as well as his achievements in terms of adventure and romance.

—Albert Murray

chapter 18

JACQUI MALONE

Jazz Music in Motion: Dancers and Big Bands

> Dancing is very important to people who play music with a beat. I think that people who don't dance, or who never did dance, don't really understand the beat. . . . I know musicians who don't and never did dance, and they have difficulty communicating.
>
> —DUKE ELLINGTON, *The World of Duke Ellington*

The infancy of jazz coincided with extensive artistic and commercial efforts to get black musical theater established on Broadway. As a result, jazz musicians had a recognized connection with professional dance acts prior to the thirties. From the orchestra pit, musicians backed professional dancers and singers in theaters across the country. Throughout the twenties, jazz musicians, singers, and dancers worked together in night clubs and cabarets; and they performed jointly in revues that toured the United States and abroad. As early as 1921, when Garvin Bushell toured with Mamie Smith and Company, his co-performers included a comedian, a dance team, a magician, and some singers. Many of America's jazz giants gained experience playing for these small revues. Bushell recalled hiring a pickup musician while appearing in Kansas City: "When we got there for the first rehearsal we met this youngster on saxophone who played all his parts and didn't miss a note. When we told him to take a solo, he took a tremendous one. We said, 'What's your name?' 'Coleman.' 'Coleman who?' 'Coleman Hawkins.' . . . We had to read our parts when we played in the pit, and Hawk never hit a bad note."[1]

Garvin Bushell was a member of Sam Wooding's orchestra when it toured Europe in 1925 with a revue called *Chocolate Kiddies* that included over thirty dancers, comedians, and chorus line members. The hit of the show was "Jig Walk," created by the choreographer Charlie Davis. According to Bushell, "That's where we got to do the Charleston." That same year the Claude Hopkins band toured Europe with the Josephine Baker Revue. These were just a few of many shows that afforded opportunities for professional dancers and jazz musicians to inspire one another.[2]

As jazz bands became increasingly popular, they moved up from the pit to take center stage. Earl Hines helped pioneer the move from the pit to the stage at the Apollo Theater:

> We had to play the show from the pit and then go up onstage for our specialty. I had written three weeks before we got there that we wanted to wear the white suits and be onstage all the time, and they had agreed. "I'm not going in the pit," I said, getting salty. The producer called the manager, and he came and said, "You *are* going in the pit!" I told all the boys to pack up then, and we left the show standing there. Next morning I went to the theater and said, "Well, what about it?" The stage manager said, "We've got you set up on the stage."[3]

Vaudeville declined rapidly around the early thirties and a new performance format called presentation evolved. By this time, radio broadcasts had helped create a demand for jazz bands throughout the country at hotels, supper clubs, theaters, colleges, nightclubs, high schools, affluent prep schools, and at such dance halls as the Savoy and Roseland in New York City. Big city movie houses also featured bands on vaudeville-like bills that were presented between motion pictures.[4] According to Cholly Atkins, a tap dancer, choreographer, and director, the most popular venues of the thirties were dance halls, hotels, and theaters. Dance halls were scattered across the United States, and any town with more than 150,000 people had at least one hotel with a reasonably sized dance floor. And though they were often presented as part of a musical package, bands were the headliners in these performance arenas. During the era of presentation, these packages were called "revues" or "units" and included dancers, solo singers, comedians, a chorus line, and, of course, a big-name band.

Many bands had two or three dancing acts that they secured through booking agencies. For example, if Cab Calloway saw an act he liked, he would have his band manager find out which agency was handling the dancers and see if they were available for a future engagement. A booking agency allowed the tap duo of Honi Coles and Cholly Atkins to take their class act on the road with numerous bands. Typically they might hook up with the Basie band for a cross-country tour on a northern route from New York to California and come back with the Billy Eckstine Band on a southern route through Oklahoma City, St. Louis, Atlanta, and then up to Washington, D.C., as a final stop. But most dance acts didn't do extended tours with big bands; rather, they were hired for "spot bookings." During the thirties, Jimmy Lunceford carried his own revue, called *The Harlem Express*.

In the thirties, the most well-known African American theater circuit was called 'Round the World. Its tour comprised such independent theaters as the Howard in Washington, D.C.; the Lafayette in Harlem; the Royal in Baltimore;

the Lincoln, Standard, and Pearl in Philadelphia; and the Regal in Chicago. Ninety-nine percent of the artists featured in this big city loop were black. Revues generally opened with a couple of numbers by the band followed by a singer, a comedy dance act, more pieces by the band, a straight dancing act, another band appearance, and a closing number that featured a popular singer.[5]

Honi Coles counted as many as fifty top-flight dance acts "in the late 20s and early 30s." Coles explained the importance of these acts: "Back a while, when show business was show business, and there were all sorts of variety presentations, the dancing act was the nucleus of every show. Dancing acts were always surefire crowd pleasers. . . . Generally speaking, [they] were used to strengthen the show." Coles insisted that at one point tap dancers were more important than any other act on most bills because they could not only open and close the show but they could also fill the trouble spots. They were "the best dressed, the best conditioned, the most conscientious performer[s] on any bill, and in spite of being the least paid, [they were] the act[s] to 'stop the show.' "[6]

The diversity of dancing acts during the thirties and forties was astonishing: ballroom, adagio, eccentric, comedy, flash, acrobatics, and tap—the most prevailing style. Harold Norton and Margot Webb, who had studied ballet and performed a repertory of rumba, waltz, tango, and bolero numbers, made up one of the most famous African American ballroom teams from 1933 to 1947. Webb's solo work included a jazz toe dance (*en pointe*). During the thirties, this team enjoyed extended bookings with the Earl Hines Band at Chicago's Grand Terrace; toured England and France with Teddy Hill's band as part of the *Cotton Club Revue*; and performed as a single act on variety stages in Italy, France, and Germany. Before meeting Norton, Webb appeared in revues choreographed by leading black "dance directors," including Clarence Robinson and Leonard Harper.[7]

"Adagio" dancers performed a style that consisted of ballroom dance with various balletic and acrobatic lifts, spins, and poses. Honi Coles referred to Anise Boyer and Aland Dixon as the "fastest . . . adagio act." They traveled extensively with the Cab Calloway Band, sharing the dance spotlight with stand-up tap single Coles and with the Chocolateers, who introduced a dance called peckin.'[8]

Eccentric dance, a favorite with many jazz band leaders, "may include elements of contortionist, legomania, and shake dancing, although these styles frequently overlap with others, and a dancer can combine something of all of them. A few involve tap, for tappers are generally regarded as the dancing elite and imitated whenever possible. . . . 'Eccentric' is a catch-all for dancers who have their own non-standard movements and sell themselves on their individual styles." One of the most famous of these dancers was Dynamite Hooker, who toured during the thirties with the bands of Cab Calloway, Duke Ellington, and Jimmy Lunceford.[9]

The big band era coincided with the most fruitful years for comedy-dancing acts. As a result, bands provided steady employment for such two-man teams as Chuck and Chuckles, Stump and Stumpy, Moke and Poke, and Cook and Brown, who combined superb dancing with acrobatics and tumbling. Straight acrobatic teams were also featured in traveling units. They combined gymnastic material with music and performed it precisely on the beat. Most of the black acrobatic acts used jazz music.[10]

By the midthirties, many dancers in search of new and exciting ideas had developed what became known as flash dancing—a compression of acrobatics and jazz dancing. The flash acts "spice their routines with *ad lib* acrobatics. Without any warning or apparent preparation, they insert a variety of floor and air steps— a spin or flip or knee-drop or split—in the midst of a regular routine, and then, without a moment's hesitation, go back to the routine."[11]

The connection between big bands and tap dancers is one that has resurfaced in the last decades of the twentieth century. As jazz music has commanded a broader and broader audience, jazz lovers have discovered again one of the most sophisticated representations of jazz music by dancers, rhythm tap, created by African American tap innovators of the twentieth century. King Rastus Brown's flatfooted hoofing preceded the legendary Bill Robinson's "up on the toes" approach. Eddie Rector added elegance and body motion, and John Bubbles's crowning achievement—dropping the heels—added extraordinary rhythmical complexity.

Baby Laurence, tap dancer extraordinaire, explained that "tap dancing is very much like jazz music. The dancer improvises his own solo and expresses himself." Rhythm tappers are jazz percussionists who value improvisation and self-expression. Jazz musicians tell stories with their instruments and rhythm tappers tell stories with their feet. In a 1973 obituary for Baby Laurence, Whitney Balliett wrote, "A great drummer dances sitting down. A great tap-dancer drums standing up."[12]

Rhythm tap's close relationship to jazz music is evident in the large number of top caliber jazz drummers who could tap: Philly Joe Jones, Buddy Rich, Jo Jones, Big Sid Catlett, Eddie Locke, and Cozy Cole, who once had a dance act along with tapper Derby Wilson. Louis Bellson, who played drums with Duke Ellington in the fifties, commented on the relationship between drumming and tapping: "You get a guy like Jo Jones, all those guys can do a time step and the shim-sham-shimmy because that's what you did in the theater. . . . We base all of our rhythms on dancing. When I play a drum solo, I'm tapping. My brother-in-law Bill Bailey, oh, what a tap dancer. I mean that's one of the greatest drum solos I've heard in my life, Bill Bailey did it on stage. All he had was a rhythm section and he danced up and down that stage. I've got films on him. I look at them every once in a while. I study those films." According to Bellson, Duke Ellington always referred to the drummers as dancers. "I remember Ellington telling me that the great thing about Africa is that the drummers and dancers are like one." He would introduce the drummer by saying, "And now Dave Black is going to perform a little dancing for you." Bellson added, "And I know every time I get ready to play the brushes, I say 'I'm going to tap dance for you now, and these are Jo Jones' licks that he taught me.' "[13]

At the start of their careers, the drummers Max Roach, Kenny Clarke, and Art Blakey were greatly influenced by rhythm tappers. Roach accompanied Groundhog and Baby Laurence and learned steps from them. He recalled performing with Laurence: "We usually did our act as an encore. I would play brushes on the snare and he would just dance and we'd exchange things, call and response. I would imitate him and then I would play time over it." In 1961, while playing with the Charlie Mingus band, Dannie Richmond enhanced his drumming technique by studying Laurence's feet every night:

The band would play the head on the theme and Baby Laurence played the breaks. Little by little we worked it where at first I was just doing stop-time, fours, so much that I'd memorized every lick of his. I learned that it wasn't just single strokes involved in the drums. My concept was that if you had the single strokes down, you could play anything. It's not true. It's almost true, but not totally. And the way Laurence would mix paradiddles along with single strokes. He could do all of that with his feet. It got to where we're doing fours together. He'd dance four, then we played threes, twos, one bar apiece, but I was copying him. I'd more or less play what he danced. I was trying to keep it in the context of melody dance and, mind you, to me that was the same as a saxophone player trying to play like Charlie Parker. He was the only one who could dance to Charlie Parker tunes. . . . It was a gas for me to duplicate what Laurence danced. When he switched up me and changed the time, there was no way I could play that.

According to Philly Joe Jones, "the drummer who has been a dancer can play better than someone who has never danced. See, the drummer catches the dancer, especially when a dancer's doing wings. And the cymbals move at the same time to catch the dancer."[14]

In the thirties and forties, rhythm tap's greatest exponents functioned in closely knit circles that included singers, comedians, jazz musicians, and chorus line dancers. The various types of performers shared rehearsal and performance spaces, jam sessions, and living quarters; they attended sports events and parties; they belonged to the same fraternal clubs. Billy Strayhorn, Duke Ellington's co-composer, was the last official president of the Copasetics, a club organized by tap dancers but with musicians such as Dizzy Gillespie and Lionel Hampton among its membership.

The impact of the jam session, or "cutting contest," on rhythm tap's evolution parallels much of what Ellison has to say about the relationship of the jam session to the development of jazz instrumentalists. Ralph Ellison called the jam session the "jazzman's true academy":

It is here that he learns tradition, group techniques and style. For although since the twenties many jazzmen have had conservatory training and were well grounded in formal theory and instrumental technique, when we approach jazz we are entering quite a different sphere of training. Here it is more meaningful to speak, not of courses of study, of grades and degrees, but of apprenticeship, ordeals, initiation ceremonies, of rebirth. For after the jazzman has learned the fundamentals of his instrument and the traditional techniques of jazz—the intonations, the mute work, manipulation of timbre, the body of traditional styles—he must then "find himself," must be reborn, must find, as it were, his soul. All this through achieving that subtle identification between his instrument and his deepest drives which will allow him to express his own unique ideas and his own unique voice. He must achieve, in short, his self-determined identity. In this his instructors are his fellow musicians, especially the acknowledged masters, and his recognition of manhood depends upon their acceptance of his ability as having reached a standard which is all the more difficult for not having been codified. This does not depend upon his ability to simply hold a job but upon his power to express an individuality in tone.[15]

In nightclubs and on street corners tap dancers participated in jam sessions—exchanging ideas, inspiring one another, and battling for a place in the rhythm tappers' hierarchy of artistic excellence. Jimmy Crawford jammed with many rhythm tap artists: "Dancers influenced the music a whole lot in those days. Sometimes we'd have jam sessions with just tap dancers, buck dancers and drums. Big Sid Catlett was one of the greatest show drummers who ever lived. He could accompany, add on, improvise, so well. And believe me, those rhythm dancers really used to inspire you."[16] No jam sessions were as exciting as those held at the legendary Hoofer's Club, where the reigning tap kings of the early thirties included Raymond Winfield, Honi Coles, Harold Mablin, and Roland Holder.

In 1932, when Baby Laurence went to New York as a singer with the Don Redman Band, he headed straight to the Hoofer's Club: "Don discouraged my dancing, but when we hit town my first stop was the Hoofer's Club—it was the biggest thrill of my life." The cardinal rule there was "Thou Shalt Not Copy Another's Steps—Exactly." Those foolish enough to break that rule in public had to suffer the consequences. Dancers lined up to get front row theater seats when tap acts performed at local theaters. According to Laurence, "they watched you like hawks and if you used any of their pet steps, they just stood right up in the theater and told everybody about it at the top of their voices."[17] Leonard Reed's first stop in New York was also the Hoofer's Club:

> You could hear dancing the minute you got in the building. There was always dancin' going on, known dancers and unknown dancers. Bubbles would come occasionally. Bill Robinson came in occasionally. . . . All the dancers would hang out, and they would trade ideas. That was affectionately called "stealin' steps." Everybody did it. That's how you learned. You would do something, and you'd say to the other dancers, "You tryin' to steal it? Alright, do it!" "Let me see you do this!" And they'd try it. Of course, when they did it, it was slightly different. But that's how it was. Everybody was always showin' steps and trying to steal steps. It was an amazing time.[18]

The very best dancers in this tradition have unique styles that are immediately recognizable aurally and visually, although the emphasis, of course, is on sound. This drive toward individual expressiveness grows right out of an African American aesthetic sense that puts supreme value on what the African Americanist John Vlach calls "freewheeling improvisation and innovation, . . . distinctive dynamism, . . . and delight in the surprise value of new, not complely anticipated discovery." What these dancers value most is not the exactness of frozen choreography and set routines developed by others, but the joy that is inherent in improvisational flights of freedom. Perhaps Baby Laurence said it best: "From my point of view, having a choreographer tell me what to do would ruin everything. I wouldn't be able to improvise or interpret the music, and I couldn't express myself."[19]

During the early sixties, Stanley Dance conducted a "Spontaneous Opinion" poll in *Metronome* of twenty-eight jazz musicians. One of the questions asked was "Who is the greatest dancer you ever saw?" Twenty-six named tap dancers and over half of the votes went to Baby Laurence—a tap artist with a jazz musician's sense of his craft.[20]

Jazz musicians and rhythm tap dancers were obviously in pursuit of identical artistic goals. Their partnership in the thirties and forties mirrored much more than a convenient musical package. Their mutual admiration grew out of a special kinship based on similar aesthetic points of view and what Albert Murray calls a shared "idiomatic orientation."

Numerous rhythm tappers performed with jazz bands during the thirties and forties. Honi Coles worked as a single with Count Basie, Claude Hopkins, Jimmy Lunceford, Fats Waller, Duke Ellington, Lucky Millinder, Louis Armstrong, and Cab Calloway. Coles felt "it was such a kick to work with the great bands, especially with guys like Fats Waller—the looser of the band leaders. . . . People like Fats Waller and Louie Armstrong were people who enjoyed and loved life and showed it every instant of the day."[21] Buster Brown toured with Count Basie, Jimmy Lunceford, and Dizzy Gillespie; Bunny Briggs with Duke Ellington, Earl Hines, Count Basie, and Charlie Barnet; Jeni LeGon with Fats Waller and Count Basie; Baby Laurence with Count Basie, Duke Ellington, and Woody Herman; the Miller Brothers and Lois with Jimmy Lunceford and Cab Calloway; Coles and Atkins with Billy Eckstine, Count Basie, and Charlie Barnet; and Peg Leg Bates with Erskine Hawkins, Claude Hopkins, Duke Ellington, Louis Armstrong, and many others.[22]

Although dancers appeared with big bands in theaters throughout the country, the premiere stage and number one testing ground in America was Harlem's Apollo Theater. Beginning in 1934, stage shows were built around such well-known jazz bands as those led by Duke Ellington, Count Basie, Don Redman, Chick Webb, Lucky Millinder, and Fletcher Henderson.[23] The Apollo opened around 10:00 A.M. and offered four to five shows per day, starting with a short film, a newsreel, and a featured film, followed by a revue. Presented in the spring of 1934, *The Golliwog Revue* was a typical show that consisted of seven acts, including Don Redman's band, the headliner; chorus line dancers; the Jack Storm Company, an acrobatic act; Leroy and Edith, the Apollo lindy hop contest winners; Myra Johnson, a singer; the Four Bobs, tap dancers; and Jazzlips Richardson, an eccentric dancer. Throughout the show Johnny Lee Long and Pigmeat Markham, comedians, joked with Ralph Cooper, the host.

In addition to their own presentations, the featured bands played for the chorus lines and for all the dance acts. Andy Kirk backed Bill Robinson at the Apollo:

"Playing the Apollo was different from playing a dance hall, because in a dance hall the dancers had to dance to your music. At the Apollo, with a star like Bojangles, we had to play music for *him* to dance to. . . . We always had regard for the artist, whatever he was doing, and our music was background. We wanted to play it right—the way he wanted it." The Apollo had a good floor for dancers. And the place was known for unusually demanding and discriminating audiences. "When big name dancers played the Apollo, there was nothing in the audience but dancers with their shoes," said Sandman Sims. "Up in the balcony, dancers, and the first six rows, you saw nothing but tap dancers, wanta-be tap dancers, gonna-be tap dancers, tried-to-be tap dancers. That's the reason a guy would want to dance at the Apollo."[24]

Under the direction of black producer-choreographers (who maintained their own chorus lines), the Apollo revues changed each week. Charlie Davis, Leonard Harper, Addison Carey, Teddie Blackman, and Clarence Robinson also took their chorus lines on the independent theater circuit 'Round the World. The Apollo chorus line was the best in New York. Honi Coles "was astounded at the dancing ability that most of these young ladies had. A dancing act could come into the Apollo with all original material and when they left at the end of the week, the chorus lines would have stolen many of the outstanding things that they did. . . . The production numbers that these girls did were often as effective as anything the stars or any of the acts would do."[25]

The role of chorus line dancers in the development of jazz has been consistently overlooked by jazz and dance historians. According to Dicky Wells, many jazz musicians felt a kinship with chorus line dancers: "They used to be the biggest lift to musicians, because we thought alike." "They were more important than people realize. You might say we composed while they danced—a whole lot of swinging rhythm. That's when we invented new things and recorded them [the] next day."[26]

The Apollo's dance contests featured some of the most dedicated big band followers in the country. Their intricate steps devised to the swinging rhythms of America's jumpingest jazz bands could only be matched in enthusiasm by the contests held further uptown at Harlem's legendary dance hall the Savoy Ballroom, known among the initiated as "the track." The artist Romare Bearden went there three nights a week during the early thirties: "The best dancing in the world was there, and the best music. . . . You'd want to be either in Harlem then or in Paris. These were the two places where things were happening."[27]

When the Savoy opened its doors on 12 March 1926, over five thousand people rocked the city block–long building to the rhythms of Fess Williams and His Royal Flush Orchestra and the Charleston Bearcats. "Few first-nighters will ever forget the dynamic Fess, whose eye-catching trade mark was a shimmering, glittering diamond studded suit and whose showmanship and musicianship eventually catapulted him to national fame from the newly-born Savoy's No. 1 bandstand."[28]

That first night, Fletcher Henderson's Roseland Orchestra made a guest appearance at the Savoy as did the legendary tap dancer Eddie Rector. Leaders of

Harlem's benevolent, social, cultural, civic, educational, and welfare groups were present along with Hollywood and Broadway stars, social leaders, church dignitaries, sports and newspaper personalities, and federal, state, and city government officials. The Savoy offered quite a showcase for this grand event: "Architecturally, the Savoy dazzled with a spacious lobby framing a huge, cut-glass chandelier and marble staircase, an orange and blue dance hall with soda fountain, tables, and heavy carpeting covering half its area, the remainder a burnished dance floor 250 feet by 50 feet with two bandstands and a disappearing stage at the end."[29]

This institution of international fame surpassed all of America's top dance halls in grandeur and impact on American music and dance. The Savoy's twenty-fifth anniversary booklet was justified in boasting: "From [the] Savoy's mammoth mahogany floor, there was launched a long succession of dance fads, styles, and crazes that 'caught fire' almost overnight, capturing the imagination of dancers in every nook and corner of this country and sweeping far to the four winds and the seven seas for universal popularity." Dances that started or were made popular at the Savoy include the lindy hop, the flying Charleston, the big apple, the stomp, the jitterbug jive, the snakehips, the rhumboogie, variations of the shimmy and the peabody, and new interpretations of the bunny hug and the turkey trot.[30]

Charles Buchanan, the Savoy's manager, paid such dancers as Shorty Snowden to come in and "perform" for his clientele. Couples went there to practice during the day, and the most skillful "rug cutters" were constantly vying for first place honors in the northeast corner of the dance floor, known as "the Corner." There an invisible rope surrounded a dancing area that met the requirements of ritual, recreation, and performance. The "Saturday night function" that is associated with affirmation, celebration, and freedom was played out in this setting, where individual expression and inventiveness were as prized as technical virtuosity and the ability to execute carefully rehearsed maneuvers. As at the Apollo, no one could copy another dancer's steps. Shorty Snowden, the self-styled introducer of the lindy, was king for many years. Although his expertise was limited to the floor lindy (as opposed to the lindy, which had aerial steps), his dancing skills still far exceeded the capabilities of the average dancer.[31]

The lindy revolutionized American dance. Its fundamental approach can still be seen in social dancing. The breakaway, its most important element, allows for improvisation that might incorporate old steps or create new ones. An influential predecessor of the lindy was the Charleston swing. Barbara Engelbrecht explains that "this 'swing' infused the Lindy Hop's basic step—the syncopated two step, with the accent on the offbeat—with a relaxed and ebullient quality. And this relaxed and ebullient style of execution gives the impression, like the music, of the beat moving 'inexorably ahead.' The dancers' feet appear to 'fly' in syncopated rhythms, while the body appears to 'hold' the fine line of balance in calm contrast to the headlong rush of the feet." According to Stearns and Stearns, the lindy flowed more smoothly and horizontally than the earlier two-step, had more rhythmic continuity, and was more complicated.[32]

At the Savoy, black musicians and dancers, armed with the musical innovations of Louis Armstrong, helped develop the formula for what was eventually called "swing music," which swept the country during the Great Depression and ricocheted far beyond the Western Hemisphere. The relationship between dance halls and jazz is eloquently explained by Ralph Ellison:

> Jazz, for all the insistence of the legends, has been far more closely associated with cabarets and dance halls than with brothels, and it was these which provided both the employment for the musicians and an audience initiated and aware of the overtones of the music; which knew the language of riffs, the unstated meanings of the blues idiom, and the dance steps developed from, and complementary to, its rhythms. And in the beginning it was in the Negro dance hall and night club that jazz was most completely a part of a total cultural expression; and in which it was freest and most satisfying, both for the musicians and for those in whose lives it played a major role.

"The Savoy Ballroom was the ultimate conferrer of postgraduate degrees in big bandsmanship," asserts Nat Hentoff. Only the best bands were allowed to return, and Charles Buchanan, the Savoy's manager, called the best bands the ones that kept the floor filled. Night after night, the dancers and musicians at the Savoy spurred one another on to greater heights and earthier depths—always with an attitude of elegance.[33]

During the forties, Dicky Wells played trombone at the Savoy for six months with Jimmy Rushing's band: "There was plenty of competition on the next stand then, with all the different bands coming and going. And the Lindy Hoppers there made you watch your P's and Q's. The dancers would come and tell you if you didn't play. They made the guys play, and they'd stand in front patting their hands until you got the right tempo."[34]

Countless jazz musicians have commented on the importance of dance to their music:

William "Cat" Anderson: "I enjoy having a floor full of dancers. It seems to me that everybody enjoys the music more, even those who are not dancing but just standing there watching the dancers. We play more swinging things then than we would at a concert, because people like to get up and move about in rhythm."[35]

Duke Ellington: "They used to have great dancers up at the Ritz, Bridgeport. Every now and then you go into a ballroom like that where they have great dancers. It's a kick to play for people who really jump and swing. On two occasions up there we were using a substitute drummer, but we didn't have to worry about him because the dancers were carrying the band and the drummer. You start playing, the dancers start dancing, and they have such a great beat you just hang on!"[36]

Pops Foster: "In about 1935 or 1936 we started playing for audiences that just sat there. I never liked this, I always liked to play for an audience that dances."[37]

Lester Young: "I wish jazz were played more for dancing. I have a lot of fun playing for dances because I like to dance, too. The rhythm of the dancers comes back to you when you're playing. When you're playing for dancing, it all adds up to playing the right tempo. After three or four tempos, you find the tempos they like. What they like changes from dance date to dance date."[38]

Baby Dodds: "When I first went to New York it seemed very strange to have people sitting around and listening rather than dancing. In a way it was similar to theater work. But it was peculiar for me because I always felt as though I was doing something for the people if they danced to the music. It never seemed the same when they just sat around and listened. We played for dancing and quite naturally we expected people to dance."[39]

Jimmy Crawford: "In ballrooms, where there's dancing like I was raised on, when everybody is giving to the beat, and just moving, and the house is bouncing—that inspires you to play. It's different when you go to those places where it's 'cool' and the people just sit listening. I don't care too much for the 'cool,' harsh pulsation. I don't like music where it's simply a matter of 'Listen to my changes, man!' and there's no emotion or swing. I think Louis Armstrong has done more to promote good feeling among earthy people than anyone. He can't speak all those foreign languages, but he lets a certain feeling speak for him. You can play too many notes, but if you make it simple, make it an ass-shaker, then the music speaks to the people."[40]

Frankie Manning, Norma Miller, and many other lindy hop experts attest to the ability of the Savoy big bands to "speak to the people." Constantly driven toward excellence and technical perfection, the Savoy Lindy Hoppers perfected the lindy in direct response to the dynamics of the musicians. According to Stearns and Stearns, the stage was set for movement innovations with the appearance of a group of Kansas City musicians in 1932. The power and drive of the Bennie Moten Band "generated a more flowing, lifting momentum. The effect on the dancers was to increase the energy and speed of execution."[41]

During the midthirties, a monumental change in the lindy took place when Frankie Manning and his partner Freida Washington introduced the first aerial or air step (called "over the back") in a Savoy dance contest against Shorty Snowden's Lindy Hoppers. What followed was the development and perfection of numerous air steps by Savoy dancers. Manning and Washington were members of Whitey's Lindy Hoppers, a group of excellent dancers organized by Herbert White, the Savoy's floor manager. In 1936, Manning developed the first ensemble routines, which made it possible to easily adapt the lindy hop to stage presentations.[42]

As the dance became airborne, its popularity spread the length and breadth of America. By the fall of 1936, White managed three teams, each comprised of three couples. Frankie Manning became the main choreographer for the first-string team; during his years with Whitey's Lindy Hoppers, they became internationally known. The Savoy dancers traveled with many great jazz bands, including those of Duke Ellington, Count Basie, Chick Webb, and Cab Calloway. Manning was a member of the teams that traveled to Europe, Australia, New Zealand, and South America. The Savoy dancers appeared in a production of *The Hot Mikado* with Bill Robinson at the 1939 World's Fair, at the Cotton Club and Radio City Music Hall in New York City, at the Moulin Rouge in Paris, and in a musical short, *Hot Chocolate* (1941), with Duke Ellington. In addition to *Hot Chocolate*, White's teams appeared in the films *A Day at the Races* (1937), *Radio City Revels* (1938), and *Hellzapoppin'* (1941). With the exception of *A Day at the*

Races, Frankie Manning was the choreographer for all of the film appearances.

Between 1935 and 1950, Savoy lindy hop teams won fourteen championships at the annual Harvest Moon Ball, a competitive dance spectacle held at Madison Square Garden in New York. During the thirties and the forties a significant number of Savoy regulars made the transition from amateur to professional. Whitey's Lindy Hoppers disbanded after Manning, and most of the group's other men were drafted during World War II.[43]

The Savoy's success owes as much to the famous "battles of the bands" staged there as it does to the music and the dancers who created visualizations of the music. For most of the thirties, the all-time favorite at the Savoy was the hard-driving band of Chick Webb. When a band battle was scheduled, Webb's musicians trained like prizefighters and had special section rehearsals to prepare for the "kill." "The brass used to be downstairs, the saxophones upstairs, and the rhythm would get together somewhere else. We had the reputation of running any band out that came to the Savoy. But just forget about Duke!" Another tough opponent was the Count Basie Band. Dicky Wells called Basie's rhythm section "nothing less than a Cadillac with the force of a Mack truck." The alto saxophonist Earle Warren recalled one occasion when the Count reigned supreme.

> *Swingin' the Blues* was built to be a house breaker. . . . "We began working on it when we were on the road and getting things together for a battle of jazz with Chick Webb at the Savoy. The battle of jazz was something to be reckoned with and we had to have something fresh and new to bring to the Savoy or we would falter at the finish line. So we proceeded to rehearse diligently. . . . By the time we got it together we were cookin'. At the Savoy we saved it until about halfway down in the program. Chick did his thing, *God Bless*, and then we reached into our bag and pulled out this powerhouse. When we unloaded our cannons, that was the end. It was one of those nights—I'll never forget it." Nor will anyone else who heard it, for that was one of the few nights at the Savoy when Chick Webb lost a battle of jazz.[44]

One of the most famous battles at the Savoy was the night the Benny Goodman Band faced Chick Webb and His Little Chicks. The Savoy was packed and many more people waited outside. For blocks, traffic was backed up in every direction—with approximately twenty-five thousand people trying to attend. Goodman pulled out all of his guns, but could not win the crowd. When Webb ended the session with a drum solo, the dancers exploded in a thunderous ovation. "Goodman and his drummer, Gene Krupa, just stood there shaking their heads."[45]

The Savoy was Webb's "musical home," and he played on and off there for ten years until his death in 1939. His phenomenal success is explained by Duke Ellington:

> Some musicians are dancers, and Chick Webb was. You can dance with a lot of things besides your feet. Billy Strayhorn was another dancer—in his mind. He was a dance-writer. Chick Webb was a dance-drummer who painted pictures of dances with his drums. . . . The reason why Chick Webb

had such control, such command of his audiences at the Savoy ballroom, was because he was always in communication with the dancers and felt it the way they did. And that is probably the biggest reason why he could cut all the other bands that went in there.[46]

Ralph Ellison has written that after the church and the school, the third most vital institution in the lives of African Americans has been the public jazz dance. There the artistry of dancers, musicians, and singers converged to create a union that personifies what jazz is all about. Ellison spent time in Oklahoma watching Jimmy Rushing on the bandstand: "It was when Jimmy's voice began to soar with the spirit of the blues that the dancers—and the musicians—achieved that feeling of communion which was the true meaning of the public jazz dance. The blues, the singer, the band and the dancers formed the vital whole of jazz as an institutional form, and even today neither part is quite complete without the rest." Wynton Marsalis's conception of an ideal forum for jazz is an intimate communal setting in which members can choose to participate by dancing or by engaging in "call and response" with the musicians: "We love to have the people get into the music even if we're in a concert hall. . . . People should be able to come in and out of the hall, it's like a community event. We're community musicians."[47]

In the late fifties, the Savoy Ballroom closed and later the building was demolished. Ralph Ellison had this to say about the Savoy's importance as a cultural institution of the thirties.

In those days, for instance, the Savoy Ballroom was one of our great cultural institutions. In the effort to build much needed public housing, it has been destroyed. But then it was thriving and people were coming to Harlem from all over the world. The great European and American composers were coming there to listen to jazz—Stravinsky, Poulenc. The great jazz bands were coming there. Great dancers were being created there. People from Downtown were always there because the Savoy was one of the great centers of culture in the United States, even though it was then thought of as simply a place of entertainment.[48]

The musicians, dancers, and singers that walked through the doors of the Savoy infused American culture with elegance and brilliance in music and movement and an unmistakable style that has been embraced by cultures worldwide. Albert Murray observed, "No institutions had more to do with the development or the sophistication, the variety, the richness and the precision of jazz than institutions like the Savoy ballroom. But dance has always been central and I always want to see jazz connected with dance. What we should try to reach in a concert hall is the same kind of ambience that one reaches in a dance hall."[49]

Vernacular Dance on Stage: An Overview

The dances that began on the farms, plantations, levees, and urban streets of colonial America evolved through minstrelsy and moved onto the "stages" of traveling shows, vaudeville, musical theater, cabarets, and nightclubs. The development and growth of this country's preeminent vernacular dance paralleled the evolution of African American music and took a giant leap forward in the twenties, thirties, and forties, when the connections between black singers, dance acts, and jazz musicians revolutionized American culture.

Throughout his life, Duke Ellington, arguably America's greatest twentieth-century composer, never severed the tie between his music and dance. Even the sacred concerts, late in his career, featured such dancers as Geoffrey Holder, Baby Laurence, Bunny Briggs, and Buster Brown. Ellington always preferred having musicians in his band who could dance: "I used to be a pretty good dancer at one time. I think it's very important that a musician should dance. . . . Dancing is very important to people who play music with a beat. I think that people who don't dance, or who never did dance, don't really understand the beat. What they get in their minds is a mechanical thing not totally unacademic. I know musicians who don't and never did dance, and they have difficulty communicating." According to Albert Murray, one of the first Ellington musicians that played and danced in front of the band was Freddy Jenkins, known as "Little Posey," but the all-time king of the dancer-musicians in this band was Ray Nance, nicknamed "Floorshow." During his years with Ellington, he was featured on trumpet and violin and as a dancer and singer.[50]

As Wynton Marsalis perceptively remarked, "Duke Ellington understood the importance of romance in body movement, the romantic aspect of body movement to jazz music." When Ellington reached his sixties, he danced in front of the band much more than he had in previous years. Still, movement was important to him all along. According to Albert Murray, earlier in his career "there was that subtle thing, the way he would walk and as [Count] Basie and those guys would say, 'It was all such a picture.' " Many jazz musicians knew how to move with style: "Ellington had that big wide-legged stride and Earl [Hines] had that flashy patent leather tip and Nat King Cole put it like his shoes were velvet, like they were socks and Basie would come out there like he didn't know what was happening. He was doing the hell out of that stuff. They all had that—Hamp [Lionel Hampton] always danced, Cab [Calloway] could sing and dance."[51]

Louis Armstrong, America's quintessential twentieth-century musician/singer/dancer, was "considered the finest dancer among the [jazz] musicians" of the twenties. During the midtwenties, at Chicago's Sunset Cafe, Armstrong played in a show that included Buck and Bubbles, Edith Spencer, Rector and Cooper, and Mae Alix. On Friday nights Charleston contests were held. The show's producer staged the finale of the main show as a dancing act for four musicians in the band: Armstrong, Earl Hines, Tubby Hall, and Joe Walker. Armstrong remembered: "We would stretch out across that floor doing the Charleston as fast as the music would play it. Boy, oh boy, you talking about four cats picking them up and laying them down—that was us."[52]

Another sparkling partnership on the dance floor consisted of the jazz singer Sarah Vaughan and Dizzy Gillespie. Vaughan recalled that during the early forties when she and Gillespie toured with Earl Hines, "we'd get to swinging so much, Dizzy would come down and grab me and start jitterbugging all over the place." Ella Fitzgerald had similar memories: "We used to take the floor over. Yeah, do the

Lindy Hop because we could do it. Yeah, we danced like mad together. . . . We'd go with the old Savoy steps." Gillespie, noted for a "snake hips" dance specialty at the start of his career, always created dances to his music: "A feeling for dancing was always a part of my music; to play it right, you've got to move. If a guy doesn't move properly when he's playing my music, he ain't got the feeling. Thelonious Monk, Illinois Jacquet, and all those instrumentalists who move a lot, are playing just what they're doing with their bodies."[53]

Thelonious Monk, like Ellington, never severed the connection between jazz music and dance. According to the pianist Randy Weston, "not only is Monk such a master pianist and composer, but when you watch him play, he does a complete ballet. He doesn't just play the piano, but he puts his whole body into the piano. . . . It's a whole dance." Monk would often rise from the piano and break into bodily visualizations of his music. "When his music was happening," according to Ben Riley, a jazz drummer, "then he'd get up and do his little dance because he was feeling good and he knew you knew where you were and the music was swinging and that's what he wanted. So, he'd say, 'I don't have to play now, you're making it happen.' "[54]

Early in his career, Count Basie played with Gonzelle White and Her Jazz Band, a stand-up act that featured dancing musicians who performed all kinds of tricks with their instruments. Basie would play behind his back, stand on one foot, play with his leg on the piano, or perform fancy tricks with his hands and arms. Gonzelle White's trumpet player, Harry Smith, was featured as a dancer who tapped, did splits, buck and wing, kicks, and the soft shoe. Basie was knocked out by the group's drummer: "Freddy Crump was a top-notch drummer, and he did all of the fancy things that show-band drummers used to, like throwing his sticks in the air and catching them like a juggler without losing a beat. He was a whole little act by himself, especially when it came to taking bows. He used to come dancing back in from the wings and hit the drum as he slid into a split. He used to grab the curtain and ride up with it, bowing and waving at the audience applauding."[55]

But the all-time experts of show-band novelties were the dancing-singing musicians that played with Jimmy Lunceford. Eddie Durham, an arranger, believed that Lunceford's band had the slickest, most precise stage presentation in the business: "There was nobody could play like that band! They would come out and play a dance routine. The Shim Sham Shimmy was popular then and six of the guys would come down and dance to it—like a tap dance, crossing their feet and sliding."[56] What followed were impersonations of other bands and glee club–like song presentations. Nat Pierce, a jazz pianist, saw Lunceford's band perform in Boston: "His four trumpet players were throwing their horns up to the ceiling. It was a big high hall, and they'd throw them up twenty or thirty feet, pick them out of the air, and hit the next chord. I was just amazed by the whole thing."[57]

Commenting on the relationship between jazz and dance, Murray observes that

> whatever else it was used for, it was always mostly dance music. Even when
> it was being performed as an act in a variety show on a vaudeville stage, the

most immediate and customary response consisted of such foot tapping, hand clapping, body rocking, and hip rolling as came as close to total dance movement as the facilities and the occasion would allow. Nor was the response likely to be anything except more of the same when the most compelling lyrics were being delivered by Ma Rainey or Bessie Smith, whose every stage gesture, by the way, was also as much dance movement as anything else.[58]

From Billy Kersands's captivating Virginia essence to the dynamic glides, spins, and splits of James Brown, African American dancing singers have captured the imaginations of people throughout the world. The long-standing tradition of dancing singers in African American culture reaches back to central and western Africa, where song was always coupled with bodily movement. Many of America's most outstanding twentieth-century singers began as dancers or included dancing in their performances.

Just after World War II, the relationship that dancers, musicians, and singers had enjoyed for so many years was fractured by federal, state, and city governments. In 1944, a 30 percent federal excise tax was levied against "dancing" night clubs. Later it was reduced to 20 percent. "No Dancing Allowed" signs went up all over the country.[59] Max Roach argues that the new tax signaled the end of variety entertainment as it had been known: "It was levied on all places where they had entertainment. It was levied in case they had public dancing, singing, storytelling, humor, or jokes on stage. This tax is the real story behind why dancing, not just tap dancing, but public dancing per se and also singing, quartets, comedy, all these kinds of things, were just out. Club owners, promoters, couldn't afford to pay the city tax, state tax, government tax."[60]

Dancers, singers, and comedians suffered. Only jazz instrumentalists were able to thrive under these conditions. According to Roach, "if somebody got up to dance, there would be 20 per cent more tax on the dollar. If someone got up there and sang a song, it would be 20 per cent more. If someone danced on the stage it was 20 per cent more." As a result jazz gradually lost its dancing audience. People began sitting down in clubs, and as agents began pushing small combos, only a few big bands were able to survive.[61]

Social dancing suffered, but as usual African Americans found other avenues for public dancing. Professional dancers, on the other hand, were faced with a serious dilemma. Many tap dancers turned away from dance to other careers. The eccentric dancer Bessie Dudley eventually found a job in a Long Island factory. By the early fifties, promoters were pushing vocal groups instead of dancers.[62] With the help of Cholly Atkins, these groups became the new disseminators of vernacular dance on stage. They comprised a new generation of dancing singers.

The extremely rich cross-fertilization of African American vernacular dance, jazz, and singing in the twenties, thirties, and forties brought character and style to American culture. The dance that evolved during that period in America's history is "classic jazz dance." Duke Ellington had this to say about a renewal of the association between jazz music and jazz dance: "With the new music that already is, and what is coming, there's no predicting what effect the disassociation from dancing will have in the future, but my own idea is that it is going to make a big fat curve and come right back to where it was, except that it will be on a slightly higher musical plane."[63]

NOTES

1. Garvin Bushell, with Mark Tucker, *Jazz from the Beginning* (Ann Arbor: University of Michigan Press, 1990), 23, 26–27, quotation from 27; William Howard Kenney III, "Influence of Black Vaudeville on Early Jazz," *Black Perspective in Music* 14, no. 3 (fall 1986): 235.

2. Bushell, *Jazz*, 54–57, quotation from 57; Thomas J. Clark, "Cotton Club," accompanying booklet to *The Original Cotton Club Orchestras* (Audiofidelity Enterprises, AFE-3-13, 1985), 9.

3. Stanley Dance, *The World of Earl Hines* (New York: Charles Scribner's Sons, 1977; reprint, New York: Da Capo Press, 1983), 71.

4. Gunther Schuller and Martin Williams, "Big Band Jazz: From the Beginnings to the Fifties," accompanying booklet to *Big Band Jazz: From the Beginnings to the Fifties* (RCA, the Smithsonian Collection of Recordings, DMM 6-0610 LP Edition R 030, 1983).

5. Cholly Atkins, telephone interview with author, 15 May 1992; LeRoy Myers and Marion Coles, interview with author, New York, N.Y., 8 Nov. 1994.

6. Honi Coles, "The Dance," in *The Apollo Theater Story* (New York: Apollo Operations, 1966), 8–9, first two quotations from 8; Ted Fox, *Showtime at the Apollo* (New York: Holt, Rinehart, and Winston, 1985), 97–98, quotation from 98.

7. Brenda Dixon-Stowell, "Between Two Eras: 'Norton and Margot' in the Afro-American Entertainment World," *Dance Research Journal* 15, no. 2 (Spring 1983): 11–20.

8. Coles, "The Dance," 8; Marion Coles, telephone interview with author, 15 May 1995; Atkins interview, 15 May 1992.

9. Marshall Stearns and Jean Stearns, *Jazz Dance: The Story of American Vernacular Dance* (New York: Macmillan, 1968), 231–36, quotation from 231–32.

10. Ibid., 244–46; Cholly Atkins, telephone interview with author, 25 July 1992.

11. Stearns and Stearns, *Jazz Dance*, 282.

12. Baby Laurence quoted in ibid., 337; Whitney Balliett, *New York Notes: A Journal of Jazz, 1972–75* (Boston: Houghton Mifflin, 1976), 142; Sally Sommer, "Tap and How It Got That Way: Feet, Talk to Me!" *Dance Magazine*, Sept. 1988, 59–60.

13. Quotations from Louis Bellson, interview with Robert G. O'Meally, San Jose, Calif., 8 June 1992, from the files of Robert G. O'Meally; Jane Goldberg, "A Drum Is a Tapdancer," in "The Village Voice Jazz Special," a special section of *Village Voice*, 30 Aug. 1988, 11–13; Stanley Dance, *The World of Swing* (New York: Charles Scribner's Sons, 1974; reprint, New York: Da Capo Press, 1979), 184; Leroy Williams, telephone interview with author, 1 May 1992.

14. Max Roach quoted in Goldberg, "A Drum Is a Tapdancer," 12; Dannie Richmond quoted in ibid., 12; Philly Joe Jones quoted in ibid., 11–12.

15. Ralph Ellison, *Shadow and Act* (New York: Random House, 1964; reprint, New York: Vintage Books, 1972), 208–9; Duke Ellington, *Music Is My Mistress* (Garden City, N.Y.: Doubleday, 1973; reprint, New York: Da Capo Press, 1976), 161–62; Myers interview.

16. Jimmy Crawford quoted in Dance, *Swing*, 124.

17. Stearns and Stearns, *Jazz Dance*, 337–38; George Hoefer, "Jazz Odyssey, Vol. 3: The Sound of Harlem," accompanying booklet to *Jazz Odyssey*, vol. 3: *The Sound of Harlem* (Columbia Records, Jazz Archive Series, Mono-C3L 33, 1964).

18. Leonard Reed, interview with Rusty Frank, Hollywood, Calif., 8 June 1988, in *Tap!* ed. Rusty Frank (New York: William Morrow, 1990), 42.

19. John Michael Vlach, "Afro-American Aesthetic," in *Encyclopedia of Southern Culture*, ed. Charles Reagan Wilson and William Ferris (Chapel Hill: University of North Carolina Press, 1989), 457; Baby Laurence quoted in Stearns and Stearns, *Jazz Dance*, 341.

20. Dance, *Swing*, 399, 402.

21. Honi Coles quoted in Melba Huber, "Tap Talk," *Dance Pages* 9, no. 4 (Spring 1992): 18.

22. This information was taken from various interviews with Cholly Atkins and Honi Coles; Stearns and Stearns, *Jazz Dance*, 351–52, 339; Frank, *Tap!* 259.

23. Hoefer, "Jazz Odyssey."

24. Fox, *Showtime*, 74–75, 80–81, 98, 100, Andy Kirk quoted on 81, Sandman Sims quoted on 98, 100.

25. Coles, "The Dance," 9; Fox, *Showtime*, 75–77.

26. Dicky Wells and Stanley Dance, *The Night People: Reminiscences of a Jazzman* (Boston: Crescendo, 1971), 53, 113.

27. Romare Bearden quoted in Jervis Anderson, *This Was Harlem: A Cultural Portrait, 1900–1950* (New York: Farrar, Straus & Giroux, 1982), 241; Fox, *Showtime*, 82.

28. *The Savoy Story*, Twenty-Fifth Anniversary of the Savoy Ballroom Brochure, 1951; Hoefer, "Jazz Odyssey."

29. Quotation from David Levering Lewis, *When Harlem Was in Vogue* (New York: Alfred A. Knopf, 1981; reprint, New York: Oxford University Press, 1989), 170; Hoefer, "Jazz Odyssey"; *The Savoy Story*.

30. *The Savoy Story.*

31. Stearns and Stearns, *Jazz Dance*, 322–23; Albert Murray, *Stomping the Blues* (New York: McGraw-Hill, 1976; reprint, New York: Vintage Books, 1982), 23–42; Frankie Manning, interview with Robert P. Crease, New York, N.Y., 22–23 July 1992, Jazz Oral History Program, Smithsonian Institution.

32. Barbara Engelbrecht, "Swinging at the Savoy," *Dance Research Journal* 15, no. 2 (Spring 1983): 7; Stearns and Stearns, *Jazz Dance*, 322–25, 329.

33. Ellison, *Shadow and Act*, 206–7; Nat Hentoff, liner notes to *Big Band at the Savoy Ballroom* (Radio Corporation of America, LPM/LSP-2543, 1958); Stearns and Stearns, *Jazz Dance*, 324; Wells and Dance, *Night People*, 59.

34. Wells and Dance, *Night People*, 77.

35. William "Cat" Anderson quoted in Stanley Dance, *The World of Duke Ellington* (New York: Charles Scribner's Sons, 1970; reprint, New York: Da Capo Press, 1981), 153.

36. Dance, *Duke Ellington*, 13.

37. Pops Foster and Tom Stoddard, *Pops Foster: The Autobiography of a New Orleans Jazzman* (Berkeley: University of California Press, 1973), 166.

38. Lester Young quoted in Nat Shapiro and Nat Hentoff, eds., *The Jazz Makers: Essays on the Greats of Jazz* (New York: Rinehart, 1957; reprint, New York: Da Capo Press, 1979), 267.

39. Baby Dodds and Larry Gara, *The Baby Dodds Story*, rev. ed. (Baton Rouge: Louisiana State University Press, 1992), 88.

40. Jimmy Crawford quoted in Dance, *Swing*, 124.

41. Stearns and Stearns, *Jazz Dance*, 325.

42. Manning interview.

43. *The Savoy Story*; Alice Irene Pifer, "Back into Swing," *20/20*, 28 July 1989, transcript; *Duke Ellington and His Orchestra, 1929–1941* (Jazz Classics, Amvest Video, Rahway, N.J., 1987); Manning interview; Norma Miller, interview with Ernie Smith, Bolton Landing, N.Y., 23–24 Sept. 1992, Jazz Oral History Program, Smithsonian Institution; Robert Crease, "Last of the Lindy Hoppers," *Village Voice*, 25 Aug. 1987, 27–32; Norma Miller, telephone interview with author, 14 Dec. 1992; Robert P. Crease, "The Lindy Hop," *Research Forum Papers: The 1988 International Early Dance Institute* (June 1988): 1–11.

44. Dance, *Swing*, 71; Wells and Dance, *Night People*, 62; Philip W. Payne, ed. "The Swing Era 1938–39: Where Swing Came From," accompanying booklet to *The Swing Era 1938–39: Where Swing Came From* (Time-Life Records, New York, STL 343, 1971), 55.

45. Samuel B. Charters and Leonard Kundstadt, *Jazz: A History of the New York Scene* (Garden City, N.Y.: 1962; reprint, New York: Da Capo Press, 1984), 257–59, quotation from 259.

46. Ellington, *Music Is My Mistress*, 100; Barry Ulanov, *A History of Jazz in America* (New York: Viking Press, 1952), 166–73.

47. Ellison, *Shadow and Act*, 243–44; Albert Murray and Wynton Marsalis, "Good Evening Blues," lecture, Alice Tully Hall, Lincoln Center for the Performing Arts, New York, N.Y., 12 May 1992.

48. Ralph Ellison, "Harlem's America," from the U.S. Senate Investigation of the Crisis in our Cities, *New Leader* 49, no. 19 (26 Sept. 1966): 22–35, quotation from 23.

49. Murray and Marsalis, "Good Evening Blues."

50. Dance, *Duke Ellington*, 13; Ellington, *Music Is My Mistress*, 264, 281; Ellison, *Shadow and Act*, 268; Albert Murray, interview with the author, New York, N.Y., 8 May 1993; Buster Brown, interview with author, New York, N.Y., 31 Oct. 1994.

51. Wynton Marsalis, interview with Robert G. O'Meally, New York, N.Y., July 1992, from the files of Robert G. O'Meally; Murray interview.

52. Tom Davin, "Conversation with James P. Johnson," in *Jazz Panorama*, ed. Martin Williams (New York: Crowell-Collier, 1962; reprint, New York: Da Capo Press, 1979), 44–61, quotation from 56; Louis Armstrong quoted in Nat Shapiro and Nat Hentoff, eds., *Hear Me Talkin' to Ya: The Story of Jazz as Told by the Men Who Made It* (New York: Rinehart, 1955; reprint, New York: Dover, 1966), 111.

53. Dizzy Gillespie with Al Fraser, *To Be or Not to Bop: Memoirs* (New York: Doubleday, 1979; reprint, New York: Da Capo Press, 1985), 26–27, 223, Sarah Vaughan quoted on 179, Ella Fitzgerald quoted on 273, and Dizzy Gillespie quoted on 42.

54. Randy Weston and Ben Riley quoted in Toby Byron and Richard Saylor, *Thelonious Monk, American Composer* (Masters of American Music Series, Toby Byron/Multiprises in association with Taurus Film, Munich, and Videoarts, Japan, 1991).

55. Count Basie and Albert Murray, *Good Morning Blues: The Autobiography of Count Basie* (New York: Random House, 1985), 85–86.

56. Eddie Durham quoted in Stanley Dance, *The World of Count Basie* (New York: Charles Scribner's Sons, 1980; reprint, New York: Da Capo Press, 1985), 65; Stanley Dance, "The Complete Jimmy Lunceford, 1939–40," accompanying booklet to *The*

Complete Jimmy Lunceford, 1939–40 (cbs Disques, France, cbs 66421, 1981).

57. Nat Pierce quoted in Dance, *Swing,* 342; Dance, "The Complete Jimmy Lunceford."

58. Murray, *Stomping the Blues,* 138.

59. Frederic Ramsey Jr., "Jazz Odyssey, Vol. 1: The Sound of New Orleans, 1917–1947," accompanying booklet to *Jazz Odyssey, Vol. 1: The Sound of New Orleans, 1917–1947* (Columbia Records, Mono-C3L 30, 1964).

60. Max Roach quoted in Goldberg, "A Drum Is a Tapdancer," 12.

61. Max Roach quoted in Gillespie, *To Be or Not to Bop,* 232–33.

62. Bessie Dudley, interview with author and Robert G. O'Meally, New York, N.Y., 23, 29 June 1992; Cholly Atkins interviews, 1988–92.

63. Dance, *Duke Ellington,* 14.

chapter 19

ZORA NEALE HURSTON

Characteristics of Negro Expression

Drama

The Negro's universal mimicry is not so much a thing in itself as an evidence of something that permeates his entire self. And that thing is drama.

His very words are action words. His interpretation of the English language is in terms of pictures. One act described in terms of another. Hence the rich metaphor and simile.

The metaphor is of course very primitive. It is easier to illustrate than it is to explain because action came before speech. Let us make a parallel. Language is like money. In primitive communities actual goods, however bulky, are bartered for what one wants. This finally evolves into coin, the coin being not real wealth but a symbol of wealth. Still later, even coin is abandoned for legal tender, and still later cheques for certain usages.

Every phase of Negro life is highly dramatized. No matter how joyful or how sad the case there is sufficient poise for drama. Everything is acted out. Unconsciously for the most part of course. There is an impromptu ceremony always ready for every hour of life. No little moment passes unadorned.

Now the people with highly developed languages have words for detached ideas. That is legal tender. "That-which-we-squat-on" has become "chair." "Groan-causer" has evolved into "spear" and so on. Some individuals even conceive of the equivalent of cheque words, like "ideation" and "pleonastic." Perhaps we might say that *Paradise Lost* and *Sartor Resartus* are written in cheque words.

The primitive man exchanges descriptive words. His terms are all close fitting.

Frequently the Negro, even with detached words in his vocabulary—not evolved in him but transplanted on his tongue by contact—must add action to it to make it do. So we have "chop-axe," "sitting-chair," "cook-pot" and the like because the speaker has in his mind the picture of the object in use. Action. Everything illustrated. So we can say the white man thinks in a written language and the Negro thinks in hieroglyphics.

A bit of Negro drama familiar to all is the frequent meeting of two opponents who threaten to do atrocious murder one upon the other.

Who has not observed a robust young Negro chap posing upon a street corner, possessed of nothing but his clothing, his strength, and his youth? Does he bear himself like a pauper? No, Louis XIV could be no more insolent in his assurance. His eyes say plainly "Female, halt!" His posture exults "Ah, female, I am the eternal male, the giver of life. Behold in my hot flesh all the delights of this world. Salute me, I am strength." All this with a languid posture, there is no mistaking his meaning.

A Negro girl strolls past the corner lounger. Her whole body panging[1] and posing. A slight shoulder movement that calls attention to her bust, that is all of a dare. A hippy undulation below the waist that is a sheaf of promises tied with conscious power. She is acting out "I'm a darned sweet woman and you know it."

These little plays by strolling players are acted out daily in a dozen streets in a thousand cities, and no one ever mistakes the meaning.

Will to Adorn

The will to adorn is the second most notable characteristic in Negro expression. Perhaps his idea of ornament does not attempt to meet conventional standards, but it satisfies the soul of its creator.

In this respect the American Negro has done wonders to the English language. This is true, but it is equally true that he has made over a great part of the tongue to his liking and has his revision accepted by the ruling class. No one listening to a Southern white man talk could deny this. Not only has he softened and toned down strongly consonanted words like "aren't" to "ain't" and the like, he has made new force words out of old feeble elements. Examples of this are "ham-shanked," "battle-hammed," "double-teen," "bodaciously," "muffle-jawed."

But the Negro's greatest contribution to the language is: (1) the use of metaphor and simile; (2) the use of the double descriptive; (3) the use of verbal nouns.

1. Metaphor and Simile

One at a time, like lawyers going to heaven.

You sho is propaganda.

Sobbing hearted.

I'll beat you till [you]: (a) rope like okra, (b) slack like lime, (c) smell like onions.

Fatal for naked.

Kyting along.

That's a rope.
Cloakers—deceivers.
Regular as pig-tracks.
Mule blood—black molasses.
Syndicating—gossiping.
Flambeaux—cheap cafe (lighted by flambeaux).
To put yo'self on de ladder.

2. *The Double Descriptive*

High-tall.
Little-tee-ninchy (tiny).
Low-down.
Top-superior.
Sham-polish.
Lady-people.
Kill-dead.
Hot-boiling.
Chop-axe.
Sitting-chairs.
De watch wall.
Speedy-hurry.
More great and more better.

3. *Verbal Nouns*

She features somebody I know.
Funeralize.
Sense me into it.
Puts the shamery on him.
'Taint everybody you kin confidence.
I wouldn't friend with her.
Jooking—playing piano or guitar as it is done in Jook-houses (houses of ill-
     fame).
Uglying away.
I wouldn't scorn my name all up on you.
Bookooing (beaucoup) around—showing off.
Won't stand a broke.
She won't take a listen.
He won't stand straightening.
That is such a compliment.
That's a lynch.

The stark, trimmed phrases of the Occident seem too bare for the voluptuous child of the sun, hence the adornment. It arises out of the same impulse as the wearing of jewelry and the making of sculpture—the urge to adorn.

On the walls of the homes of the average Negro one always finds a glut of gaudy calendars, wall pockets and advertising lithographs. The sophisticated white man or Negro would tolerate none of these, even if they bore a likeness to the Mona Lisa. No commercial art for decoration. Neither the calendar nor the advertisement spoils the picture for this lowly man. He sees the beauty in spite of the declaration of the Portland Cement Works or the butcher's announcement. I saw in Mobile a room in which there was an over-stuffed mohair living-room suite, an imitation mahogany bed and chifferobe, a console victrola. The walls were gaily papered with Sunday supplements of the *Mobile Register*. There were seven calendars and three wall pockets. One of them was decorated with a lace doily. The mantel-shelf was covered with a scarf of deep home-made lace, looped up with a huge bow of pink crepe paper. Over the door was a huge lithograph showing the Treaty of Versailles being signed with a Waterman fountain pen.

It was grotesque, yes. But it indicated a desire for beauty. And decorating a decoration, as in the case of the doily on the gaudy wall pocket, did not seem out of place to the hostess. The feeling back of such an act is that there can never be enough of beauty, let alone too much. Perhaps she is right. We each have our standards of art, and thus we are all interested parties and so unfit to pass judgment upon the art concepts of others.

Whatever the Negro does of his own volition he embellishes. His religious service is for the greater part excellent prose poetry. Both prayers and sermons are tooled and polished until they are true works of art. The supplication is forgotten in the frenzy of creation. The prayer of the white man is considered humorous in its bleakness. The beauty of the Old Testament does not exceed that of a Negro prayer.

301

Angularity

After adornment the next most striking manifestation of the Negro is Angularity. Everything that he touches becomes angular. In all African sculpture and doctrine of any sort we find the same thing.

Anyone watching Negro dancers will be struck by the same phenomenon. Every posture is another angle. Pleasing, yes. But an effect achieved by the very means which a European strives to avoid.

The pictures on the walls are hung at deep angles. Furniture is always set at an angle. I have instances of a piece of furniture in the *middle* of a wall being set with one end nearer the wall than the other to avoid the simple straight line.

Asymmetry

Asymmetry is a definite feature of Negro art. I have no samples of true Negro painting unless we count the African shields, but the sculpture and carvings are full of this beauty and lack of symmetry. It is present in the literature, both prose and verse. I offer an example of this quality in verse from Langston Hughes:

> I ain't gonna mistreat ma good gal any more,
> I'm just gonna kill her next time she makes me sore.

I treats her kind but she don't do me right,
She fights and quarrels most every night.

I can't have no woman's got such low-down ways
Cause de blue gum woman ain't de style now'days.

I brought her from the South and she's goin on back,
Else I'll use her head for a carpet tack.

It is the lack of symmetry which makes Negro dancing so difficult for white dancers to learn. The abrupt and unexpected changes. The frequent change of key and time are evidences of this quality in music (Note the St. Louis Blues).

The dancing of the justly famous Bo-Jangles and Snake Hips are excellent examples.

The presence of rhythm and lack of symmetry are paradoxical, but there they are. Both are present to a marked degree. There is always rhythm, but it is the rhythm of segments. Each unit has a rhythm of its own, but when the whole is assembled it is lacking in symmetry. But easily workable to a Negro who is accustomed to the break in going from one part to another, so that he adjusts himself to the new tempo.

Dancing

Negro dancing is dynamic suggestion. No matter how violent it may appear to the beholder, every posture gives the impression that the dancer will do much more. For example, the performer flexes one knee sharply, assumes a ferocious face mask, thrusts the upper part of the body forward with clenched fists, elbows taut as in hard running or grasping a thrusting blade. That is all. But the spectator himself adds the picture of ferocious assault, hears the drums and finds himself keeping time with the music and tensing himself for the struggle. It is compelling insinuation. That is the very reason the spectator is held so rapt. He is participating in the performance himself—carrying out the suggestions of the performer.

The difference in the two arts is: the white dancer attempts to express fully; the Negro is restrained, but succeeds in gripping the beholder by forcing him to finish the action the performer suggests. Since no art can ever express all the variations conceivable, the Negro must be considered the greater artist, his dancing is realistic suggestion, and that is about all a great artist can do.

Negro Folklore

Negro folklore is not a thing of the past. It is still in the making. Its great variety shows the adaptability of the black man: nothing is too old or too new, domestic or foreign, high or low, for his use. God and the Devil are paired, and are treated no more reverently than Rockefeller and Ford. Both of these men are prominent in folklore. Ford being particularly strong, and they talk and act like good-natured stevedores or mill-hands. Ole Massa is sometimes a smart man and often a fool.

The automobile is ranged alongside of the oxcart. The angels and the apostles walk and talk like section hands. And through it all walks Jack, the greatest culture hero of the South; Jack beats them all—even the Devil, who is often smarter than God.

Culture Heroes

The Devil is next after Jack as a culture hero. He can outsmart everyone but Jack. God is absolutely no match for him. He is good-natured and full of humour. The sort of person one may count on to help out in any difficulty.

Peter the Apostle is third in importance. One need not look far for the explanation. The Negro is not a Christian really. The primitive gods are not deities of too subtle inner reflection; they are hard-working bodies who serve their devotees just as laboriously as the suppliant serves them. Gods of physical violence, stopping at nothing to serve their followers. Now of all the apostles, Peter is the most active. When the other ten fell back trembling in the garden, Peter wielded the blade on the posse. Peter first and foremost in all action. The gods of no peoples have been philosophic until the people themselves have approached that state.

The rabbit, the bear, the lion, the buzzard, the fox are culture heroes from the animal world. The rabbit is far in the lead of all the others and is blood brother to Jack. In short, the trickster-hero of West Africa has been transplanted to America.

John Henry is a culture hero in song, but no more so than Stacker Lee, Smokey Joe or Bad Lazarus. There are many, many Negroes who have never heard of any of the song heroes, but none who do not know John (Jack) and the rabbit.

Examples of Folklore and the Modern Culture Hero

WHY DE PORPOISE'S TAIL IS ON CROSSWISE   Now, I want to tell you 'bout de porpoise. God had done made de world and everything. He set de moon and de stars in de sky. He got de fishes of de sea, and de fowls of de air completed. He made de sun and hung it up. Then He made a nice gold track for it to run on. Then He said, "Now, Sun, I got everything made but Time. That's up to you. I want you to start out and go round de world on dis track just as fast as you kin make it. And de time it takes you to go and come, I'm going to call day and night." De Sun went zoomin' on cross de elements. Now, de porpoise was hanging round there and heard God what he told de Sun, so he decided he'd take dat trip round de world hisself. He looked up and saw de Sun kytin' along, so he lit out too, him and dat Sun!

So de porpoise beat de Sun round de world by one hour and three minutes. So God said, "Aw naw, this aint gointer do! I didn't mean for nothin' to be faster than de Sun!" So God run dat porpoise for three days before he runs him down and caught him, and took his tail off and put it crossways to slow him up. Still he's de fastest thing in de water. And dat's why de porpoise got his tail on crossways.

ROCKEFELLER AND FORD   Once John D. Rockefeller and Henry Ford was woofing at each other. Rockefeller told Henry Ford he could build a solid gold road round the world. Henry Ford told him if he would he would look at it and see if he liked it, and if he did he would buy it and put one of his tin lizzies on it.

Originality

It has been said so often that the Negro is lacking in originality that it has almost become a gospel. Outward signs seem to bear this out. But if one looks closely its falsity is immediately evident.

It is obvious that to get back to original sources is much too difficult for any group to claim very much as a certainty. What we really mean by originality is the modification of ideas. The most ardent admirer of the great Shakespeare cannot claim first source even for him. It is his treatment of the borrowed material.

So if we look at it squarely, the Negro is a very original being. While he lives and moves in the midst of a white civilization, everything that he touches is re-interpreted for his own use. He has modified the language, mode of food preparation, practice of medicine, and most certainly the religion of his new country, just as he adapted to suit himself the Sheik haircut made famous by Rudolph Valentino.

Everyone is familiar with the Negro's modification of the whites' musical instruments, so that his interpretation has been adopted by the white man himself and then re-interpreted. In so many words, Paul Whiteman is giving an imitation of a Negro orchestra making use of white-invented musical instruments in a Negro way. Thus has arisen a new art in the civilized world, and thus has our so-called civilization come. The exchange and re-exchange of ideas between groups.

Imitation

The Negro, the world over, is famous as a mimic. But this in no way damages his standing as an original. Mimicry is an art in itself. If it is not, then all art must fall by the same blow that strikes it down. When sculpture, painting, dancing, literature neither reflect nor suggest anything in nature or human experience we turn away with a dull wonder in our hearts at why the thing was done. Moreover, the contention that the Negro imitates from a feeling of inferiority is incorrect. He mimics for the love of it. The group of Negroes who slavishly imitate is small. The average Negro glories in his ways. The highly educated Negro the same. The self-despisement lies in a middle class who scorns to do or be anything Negro. "That's just like a Nigger" is the most terrible rebuke one can lay upon this kind. He wears drab clothing, sits through a boresome church service, pretends to have no interest in the community, holds beauty contests, and otherwise apes all the mediocrities of the white brother. The truly cultured Negro scorns him, and the Negro "farthest down" is too busy "spreading his junk" in his own way to see or care. He likes his own things best. Even the group who are not Negroes but belong to the "sixth race," buy such records as "Shake dat thing" and "Tight lak dat." They really enjoy hearing a good bible-beater preach, but wild horses could drag no such admission from them. Their ready-made expression is: "We done got away from all that now." Some refuse to countenance Negro music on the grounds that it is niggerism, and for that reason should be done away with. Roland Hayes was thoroughly denounced for singing spirituals until he was accepted by white audiences. Langston Hughes is not considered a poet by this group because he writes of the man in the ditch, who is more numerous and real among us than any other.

But, this group aside, let us say that the art of mimicry is better developed in the Negro than in other racial groups. He does it as the mocking-bird does it, for the love of it, and not because he wishes to be like the one imitated. I saw a group of small Negro boys imitating a cat defecating and the subsequent toilet of the cat. It was very realistic, and they enjoyed it as much as if they had been imitating a coronation ceremony. The dances are full of imitations of various animals. The buzzard lope, walking the dog, the pig's hind legs, holding the mule, elephant squat, pigeon's wing, falling off the log, seaboard (imitation of an engine starting), and the like.

Absence of the Concept of Privacy

It is said that Negroes keep nothing secret, that they have no reserve. This ought not to seem strange when one considers that we are an outdoor people accustomed to communal life. Add this to all-permeating drama and you have the explanation.

There is no privacy in an African village. Loves, fights, possessions are, to misquote Woodrow Wilson, "Open disagreements openly arrived at." The community is given the benefit of a good fight as well as a good wedding. An audience is a necessary part of any drama. We merely go with nature rather than against it.

Discord is more natural than accord. If we accept the doctrine of the survival of the fittest there are more fighting honors than there are honors for other achievements. Humanity places premiums on all things necessary to its well-being, and a valiant and good fighter is valuable in any community. So why hide the light under a bushel? Moreover, intimidation is a recognized part of warfare the world over, and threats certainly must be listed under that head. So that a great threatener must certainly be considered an aid to the fighting machine. So then if a man or woman is a facile hurler of threats, why should he or she not show their wares to the community? Hence, the holding of all quarrels and fights in the open. One relieves one's pent-up anger and at the same time earns laurels in intimidation. Besides, one does the community a service. There is nothing so exhilarating as watching well-matched opponents go into action. The entire world likes action, for that matter. Hence prize-fighters become millionaires.

Likewise love-making is a biological necessity the world over and an art among Negroes. So that a man or woman who is proficient sees no reason why the fact should not be moot. He swaggers. She struts hippily about. Songs are built on the power to charm beneath the bed-clothes. Here again we have individuals striving to excel in what the community considers an art. Then if all of his world is seeking a great lover, why should he not speak right out loud?

It is all in a view-point. Love-making and fighting in all their branches are high arts, other things are arts among groups where they brag about their proficiency just as brazenly as we do about these things that others consider matters for conversation behind closed doors. At any rate, the white man is despised by Negroes as a very poor fighter individually, and a very poor lover. One Negro, speaking of white men, said, "White folks is alright when dey gits in de bank and on de law bench, but dey sho' kin lie about wimmen folks."

I pressed him to explain. "Well you see, white mens makes out they marries wimmen to look at they eyes, and they know they gits em for just what us gits em for. 'Nother thing, white mens say they goes clear round de world and wins all de wimmen folks way from they men folks. Dat's a lie too. They don't win nothin, they buys em. Now de way I figgers it, if a woman don't want me enough to be wid me, 'thout I got to pay her, she kin rock right on, but these here white men don't know what to do wid a woman when they gits her—dat's how come they gives they wimmen so much. They got to. Us wimmen works jus as hard as us does an come home an sleep wid us every night. They own wouldn't do it and its de mens fault. Dese white men done fooled theyself bout dese wimmen.

"Now me, I keeps me some wimmens all de time. Dat's whut dey wuz put here for—us mens to use. Dat's right now, Miss. Y'll wuz put here so us mens could have some pleasure. Course I don't run round like heap uh men folks. But if my ole lady go way from me and stay more'n two weeks, I got to git me somebody, ain't I?"

The Jook

Jook is the word for a Negro pleasure house. It may mean a bawdy house. It may mean the house set apart on public works where the men and women dance, drink and gamble. Often it is a combination of all these.

In past generations the music was furnished by "boxes," another word for guitars. One guitar was enough for a dance; to have two was considered excellent. Where two were playing one man played the lead and the other seconded him. The first player was "picking" and the second was "framming," that is, playing chords while the lead carried the melody by dexterous finger work. Sometimes a third player was added, and he played a tom-tom effect on the low strings. Believe it or not, this is excellent dance music.

Pianos soon came to take the place of the boxes, and now player-pianos and victrolas are in all of the Jooks.

Musically speaking, the Jook is the most important place in America. For in its smelly, shoddy confines has been born the secular music known as blues, and on blues has been founded jazz. The singing and playing in the true Negro style is called "jooking."

The songs grow by incremental repetition as they travel from mouth to mouth and from Jook to Jook for years before they reach outside ears. Hence the great variety of subject-matter in each song.

The Negro dances circulated over the world were also conceived inside the Jooks. They too make the round of Jooks and public works before going into the outside world.

In this respect it is interesting to mention the Black Bottom. I have read several false accounts of its origin and name. One writer claimed that it got its name from the black sticky mud on the bottom of the Mississippi River. Other equally absurd statements gummed the press. Now the dance really originated in the Jook section of Nashville, Tennessee, around Fourth Avenue. This is a tough neighborhood known as Black Bottom—hence the name.

The Charleston is perhaps forty years old and was danced up and down the Atlantic seaboard from North Carolina to Key West, Florida.

The Negro social dance is slow and sensuous. The idea in the Jook is to gain sensation, and not so much exercise. So that just enough foot movement is added to keep the dancers on the floor. A tremendous sex stimulation is gained from this. But who is trying to avoid it? The man, the woman, the time and place have met. Rather, little intimate names are indulged in to heap fire on fire.

These too have spread to all the world.

The Negro theatre, as built up by the Negro, is based on Jook situations, with women, gambling, fighting and drinking. Shows like "Dixie to Broadway" are only Negro in cast, and could just as well have come from pre-Soviet Russia.

Another interesting thing—Negro shows before being tampered with did not specialize in octoroon chorus girls. The girl who could hoist a Jook song from her belly and lam it against the front door of the theatre was the lead, even if she were as black as the hinges of hell. The question was "Can she jook?" She must also have a good belly wobble, and her hips must, to quote a popular work song, "Shake like jelly all over and be so broad, Lawd, Lawd, and be so broad." So that the bleached chorus is the result of a white demand and not the Negro's.

The woman in the Jook may be nappy headed and black, but if she is a good lover she gets there just the same. A favorite Jook song of the past has this to say:

SINGER: It aint good looks dat takes you through dis world.
AUDIENCE: What is it, good mama?
SINGER: Elgin[2] movements in your hips. Twenty years guarantee. And it
            always brought down the house too.

> Oh de white gal rides in a Cadillac,
> De yaller girl rides de same,
> Black gal rides in a rusty Ford
> But she gits dere just de same.

The sort of woman her men idealize is the type put forth in the theatre. The art-creating Negro prefers a not too thin woman who can shake like jelly all over as she dances and sings, and that is the type he put forth on the stage. She has been banished by the white producer and the Negro who takes his cue from the white.

Of course a black woman is never the wife of the upper class Negro in the North. This state of affairs does not obtain in the South, however. I have noted numerous cases where the wife was considerably darker than the husband. People of some substance, too.

This scornful attitude towards black women receives mouth sanction by the mud-sills.

Even on the works and in the Jooks the black man sings disparagingly of black women. They say that she is evil. That she sleeps with her fists doubled up and ready for action. All over they are making a little drama of waking up a yaller[3] wife and a black one.

A man is lying beside his yaller wife and wakes her up. She says to him, "Darling, do you know what I was dreaming when you woke me up?" He says, "No honey, what was you dreaming?" She says, "I dreamt I had done cooked you a big fine dinner and we was setting down to eat out de same plate and I was setting on yo' lap jus huggin you and kissin you and you was so sweet."

Wake up a black woman, and before you kin git any sense into her she be done up and lammed you over the head four or five times. When you git her quiet she'll say, "Nigger, know whut I was dreamin when you woke me up?"

You say, "No honey, what was you dreamin?" She says, "I dreamt you shook yo' rusty fist under my nose and I split yo' head open wid a axe."

But in spite of disparaging fictitious drama, in real life the black girl is drawing on his account at the commissary. Down in the Cypress Swamp as he swings his axe he chants:

> Dat ole black gal, she keeps on grumblin,
> New pair shoes, new pair shoes,
> I'm goint to buy her shoes and stockings
> Slippers too, slippers too.

Then adds aside: "Blacker de berry, sweeter de juice."

To be sure the black gal is still in power, men are still cutting and shooting their way to her pillow. To the queen of the Jook!

Speaking of the influence of the Jook, I noted that Mae West in "Sex" had much more flavor of the turpentine quarters than she did of the white bawd. I know that the piece she played on the piano is a very old Jook composition. "Honey let yo' drawers hang low" had been played and sung in every Jook in the South for at least thirty-five years. It has always puzzled me why she thought it likely to be played in a Canadian bawdy house.

Speaking of the use of Negro material by white performers, it is astonishing that so many are trying it, and I have never seen one yet entirely realistic. They often have all the elements of the song, dance, or expression, but they are misplaced or distorted by the accent falling on the wrong element. Everyone seems to think that the Negro is easily imitated when nothing is further from the truth. Without exception I wonder why the black-face comedians *are* black-face; it is a puzzle—good comedians, but darn poor niggers. Gershwin and the other "Negro" rhapsodists come under this same axe. Just about as Negro as caviar or Ann Pennington's athletic Black Bottom. When the Negroes who knew the Black Bottom in its cradle saw the Broadway version they asked each other, "Is you learnt dat *new* Black Bottom yet?" Proof that it was not *their* dance.

And God only knows what the world has suffered from the white damsels who try to sing Blues.

The Negroes themselves have sinned also in this respect. In spite of the goings up and down on the earth, from the original Fisk Jubilee Singers down to the present, there has been no genuine presentation of Negro songs to white audiences. The spirituals that have been sung around the world are Negroid to be sure, but so full of musicians' tricks that Negro congregations are highly entertained when they hear their old songs so changed. They never use the new style songs, and these are never heard unless perchance some daughter or son has been off to college and returns with one of the old songs with its face lifted, so to speak.

I am of the opinion that this trick style of delivery was originated by the Fisk Singers; Tuskegee and Hampton followed suit and have helped spread this misconception of Negro spirituals. This Glee Club style has gone on so long and become so fixed among concert singers that it is considered quite authentic. But I say again, that not one concert singer in the world is singing the songs as the Negro songmakers sing them.

If anyone wishes to prove the truth of this let him step into some unfashionable Negro church and hear for himself.

To those who want to institute the Negro theatre, let me say it is already established. It is lacking in wealth, so it is not seen in the high places. A creature with a white head and Negro feet struts the Metropolitan boards. The real Negro theatre is in the Jooks and the cabarets. Self-conscious individuals may turn away the eye and say, "Let us search elsewhere for our dramatic art." Let 'em search. They certainly won't find it. Butter Beans and Susie, Bo-Jangles and Snake Hips are the only performers of the real Negro school it has ever been my pleasure to behold in New York.

Dialect

If we are to believe the majority of writers of Negro dialect and the burnt-cork artists, Negro speech is a weird thing, full of "ams" and "Ises." Fortunately, we don't have to believe them. We may go directly to the Negro and let him speak for himself.

I know that I run the risk of being damned as an infidel for declaring that nowhere can be found the Negro who asks "am it?" nor yet his brother who announces "Ise uh gwinter." He exists only for a certain type of writers and performers.

Very few Negroes, educated or not, use a clear clipped "I." It verges more or less upon "Ah." I think the lip form is responsible for this to a great extent. By experiment the reader will find that a sharp "i" is very much easier with a thin taut lip than with a full soft lip. Like tightening violin strings.

If one listens closely one will note too that a word is slurred in one position in the sentence but clearly pronounced in another. This is particularly true of the pronouns. A pronoun as a subject is likely to be clearly enunciated, but slurred as an object. For example: "You better not let me ketch yuh."

There is a tendency in some localities to add the "h" to "it" and pronounce it "hit." Probably a vestige of Old English. In some localities "if" is "ef."

In story telling "so" is universally the connective. It is used even as an introductory word, at the very beginning of a story. In religious expression "and" is used. The trend in stories is to state conclusions; in religion, to enumerate.

I am mentioning only the most general rules in dialect because there are so many quirks that belong only to certain localities that nothing less than a volume would be adequate.

NOTES
1. From "pang."
2. Elegant (?). [from the Elgin Watch, Ed.]
3. Yaller (yellow), light mulatto.

chapter 20

ROBERT FARRIS THOMPSON

African Art and Motion

When he wanted to show that I was many he would say that I have a right and a left side and a front and a back and an upper and a lower half, for I cannot deny that I partake of multitude.   —PLATO, *Parmenides*

Both space and motion can be manipulated rhythmically. Existence can also be manipulated in like manner; but we'll deal with that some other time when we are discussing contests that involve more than four persons. If we went into that now, we would have to discuss history, and that bitch is not the subject of my discussion.

—LARRY NEAL, "UNCLE RUFUS RAPS ON THE SQUARED CIRCLE," *Partisan Review*

Shared evaluations are vital to the understanding of African traditional art and dance. I, therefore, start with the norms of these traditions: the canons of fine form in art and dance, with occasional reference to music and to dress, and the persistence in time of some of these themes.

An aesthetic is a mode of intellectual energy that only exists when in operation, *i.e.*, when standards are applied to actual cases and are reasoned. Criticism by Africans is largely verbal, deepened by subjectivity of mind and expressive of a double admonition: improve your character to improve your art. Art and goodness are combined. The road to social purification and destiny is predicated upon a process through which the person takes on the essential attributes of aesthetically defined perfection in order to live in visible proximity to the divine.[1] The process can start in childhood, as when a black mother tells her child, "the way you walk signals your station in life."

Criticism of visual traditions has been identified in Africa,[2] but the canons of motion remain to be established. The next step is to discover and define artistic criticism of the dance in Africa in order to complete a dimension of critical awareness.

Dance Criticism in Africa

In 1912 Robert Schmitz noted artistic evaluation of dancing among the Baholoholo of Central Africa: "the spectators commented, one to the other, on the aesthetic qualities of the dancers, and upon the choreographic expertise of each person."[3] In 1938 Jomo Kenyatta showed Kikuyu children in Kenya were subject to close critical scrutiny by their parents when they danced.[4] Jean Rouch published in 1950 fragments of dance criticism from Timbuktu. He found that, "the slightest errors are criticized by interminable pleasantry" and that, "where pure figures, free and abstract, linked in a dazzling series of variations, are finally finished by the dancer, stopping in a pirouette phrased close to the surface of the earth, there mounts from the enchanted gathering that indescribable murmur by which blacks traditionally applaud."[5]

Margaret Read reported, from what is now Malawi, Ngoni thoughts about the dance in 1960. Ngoni define the dance as a force revealing manhood, character, and birth-right. Ngoni elders praise dancing on the score of strength and perfect timing. Interest seems to focus on the beating of the earth by bare male feet. A Ngoni dance of men is not a dance unless forcefully asserted.[6]

By 1967 evidence had accumulated sufficient to show dance criticism south of the Sahara existed in its own right. New sources included research among the Akan of Ghana, Tiv of Nigeria, and Dan of northeastern Liberia. As to the Akan, Kwabena Nketia discovered distinct qualities lauded in dancing, especially creative self-absorption. The ideal dancer, Akan say, never seeks applause while dancing, but spontaneously incites enthusiasm through total commitment to his footwork and kinetic flair. It is never to be said, in Akan culture, that a dancer performed "throwing glances at people" (*n'asa nhwehwewanimu*), i.e., disgracefully begging support or praise. Nor will Akan connoisseurs tolerate the one-style dancer. "He has only one style," a critic might pointedly remark, "and yet he [has the effrontery to go] round and round" (*n'asa fua, nso na ode reko anwan*).[7]

Charles Keil, in a report entitled, *Tiv Dance: A First Assessment* (1966), focused on Tiv adverbs of motion analysis:

> *Girnya*, the traditional warriors' dance, should be danced quickly (*ferefere*), light on the feet (*gendegende*) with strength (*tsoghtsogh*), and vigorously, as a hen scratches (*sagher-sagher*).
>
> Some men's and all women's dances should be done smoothly, cool, "like sleeping on a new mattress" (*lugh-lugh*), deep, steady, respectfully, as if pressing down the earth (*kindigh-kindigh*), slowly, steadily, controlled (*kule-kule*), and carefully, soothingly, and persuasively (*legh-legh*).
>
> Whatever the dance being done, it should be executed perfectly, com-

pletely, clearly, without mistake (*tsembele-tsembele*) in an orderly manner (*shanja-shanja*) and in detail (*vighe-vighe*).[8]

There is much meaningful substance here, sexually distinguishable ideals of strength (men) and coolness (women) and clarity (all dancing), but we will defer discussion and pass on to one further demonstration of the vitality of dance criticism in traditional Africa.

George Tabmen, a Dan from the northeast of Liberia, asserts that Dan people live in a state of constant critical awareness of bodily motion. He gives, as partial evidence, the readiness of Dan to criticize even a good-looking youth if the way he walks is incommensurate with the beauty of his body: "He is fine," a critic might say, "but he bends his head when walking" (*E sa ka a gagban tay gu*).[9] Artistic criticism is deemed so important in this African civilization that the process of judging music and dance can become a performance in its own right, entertaining and informing the inhabitants of an entire village. Thus the village of Blimiple, near the river dividing Liberia from the Ivory Coast, is said to be famed for its critical code:

> If a band of performers comes to the town of Blimiple, and attempts to perform in the town square, but has no talent whatsoever, the town chief, or the quarter chief, will tell them to go to the house of *Woya* (Bad Singer) and the town will have been informed to ignore these men because of their lack of musical quality.
>
> If there is a play and they discover that the performers are repeating and repeating, singing and dancing the same phrase over and over again, then a citizen of the town will stop the music, and say, "let's go before one of our elders' houses," his name is *Pindou* (Repetitious).
>
> Singers whose voices are not smooth will be invited to visit the house of *Zoogbaye* (Harsh Singing).
>
> If the singers begin to sense that their efforts are not appreciated and become belligerent, they are led to *Nyazii* . . . (Frankness) . . . [who will frankly tell them they are] terrible and to pack their things and move on. . . .[10]

The young Dan dancer runs a fascinating gauntlet between the peremptory challenges of a master drummer and his peers. He enters the dancing ring in the village square first to salute the master drummer, "to get his motion," *i.e.*, to settle the basic rhythm. He then begins a toe-dragging sequence, kept simple, because the drummer is studying his motion. Slowly he develops his dance; he must keep the drummer active with counter-challenges of percussive footwork. If he is excellent he will win applause, which among Dan takes the form not of handclapping, but symbolic outstretching of both arms, palms open and parallel, "as if to embrace the dancer, you want to embrace him as a sign of deep respect." This gesture may be underscored by the cry, "*Yaaa titi*!! reserved for something exciting, for the pleasure of the people."[11]

This is the crucial moment of the dancer's entrance; if he rests on his accomplishments, and lets the mark of his pleasure show upon his lips, without returning immediately to the task of discovering fresh patterning, he may suffer a fate identical to that of the Akan one-style dancer. He must search for fresh vision with determination: "When the applause mounts, the smile dies down, and you pay more attention to the footwork."[12]

Consulting the Experts, Traditional and Modern: Remarks on Method

The smile of the writer dies down, too, when he considers the problems of translation of motion, as an aesthetic criterion in the history of African art. It is a sobering experience. There are fortunately a number of sources at my disposal: (1) the traditional expert in Africa, defined as any person who holds a strong and reasoned opinion about dance and who, himself, is a member of a traditional society (2) modern experts on music, dance, and art in Africa (3) the White Collection. Let me discuss and reason these sources.

The aim of this book [*African Art in Motion*] is an existential definition of African art in motion. Accordingly, the work begins with the opinions of those who live these traditions. They are the existential experts. I identify them as such, citing in the process some of their own terms for expertise, *e.g.*, *amewa* (Yoruba: "knower of beauty"), *edisop* (Efik: "acute in hearing and seeing"), *nganga* (Ki-Kongo: "traditional priest, doctor, savant, expert").[13] Meeting people and hearing their opinions demands discretion. In the spring of 1967 I asked some of the elders of Butuo, a Liberian Dan village, which of several dancers performing were the finest. The answer was immediate: "we know which children are best but they are *our* children."[14] The situation resembles the Yoruba evaluation of the finest singers of the ballads of the hunters (*ijala*): "usually members of the audience do not speak out, on the spot, their opinions about the relative merits of the performing *ijala* artists. But later on, in private conversation on the subject of who is who in *ijala* chanting in the area, each person speaks out his mind and thus the reputations of the best *ijala* artists are established."[15]

African traditions of artistic criticism, in some important instances at least, tend to favor discretion. I therefore discussed such matters in private, as with my best Dan informant, or in public in the most diplomatic manner, *i.e.*, through positive criticism within the traditions ("why is this dance beautiful?") and positive or negative criticism outside tradition ("describe what I am doing wrong"—where the writer attempted traditional steps and motions—and "what do you think of this dance?" *i.e.*, inviting criticism of foreign modes). The intent was to avoid at all costs seeking criticism of lineage members within the lineages.

The comments of the local observers were never so technical as to destroy the flavor of the motion as a work of art. They spoke in their own voices with a sensible, non-pretentious vocabulary. Characteristically, phrasing was lexically simple but conceptually rich, shared by cultivators and kings alike. This was popular expertise.

Traditional opinion potentially exists everywhere, brought to brilliant focus by men and women of special perceptiveness. I was fortunate to meet several informants who operated on the highest levels of intellectual discourse, notably George Tabmen of Liberia and Sukari Kahanga of Zaire.

Throughout this [article] when I speak of "Africa" it is shorthand for those West and Central African civilizations I have visited, together with Bantu societies for which the literature yields pertinent material on art and dance. Islamic North Africa, Ethiopia and the Horn, and most of East and South Africa are lamentably omitted from the scope of this study.

I have visited the following cultures: Liberian Dan, Popo, Fon and Yoruba of Dahomey, Yoruba and Abakpa of Nigeria, Banyang and Ejagham of Cameroon, Kongo of Zaire. In addition, in two Cameroon towns (Douala, Kumba) I interviewed migrant workers from rural areas, and did the same in Kinshasa, Zaire. The number of informants in each particular culture varied, *i.e.*, Bariba (1), Kossi (1), Yoruba (31), Banyang (16). The following is a list showing nation, date of work, and number of informants interviewed: Liberia, March–June 1967, 5; Dahomey, August 1972, June 1973, 24; Nigeria, summers 1964, 1965, 1966, 14; Cameroon, March–June 1973, 43; Zaire, March, June 1973, 10. The total sample was, therefore, ninety-six. Most informants were cultivators and often religiously bi-lingual, that is, they were official Christians who, nevertheless, continued to honor some of the ancient forms of ritual. Lest the impression be given that the sampling was entirely rural, I ought to recall that all Zairois interviewed, though often from savannah villages where traditional flavor still exists, were, nevertheless, now residents of the city of Kinshasa. By contrast, Dahomean, Nigerian, Liberian, and Cameroon informants were predominantly rural.

In the villages of the interior informants were identified and gathered by traditional chiefs or headmen after careful prior consultation; these rulers did their best to bring together a representative sampling, but most of the respondents, perforce, were cultivators, leavened with a sprinkling of traditional priests and leaders.

The pace of the research stepped up in June 1973, when I met seventy traditional experts on dance. This last voyage was also distinguished by an experimental usage of the medium of videotape. A portable videotape unit is an instrument with several advantages for aesthetic fieldwork. Unlike photography and film, picture-*taking* media, literally removing the images from the world of the informant (excepting the Polaroid process), and transporting them to foreign or locally distant processing stations, videotape is picture-*giving*.[16] The image is now. It is immediate. Africans observe the image of their kinsmen performing, on the two-inch monitor screen of the portable (Akai) recorder, while they are performing. They shared in the pleasures of the instant-replay, an expression of the video revolution whose usefulness to the focusing of discussion on the fine points of dance can be well imagined.

I played sequences of traditional African dances, taped during prior voyages, and solicited responses, in the vernacular wherever possible, on form and quality in the motions. I had these comments written down on the spot. I played Zaire dances to Cameroon audiences, Yoruba dances to Dahomeans, and so on, in order to avoid the problems emergent in asking a person to criticize his own tradition.

I also played culturally intra-mural materials (*i.e.*, Ejagham dancing to Ejagham, Yoruba to Yoruba), but never from the same village and always in positive terms, inviting reasons for the beauty of a given dance. By paying careful attention to local protocol I was rewarded by full and interesting discussions in nearly every case, though doubtless the novelty of the medium and the beauty of the dances flashing on the screen also informed immediacy and gusto of response.

Only two persons refused to criticize dances outside their culture, on the score of their formal strangeness: "they dance like devils," one said. All the rest (94 informants) discussed style with saliency, voicing comments about timing, finish, dress, thematic balance, and so forth without hesitation. Foreign dress or exotic iconography did not distract informants from the basic issues of bodily motion and qualitative phrasing. In fact, I have the distinct impression that the informants were proud of the parallels they spotted between the distant videotaped dances and the dances of their own villages. Without question, among the many winds of change sweeping tropical Africa is a sense of artistic cultural solidarity, and not a few of the respondents talked about the beauty of the dances in terms of their *being African*. Some respondents broke into sympathetic body motions to demonstrate the closeness of their traditional dances to those filmed and visible on the screen. Zaire (Pende) circumcision knitted costumes caused a minor sensation in the Ejagham (Cameroon) village of Otu where a general similarity in weave and striped pattern was immediately remarked and compared to local Ngbe Society traditions.

These experiences suggest that the assumption that Africans cannot, or are unwilling to, evaluate art or dance from outside their immediate cultural universe is untrue.

The words written down were but an abstraction of a larger affective response, including laughter, smiling, brightness of eye, sympathetic bodily response, and gossip of many sorts. The most exciting finding in my opinion was: village after village evaluated dance from areas hundreds of miles away precisely as if the dances stemmed from their own traditions.

Men and women working within Western academic disciplines have also been in touch with the world represented by the field informants. When I reread the researches of Kwabena Nketia, Alan Lomax, *et al.*, upon return from Africa in June 1973, I noted concordance between traditional criteria of fine form and scholarly definition of important musical and dance structure. Field and academic data, therefore, often mesh in an interesting way and reinforce each other.

Agreement between the two worlds forms the basis of this chapter. In every instance, save one, the criteria of fine form in the dance exist as realities, both in the mind of the traditional folk who elaborate them, and of the persons who have studied African aesthetics professionally.

The rationale for the inclusion of a criterion is, therefore, consensus—both intramurally African and extramurally academic. The one exception is the canon of suspending the beat in music and in dance. This trait has been objectively documented by Waterman and Jones in music and dance; its absence in field commentary perhaps reflects the fact that it is so deeply ingrained a habit-of-performance that it is thoroughly taken for granted. It certainly exists. I am attempting to show that the trait of suspending the beat characterizes footwork, bodily phrasing, and, as a promising metaphor, some aspects of rhythmized color patterning in parts of West Africa, notably Akan.

All the other criteria generally represent the writer's synthesis of inside and outside opinion. The intent of marshalling the materials in this way is to suggest a given body of instruments by which to comprehend stylized motion and arrest in the figural sculpture of Black Africa. Attitudes, or positions of the body, as realized in African sculpture, often betray choreographic implications. On close inspection, the relation between the bent knees of the black dance and the identical expression of flexibility in the corpus of black sculpture can immediately be grasped.

I also hope to use these criteria to define, in part, the means by which African icons of repose (sitting, standing, balancing) are reconciled with the fullness of human motion when carried in the dance. . . .

If a private collection of African sculpture is truly representative, points can be made in intellectual argument in terms of the holdings, in spite of the fortuitous manner by which collections ordinarily are assembled. The White Collection, one of the major private gatherings of subsaharan sculpture and textiles in the world, sustains, in most cases, the sort of inquiry we wish to make. In addition, icons of balance and repose . . . are so pervasive in African sculpture that, given the breadth of the collection, most are present here. Most felicitously, it was agreed, when I undertook to write [the book in which this essay appears], that I would be free to omit those objects in the collection which were not germane. It was also agreed that I might add photographs of objects from other collections to illustrate, optimally, a given point and that special accessions would be made. I have thus been able to concentrate on people and ideas in interaction with works of art, instead of, idolatrously, on the statuary alone. The two realms, art and motion, must be brought together. We now come to the canons of fine form.

1. Ephebism: The Stronger Power that Comes from Youth

Beauty blazes out of bodies which are most alive and young. Ephebism, or youthfulness (cf. ephebe, "in ancient Greece, a youth between eighteen and twenty years of age"),[17] is universally admired in Africa as an aspect of fine form. A terracotta head (Plate 1) from Akan antiquity, found in the southern region of modern Ghana, represented an important priest or royal person, i.e., a senior person, a person who had attained his rank advanced in years. Yet there is not a single trace of age or stress. The visage is a flawless seal. The lips are discreet. The surface of the skin is smooth and strong. This image is beautiful, in Akan terms, precisely because it makes the subject look both honorable and strong.[18]

Traditional people among the Mende, Baoule, Yoruba, Fang, and Chokwe share the cherishing of newness and youthfulness in artistic expression.[19] Chokwe in Angola, Crowley shows, distinctly prefer new masks over old, because the former have the, "stronger power that comes from youth."[20] Without this, an object cannot shine within its force, and without vital aliveness we are no longer talking about African art.

This point richly applies to the dance. People in Africa, regardless of their actual age, return to strong, youthful patterning whenever they move within the streams of energy which flow from drums or other sources of percussion. They obey the implications of vitality within the music and its speed and drive. Some Western observers fail to see this; they miss the magic act of grace when men and

PLATE 1
Ghana, Akan, head, terra cotta, 10"

women find their youth in dance (compare Athena's loving restoration of the youthful frame of Odysseus at crucial points within his life). André Gide, for example, has written:

> the women dance at the entrance of every village. This shameless jigging of elderly matrons is extremely painful to look at. The most aged are the most frenzied. . . .[21]

How different is the tone and quality of testimony from the inside. Thus an old member of a Cameroon Ngbe society:

> I like him because he uses the conversation with his body. Even an old man can dance conversation, using the whole body; that old man, why he so dance?—to show still get power![22]

The power of youth is suggested by other traits of African art and dance:

a. "Swing" Every Note and Every Color Strong

Most dancers in Africa (elderly kings are sometimes an exception) step inside rhythms which are young and strong, and to this extent their bodies are general-

PLATE 2
Cameroon, Wum, mask, wood, 13 ½"

ized by vital rhythmic impulse. This necessitates phrasing every note and step with consummate vitality. This is a uniquely African quality, dubbed "swing" by jazzmen in the United States. "Swing," Gunther Schuller suggests, is a force in music that perfectly maintains an equilibrium between melodic and rhythmic relationships.[23] In the music of the West, in contrast to this history, pitch is considered more important than rhythm. A classical musician is mindful only of vertical accuracy and pays no heed to propulsive flow nor motion; he does not become involved in the horizontal, rhythmic demands of music.

In Africa, pitch is unthinkable without a correspondingly strong impulse in rhythm. Pitch and accent are phrased with equal strength, equal force, creating a youthful buoyancy and drive. Jazzmen call this quality swing, but Schuller rephrases it "democratization of rhythmic values," and explains what he means:

> in jazz so-called weak beats (or weak parts of rhythmic units) are *not* underplayed as in "classical" music. Instead, they are brought up to the level of strong beats, and very often even emphasized *beyond* the strong beat. The jazz musician does this not only by maintaining an equality of dynamics among "weak" and "strong" elements, but also by preserving the full sonority of notes even though they may happen to fall on weak parts of a measure. . . . This consciousness of attack and sonority makes the jazz horn player tongue almost all notes, even in the fastest runs, though the effect may be that of slurring. A pure "legato" is foreign to him because he cannot then control as well the attack impulse.[24]

It is precisely an "attack impulse," in the staccato handling of solid and void, that distinguishes the "Africanness" of a Wum carved head from the north of the Cameroon Grasslands (Plate 2). The hollowed spaces under the brow which suggest the eyes, rich in expressive shadow, become as important, as "strong elements," as the firm cheeks or the bristling fence of teeth. The lines of the hair might have been treated with realistic softness in a Western carving, but nothing here is allowed to project weakly from the surface of the object. Consciousness of fully realized strength of expression, as part of the canon of vitality, caused the carver to make a sharp series of accents to represent coiffure.

Equality of dynamics, in the handling of the masses, characterizes an exquisitely strong piece from the Kom style of the Cameroon Grasslands (Plate 3). The plastic order of the eye, strongly outlined, is matched by the intensity of line which marks the ears; crown and facial surfaces are strongly equalized.

A. M. Jones has observed: "the African normally makes no noticeable physical stress on any note and sings all the notes in a steady outpouring of even tone."[25] The same point applies to the strong use of color in African textiles. There are two ways of preserving the full sonority of colors in textile patterning: either through contrastive colors, hot and cool, of equal strength, or by maintaining equality of dynamics in the phrasing of light and dark colors (the textiles of the Akan of Ghana are excellent examples) (Plate 4). Either way, full sonority and attack in the handling of color means that every line is equally emphasized. For this reason, many or most of the textile traditions of Africa seem "loud" by conventional

Western standards, but this is precisely the point. Equal strength of every note parallels equal strength of every color. Yet there are probably differential limits to the amount of intensity in color preferred by different African societies, as suggested by an interlude in Bida, Nigeria, on 18 July 1965, when an Eket Ibibio migrant in Nupeland criticized red Nupe cloth on the ground that "the sun, which is red, makes such cloth brighter than it really is, and the designs on the cloth may disappear. The cloth is too bright."[26] In general, however, the African usage of color in cloth is splendidly vital, as evidenced by textiles from the Ivory Coast (Plate 5).

PLATE 3
Cameroon, Kom, mask, wood, 16"

PLATE 4
Ghana, Ashanti, Kente cloth (detail)

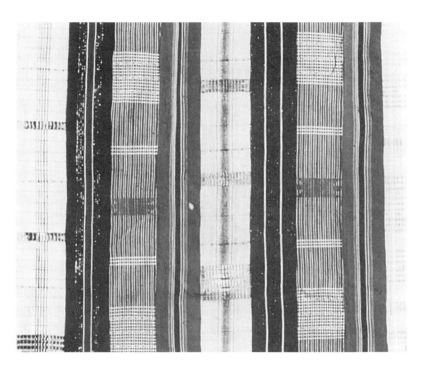

PLATE 5
Ivory Coast, textile (detail)

b. Vital Aliveness: Playing the Body Parts with Percussive Strength

Intensity in African color is paralleled by percussive attack in African musical and choreographic performance principles. Never is the stronger power that comes from youth more evident than in the canon of vital aliveness. Commentators on the dance in traditional areas are concerned with the quality, which might also be described as full power in response to percussion. Here are some of the voices of the Africans—Yoruba, "[Agbeke] has a great deal of power, more than anyone else"; "dance brings vitality to the body; this dance intensifies the honor and memory of our lord, the God of Iron"; Ejagham, "he turns round, round, round, to show he has power in dancing."[27]

African dance is seen in the eyes of its performers as an instrument of strong expression. The dancer must be strong. He must shake his being with vigor, creating a vision "terrible to watch" in the words of a Bangwa hunter. Vital aliveness, high intensity, speed, drive—these are some of the facets of artful muscularity and depth of feeling that characterize the dances of this continent.

The concept of vital aliveness leads to the interpretation of the parts of the body as independent instruments of percussive force. It is usually not permissible to allow the arms to lapse into an absent-minded swaying while the legs are stamping fiercely. The dancer must impart equal life, equal autonomy, to every dancing portion of his frame. He dances his shoulders strongly; he shakes his hips strongly; he does many strong things besides move his feet. The verbs used by traditional commentators on the dance underscore the transparent value of joyous play that is involved in the remarkable process of infusing, democratically, equal life to different body parts.

Thus one Yoruba talked about *making* the shoulders, with forcefully marked activations; a Banyang mentioned his father *playing* his toes; and an Ejagham remarked on dancing "with the things where they *make* 'em," *i.e.*, the transformation of upper and lower parts of the body into zones of independently enlivened motion.[28]

The representation of the youthful strength of the body in abstract pulsations is carried forward section by section. The same logic of analysis applies to sculpture criticism. Susan Vogel finds Baoule critics in the interior of the Ivory Coast admire the human body, as represented in traditional sculpture, by examining the parts of the frame, one by one, and commenting on each, separately. She concludes: "the very way the Baoule look at their art reflects one of its cardinal features: segmented quality."[29] The same method of analysis is used by rural, traditional Yoruba. Generalizing for most of Black Africa, Alfons Dauer maintains in fact that there are always points of the body which are most emphasized, rhythmically, in the dance and that these points of percussive emphasis can be identified by clustering of feathers, raffia fringing, bells, and other elements. In sum, I think the segmenting of the strength of the human frame, the playing of the musculature as if it were a series of notes in a melody of youthful stamina and force is one of the cardinal unifying aspects of the presentation of the self in sculpture and the dance in Africa.

The visual side to the dimension was carefully described by Robert Goldwater:

The African sculptor, whether his forms were rectangular, elliptical, or round in outline, and whether he cut back little or much into the cylinder of fresh wood with which he began, was content to show one aspect of the figure at a time. He achieved his "instinctive" three-dimensional effect by calculated simplification and separation of parts that allowed the eye to grasp each one as a unified coherent mass.[30]

The image of a standing nubile woman with extended arms (Plate 6), attributed to the Guro, visually corroborates Goldwater's point. But the body parts are not only independently rhythmized and lent strength in African presentation, they are coherently realized within a larger dimension. The dynamic aspects are couched in a flexibly buoyant manner, for youth is also characterized by ability to bend. Thus the Guro woman stands with partially relaxed arms, elegantly bent knees.

c. Flexibility: "les trésors de souplesse"

Africans refer to a priceless cultural resource, the suppleness of their dancers, by comparing them to beings who have no bones. To say that a person dances as if she or he had no bones is one of the highest compliments a Liberian Dan, Nigerian Tiv, or Zairois Yanzi can bestow (echoed, in a ribald vein, by Lightning Hopkins: "Rock me baby, like your back ain't got no bones"). Dan in Liberia also strongly criticize lack of flexibility in standing; Yoruba do too, and Luba in Zaire simply say, virtually as a matter of choreographic law, that a person must move his hips in as supple a manner as possible. The Luba dancer, a young Luba told me in Kinshasa, must manifest his suppleness with bent knees, bent elbows, and suave oscillations to the music.[31]

The Kongo sense of flexibility in the dance is stark: dance with bended knees, lest you be taken for a corpse.[32] Africans, in short, are very much aware of the import of flexibility as a sign of youth in life, as a demonstration of the bright willingness to respond to change in music and in speech. Such are the African *trésors de souplesse*.

Flexible dancing demands a complicated series of transitions, especially from life to art. Thus Peggy Harper:

the practice among rural women of carrying loads on the head results in a walk in which the undulations of the ground surface are taken up in the flexibility of the hips and knees whereas the ankles remain relatively rigid and the head remains in a consistently upright position so as not to upset the objects carried. This practice strengthens the muscles of the neck and back, contributes towards the habit of the straight-backed torso with the head and neck carried as an extension of the line of the back, and develops a marked flexibility in the pelvic region.

These and many other occupation patterns of movement are reflected in the basic body positions which recur in many forms of Nigerian dance. A characteristic body posture in dance consists of a straight-backed torso with

PLATE 6
Ivory Coast, Guro, standing female, wood, 16 $\frac{1}{2}$"

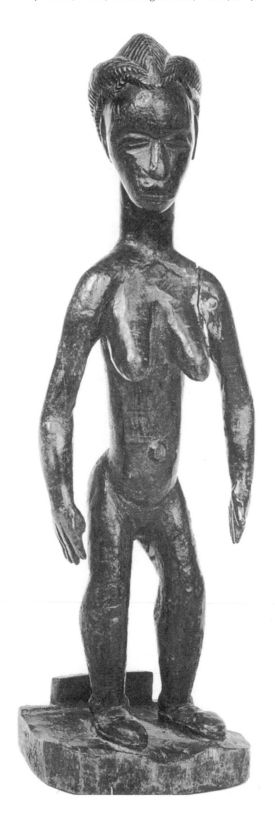

PLATE 7
Nigeria, Montol, standing female, wood, 12"

the legs used as springs, the knees bending and stretching in fluidly executing the rhythmic action patterns of the dance, and feet placed firmly on the ground.[33]

This fits perfectly the pelvic thrust and spring-like knees under pridefully held straight-backed torso characterizing a minor masterpiece of northern Nigerian sculpture (Plate 7). The point applies, as well, to a figure of a woman attributed to the Kossi (Plate 8), an ethnic group who live in and around the Cameroon town of Kumba, northwest of Douala. This figure, allegedly from a village altar and of undocumented function,[34] extends the straight line of the back through the neck and head, set over buoyant knees and stable feet. The implication of flexible potency at the hips and knees is striking.

2. "Afrikanische Aufheben": Simultaneous Suspending and Preserving of the Beat

Hegel shows that the German verb *aufheben* resonates with a double meaning: to cancel and to affirm. "By this suspension and preservation," he writes, "[we gain] an affirmative and indeed richer and more concrete determination."[35] This perfectly describes suspending the beat in art and dance in Africa, *i.e.*, in some African styles art and music forms are enlivened by off-beat phrasing of the accents. Let me begin with a concrete example from the visual arts of Ghana. A state sword from, to judge from the quality of the openwork, the Akwamu area (Plate 9) is constructed in an unusual way, so that the expected continuum of unbroken surface leading from the pommel to the end of the blade is suspended and replaced by three kinds of symbolic chainwork (two representing the royal knot of wisdom and one probably signifying the unifying power of the royal or priestly owner of the sword). Two of these lengths are in openwork, one is not. Suspending the expected continuum of blade surface preserves, at a higher symbolic level, the importance of the owner.

The handle of an Ashanti spoon (Plate 10) is also interrupted by symbolic openwork patterning, suspending utilitarian simplicity of form with complicated and choppy geometric shapes—ellipse, diamond, and rectangle. The base of the handle is also decorated with an apparent representation of the "wisdom knot" (*nyansapo*), the knot that only the wise leaders know how to unravel.[36] Such special spoons were sometimes placed over a clay pot on the grave of an important person on the fifth day after burial. The impression gained is that of richness of life, surrounding the honorable person in Akan society, here expressed with objects whose ordinary outlines are cancelled with proverbial allusions and other speech-implying units. The mass is modified and perforated with openwork, and thus seems more powerfully sustained and meaningful. It is for this reason that I call the process *afrikanische aufheben*, noting, as I do so, that it takes one of the most brilliant minds of the West, Hegel, to produce a term commensurate with the complexity.

The regularity of striped patterning in Upper Volta weaving is sometimes spec-

PLATE 8
Cameroon, Kossi standing female, wood, 9"

tacularly complicated by vibrant suspensions of expected placement of the pattern (Plate 11). Sieber comments, concerning this staggered pattern, that, "careful matching of the ends of the cloth dispels the impression of an uncalculated overall design."[37] Staggered motifs on certain chiefly cloths can be profitably compared with off-beat phrasing in music, dance, and decorative sculpture. In her recent study, *Textilien Aus Westafrika*, Brigitte Menzel illustrates a number of traditional cloths emblazoned with suspensions of symmetrical pattern. The narrow bands which make up these textiles are sewn together so that what is "on beat" at one level of the cloth is immediately "off beat" in terms of another (*cf.* her illustrations, Vol. II, 523, 529, 535, 688, 765, Hausa and Akan examples). There is an

PLATE 10
Ghana, Ashanti, spoon, wood, 14"

PLATE 9
Ghana, Ashanti,
state sword, wood
and iron, 41"

interesting further example of this quality in the White Collection of Akan textiles (Plate 4).

If there is a social meaning to be extracted from this element of West African visual expertise, perhaps the knot of wisdom motif provides a clue. It may be that the chiefly person who wears a cloth with staggered pattern in effect promises to rediscover wholeness in perfecting uneven human relationships, even as he unties the knot of trouble and obstruction. Suspending the beat hints that to dwell at one level is to lose the precious powers of balance inherent in human capability.

Certainly learning to walk with objects balanced on the head, in Africa, depends upon confident absorption of the undulations of the ground, *i.e.*, suspensions of the normal flatness of the earth within the spring-like hips and flexible knees, so that whatever is carried on the head remains safely in repose.

And there is a further dimension to control of off-beat phrasing in African art and life, and that is music. When Western musicians think of cancelled beats or rhythmic elision, they normally think of syncopation, defined as the shift of accent in a passage or composition that occurs when a normally weak beat is stressed. Yet "swing" is prevalent in Africa and musicians characteristically impart equal stress to every note; what is unusual north of the Sahara is a commonplace south. The structuring of the pulse in African music is more complicated than syncopation. Thus Waterman:

> Melodic tones, and particularly accented ones, occur between the sounded or implied beats of the measure with great frequency. The beat is, so to

jazz is a dance

PLATE 11
Upper Volta, textile, 87"

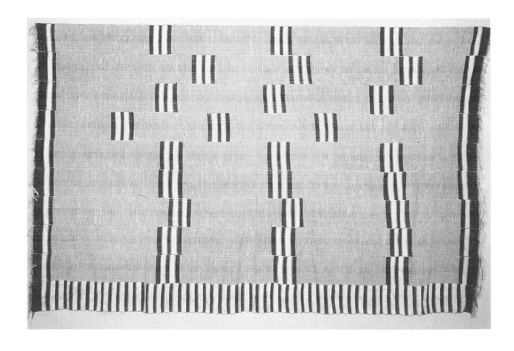

speak, temporarily suspended, *i.e.*, delayed or advanced in melodic execution, sometimes for single notes (syncopation), sometimes for long series of notes. The displacement is by no means a random one, however, for the melodic notes not coinciding with the beat are invariably sounded, with great nicety, precisely on one of the points of either a double or a triple division of the beat.[38]

Waterman thus makes the same observation about offbeat melodic phrasing that Sieber did about patterning, *i.e.*, it is not random, but deliberate. I am not arguing, however, that musical quality is consciously suggested by textile-makers, for there is no evidence to that effect, nor am I suggesting this visual quality is transcendentally African (it seems specially present among the Akan). Nevertheless, it seems to me that it would be irresponsible not to attempt to sharpen awareness of staggered and suspended pattern in some forms of African cloth by reference to off-beat phrasing of melodic accents in music, or in dance, for A. M. Jones shows that foot and hand movements are staggered in the Ewe *adzida* club dance in Ghana and also in the modern *makwaya* dancing of Central Africa.[39]

3. The "Get-Down Quality": Descending Direction in Melody, Sculpture, Dance

The nature of tropical African melody has been characterized:

Broadly speaking, the outline of an African tune is like a succession of the teeth of a rip-saw; a steep rise (not usually exceeding a 5th) followed by a gentle sloping down of the tune; then another sudden rise—then a gentle sloping down and so on. The tendency is for the tune to start high and gradually work downwards in this saw-like manner.[40]

Opposition of high and low, gentle and sudden, fits the familiar African taste for high-affect combinations, *i.e.*, hot-against-cool, male-within-female, angles and curves, "loud" colors against "dark." The trend from high to low sets up a basic opposition, inexorably resolved in favor of descent. "Getting down" would seem to be a most important concept, and an ancient one, too, as suggested by the fact that the music of descendants of seventeenth and eighteenth century slaves in Surinam, on the north coast of South America, is characterized precisely by a predominantly descending course in melody.[41]

There are some interesting parallels to this quality in dance. First, waterspirit dancers in southern Yorubaland insist that when the sound of the master drummer ascends in pitch the dancers correspond by dancing "high," *i.e.*, upon their toes, to the maximum vertical extent of their frame.[42] But they bend, gradually, closer to the earth as they dance until, at one point, they crouch and whirl. In addition, there is a hint of correspondence between rising and falling spears in a certain northeastern Zairois dance of the last century and the rise and fall of the level of the singing,[43] but in the latter instance we cannot be certain in the absence of objective filmed and taped means of documentation.

What is apparently true, however, is that the use of "get-down" sequences in the dance, where a performer or a group of performers assume a deeply inflected, virtually crouching position, thus moving in proximity to the level of the earth, is important in Africa and found in a number of societies of the western and central portions of the continent. Here is field evidence: Anago Yoruba—"step . . . finished at a level superbly low"; Dahomean Yoruba—"if the drum strikes *strong*, you bend down"; Nigerian Yoruba—"bend down, to complete the dance"; Mbam, Cameroon—"close to the earth, similar to our own *ganga* dance"; Luba—"dance bending deep."[44] In addition to these sources, Jean Rouch, in contemplating the dance as an art form among the blacks of the region of Timbuktu, noted a masterly sequence in which the virtuoso strung a sizzling line of improvisations together and then polished them off with a "pirouette" executed virtually at earth level.

There is more, however, to getting down than sheer proximity to the ground. In a recent study, Ladzekpo and Pantaleoni show that dancing in relation to Takada drumming is characterized by a "flexing torso at one height above the ground *unless the intensity of the movement changes* [my italics], *greater vigor being reserved for more of a crouch.*"[45] This is precisely the situation among the Fon of Ouidah, dancing for the god of smallpox. In the late summer of 1972 I observed this style at a festival in which the finest dancer distinguished herself by the usage of the get-down range. She saved for this level, not only the high intensity passage of her dance, but also her most inventive shoulder-work, kicks, and whirls (Plate 12).

Compare her posture to an Ibibio sculpture which seems to have been carved with something like the get-down range in mind (Plate 13). The vigor that accompanies the gesture is powerfully conveyed, but the sculptural rendering shows a straight back that indicates a blend of standing and bending low.

In Surinam, the blacks of the interior, notably on the Piki Lio, mark time at a

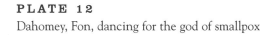

PLATE 12
Dahomey, Fon, dancing for the god of smallpox

jazz is a dance

PLATE 13
Nigeria, Ibibio, female figure, wood, 19 ¹/₂"

dance with what Richard Price calls a kind of "holding pattern"[46] until they decide that the psychological moment to improvise has come. Then they crouch, bursting into choreographic flames, showing off marvels of footwork and muscular expression. Such displays normally last, in West Africa and Surinam, for two or three seconds. They are subject to what might be termed the aesthetic parsimony of the call-and-response form of dancing, assuring, in the overlapping, that everyone who wants to dance can have his turn at getting down.

Get-down sequences are, therefore, virtuosic. They seem to be frequently correlated in Africa with showing honor and respect, either to a fine drummer, in response to the savor of his phrasing, or to a deity, as in the case of the descent of the Ouidah dancer before the drums. Getting down encloses a dual expression of salutation and devotion. Among the southern Egbado of Yorubaland in Nigeria, when mothers dance with statuettes representing dead twins in their hands, begging the departed spirits for the blessing of continuing fertility, there is a get-down sequence:

> Style shifted . . . from group structure to solo, from calm to energy . . . from full posture to low. The mother broke the expected patterns of the dance and bent low, close to the earth, carrying the single image with her in one strong single sweep that brought the image parallel to the ground and then up. . . . She had danced an abstract rendering of the lowering of the body of the Yoruba woman on first one elbow and then the other, as special obeisance, when in the presence of a king. . . . "We are begging the twins not to trouble us, we are saying mo *degbe O!*—I prostrate myself—as the royal wives do before the king."[47]

Thus getting down, structurally, it would seem, correlates with solo dancing, as opposed to choral, with an important part of the dance as opposed to an indifferently selected moment in transition, with vigor and intensity. Iconographically, getting down would seem to correlate with kneeling (Plate 14) or prostration in at least one African society, *i.e.*, as a sign of worship in sacred contexts and salutation in ordinary realms.[48] But in Surinam, Price tells us, getting down is a purely aesthetic phenomenon, the ultimate form of dance virtuosity for a man. When he whirls down, people concentrate on him. Then he gets back up, then he goes back into it. But the sequence never lasts more than seconds.[49]

By contrast to this Afro-American development, the African form seems, provisionally, more symbolic and honorific. Compare the Tiv phrase, "he bends in dancing" (*a ngurum ishol*) in which the verb can also mean "to bow to a person."[50] Downward descending melody in Africa leads to the same position dancers in Africa assume to prove openness to talent or authority. Getting down is honoring with virtuosic art and total presence.

4. Multiple Meter: Dancing Many Drums

African music is distinguished from other world traditions by the superimposition of several lines of meter. Thus Ward in 1927: "Broadly speaking, the differ-

PLATE 14
Ivory Coast, Senufo, box with kneeling figure,
wood, 9 $\frac{1}{2}$"

ence between African and European rhythms is that whereas any piece of European music has at any one moment one rhythm in command, a piece of African music has always two or three, sometimes as many as four."[51] The transfer of this extraordinary complexity to the frame of the human body is implied in the following statement:

> An African learns to be conscious mentally of every instrument employed in an African orchestra and this has a tremendous influence on his dance, all the various muscles of the body act differently to the rhythms of the instruments.[52]

Richard Alan Waterman has given us a theoretical account of the interrelationship governing music and the dance in Africa. He talks about response to each metrical thread, within the total percussive whole of the music, without separation from multi-metric context.[53] But he does not tell us how this marvel is achieved. It remained for an anthropologist reconsidering her field experiences in novelistic form, *i.e.*, Laura Bohannan's *Return to Laughter*, to arrive at the existential truth of the matter. The author was directly challenged to dance at a (thinly disguised) Tiv wedding in northern Nigeria in order to demonstrate allegiance to the involved lineages. " 'Teach me, then,' I retorted. Duly she and the other senior women began my instruction: my hands and my feet were to keep time with the gongs, my hips with the first drum, my back and shoulders with the second." Whenever she lapsed into an absent-minded shuffle, elderly women poked her in the ribs and commanded her to return to what she was supposed to be doing, *i.e.*, *dance*.[54] Charles Keil has later shown that one of the key Tiv musical terms can be variously interpreted to mean "respond," "sing in chorus," or "dance multi-metrically," according to context and to phrasing.[55] This implies, I think, Tiv consciously elaborate multiple meter in the dance as a form of full response to vitality and human presence in the music. Multi-metric dancing seems to refer to shared complexity of response, the giving of the person to more than one musical argument, to more than one musician, to more than one source of musically elaborated form of speech. No wonder the crones poked the anthropologist in the ribs. She was slighting everybody.

Ideally speaking, multiple meter in the dance is a means of articulating the human body more fully than is possible in ordinary discourse; it makes a person blaze as a live entity at the center of understanding. Quite clearly, however, the gift is beyond the reach of the lazy and the distracted. And even among those of talent and imagination there are theoretical limits:

> It is common for an individual dancer to combine two rhythms simultaneously in his dance movement; a combination of three distinct rhythms may be used by a highly skilled dancer, and four simultaneous rhythms are rarely observed.[56]

Tiv multi-metric dancing restores music to muscular notation in which "notes" are written in the flesh and can be followed by attention to different body parts.

In the following diagram (Fig. 1), based on the episode in Laura Bohannan's novel, the dancer stands in characteristic posture: whole foot on the ground, knees bent, arms bent, torso forward, buttocks out, face composed. A pattern of four equal diamonds represents a rhythmic motif on gong, answered in the feet and hands; three circles represent another motif, this one simultaneously sounded by first drum and the hips; second drum produces a combined pattern of two and three pulsations, simultaneously embodied in the shoulders and the back; these last pulsations are symbolized by squares.

The contrastive logic of multiple meter in the dance "plays" the parts of the body as virtual instruments of music, so that, as Professor John Szwed has told me in conversation, "shaking that thing" in jazz parlance in the United States can refer, as an element of African influence, either to the tambourine, or to the hips, or to another body part, the point being that all are detached media for the expres-

FIGURE 1

Diagram of Tiv dancer, based on an episode in Laura Bohannon's novel Return to Laughter.

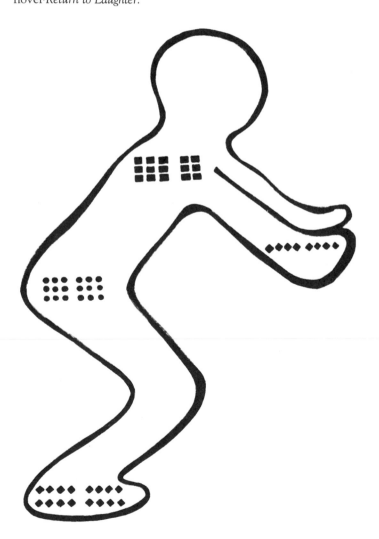

sion of autonomy in vitality.[57]

The phenomenon fills in and actualizes a theoretical statement of potentiality signalized centuries ago by Plato: "when he wanted to show that I was many he would say that I have a right and a left side and a front and a back and an upper and a lower half, for I cannot deny that I partake of multitude."[58]

Africans are very much aware of such potentiality. Their grasp of dancing to various metric lines is sophisticated and clear. Thus Chokwe say, "dance all the drums in your body." They talk about absorbing one tasty "drum bit" after another until all are digested within a strongly moving single frame. People in Africa further suggest that dance is defined as a special intricacy built of superimposed motions. The following are their words: "dance while activating the shoulders, and stamping the feet"; "goes around while shaking the body"; "they dance shaking themselves and breaking at the same moment"; "I like the way he moves because he is always listening to something"; "bending down and hitting."[59]

The inferential leap from complexity in motion to complexity in sculptural rendering must be handled gingerly. Sculpture stops time. This makes impossible the objective determination of multiple meter in the plastic arts even if it were implied. Yet traditional commentary makes us sensitive to simultaneity as an objective criterion in the phrasing of a dance, *e.g.*, combined bending low, circling near, and reaching high in the Sato dance of Dahomey (Plate 15). Accordingly, we note a corresponding complexity in the stopping of various implied acts in some forms of African statuary. To contemplate an image of a Yoruba woman with child (Plate 16) and then paraphrase her impact in the following words—"seated figure, female, Yoruba, 20th century"—destroys the simultaneity of suggested action which makes the image function as poetic act. One young African, looking

PLATE 15
Dahomey, Sato dance

PLATE 16
Nigeria, Yoruba, mother and child, wood, 17"

at a similar object, taught me to recognize an implied combination of five discrete actions in one: sitting nobly, giving generously with both hands, joyously supporting a new-born child upon the back, and supporting fire from heaven upon the head (a pair of thunderstones), while disciplining the face so that pleasure does not reveal itself.[60] If multi-metric dancing is impossible to convey in figural art, nevertheless, in highly sophisticated African civilizations, many acts can be intuited within a single piece of sculpture.

5. Looking Smart: Playing the Patterns with Nature and with Line

The African dancer not only dances many drums. He plays many patterns. In so doing, he is *looking smart*. The phrasing is in African English, based on traditional concern with brilliance of phrasing and vividness of enactment. Thus Yoruba comment: "they put on their costumes, tumbled, and looked smart"; Yoruba again, "whirled like the wind and looked smart."[61] The equivalent construction in the Dan language of northeastern Liberia, is *nyaa ka*, roughly translated as "moving with flair," which means the same thing and which can be provisionally glossed by contextual usage: "This is a quality which must be added to all his actions. With *nyaa ka* I have added something to my dance or walking, to show my beauty to attract the attention of all those around me, even if they should be thinking of something else."[62]

Looking smart, therefore, partially is defined in strikingly attractive use of style, loaded with notions of preening and the making of the person sexually attractive. A. M. Jones simply calls the process "showing off" and adds: "this spirit of emulation should be noted. We believe it is quite an important element in African dancing as a whole: in fact 'showing off' seems to be one of the vitalizing factors in good dancing."[63]

Continuing with the glossing of the term, another Dan commentator was struck by the beauty of the vibration of the back and chest of two young women dancing and said, "this shows a certain flair; they know how to cut (*i.e.*, properly finish or round off the pattern)."[64] In other words, the vibration looked smart, in part, because it was crisply ended, marked off as a segmentary part of pattern. Looking smart has to do with line in dance. But it also has to do with nature. Thus Bangwa, from the west of the Cameroon Grasslands: good dancing there is compared to the "smart" (strong, graceful, masterly) motion of the leopard in the forest or to the iridescent vibration of the feathers of the Pin-Tailed Whydah, when shaking his plumage during the mating season to display his feathers to full effect.[65] Animal qualities of motion, glitter, and vitality are very much part of the attraction. Ejagham's comment adds further dimensions: "their dance looked very attractive because they looked smart and danced very well."[66] To this observer, looking smart meant multiple enactment and variety ("they jump and turn themselves"), multiple usage of color (*ita m naring*, lit. cap with colors), and embodiment of tradition.

The vibrations of color and muscle in looking smart make human patterning resonate with inner life; it is playing the patterns as if they were autonomous forces of their own, in one instance, part-leopard, in another, bird-like quivering, while at the same time shaped by ordering consideration of limit and of line. The concept involves the idea of nature and line cast in vivid equilibrium. Looking smart carries us within an existential African sense of "art."

The Yoruba word for "art," for example, refers to the shaping of natural elements with craftsmanship: cicatrization of the skin, splitting open and shaping of wood, the cutting and dyeing of animal hide, and even making towns by cutting habitable pattern out of forests.[67] These patterns are all cut from nature by means of line, thus intersecting with the verb, incise (*la*), which partially qualifies the making. *La* means to cut, draw line, open up with line.[68] A crucial rendering of natural force with human line defines the artistic process.

Similar modes of thought characterize the Efik of the southeast state of Nigeria. There the word for "art" really refers to decoration and to pattern, *viz.* painting, textile-making, marking, shaping, impressing, representing.[69] The lined patterning defined by "art" overlaps the Yoruba concept, *i.e.*, splitting wood, marking earth, engraving calabashes, cutting villages out of the forest, in short, "colonizing," making civilization. The aesthetic of the Baoule of the Ivory Coast is summed up in broadly similar terms, as is the aesthetic of the Tiv, the latter society drawing a connection between the verb to sing (*gber*) and secondary senses, "to cut, to incise," which brings craftsmanship, song, and line into even tighter grouping.[70]

"Art" is, therefore, becoming civilized through the vital patterns drawn on or within objects taken direct from nature, acts so vital in themselves they can be referred back to nature, to the grace of the leopard, to the fluttering of the plumage of a bird. Just as a traditional person in Africa divines or cures by means of objects taken direct from nature, raw herbs, water from the sea, bone and branch, so some informants see pattern in music converted into fleshly terms: "fine on a person . . . like sumptuously patterned cloth."[71] Looking smart is confirmed in making the body glitter with multiple response to multiple meter, with playing the body parts as patterns, with wearing design upon, or deep within the flesh, all elements rhythmized with speed and strength.

Even in the stillness of sculpture this remarkable quality can be partially conveyed, rendering the head or the muscles of the trunk as autonomous units of design. Consider the famous *eyima bieri* sculptures of the Fang of Gabon and Equatorial Guinea (Plate 17). These images once presided over the bones of the ancestors, stored in receptacles placed beside the image. These guardian images therefore "wore" their stylized muscle as communications of transcendent strength and determination, just as certain parts of the human frame are rhythmized and filled with strength in the sculpture of the Mende of Sierra Leone to portray the power of woman in the Sande Society (Plate 18). Rich feminine curves shape the head and yield below to the strong repeating of the creases in the neck of the represented important woman. The subject "wears" her neck as extraordinary orna-

PLATE 17
Gabon, Fang, "bieri" figure, wood, 19 ¾"

PLATE 18
Sierra Leone, Mende, staff, wood, 46 ¾"

ment, representing, according to Warren d'Azevedo: "voluptuousness; indulgence; luxury; abundance; fecundity; sexual attraction; wealth; status; and the fattening process within the female secret society." And again, the strength with which the human image in Fang sculpture "wears" his chest, and "wears" his arms, defines his power in deep embodied patterning. The sculptor of style, like the "man of words,"[72] and the dancer of flair, turns his phrases, keeping them brilliant, by making line visible, without destroying natural rhythms.

One final example: in December 1962 in the northern Egbado village of Joga-Orile, in southwestern Nigeria, I saw a group of masked dancers gathered in the market. They postured in honor of departed rulers, making bizarre patterns with their arms and hands, and flashing multi-colored textiles as they turned and jumped and ran. "What do you think?" I asked an English-speaking schoolboy. "They look smart," he replied.

6. Correct Entrance and Exit: "Killing the Song," "Cutting the Dance," "Lining the Face"

Every pattern must have clear boundaries. This is a very important rule in Diola-Fogny singing in Senegal. The Diola soloist controls the song and has the right to "kill," or end properly a given phrase. If he does this correctly, *i.e.*, crisply and unambiguously, then the chorus will sing the response in unison and in time. If he does not, he invites confusion.[73]

The importance of "killing" the song parallels the "cutting" of the dance among the Dan of northeastern Liberia. Each dancer must know how to *yia*, or "cut" his dance. Consider the following Dan testimony: "a good dancer is the dancer who cuts his dance in time to the rhythm of the instrument, *i.e.*, in our tribal dancing, you can be a good dancer with all the requirements I have mentioned in your performance, but if you are dancing and do not *yia*, end things properly, you are not a good dancer."[74] Cutting the motion is correlated with making sharp pattern. Agreement with this line of thought can be readily found among Dahomean and Yoruba dancers, the latter stating the importance of ending the motion when the phrasing of the master drummer stops.[75]

The Akan of Ghana make this criterion an explicit measure of performance:

When at an appropriate moment the dancer stretches his hands sideways, jumps up and crosses his legs in the landing, the master drummer begins the piece proper . . . for the crossing of the legs is the sign that the dancer is ready to dance vigorously. From this point the dancer must follow the drumming closely for the cue to end the dance in a posture or appropriate gesture carefully timed to the end beats . . . both hands or right hand pointing skywards—*I Look to God* . . . right forefinger touching the head (other fingers clenched) *It is a matter for my head.*

The timing of the end gesture is very important, for it is one of the fine points in the collaboration between drummers and dancers to which every spectator looked forward. If a dancer misplaces it, he exposes himself to ridicule and booing. After a dancer has had enough rounds of dancing—each marked by an end gesture—he leaves the ring for another person to step in.[76]

In other words, the end gestures are proverbs. Figurated Akan gold-weights are also enlivened with accurately gestural suggestions of proverbial wisdom. For example, one gold-weight in brass (Plate 19) is said to represent Adu and Amoako, old friends meeting after long absence, recounting their misfortunes.[77] These images are rendered in miniature, with a charming sinuosity of expression far transcending the normal straightforward verticality of African figural sculpture. One figure suggests the act of greeting, the other meditative reaction, hand on chin. Just as end gestures in the Akan dance transform the dancer in fleeting asymmetric sculpture, so figuration of a proverb in the metal arts enlivens sculptural stance with relative realism of suggested motion. Narrowing the gap between media shows what can happen when two traditions converge on similar function, communication through proverb, within the same cultural universe. The end gesture in the dance and the proverbial stance of the figurated gold-weight also share their stillness, fleeting in the dancing ring, permanent in the metal art. The finishing of these related arts completes iconic communication.

PLATE 19
Ghana, Ashanti, gold-weight, brass, 1 ¹/₄"

jazz is a dance

The beginning is also important. Yoruba state that dancers must prepare for the opening beat of the dance before moving—like a boxer, bracing for the punch.[78] The Yoruba dancer is supposed to "come in" correctly, effortlessly, one with the phrasing of the master drummer. The Cameroon Bangwa judge choreography the same way, looking to see if performers make a proper entrance in relation to the beat.[79] Luba demand that a dancer determine the position of his body, as a quasi-sculptural force with bent knees and arms held close to the trunk, before actually dancing.[80] Other societies I have been citing, notably the Tiv, also apply this criterion.

To return to the Dan, ever precise in their phrasing of the criteria of fine dance: the proper dancer initiates his motion from a flexible, knees-bent, arms-bent position. This attitude also characterizes fine standing in Dan culture. The dancer begins to improvise, sometimes crouching, at the end of his phrase. Then he strikes the last gesture of his dance timed to the last syllable of the master drummer's phrase.

It is interesting that correct starting position, from a base of relaxed power, is similar from culture to culture, but that end gestures vary. This might be compared to process in wood carving, where the initial stages of the work, all the masses attacked, seemingly simultaneously, show a rough similarity (indeed provincial styles of wood carving, even when finished, sometimes seem never to transcend the initial stage of blocking-out the masses).[81] But the finished, polished forms vary enormously, from society to society. This observation also applies to dance. Dahomean girls end each phrase of the Aguele Yeye dance with a strong hurling of the arms; Yoruba male dancers for the cult of Gelede at Ketu end each phrase sounded by the master drummer with a kick of the right leg; and Akan strike moralistic poses.

We might compare shaping and finishing in sculpture and the dance in traditional Africa. Beginning, the dancer enters flexed and attentive, body inflected, usually into two or more expressions according to the multi-metric structure of the music, e.g., chest vibrated by one meter, hips by another. This might be compared to the first stage in carving, called among Yoruba Ekiti "hard pattern" (Plate 20), the blocking-out of the initial mass. Then, as he improvises, he further divides his frame. He can get down in a crouch, he can move his head and arms to staggered patterns, he can, with inimitable hauteur, make his muscles shine with brilliant motions set against his facial calm. This might be compared to second and third stages of carving, where the frozen quality of the face becomes apparent and the main body forms are broken into smaller masses (Plate 21) and smoothed and made more luminous (Plate 22).

It is the last stage where mass contends with line, where the face is "lined"—i.e., when eyelids are cut, lips lined, cicatrized descent markings added, and so forth. The final stage of "lining" (Plate 23) completes the figural shaping of the wood, the civilizing impact of the art of line. Similarly, the end of the dance, sharp, dynamically precise, establishes a clear boundary between one improvisation and the next. The "kill" of the Diola song, the "cut" of the dancer's phrasing in the ring, the "end

PLATE 20
Nigeria, Yoruba

PLATE 21
Nigeria, Yoruba

PLATE 22
Nigeria, Yoruba

PLATE 23
Nigeria, Yoruba

gesture" among the Akan, and "lining" in the final stages of Ekiti Yoruba carving—each is an instrument by which to realize perfected sequence.

7. Vividness Cast into Equilibrium: Personal and Representational Balance

African design is, quite often, rendered vivid by rhythmized, contrastive, changing elements within the pattern. Compare the wholly predictable alternation of the checkerboard (Plate 24) with the checkerboard-like cloth in Ghana known as *kente* (Plate 25). Balance in the latter case is struck by, first of all, the richness of the oppositions—horizontal sections versus vertical; uncomplicated blue against linear complexity in golds, blacks, greens, and reds; simplicity beside elaboration. One of the master craftsmen of this tradition, Nana Ntiamoah Mensah, of Adagomase quarter, Bonwire, northern Ashanti, has concisely summarized the form: "designs combined to show beauty and meaning" (*adwinie ahorow a yaka bonu na ema eye fe efirise ebiara wo ase*).[82]

Ntiamoah further says kente design rests in part on artful phrasing of stripes (*nsensaaye*) whose colors are rendered powerful by the richness of their associated meanings. Kente are thus balanced patterns made doubly brilliant in iconic usage. Our example (Plate 25) is superb, a relatively old cloth from perhaps the first quarter of this century. This kente displays, within the gleaming sections dominated by stripes of gold, black, green, and red, a double motif in gold and red called *nkyemfre*.[83] The *nkyemfre* motif is flanked by brilliant stripes and divided from them by pinstripes of white.

PLATE 24
Checkerboard

Instead of discussing the meaning of these design units and their combination without specific field information, I prefer to repeat Nana Ntiamoah's exegetic commentary apropos of a somewhat similar cloth: "the sections with gold and red thread have kingly meaning. For example, one pattern is called Mixed-Together-From-Left-To-Right (*emotewa*), whose deep meaning is: wisdom does not stem from a single person. Another pattern [brilliantly stepped, in gold and red, *cf.* Menzel, Vol. II, fig. 942] is called 'cannon' (*apremo*)—the power of the king."[84] The gold-tinged sections of this kente, as in the illustrated example, varied in small or large details, while the blue sections, as again in the . . . illustration, remained more or less constant. The rectangles dominated by blue, Ntiamoah gives as "playing" (*ahwepan*) or "playful, cheerful people." In sum, the gold sections are filled with references to governmental might; the blue, freshness, humor, and simplicity. Set in suggested alternation, therefore, are: work and play, social heat and social coolness, responsibility and pleasure. It is interesting that Ntiamoah names the entire cloth Everyone-Depends-Upon-Somebody (*obi nkye obi kwan musi*), thus not only rephrasing John Donne, *i.e.*, "no man is an island," but showing the necessity of persons of caprice and humor within the shaping of human viability. We must accept composure and control, but not at the price of humor—the gift of refusal to suffer.

Thus much more than brilliant color is cast into equilibrium by kente design tradition. Nana Ntiamoah has suggested, following the teaching of his ancestors, that the peace which makes possible human interaction is founded on respect for variety and the rights of others. This is one kind of balance memorably struck in

PLATE 25
Ghana, Ashanti, Kente cloth (detail)

African art. Other forms of equipoise are equally rich in nuance and communicative power.

a. Stability or Straightness: Personal Balance

The human image in African art and dance rises, in the main, from feet set flat and firm upon the earth (Plates 26 and 27). The distinctive, continuing Western manner, a preference for asymmetrical posture or stylized instability, remains clear in United States dancing. Bessie Jones and Bess Lomax Hawes have noted the contrast between Sea Island black dancing and mainland white: "all [black] dancing is done flat-footed; this is extremely difficult for [white] Americans, whose first approach to a dancing situation is to go up on their toes."[85]

If Gothic architects sought God through "anagogic"[86] finials, pointed towards heaven, later to be mirrored, in a sense, by the desire of the ballet dancer to soar through the air, West Africans cultivate divinity through richly stabilized traditions of personal balance. Presentation of the self through stability is sometimes phrased as "straightness," as among Ekiti Yoruba where a king viewed an Epa rite in which towering wooden headdresses were moving in the dance and commented, "keep the Epa image *straight*. It's very dangerous to carry those heavy images and they must be kept aright."[87] In a variety of documented verbal instances of artistic criticism in West Africa, the notion of "straightness," in the sense of the maintaining of the commanding vertical position of the human body, has consistently loomed as an important issue.

However, the convention would doubtless soon wax boring, were it not honored so magnificently in the breach by kicks, spins, and leaps of certain of the men's dances in Africa. In addition, the image of the trickster, defying gravity in every sense, is considered, at least covertly, admirable in some societies. One trickster spirit in Yorubaland is called Eshu Alabada. He dances on one leg (mirrored by his single horn) (Plate 28): when he does so, trouble is supposed to break out.[88] When he returns to dancing on both feet, trouble ceases. In other words, normative stability of stance and balance in art and sculpture, at least in one African society, is correlated with social stability and calm. So pervasive is the richly stabilized tradition of the dance and statuary south of the Sahara that departures can be cultivated and admired. Trickster merely confirms the rule.

b. Mid-Point Mimesis: Representational Balance

The African image stands not only fully upright, but is evocative of balance in another sense—degree of realism. Representational balance is as important as stability *per se*, and can be identified in imagery which is not too real and not too abstract, but somewhere in between. I call this remarkable quality *mid-point mimesis* to convey what Africans have taught me, *i.e.*, that beauty is a mean. Thus Tutuola:

neither too tall and not too short,
not too black and not [too] yellow.[89]

The last citation was Yoruba folk. The Akan of the Ivory Coast similarly believe

PLATE 26
Upper Volta, Mossi,
standing female,
wood, 16"

that the beautiful woman is moderate in height, neither as tall as a giraffe nor as short as a pygmy. The Bete in the same African nation adore eyes that are neither white, the color of death, nor red, the color of cruelty, but shaded and smiling. Bete like noses which are neither too snubby nor too aquiline; and they desire ears neither too large nor too small.[90] Correspondingly, the Kongo find prominent eyes, swollen or staring, distasteful; neither do they like reddened eyes, immediately associated with violence of temper. The perfect eyes are moderate: small, bright, and clear. Kongo skin color is also very carefully judged in terms of moderation: "a very darkly pigmented skin is not considered beautiful, nor is a fair complexion. But a person with a shining brown complexion, like the fish *ngola zanga*, is pleasant to look upon. If the skin is too dark, it is likened to the sooty *mfilu*-trees, where a prairie fire has passed. If a person has too fair a complexion, the mother is considered to have come into contact, for example when bathing, with *nkisi Funza* or *simbi*-spirits."[91] Throughout West Africa, wherever data are available, moderation seems important.

English-speaking informants in western Nigeria use the word "normal" when remarking such qualities and the word *niiwon* ("expressed in moderation")[92] when speaking in Yoruba and discussing images which are pleasingly phrased at the middle point of representative realism. African connoisseurs savor moderation of resemblance, avoiding puzzling abstractions or glaring realism. The Kalabari Ijaw of the Niger Delta use the criterion of "resemblance" in judging wood sculpture; the canon is mid-way between excessive abstraction ("if an object is so crudely

354

PLATE 27
Nigeria, Yoruba, standing male in Western dress, wood, 16"

PLATE 28
Nigeria, Yoruba, "elegba" staff, wood, 20"

carved as to be virtually unrecognizable, it will certainly be rejected") and undue resemblance ("no cult object should resemble that of any other spirit more than it resembles its own previous versions").[93] Why is this preoccupation with avoiding, on the one hand, photographic or undue likeness, and extreme abstraction, on the other, so important? Bassa tradition, from the interior of Liberia, in effect affords a partial answer to this problem:

> Individual likenesses are virtually non-existent in the ritual masks of the Liberian hinterland. Men living in groups tend to identify primarily with clan symbols, rather than with their existence as separate entities. There is the story of a carver who was so fond of his young wife that he took her with him to a secluded place and kept a loving eye on her while he carved a mask. The result was a likeness of the girl so exact that it created a furor when the mask came out for its first public function. "That's Kwa-za," shouted the people, not knowing whether to rejoice or be frightened. But the elders were not amused; by his lack of self-control, the artist had betrayed the myth of the mask, thus revealing that masks were man-made and subject to the vagaries of human emotion. The mask was "retired" and the carver punished.[94]

The possibility of photographic likeness does exist in the traditional imagination, but it is not tolerated because it is dangerous, as an absolute, as an extreme. Some Ashanti, for example, are moved to tears by the sight of a photograph of a departed loved member of a lineage: "in fact, such likenesses are often turned face to the wall and only turned around on the occasions when the funeral custom is being revived."[95] Mirrors are subject to cognate cautions. The mirror's glare is often associated with danger and death, and mirrors are carefully covered except when used in some traditional Yoruba and Zulu families in order to avoid the attraction of lightning from the sky during stormy periods in the rainy season. A carved face is much more moderate and its glitter can be carefully controlled.

Preoccupation with moderation applies in the phrasing of the dance, as well. Yoruba say good dancing occurs *olele*, "not too fast and not too slow,"[96] and where Yoruba refer to moderation of tempo, Luba in Zaire talk about restraint in effort and the cutting-through of space: do not go too far out with gestures of the legs or arms; keep the movement self-contained and moderate.[97] However, regardless of the moderation of speed and dynamics, the speed of most African dancing is remarkable by Western standards because the sliding scale of judgment is weighted in the direction of strength and full intensity.

Mid-point mimesis or balance in the mode of representing visual reality defines the African aesthetic as a mediating force. The canon also explains, I think, the preference for the generalization of humanity in the dancing ring. Humanity generalized by rhythmic impulse, in sculpture and the dance, is humanity divested momentarily of the heat of personal ambition and individualism, detached from emotion, and shaped within repeated images of ideal vital character. The person of moral perfection is the subject of African art and dance, not the representation of the individual. To find identity through merger with a larger social whole is also important in the formal structure of singing south of the Sahara, the form called call-and-response or leader-and-ensemble.

8. Call-and-Response: The Politics of Perfection

Evans-Pritchard has observed: "most African songs are antiphonal, that is, they are sung by a soloist and a chorus. . . . If there are several verses then the soloist begins the [solo] while the chorus is still finishing. This overlapping is a common feature of all songs."[98] The characterization extends to most of Black Africa. Thus Waterman: "a peculiarity of the African call-and-response pattern, found but infrequently elsewhere, is that the chorus' phrases regularly commence while the soloist is still singing; the leader, on his part, begins his phrase before the chorus has finished."[99] Alan P. Merriam has noted a clear instance, among Bulu in southern Cameroon, where the song leader initiates his phrase considerably before the chorus completes their own melodic line. Overlapping call-and-response south of the Sahara is linked to a percussive concept of performance:

> the entrance of the solo or the chorus part on the proper beat of the measure is the important thing, not the effects attained through antiphony or polyphony. Examples of call-and-response music in which the solo, for one reason or another, drops out for a time, indicate clearly that the chorus part, rhythmical and repetitive, is the mainstay of the song and the one really inexorable component of their rhythmic structure. The leader, receiving solid rhythmic support from the metrically accurate rolling repetition of phrases by the chorus, is free to embroider as he will.[100]

Thus the chorus forms a kind of melodic handclap, testing and supporting the soloist and his ingenuity.

South of the Sahara, solo-and-circle, or solo-and-line, or solo-and-solo forms of dancing mirror melodic call-and-response.[101] Dance and music are very closely interwoven in African cultures, and persons singing the chorus frequently double as the circling group who surround or are led by the master singer.[102] Unsurprisingly, the leader of the dancers is, often, the leader of the song. Often the overlapping danced responses to the calls are enthusiastic and very strong. Rising eloquence can cause the size of the chorus dramatically to swell. But it is not just aesthetic impact that is at issue here, but also the moral condition of the singer or the dancer. Thus a Yoruba refrain:

> You are rejected in the town
> Yet you continue to sing for them.
> If you learn a new song
> Who will sing the chorus?[103]

The rights and feelings of others loom very large in African creativity. It does not matter, according to the canon of African call-and-response, how many new steps or verses the person elaborates in his head; if he is of ugly disposition or hatefully lacking in generosity or some other ideal quality, then he may never be given a chance to elaborate his ideas in public. His creativity may be void if the chorus finds him beneath contempt in a social sense. The chorus, as in ancient Attic tragedy, is therefore, a direct expression of public sanction and opinion. Call-and-response goes to the very heart of the notion of good government, of popular response to the actions of the ideal leader.

At this level of discourse it is not difficult to understand in what sense the visual motif of master-and-entourage, highly and memorably developed among certain West African civilizations (*e.g.*, Akan, Fon, Yoruba, and Cameroon Grasslands)[104] seems an analogue in the history of art to the musical and choreographic solo-chorus theme. Master-and-entourage themes in visual art in Africa are usually characterized by a dominant central figure flanked by symbolically small-scale human attendants.

Consider in this vein a Yoruba divination cup (Plate 29) which shows a mounted master accompanied by a portion of his entourage. The spacing of the latter in a semi-circle before his horse is not unlike the circling of handclappers and singers about the master dancer in the ring. This solution brings sculpture close to the

PLATE 29
Nigeria, Yoruba, "ifa" bowl, wood, 10 ¹/₂"

structure of call-and-response, closer than the related frontal dispositions of similar themes of leader-follower interaction in the courtly styles of ancient Benin.

I have on several occasions in West Africa observed traditional mounted rulers accompanied by followers who chanted the praises of their master, while the latter, for his part, led them forward in regal silence. This was a most refined instance of the genre—the ruler who sets the song in motion by sheer force of personality, a tacit "call" that brings out a full and explicit mode of choral response. This poetic refinement of the structure of call-and-response, subtle and unsuspected, is exactly mirrored by the imperatives of gravity, dignity, and composure which mark the face of the mounted ruler who organizes the richly differentiated following (a mother with child, a pressure-drummer, and a soldier and his captive). His silence is confirmed by the visual "noise" of their energetic roles.

There are proverbs galore to warn the ruler, mounted or otherwise, that he can be replaced, should he prove despotic. Herein another telling point of connexion between life and art, between call-and-response and the phenomenon of master-and-entourage in the urban states of traditional West Africa. The arrogant dancer, no matter how gifted or imaginative, may find that he dances to drums and handclaps of decreasing strength and fervor. He may find, and this is damaging to his reputation, that the chorus will crystallize around another person, as in the telling of tales among the Tiv of northern Nigeria. There, we are told by Laura Bohannan, the poor devil who starts a tale without proper preparation or refinement will find the choral answering to his songs becomes progressively weaker until they ultimately reform about a man with stronger themes and better aesthetic organization. He is soon singing to himself. The terror of losing one's grip on the chorus is a real one in some African societies, a poignant dimension of social interaction that for some reason is not mentioned in discourse on singing in African music. Consider the following Azande evidence:

> Sometimes also a man will have a magic whistle and then blows it before going to sing his songs at a dance. When addressing the whistle he says: "You are a whistle of song. I am going to sing my songs. Men back up my songs very much. Don't let people remain silent during my songs."[105]

Thus call-and-response and solo-and-circle, far from solely constituting matters of structure, are in actuality levels of perfected social interaction. The canon is a danced judgment of qualities of social integration and cohesion. Call-and-response, essentially hierarchic in aesthetic structure, nevertheless perennially realizes, within the sphere of music and of dance, one of the revolutionary ideals of the last century:

> . . . revolutions . . . criticize themselves constantly, interrupt themselves continually in their own course, come back to the apparently accomplished in order to begin it afresh, deride with unmerciful thoroughness the inadequacies, weaknesses, and paltrinesses of their first attempts, seem to throw down their adversary only in order that he may draw new strength from the earth and rise again, more gigantic, before them, recoil ever and anon from

the indefinite prodigiousness of their own aims, until a situation has been created which makes all turning back impossible.[106]

9. Ancestorism: Ability to Incarnate Destiny

Destiny is achieved where man knows what is good and builds on what is right, what ought to be.[107] The sequence depends upon a supposition: the person of character and the ancestors are one. Ancestorism is the belief that the closest harmony with the ancient way is the highest of experiences, the force that enables a man to rise to his destiny, for, as John S. Mbiti points out, the person in Africa can only say, "I am, because we are; and since we are, therefore I am."[108]

"Our ancestors gave us these dances," a Kongo taxi-driver told me in Kinshasa, "we cannot forget them."[109] In Dahomey a man from Ajashe admired a dance and said, "it is our blood that is dancing."[110] There is further evidence on this point, centered on the notion that the ancestors, in ways varying with every culture, continue their existence within the dancer's body. They created the steps; the dancer moves, in part, to bring alive their name.

Thus African art and dance partially are defined as social acts of filiation, extending human consciousness into the past and the time of the founding fathers. It is essentially a timeless tradition, shaping ultimate values. Evidence of this is found in the widespread belief in reincarnation in West and Central Africa, a belief which dissolves the primacy of time. For a single dramatic example, among the Ga of Ghana when a person is possessed by an ancient spirit she "looks quite young while dancing"; the marks of old age resume when she steps back into real time.[111] Vansina calls this timelessness, this unity with the ancestors and the sources of vitality, Great Time.[112]

Ancestral presence in the dance diminishes the destroying force of time:

> the historic event is thus the descent of Great Time into the passage of time, that is to say, a degradation. But to deny time, or at least to limit its effect, does not mean a rejection of history as such.[113]

On the contrary, traditional people in Africa select those noble persons in actual life who deserve extended life in history and praise-singing. We realize that Africans, moving in their ancient dances, in full command of historical destiny, *are* those noble personages, briefly returned. The more traditional and ancient forms of dance "transforms one into a noble person among the people of this world."

I can document ancestorism as an empirical fact, as well as mystic assumption, in the sense that many or some of the gross structural traits of African performance have been in existence for at least four hundred years. . . .

a. Black Performance in Time Perspective

Certain traits thus have existed for centuries; call-and-response (soloist and handclapping chorus), balance of many kinds, youthful power. To be added to this list are facial serenity, noted in the seventeenth century, descent in melodic and choreographic structure, and a possible medieval notice of suspending the beat. Zero allusion to incarnation of ancestral presence, multiple meter, and rhythmized play with pattern in music and in art ("looking smart") reflects, in all probability, lack of sophistication in observation.

It seems reasonable to suggest that notice of one or more of the traits of African creativity implies the presence of others. These notices were doubtless abstracted from a larger whole of socially aesthetic happening and intelligibility.

The history of the dance in Africa cannot be characterized solely as a phenomenon of individualist will or totally communal effort, but has to recognize the mutual play of both these forces. There were individual masters of form and their accomplishments could and did occur within objective time, viz., the imposition of a tax, a solar eclipse, the visit of a caravel.

But there were also choral dancers, like the women who met Towerson in the sixteenth century and who chanted in his honor, or so he would have us believe. Ensemble expressions of motion on the Gambia circa 1601 and in mid-eighteenth century Senegal belong more to the realm of ontological time—for they were communal events stylized by ideal past perfection, even though they, too, actually happened.

Two kinds of time, the real time of individual variation and the mythic time of choral enactment, seem commingled in the documents of exploration and missionary effort. We guess at their mutual interpenetration each time the call-and-response form seems to appear. This overlap situation combines innovative calls (or innovative steps, of the leader) with tradition (the choral round, by definition blurring individuality). Solo-ensemble work, among the many things it seems to accomplish, is the presentation of the individual as a figure on the ground of custom. It is the very perception of real and mythic time.

The sophistication of all this clearly hints of deeper sources of inspiration, the mediating processes of worldview. A common ground of basic philosophical assumptions, for example, would explain the apparent concordance between observations on the art of certain civilizations in Mali with art among traditional societies in Tanzania and other regions of East Africa. Let us start with art in Mali:

> an antelope head will be carved with the idea of continuing the vital force of the whole species . . . or a human head will be sculptured as a support for the force of some human group or of a certain ancestor.[114]

and continue with East Africa:

> Emotions are expressed by gestures and positions while the faces themselves are generally stereotyped. The reason, in my submission, may be found in the absence of any valuation of the individual within the social structure of a [traditional] society where all are basically equal . . .[115]

The image of a person or an animal in Mali or East Africa therefore is: an expression of aesthetic or spiritual principles. Such principles explain in part the midpoint mimesis which we find virtually everywhere within the African aesthetic universe. The East African art expert continues:

Thus the artists, with few exceptions, correctly express the common faith in the small importance of individual characteristics by the conspicuous absence of individual features. They saw human beings as types and not as individuals. For it is difficult to believe that men who were capable of forming anatomically correct torsos lacked the skill to give expression to the faces.

Generalization by style reflects a cultural preference for ideal substance and spirit, setting aside the possibility of naturalism. It identified another kind of realism, a concern with abiding concepts. This leads us to the most metaphorical, perhaps, of the ten suggested canons of African performance, "coolness." It is this trait which grants a person the power to incarnate the destiny of his tradition.

10. Coolness: Truth and Generosity Regained

Cool philosophy is a strong intellectual attitude, affecting incredibly diverse provinces of artistic happening, yet leavened with humor and a sense of play. It is an all-important mediating process, accounting for similarities in art and vision in many tropical African societies. It is a matrix from which stem ideas about being generous, clear, percussively patterned, harmonized with others, balanced, finished, socially perfected, worthy of destiny.[116] In other words, the criterion of coolness seems to unite and animate all the other canons.

This becomes evident when considering the semantic range of the concept, "cool" in thirty-five Niger-Zaire languages, from Woloff of Senegal to the Zulu of South Africa: calm, beauty, tranquility of mind, peace, verdancy, reconciliation, social purification, purification of the self, moderation of strength, gentleness, healing, softness (compared to cushions, silk, even the feel of a brand-new mattress), silence, discretion, wetness, rawness, newness, greenness, freshness, proximity to the gods.[117]

Language in Africa and Europe shares notions of self-control and imperturbability expressed under a metaphoric rubric of coolness, *viz.* notions of cool-headedness and *sang-froid*. But, in traditional Africa it is customary to talk about *cool country* meaning peace, and *cool heart*, meaning collectedness of mind. These expressions would clearly be anomalous in standard English.[118] The metaphor of the cool in tropical African symbolism far exceeds notions of moderation in coldness and degree of self-control and imperturbability. In Africa coolness is an all-embracing positive attribute which combines notions of composure, silence, vitality, healing, and social purification.

Composure intersects with silence; vitality intersects with healing in the sense of restoration of shining health; the body politic is "healed" in social reconciliations. Ideas of silence and calm are strongly indicated. Vitality connotes the strength of the young, while discretion, ability to heal, and good government connote the seasoned members of society. Coolness thus emerges as a metaphor of right living, uniting the special strengths of the elder with the warrior, women with men. In other studies I have shown the impact of this concept on visual art.[119] Here I illustrate [and] comment on coolness in the dance: "it cools the town when you dance . . . when you finish . . . you are restored to repose . . . and reconciliation with your family. They (the chiefs) keep themselves peaceful when they are dancing—this is reassuring to the townsmen"; "the heads of the dance cult are people who are 'cool,' who like 'to laugh and play' and who do not look for 'cases' (*i.e.*, litigation)."[120]

If coolness is a cardinal tenet, then realization of its facets can transform a person into a purified source of power. But there are a number of canons under its rubric which remain to be explained and identified before we move on to nuance and semantic form in the gestures, attitudes, and motions of African visual art. Three of these are qualified by light.

a. Visibility

A cool person does not hide. The Tiv in Nigeria demand that a person dances clearly.[121] The Yoruba use the arms to make the direction of the dance visible.[122] Bamenda like display, in the sense of making the dancers and their motions fully visible.[123] Diola-Fogny require the voice of the singer to be clear.[124]

Although there are exceptions, such as the king who must work in secrecy to combat the secretive forces of witchcraft in behalf of his people and embody to a certain extent their mystic heart, in general, visibility is an embodiment of the resolving power of the cool, *i.e.*, moderation of force in discovery of the mean between that which is faint and that which is conspicuous. The aliveness of the concept among the Igbo of southeastern Nigeria is apparent in the need, in this society, to be "transparent" or "open" in one's actions.[125] Visibility in the sense of aesthetic clarity governs the thought of artists among the Chokwe of Angola.[126] The Manding of Mali, according to Charles S. Bird, associate the forest with darkness and the unknown.[127] Areas under cultivation and within the town are *clear*; open to the sky and visible.

The criterion of clarity under the rubric of social coolness (people who have things to hide often generate heat, dissension, and bloodshed) is of importance for the further understanding of the significance of "danced" sculpture, *i.e.*, the sculpture is removed from the secrecy or relative privacy of the shrine or grove and restored to the public view. Compare the Yoruba proverb: "if the secret is beat upon the drum, that secret will be revealed in dance."[128] Nothing should or can remain unrevealed in viable society. This is also a basic premise among the Ndembu of Central Africa, where it is believed that what is clearly seen can be accepted as valid ground for knowledge.[129]

b. Luminosity

It follows that that which is clear is also brilliant. The Tiv have the strangely beautiful concept of the good dancer "shooting darkness,"[130] *i.e.*, reducing the powers of darkness and social heat by means of his shining athletic grace. Yoruba maintain that some forms of artistic motion positively shine,[131] a belief perhaps continuing, in change, within the Yoruba barrios of Bahia, where it is believed that varnished, shining drums produce more brilliant tones than drums without varnish or shining surfaces.[132] In Angola the Chokwe very decidedly prefer bright colors over dull.[133] Onitsha Igbo take the famous ozo title dressed in immaculate white and wear white feathers as essential attributes of shining purity in proximity to the gods.[134]

c. Smoothness

This is again a function of perfected clarity because that which has been properly smoothed and finished will shine and become brilliantly visible. Diola-Fogny laud the smooth-sounding voice, not scratchy or "shrill and hard like unripened fruit."[135] Mbam in Cameroon demand dancing that is smooth and not harsh or brutal and Yoruba compare fine motion with the spinning of the agbaarin seed in a game played by children.[136] Liberian Dan in effect gloss what is meant by this last image when they praise the good dancer by comparison to a spinning top: "because no part of a top will wait; the whole is going."[137] Smoothness is thus identified in unified aesthetic impact; seams do not show, the whole is moving towards generous conclusions based on total givings of the self to music and to society. The analogous smoothing of the surfaces of most forms of African sculpture is so obvious that it will not be belabored.

d. Rebirth and Reincarnation

In another work I have shown how the concept of the cool is often apparent in crisis situations and points of transition. In African ritual, as in ritual in many places in the traditional world, a person "dies" in order to be reborn in new strength and insight. Motion arts in Africa bring pleasure precisely because many people see the founders of the nation or lineage returning in these styles. The pleasure taken in viewing vitally inflected sculpture or the dance therefore stems, in part, from sensations of participation in an alternative, ancient, far superior universe. Richard Henderson points out that attributes appropriate to descent tend to be defined in Onitsha Igbo culture by emotion: "indeed the affective components of filiation are often symbolically elaborated."[138] African dance and art, we saw in the concept of ancestorism, are vitalized by embodiment of superior mind from the past; conversely, the ancient elders are united again with strong means of realization of their principles, in the bodies of the dancers or sculpted image. It is a remarkable synthesis.

e. Composure of the Face: Mask of the Cool

The mind of an elder within the body of the young is suggested by the striking African custom of dancing "hot" with a "cool" unsmiling face. This quality seems to have haunted Ten Rhyne at the Cape in 1673, and it struck the imagination of an early observer of strongly African-influenced dancing in Louisiana in the early nineteenth century, who noted "thumping ecstasy" and "intense solemnity of mien."[139] The mask of the cool, or facial serenity, has been noted at many points in Afro-American history.

It is interesting that what remains a spiritual principle in some parts of Africa and the rare African-influenced portions of the modern U.S.A., such as tidewater

Georgia, becomes in the mainline Afro-American urban culture an element of contemporary street behavior:

> Negro boys . . . have a "cool" way of walking in which the upper trunk and pelvis rock fore and aft while the head remains stable with the eyes looking straight ahead. The . . . walk is quite slow, and the Negroes take it as a way of "strutting" or "showing off." . . .[140]

In the fast-moving urban world of Black America this citation is already dated. The 1974 cool style of male walking in the United States is called *bopping*; but, it is still a mode of asserting strength of self, broadly dove-tailing with portions of the African mode of "looking smart." Mystical coolness in Africa has changed in urban Afro-American assertions of independent power. But the functions, to heal and gather strength, partially remain. And the name, *cool*, remains. And the body is still played in two patterns, one stable, the other active, part energy and part mind. This image would seem indelible, as resistant to destruction by Western materialist forces as the similar shaping of the melodies of Africa. Thus A. M. Jones:

> melody in the old folk-music is markedly impersonal; time is not used to express emotion—a very sad subject may well be sung allegro . . .[141]

Time in African music and dance cannot, of course, be contaminated by descent into real time, the sources of petty stress and perturbation. Dance is Great Time, the time in which coolness ideally is realized. Vitality and mind must be made to correspond, like the use of stress in "swinging" music, in order to approach the gods. Coolness, the Songhai of the Niger say, comes in lightning and rain securing human life within spiritually insured calm.[142] Men are cooled by the flash of the gods' magnificence, and the gods are cooled by promises made and kept. The basis is power, generosity, and truth.

NOTES

1. For example, see Richard N. Henderson, *The King in Every Man* (New Haven: Yale University Press, 1972) p. 266: "purification of self transforms one's general identity to bring a man close to the divine order of things."
2. *Cf.* Frank Willett, *African Sculpture* (New York: Praeger, 1971) pp. 208–222, for a good survey of available data on African aesthetics.
3. Robert Schmitz, *Les Baholoholo* (Brussels: A. Dewit, Collection de Monographies Ethnographiques, 1912) p. 410.
4. Jomo Kenyatta, *Facing Mt. Kenya* (New York: Vintage Books, 1962) pp. 100–1.
5. Jean Rouch, "La Danse," *Le Monde Noir*, Numéro Spécial 8–9, *Présence Africaine*, 1950, pp. 223–4.
6. Margaret Read, *Children of Their Fathers* (New Haven: Yale University Press, 1960) p. 147. *Cf.* also Alvin Wolfe, *In The Ngombe Tradition* (Evanston: Northwestern University Press, 1961) p. 16.
7. Kwabena Nketia, *Drumming in Akan Communities* (London: Thomas Nelson, 1963) p. 169.

8. Personal communication to the author, 1 February 1966.

9. Informant 1.

10. *Ibid.*

11. *Ibid.*

12. *Ibid.*

13. R. C. Abraham, *A Dictionary of Modern Yoruba* (London: University of London Press, 1958) p. 424, *mon* "know" and p. 199, *ewa* "beauty." See also T. J. Bowen, *Grammar and Dictionary of the Yoruba Language* (Washington: Smithsonian Contributions to Knowledge, 1858): "*amewa*: a judge of beauty." For Efik evidence, see Hugh Goldie, *Dictionary of the Efik Language* (Ridgewood: The Gregg Press, 1964) reprint, p. 66, Kikongo, K. E. Laman, *Dictionnaire Kikongo-Française* (Hants: The Gregg Press, 1964) reprint, p. 683.

14. Butuo, Nimba Country, Liberia, 30 March 1967.

15. S. A. Babalola, *The Content and Form of Yoruba Itala* (Oxford: Oxford University Press, 1966) p. 51.

16. I am indebted to John Neuhart of the UCLA Department of Art for these insights, Los Angeles, 19 November 1972.

17. *The American Heritage Dictionary*, William Morris, ed. (Boston and New York: American Heritage Publishing Co. and Houghton Mifflin Company, 1969) p. 439.

18. Shown a photograph of this object, one of the "linguists" to the Agogohene of Agogo remarked, "This one is most beautiful to me. If you look at the neck it is befitting to him. The Ashanti have a saying, 'a handsome person is a person who has respectability' " (*eno na eye me fe esiane se nanim fere. Wohwe ne kon a efeta no paa. Asante foo ka see obi ho ye fe a na owo animnonyan*). Agogo, Northern Ashanti, 2 January 1971. The Agogohene was pleased by the implication of youth in the firm curve of the jaw and the smoothness of the skin.

19. Daniel Crowley, "An African Aesthetic" in: *Art and Aesthetics in Primitive Societies*, ed. Carol Jopling (New York: Dutton, 1971) p. 328. "Hence old and worn masks are thrown away or allowed to be eaten by termites. Similarly bright colors are preferred to dull. . . ." The Mende and Baoule cases come from unpublished field work shared by Frank Dubinakas and Susan Vogel. The Fang evidence, collected by James Fernandez, also appears in the Jopling anthology on p. 366: "the statue presents both an infantile and an ancestral aspect." Note that Fang seem to bracket infancy and old age within shining muscularity.

20. Crowley, *ibid.*

21. André Gide, *Travels in the Congo* (Berkeley and Los Angeles: University of California Press, 1962) p. 80.

22. See Informant 60.

23. Gunther Schuller, *Early Jazz* (New York: Oxford University Press, 1968) pp. 7–9.

24. *Ibid.*, p. 8.

25. A. M. Jones, "African Rhythm," *Africa*, Vol. XXIV, No. 1 (January 1954) p. 28.

26. Informant: "James," from Eket District, Ibibio country, Nigeria, at the central market, Bids, 18 July 1965. He did not like the designs of Nupe cloths either, and criticized their off-beat phrasing: "it's scattered, not properly aligned."

27. Informants 40, 36, 59.

28. Informants 43, 47, 68.

29. Susan Vogel, "Yoruba and Baoule Art Criticism," unpublished research paper, March 1971.

30. Robert Goldwater, *Primitivism in Modern Art*. Revised Edition (New York: Vintage Books, 1967) p. 230.

31. Informant 87.

32. I am indebted to Professor Wyatt MacGaffey of Haverford College for this information. Personal communication, 3 May 1972.

33. Peggy Harper, "Dance in Nigeria," *Ethnomusicology*, Vol. XIII (May 1969) pp. 288–9.

34. Source: Katherine Coryton White archive.

35. *The Philosophy of Hegel*, ed. Carl J. Friedrich (New York: Modern Library, 1953) p. 28.

36. For information on the "knot of wisdom" motif, see Kofi Antubam, *Ghana's Heritage of Culture* (Leipzig: Koehler & Amelang, 1963) p. 176. However, Antubam's interpretations of Akan motifs should not be taken as universally applicable. The reef-knot motif he interprets, for example, as "the detection of the secret motive underlying a diplomatic move," whereas at Agogo I was told that the motif refers to "unusual kingly knowledge," "ability to unlock that which common men cannot." Brigitte Menzel, *Goldgewichte Aus Ghana* (Berlin: Museum für Volkerkunde, 1968) p. 68. At p. 69 Menzel reports her own informants' interpretation of the wisdom knot motif: "only a wise man would be able to tie or loosen that kind of knot."

37. Roy Sieber, *African Textiles and Decorative Arts* (New York: The Museum of Modern Art, 1972) p. 190.

38. Richard Alan Waterman, "African Influence on the Music of the Americas," *Mother Wit from the Laughing Barrel*, ed. Alan Dundes (Englewood: Prentice-Hall, 1973) p. 88.

39. A. M. Jones, *Studies in African Music*. Vol. I (London: Oxford University Press, 1959) pp. 149, 274.

40. A. M. Jones, *African Music in Northern Rhodesia and Some Other Places* (Livingstone: The Rhodes-Livingstone Museum, 1958) p. 11.

41. Melville J. Herskovits and Frances S. Herskovits, *Suriname Folklore* (New York: AMS Press, 1969). Reprint of the 1936 edition, p. 518.

42. Informant 34.

43. Henry Stanley, *In Darkest Africa* (New York: Scribners, 1890) pp. 436–8.

44. Informants 22, 27, 37, 50, 87.

45. S. Kobla Ladzekpo and Hewitt Pantaleoni, "Takada Drumming," *African Music*, Vol. 4, No. 4 (1970) p. 12.

46. Personal communication, 15 August 1973.

47. Robert Farris Thompson, *Black Gods and Kings* (Los Angeles Museum and Laboratories of Ethnic Arts and Technology, 1971) p. 13/5.

48. Clara Odugbesan, "Femininity in Yoruba Religious Art," *Man in Africa*, ed. Mary Douglas and Phyllis M. Kaberry (London: Tavistock, 1969) p. 202.

49. Personal communication, 10 September 1973.

50. Charles Keil, *Tiv Song*, 21 May 1973, mimeographed, p. 39.

51. Quoted in Alan P. Merriam, "African Music," *Continuity and Change in African Cultures*, ed. William Bascom and Melville J. Herskovits (Chicago: University of Chicago, 1959) p. 58.

52. Philip Gbeho, "The Indigenous Gold Coast Music," *Journal of the African Music Society*, I (5) 1952, p. 31.

53. Waterman, "Hot Rhythm in Negro Music," *Journal of the American Musicological Society*, Vol. I, No. 1 (Spring 1948) p. 26.

54. Laura Bohannan (pseud. Eleanor Bowen Smith), *Return to Laughter* (Garden City, N.Y.: Doubleday and Co., 1964) p. 123.

55. Keil, *op. cit.*, p. 22: "*a vine a tsorogh* might be translated she is dancing polymetrically."

56. Harper, *op. cit.*, p. 290. In addition, I mention a letter from Joann Wheeler Kealiinohomoku, dated 1 October 1966, in which she points out the necessity of distinguishing between polymetric and polyrhythmic, something that is not always done in writings on African music and dance: "when, for example, a ballet dancer moves rapidly across the stage in *bourée* while performing an *adagio port de bras* she is using polyrhythms. Using 3/4 against 12/8 *is* polymetric . . . dancing with the right hand moving in a 5/4 meter and the feet performing a strong 3/4 beat is also polymetric. In other cases, where there is really only one meter, as in Western music, the dancer feels that pervading meter, and the different body parts select different portions of the overall organization for expression."

57. Personal communication, 21 August 1973.

58. *The Republic and Other Works*, translated by B. Jowett (New York: Doubleday & Co., 1960) p. 372.

59. Informants 22, 53, 56, 58, 64.

60. Informant: Adisa Fagbemi, Ajilete, southern Egbado, Yorubaland.

61. Commentary collected at Ilaro, capital of the Egbado Yoruba, June 1963.

62. Informant 1.

63. A. M. Jones, 1959, Vol. I, p. 94.

64. Informant 5.

65. Informant 44.

66. Informant 66.

67. R. C. Abraham, pp. 522, 399.

68. *Ibid.*, p. 399.

69. Goldie, p. 237, *nwet* "pattern"; p. 268, *siak*, "to divide."

70. Charles Keil, Abstract, *Tiv Song*, mimeographed, 21 May 1973, p. 2.

71. Informant 5.

72. See Roger Abrahams, "Patterns of Performance in The British West Indies," *Afro-American Anthropology*, ed. Norman E. Whitten and John F. Szwed (New York: The Free Press, 1970) p. 164.

73. J. David Sapir, "Diola-Fogny Funeral Songs and the Native Critic," *African Language Review* (1969) p. 178.

74. Informant 1, criterion vii.

75. Informant 37.

76. Kwabena Nketia, "The Role of the Drummer in Akan Society," *African Music*, Vol. I, No. 1 (1954) p. 42. I have inserted Nketia's footnote 3 after the phrase "timed to the end beats" and before the next paragraph of the citation.

77. See M. D. McLeod, "Goldweights of Asante," *African Arts*, Vol. V, No. 1 (Autumn 1971). The description of this piece appears beside the masthead of the magazine, p. 4.

78. Informant 36.

79. Informant 45.

80. Informant 87.

81. Kevin Carroll, *Yoruba Religious Carving* (New York: Praeger, 1967) pp. 96–97.

82. Interviewed at Agogo, Ghana, 2 January 1971.

83. Brigitte Menzel, *Textilien Aus Westafrika* (Berlin: Museum für Volkerkunde, 1972) Fig. 982.

84. Nana Ntiamoah Mensah, interview, Agogo, Ghana, 2 January 1971.

jazz is a dance

85. Bessie Jones and Bess Lomax Hawes, *Step It Down* (New York: Harper and Row, 1972) p. 44. They add: "a clear mental picture of the difference in basic foot position might be gained if Bill Robinson's and Fred Astaire's tap dancing styles could be visualized."

86. See Irwin Panofsky, *Meaning in the Visual Arts* (Garden City: Doubleday Anchor Books, 1955) p. 128. Panofsky shows that: "This ascent from the material to the immaterial world is what the Pseudo-Areopagite and John the Scot describe—in contrast to the customary theological use of this term—as the 'anagogical approach' (*anagogicus mos*, literally translated: 'the upward-leading method'); and this is what Suger professed as a theologian, proclaimed as a poet, and practiced as a patron of the arts."

87. Informant 33.

88. *Ibid.*, Informant 41.

89. Amos Tutuola, *Feather Woman of the Jungle* (London: Faber and Faber, 1962) p. 49.

90. Harris Memel-Fote, "The Perception of Beauty in Negro-African Culture," *Colloquium on Negro Art* (Paris: Présence Africaine, 1968) pp. 51–2.

91. Karl Laman, *The Kongo, I* (Upsala: Studia Ethnographica Upsaliensia, 1953) pp. 41–2.

92. R. C. Abraham, p. 671. See *won*, as in the phrase, *o mun oti niiwon*: "He drank liquor in moderation."

93. Robin Horton, *Kalabari Sculpture* (Lagos: Department of Antiquities, 1965) p. 22.

94. Mario Meneghini, "The Bassa Mask," *African Arts*, Vol. VI, No. 1 (Autumn 1972) p. 47.

95. Capt. R. S. Rattray, *Religion and Art in Ashanti* (Oxford: Clarendon Press, 1927) p. 110.

96. Informant 37.

97. Informant 87.

98. E. E. Evans-Pritchard, "The Dance," *Africa 1*, 4 (October 1928) p. 450.

99. Waterman, *op. cit.*, p. 90.

100. *Ibid.*

101. See Robert Farris Thompson, "An Aesthetic of the Cool West African Dance," *African Forum*, Vol. 2, No. 2, Fall 1966.

102. A phenomenon I have observed at Sebikotan, Senegal, Butuo, Liberia, throughout Yorubaland, in West Cameroon, and in Zaire.

103. Ulli Beier and Bakari Gbadamosi, *Yoruba Poetry* (Lagos: Black Orpheus, 1959) p. 62.

104. For an excellent study, see Esther Pasztory, "Hieratic Composition in African Art," *Art Bulletin*, Vol. III, No. 3 (September 1970) pp. 299–304.

105. E. E. Evans-Pritchard, *op. cit.*, pp. 455–6.

106. K. Marx, *The 18th Brumaire of Louis Bonaparte* (New York: International Publishers, 1963) p. 19.

107. See R. F. Thompson, *Black Gods and Kings*, p. 20–3.

108. John S. Mbiti, *African Religions and Philosophy* (Garden City, N.Y.: Anchor Books, 1970) p. 141.

109. Informant 89.

110. Informant 14.

111. Mbiti, *op. cit.*, p. 277.

112. *The Historian in Tropical Africa*, ed. Jan Vansina, Raymond Mauny, and L. V. Thomas (London: Oxford University Press, 1964) pp. 372–3.

113. *Ibid.*, p. 373.

114. Marcel Griaule, *Folk Art of Black Africa* (New York: Tudor, 1950) p. 58.

115. H. Cory, *African Figurines* (London: Faber and Faber, 1956) p. 153.

116. R. F. Thompson, "Aesthetic of the Cool," *African Arts*, Vol. VII, No. 1 (Autumn 1973) pp. 41–3, 64–67, 89–91.

117. *Ibid.*, pp. 90–91, Table.

118. I have in mind here a parallel with the use of the verb, "signifying" in Black and Standard English: "What is unique in Black English usage is the way in which signifying is extended to cover a range of meanings and events which are not covered in its Standard English usage." For details, see Claudia Mitchell-Kernan, "Signifying" in: *Mother Wit from the Laughing Barrel*, ed. Alan Dundes (Englewood Cliffs: Prentice-Hall, 1973) p. 313.

119. *E.g., Black Gods and Kings* (1971).

120. Informant 15, 66. See also, Robin Horton, for last reference, which is Ijaw, "The Kalabari Ekine Society: A Borderland of Religion and Art," *Africa*, Vol. XXXIII, No. 2 (April 1962) p. 103: "by people, i.e. who are in many ways the antithesis of the aggressive thrusting politician. The same is often true of the core of dancing enthusiasts who give the society its real vitality." Cool people, Horton says, are able to stand back from life and portray it in the masquerade; his data coincide closely with the idea of detachment and humor (refusal to suffer) embedded in the cool of many forms of African philosophy.

121. Keil, *op. cit.*

122. Informant 35.

123. Informant 81.

124. David Sapir, *op. cit.*, p. 183.

125. Quoted in Karl Riesman, "Remarks on Sama Vocabulary," paper read at Northeastern Anthropological Association Annual Meeting, April 27, 1973, p. 13.

126. For details, see Crowley's contribution to the forthcoming *The Traditional Artist in African Society*, ed. Warren d'Azevedo (Bloomington: Indiana University Press, 1973).

127. Personal communication, 3 April 1973. I am indebted to Professor Charles S. Bird for sharing his rich knowledge of Manding culture.

128. Abraham, p. 80.

129. Victor Turner, *The Forest of Symbols* (Ithaca: Cornell University Press, 1967) p. 76.

130. Charles Keil, personal communication, March 1966.

131. Informant 38. He says this by indirection—"the style of some people will not shine well."

132. Melville J. Herskovits, *The New World Negro* (Bloomington: Indiana University Press, 1966) p. 187,

133. Crowley, *op. cit.*, p. 323.

134. Henderson, *op. cit.*, p. 263.

135. Sapir, *op. cit.*, p. 183.

136. S. A. Babalola, *The Content and Form of Yoruba Itala* (Oxford: Oxford University Press, 1966) p. 75.

137. Informant 1.

138. Henderson, *op. cit.*, p. 14.

139. Quoted in Kenneth M. Stampp, *The Peculiar Institution* (New York: Vintage Books, 1956) p. 366.

140. Gerald D. Suttles, *The Social Order of the Slums: Ethnicity and Territory in the Inner City* (Chicago: University of Chicago Press, 1968) pp. 62, 66. I thank Roger Abrahams for this reference.

141. A. M. Jones, *Studies in African Music*, Vol. I, p. 264.

142. Jean Rouch, *La Religion et la Magie Songhai* (Paris: Presses Universitaires de France, 1960) p. 223.

chapter 21

Be Like Mike?
Michael Jordan and the Pedagogy of Desire

Michael Jordan is perhaps the best, and best-known, athlete in the world today. He has attained unparalleled cultural status because of his extraordinary physical gifts, his marketing as an icon of race-transcending American athletic and moral excellence, and his mastery of a sport that has become the metaphoric center of black cultural imagination. But the Olympian sum of Jordan's cultural meaning is greater than the fluent parts of his persona as athlete, family man, and marketing creation. There is hardly cultural precedence for the character of his unique fame, which has blurred the line between private and public, between personality and celebrity, and between substance and symbol. Michael Jordan stands at the breach between perception and intuition, his cultural meaning perennially deferred from closure because his career symbolizes possibility itself, gathering into its unfolding narrative the shattered remnants of previous incarnations of fame and yet transcending their reach.

Jordan has been called "the new DiMaggio" (Boers 1990, 30) and "Elvis in high-tops," indications of the herculean cultural heroism he has come to embody. There is even a religious element to the near worship of Jordan as a cultural icon of invincibility, as he has been called a "savior of sorts," "basketball's high priest" (Bradley 1991–92, 60), and "more popular than Jesus," except with "better endorsement deals" (Vancil 1992, 51). But the quickly developing cultural canonization of Michael Jordan provokes reflection about the contradictory uses to which Jordan's body is put as a seminal cultural text and ambiguous symbol of fantasy, and the avenues of agency and resistance available especially to black youth who make symbolic investment in Jordan's body as a means of cultural and personal possibility, creativity, and desire.

I understand Jordan in the broadest sense of the term to be a public pedagogue, a figure of estimable public moral authority whose career educates us about productive and disenabling forms of knowledge, desire, interest, consumption, and culture in three spheres: the culture of athletics that thrives on skill and performance, the specific expression of elements of African-American culture, and the market forces and processes of commodification expressed by, and produced in, advanced capitalism. By probing these dimensions of Jordan's cultural importance, we may gain a clearer understanding of his function in American society.

Athletic activity has shaped and reflected important sectors of American society. First, it produced communities of common athletic interest organized around the development of highly skilled performance. The development of norms of athletic excellence evidenced in sports activities cemented communities of participants who valorized rigorous sorts of physical discipline in preparation for athletic competition and in expressing the highest degree of athletic skill. Second, it produced potent subcultures that inculcated in their participants norms of individual and team accomplishment. Such norms tapped into the bipolar structures of competition and cooperation that pervade American culture. Third, it provided a means of reinscribing Western frontier myths of exploration and discovery-as-conquest onto a vital sphere of American culture. Sports activities can be viewed in part as the attempt to symbolically ritualize and metaphorically extend the ongoing quest for mastery of environment and vanquishing of opponents within the limits of physical contest.

Fourth, athletic activity has served to reinforce habits and virtues centered in collective pursuit of communal goals that are intimately connected to the common good, usually characterized within athletic circles as "team spirit." The culture of sport has physically captured and athletically articulated the mores, folkways, and dominant visions of American society, and at its best it has been conceived as a means of symbolically embracing and equitably pursuing the just, the good, the true, and the beautiful. And finally, the culture of athletics has provided an acceptable and widely accessible means of white male bonding. For much of its history, American sports activity has reflected white patriarchal privilege, and it has been rigidly defined and socially shaped by rules that restricted the equitable participation of women and people of color.

Black participation in sports in mainstream society, therefore, is a relatively recent phenomenon. Of course, there have existed venerable traditions of black sports, such as the Negro (baseball) Leagues, which countered the exclusion of black bodies from white sports. The prohibition of athletic activity by black men in mainstream society severely limited publicly acceptable forms of displaying black physical prowess, an issue that had been politicized during slavery and whose legacy extended into the middle of the twentieth century. Hence, the potentially superior physical prowess of black men, validated for many by the long tradition of slave labor that built American society, helped reinforce racist arguments about the racial regimentation of social space and the denigration of the black body as an inappropriate presence in traditions of American sport.

Coupled with this fear of superior black physical prowess was the notion that inferior black intelligence limited the ability of blacks to perform excellently in those sports activities that required mental concentration and agility. These two forces—the presumed lack of sophisticated black cognitive skills and the fear of superior black physical prowess—restricted black sports participation to thriving but financially handicapped subcultures of black athletic activity. Later, of course, the physical prowess of the black body would be acknowledged and exploited as a supremely fertile zone of profit as mainstream athletic society literally cashed in on the symbolic danger of black sports excellence.

Because of its marginalized status within the regime of American sports, black athletic activity often acquired a social significance that transcended the internal dimensions of game, sport, and skill. Black sport became an arena not only for testing the limits of physical endurance and forms of athletic excellence—while reproducing or repudiating ideals of American justice, goodness, truth, and beauty—but it also became a way of ritualizing racial achievement against socially imposed barriers to cultural performance.

In short, black sport activity often acquired a heroic dimension, as viewed in the careers of figures such as Joe Louis, Jackie Robinson, Althea Gibson, Wilma Rudolph, Muhammad Ali, and Arthur Ashe. Black sports heroes transcended the narrow boundaries of specific sports activities and garnered importance as icons of cultural excellence, symbolic figures who embodied social possibilities of success denied to other people of color. But they also captured and catalyzed the black cultural fetishization of sport as a means of expressing black cultural style, as a means of valorizing craft as a marker of racial and self-expression, and as a means of pursuing social and economic mobility.

It is this culture of black athletics, created against the background of social and historical forces that shaped American athletic activity, that helped produce Jordan and help explain the craft that he practices. Craft is the honing of skill by the application of discipline, time, talent, and energy toward the realization of a particular cultural or personal goal. American folk cultures are pervaded by craft, from the production of cultural artifacts that express particular ethnic histories and traditions to the development of styles of life and work that reflect and symbolize a community's values, virtues, and goals. Michael Jordan's skills within basketball are clearly phenomenal, but his game can only be sufficiently explained by understanding its link to the fusion of African-American cultural norms and practices, and the idealization of skill and performance that characterize important aspects of American sport. I will identify three defining characteristics of Jordan's game that reflect the influence of African-American culture on his style of play.

First, Jordan's style of basketball reflects the will to *spontaneity*. I mean here the way in which historical accidence is transformed into cultural advantage, and the way acts of apparently random occurrence are spontaneously and imaginatively employed by Africans and African-Americans in a variety of forms of cultural expression. When examining Jordan's game, this feature of African-American culture clearly functions in his unpredictable eruptions of basketball creativity. It was apparent, for instance, during game two of the National Basketball Association 1991 championship series between Jordan's Chicago Bulls and the Los Angeles

Lakers, in a shot that even Jordan ranked in his all-time top ten (McCallum 1991, 32). Jordan made a drive toward the lane, gesturing with his hands and body that he was about to complete a patent Jordan dunk shot with his right hand. But when he spied defender Sam Perkins slipping over to oppose his shot, he switched the ball in midair to his left hand to make an underhanded scoop shot instead, which immediately became known as the "levitation" shot. Such improvisation, a staple of the will to spontaneity, allows Jordan to expand his vocabulary of athletic spectacle, which is the stimulation of a desire to bear witness to the revelation of truth and beauty compressed into acts of athletic creativity.

Second, Jordan's game reflects the *stylization of the performed self*. This is the creation and projection of a sport persona that is an identifying mark of diverse African-American creative enterprises, from the complexly layered jazz experimentation of John Coltrane, the trickstering and signifying comedic routines of Richard Pryor, and the rhetorical ripostes and oral significations of rapper Kool Moe Dee. Jordan's whole game persona is a graphic depiction of the performed self as flying acrobat, resulting in his famous moniker "Air Jordan." Jordan's performed self is rife with the language of physical expressiveness: head moving, arms extending, hands waving, tongue wagging, and legs spreading.

He has also developed a resourceful repertoire of dazzling dunk shots that further express his performed self and that have garnered him a special niche within the folklore of the game: the cradle jam, rock-a-baby, kiss the rim, lean in, and the tomahawk. In Jordan's game, the stylization of a performed self has allowed him to create a distinct sports persona that has athletic as well as economic consequences, while mastering sophisticated levels of physical expression and redefining the possibilities of athletic achievement within basketball.

Finally, there is the subversion of perceived limits through the use of *edifying deception*, which in Jordan's case centers around the space/time continuum. This moment in African-American cultural practice is the ability to flout widely understood boundaries through mesmerization and alchemy, a subversion of common perceptions of the culturally or physically possible through the creative and deceptive manipulation of appearance. Jordan is perhaps most famous for his alleged "hang time," the uncanny ability to remain suspended in midair longer than other basketball players while executing his stunning array of improvised moves. But Jordan's "hang time" is technically a misnomer and can be more accurately attributed to Jordan's skillful athletic deception, his acrobatic leaping ability, and his intellectual toughness in projecting an aura of uniqueness around his craft than to his defiance of gravity and the laws of physics.

No human being, including Michael Jordan, can successfully defy the law of gravity and achieve relatively sustained altitude without the benefit of machines. As Douglas Kirkpatrick points out, the equation for altitude is $1/2 \; g \times t2 = VO \times t$ ("How Does Michael Fly?"). However, Jordan appears to hang by *stylistically* relativizing the fixed coordinates of space and time through the skillful management and manipulation of his body in midair. For basketball players, hang time is the velocity and speed with which a player takes off combined with the path the player's center of gravity follows on the way up. At the peak of a player's vertical jump, the velocity and speed is close to, or at, zero; hanging motionless in the air is the work of masterful skill and illusion ("How Does Michael Fly?"). Michael Jordan, through the consummate skill and style of his game, only appears to be hanging in space for more than the one second that human beings are capable of remaining airborne.

But the African-American aspects of Jordan's game are indissolubly linked to the culture of consumption and the commodification of black culture.[1] Because of Jordan's supreme mastery of basketball, his squeaky-clean image, and his youthful vigor in pursuit of the American Dream, he has become, along with Bill Cosby, the quintessential pitchman in American society. Even his highly publicized troubles with gambling, his refusal to visit the White House after the Bulls' championship season, and a book that purports to expose the underside of his heroic myth have barely tarnished his All-American image.[2] Jordan eats Wheaties, drives Chevrolets, wears Hanes, drinks Coca-Cola, consumes McDonald's, guzzles Gatorade, and, of course, wears Nikes. He and his shrewd handlers have successfully produced, packaged, marketed, and distributed his image and commodified his symbolic worth, transforming cultural capital into cash, influence, prestige, status, and wealth. To that degree, at least, Jordan repudiates the sorry tradition of the black athlete as the naif who loses his money to piranha-like financial wizards, investors, and hangers-on. He represents the new-age athletic entrepreneur who understands that American sport is ensconced in the cultural practices associated with business, and that it demands particular forms of intelligence, perception, and representation to prevent abuse and maximize profit.

From the very beginning of his professional career, Jordan was consciously marketed by his agency Pro-Serv as a peripatetic vehicle of American fantasies of capital accumulation and material consumption tied to Jordan's personal modesty and moral probity. In so doing, they skillfully avoided attaching to Jordan the image of questionable ethics and lethal excess that plagued inside traders and corporate raiders on Wall Street during the mideighties, as Jordan began to emerge as a cultural icon. But Jordan is also the symbol of the spectacle-laden black athletic body as the site of commodified black cultural imagination. Ironically, the black male body, which has been historically viewed as threatening and inappropriate in American society (and remains so outside of sports and entertainment), is made an object of white desires to domesticate and dilute its more ominous and subversive uses, even symbolically reducing Jordan's body to dead meat (McDonald's McJordan hamburger), which can be consumed and expelled as waste.

Jordan's body is also the screen upon which is projected black desires to emulate his athletic excellence and replicate his entry into reaches of unimaginable wealth and fame. But there is more than vicarious substitution and the projection of fantasy onto Jordan's body that is occurring in the circulation and reproduction of black cultural desire. There is also the creative use of desire and fantasy by young blacks to counter, and capitulate to, the forces of cultural dominance that attempt to reduce the black body to a commodity and text that is employed for entertainment, titillation, or financial gain. Simply said, there is no easy correlation between the commodification of black youth culture and the evidences of a completely dominated consciousness.

Even within the dominant cultural practices that seek to turn the black body into pure profit, disruptions of capital are embodied, for instance, in messages circulated in black communities by public moralists who criticize the exploitation of black cultural creativity by casual footwear companies. In short, there are instances of both black complicity and resistance in the commodification of black cultural imagination, and the ideological criticism of exploitative cultural practices must always be linked to the language of possibility and agency in rendering a complex picture of the black cultural situation. As Henry Giroux observes:

> The power of complicity and the complicity of power are not exhausted simply by registering how people are positioned and located through the production of particular ideologies structured through particular discourses. . . . It is important to see that an overreliance on ideology critique has limited our ability to understand how people actively participate in the dominant culture through processes of accommodation, negotiation, and even resistance. (GIROUX 1992, 194–95)

In making judgments about the various uses of the black body, especially Jordan's symbolic corporeality, we must specify how both consent and opposition to exploitation are often signaled in expressions of cultural creativity.

In examining his reactions to the racial ordering of athletic and cultural life, the ominous specificity of the black body creates anxieties for Jordan. His encounters with the limits of culturally mediated symbols of race and racial identity have occasionally mocked his desire to live beyond race, to be "neither black nor white" (Patton 1986, 52), to be "viewed as a person" (Vancil 1992, 57). While Jordan chafes under indictment by black critics who claim that he is not "black enough," he has perhaps not clearly understood the differences between enabling versions of human experience that transcend the exclusive gaze of race and disenabling visions of human community that seek race neutrality.

The former is the attempt to expand the perimeters of human experience beyond racial determinism, to nuance and deepen our understanding of the constituent elements of racial identity, and to understand how race, along with class, gender, geography, and sexual preference, shape and constrain human experience. The latter is the belief in an intangible, amorphous, nonhistorical, and raceless category of "person," existing in a zone beyond not simply the negative consequences of race, but beyond the specific patterns of cultural and racial identity that constitute and help shape human experience. Jordan's unclarity is consequential, weighing heavily on his apolitical bearing and his refusal to acknowledge the public character of his private beliefs about American society and the responsibility of his role as a public pedagogue.

Indeed it is the potency of black cultural expressions that not only have helped influence his style of play, but have also made the sneaker industry he lucratively participates in a multi-billion-dollar business. Michael Jordan has helped seize upon the commercial consequences of black cultural preoccupation with style and the commodification of the black juvenile imagination at the site of the sneaker.

At the juncture of the sneaker, a host of cultural, political, and economic forces and meanings meet, collide, shatter, and are reassembled to symbolize the situation of contemporary black culture.

The sneaker reflects at once the projection and stylization of black urban realities linked in our contemporary historical moment to rap culture and the underground political economy of crack, and reigns as the universal icon for the culture of consumption. The sneaker symbolizes the ingenious manner in which black cultural nuances of cool, hip, and chic have influenced the broader American cultural landscape. It was black street culture that influenced sneaker companies' aggressive invasion of the black juvenile market in taking advantage of the increasing amounts of disposable income of young black men as a result of legitimate and illegitimate forms of work.

Problematically, though, the sneaker also epitomizes the worst features of the social production of desire and represents the ways in which moral energies of social conscience about material values are drained by the messages of undisciplined acquisitiveness promoted by corporate dimensions of the culture of consumption. These messages, of rapacious consumerism supported by cultural and personal narcissism, are articulated on Wall Street and are related to the expanding inner-city juvenocracy, where young black men rule over black urban space in the culture of crack and illicit criminal activity, fed by desires to "live large" and to reproduce capitalism's excesses on their own terrain. Also, sneaker companies make significant sums of money from the illicit gains of drug dealers.

Moreover, while sneaker companies have exploited black cultural expressions of cool, hip, chic, and style, they rarely benefit the people who both consume the largest quantity of products and whose culture redefined the sneaker companies' raison d'être. This situation is more severely compounded by the presence of spokespeople like Jordan, Spike Lee, and Bo Jackson, who are either ineffectual or defensive about or indifferent to the lethal consequences (especially in urban black-on-black violence over sneaker company products) of black juvenile acquisition of products that these figures have helped make culturally desirable and economically marketable.

Basketball is the metaphoric center of black juvenile culture, a major means by which even temporary forms of cultural and personal transcendence of personal limits are experienced. Michael Jordan is at the center of this black athletic culture, the supreme symbol of black cultural creativity in a society of diminishing tolerance for the black youth whose fascination with Jordan has helped sustain him. But Jordan is also the iconic fixture of broader segments of American society, who see in him the ideal figure: a black man of extraordinary genius on the court and before the cameras, who by virtue of his magical skills and godlike talents symbolizes the meaning of human possibility, while refusing to root it in the specific forms of culture and race in which it must inevitably make sense or fade to ultimate irrelevance.

Jordan also represents the contradictory impulses of the contemporary culture of consumption, where the black athletic body is deified, reified, and rearticulated within the narrow meanings of capital and commodity. But there is both resistance and consent to the exploitation of black bodies in Jordan's explicit cultural symbolism, as he provides brilliant glimpses of black culture's ingenuity of improvisation as a means of cultural expression and survival. It is also partially this element of black culture that has created in American society a desire to dream Jordan, to "be like Mike."

This pedagogy of desire that Jordan embodies, although at points immobilized by its depoliticized cultural contexts, is nevertheless a remarkable achievement in contemporary American culture: a six-foot-six American man of obvious African descent is the dominant presence and central cause of athletic fantasy in a sport that twenty years ago was denigrated as a black man's game and hence deemed unworthy of wide attention or support. Jordan is therefore the bearer of meanings about black culture larger than his individual life, the symbol of a pedagogy of style, presence, and desire that is immediately communicated by the sight of his black body before it can be contravened by reflection.

In the final analysis, his big black body—graceful and powerful, elegant and dark—symbolizes the possibilities of other black bodies to remain safe long enough to survive within the limited but significant sphere of sport, since Jordan's achievements have furthered the cultural acceptance of at least the athletic black body. In that sense, Jordan's powerful cultural capital has not been exhausted by narrow understandings of his symbolic absorption by the demands of capital and consumption. His body is still the symbolic carrier of racial and cultural desires to fly beyond limits and obstacles, a fluid metaphor of mobility and ascent to heights of excellence secured by genius and industry. It is this power to embody the often conflicting desires of so many that makes Michael Jordan a supremely instructive figure for our times.

NOTES

1. I do not mean here a theory of commodification that does not accentuate the forms of agency that can function even within restrictive and hegemonic cultural practices. Rather, I think that, contrary to elitist and overly pessimistic Frankfurt School readings of the spectacle of commodity within mass cultures, common people can exercise "everyday forms of resistance" to hegemonic forms of cultural knowledge and practice. For an explication of the function of everyday forms of resistance, see Scott, *Domination and the Arts of Resistance*.

2. For a critical look at Jordan behind the myth, see Sam Smith, *The Jordan Rules* (New York: Simon and Schuster, 1992).

WORKS CITED

Boers, Terry. "Getting Better All the Time." *Inside Sports*, May 1990, pp. 30–33.

Bradley, Michael. "Air Everything." *Basketball Forecast*, 1991–92, pp. 60–67.

Giroux, Henry. *Border Crossings: Cultural Workers and the Politics of Education*. New York: Routledge, 1992.

"How Does Michael Fly?" *Chicago Tribune*, February 27, 1990, p. 28.

McCallum, Jack. "His Highness." *Sports Illustrated*, June 17, 1991, pp. 28–33.

Patton, Paul. "The Selling of Michael Jordan." *New York Times Magazine*, November 9, 1986, pp. 48–58.

Scott, James. *Domination and the Arts of Resistance*. New Haven, Conn.: Yale University Press, 1990.

Vancil, Mark. "Playboy Interview: Michael Jordan." *Playboy*, May 1992, pp. 51–164.

jazz is a dance

chapter 22

MARGO JEFFERSON

"Noise" Taps a Historic Route to Joy

Every art form made or mass produced in America is a hybrid. Jazz, the movies, blues, musical theater and gospel songs; vernacular dance, from square dancing to break dancing; even modern dance, with its high-art manners and mongrel vocabulary. They all serve hybrid functions, for they have been and can be folk art, popular art or high art. They are rich forms that an artist can spend a lifetime perfecting, but they can serve as passing styles too, to be lightly sampled or briefly savored.

Tap is a quintessential multipurpose form. It is dance, music and theater, suitable for clubs, studios, street corners, chorus lines and concert halls. It is aural, visual and dramatic: it can tell a story about people, places and emotions, or about rhythm, movement and a body talking to no one but itself.

Tap is and does all of these things—and with such splendor, such valor and such delight—in "Bring in da Noise, Bring in da Funk." "Noise and Funk" opened 11 days ago at the Joseph Papp Public Theater. It is directed by George C. Wolfe and choreographed by Savion Glover. You many have seen Mr. Glover as a Wunderkind dancer in Mr. Wolfe's Broadway musical, "Jelly's Last Jam" or, back in the 80's, in "Black and Blue" or "The Tap Dance Kid." But now, at just 21, that Wunderkind dancer has become a brilliant choreographer.

Exactly what is "Noise and Funk"? It is dance theater. It is musical theater. It is epic theater (think Brechtian devices like film projections, cutouts, slides and titles; think a taut progression of scenes that are linked but self-sufficient). And it is black theater, by which I mean its form and content are grounded in black, Negro and African-American history. But when I say history, I don't mean history as an assemblage of social and political facts, though they're here. I mean black, Negro and African-American history as a series of experiments (driven, desperate, crafty, witty, ebullient) in style and esthetics.

Newspapers and magazines these days are filled with anxious and portentous talk of "race relations." Let's talk about race esthetics instead, which turn culture into a series of evolving performance traditions rather than a set of eternal socio-logical maxims; and where terms like "primitive," "sophisticated," "folk," "popular and "high" art become styles meant to be used, discarded and made over, not set categories meant to arouse smug, set responses.

Capital letters projected above the stage announce "in the beginning there was . . . da beat!" No sooner said than done. Five musicians are setting the beat in the pit, and as it multiplies and diversifies, they are joined by five dancers (Mr. Glover, Baakari Wilder, Jimmy Tate, Vincent Bingham, Dulé Hill), a singer (Ann Duquesnay) and a rapper-poet (Reg E. Gaines). There they are, bodies and voices in unison and syncopation, doing . . . well, let me quote Mr. Gaines as to what they're doing:

> Be boppin/toe tappin
> Hip hoppin/crackin—snappin
> Juba pattin/soft sole shufflin—
> Lindy hoppin—West Coast poppin
> Charleston chica—hustlin—cakin—
> Twistin—jerkin—East Coast breakin
> Blackened bottoms doing da bump
> Cuz when you bring in da noise
> You gots to bring da funk.

The word and the beat made a glorious beginning, but in the beginning there was slavery too, and while history can record it, theater has to reinvent it.

Here on the film screen is a calm sea; here are regal ships on a prosperous voy-age. And here below is a box with a man crouched inside. A cone of blue light shines down on him as he begins, with one leg (the tap sounds like a chain), to trace the rhythm on the floor and listen to it. The singer recites the ships' names, "the *Medusa*, the *Othello*, the *Enterprise*, the *Jesus of Lubeck*"; the dancer acceler-ates, pauses, elaborates, then draws back into himself.

A terrible beauty is born.

Moments later, Ms. Duquesnay is lounging at the side of the stage, fanning her-self and singing a cappella as four young men (four young slaves, four young bucks) stand before us in field-hand garb and straw hats, each tracing the movement of a work task with a kind of precision and delicacy that you can see in silent movies, when actors like Chaplin or Keaton or the young Will Rogers execute physical tasks and encounter inanimate objects.

(Even the ill-used and much-maligned Stepin Fetchit has brief moments—he actually was a physically skilled performer—that erase shame. And watching the long-faced Baakari Wilder work with his witty but mournful limbs, I felt that those moments were being claimed and redeemed.)

Good and great art do redeem bad—or vicious—entertainment: as can be seen when two clowns stroll in with a well-stocked cart of pots and pans. They themselves are covered with pots and pans: pans tied around their waists, pans strapped to their backs, pans jutting out from their stomachs and backsides. And these doofus-looking little panhandlers proceed to turn out a percussion concert—playing on themselves and on each other's bodies, and on the kitchen utensils behind them (so many tones, so many *kinds* of sounds)—with solemn skill and wonder. Scenes shift, moods change and whenever history does its worst, art and craft answer back with their best, thanks to these extraordinary performers, thanks to Mr. Wolfe's direction, but thanks also to the sets, costumes, lighting and sound (not least the miking of the taps), the work of Riccardo Hernandez, Karen Perry, Jules Fisher and Peggy Eisenhauer, and Dan Moses Schreier, respectively.

How do you use tap to show a lynching? Make the rhythm of the hanged man's feet go jagged and scratchy, like muscles going into spasms.

A factory up North in Chicago becomes a jungle gym of men in synchronized motion; limbs, chains, drumsticks beating the soles of outstretched feet at metronomic intervals. You've seen something similar in videos by Madonna and Janet Jackson; all of them are taking from Fritz Lang's "Metropolis." But "Noise and Funk" isn't just borrowing these images; it's making them new again.

It even manages to make something new of the old and bitter tale of how Hollywood musicals misused, underused or just refused to use so many gifted black performers. (Sure, the performers lost, but the movies lost more.) When Mr. Baakari's bespangled Uncle Huck-a-Buck does his duet with Mr. Glover's beribboned and beruffled Lil Dahlin doll, Bill (Bojangles) Robinson and Shirley Temple live again, giving off rhythms, contradictions and complexities that they both knew they could never express on camera.

"Street Corner Symphony" takes us through the raucous 1950's, 60's and 70's, and the last three dances take us up to the here and now. The dancers, the drummers and the musicians all undertake, understand and extend the styles of the past. And they do so with their own postmodern will, intellect and edge. Watch them work and play with hoofing, hip-hop and ballet moves in "Hittin'." And listen to and with Ms. Duquesnay as she delivers her own version of a Bessie Smith—Mahalia Jackson gospel blues, or pitches a Jazz Age twitter somewhere between naughty Trixie Smith and girlish Rose (Chi Chi) Murphy. (Ms. Duquesnay did her own vocal arrangements; Zane Mark and Daryl Waters wrote the music.)

Mr. Glover does a gorgeous solo tribute to the four tap masters who were his mentors: Chuck Green, Lon Chaney, Buster Brown and Jimmy Slyde. But his choreography is not about his vision of himself as a soloist, it is choreography for five inventive, resourceful dancers, each with tones, rhythms and lines of his own.

The poet-rapper Reg E. Gaines doesn't yet have the performing skills that the others have, and more than once I felt his words distracted me from the dance the way fussy camera angles in movie musicals and videos do. But he got better—more varied, more textured—as he went along; I felt he was watching, listening and learning from the dancers. (Once, he even tried to balance on his toes, like they do.)

The history of American art and entertainment, from the stage to movie and television screens, is all bound up with how we dramatize racial and ethnic styles. Who can think of jazz without thinking of African-Americans, or musical comedy without thinking of Jews, or romantic comedies without visions of those Anglo-Americans we call high or middling-high *wasps*? Thrillers and crime dramas, having long fed on the Irish and the Italians, are now extending their appetites to blacks, Latins and Asians; vaudeville and situation comedies have gone the same route.

And yet these things are so bound up with shame too, all kinds of shame, and with ignorance. Say "black tap," and for all its inventiveness and experimentation—John Bubbles, the Nicholas Brothers, Baby Laurence, Honi Coles and Cholly Atkins, Charles (Cookie) Cook, Gregory Hines and so many others—you can still conjure up the sad, stale clichés of stoop-shouldered, ingratiating shuffles, preposterously fixed in wide grins and compulsive acrobatics with rhythm to burn and no brains or emotional subtlety to spare.

May "Bring in da Noise, Bring in da Funk" put an end to these traumas and prejudices once and for all. As dance, as music, as theater, as art, history and entertainment, there's nothing it cannot and should not do.

"Jam on the Groove"

Tap may have started as a folk art and become a popular art, but at this point it is also a fine art. It overlapped with popular dances like the Charleston and the Lindy Hop, it was taken up by jazz dance, but it always kept a separate identity, bound up with musical experiment and improvisation.

Break dancing began as an urban folk art in the 70's and, thanks to the media, it has become a form of mass entertainment, like the Charleston and the Lindy.

But popular dance finds its way into theaters long after it has made its name in clubs, videos and movies. And that is what has finally happened with "Jam on the Groove," a kinetic hip-hop revue brought to the Minetta Lane Theater by the 10-man, 4-woman troupe that calls itself GhettOriginal Productions.

Break dancing is all youthful explosions, with its martial-arts moves, head and shoulder spins, crazy-leg kicks and twists and perpetual-motion arms (sometimes they look like jolts of electricity; sometimes they look like oars; sometimes they look like bowling pins). But it's also otherworldly, wrapped up in science fiction and Walt Disney movies. In fact, you could say that break dancing, with its endless, improbable mobility, is the only known human extension of cartoon animation.

The 10 numbers in "Jam on the Groove" greedily and happily play with all kinds of forms: "Concrete Jungles," with outlaw street dancers shot down by policemen, then brought back to life by music, is Jerome Robbins's "West Side Story" and Talley Beatty's "Stack-Up," taken back to the streets where they came from. "Puppet" is a hip-hop mini-"Pinocchio," with the tables turned on the puppeteer, while "The Shadow Knows" harks back to Fred Astaire dancing with and against his black Bill Robinson—like shadow in the "Bojangles of Harlem" number from the movie "Swing Time." "Moments," with its bare-chested men moving through, in and out of liquid "Oriental" attitudes will remind you of Ted Shawn and Ruth St. Denis in vaudeville.

There's a fun but overlong parody of Jackie Chan's kung fu movies, and a not-fun, overlong parody of "Slaughter on 10th Avenue"—gangster-and-moll ballets. These last two didn't really work, though, because there is no real shape to them.

You don't need to bring these entertainment associations to "Jam on the Groove." You just need to watch these hard-working, well-prepped young dancers. In fact, I wish that there were fewer such old-time associations in the opening and closing numbers; less of that "Hi, here we are, just a bunch of vivacious, outgoing, show-stopping kids" manner we know so well. The piece I liked best was a mysterious, abstract set of squatting, scooping, rolling, twisting movements and friezes called "Portrait of a Freeze." It was utterly self-contained, and I wish they had taken it further.

Hip-hop is still a very young form. Where it will go, as dancers, choreographers and directors develop it further, is anybody's guess. For now, "Jam on the Groove" goes for nothing less—and nothing more—than a good time.

part 5

tell the story: jazz, history, memory

introduction

a. Among this music's most magical words are those reminding its players to "tell the story." This is jazz's profoundest invocation, its most deep-voiced invitation and witness, amen-ing those who have achieved more than technical fluency and tricks of the trade; exhorting and high-praising those who have reached jazz's highest goal of attaining a personal artistic voice. Max Roach tells one on himself, the young drummer, new in town from North Carolina, the teenage virtuoso sitting in with elder statesman Lester Young and showing off his talent by playing master drummer Jo Jones's style to a fare-thee-well, a perfect copy. When the set broke, Max waited for a good word from Prez, who at first remained silent as he packed his horn, his face a distracted mask. Then he turned to look at Max and shook his head as he sing-songed his warning: "You can't join the throng . . . till you got your own song." Roach's graduate study of jazz had begun.

If to "tell the story" means to find an artistic voice and language of one's own and to recite with style one's personal history, it also means to tell something more than one's own private tale. I refer to the capacity to tell one's story with resolution and resonance, with a sense of the fullness of the jazz tradition. Had the young Max Roach used his tubs and sticks to *invoke* Papa Jo (and thus Papa's influences back to Baby Dodds and master tap dancers like Pete Nugent and on back to Africa) at the same time that he turned the invocation into a statement in Max Roachese, then Lester might have given him a Presidential nod and said, "Go 'head, Youngboy, tell the story!" Then, too, jazz's greatest storytellers know how to comment and blend not just with past but with present jazz players as they tell their stories and together create an ensemble statement, a cascading, intertwining set of stories that add up to new tellings of The Story. In this context, "to swing" means to converse across barriers of time and space, to play with and against the jazz tradition. One thinks of Faulkner's "compound novels," single novels made up of a mosaic of narratives that could (and, in the case of Faulkner's stories that turn up as parts of novels, do) stand on their own. Or more to the point, think of Mingus's big works like *Let My Children Hear Music* and how they tell their elegant patchwork quilt story.

Jazz music also tells its own version of history. (Recall the close association between the words *story* and *history*; in French the same word, *histoire*, conveys both meanings.) In a sense "Tell the Story" means "Tell the History," and let's get it right this time: Put in the parts the historians don't know or can't face or don't understand. The subtle, funky, evil, funny, contradictory, tragic parts, the Ellisonian invisible history that words generally can't quite (or just won't) express, the parts even the best historians had forgotten to ask for—history's now sad, now farcical continuities and discontinuities. Get the rhythm and the tone of the experience into the telling. Dance a jazz attitude into the telling. Tell it all, or nearly all. Without romanticizing art, one might do well to study jazz music's version(s) of American history—the Gospel according to "the Throng": Monk, Hawk, Bird, Betty, Sweets, Rabbit, Prez, and yes, Max. No wonder more and more historians are writing about jazz music and musicians. There's a (hi)story in a Johnny Hodges solo (is not every solo a form of narration?) to enlighten (as well as to enrapture and terrify) us all.

This figure of the jazz player as historian hovers (perhaps with a faraway Hodges look of dubiousness) in the background of this section on historians' efforts to tell jazz's story. Social myths and insistent prejudices combine with America's traditional undervaluing of its vernacular products to keep this part of history from being told well, generally speaking. It is striking that no satisfactorily comprehensive history of jazz in America has been written. Focusing on the jazz tradition writ large, on bebop, and, in Hazel Carby's article, on blues women, this section of *Jazz Cadence* challenges historians to do what jazz musicians make each other do: Tell the story, tell it with style and resonance, tell it all, or nearly all. At the very least, as the Max story insists, tell it in your own way, in your own voice.

jm: Those emotions have their own life and need to be taken in different directions. The narrative, or the story—to think of that ballad notion—is not just the song being played right now. It's a larger story and extends between pieces to link them.

jw: That's true. With regard to that, when Lunceford played ballads, and there were people left on the dance floor, he had to pick the right ballad. Something that's going to touch them here, to keep them out there dancing. It's a fantastic thing, but its a very difficult thing to describe.

jm: Gil Evans, in some of those classic fifties recordings of his, like *Pacific Standard Time* and *Old Wine, New Bottle*—you know the ones I'm talking about . . . Gil put those pieces together by the "inner songs," whatever you want to call them. What do you call the linking of two songs like that? There's a simple term for it. At any rate, jazz and its performance can be a large lyrical canvas and tell a wider story than any one piece.

—Joe Wilder and Jim Merod

Albert Wilkes's song [is] so familiar because everything she's ever heard is in it, all the songs and voices she's ever heard, but everything is new and fresh because his music joined things, blended them so you follow one note and then it splits and shimmers and spills the thousand things it took to make the note whole, the silences within the note, the voices and songs.

—John Wideman

The blues are rooted in the slave songs: the slaves discovered something genuinely terrible, terrible because it sums up the universal challenge, the universal hope, the universal fear:

The very time I thought I was lost

My dungeon shook and my chains fell off.   —James Baldwin

Even though you go through these terrible experiences, you come out feeling good. That's what the blues say and that's what I believe—life will prevail. That's why I've gone back to the South and to jazz.

—Romare Bearden, *1994 Calendar*

I lay back and tried to sleep, but couldn't. I started humming the part about taking my rocking chair down by the river and rocking my blues away. What she said about the voice being better because it tells what you've been through. Consequences. It seems as if you're not singing the past, you're humming it. Consequences of what? Shit, we're all consequences of something. Stained with another's past as well as our own. Their past in my blood. I'm a blood. *Are you mine, Ursa, or theirs?*   —Gayl Jones

We had to give up the Spanish guitar for the industrial one, the urban worker's guitar that needed electricity to tell its tale. In my generation we came up with the rise of rhythm and blues, the big-city blues of screaming horns and endless riffs. The big bands were actually big blues bands, and even the jazz bands were blues bands that also had another kind of story, one that included deeper histories and music so heavy it could call on an ology if it needed to explain itself.

—Amiri Baraka, The Autobiography of LeRoi Jones

The train is hunkering down, its wheels grabbing tighter. What sings and dances in the hurry of the train starts to get to him. He has been sitting a long time, watching through the face a long time hearing nothing but the wheels saying I'm tired and still got a long way to go. He wouldn't listen because there was no play in the sound, nothing but a flat, lonely, almost moan like somebody telling the same sad story over and over again in the same tired voice and the wheels couldn't do nothing but keep on telling the tale. Now he hears a beat, a gallop. The steel wheels rising and set down one at a time so it's boogity, bop, boogity boopin a little different each measure.

—John Wideman

What do blues do for you?
It helps me to explain what I can't explain.   —Gayl Jones

chapter 23

GERALD EARLY

Pulp and Circumstance:
The Story of Jazz in High Places

Prologue: Plain Dirt

My master is sick outdoors.

—SHIRLEY CAESAR, RECOUNTING THE STORY OF
NAAMAN IN HER SERMON "GO TAKE A BATH"

Sometime between 1966 and 1967, after she had left the Caravans for good, gospel singer and evangelist Shirley Caesar made a recording of her sermon entitled "Go Take a Bath," a fairly difficult record to find these days. In this twenty-five-minute homily, Caesar recounts the story of Naaman from the fifth chapter of Second Kings. Naaman is the captain of the army of Syria and "a great man with his master, and honorable," but Naaman is also a leper. During one of their battles with Israel, Naaman's company had captured an Israelite girl who tells Naaman's wife that Naaman can be cured of his leprosy by a great Israelite prophet, Elisha. Naaman goes forth to Israel to the house of Elisha and is told, not by Elisha but by a messenger, that he must wash in the Jordan River seven times if he wishes to be cured of his leprosy. The King James version continues the account in this manner.

> But Naaman was wroth, and went away, and said, Behold, I thought, he will surely come out to me, and stand, and call on the name of the Lord his God, and strike his hand over the place, and recover the leper.
>
> Are not Abana and Pharpar, the rivers of Damascus, better than all the waters of Israel? May I not wash in them, and be clean? So he turned and went away in a rage.

And his servants came near, and spake unto him, and said, My father, if the prophet had bid thee do some great thing, wouldst thou not have done it? how much rather then, when he saith to thee, Wash, and be clean?

Then went he down, and dipped himself seven times in Jordan, according to the saying of the man of God: and his flesh came again like unto the flesh of a little child, and he was clean.

And he returned to the man of God, he and all his company, and came, and stood before him: and he said, Behold, now I know that there is no God in all the earth, but in Israel; now therefore, I pray thee, take a blessing of thy servant.

Elisha refused Naaman's offer of a gift. The essential message that Caesar conveys through her sermon, its moral, if you will, is that of the reduction of the pride of the mighty exemplified by Naaman's possessions (he left Syria for Israel with "ten talents of silver, and six thousand pieces of gold, and ten changes of raiment") and Naaman's attitude when Elisha refused to cure him personally. But the story of the pride of the mighty being humbled by the prophecy of the weak resonates and signifies particularly when one considers that this sermon was delivered in the mid-sixties when the civil rights battles, urban riots, and concerns about racial matters were at their height and when one considers that this sermon was meant specifically for a black audience that is both on the record responding to the sermon and the consumer for whom the record is marketed. There is a double message and, consequently, a layered complexity, in Caesar's message. She tells her black audience that they must, like Naaman, go take a bath because, in one of her many consumer-culture, womanly allusions, "Oxydol cannot make a soul white."[1] This, of course, implies overtly that her audience must wash the leprosy of sin from their souls but also, as has always been the case when blacks have had to mouth the cliché about being washed in the blood of the Lamb in a culture that for so very long saw their blackness as the outward mark of their inward depravity. There is nothing especially noteworthy in this, and along with the sermon itself, it can be dismissed as the peculiar dilemma of the Afro-Christian's struggle with theological rhetoric. But it must not be forgotten that while Caesar is telling her black audience to take a bath, she is telling the story of how the high and mighty Naaman was healed by the God of a despised people, so, in effect, the sermon has two messages: the standard cry for Christian salvation and repentance from the sinner and another covert message that tells the tale of two peoples, one strong and the other weak, and that would have a pointed significance in the mid-1960s era of race consciousness.

Caesar calls on God at the beginning of her sermon to "give us the Gospel" so that it might "root up and tear down," interesting language, indeed, in the days of Watts and the March on Selma. Some might say that the Gospel or its absence was certainly rooting up and tearing down a great deal of America's social fabric in those days. At the end of her sermon, she tells her audience of "the modern day bathroom. We got a face bowl, we got a shower, we got a bath tub." What is remarkable here is that it is in this modern bathroom that total transformation takes place, where one truly becomes clean, as the face bowl represents conversion, the shower sanctification, and the bathtub being washed in the blood of Jesus. It was on southern restrooms and public bathhouses that White and Colored signs were most commonly hung, and having the very type of modern indoor bathroom of which Caesar speaks was a mark of distinction that separated the rich from the poor in this country for a very long time. So it is greatly politically suggestive to speak of a major transformation of the soul taking place in the modern bathroom for, metaphorically, such a battle—between classes and between the races—for the transformation of the House of America was taking place in that very room.

Finally, and most important for her audience, when Caesar shouts what Elisha's servant tells Naaman, "Go wash, Go Wash, Go Wash down in the Jordan," to which the listeners shriek, the message is clearly that only the prophecy of the lowly can save the high from white leprosy. (Leprosy was often described in the Bible as a kind of whiteness; see the story of the leprosy of Miriam in Numbers 12:10: "Behold, Miriam became leprous, white as snow.") So to wash in the Jordan, in effect, washes the whiteness from Naaman while revealing to him the fundamental truth that the lowly Jordan is greater than the mighty rivers of Syria, and it is on this irony about the change that results from the act of washing, to become white or to become unwhite, that the true signifying power of Caesar's sermon depends. Since at least the early nineteenth century and certainly since the 1852 publication of Harriet Beecher Stowe's *Uncle Tom's Cabin*, the life of blacks, their presence, the very myth that has charged and inspired the nature of their condition have served as the spiritual waters of the Jordan in which whites have washed themselves clean of their whiteness, their civilization, their inhibitions, where, in fact, they have gone, from time to time, to refresh their consciousness. It is a truism in American cultural history that the African American is both a greater demon and a greater soul, from Stowe's Uncle Tom to Mailer's black prizefighters, from Fannie Hurst's Delilah to Margaret Mitchell's Mammy to Alice Walker's Shug Avery and Celie, is the authenticating consciousness that the white, trapped by a false whiteness, seeks. Blacks become the spiritual pools in which somehow the whites must transform their own souls. This myth has been nowhere so recurrent or so powerful in our country as in the making and performance of popular music. With only those few exceptions such as country and western or easy listening music in which whites do not share much performance space with blacks, virtually every popular music in this country is considered the authentic expression of blacks, and if whites play these forms of music they must somehow, like Naaman, wash themselves in the black Jordan to validate their right to play this music.

Old Rockin' Chair's Got Me

In the entire history of jazz music, there have been two musicians who have become known to both their colleagues and their fans by the nickname Pops, signifying, for at least a certain time, the range of influence and the fervency of respect that each man generated. Oddly, one has become a permanent fixture in American popular music, his genius unquestioned, his popularity undiminished by the passage of time. The other is virtually forgotten nowadays, and when he is remembered it is largely thought that he had no genius and that his popularity was largely of the moment when his band enjoyed its heyday in the 1920s. The former is Louis Armstrong, the great black jazz musician from New Orleans who so thoroughly reshaped American music in the 1920s. The other is Paul Whiteman, the white bandleader from Denver who also, in his way, thoroughly reshaped not American music so much as American musical taste with his very popular dance band. These are the twin father figures of American popular music, both reaching their stride and producing their most important work in the 1920s; both considered old heads in this business even when they were young, men without youths; both heavy and both popular as personalities as much as for their musical abilities. While we may speak of several mothers of American popular music—Bessie Smith and Ruth Etting, Ethel Waters and Sophie Tucker, Josephine Baker and Fanny Brice, Black Patti and Aretha Franklin—only one woman has ever been popularly called a mother in American music: (Gertrude) Ma Rainey, the Mother of the Blues. Perhaps it is fitting, since we see popular American music so much in terms of its influential male musicians, that it should have two fathers, one black and one white: Pops Armstrong and Pops Whiteman.[2]

Pomp and Circumstance; Pulp and Circumstance

The only thing that is different from one time to another is what is seen and what is seen depends upon how everybody is doing everything. This makes the thing we are looking at very different and this makes what those who describe it make of it, it makes composition, it confuses, it shows, it is, it looks, it likes it as it is, and this makes what is seen as it is seen. Nothing changes from generation to generation except the thing seen and that makes a composition. . . .

Those who are creating the modern composition authentically are naturally only of importance when they are dead because by that time the modern composition having become past is classified and the description of it is classical. That is the reason why the creator of the new composition in the arts is an outlaw until he is a classic, there is hardly a moment in between and it is really too bad very much too bad naturally for the creator but also very much too bad for the enjoyer, they all really would enjoy the created so much better just after it has been made than when it is already a classic, but it is perfectly simple that there is no reason why the contemporaries should see, because it would not make any difference as they lead their lives in the new composition anyway.

—GERTRUDE STEIN, "COMPOSITION AS EXPLANATION"

And whether there is Negro art or not, it is indisputable there is a certain spiritual something that has been deposited by the Negro in America, a certain buoyancy, spontaneity, and joy of living that has re-inspired the staid, mechanical, intellectualized Caucasian, stirring him to a merrier mood, and causing the blood to course with joyous rhythm through his veins. The Negro spirit, if I may use the phrase, practically dominates the amusement world in America and Europe today. Mr. Whiteman has brought out this art excellently, and given full justice to the Negro.

—J. A. ROGERS, FROM HIS REVIEW OF WHITEMAN'S BOOK, *Jazz*, IN THE
DECEMBER 1926 ISSUE OF *Opportunity*

On the evening of February 12, 1924, a major cultural event occurred in New York City. A concert was performed at the Aeolian Hall by Paul Whiteman, rotund band leader ("He trembles, wobbles, quivers—a piece of jazz jelly," wrote Olin Downes of the *New York Times*). Whiteman, like Jack Dempsey, the great heavyweight champion of this era, roared in from the west, Colorado being the birthplace of both men and San Francisco being the place of critical juncture in their careers, and succeeded in establishing not just one thriving dance band but, by the mid-twenties, a cohort of them. The Whiteman sound was the sound of the age, the sound of the 1920s. On February 12, Whiteman gave what he called a "jazz" symphonic concert. Whiteman was not without misgivings about the entire enterprise. Just an hour or so before the concert he felt this way according to his 1926 autobiography, *Jazz*:

> I went back stage again, more scared than ever. Black fear simply possessed me. I paced the floor, gnawed my thumbs and vowed I'd give $5,000 if we could stop right then and there. Now that the audience had come, perhaps I had really nothing to offer after all. I even made excuses to keep the curtain from rising on schedule. But finally there was no longer any way of postponing the evil moment. The curtain went up and before I could dash forth, as I was tempted to do, and announce that there wouldn't be any concert, we were in the midst of it.

Whiteman, whose father was the supervisor of music education for the Denver public school system, was reared in a fairly strict, quite religious, and typically middle-class home where, of course, he received considerable instruction in music. He was a rather aimless and somewhat indolent young man, which apparently infuriated his father, who decidedly and decisively pushed his son from the nest when he tired of his lack of ambition. Eventually, Whiteman became an indifferent viola player with, first, the Denver Symphony Orchestra and, later, the San Francisco Symphony Orchestra. But he had a great deal more ambition or more desire to be noticed and make money than could be accommodated by being an orchestra player whose meager pay often had to be supplemented by teaching. Whiteman began to investigate the possibilities of playing popular music and often went to dives and taverns around San Francisco to hear the locals play. And it was during these years, before World War I and before he formed his first band, that Whiteman first heard jazz music. Contrary to popular belief, jazz did not move up the river from New Orleans to Chicago in a straight line; some of the musicians went west, and the Barbary Coast became a very active hive of Dixieland or hot jazz music. Whiteman discovered, when he tried to play with a jazz band, that he could not play in the new idiom very well, but that if the music could be scored and played by better-trained musicians it could have broad appeal.

"Jazz it up. Jazz it up," the conductor would snort impatiently at about this point in my reflections. And I would try, but I couldn't. It was as if something held me too tight inside. I wanted to give myself up to the rhythm like the other players. I wanted to sway and pat and enjoy myself just as they seemed to be doing. But it was no good.

The second day the director fired me. . . .

After many attempts, I finally worked out an orchestration and learned what I wanted to know about faking. Faking was what the early jazz orchestras relied upon. That is, they had no scores, each man working out his part for himself, "faking" as he went along. Up to that time, there had never been a jazz orchestration. I made the first and started into the jazz orchestra business.

Whiteman, not a terribly sophisticated or intellectual man, certainly no highbrow, was, due to his middle-class background, uneasy about playing a low-class music, a music, he goes to great pains to point out, that his father disapproved of, although his mother seemed to have liked it well enough; indeed, she used to sing the popular songs of the day to him when the father was out of the house. It was, obviously, not a conflict with his mother that Whiteman wanted both to resolve and to win by playing jazz music successfully, but an issue with his father. This is very important in understanding why Whiteman was attracted to the idea of jazz composition or highly arranged jazz music. Also, we know that Ferde Grofe was in San Francisco at the same time as Whiteman, writing arrangements for the Art Hickman band that people were describing as "new music." In 1915 the Hickman band was playing at the St. Francis Hotel and the Whiteman band at the Fairmount. Sometime after the war, before Whiteman took his band east, he hired Grofe as an arranger. As Whiteman writes: "For quite a while I did the arrangements and orchestrations, as well as the conducting, but it was too much for one man, so we took on Ferde Grofe, talented symphony player and composer." Although born in New York City, Grofe had played viola with the Los Angeles Symphony before turning to popular music. At the 1924 Aeolian Hall concert, the most important piece of music performed, George Gershwin's *Rhapsody in Blue*, was arranged—virtually shaped and molded—by Grofe, as Gershwin at that point knew very little about orchestrating music. As the story goes, Whiteman went from being a string player in a symphony orchestra to becoming, after the First World War, the highest paid dance band leader in the country, achieving both fame and money but not quite respect. A concert "to make a lady of jazz," as the critics put it, implying that jazz was actually no mere dame but an outright whore, would be an inevitable preoccupation to someone of Whiteman's background. As Gilbert Seldes, a critic and friend of Whiteman who helped write the program notes for the Aeolian Hall concert, said in his 1924 book, *The Seven Lively Arts*,

"Paul Whiteman . . . wanted to 'elevate' jazz and thought the right way was to give a concert at Aeolian Hall."

In short, the source of Whiteman's motivation for holding a jazz concert in a symphony hall was the twin diseases of the American middle-class mind: self-consciousness and class anxiety. Throughout most of his life, Whiteman constantly suffered from stage fright, although seldom as severely as before the Aeolian Hall concert. His acute distress may have been the reason for his alcoholic and eating binges, which would last for weeks. The class anxiety is evidenced in other passages in his autobiography:

To the Palais Royal [the New York club which Whiteman used as a base of operations during the height of his fame in the 1920s] came all the country's great names and foreign visitors of renown, too. Any night at all, we could look out and see Vanderbilts, Drexel Biddles, Goulds and the rest dancing to our music. Lord and Lady Mountbatten, cousins of the Prince of Wales, were among the distinguished guests one night. They had just arrived in this country to spend their honeymoon.

After that night, they came often, for they adored dancing. They were such a friendly, jolly pair that when they were in the room, we invariably played almost nothing but their favorite pieces. We had many conversations and Lord Mountbatten got to be friends with every boy in the band.

This is Whiteman's account of meeting the Prince of Wales during his band's first European tour:

The Prince had already arrived when I went into the room, but I was so nervous that I couldn't tell him from any of the others. I had a bad attack of stage fright and I wished I were somewhere else. Lord Mountbatten was disgusted with me. He is such a democratic, unassuming chap himself that he can't imagine anybody getting into what he calls a "funk" over a mere meeting with a prince. . . .

I hope I was natural, but if I wasn't at first, I was later; for the Prince put me instantly at ease with some flattering comment about the orchestra. He was wearing evening clothes and I thought I had never seen a man's shoulders look better in such dress. The Prince of Wales is really small, but for some reason, partly the way he carries himself, I suppose, you never realize it, even in his pictures.

I saw him many times after that evening. Sometimes we played for parties he or others gave at private houses; and whenever he wanted me, instead of sending an equerry to "command" my presence, he would come himself and ask in friendly fashion if it would be convenient for us to play.

We never accepted any pay from him.

Whiteman, like most of the middle class, is ambivalent in his feelings toward the aristocracy. There is always revealed the expressly astonished admiration that they, the royalty, are like everyone else, just ordinary-acting people; contrarily a great deal of pride is expressed that these quite extraordinary people, the royalty, are not above noticing a mere nobody, which, of course, is indicative, this act of noticing, that one is not a nobody after all. ("I didn't want you to think I was just some nobody," Gatsby tells Nick, but in the end he is actually what Tom Buchanan accuses him of being: "Mr. Nobody from Nowhere." In the age of the crystallization of modern mass culture, anonymity is a sin, the escape from it an obsession.) It is not that the aristocrats deign to acknowledge Whiteman's existence; what impresses Whiteman is that they seem truly pleased to meet him. Whiteman was sensitive about the idea of being a nobody, when his band was asked to play at "the home of a very rich, very well-known New Yorker" they were not permitted to mingle with the guests, were not in fact permitted to be seen as they were requested to play behind a screen, unlike in California where the band had played for and played with the rich and famous, especially the Hollywood crowd. Whiteman casually but cuttingly straightened the matter out with the host. But here is the class problem manifesting itself not simply because Whiteman is a popular bandleader but because he is a musician, which to many of the rich made him little better than a tradesman no matter what sort of music he played. Among the rich, to be a musician, black or white, especially a player of popular music, made one little better than a mere Negro domestic of the period. The fact that Whiteman never accepted any fee from the Prince of Wales only underscores this ambivalence of wishing to level class differences while using the existence of class differences to egoistic, if groveling, advantage. There was great pride for Whiteman in the fact that the Mountbattens came to hear his band, for they were, after all, dancing to *his* music; but Whiteman was nervous in meeting the Prince, just as nervous perhaps as on the night of the Aeolian Hall concert. In the audience on the night of the concert were Damrosch, Godowsky, Heifetz, Kreisler, Stokowski, McCormack, Rachmaninoff, Rosenthal, and Stravinsky, all prominent classical musicians. (Walter Damrosch was to be so impressed by Gershwin's *Rhapsody* that he commissioned Gershwin to write the *Concerto in F* and conducted the New York Symphony in Gershwin's orchestration at the work's premiere, with Gershwin at the piano.) Also present were such noted writers as Fannie Hurst, Heywood Broun, Frank Crowninshield, S. J. Kaufman, Karl Kitchin, Leonard Liebling, O. O. McIntyre, Pitts Sanborn, Gilbert Seldes, Deems Taylor, and Carl Van Vechten. The striking similarity between Whiteman's response to meeting the Prince of Wales and his giving the Aeolian Hall concert is largely that he wanted to please both audiences as a sign of having made it, of being more than a mere parvenu socially or artistically. At the same time he wished to thumb his nose at convention, to level down, to democratize by bringing these European or Eurocentric aristocracies, one national and racial, the other critical and conformist, to his level, by making them dance to his music. It is an odd moment in the history of American popular culture that perhaps explains, more than any other, the precise nature of both rebellion and accommodation that is inherent in our music. Our popular artists become a sort of aristocracy for us while they seek audiences with the real aristocracy but still desire respect from legitimate or highbrow critical circles. Whiteman wanted to challenge and appease current social and critical conventions, as conflicted as the bourgeoisie has always been conflicted, with two relatively feeble weapons: first, his urge to democratize and second, his urge to cultural artifice that would make him acceptable to the aristocracies that torment the bourgeoisie by always making them aware that they, the middle classes, must sweat to live as much as the lower classes do. On the one hand, this explains why the concert took place on February 12, Lincoln's birthday, a day signifying both freedom and salvation and the triumph of the common man, in this case, specifically, the common midwestern man who had come east. (Of course, the February 12 date has a special significance to blacks as Lincoln himself bears a sort of mythical, if ambivalent, stature among blacks as the man who freed the slaves—Richard Wright used this date, for instance, as an important thematic device in his first novel, *Lawd Today*, written in 1936 but not published until 1963, three years after his death. The date for Whiteman's jazz concert would resonate in an ironic way for blacks since it is on this day that Whiteman, playing essentially a bowdlerized black, lower-class music, wishes to reinvent white bourgeois American music and white bourgeois American musical tastes.) On the other hand, that is why Whiteman had what must be, in some respects, a very unusual musical outfit: a jazz band with strings.

We all know what strings have come to mean for jazz and American popular music generally. Bebop alto saxophonist Charlie Parker's bestselling records were those he recorded with strings; in his later years, Louis Armstrong often sang pop songs against a string orchestra backdrop; Wynton Marsalis has not only recorded with symphony orchestras, he has also made a jazz album with strings entitled *Hot House Flowers*; horn players from Warren Vaché to Ornette Coleman, and the traditions they embody—and there is a tradition for every jazz taste—have recorded at least one record with strings; jazz guitarists ranging from Wes Montgomery to Earl Klugh and jazz pianists from Oscar Peterson to Errol Garner to McCoy Tyner to Keith Jarrett have made records with strings; the first, true rhythm and blues as Rock-and-Roll ballad record with strings (the Platters and Dinah Washington recorded with strings earlier but represent something different), the Drifters' 1959 *There Goes My Baby*, produced a veritable movement in both black and white popular music in which recordings with strings were meant to cut the barrier between easy listening and rock and roll. In this respect, Johnny Mathis becomes a more intriguing and suggestive crossover artist than Chuck Berry; his first string recordings, made just a few years after Berry's first successful records, suggest that ur-rock was not truly the political supersession of previous black American popular musics or that ur-rock was the music of the age of racial integration. The presence of strings is both aurally and symbolically a trip to both a pop culture and a high-culture heaven. The strings "sweeten" the music, as musicians so often put it, which means that the music can approach the generally understood idea among the populace of a sentimental and sentimentalized sound for music. But the strings not only popularize popular music, if such a redundancy can be acceptable; they also make it profound by making it a music that seems more Eurocentric, more closely associated with high-culture art music, requiring trained musicians to read a score. And a score was what Whiteman felt distinguished his music from ur-jazz or hot Dixieland jazz, which was almost exclusively a small combo music. "The greatest single factor in the improvement of American music has been the art of scoring. Paul Whiteman's orchestra was the first organization to especially score each selection and to play it according to the score." So wrote Whiteman supporter Hugh C. Ernst, in the program notes of the Aeolian Hall concert. We have currently in jazz the growing phenomenon of the jazz string quartet: the Kronos Quartet, the Turtle Island String Quartet, the Uptown String Quartet, this last being composed of four black women, led by jazz drummer Max Roach's daughter. Conceptually speaking, these groups are largely the offspring of two strains of jazz: the traditionalist string players such as violinist Joe Venuti, who early in his career played with Whiteman; Ray Nance, violinist, singer, and cornet player with the Duke Ellington Orchestra; Stephane Grappelli, the noted violinist who played with Gypsy guitarist Django Reinhardt during the thirties; and Stuff Smith, who combined both swing and country in his playing; and the new-school players such as cellist Doug Watkins, Ellington bassist Jimmy Blanton, Charles Mingus, Richard Davis, Jean-Luc Ponty, Michael White, and Billy Bang. The particular branch of modern popular music known as jazz, in its search for respectability and its anguish to achieve a sound of European art music, may have finally achieved its end with this amalgam of small-group jazz and chamber string quartet. Whiteman missed the boat a little. We have not quite reached symphonic jazz yet, but we do have finally and literally classical jazz.

In regard to the presence of strings in Whiteman's band, nothing so underscores his ambivalence about the nature of the artistic revolt he was leading or at least "fronting" than his attitude toward classical music, the use of which was one of the major reasons Whiteman's band had strings:

> Until we went to Atlantic City, the only recognition we had won, aside from the approval of those who danced to our music, came from persons interested in our trick of jazzing the classics—that is, of applying our peculiar treatment of rhythm and color to well-known masterpieces.
>
> The notice this brought us was not always of the pleasantest. Certain correspondents called us scoundrels and desecrators and one man described us as ghouls "bestializing the world's sweetest harmonies," rather a mixed metaphor, it seemed to me. A woman with a gift of epithet termed us "vultures, devouring the dead masters."
>
> I don't get mad at these communications and I always read them. Sometimes I can even see justice in them. Besides, it's good to know the worst that people think of us. But of course I don't agree that we have done such very terrible things to the classics. I don't think we've even insulted them much.
>
> I worship certain of the classics myself and respect them all. But I doubt it hurts Tschaikowsky or even Bach when we rearrange what they have written—provided we choose appropriate compositions of theirs—and play to people who haven't heard good music before.
>
> I have never had the feeling that I must keep my hands off the "dead masters," as people feel they must not speak the truth of the dead unless it

is a complimentary truth. The masters are not dead to me. I think of the great writers of music, not as gods who finished their jobs forever in seven days, but as plain human men, as human as any of the rest of us. They were working on a job that will never be finished as long as human beings live, for music is as much a part of life as the heart beat. . . .

Not that I mean to imply that there was any real musical value in our jazzing the classics. Of course not. It was partly a trick and partly experimental work. We were just fooling around with the nearest material, working out our methods.

Here is Whiteman clearly thumbing his nose at the convention of apotheosizing European art composers. On the one hand, he suggests that existing compositions are made to be used and reinterpreted by musicians. On the other hand, "jazzing" the classics amounts for him to nothing more than a schoolboy's prank, rather like rearranging the periodic table—queer, quaint, humorous, but ultimately worthless. Whiteman believes this because he believes that jazz really is not music but only a modernistic technique of treating music and coloring composition. As he says elsewhere in *Jazz*: "With a very few but important exceptions, jazz is not as yet the thing said; it is the manner of saying it." (One of those exceptions would be George Gershwin's *Rhapsody in Blue*.) Jelly Roll Morton, the famous black New Orleans pianist who recorded some of his most important work in the 1920s, said much the same thing: "Ragtime is a certain type of syncopation and only certain tunes can be played in that idea. But jazz is a style that can be applied to any type of tune." When one hears such modern jazzers as Miles Davis, the Modern Jazz Quartet, and Chet Baker and Paul Desmond play the Adagio movement from Joaquin Rodrigo's *Concierto* or listens to the number of times Bach's music has been jazzed up (the Jacques Loussier trio and the John Lewis Group are the latest in this trend; Keith Jarrett's un-jazzed-up *Goldberg Variations* and *Well-tempered Clavier* are a variant of the Benny Goodman school of the respectable jazzer playing classical music straight up), one thinks that on one level both Whiteman and Morton are right. But jazz is also rightly understood by such younger musicians as trumpeter Wynton Marsalis and saxophonist Christopher Hollyday as a demanding and tradition-laden discipline, a vision with certain accompanying sets of implementations. Whiteman and other noted jazz musicians of the era saw jazz not as an independent art form that proposed very specific solutions to the problem of creating composition and proposed very specific roles that the musician and the composer were to play not only in relation to the creation of this music but in relation to their audience and to the larger society in which they functioned, but largely as a way of spicing up dance music or making classical music more palatable to the hoi polloi. This ultimately blunts the political implication of jazz as an assault on Eurocentric cultural hegemony, which, as historian Cathy Ogren has pointed out in *The Jazz Revolution: Twenties America and the Meaning of Jazz*, is precisely what jazz in the twenties really was. Whiteman himself was at least partly aware of the revolutionary scope of the new music; he discussed in an early chapter in *Jazz* the makeup of his orchestra as something really new, not simply an amalgam of already existing musical configurations: "The usual jazz orchestra was no good for my purpose and neither were the more set-in-their-way symphony players. I needed musically trained youngsters who were ambitious, slightly discontented and willing to adventure a little." But Whiteman did not want to go so far as to propose turning the culture on its head and on its ear by questioning the very cultural assumptions that gave Eurocentric art and values their unquestioned validity. Few musicians, black or white, were ready to do that or even thought that by making a music called jazz they were doing so. (Indeed, few of the musicians thought of themselves as artists or of their work as art. It was not until the emergence in 1923 of drummer Dave Tough and the white Austin High that included Eddie Condon, Bud Freeman, Jimmy McPartland, and others that the idea of the jazz man as a romantic tragic artist began to be articulated. And with the mental breakdown of New Orleans Rhythm Kings' clarinetist Leon Roppolo in the mid-1920s, and the deaths of cornetist Bix Beiderbecke in 1931 of acute alcoholism and clarinetist Frank Teschemacher in 1932 in an auto accident—three promising careers cut short—jazz, by the mid-thirties, had the full-blown myth of the tragic white jazz artist. It was not until the 1950s, with the deaths of Charlie Parker, Billie Holiday, and Lester Young, coinciding with the push for racial integration in this country, that jazz was to have a comparable black version of that myth.)

Whiteman's Aeolian Hall concert was apparently the first of its kind, and probably many people of the day found the term "symphonic jazz," which Whiteman seems to have made up, to be a contradiction, an oxymoron that could not fuse the chasm it appeared to create. Jazz, in whatever form, was not a completely respectable music in the twenties. In part, this attitude might be attributed to the music's lowly origins. As Whiteman reminds us on the very first page of his autobiography: "Jazz came to America three hundred years ago in chains. The psalm-singing Dutch traders, sailing in a man-of-war across the ocean in 1619, described their cargo as 'fourteen black African slaves for sale in his Majesty's colonies.' But priceless freight destined three centuries later to set a whole nation dancing went unnoted and unbilled by the stolid, revenue-hungry Dutchmen." Whiteman here is offering a restatement of the original oxymoron in historical terms: the psalm-singing European and the rhythmic blacks, the masters above deck and the slaves below, fused in a commercial enterprise. That is, in part, what "symphonic jazz" as a concept means, the fusion of the black primitive and the white civilized. Jazz was suspect or disliked simply because its origins lie with a group of degraded and socially outcast people who performed this music in its inception in whorehouses or on streetcorners or at African-American parades. After all, most whites in the twenties who had heard of jazz at all were likely to know it only through Whiteman or through the Original Dixieland Jazz Band, the New Orleans Rhythm Kings, Vincent Lopez, or Jean Goldkette, all white bands that, in some sense or the other, were jazz bands. (To know black bands meant traveling to black neighborhoods to hear the music live in bars and clubs or to purchase black records, known in the twenties as "race records," from black record stores. Whites scarcely frequent black neighborhoods now and there is little reason to think, with

Jim Crow as strong as it was, that they were any less reluctant to do so in the twenties.) Since jazz was understood in dominant white culture circles as at least in good measure a white artistic enterprise, race does not entirely or satisfactorily explain its status. Therefore, we must conclude that, in part, jazz was looked down upon because it was, as Whiteman points out, American: "Americans were ashamed of the upstart. They kept humming it absent-mindedly, then flushing and apologizing. Nothing so common could be esthetic, insisted the highbrows. Like everything else that was our own, its merits were, we thought, questionable. So it was left to Europe to discover the possibilities of our creature." The oxymoron acquires another distinct level: Symphonic jazz becomes the fusion of the European with the American. But there is more here than meets the eye: Americans disliked jazz because as rib-rock Protestants they were uncomfortable with the idea of music's existing for sensual pleasure, for the joy of the vulgarity that it symbolized and elicited. This fear transcended color; many blacks ostracized their brothers and sisters who played this music, and it was common for the believers to call jazz and blues "the devil's music." But if the lowbrow black or white heard jazz simply as "sin din," the highbrow heard it as "depraved dissonance." If the uncultivated Protestant heard jazz with disgust, the more intellectual Jew of the period heard it as despair, and in a kind of sweeping critical continuum jazz goes from trash to tragedy. In the 1927 film *The Jazz Singer*, the first feature-length talking film (the title alone is indicative of the popularity of both the term "jazz" and some form of popular music that went under that name), we have one form of fusion merging the Jew and the black, and the supposed linkage of minstrelsy and jazz (this latter being largely untrue as jazz was generally neither a music played by whites in blackface nor a music whites used to ridicule or parody blacks). Al Jolson plays a Jewish cantor's son who, when masked in blackface, becomes a successful blackface popular singer. What is interesting here is what Samson Raphaelson, author of "The Day of Atonement" and *The Jazz Singer*, the story and play upon which the film is based, said about jazz in explaining the title of his play in 1925:

> In seeking a symbol of the vital chaos of America's soul, I find no more adequate one than jazz. Here you have the rhythm of frenzy staggering against a symphonic background—a background composed of lewdness, heart's delight, soul-racked madness, monumental boldness, exquisite humility, but principally prayer.
>
> I hear jazz, and I am given a vision of cathedrals and temples collapsing and, silhouetted against the setting sun, a solitary figure, a lost soul, dancing grotesquely on the ruins. . . . Thus do I see the jazz singer.
>
> Jazz is prayer. It is too passionate to be anything else. It is prayer distorted, sick, unconscious of its destination. The singer of jazz is what Matthew Arnold said of the Jews, "lost between two worlds, one dead, the other powerless to be born."

This may have been the first time jazz was described as a kind of sacred music, but it was surely not to be the last. In effect, what Raphaelson is describing is not music of transcendence but an art form that mirrors the dysfunction and anguish of the culture that produced it. What Raphaelson defines is not a creative art form but a failed one that is incapable of articulating anything but its own inarticulation, its own inability to be art or to be religion. The highbrow criticism of jazz during these years supported the general idea that it was a dysfunctional art, a music that was both the sign and signifier of dysfunction. A variant of Raphaelson's observations on jazz was to become—and very much remain, ironically—the basis of jazz's critical acceptance among the highbrows as a profound art form: namely, jazz functions as holistic spirituality in a dysfunctional world, even if some of its finest players have themselves been unstable, depressed, or disturbed personalities. In the twenties, highbrows thought of jazz as simply symbolic of contemporary dysfunction; nowadays, according to the highbrow critic, jazz, like all great art, transcends dysfunction, even the dysfunctional tendency inherent in its process of creation. Today, jazz, like all accepted highbrow art, is a religion. The implications of Raphaelson's remarks were ahead of their time.

There had always been popular music in America since the inception of some form of theater in the eighteenth century, but jazz was particularly unnerving because it threatened completely to engulf the business, the aesthetic, the purpose, the very consciousness of music-making and music listening. With records, the beginnings of radio, and the urbanization of Americans, particularly blacks, jazz may have appeared more threatening and more pervasive than it really was. It was surely indicative of a frightening change, for if the rise of the nineteenth-century sentimental woman's novel could be called the feminization of American culture, the rise of jazz was in a real sense the primitivization of American culture. In early-twentieth-century highbrow culture criticism of American society, the terms "philistine" and "barbarian" were used interchangeably; in culture criticism terms, the 1920s was about the clash between the philistine and the barbarian. H. L. Mencken even continued to use these terms in the 1920s, although since the coming of jazz the two terms had come to signify quite distinct states of the American character. Once again, as had become the common cultural dialectic in American life since the middle of the nineteenth century, it was city versus small town, agrarian values versus urban trends. It was just these forces of opposition that clashed during the struggle over Prohibition in the late nineteenth and early twentieth centuries. In the instance of Prohibition, small town agrarianism, and the conservative Christian reformism instinct won. In the case of jazz, it was the urban, secular, more liberal element of the culture that won. It is no accident that, of course, these two gigantic cultural movements should meet head-to-head in the 1920s, when jazz entered popular culture in a big way, largely through recordings and the burgeoning nightclub and speakeasy business (the latter made possible, in large part, by Prohibition), when the grandest social reform movement since abolitionism and Reconstruction was in effect. Symphonic jazz was not simply a bow to the highbrow culture that condemned jazz as unartistic noise but to the frightened small-towner, philistine and otherwise, who was alarmed by a secular music that seemingly had no restraints and no aim but seemed to possess enormous emotional and commercial power. Symphonic jazz was an attempt to make jazz less the cultural assault against white, middle-class, Christian, small-town taste than it appeared to be. There was a great fear of mongrelization among this very class of people, the small-town philistine; after all, during the Ku Klux Klan's resurgence as a political and social force in American life in the 1920s, it was just this mass group of Americans who were attracted to the insignias, the regalia, the idea of mythical American purity. The twenties symbolized acceleration (which is perhaps why a novel like *Gatsby* turns so much on the speed of automobiles): automobiles, airplanes, trains, telegraph, telephone, the era of instant communication. And what is jazz, in the end, but, as one musicologist told me, abrupt and explosive composing. (Cathy Ogren points out in her study of jazz in the 1920s that both detractors and admirers of the music often commented on how the music was both the cause and effect of the age of the motor and speed. She quotes Irving Berlin, who compared jazz to the "rhythmic beat of our everyday lives. Its swiftness is interpretive of our verve and speed and ceaseless activity. When commuters no longer rush for trains, when taxicabs pause at corners, when businessmen take afternoon siestas, then, perhaps jazz will pass." Ogren writes: "By indicating that jazz was a music of the city and industrial life, Berlin implied that it was clearly tied to increased mechanization.")

As early as 1917, in an article entitled "The Appeal of Primitive Jazz" that appeared in *Literary Digest*, "jazz" was defined by Walter Kingsley as an African word that meant "speeding things up. . . . In the old plantation days," Mr. Kingsley writes, "when the slaves were having one of their rare holidays and the fun languished, some West-Coast African would cry out, 'Jazz her up,' and this would be the cue for fast and furious fun." Considering the fact that jazz's black origin was the source of a great deal of the white critical contempt and discontent during the twenties, it is a sort of wild irony that a people normally associated with agrarianism and slowness (think of the Hollywood stereotypes of Stepin Fetchit and Willie Best as examples of the dominant cultural idea that blacks were slow in movement, slow in speech, and slow in thought) were now the creators of a music that symbolized machines and speed.

The musician has always been a charismatic being in Western culture, but with the coming of jazz he (gender specificity is important here because of the male dominance in music) becomes a magical primitive, in a sense, making music without a score, producing art without a text, based entirely upon his inspiration of the moment. Jazz was supposed to touch a more authentic, more primal core of creative consciousness. Jazz, in effect, has given us the newly stated old myth of the energetic barbarian, and the rest of the history of popular dance music in this country has simply reiterated this. Early jazzmen cashed in on this myth of the jazzer as the artist of the moment by often believing the fiction that learning to read music would ruin their ability to improvise. Symphonic jazz, with its emphasis on scoring, is at last the ultimate American oxymoron as it wishes to fuse both the past and the future, which was very much on the minds of intellectuals of the day. Consider T. S. Eliot's 1933 lecture on Matthew Arnold:

> What I call the "auditory imagination" is the feeling for syllable and rhythm, penetrating far below the conscious levels of thought and feeling,

invigorating every word; sinking to the most primitive and forgotten, returning to the origin and bringing something back, seeking the beginning and the end. It works through meanings, certainly, or not without meanings in the ordinary sense, and fuses the old and obliterated and the trite, the current, and the new and surprising, the most ancient and the most civilized mentality.

Inasmuch as jazz was a primitive music (and it was certainly almost always referred to in that way by the white press and sometimes by the black press too), it could be seen as an artistic and cultural ritual meant to replicate a past, more primeval, archetypical consciousness in the modern world. Broadly considered, it was a new way to bring about a sort of racial syncretism by allowing whites to pretend that they were primitives of some sort, not through sight, not visually through picture imagination as blackface minstrelsy suggested, but through sound and one's response to the sound both as adventuresome musician and as adventuresome audience. It was during the jazz age of the twenties that blackface minstrelsy died as a mass form of American entertainment, died as America's most powerful theater. "Amos 'n' Andy" became a huge success on radio, and when it was finally brought to a visual medium, television, black actors played the roles. When Jolson made *The Jazz Singer*, the blackface performer was already an anachronism. One white writer of the period wrote that "jazz differs from other music, as it wants to appeal to the eye as much as to the ear." But this was quite incorrect. Until the coming of rock, no popular American music was as vision-centered, as voyeur-obsessed as minstrelsy. Perhaps the Whiteman concert was both the sign and signifier, the deconstructive text of the auditory imagination.

In *The Great Gatsby* we have one of the few references that Fitzgerald, who named the twenties "The Jazz Age," ever made to jazz. The first time that Nick, the book's narrator, attends a grandiose Gatsby at-home he and the other guests are treated to some interesting music:

> There was the boom of a bass drum, and the voice of the orchestra leader rang out suddenly above the echolalia of the garden.
>
> "Ladies and gentlemen," he cried. "At the request of Mr. Gatsby we are going to play for you Mr. Vladimir Tostoff's latest work, which attracted so much attention at Carnegie Hall last May. If you read the papers you know there was a big sensation." He smiled with jovial condescension, and added: "Some sensation!" Whereupon everybody laughed.
>
> "The piece is known," he concluded lustily, "as Vladimir Tostoff's *Jazz History of the World*."

Knowing that the *Gatsby* manuscript was not submitted to Scribner's until September 1924, nearly seven months after the Whiteman concert, and knowing how much notice the concert received, it is not unwarranted to suppose that Fitzgerald, even though he was abroad when he wrote most of his novel, had the Whiteman concert in mind when he made a reference to *Jazz History of the World*. The orchestra certainly has the same instrumentation as Whiteman or a

Whiteman clone, "a whole pitful of oboes and trombones and saxophones and viols and cornets and piccolos, and low and high drums." And certainly the Whiteman Aeolian Hall concert was, in effect, the Jazz History of the World. Starting from the earliest white jazz, *Livery Stable Blues*, recorded by the Original Dixieland Jazz Band in 1917, the first jazz record, Whiteman's band worked its way in a clearly evolutionary manner to Victor Herbert's Serenades and George Gershwin's *Rhapsody in Blue*. The concert actually ended with Elgar's "Pomp and Circumstance," but Whiteman, even during this very first performance, thought the Elgar piece to be an anticlimax following Gershwin, and in subsequent concerts "Pomp and Circumstance" was either deleted or moved to the middle of the program, thus emphasizing even more intensely the evolutionary nature of a program meant to display the growth of an American art form. As Whiteman wrote: "I still believe that 'Livery Stable Blues' and 'A Rhapsody in Blue' . . . are so many millions of miles apart, that to speak of them both as jazz needlessly confuses the person who is trying to understand modern American music." If, however, Whiteman's concert is a jazz history of the world or a history of the jazz world, it is a revisionist history that has excised the presence of blacks as creators of this music. There are no references to blacks in the entire concert. We know, of course, that *Gatsby* is a novel filled with theories of history, from Tom Buchanan's suggestion that the colored races are on the verge of overrunning the world to the European discovery of the New World being, in some measure, equivalent to or signifying Gatsby's own puerile idealism that is so compellingly represented by the *Hopalong Cassidy* novel with Gatsby's schedule for self-improvement printed inside the cover that is found among his effects after his death. In a novel obsessed with various geographical myths of America (southern belles, midwesterners, and westerners all meeting in the East), this boyhood novel with the printed schedule collapses east and west, as western cowboy hero meets Ben Franklin in what signifies not an evolution but a repetition. But there may be more in the theory of American culture history that Whiteman's concert tried to explicate and symbolize than simply easterner meets westerner or a falsified set of circumstances meant to signify progress and evolution.

After all, Whiteman was no more racist than other whites of his era, and there is, indeed, evidence to indicate that he may have been less so. He wanted to hire black musicians to play in his band in the mid-twenties but was talked out of it by other band members and commercial sponsors. He did hire black arrangers William Grant Still and Don Redman before any other white band was known to do so. What Whiteman's 1924 concert was trying to establish was the idea that from its beginnings to its most fully realized form as symphonic concert music, jazz was and is an undeniable *American* music; and inasmuch as Whiteman wanted to convince himself and his audience that it was an American music, he was bound to convince both himself and others that it was, officially, a white music. Otherwise, history taught him that the only way he could perform black music would be in blackface or as a kind of minstrel. Whiteman, whatever his faults, did not want jazz to become another minstrel music, and it is, in part, through his popularizing efforts that the music did not become that. As Neil Leonard pointed out in his *Jazz and the White Americans*, jazz signified, in its speeded-up rhythms, a rapid, almost dizzying change in American conventions. "This surprisingly quick change of taste resulted from the breakdown of traditional values, the esthetic needs jazz seemed to fulfill, its increased diffusion by new sound reproducing devices and the modifications that made it increasingly acceptable." Whiteman mediated a major shift in American culture. And while his concert could attempt to deny a mongrelized American cultural past, it could not ultimately deny a kind of racial syncretism that suggested that the sharing of art between black and white, from commercial co-option to friendly collaboration, would not be used exclusively as a method to further denigrate and oppress blacks within the culture. Whiteman's concert is evidence that whites felt no less threatened by black artistic expression and its charismatic power, but the whole business of how black artistic expression related to the dominant white culture changed, and Whiteman, inadvertently, symbolized that change.

People who have never heard Whiteman's band often ask if the music was good. Gunther Schuller probably provides the fairest analysis of the musical Whiteman:

> On purely musical terms . . . the Whiteman orchestra achieved much that was admirable, and there is no question that it was admired (and envied) by many musicians, both black and white. For it was an orchestra that was overflowing with excellent musicians and virtuoso instrumentalists. Its arrangers—Lennie Hayton, Ferde Grofe, and particularly Bill Challis—wrote complex, demanding scores that took everything these musicians could give. It was not jazz, of course—or perhaps only intermittently so. Many of the arrangements were overblown technicolor potpourris, eclectic to the point of even quoting snatches of *Petrushka* and *Tristram and Isolde*. . . . But often enough—to make the point worth making—the arrangements were marvels of orchestrational ingenuity. They were designed to make people listen to music, not to dance . . . the resultant performances were often more than merely slick. Excellent intonation, perfect balances, and clean attacks do not necessarily equate with superficiality. There is in the best Whiteman performances a feeling and a personal sound as unique in its way as Ellington's or Basie's.

In an interview for the December 1936 number of *The Brown American*, a leading black magazine of the day, Duke Ellington, when asked what was his favorite band, said it was Paul Whiteman's.

Everybody's Doing It Now

Mumbo Jumbo is the god of jazz; be careful how you write of jazz, else he will hoodoo you.

—WALTER KINGSLEY, "THE APPEAL OF PRIMITIVE JAZZ"

I feel like a whore in church.

—TRUMPETER HARRY JAMES MOMENTS BEFORE THE 1938
BENNY GOODMAN CARNEGIE HALL CONCERT

But one night Helen [Oakley] came into the room and started talking about a concert. It seems she thought it would be a swell idea for people to get together and just listen to the band play, without a lot of waiters rattling dishes and people talking.

"Hell, no!" I said. "After all, this is just dance music. What's the use of trying to make something fancy and formal out of it."

—BENNY GOODMAN, *The Kingdom of Swing*

The negro loves anything that is peculiar in music.

—JAMES REESE EUROPE, 1919

But this analysis of the Whiteman concert has only scratched the surface; there are greater and more intricate complexities that we must confront if we are to come to some understanding of the connection between the meaning of popular music and the place where it is played and if we are to come to an understanding of how racial syncretism works in our culture. First, let us return to *The Great Gatsby* and Tom Buchanan's reference to a history book in a conversation he has with Nick Carraway:

> "Civilization's going to pieces," broke out Tom violently, "I've gotten to be a terrible pessimist about things. Have you read *The Rise of the Colored Empires* by this man Goddard?"
>
> "Why, no," I answered, rather surprised by his tone.
>
> "Well, it's a fine book and everybody ought to read it. The idea is if we don't look out the white race will be—will be utterly submerged. It's all scientific stuff; it's been proved."

The book Tom is referring to, as has been pointed out by several scholars, is Lothrop Stoddard's *The Rising Tide of Color Against White World Supremacy* published by Scribner's (Fitzgerald's publishing house) in 1919. While it may not be terribly surprising that the fictional Tom Buchanan—a selfish, racist, stupid, and brutal rich white man—is recommending the book, it may be a bit more remarkable that Hubert H. Harrison, one of the leading black nationalist intellectuals of the 1920s, was also recommending Stoddard's book—to black readers. Harrison, a fervent Marcus Garveyite, was both member and fellow traveler of the United Negro Improvement Association and one of the editors of *Negro World*, Garvey's paper, back during the early twenties, the peak days of Garvey's movement. In his *When Africa Awakes*, published in 1920 and a quite popular book in black circles, Harrison writes about Stoddard's work: "Here is a book written by a white man which causes white men to shiver. For it calls their attention to the writing on the wall. It proves that the white race in its mad struggle for dominion over others has been exhausting its vital resources and is exhausting them further." "Mr. Stoddard's thesis," Harrison continues, "starts from the proposition that of the seventeen hundred million people on our earth today the great majority is made up of black, brown, red, and yellow people. The white race, being in the minority, still dominates. . . . In the course of this dictatorship and domination the white race has erected the barrier of the color line. . . . But this barrier is cracking and giving way at many points and in the flood of racial self-assertion." He ends the chapter by recommending Stoddard's book, despite the fact that Stoddard is "an unreconstructed Anglo-Saxon," writing that "intelligent men of color from Tokio [sic] to Tallahassee" should read it. Of course, at least for Tom Buchanan and for the millions of other whites who either bought or read *The Rising Tide of Color Against White World Supremacy*, the fact that Stoddard was an unreconstructed Anglo-Saxon was the whole reason for the message of the book. To paraphrase Marshall McLuhan, in this instance, the messenger is the message. Nonetheless, we have this mad irony that gives us a fictional white racist and a black nationalist, one who never reads and the other who writes editorials in his black nationalist newspapers exhorting his people to "read, read, read," recommending a book by a white New Englander who wishes to warn the white world of its impending doom. This should not seem as unusual as it might at first glance. In the 1920s there was a conflict occurring about the racial origins and the racial future of the American self. It was largely a battle about authenticity and authenticating a glorious or at least praiseworthy heritage of achievement. This authenticating heritage became, in effect, an authenticating essence of some sort of national or racial peoplehood. Jazz became one of the major cultural happenings of the twenties in which this preoccupation with authenticating the American self in racial and national ways was most intense. Indeed, Fitzgerald himself was aware that, by 1925, there were clearly two competing theories of history or theories of authenticating the American racial and national self. One was the pseudoscience of pure racial origins espoused by Stoddard and the like, and the other was satirized in the passage I quoted earlier about the jazz band playing a "Jazz History of the World." There were a number of people who were trying to authenticate something about the American racial and national character through the development of American popular music. But in order to understand this fully we must, within the flow of this discussion, examine some events that happened both before and after the 1920s, and we must look at art forms other than jazz.

Stoddard was simply the most popular of a line of white racist scientific theorists writing around the time of World War I. Madison Grant's *The Passing of the Great Race* (1916), Dr. Carl C. Brigham's *A Study of American Intelligence* (1923), Dr. William MacDougall's *Is America Safe for Democracy?* (1921), and Stoddard's book were all part of a larger overall assault (as were the creation of the intelligence quotient—the IQ—in 1912 by William Stern and the introduction of the Stanford-Binet intelligence test in 1916 by Lewis Terman) against the incursion of not only dark-skinned people in American life and culture but also an attempt to stop the further immigration of eastern and southern Europeans to this shore. The authentic American was the Anglo-Saxon or, as these writers designated, "the Nordic" (there were, according to these theorists, three classes of Europeans: the Nordic or highest class, the Alpine or next highest, and the Mediterranean or the lowest), and the Nordic American's hegemony must be protected and fortified against the hordes, so this scientific racist movement asserted. Stoddard's book is particularly interesting in this regard, for not only did he argue for the authentic superiority of the Nordic over the other whites as well as over dark-skinned peoples, he further argued that the downfall of the white race was rooted in its acceptance of the doctrines of Jean-Jacques Rousseau, because through Rousseau the white world embraced the concept of the noble savage and the natural equality of all people. Certainly, Stoddard's argument has some validity when we think of the relationship of white and black in America, where so often the white has looked upon the black as a kind of primitive alter ego; but the danger rested in the very idea of the primitive or uncivilized nature of the black, for inasmuch as that nature represented a predating, prehistorical, or primeval consciousness, it became a kind of undeniable and compelling authentication of the human soul, the human essence. In a dangerous and ironic, yet mutually exploited, way, the black became the white's authenticating self; thus the cultural rite of having periodic performances of concerts called "The Jazz History of the World," which seem to be nothing more, on one grand level, than to ask: Where is the Negro located in American popular culture, where is he located in the origins of the American self?

If, around the time of the war, many white intellectuals were engaged in authenticating something called white history and the white historical mission through science, blacks were concerned with authenticating themselves through the location and discovery of the history that had been denied them. For whites this was expressed through a voracious and rampant deconstructive expropriation of everything that was called civilization during the entire course of human history, while for blacks it was the hopeful archaeological hunt for anything that was black and civilized in the past, anything that would support an ideological conception of blackness as something other than a sign of degradation in the world. (It must be understood that this is why the Harlem Renaissance occurred after the war. There was, finally, a critical mass number of black intellectuals and a sufficiently literate black bourgeois population to begin the engagement of this issue that the Negro could authenticate himself through his past. Countee Cullen asked the most relevant question of the age in his poem "Heritage": "What is Africa to me?" Or as black bibliophile Arthur A. Schomburg put it, "The American Negro must remake his past in order to make his future." The most important intellectual/historical formation of this period for blacks was Garvey's and Du Bois's separate developments of Pan Africanism.) In 1915, Carter G. Woodson formed the Association for the Study of Negro Life and History and started *The Journal of Negro History*. During the Harlem Renaissance of the 1920s, a spate of anthologies—some edited by blacks, others by whites—were published in an attempt to authenticate the black history and cultural contributions to America. Between 1922 and 1927, for instance, five anthologies of Negro poetry were published: James Weldon Johnson's *The Book of American Negro Poetry* (1922), Robert T. Kerlin's *Negro Poets and Their Poems* (1923), White and Jackson's *An Anthology of Verse by American Negroes* (1924), Alain Locke's *Four Negro Poets* (1926), and Countee Cullen's *Caroling Dusk* (1927). What makes this even more striking is that before the decade of the twenties, excepting Arthur Schomburg's *A Bibliographical Check List of American Negro Poetry* (1916), which made these anthologies possible, no one ever attempted an anthology of black literature of any sort. There were also several collections of black music during this decade, including James Weldon Johnson and J. Rosamond Johnson's *The First Book of Negro Spirituals* (1925) and *The Second Book of Negro Spirituals* (1926), Howard W. Odum and Guy B. Johnson's *The Negro and His Songs* (1925), and *Negro Workaday Songs* (1926), Dorothy Scarborough's *On the Trail of Negro Folksongs* (1925), and Abbe Niles and W. C. Handy's *Blues* (1926). Just as Schomburg's pathbreaking work made the black poetry anthologies possible, so did Henry Edward Krehbiel's seminal 1914 study, *Afro-American Folksongs*, make the music books possible. Finally, the major anthologies of African-American literature and culture were Howard University professor of philosophy Alain Locke's *The New Negro*, published in 1925, and National Urban League Executive Director Charles S. Johnson's *Ebony and Topaz*, which appeared in 1927. This brief summary of anthologies of black life and culture in the 1920s certainly does not exhaust the list. Digging up the Negro's past became something of an obsession with both blacks themselves and many liberal white intellectuals.

The most important of all these anthologists was James Weldon Johnson, former school principal, Atlanta University graduate, popular songwriter, poet, former U.S. consul to Nicaragua and Venezuela, novelist, and, during the 1920s, field secretary of the NAACP. As early as 1905 Johnson and his brother Rosamond, composers of "Lift Every Voice and Sing," the song that became known as the Black National Anthem, were propagandizing for blacks as creators of American popular music in one of the most important and popular bourgeois magazines in America: *Ladies Home Journal*. Under the title, "The Evolution of Ragtime," *Ladies Home Journal* published four songs written by the Johnson brothers and Bob Cole that demonstrated the growth of a musical form. An interesting sign of that growth is that the first three songs in the series—"Lay Away Your Troubles," a minstrel song about plantation work, "Darkies' Delights," a minstrel tune about blacks eating possum, and "The Spirit of the Banjo!" a tune celebrating "the old-time banjo song of the cotton-fields"—have lyrics in dialect, while the final and best song, "Lindy: A Love Song," does not (Johnson, who wrote dialect song lyrics during the very early 1900s and who wrote dialect poetry for his first collection of poems, "Fifty Year and Other Poems," published in 1917, was to turn away from dialect in the 1920s and, indeed, in his writings, discourage other black writers from using it. In his 1927 book of poems, *God's Trombones*, Johnson had, like Langston Hughes and Sterling Brown, solved the problem of dialect by re-creating black speech through idiomatic expressions, syntax, and rhythm.) As early as January 1909, J. Rosamond Johnson, in an article in *The Colored American Magazine* entitled "Why They Call American Music Ragtime," wrote:

> The happy expressions of the Negro's emotions in music have been dubbed "ragtime," while his more serious musical expressions have been called "plantation" and "Jubilee" songs, and these two styles of his expressions in

music are all that I can see that is distinctively American music. It is the only music that the musical centers of the world and great musicians of the world recognize as American music.

James Weldon Johnson went still further in promoting the range of influence blacks exercised in music in an earlier 1905 article in *Charities* entitled "The Negro of Today in Music" in which he discussed the works of serious black composers Samuel Coleridge-Taylor and Harry T. Burleigh as well as the show music of black minstrel Ernest Hogan, then the highest paid black performer on the American stage and composer of the song "All Coons Look Alike to Me," Black Patti, and Walker and Williams.[3] The black presence in contemporary music was ubiquitous; the black's magnetism was pervasive and encompassing. If whites were going to stereotype blacks through their so-called "natural" gifts of rhythm and song, black propagandists like the Johnson brothers, Du Bois, and others decided to make a virtue of a necessity and authenticate the black as a vital presence in American culture through music.

So, in reading the lengthy preface Johnson wrote for his anthology of American Negro poetry, probably one of the most important and, surely, one of the most brilliant cultural and historical evaluations of Black America ever written, a stunning manifesto of the African-American origins of the modern American self, there was really no surprise to any knowledgeable black reader of the 1920s who came across these passages:

> I make here what may appear to be a more startling statement by saying that the Negro has already proved the possession of these powers [of creating that which has universal appeal and influence] by being the creator of the only things artistic that have yet sprung from American soil and been universally acknowledged as distinctive American products.
>
> These creations by the American Negro may be summed up under four heads. The first two are the Uncle Remus stories, which were collected by Joel Chandler Harris, and the spirituals or slave songs. . . .
>
> The other two creations are the cakewalk and ragtime. We do not need to go very far back to remember when cakewalking was the rage in the United States, Europe and South America. . . .
>
> The influence which the Negro has exercised on the art of dancing in this country has been almost absolute. For generations the "buck and wing" and the "stop-time" dances, which are strictly Negro, have been familiar to American theatre audiences. A few years ago the public discovered the "turkey trot," the "eagle rock," "ballin' the jack," and several other varieties that started the modern dance craze. These dances were quickly followed by the "tango," a dance originated by Negroes of Cuba and later transplanted to South America.
>
> As for Ragtime, I go straight to the statement that it is the one artistic production by which America is known the world over. It has been all-conquering. Everywhere it is hailed as "American music. . . ."

The power of the Negro to suck up the national spirit from the soil and create something artistic and original, which, at the same time, possesses the note of universal appeal, is due to a remarkable racial gift of adaptability; it is more than adaptability, it is a transfusive quality.

Thus, in the 1920s, the battle was about locating a usable American past; the white racists argued that the American past was white and the black cultural promoters argued that the American past was, at least, significantly, black. The fact that Johnson and other blacks chose to argue the importance of the black presence through the very line of stereotype that had been used to denigrate the black in Western culture—the black as instinctive, pagan, sensual, imitative—was in some ways a stroke of genius; in other ways, it revealed the limitations of the black intellectual's ways of conceiving the cultural paradoxes and contradictions of American culture.[4] In effect, the black propagandists won a victory—that is, succeeded all too well in making the general population of this country think of the black as the noble savage of American music, the authenticating soul of American instinctive artistic expression—that was to prove the creation of the very matrix of confinement and dilemma that bedevils the black intellectual today.

The Whiteman concert, as a cultural phenomenon, was largely both a result and a cause of this quest for sources, an evolutionary spiral of history, a teleological authentication, and a politicization of culture as battle between the oppressor and the oppressed. Whiteman's concert was the one supreme moment of the authentication of white jazz and thus of a white hegemony over American popular music and its sources. It was a false authentication in some very important respects. And yet it was a true authentication because the concert demonstrated so well how racial syncretism in American culture works and why it works in the way it does that ultimately is acceptable to both races.

"I have come back from France more firmly convinced than ever that negroes [sic] should write negro music," said black bandleader James Reese Europe in the *New York Tribune* in 1919. "We have our own racial feeling and if we try to copy whites we will make bad copies. . . . Our musicians do their best work when using negro material. Will Marion Cook, William Tires, even Harry Burleigh and Coleridge-Taylor are not truly themselves in the music that expresses their race. The music of our race springs from the soil, and this is true with no other race, except possibly the Russians." Perhaps it is this view of hegemony through the artistic realization of a racial consciousness that makes Europe, in the same article, give his version of the origin of the word "jazz," which differs quite significantly than the earlier version I quoted from white writer and stage performer Walter Kingsley:

> I believe the term "jazz" originated with a band of four pieces which was founded about fifteen years ago in New Orleans, and which was known as "Razz's Band." This band was of truly extraordinary composition. It consisted of a baritone horn, a trombone, a cornet, and an instrument made out of the china-berry tree. This instrument is something like a clarinet, and is made by the Southern negroes themselves. . . . The four musicians of Razz's Band had no idea at all of what they were playing; they improvised as they

went along, but such was their innate sense of rhythm that they produced something which was very taking. From the small cafes of New Orleans they graduated to the St. Charles Hotel, and after a time to the Winter Garden, in New York, where they appeared, however, only a few days, the individual musicians being grabbed up by various orchestras in the city. [Black dance bands dominated popular music in the very early 1900s, and there were scarcely enough musicians to go around. It would hardly be surprising that if these players were in any way competent they would be employed by the larger bands. In the 1920s, the star players of both black and white bands were constantly being recruited and wooed and earned unbelievable salaries, although most of them were virtually unknown to the record-buying public.] Somehow in the passage of time Razz's Band got changed into "Jazz's Band," and from this corruption arose the term "jazz."

Europe's etymology shows how the politicalization of American popular culture was moving apace: Here, the idea that jazz is connected with either Africa or slavery is eliminated. Jazz refers to something that is purely Negro-American and is purely unconnected with a degraded past. Here, jazz is not associated with bars and whorehouses and places of ill-repute; the places where the Razz Band played were all quite respectable venues. Europe realized, as did Whiteman, that the status of a particular form of music has little to do with what it is and much to do with where it is played.

Whiteman's band is considered the first to perform some sort of symphonic jazz concert in a hall known only for permitting the performance of classical European art music, but this is not actually so. James Reese Europe, organizer of New York's black musicians into something called the Clef Club, which someone remarked at the time to be an odd name as most of its members could not read music, led 125 black musicians in a concert of ragtime-based popular music at Carnegie Hall in May 1912. James Weldon Johnson described the concert in his history of Harlem, *Black Manhattan*:

> There were a few strings proper, the most of them being 'cellos and double-basses; the few wind-instruments consisted of cornets, saxophones, clarinets, and trombones; there was a battery of drums; but the main part of the orchestra was composed of banjos, mandolins, and guitars. On this night all these instruments were massed against a background of ten upright pianos. In certain parts the instrumentation was augmented by voices. New York had not yet become accustomed to jazz; so when the Clef Club opened its concert with a syncopated march, playing it with a biting attack and an infectious rhythm, and on the finale bursting into singing, the effect can be imagined. The applause became a tumult.

There is evidence that Europe may have performed more than one such concert at Carnegie Hall; there is a review of a Carnegie Hall concert by the Clef Club in the March 1913 issue of *The Craftsman* that would seem a bit late for a review of a concert that took place in May of the previous year. Europe, who often wore a white suit and matching white shoes, and small, round, wire-framed glasses, was doubtless the first black band leader to play symphonic jazz in a European art-music hall.[5] Indeed, he seems to have been the first American of any color to have done so. The fact that he did is virtually forgotten in the history of American popular music. The fact that Whiteman did is not. But there is one crucial difference, aside from the primary one of race, that must be kept in mind when considering Europe and Whiteman. It has been suggested that few members of Europe's band could read music (although Europe insisted on his musicians' being disciplined and dedicated; as he said, "It takes a lot of training to develop a sense of time and delicate harmony"), whereas it was almost impossible to be a member of Whiteman's band unless one could sight-read well.[6] (When Bix Beiderbecke joined Whiteman in 1927, he played his solos brilliantly but struggled with the often demanding ensemble parts because he was such a poor reader.) With Whiteman we cannot overlook his emphasis on scoring and composition as the essence of the new American popular music. However challenging and innovative Europe's music may have been, it could not have been, conceptually, a music that saw or realized its essence as a score. In this sense, Europe's music lacked a certain legitimating power that Whiteman's had. Thus, Whiteman's band was really and truly modern, and Europe's was still a throwback to a kind of ur-jazz, primitive black music, although, apparently, Europe's music was far from sounding primitive and Europe himself, reared in the same black middle-class environs of Washington, D.C., that was later to produce Duke Ellington, was classically trained and came from a family of classically trained musicians.

Later, in 1914, Europe formed the Temp Club and played and wrote music for Irene and Vernon Castle for the next three years. (His associate, Ford Dabney, organized and directed a jazz orchestra featured at Florenz Ziegfeld's roof-garden shows.) It may have been that blacks, as James Weldon Johnson argued, invented the popular dances of the 1910s that took the country by storm, but a white upper-middle-class theatrical couple, the Castles, popularized them and helped to spread Europe's music to wider circles than those of New York High Society. Once again, an example of the racial syncretism of American popular music is illustrated by how the Castles and Europe were able to work together quite well and to their mutual benefit. Despite the fact that the Castles were white, they were still seen as threatening to many conservative, small-town Americans who feared the new dancing craze. There were cases of women being arrested for dancing in public and of being fired from jobs for dancing during their lunch breaks. When Edward Bok tried to run a series of dance instruction articles with accompanying photos of the Castles in his *Ladies Home Journal* in 1914, the outcry from his readers and segments of the general public was so great that he discontinued the feature after only one installment. If such significant pockets of the country were that resistant to white dancers performing quite respectable and chaste versions of black dances, how much more resistant would that public have been to black dancers trying to do the same thing? Here is the paradox: Blacks may very well have created most American forms of music and dance, but they certainly could not popularize them. This means, strictly speaking, that they never created American popular music and dance but rather contributed a lion's share of the ideas that helped to shape an American popular imagination. They constantly needed whites as brokers, intercessors, collaborators, and promoters in order to help introduce them to wider audiences and to make the music truly popular. This very idea that modern black art not only is created but in some vital senses is conceptualized as having its presence through the mediating patronage of whites is the informing and controversial message of Zora Neale Hurston's 1942 autobiography, *Dust Tracks on a Road*, and of her essay "The 'Pet Negro' System," which appeared in *The American Mercury* in May 1943. For Hurston, the political question of whites' ultimately exercising control over the nature and shape of black art was obviously of importance, but her point was that art was being created only partially for blacks themselves. It could reach its final if diminished realization only if it came to mean something for whites as well. In the way popular black arts developed, blacks may have had to share much with the whites who, in some instances, may not have contributed much to their creation, but the blacks ultimately gained immeasurably as well; so much so, in fact, that by the 1920s, there was a literary and artistic movement called the Harlem Renaissance in which blacks such as James Weldon Johnson spoke of the renovation of the black's political, social, and psychic status through the creation and acceptance of art.

"The music world is controlled by a trust, and the negro must submit to its demands or fail to have his compositions produced," James Reese Europe said in 1914. "I am not bitter about it. It is, after all, but a small portion of the price my race must pay in its, at times, almost hopeless fight for a place in the sun. Some day it will be different and justice will prevail." But the future brought no real change except the institutional and legal breakdown of segregation, and, despite that cataclysmic cultural change in America, the ties that bind blacks and whites and American popular artistic forms simply have become more intricate. We may conclude from this either that segregation as the operating ideology in this culture is not dead because whites or blacks or both do not wish it to die, or that how blacks and whites relate to each other as ritual, as anthropological reality, as psychokinetic construct, is far stronger than anything that was ever embedded in the codes created to govern that relationship.

Perhaps nothing better illustrates this problem of how black artists should relate to whites than the entire discussion that took place in the 1920s and earlier among blacks as to whether they should indeed be engaged in creating a race-based or racially conscious art. This is far too complex a topic for me to explore at length in this essay, but there are two relevant instances that need to be reviewed here. First, Europe, whom I have already quoted as expressing an interest in creating a distinctly "Negro music," was attacked by Will Marion Cook, whom Europe singled out in his comments on "serious" black composers, for creating a cheap commercial music that was insufficiently elevated. Cook himself, at the time of Europe's popularity, was leading a fifty-piece popular music band called the New York Syncopated Orchestra and had provided music for Bert Williams's stage shows as well as having written several pop standards, including "I'm Coming Virginia," which became a favorite of Bix Beiderbecke in the 1920s. So, on one level, the source of the criticism might seem a bit more than disingenuous; however, Cook had done rather over-Europeanized arrangements of Negro spirituals and had written extended scores using Negro folk themes. As Gunther Schuller writes, Cook thought of "both Europe's band of brassy jazz and the novelty bands on Broadway, which claimed to represent the Negro's music from New Orleans, as unworthy reflections upon the dignity of Negro music." But Cook was not alone. Other serious composers felt the same way: Harry T. Burleigh, the British black musician Samuel Coleridge-Taylor, even popular songwriter James Weldon Johnson, whose 1912 novel, *The Autobiography of an Ex-Colored Man*, is, in part, about a very light-skinned black musician who hopes to elevate ragtime to a "serious" art through the creation of elaborate scores. If there was to be a distinctive Negro music, first, it would be scored and self-consciously composed and not just intuitively created, indeed, it would require extremely well-trained, sight-reading musicians. Second, it would be, in some sense, an amalgam of an African sensibility with a Eurocentric method. In short, it would be some sort of symphonic black music. Despite the symphonic pretensions of Europe's Clef Club, it was not quite regarded, in some circles, as what black music was aspiring to be.

In 1926, this controversy was articulated in another way between the two leading young black literary figures of the day, Countee Cullen and Langston Hughes. By then one of most celebrated literary figures of the Renaissance, Cullen, who wrote poetry of a strictly metered, well-schooled Eurocentric form largely inspired by Keats, Shelley, Houseman, and Edna St. Vincent Millay, reviewed Hughes's first volume of poetry, *The Weary Blues*, in the February issue of *Opportunity*, one of the leading black magazines of the day. In what was otherwise a very favorable review, he took Hughes to task for writing jazz poems:

> I regard these jazz poems as interlopers in the company of the truly beautiful poems in other sections of the book. They move along with the frenzy and electric heat of a Methodist or Baptist revival meeting, and affect me in such the same manner. The revival meeting excites me, cooling and flushing me with alternate chills and fevers of emotion; so do these poems. But when the storm is over, I wonder if the quiet way of communing is not more spiritual for the God-seeking heart; and in the light of reflection I wonder if jazz poems really belong to that dignified company, that select and austere circle of high literary expression which we call poetry.

Like Raphaelson earlier, Cullen connects jazz and religion. But in his case, the very atavistic, pagan quality of the jazz poems summons forth the more pagan, atavistic quality of black Christian worship that disturbs him—not from fear that the entire expression of jazz is dysfunctional, but that it is a kind of infantile obsession with something orgasmic that pulls the black writer away from the entire purpose of writing, from the script or the score, which demands permanency. The conflict between what Cullen felt were the pagan and Christian impulses of Black-American consciousness was the constant theme of most of his poetry. This is not surprising, as he was the foster son of Frederick A. Cullen, one of the most important African Methodist Episcopal ministers in 1920s Harlem.

In his famous June 1926 *Nation* article, "The Negro Artist and the Racial Mountain," Hughes, known for writing poems based on blues and jazz themes, supposedly responding to an article written the previous week by black conservative satirist George S. Schuyler called "The Negro-Art Hokum," was clearly responding directly to Cullen's criticism: "One of the most promising of the young Negro poets said to me once, 'I want to be a poet—not a Negro poet,' meaning, I believe, 'I want to write like a white poet'; meaning subconsciously, 'I would like to be a white poet'; meaning behind that, 'I would like to be white.' " Of course, every black reader and some of the more knowledgeable white ones knew instantly that Hughes was referring to Cullen, who had, in nearly every public forum available to him, repeatedly said that he did not wish to be known as a Negro poet or purely as a racial poet. After dealing succinctly with what he felt to be Cullen's racial neurosis, Hughes discussed why he wrote jazz poems:

> Most of my own poems are racial in theme and treatment, derived from the life I know. In many of them I try to grasp and hold some of the meanings and rhythms of jazz. . . . What makes you do so many jazz poems? [Hughes is asked by his incredulous and sometimes unappreciative black public.]
>
> But jazz to me is one of the inherent expressions of Negro life in America; the eternal tom-tom beating in the Negro soul—the tom-tom of revolt against weariness in a white world, a world of subway trains, and work, work, work; the tom-tom of joy and laughter, and pain swallowed in a smile. Yet the Philadelphia clubwoman is ashamed to say that her race created it and she does not like me to write about it. The old subconscious "white is best" runs through her mind.

Hughes moves neatly from the opening image of the neurotic, inferior-feeling, assimilative black poet of the beginning of the piece—old Uncle Tom of the literary world—to the jazzman as race poet and the tom-tom of revolt. The piece, more cleverly designed than necessarily intellectually convincing, was an attack against the black bourgeois concept of a race-based or racially conscious art as being necessarily centered in some sort of recognizable mastered Eurocentric method or discipline. Yet the answer for blacks was never as simple as the Hughes–Cullen debate would suggest. As the symphonic jazz music movement continued beyond the 1920s, Duke Ellington became one of its leaders. One can scarcely imagine a more bourgeois-minded black artist: reared in a home of such conventionality that he heard little hot music or jazz, growing up adopting the same kind of mass bourgeois, popular taste as Paul Whiteman. Yet Ellington, in his blackness, was to have one of the most successful dance bands and swing music aggregations in the 1920s and the 1930s. Ellington was an almost completely unschooled musician; he never finished high school and never formally studied music, much like many of the ordinary lower-class black musicians of his day. He was indeed the least musically educated of the major black big band leaders and arrangers of the 1920s and 1930s, with the exception of Count Basie. He was certainly far less musically educated than Don Redman, Fletcher Henderson, Andy Kirk, Bennie Moten, and others. Yet he was to write, and have performed, more jazz concertos, symphonylike jazz compositions, ballets, and the like than virtually any other black or white jazz musician in the history of American popular music, and it was in these extended compositions that Ellington tended to be his most racially conscious. He symbolizes the paradox of the black artist in American popular culture and the contradictory and contrary idea of what a black art in relation to a larger white cultural framework really is.

There were two Jews whose parents were part of that mass that escaped the ghettos of Russia in the late nineteenth century to come to America whose spectacular success in popular music was part of the larger infusion of Russian and Eastern European Jews in the workings of American popular culture of the late nineteenth and early and middle twentieth centuries that so changed the entire course of the culture. The success of these two Jewish men in particular has a great deal to do with the entire business of white jazz and racial syncretism and our understanding of it. First, let us consider the case of clarinetist Benny Goodman, who became the extremely successful leader of a swing jazz band during the 1930s. Goodman, born in Chicago in 1909, had fewer than two years of formal musical instruction yet became one of the most compelling and accomplished hot jazz musicians of his generation. Forming his own band in March 1934 after an apprenticeship of nearly a dozen years as a sideman and studio player, Goodman struggled until, while on a national tour, the band clicked in California at the Palomar Club in 1935. Like Whiteman, when Goodman came back east he seemed like a triumphant, newfangled westerner. (Also like Whiteman, Goodman was to write his autobiography shortly after his Carnegie Hall concert, signifying that reaching that venue was a kind of pinnacle.) The band stopped in Chicago to play the Congress Hotel before going on the legendary Paramount engagement in New York City in 1937, where the kids danced in the aisle, and finally to the swing concert at Carnegie Hall. Because the band had built its popularity in the West and the Midwest, there was a sense, once again, of the displaced westerner coming east, intensified by the fact that Goodman was from Chicago. But the fact that his ancestry was Eastern European added a reversed image to the myth, as he was also the easterner come west for freedom, and what better way to symbolize that quest than by playing an art form noted for its freedom of expression?

The January 16, 1938, Carnegie Hall concert has always been seen as an analogue to the Whiteman concert that took place fourteen years earlier. And inasmuch as the former can be viewed as a major event in the history of American popular music, such a reading is actually correct—despite the fact that Vincent Lopez and His Orchestra performed a symphonic jazz concert at the Met on November 23, 1924, and included the work of black blues pioneer W. C. Handy, whose "St. Louis Blues" had been plugged by Lopez's band several years earlier; and despite the fact that Fats Waller performed James P. Johnson's *Yamekraw (Negro Rhapsody)*, orchestrated by black composer William Grant Still, at Carnegie Hall with W. C. Handy conducting in 1928. The Goodman band was clearly the most popular and remarkable band to play a popular music concert at Carnegie Hall. It differed from all previous popular music concerts at classical European art halls in two ways: First, Goodman was not playing symphonic jazz but rather swing or hot jazz; second, his band was racially integrated, at least in the small group portion that featured Lionel Hampton on vibes and Teddy Wilson on piano. Unlike Whiteman, Goodman devoted only a portion of his concert to an evolutionary historical look at the development of jazz, and this portion was a mixture of songs associated with and written by both black and white musicians, including pieces by Will Marion Cook and Ford Dabney from the James Reese Europe era. Moreover, for several of these selections, Goodman was accompanied by black musicians from the Duke Ellington and Count Basie bands, therefore presenting the entire historical scope of the music as an integrated, openly racially syncretized art instead of as a subversively racially syncretized art. The article that ran in the *New York Times* magazine on the day of the concert entitled "Swing It! And Even in a Temple of Music" emphasized the comparison with the symphonic jazz concerts of an earlier day and saw a kind of evolution in the entire nature of popular music concerts at European art music halls: One might say, with Goodman at Carnegie Hall, that the country had officially gone "into the hot." As writer Gama Gilbert states:

> The occasion is a landmark in the growth and recognition of a species of music that was reborn after the halcyon days of symphonic jazz some ten years ago. . . .
>
> The salient impression of orchestra music and performance was one of order, decorum, and control. Jazz was congratulating itself, and receiving the congratulations of polite society, that it had shed every vestige of its uncouth and disreputable origins and had taken on the odor of respectability. It had disowned and erased from its memory its forebears and ancestral homes—the darky workers on the levees of the lower Mississippi, the hellholes of New Orleans, the riverboat bands with Bix Beiderbecke, King Oliver and Satchelmouth Armstrong, Memphis and its blues, the sawdust and smoke-beery air of the Chicago joints. . . .
>
> But the germ of its undoing was implicit in its irreconcilable elements and in its flagrant artificiality. Divorced from the urgency of human emotion, lost to the lusty world from which it had exiled itself, its cleverly fabricated, sterile music began to ail and pall.

Clearly, this analogue recapitulates the concern that the culture had been expressing all along throughout the twenties: authentication. Jazz had lost its own authenticating voice by having, through the corruption of bourgeois, philistine appeasement, denied its own origins. Through Goodman, it had come back in a sort of loop to its own authority through its own primitiveness, its own lack of presumption or lack of unease about its disreputable origins. Yet there are a number of problems with this thesis: First, virtually all of the symphonic jazz bands, Europe's in some sense, Whiteman's, Lopez's, and others, were also dance bands playing arranged music that could only be played by highly skilled players, whether sight-readers or not. Indeed, the introduction of the saxophone as an innovative, virtuosic instrument in jazz can be credited not to black hot bands in

New Orleans or on the Barbary Coast or in Chicago but to sophisticated black and white big dance bands, particularly Whiteman's, and was precisely what the Goodman band was. Moreover, the idea that the great musical theorists, organizers, and bandleaders were not concerned with composition, with achieving the entire range of musical effects and possibilities available through a highly arranged music executed with discipline, is false. In other words, symphonic jazz, as an extension of the American dance band tradition, was not an aberration but a serious if occasionally unsuccessful exploration of the possibility that dance music could be metamorphosed into an art music. Goodman's concert was the culmination of the acceptance of jazz music with whites as popularizers and blacks as cocreators, coperformers, and atavistic spiritual source. Goodman also made people listen to dance music and thus, even more than the beboppers who came later, he effected the transformation of hot jazz music to an art music and reoriented the public to accepting jazz as high art without the trappings of classical European art music. The irony is that Goodman elevated jazz while he himself, despite being white, was to the Anglo-Protestant public nothing more than a lower-class Eastern European Jewish immigrant, the very kind of ethnic who, along with the blacks, the white racist writers of the 1920s kept saying, was going to swamp American civilization. If Goodman's Carnegie Hall concert was any indication, the white racist theorists were right at last:

> That night at Carnegie Hall was a great experience, because it represented something—a group of musicians going on that stage and playing tunes by Gershwin and Berlin and Kern in arrangements by Fletcher and Edgar Sampson, getting up and playing the choruses the way they wanted to, each of them just being himself—and holding the attention of all those people for two hours and a half.
>
> When the thing was first put up to me, I was a little bit dubious about it, not knowing just what would be expected of us. But as soon as it was understood that we could handle the thing in our own way, and let the people listen to it as they would any other kind of music, the proposition really began to mean something. Certainly if the stuff is worth playing at all, it's worth playing in any hall that presents itself. I didn't have the idea of putting across a "message" or anything like that—I was just satisfied to have the kids in the band do what they always had done, and the way they did it was certainly wonderful. Personally, it was the thrill of my life to walk out on that stage with people just hemming the band in [some of the overflow audience sat on the stage], and hear the greeting the boys got. We were playing for "Bix" and the fellows on the riverboats, in the honky tonks and ginmills that night.

While the end of this passage from Goodman's autobiography sounds suspiciously as if it were lifted from the *New York Times* magazine article, one particular observation needs to be made: Goodman described the creative configuration of jazz as being the songs of Jewish Tin Pan Alley songwriters (Berlin, Gershwin, Kern) and the arrangements of black arrangers (Fletcher Henderson and Edgar

Sampson) who, apparently, could make the songs swing. This brings me to the other Jew we must consider, popular songwriter Irving Berlin. Born Israel Baline in Temun, Russia, in 1888, Berlin started his musical career as a singing waiter in the Bowery, making a name for himself at Nigger Mike Salter's Saloon and dance hall at 12 Pell Street in the heart of Chinatown. Nigger Mike was not black; he was, like Berlin, a Russian Jew whose dark skin earned him his extremely distasteful, if vivid, nickname. It was at Nigger Mike's that Berlin began his songwriting career, and it was during the early stages of his career that his name underwent a change from Israel Baline to I. Berlin and, finally, Irving Berlin, "a Jew boy that had named himself after an English actor and a German city," so jocularly said George M. Cohan. Cohan said this at a banquet in honor of Berlin, who had, by the early 1910s, become the most prolific and the most successful songwriter in America. In 1911, Berlin had one of his biggest hits with "Alexander's Ragtime Band," which, for a time, was the song that he was known by, despite his other hits. The success of "Alexander's Ragtime Band" led to a spate of ragtime songs from Berlin: "That Mysterious Rag," "Whistling Rag," "The Dying Rag," "The Ragtime Jockey Man," "The Ragtime Soldier Man," "That International Rag," and the huge hit "Everybody's Doin' It Now." All of these songs were written between 1912 and 1917. Berlin is the linchpin that, finally, ties everything together, for his songs appeared on the bill of the two major jazz concerts at European art music halls between 1924 and 1938—Whiteman's 1924 Aeolian Hall concert and Goodman's 1938 Carnegie Hall concert. Berlin's music not only ties together both symphonic and swing or hot jazz, it also ties together virtually the entire era of American popular music from nearly the turn of the century to the Goodman concert, since Berlin's music and the musical traditions it represents—both African-American and East European Jewish as well as the ethnic song of the minstrel and Yiddish theaters—goes back that far. Berlin's music confirmed that any "serious" American art form, be it inspired by some symphonic form or the energy of the popular dance, was going to be based on the largely Jewish-created Tin Pan Alley song. (The apotheosis of the American popular song and its writer occurred shortly after Whiteman's concert, when drama critic Alexander Woolcott, of Algonquin Roundtable fame, wrote a biography of Berlin published in 1925 when Berlin was just thirty-six years old.) Certainly jazz has developed largely and recognizably as an art form built on the chord changes of the Tin Pan Alley song. For instance, modernist trumpeter Wynton Marsalis's symphonic jazz album, *Hot House Flowers*, is not a collection of concertos or European derived forms, but a series of string settings of a bunch of evergreen popular songs familiar to nearly everyone in America who is aware of show music. There are, of course, compositions by jazz composers from Jelly Roll Morton to Duke Ellington to Thelonious Monk that have become part of the stock repertoire of the jazz performer, but most frequently it is a specific group of Tin Pan Alley pop tunes that are called "standards," implying the very foundation upon which the art is built. And many compositions by noted jazz players have merely been variations of the chord changes of these standards.

It might be unnerving to some blacks and even some liberal whites that

Whiteman was called the King of Jazz, that Berlin was called the King of Ragtime, and that Goodman was called the King of Swing. The titles on the one hand, signify a kind of white cultural hegemony, a white cultural imperialism, some might argue. And while the story is, perhaps, as simple as that (for theft explains a great deal of the phenomenon of the popularization and racial politicalization of American popular art), it is in the end a great deal more complicated, too. The growth of syncopated rhythmic American popular music has been the growth of racially inclusive art, virtually the only racially inclusive art in America where whites, as a commonplace, acknowledge the work of blacks. Moreover, the impulse of this music was also to battle against the conventions of the day; the impulse of the music was always to bring the races and classes closer together even if, meeting the walls of commercialism and stubborn social and political customs, it did not succeed. Where else, other than in the popular culture arenas of sports and music, have the races really come together, really syncretized their being? And has it not been, in many compelling ways, that society has experienced its greatest changes for the better through just these avenues of marginalized popular culture suddenly taking center stage in the culture for one crucial moment? Popular culture has changed us and how we see ourselves, and how we relate to ourselves as blacks and whites and to each other, more than any other single force or combined forces in this country. Let us not forget that it is impossible for American culture, popular or otherwise (and in a real sense America has no other culture but popular culture), to authenticate *anything*, since American culture exists from its very inception, to authenticate *everything*. As Kierkegaard argued about the relationship of paganism and Christianity, when whites in America tried to define the culture by their whiteness, it only intensified their realization that it must exclude blackness, and as it fought to exclude blackness, it only, paradoxically, continued to include it by recognizing it as a power, a symbol, a threat, a principle, that had to be excluded. In the end, Hubert H. Harrison more properly assessed Stoddard's book than Tom Buchanan ever did. American culture is the one human aggregate that will support any proposition you wish, because its energy is its willingness to try to sell anything at least once.[7] The King of Swing, the King of Ragtime, the King of Jazz—these titles are a sign of cultural hegemony, to be sure, but also of the racial syncretism that gives American popular music its distinctiveness and its power. White guitarist Eddie Condon organized a jazz concert on January 14, 1942, at Carnegie Hall as a tribute to black jazzman Fats Waller, and the program included many of the famous songs Waller composed and other songs he did not write but made famous through performance, such as "I'm Gonna Sit Right Down and Write Myself a Letter." It was the first concert in tribute to a black jazz musician ever held at Carnegie Hall. Jazz had been reauthenticated through its blackness and the entire cycle had moved fully around from Whiteman and symphonic jazz and popular song in 1924 to Waller and Harlem stride piano and the popular song in 1942. Waller had been drinking heavily both before and during the concert and was a bit unsteady at times, and Condon kept wondering why so many of the tunes played had snatches of Gershwin in them.

It might be that Duke Ellington said it right in his 1931 song title: "It Don't

Mean a Thing, If It Ain't Got That Swing." But considering how mongrelized our culture really is and how our popular music constantly celebrates the wonder and glory of our mixed-up selves, Berlin said it even better in 1916: "Everything in America is Ragtime."

Epilogue: It Could Happen to You

The Carnegie concert was the biggest thing that ever happened to me.

— BILLIE HOLIDAY, *Lady Sings the Blues*

Billie Holiday gave two concerts at Carnegie Hall. The first, which she describes in her autobiography, *Lady Sings the Blues*, took place on March 27, 1948, ten days after her release from prison, where she served nine and a half months of a year and a day sentence for the possession of narcotics. It was a midnight concert, the night before Easter, a bad night for business according to Holiday, and it was the only time in her life that she fainted.

> Just before I was set to go on for the second set a big mess of gardenias arrived backstage. My old trademark—somebody had remembered and sent it for luck. I took them out of the box and fastened them smack to the side of my head without even looking twice. I hadn't noticed, but there was a huge hatpin and I stuck it deep into my head. I was so numb from excitement I didn't even feel anything until the blood began running down in my eyes and ears.

It was, one supposes, as a result of this wound and the general excitement of doing her "welcome back" concert at such a prestigious forum that Holiday fainted, although she ultimately performed a show of twenty-one tunes and six encores.

Holiday's second and last Carnegie Hall concert took place nearly eight years later—on November 10, 1956, more than a year after the highly publicized drug death of Charlie Parker. Her autobiography had just been published and, between groups of numbers she sang, Gilbert Millstein, a writer for the *New York Times*, read lengthy though not profane excerpts from Holiday's book. (There is a recording of this concert available on Verve Records.) Perhaps the readings from the autobiography would have been more effective had Holiday read the book herself, or perhaps had any woman at all read it. The overall effect of hearing these passages between the songs is strange and dislocating, the sort of victory-in-defeat that was, at points, the hallmark of Holiday's life, the hallmark of the black jazzer's life, the singular triumph of vulgarity, bad taste, feminized artifice, politicized artifact, and profound art. At the second concert an excerpt from her book about her first Carnegie Hall concert was read, giving a tremendous sense of performance as both replication and reification. Jazz had, at last, acquired a text; it had become a narrative art, an epic. In both concerts, it was Holiday's life or rather the myth of her victimization as woman (her bad marriages and the publicly known fact that her drug addiction was caused by men she knew), artist (one of the reasons she was performing in Carnegie Hall was because she lost her cabaret card as a result of her arrest and imprisonment and could, therefore, no longer perform in nightclubs and bars in New York), and black (she was the victim of racism, segregation, limited life choices, and a bad education) as much as her art that was being celebrated. Holiday's concerts were the final public acceptance of jazz as an art form and of the black performer as artist: The life and the art had become interchangeable. And the life and the art had become a kind of voyeuristic tragedy for the audience and a self-conscious tragedy for the artist. Indeed, as embodied by Holiday, jazz had, ironically, ceased to be art while being swallowed by the weight of its artistic pretensions; jazz had now become a sort of postmodernist negritude, a stance, a stunt, which means that it had become both more and less than it had been, existing somewhere between Walt Whitman's "barbaric yawp" and an existential aria. If jazz had once symbolized the revolt of modernity, it had now come to symbolize modernity as absurd. Jazz had become a forlorn and fashionable pulp, and Billie Holiday had become our greatest, most stirring pulp heroine. After all, only in America could someone sin so helplessly and yet be given a second chance, be granted the great buildup for the Grand Comeback. Billie Holiday, demonstrating at last the new and ultimate arrival of the black jazz artist in the mainstream and wanting so much to prove that she was loved in America and did not need to escape to Europe, showed that redemption of that sort could happen to anyone.

NOTES

1. Caesar makes other references that would be particularly striking and relevant for the women in her audience such as "They got all kinds of perfumes like Avon, Matchabelli, and Chanel No. 5 but none of them can reach where we're going tonight." And later, toward the very end of the sermon: "I saw something else on television. I'm always catching things. One day I was sitting at home I saw a bald headed man come on the screen with one earring in his ear say my name is Mr. Clean and Mr. Clean hates dirt. But I wish he'd walk in here tonight so I can tell him that I know a man named Mr. Clean." I am not suggesting here that Caesar's sermon was feminist but clearly she expresses that salvation from God and thus empowerment by the holy spirit means rejecting the carnality of this world and specifically for women the products that have defined their role and their spiritual (and, ironically for feminists and female evangelists alike, their earthly) enslavement.

    One other point that needs to be mentioned here is that Billie Holiday cowrote a song entitled "Don't Explain" inspired by discovering strange lipstick on her first husband's, Jimmy Munroe's, collar. " 'Take a bath, man,' I said, 'don't explain,' " she writes as her reply to him in her autobiography, *Lady Sings the Blues*. So, Holiday the jazz singer gives us the profane rhetorical analogue to the sacred sermon on bathing by Caesar.

2. Earl Hines, the famous black pianist and bandleader from Pittsburgh who played in Chicago during the heyday of the 1920s and 1930s, was called Fatha, and Sonny was a not uncommon sobriquet for black men. Hines did not acquire the name under circumstances that are indicative of the sort of endearment that the Pops nickname suggests. See Stanley Dance's *The World of Earl Hines*—and despite his importance in the history of jazz, Hines does not have the same historical magnitude as either Armstrong or Whiteman.

3. In the same year, black writer and activist Mary Church Terrell wrote a piece on Samuel Coleridge-Taylor's tour of the United States for *The Voice of the Negro*, a short-lived but important black magazine of the period.

4. Harold Cruse develops this line of reasoning further in his seminal work, *The Crisis of the Negro Intellectual* (1967), and trying to negotiate the interpretive quagmire that the earlier black intellectuals such as Johnson and Du Bois stumbled into is largely what Ralph Ellison's *Shadow and Act* (1964) is all about.

5. Europe was apparently a very impressive man and his music was quite compelling. Arthur W. Little, in *From Harlem to the Rhine* (1936), his book on the Fifteenth Colored Infantry known as Harlem's Hell Fighters, describes the effect of Europe's band on an audience of hostile southern whites in Spartanburg, South Carolina. The regiment, of which Europe was a member, had been stationed in Spartanburg shortly after the famous race riot involving black troops (the 24th Infantry) in Houston, Texas.

   The talk which some of us overheard through that crowd, during the early stages of the concert, was by no means reassuring. At first it seemed, almost, as if an error of judgment had been made in forcing the colored regiment into prominence at so early an hour after our arrival. But there must be something in the time-honored line about music and its charms; for, gradually, the crowd grew larger, but the noises of the crowd grew less and less, until finally, in that great public square of converging city streets, silence reigned. Lieutenant Europe conducted, as was his custom, with but a few seconds between numbers, and the program appeared to be short. When the final piece had been played and the forty or fifty bandsmen had filed out of the stand in perfect order with the "Hep-Hep-Hep" of the sergeants as the only sound from their ranks, the flower of Spartanburg's citizenry looked at each other foolishly, and one could be heard to say:—"Is that all?" while another would say:—"When do they play again?"

   Little, the white commander of the regiment, described both Europe and Noble Sissle as "artists of genius and of high musical education, and gentlemen, by instinct and by bearing," and he recounts how Europe maintained both his dignity and his common sense after both he and Sissle were verbally abused and assaulted by a white tavern owner in Spartanburg. Little reveals his respect for the two men by not having them speak in the rather overwrought Negro dialect he uses for the speech of most of the other black soldiers.

6. Whether Europe's musicians could generally read scores well is open to dispute. Irene Castle wrote: "He would not employ a man who could not read music and he would not tolerate dissipation or irresponsibility" (from "Jim Europe—A Reminiscence" in *Opportunity Magazine*, March 1930). Generally, her description of Europe matches that of Little. Ironically, she refers to him as "the Paul Whiteman of the colored race," revealing the closeness in both aesthetic vision and organizational abilities between the two men. Perhaps it would have been more apt to refer to Paul Whiteman as the James Reese Europe of the white race.

7. The obvious penalty for this is the wholesale justification of vulgarity as an art form that rock and roll music has given us. Here blacks stand uneasily, as they always have, as the symbolic basin or sink of vulgar expression from which whites can draw inspiration and through which they can justify their own preoccupation with vulgarity-as-freedom-expression and as the lowest common denominator of expression. Instead of

symbolizing a sort of sophisticated stylization of art, the contemporary black rapper, for instance, is only the stylization of vulgarity now defined by white liberals, not as symptomatic urge to profanity that afflicts culture generally, but as the special, charismatic, and skillful expressions of "ethnicity."

chapter 24

LAWRENCE W. LEVINE

Jazz and American Culture

In early 1987 Willard B. Gatewood, Jr., president of the Southern Historical Association, and Ed Harrell, chairman of its Program Committee, were kind enough to invite me to give the opening night address at the Association's annual meeting in New Orleans in November. They wanted me to speak on any aspect of jazz history that interested me, and they lured me with the promise that my paper would not be followed by the customary critiques of commentators but by "a one hour complimentary cocktail reception" and a performance by the Preservation Hall Jazz Band. In spite of these enticements, I was hesitant to accept. The invitation came at an extremely busy time; I was struggling to complete my book, *Highbrow/Lowbrow*, which I had promised to send in final form to the publisher that coming summer. I ultimately agreed for two reasons: The moment they told me what they wanted, I knew exactly what I would speak on—the relationship of jazz to the new hierarchical concept of Culture that made its appearance in the United States at the turn of the century.

I was dealing with this cultural phenomenon in the book I was finishing, and the idea of fitting jazz into the larger cultural framework intrigued me. More crucially, I was loath to do anything to discourage or undermine those of my colleagues who were striving to take seriously such aspects of American culture as jazz which had suffered neglect at the hands of historians for so long. The notion of having jazz as the centerpiece of the opening night session delighted me. The enormous amount of pressured work my decision cost me was more than compensated for by the large, enthusiastic group of historians who gathered in the Clarion Hotel on the night of November 11, and by the warm—and wet—reception and wonderful music that followed. As a friend commented at the time, "This *is* a lot better than criticism!" Inevitably, of course, the criticism came anyway—abundantly and helpfully—before a slightly expanded version of the paper was published in the *Journal of American Folklore*, 102 (January–March 1989).

The increasing scholarly interest in jazz symbolizes what I trust is an ongoing reversal of a long-standing neglect by historians and their colleagues in many other disciplines of a central element in American culture. The neglect, of course, has not been an aberration on the part of academics. In neglecting or ignoring jazz, scholars have merely reflected the values and predispositions of the larger society in which they operated. But even this simple statement belies the true complexity of the problem: American society has done far more than merely neglect jazz; it has pigeonholed it, stereotyped it, denigrated it, distorted its meaning and its character. The nature and significance of the type of attention our society has paid to jazz reveal a great deal about our culture.

Anthropologically, perhaps, my title—"Jazz and American Culture"—doesn't make a great deal of sense since Jazz is an integral part of American culture. But it is not culture in the anthropological sense that I'm dealing with here, since in fact that's not what culture meant to the society at the time jazz came upon the scene as a recognizable entity. When jazz became an identifiable form of music to the larger society, it was held to be something quite distinct from *Culture* as that term was then understood. It is the dialectic between the two—between jazz and Culture—that forms the subject of this article.

One can debate at great length the specific origins of the music we have come to know as jazz: *when* it first appeared, *where* it first appeared, *how* it was diffused, *what* its relationships to other forms of American music were. For my purposes, it is sufficient to observe that roughly during those decades that spanned either side of the year 1900, that period we call the Turn of the Century, a music or musics that came to be known as jazz appeared in and were quickly diffused throughout the United States at the same time that a phenomenon known as Culture (with a capital C) made its appearance.

America emerged from the 19th century with most of the cultural structures that have become familiar to us in place, or in the process of being put into place. Adjectival categories were created to box and identify expressive culture: High, Low, Highbrow, Lowbrow, Popular. Though these terms lacked, and continue to lack, any genuine precision, they were utilized with some consistency though always with a degree of confusion since the terms themselves were confusing and deceptive. That is, Popular Culture, in spite of its name, did not have to be truly *popular* in order to win the title. It merely had to be considered to be of little worth aesthetically, for that became the chief criterion: the cultural categories that became fixed around the turn of the century were aesthetic and judgmental rather than descriptive terms. So pervasive did this system of adjectival boxes become, that from the early years of this century, if one used the word "culture" by itself, it was *assumed* to carry the adjective "high" with it. The notion of culture was lifted out of the surrounding world into the universe of gentility. The word "culture" became equated with the word "refinement," which in fact was precisely the definition it carried in the single-word definition pocket dictionaries popular at the turn of the century.[1]

Thus at approximately the same time, two new words—or more accurately, two older words with new meanings—came into general usage. Their dual appearance is significant because the two—Culture and Jazz—helped to define one another. That is, they served as convenient polar points, as antitheses. One could understand what Culture was by looking at the characteristics of jazz and reversing them.

Jazz was, or at least seemed to be, the new product of a new age; Culture was, or at least seemed to be, traditional—the creation of centuries.

Jazz was raucous, discordant; Culture was harmonious, embodying order and reason.

Jazz was accessible, spontaneous; Culture was exclusive, complex, available only through hard study and training.

Jazz was openly an *interactive*, participatory music in which the audience played an important role, to the extent that the line between audience and performers was often obscured. Culture built those lines painstakingly, establishing boundaries that relegated the audience to a primarily passive role, listening to, or looking at the creations of true artists. Culture increased the gap between the creator and the audience, jazz narrowed that gap. Jazz was frequently played in the midst of noisy, hand-clapping, foot-stomping, dancing and gyrating audiences. Those who came to witness Culture in art museums, symphonic halls, opera houses, learned what Richard Sennett has called "Silence in the face of Art."[2]

If jazz didn't obliterate the line between composer and performer, at the very least it rendered that line hazy. Culture upheld the differentiation between the composer and the performer and insisted that the performer take no liberties with the work of the creator, who in Culture assumed a central, often a sacred, position. Jazz was a performer's art; Culture a composer's art.

Jazz seemed uniquely American, an artistic form that, if Frederick Jackson Turner and his followers had only known it, might have reinforced their notions of indigenous American development and divergence from the Old World. Culture was Eurocentric—convinced that the best and noblest were the products of the Old World which the United States had to learn to emulate.

These two very different entities were expressions of radically divergent impulses in America. Culture was the product of that side of ourselves that craved order, stability, definition. It was the expression of a colonial side of ourselves that we have not done nearly enough to understand. I am convinced that we would know ourselves better if we understood our past more firmly as the history of a people who attained political and economic independence long before we attained cultural independence. Culturally we remained, to a much larger extent than we have yet recognized, a colonized people attempting to define itself in the shadow of the former imperial power. Jazz was an expression of that other side of ourselves that strove to recognize the positive aspects of our newness and our heterogeneity; that learned to be comfortable with the fact that a significant part of our heritage derived from Africa and other non-European sources; and that recognized in the various syncretized cultures that became so characteristic of the United States an embarrassing weakness but a dynamic source of strength.

It is impossible, then, to understand the place jazz occupied in America—at least until the years after World War II—without understanding that its emergence as a distinct music in the larger culture paralleled the emergence of a hierarchized concept of Culture with its many neat but never precisely defined adjectival boxes and categories.

In the *Edinburgh Review* in 1820 the Reverend Sydney Smith asked a question that was to haunt a substantial number of influential Americans for the remainder of the 19th century: "In the four quarters of the globe, who reads an American book? or goes to an American play? or looks at an American picture or statue?"[3] Who, Smith was demanding, paid any attention to American culture at all? The question was quickly converted into an even more tortured query: *was* there an American culture worth paying attention to in the first place? As the century progressed an impressive number of Americans asked themselves some version of this question.

In his 1879 biography of Nathaniel Hawthorne, Henry James created his famous litany of American cultural deficiencies which read in part: "no cathedrals, nor abbeys, nor little Norman churches; no great Universities nor public schools—no Oxford, nor Eton, nor Harrow; no literature, no novels, no museums, no pictures." Americans, James concluded, had "the elements of modern man with *culture* quite left out."[4]

Culture was quite left out because it required standards and authority of a kind that was difficult to find in a country with America's leveling, practical tendencies. The real peril America faced, "The Outlook" declared in 1893, was not a dearth of art but the acceptance of inferior standards. "We are in danger of exalting the average man, and rejoicing in . . . mediocrity."[5]

Increasingly, in the closing decades of the 19th century the concept of culture took on hierarchical connotations along the lines of Matthew Arnold's definition of culture—"the best that has been thought and known in the world."[6] This practice of distinguishing "culture" from lesser forms of expression became so common that by 1915 Van Wyck Brooks concluded that between the highbrow and the lowbrow "there is no community, no genial middle ground."[7]

The new concept of Culture that became powerful in these years took its inspiration and its standards from Europe as the young Charles Ives discovered when he attempted to inject American idioms into his Second Symphony, which he completed in 1901 or 1902. "Some of the themes in this symphony suggest Gospel Hymns and Steve Foster," Ives noted. "Some nice people, whenever they hear the words 'Gospel Hymns' or 'Stephen Foster,' say 'Mercy Me,!' and a little high-brow smile creeps over their brow—'Can't you get something better than that in a symphony?' "[8]

So little did the arbiters of musical taste think of their own country's contributions that in 1884, when the critic Richard Grant White was invited to write a history of American music, he refused for lack of an American music to write about. American psalmbook-makers and singing-school teachers were, White declared, "about as much in place in the history of musical art as a critical discussion of the whooping of Indians would be."[9]

There were some who began to see in American and, particularly, Afro-American folk music evidence of an indigenous American musical tradition. After hearing the Jubilee Singers in 1897, Mark Twain wrote a friend, "I think that in the Jubilees and their songs America has produced the perfectest flower of the ages; and I wish it were a foreign product, so that she would worship it and lavish money on it and go properly crazy over it."[10] The most famous of these voices was that of the Czech composer Antonín Dvořák, who was teaching and composing in the United States when he made his striking statement in 1893:

> I am now satisfied that the future music of this country must be founded upon what are called the negro melodies. This must be the real foundation of any serious and original school of composition to be developed in the United States.[11]

These notions flew too directly in the face of the comfortable evolutionary predispositions of the day which simply ruled out the possibility that those at the top of society had anything to learn from the "plantation melodies" of Afro-Americans firmly ensconced in "the lowest strata of society." In the 1890s the Boston critic William Apthorp declared that such compositions as Dvořák's *New World Symphony* and Edward MacDowell's *Indian Suite* were futile attempts "to make civilized music by civilized methods out of essentially barbaric material," resulting in "a mere apotheosis of ugliness, distorted forms, and barbarous expression."[12]

These were the voices that prevailed. John Philip Sousa, America's preeminent bandmaster at the turn of the century, complained of the "artistic snobbery" that had plagued his career. "Notwithstanding the credo of musical snobs," he asserted, " 'popular' does not necessarily mean 'vulgar' or 'ephemeral.' " To touch "the public heart" required inspiration and the "stamp of genius." "Many an immortal tune has been born in the stable or the cottonfield. *Turkey in the Straw* is a magic melody; anyone should be proud of having written it, but, for musical high-brows, I suppose the thing is declassée. It came not from a European composer but from an unknown negro minstrel."[13] The stamp of European approval remained the *sine qua non* for true culture. "Either we do not believe in our own opinions, or we feel that we do not know enough to make them," *Putnam's Magazine* complained. "How long will it be," it asked wistfully, "before London applauds *because* New York approves?"[14] Thomas Wentworth Higginson agreed. The discussion over whether the United States had a distinct culture would cease, he insisted, "when Europe comes to America for culture, instead of America's thronging to Europe."[15]

The primary obstacle to the emergence of a worthy American music, Frederick Nast asserted in 1881, "lies in the diverse character of our population. . . . American music can not be expected until the present discordant elements are merged into a homogeneous people."[16] It was obvious under whose auspices the "merger" was to take place. In 1898 Sidney Lanier argued that it was time for

Americans to move back "into the presence of the Fathers" by adding the study of Old English to that of Greek and Latin, and by reading not just Homer but Beowulf. "Our literature needs Anglo-Saxon iron; there is no ruddiness in its cheeks, and everywhere a clear lack of the red corpuscles."[17] American society, Henry Adams observed in his autobiography, "offered the profile of a long, straggling caravan, stretching loosely towards the prairies, its few score of leaders far in advance and its millions of immigrants, negroes, and Indians far in the rear, somewhere in archaic time."[18]

It should hardly surprise us that such attitudes informed the adjectival categories created in the late 19th and early 20th centuries to define types of culture. "Highbrow," first used in the 1880s to describe intellectual or aesthetic superiority, and "lowbrow," first used shortly after 1900 to mean someone or something neither "highly intellectual" or "aesthetically refined," were not new terms; they were derived from the phrenological terms "highbrowed" and "lowbrowed" which were prominently featured in the 19th-century practice of determining intelligence and racial types by measuring cranial shapes and capacities. A familiar illustration of the period depicted the distinctions between the lowbrowed Ape and the increasingly higher brows of the "Human Idiot," the "Bushman," the "Uncultivated," the "Improved," the "Civilized," the "Enlightened," and, finally, the "Caucasian," with the highest brow of all. The categorization did not end this broadly, of course, for within the Caucasian circle there were distinctions to be made: the closer to Western and Northern Europe a people came, the higher their brows extended. From the time of their formulation, such cultural categories as Highbrow and Lowbrow were openly associated with and designed to preserve, nurture, and extend the cultural history and values of a particular group of peoples in a specific historical context.[19]

It was into this world of rapidly accelerating cultural hierarchy that jazz was born or at least in which it became a widely diffused music. In 1918 the *New Orleans Times-Picayune* described the "many mansions in the houses of the muses." There was the "great assembly hall of melody" where "most of us take our seats," while a smaller number pass on to the "inner sanctuaries of harmony" where "nearly all the truly great music is enjoyed." Finally, there was still one more apartment

> down in the basement, a kind of servants' hall of rhythm. It is there we hear the hum of the Indian dance, the throb of the Oriental tambourines and kettledrums, the clatter of the clogs, the click of Slavic heels, the thumpty-tumpty of the negro banjo, and, in fact, the native dances of the world.

Rhythm, though often associated with melody and harmony, "is not necessarily music," the *Times-Picayune* instructed its readers. Indeed, when rhythm took such forms as ragtime or jazz it constituted an "atrocity in polite society, and . . . we should make it a point of civic honor to suppress it. Its musical value is nil, and its possibilities of harm are great."[20]

This was the paradigmatic response the upholders of "Culture" accorded jazz in the decades in which it was establishing itself as a familiar form of American music. As early as 1901 the American Federation of Musicians ordered their members to refrain from playing ragtime: "The musicians know what is good, and if the people don't, we will have to teach them."[21] On a January Sunday in 1922 the Reverend Dr. Percy Stickney Grant used his pulpit in New York's Episcopal Church of the Ascension on Fifth Avenue to advise his parishioners that jazz "is retrogression. It is going to the African jungle for our music. It is a savage crash and bang."[22] Jazz, the *New York Times* editorialized in 1924,

> is to real music exactly what most of the "new poetry," so-called, is to real poetry. Both are without the structure and form essential to music and poetry alike, and both are the products, not of innovators, but of incompetents. . . . Jazz, especially when it depends much on that ghastly instrument, the saxophone, offends people with musical taste already formed, and it prevents the formation of musical taste by others.[23]

The *Times* returned to the subject again and again insisting that jazz "is merely a return to the humming, hand-clapping, or tomtom beating of savages."[24]

A writer in *Collier's* dismissed jazz as "trash" played on "lowbrow instruments."[25] Once America regained its soul, Rabbi Stephen Wise proclaimed, jazz "will be relegated to the dark and scarlet haunts whence it came and whither unwept it will return."[26] Condemnation by analogy became a favorite sport. Jazz, various critics insisted, bore the same relationship to classical music as a limerick did to poetry, or a farmhouse to a cathedral, or a burlesque show to legitimate drama.[27] Jazz was attacked not only for returning civilized people to the jungles of barbarism but also for expressing the mechanistic sterility of modern urban life. Jazz, the composer and teacher Daniel Gregory Mason charged, "is so perfectly adapted to robots that the one could be deduced from the other. Jazz is thus the exact musical reflection of modern capitalistic industrialism."[28] H. L. Mencken put it more succinctly when he described jazz as the "sound of riveting."[29]

The denigration of jazz was not confined to white critics. Jazz music and musicians bordered too closely upon the racial stereotypes of rhythmic, pulsating, uninhibited blacks for many race leaders. Maud Cuney-Hare, the music editor of *The Crisis*, criticized the "common combination of unlovely tones and suggestive lyrics" that characterized much of jazz. "Music should sound, not screech; Music should cry, not howl; Music should weep, not bawl; Music should implore, not whine."[30] The advice that Dave Peyton, the music critic for the politically militant *Chicago Defender*, gave to aspiring pianists was to "put two or three hours a day on your scale work, [and] stay away from jazz music." Peyton complained consistently that "heretofore our orchestras have confined themselves to hot jazzy tunes" too exclusively and that in general blacks remained too firmly within their own musical universe:

> We have played music as we think it should be played without trying to find out if we are playing it correctly. So few of us have the time to visit the grand symphony orchestras, the de luxe picture houses and other places where things musically are done correctly.[31]

Lucien H. White, the music critic for the Harlem paper, *New York Age*, excoriated jazz as music "producing a conglomerate mixture of dissonances, with a swing and a lilt appealing only to the lover of sensuous and debasing emotions." White joined forces with the National Association of Negro Musicians, Hampton Institute's journal *The Southern Workman*, and many prominent blacks in attacking those who played jazz versions of the old spirituals. A Jewish musician who dared to transform the Hebrew's despairing cry *Eli, Eli* into a jazz number "would be cast out by his people as unorthodox and unclean," White charged. So should it be with black musicians who transgressed "upon the outpourings of the racial heart when it was wrung and torn with sorrow and distress."[32] There was comparable anger on the part of whites when jazz musicians utilized themes from classical composers. Frank Damrosch was typical in denouncing the "outrage on beautiful music" perpetrated by jazz musicians who were guilty of "stealing phrases from the classic composers and vulgarizing them."[33] Jazz musicians, a critic warned, had better "keep their dirty paws off their betters."[34] Throughout the early history of jazz, its practitioners were treated consistently as low-caste defilers of the clean and sacred classic music of both the white and the black societies they inhabited.

Not all the reactions to jazz were necessarily negative. In 1924 Leopold Stokowski, the conductor of the Philadelphia Orchestra, attributed the "new vitality" of jazz to black musicians: "They have an open mind, and unbiased outlook. They are not hampered by traditions or conventions, and with their new ideas, their constant experiments, they are causing new blood to flow in the veins of music."[35] A number of critics praised jazz as a perfect idiom for articulating personal feelings. In one of the first books devoted exclusively to jazz, Henry Osgood called it "a protest against . . . the monotony of life . . . an attempt at individual expression."[36] Interestingly, jazz was also lauded for being a form of *national* expression. "No matter what is said about it," the *Literary Digest* proclaimed, "jazz is a native product. . . . Jazz is completely American."[37] In his influential *The Seven Lively Arts*, Gilbert Seldes called jazz "our characteristic expressions," which appeared to agree with those who felt it was "about the only native music worth listening to in America," and, with the mixed admiration and condescension characteristic of the time, praised black Americans for articulating and keeping alive "something which underlies a great deal of America—our independence, our carelessness, our frankness, and gaiety."[38]

There was no real contradiction between these apparently divergent sets of views. In fact, jazz was often praised for possessing precisely those characteristics that made it anathema to those who condemned it: it was praised *and* criticized for being innovative and breaking with tradition. It was praised *and* criticized for being a form of culture expressing the id, the repressed or suppressed feelings of the individual, rather than submitting to the organized discipline of the superego which enforced the attitudes and values of the bourgeois culture. It was praised *and* criticized for breaking out of the tight circle of obeisance to Eurocentric cultural forms and giving expression to indigenous American attitudes articulated through indigenous American creative structures. It was, in short, praised *and* criticized for being almost completely out of phase with the period's concept of Culture.

It was this quality of course that made jazz one of those houses of refuge in the 1920s for individuals who felt alienated from the central culture. We have come to understand the importance of such actual and symbolic cultural oases as Paris and Greenwich Village for those who sought relief from the overwhelming sense of Civilization in the post–World War I years. We need to continue to develop our understanding of the ways in which Afro-American culture, and especially jazz, served as a crucial alternative as well.

As I have argued elsewhere, many of those who found jazz and blues stimulating and attractive in the 1920s and 1930s did so because these musical forms seemed to promise them greater freedom of expression, both artistically and personally. This was especially true of young people, who, Louis Armstrong observed, were among the most numerous and avid followers of the bands he played with. In the early 1920s, a group of young whites who were born or raised in and around Chicago and who were to become well-known jazz musicians—Benny Goodman, Bud Freeman, Dave Tough, Eddie Condon, Milton "Mezz" Mezzrow, Gene Krupa, Muggsy Spanier, Jimmy McPartland, Frank Teschemacher, Joe Sullivan, George Wettling—were stunned by the music of such black jazzmen as Joe Oliver, Jimmie Noone, Johnny and Baby Dodds, and Louis Armstrong, all of whom were then playing in clubs on Chicago's South Side. These white youngsters spoke about jazz, Condon recalled, "as if it were a new religion just come from Jerusalem."[39]

The analogy was not far-fetched: in their autobiographies these musicians often described what amounted to conversion experiences. In 1924 Eddie Condon, Jimmy McPartland, and Bud Freeman dropped in to a club where Joe Oliver's band was playing: "Oliver lifted his horn and the first blast of Canal Street Blues hit me," Condon has written.

> It was hypnosis at first hearing. Everyone was playing what he wanted to play and it was all mixed together as if someone had planned it with a set of micrometer calipers; notes I had never heard were peeling off the edges and dropping through the middle; there was a tone from the trumpets like warm rain on a cold day. Freeman and McPartland and I were immobilized; the music poured into us like daylight running down a dark hole.[40]

From these encounters the young white musicians absorbed a new means of expressing their musical individuality. But it was more than musical individuality; it was also the cultural freedom, the ability to be and express themselves—which they associated with jazz—that many of these young musicians found attractive. World War I was over, Hoagy Carmichael recalled, but the rebellion against "the accepted, the proper and the old" was just beginning. "And for us jazz articulated. . . . It said what we wanted to say."[41]

This view was not confined to jazz musicians. Jazz, Sigmund Spaeth wrote in 1928, "is a distortion of the conventional, a revolt against tradition, a deliberate twisting of established formulas."[42] The vogue of jazz, Alain Locke insisted, should be regarded as the symptom of a profound cultural unrest and change, first a reaction from Puritan repressions and then an escape from the tensions and monotonies of a machine-ridden, extroverted form of civilization.[43]

For younger black musicians, especially those whose careers began in the late 1930s and 1940s, jazz performed many of the same functions. "Jazz has always been a music of integration," the saxophonist Sonny Rollins commented some years later.

> Jazz was not just a music; it was a social force in this country, and it was talking about freedom and people enjoying things for what they are and not having to worry about whether they were supposed to be white, black, and all this stuff. Jazz has always been the music that had this kind of spirit.[44]

For black musicians jazz also provided a sense of power and control, a sense of meaning and direction, in a world that often seemed anarchic. In his autobiography Sidney Bechet thought about the ups and downs of his life and concluded: "The onliest thing I've ever been sure of how it was going is the music; that's something a man can make himself if he has the feeling."[45] In the 1930s a young William Dixon looked around his neighborhood and concluded that even in Harlem whites were everywhere in control; "it did seem, to a little boy, that these white people *really* owned everything. But that wasn't entirely true. They didn't own the music that I heard played."[46]

The striking thing about jazz is the extent to which it symbolized revolt wherever it became established. In Denmark, according to Erik Wiedemann, "From 1933 on advocating jazz became part of the anti-fascist culture-radical movement."[47] Marshall Stearns, after lecturing at the Zagreb Conservatory of Music in 1956, reported that the Yugoslav students and faculty agreed that "jazz symbolized an element of unconscious protest which cut through the pretenses of tradition and authority."[48] As recently as March 1987, two leaders of the Jazz Section of the Czech Musicians' Union were sentenced to jail for "unauthorized" activities. Karel Srp, who was not released until January 1988, was forced to spend 20 days in solitary confinement in a cell whose floor was covered with excrement.[49] Thus the phenomenon of jazz as a potent and potentially dangerous form of alternative culture became well established throughout the world.

But the primary impact jazz had was not as a form of revolt; it was as a style of music, a medium of culture. That this music which was characterized as vulgar at best and as harmful trash at worst by the Guardians of Culture and that for a long time was appreciated largely by those on the margins of American society; that this form of music which seemed so firmly ensconced on the American cultural periphery should become the most widely identifiable and emulated symbol of American culture throughout the world by the mid-20th century is one of the more arresting paradoxes of modern American history. For so many decades the Keepers of the Flame had predicted that when Europe took an interest in our expressive arts as well as in our machine shops, that when Europe looked to the United States for culture as well as for technology, then and only then would we know we had truly arrived as an equal entity. And, as they hoped, Europe ultimately did come to America for culture—and the culture they came for was jazz.

"It required the stubbornness of Europeans," the Frenchman Phillipe Adler wrote in 1976, "to convince America that she had . . . given birth to one of the most dazzling arts of the twentieth century."[50] This is not to say that there was universal acceptance of jazz across the Atlantic. Many of the responses were familiar: in England in the 1920s Harold Spender worried that music in the United States might be "submerged by the aboriginal music of the negro."[51] In France the poet Georges Duhamel dismissed jazz as "a triumph of barbaric folly."[52]

Nevertheless, jazz was accorded a more positive critical reception in Europe during those early years than it was in its own country. "Jazz is a philosophy of the world, and therefore to be taken seriously," the German critic George Barthelme wrote in a Cologne newspaper in 1919. "Jazz is the expression of a *Kultur* epoch. . . . Jazz is a musical revelation, a religion, a philosophy of the world, just like Expressionism and Impressionism."[53] Jazz, the Austrian musician Ernst Krenek maintained, "has revived the art of improvisation to an extent unknown by serious musicians since . . . the contrapuntal extemporization of the fifteenth century."[54] In France Hughes Panassié placed the jazz band on a higher plane than the symphony orchestra, for while the latter "functions only as a transmitter," the musicians in jazz "are *creators*, as well."[55]

In the United States, the types of jazz that were most easily and widely accepted initially were the filtered and hybridized versions that created less cultural dissonance. Listening to Paul Whiteman's jazz band in 1926 Edmund Wilson complained of the extent to which Whiteman had "refined and disciplined his orchestra" and thus reduced the music he was playing "to an abstract pattern."[56] The degree to which blacks could be left out of this musical equation was stunning. In the mid-1920s the composer John Alden Carpenter praised jazz as "the first art innovation originating in America to be accepted seriously in Europe," and predicted that "the musical historian of the year 2,000 A.D. will find the birthday of American music and that of Irving Berlin to have been the same."[57] After hearing the black pianist Earl Hines perform, Paul Whiteman went up to him and commented wistfully: "If you were only white."[58] For all her dislike of jazz, Maud Cuney-Hare disliked preemption even more. "Just as the white minstrels blackened their faces and made use of the Negro idiom," she complained in the 1930s, "so have white orchestral players today usurped the Negro in Jazz entertainment."[59]

But here too the preemption was limited by the fact that jazz was not for long an exclusively *American* affair. Eric Hobsbawm has written of the "extraordinary expansion" of jazz "which has practically no cultural parallel for speed and scope except the early expansion of Mohammedanism."[60] By the mid-20th century jazz was no longer exclusively American any more than classical music was exclusively European. Americans found that one of the results of creating a truly international culture is that you lose control over the criteria of judgment and categorization. The recognition that black musicians received throughout the world had its effect in their own country as well.

If André Levinson's declaration in the *Theatre Arts Monthly* in 1927 that "jazz is henceforth admitted into the hierarchy of the arts" was premature, and it was, it certainly understood the direction American culture was taking.[61] Transitions are by definition almost impossible to identify with precision; they are most often gradual and cumulative. As early as 1925 the great apostle of classical music, the *Times'* critic, W. J. Henderson, admitted that jazz was the only original American music not based on European models, which explained why Europe had stretched out its arms not toward the American composers of art music but to ragtime and jazz.[62] Though there were others who perceived what Henderson did, I would argue that for most Americans the decisive transitional moment was not until after World War II, when the cultural significance of jazz could no longer be denied. The highly successful tours of musicians like Dizzy Gillespie, Benny Goodman, and Louis Armstrong through Asia, the Middle East, and Africa, as well as Europe, brought national attention to the stature of jazz music, *American* jazz music, *Afro-American* jazz music, throughout the world.

It did not take the State Department long to understand that the visit of a musician like Gillespie to Pakistan stimulated interest not only in jazz but in American culture in general.[63] "United States Has Secret Sonic Weapon—Jazz," a *New York Times* headline proclaimed in 1955, and its subhead added: "Europe Falls Captive as Crowds Riot to Hear Dixieland." What most surprised the *Times* reporter was not that jazz was popular but that it was taken so seriously. The European approach, he noted, "is what most Americans would call a 'long-haired approach.' They like to contemplate it, dissect it, take it apart to see what makes it what it is." He was informed by one European fan that jazz contained a tension between musical discipline and individual expression which "comes close to symbolizing the conditions under which people of the atomic age live." Jazz, he was told in Switzerland, "is not just an art. It is a way of life." To his own surprise the reporter concluded that "American jazz has now become a universal language."[64] The accumulation of these experiences ultimately made it common for national magazines to say matter-of-factly, as *Newsweek* did in 1973: "The U.S. wouldn't have an art form to call its own without jazz."[65]

All of this recognition did not mean the total extinction of the easy responses of the past which had either denigrated jazz or explained its accomplishments away. Amidst the tributes there was still condescension. In his *Music in American Life* Jacques Barzun could state that jazz "is our one contribution to music that Europe knows about and honors us for," even as he ranked it with "sports and philately as the realm of the self-made expert," spoke darkly of its characteristic "repetition and the excitement that precedes narcosis," and concluded that "jazz is more symptom and pastime than unperishable utterance."[66] Nor had Americans fully outgrown the convenient racial explanations for jazz that denied blacks any credit for hard work, application, or talent in acquiring musical skills, which were generally attributed to genes rather than genius. As late as 1974 a man of Virgil Thomson's stature could marvel at black music's ability to incorporate every imaginable form of music: "European classical composition, Anglo-Saxon folklore, Hispanic dance meters, hymns, jungle drums, the German lied, Italian opera, all are foods for the insatiable black hunger," he wrote, and then, whether he intended to or not, he nullified his tribute by observing: "As if inside all U.S. blacks there were, and just maybe there really is, some ancient and African enzyme, voracious for digesting whatever it encounters in the way of sound."[67]

To say that by our time jazz has become part of that entity we call art is only part of the truth. Jazz in fact is one of those forces that have helped to transform our sense of art and culture. In the early 1930s the Englishman Constant Lambert argued that jazz was the first music "to bridge the gap between highbrow and low-brow successfully."[68] One could go further and perceive jazz as a music that in fact bridged the gap between all of the categories that divided culture; a music that found its way through the fences we use to separate genres of expressive culture from one another. When Duke Ellington predicted that, "Soon it'll all be just music; you won't have to say whether it's jazz or not, just whether you like it," he was articulating a feeling with deep roots in the jazz community.[69] "There is no point in talking about different kinds of jazz," Charlie Parker told a reporter. "The most important thing for us is to have our efforts accepted as music." When he was asked about the differences between jazz and European "art" music, Parker's answer was characteristic: "There is no boundary line to art."[70] "We never labeled the music," the drummer Kenny Clarke told an interviewer. "It was just modern music. . . . We wouldn't call it anything, really, just music."[71] In his memoirs, Dizzy Gillespie was willing to recognize only two categories of music: "there's only good and bad."[72]

From the beginning jazz musicians refused to limit themselves; they reached out to embrace the themes, the techniques, the idioms of any music they found appealing and they did so with a minimum of fuss or comment. As early as the second decade of this century, the stride pianist James P. Johnson, who was to have a major influence upon Fats Waller and Duke Ellington, was paying little attention to the boundary lines: "From listening to classical piano records and concerts . . . I would learn concert effects and build them into blues and rags. . . . When playing a heavy stomp, I'd soften it right down, then I'd make an abrupt change like I heard Beethoven do in a sonata."[73] When the pianist Earl Hines discussed the formative influences upon his music, he included both the Baptist church and Chopin.[74] When Gil Evans was asked if the *Sketches of Spain* score he wrote for Miles Davis, which was influenced by the Spanish composers Joaquin Rodrigo and Manuel de Falla, was classical or jazz music, he responded: "That's a merchandiser's problem, not mine."[75] When Miles Davis was asked the same question, he responded similarly: "It's music."[76]

None of this is to suggest that jazz musicians merely wanted to blend into the larger pool of musicians. They understood they had something special to contribute to the musical world. When the drummer Max Roach enrolled in the Manhattan School of Music and the trumpeter Kenny Dorham entered New York University, they were both told that they approached their instruments incorrectly. Roach understood that this was a reflection of the differences between jazz and classical music. Conservatories taught brass players a sonority meant to allow them to blend with other instruments while jazz musicians learned to seek a distinctive voice geared to the fact that in jazz individual interpretation is far more central than in classical music.[77] This is precisely what Benny Goodman was trying to express when he discussed his double life as a jazz musician and a classical clarinetist. "Expression," he maintained, was the great difference between the two kinds of music: "The greatest exponents of jazz are those with the most originality in ideas plus the technique to express them. In classical music . . . the musician must try and see into the composer's mind and play the way he believes the composer meant the piece to be played."[78] Mezz Mezzrow said the same thing less politely: "to us . . . a guy composed *as* he played, the creating and performing took place at the same time—and we kept thinking what a drag it must be for any musician with spirit to have to sit in on a symphonic assembly-line."[79]

For black musicians especially, jazz was also a form of communal expression. Even as formally trained a musician as John Lewis of the Modern Jazz Quartet could insist, "We have to keep going back to the goldmine. I mean the folk music, the blues and things that are related to it."[80] When the contemporary composer John Cage criticized jazz music for relying too heavily on emotions, the pianist Cecil Taylor refused to listen:

> He doesn't have the right to make any comment about jazz, nor would Stravinsky. . . . I've spent years in school learning about European music and its traditions, but these cats don't know a thing about Harlem except that it's there. . . . They never subject themselves to, like, what are Louis Armstrong's criteria for beauty, and until they do that, then I'm not interested in what they have to say. Because they simply don't recognize the criteria.[81]

In their refusal to be governed by the categorical orthodoxies that prevailed, in their unwillingness to make absolute distinctions between the vernacular and classical traditions, in their insistence that they were just attempting to play *music* and just wanted to be accepted as musicians, in their determination to utilize the *entire* Western tradition, as well as other cultural traditions, jazz musicians were revolutionizing not only music but also the concept of culture. No one has put this better, again and again, than Duke Ellington, as he did in 1957 when he attempted to explain the impact that the Shakespeare Theatre in Stratford, Ontario, had upon his composition *Such Sweet Thunder*, a title he took from *A Midsummer Night's Dream*: "I never heard so musical a discord, such sweet thunder" [IV, 1]:

> I have a great sympathy with Shakespeare because it seems to me that strong similarities can be established between a jazz performance and the production of a Shakespeare play—similarities between the producers, the artists, and the audiences.
>
> There is an increasing interrelationship between the adherents to art forms in various fields. . . . It is becoming increasingly difficult to decide where jazz starts or where it stops, where Tin Pan Alley begins and jazz ends, or even where the borderline lies between classical music and jazz. . . . I suspect that if Shakespeare were alive today, he might be a jazz fan himself—he'd appreciate the combination of team spirit and informality, of academic knowledge and humor.[82]

Ellington's outlook can help us to find our way amidst and through the cultural boxes and categories and fences with which we have so unnecessarily burdened ourselves. To understand what Americans since the turn of the century thought of jazz is crucial if we are to understand how they reacted to it or how the music and its practitioners were treated. But if we are to comprehend American culture, we can no longer afford to assume jazz really *was* what many Americans thought it was. We have to make that empathetic leap and allow ourselves to see jazz as an integral vibrant part of American culture throughout this century; to realize that before even the most prescient Europeans and long before any appreciable number of Americans thought of jazz as an indigenous American contribution to the culture of the world, jazz was precisely that. Jazz tells us much about what was original and dynamic in American culture even as it reveals to what extent our culture, or more correctly, our cultural attitudes had not yet weaned themselves from the old colonial patterns of the past. Jazz has much to tell us about our history and, indeed, much to tell us about ourselves if only we have the wisdom and the skill to listen to it and learn from it.

NOTES

1. Lawrence W. Levine, *Highbrow/Lowbrow: The Emergence of Cultural Hierarchy in America* (Cambridge, Mass., 1988), 224–225.

2. Richard Sennett, *The Fall of Public Man* (New York, 1978), 230, 261.

3. Sydney Smith, "Review of Adam Seybert, Statistical Annals of the United States of America," *Edinburgh Review* 33 (1820):79–80.

4. Henry James, *Hawthorne* (1879; New York, 1967), 34–35; Marc Pachter, "American Cosmopolitanism, 1870–1910," in *Impressions of a Gilded Age: The American Fin de Siècle*, eds. Marc Chenetier and Rob Kroes (Amsterdam, 1983), 29.

5. "Criticism in America," *The Outlook* 48 (1893):990.

6. Matthew Arnold, *Culture and Anarchy* (New York, 1875), 44–47.

7. Van Wyck Brooks, *America's Coming-of-Age* (New York, 1915), 6–7.

8. Charles E. Ives, *Memos*, ed. John Kirkpatrick (New York, 1972), 52, 71, 131–32.

9. Joseph A. Mussulman, *Music in the Cultured Generation: A Social History of Music in America* (Evanston, Ill., 1985), 109.

10. Ives, *Memos*, 88–89.

11. Antonín Dvořák, "Real Value of Negro Melodies," *New York Herald*, 21 May 1893.

12. Mussulman, *Music in the Cultured Generation*, 115.

13. John Philip Sousa, *Marching Along: Recollections of Men, Women and Music* (Boston, 1928), 341.

14. "Our Window," *Putnam's Magazine* 10 (1857):133.

15. Thomas Wentworth Higginson, "A Plea for Culture," *Atlantic Monthly* 19 (1867):33.

16. Mussulman, *Music in the Cultured Generation*, 106.

17. Sidney Lanier, "The Proper Basis of English Culture," *Atlantic Monthly* 82 (1898):165–74.

18. Henry Adams, *The Education of Henry Adams* (1918; New York, 1931), 237.

19. Levine, *Highbrow/Lowbrow*, 221–23.

20. "Jass and Jassism," *New Orleans Times-Picayune*, 20 June 1918.

21. Macdonald Smith Moore, *Yankee Blues: Musical Culture and American Identity* (Bloomington, 1985), 75.

22. "Rector Calls Jazz National Anthem," *New York Times*, 30 January 1922.

23. "A Subject of Serious Study," *New York Times*, 8 October 1924.

24. "His Opinion Will Not Be Accepted," *New York Times*, 13 November 1924.

25. Robert Haven Schauffler, "Jazz May Be Lowbrow, But—," *Collier's* 72 (1928):10.

26. "Where Is Jazz Leading America?: Part II of a Symposium," *The Etude* 42 (1924):595.

27. Don Knowlton, "The Anatomy of Jazz," *Harper's* 152 (1924):578; *The Etude* 42 (1924):593.

28. Moore, *Yankee Blues*, 106.

29. *Ibid.*, 108.

30. Maude Cuney-Hare, *Negro Musicians and Their Music* (Washington, D.C., 1936), 156.

31. Dave Peyton, "The Musical Bunch," *Chicago Defender*, 28 January 1928.

32. Lucien H. White, *New York Age*, 23 April, 7 May, 23 July 1921, 8 July 1922; Richard Aldrich, "Drawing a Line for Jazz," *New York Times*, 10 December 1922, sec. VIII.

33. "Where Is Jazz Leading America?: Opinions of Famous Men and Women in and out of Music," *The Etude* 42 (1924):518.

34. Moore, *Yankee Blues*, 90.

35. "Where Is Jazz Leading America?," 595.

36. Henry O. Osgood, *So This Is Jazz!* (Boston, 1926), 247.

37. "Buying American in Music," *Literary Digest* 118 (1934):24.

38. Gilbert Seldes, *The Seven Lively Arts* (New York, 1924), 83–84, 95–97.

39. Lawrence W. Levine, *Black Culture and Black Consciousness: Afro-American Folk Thought from Slavery to Freedom* (New York, 1977), 294.

40. *Ibid.*, 294–95.

41. *Ibid.*, 295.

42. Benjamin Brawley, *The Negro Genius* (New York, 1937), 10.

43. Alain Locke, *The Negro and His Music* (Washington, D.C., 1936), 88.

44. Ira Gitler, *Swing to Bop: An Oral History of the Transition in Jazz in the 1940s* (New York, 1985), 303, 311.

45. Sidney Bechet, *Treat It Gentle* (New York, 1960), 102.

46. William R. Dixon, "The Music in Harlem," in *Harlem: A Community in Transition*, ed. John Henrik Clarke (New York, 1964), 70; emphasis in original.

47. Erik Wiedemann, *Jazz i Danmark—ityverne, trediverne og fyrrerne* [Jazz in Denmark—Past, Present, and Future] (Copenhagen, 1985), 395.

48. Dizzy Gillespie with Al Fraser, *To Be, or Not . . . to Bop: Memoirs* (New York, 1979), 424 n.

49. Josef Skvorecky, "Jamming the Jazz Section," *New York Review of Books* 30 June 1988:40–42.

50. Phillipe Adler, "La Saga du Jazz," *L'Express* 17 May 1976:52–56.

51. George Harmon Knoles, *The Jazz Age Revisited: British Criticism of American Civilization During the 1920s* (New York, 1968), 120.

52. Georges Duhamel, *America the Menace: Scenes from the Life of the Future* (London, 1931), 121–22.

53. S. Frederick Starr, *Red and Hot: The Fate of Jazz in the Soviet Union, 1917–1980* (New York, 1983), 12.

54. Ernst Krenek, *Music Here and Now*, trans. Barthold Fles (New York, 1939), 260.

55. Hughes Panassié, *Hot Jazz: The Guide to Swing Music*, trans. Lyle and Eleanor Dowling (New York, 1936), 2; emphasis in original.

56. Edmund Wilson, *The American Earthquake: A Documentary of the Twenties and Thirties* (Garden City, 1958), 114.

57. Osgood, *So This Is Jazz!*, 249–50; *New York Times*, 11 August 1924.

58. Stanley Dance, *The World of Earl Hines* (New York, 1977), 74.

59. Cuney-Hare, *Negro Musicians and Their Music*, 148.

60. Francis Newton [Eric Hobsbawm], *The Jazz Scene* (Harmondsworth, Eng., 1961), 41.

61. Margaret Just Butcher, *The Negro in American Culture* (New York, 1966), 95.

62. "He Has No Scorn for Jazz?," *New York Times*, 28 January 1925.

63. U.S. State Department, *Semi-Annual Reports* (Washington, D.C., 1956), 5–6.

64. "United States Has Secret Sonic Weapon—Jazz," *New York Times*, 6 November 1955.

65. Margo Jefferson, "Jazz Is Back," *Newsweek* 82 (1973):52.

66. Jacques Barzun, *Music in American Life* (Garden City, N.Y., 1956), 85–86.

67. Virgil Thomson, *A Virgil Thomson Reader* (Boston, 1981), 498–500.

68. Constant Lambert, *Music Ho!: A Study of Music in Decline* (London, 1934), 206.

69. "Jazz Goes to College," *Time* 97 (1971):67.

70. Ross Russell, *Bird Lives!: The High Life and Hard Times of Charlie (Yardbird) Parker* (New York, 1973), 293.

71. Gillespie, *To Be, or Not . . .*, 142.

72. *Ibid.*, 492–93.

73. Scott E. Brown, *James P. Johnson: A Case of Mistaken Identity* (Metuchen, N.J., 1986), 86–87.

74. Dance, *The World of Earl Hines*, 14.

75. Gene Lees, "Jazz: Pop or Classical," *High Fidelity* 27 (1977):22.

76. Ian Carr, *Miles Davis: A Biography* (New York, 1982), 115.

77. Bernard Holland, "By Head or by Heart?: A Musician's Dilemma," *New York Times*, 30 May 1987.

78. Benny Goodman, "I Lead a Double Life," *House and Garden*, April 1951, p. 181.

79. Milton "Mezz" Mezzrow and Bernard Wolfe, *Really the Blues* (New York, 1946), 124–25; emphasis in original.

80. Carr, *Miles Davis*, 77.

81. A. B. Spellman, *Four Lives in the Bebop Business* (New York, 1966), 34.

82. Edward Kennedy Ellington, *Music Is My Mistress* (Garden City, N.Y., 1973), 192–93.

chapter 25

RALPH ELLISON

The Golden Age, Time Past

That which we do is what we are. That which we remember is, more often than not, that which we would like to have been, or that which we hope to be. Thus our memory and our identity are ever at odds, our history ever a tall tale told by inattentive idealists.

It has been a long time now, and not many remember how it was in the old days, not really. Not even those who were there to see and hear as it happened, who were pressed in the crowds beneath the dim rosy lights of the bar in the smoke-veiled room, and who shared, night after night, the mysterious spell created by the talk, the laughter, grease paint, powder, perfume, sweat, alcohol and food—all blended and simmering, like a stew on the restaurant range, and brought to a sustained moment of elusive meaning by the timbres and accents of musical instruments locked in passionate recitative. It has been too long now, some seventeen years.

Above the bandstand there later appeared a mural depicting a group of jazzmen holding a jam session in a narrow Harlem bedroom. While an exhausted girl with shapely legs sleeps on her stomach in a big brass bed, they bend to their music in a quiet concatenation of unheard sound: a trumpeter, a guitarist, a clarinetist, a drummer, their only audience a small, cock-eared dog. The clarinetist is white. The guitarist strums with an enigmatic smile. The trumpet is muted. The bare-footed drummer, beating a folded newspaper with whisk-brooms in lieu of a drum, stirs the eye's ear like a blast of brasses in a midnight street. A bottle of port rests on a dresser, but like the girl it is ignored. The artist, Charles Graham, adds mystery to, as well as illumination within, the scene by having them play by the light of a kerosene lamp. The painting, executed in a harsh documentary style reminiscent of W.P.A. art, conveys a feeling of musical effort caught in timeless and unrhetorical suspension, the sad remoteness of a scene observed through a wall of crystal.

Except for the lamp, the room might well have been one in the Hotel Cecil, the building on 118th Street in which Minton's Playhouse is located, and although painted in 1946, some time after the revolutionary doings there had begun, the mural should help recall the old days vividly. But the décor of the place has been changed, and now it is covered most of the time by draperies. These require a tricky skill of those who would draw them aside. And even then there will still only be the girl who must sleep forever unhearing, and the men who must forever gesture the same soundless tune. Besides, the time it celebrates is dead and gone, and perhaps not even those who came when it was still fresh and new remember those days as they were.

Neither do those remember who knew Henry Minton, who gave the place his name. Nor those who shared in the noisy lostness of New York the rediscovered community of the feasts, evocative of home, of South, of good times, the best and most unself-conscious of times, created by the generous portions of Negro American cuisine—the hash, grits, fried chicken, the ham-seasoned vegetables, the hot biscuits and rolls and the free whiskey—with which, each Monday night, Teddy Hill honored the entire cast of current Apollo Theatre shows. They were gathered here from all parts of America, and they broke bread together, and there was a sense of good feeling and promise, but what shape the fulfilled promise would take they did not know, and few except the more restless of the younger musicians even questioned. Yet it was an exceptional moment and the world was swinging with change.

Most of them, black and white alike, were hardly aware of where they were or what time it was; nor did they wish to be. They thought of Minton's as a sanctuary, where in an atmosphere blended of nostalgia and a music-and-drink-lulled suspension of time they could retreat from the wartime tensions of the town. The meaning of time-present was not their concern; thus when they try to tell it now the meaning escapes them. For they were caught up in events which made that time exceptionally and uniquely *then*, and which brought, among the other changes which have reshaped the world, a momentous modulation into a new key of musical sensibility—in brief, a revolution in culture.

So how *can* they remember? Even in swiftly changing America there are few such moments, and at best Americans give but a limited attention to history. Too much happens too rapidly, and before we can evaluate it, or exhaust its meaning or pleasure, there is something new to concern us. Ours is the tempo of the motion picture, not that of the still camera, and we waste experience as we wasted the forest. During the time it was happening the sociologists were concerned with the riots, unemployment and industrial tensions of the time, the historians with the onsweep of the war, and the critics and most serious students of culture found this area of our national life of little interest. So it was left to those who came to

Minton's out of the needs of feeling, and when the moment was past no one retained more than a fragment of its happening. Afterward the very effort to put the fragments together transformed them, so that in place of true memory they now summon to mind pieces of legend. They retell the stories as they have been told and written, glamorized, inflated, made neat and smooth, with all incomprehensible details vanished along with most of the wonder—not how it was as they themselves knew it.

When asked how it was back then, back in the forties, they will smile; then, frowning with the puzzlement of one attempting to recall the details of a pleasant but elusive dream, they'll say: "Oh, man, it was a hell of a time! A wailing time! Things were jumping, you couldn't get in here for the people. The place was packed with celebrities. Park Avenue, man! Big people in show business, college professors along with the pimps and their women. And college boys and girls. Everybody came. You know how the old words to the 'Basin Street Blues' used to go before Sinatra got hold of it? *Basin Street is the street where the dark and the light folks meet*—that's what I'm talking about. That was Minton's, man. It was a place where everybody could come to be entertained because it was a place that was jumping with good times."

Or some will tell you that it was here that Dizzy Gillespie found his own trumpet voice; that here Kenny Clarke worked out the patterns of his drumming style; where Charlie Christian played out the last creative and truly satisfying moments of his brief life, his New York home; where Charlie Parker built the monument of his art; where Thelonious Monk formulated his contribution to the chordal progressions and the hide-and-seek melodic methods of modern jazz. And they'll call such famous names as Lester Young, Ben Webster and Coleman Hawkins; or Fats Waller, who came here in the after-hours stillness of the early morning to compose. They'll tell you that Benny Goodman, Art Tatum, Count Basie and Lena Horne would drop in to join in the fun; that it was here that George Shearing played on his first night in the United States; or of Tony Scott's great love of the place; and they'll repeat all the stories of how, when and by whom the word "bebop" was coined here—but, withal, few actually remember, and these leave much unresolved.

Usually music gives resonance to memory (and Minton's was a hotbed of jazz), but not the music then in the making here. It was itself a texture of fragments, repetitive, nervous, not fully formed; its melodic lines underground, secret and taunting; its riffs jeering—"Salt peanuts! Salt peanuts!"—its timbres flat or shrill, with a minimum of thrilling vibrato. Its rhythms were out of stride and seemingly arbitrary, its drummers frozen-faced introverts dedicated to chaos. And in it the steady flow of memory, desire and defined experience summed up by the traditional jazz beat and blues mood seemed swept like a great river from its old, deep bed. We know better now, and recognize the old moods in the new sounds, but what we know is that which was then becoming. For most of those who gathered here, the enduring meaning of the great moment at Minton's took place off to the side, beyond the range of attention, like a death blow glimpsed from the corner of the eye, the revolutionary rumpus sounding like a series of flubbed notes blasting the talk with discord. So that the events which made Minton's *Minton's* arrived in conflict and ran their course; then the heat was gone and all that is left to mark its passage is the controlled fury of the music itself, sealed pure and irrevocable, banalities and excellencies alike, in the early recordings, or swept along by our restless quest for the new, to be diluted in more recent styles, the best of it absorbed like drops of fully distilled technique, mood and emotions into the great stream of jazz.

Left also to confuse our sense of what happened is the word "bop," hardly more than a nonsense syllable, by which the music synthesized at Minton's came to be known. A most inadequate word which does little, really, to help us remember. A word which throws up its hands in clownish self-deprecation before all the complexity of sound and rhythm and self-assertive passion which it pretends to name, a mask-word for the charged ambiguities of the new sound, hiding the serious face of art.

Nor does it help that so much has come to pass in the meantime. There have been two hot wars and that which continues, called "cold." And the unknown young men who brought a new edge to the sound of jazz and who scrambled the rhythms of those who used the small clear space at Minton's for dancing are no longer so young or unknown; indeed, they are referred to now by nickname in even the remotest of places. And in Paris and Munich and Tokyo they'll tell you the details of how, after years of trying, "Dizzy" (meaning John Birks Gillespie) vanquished "Roy" (meaning Roy Eldridge) during a jam session at Minton's, to become thereby the new king of trumpeters. Or how, later, while jetting over the world on the blasts of his special tilt-belled horn, he jammed with a snake charmer in Pakistan. "Sent the bloody cobra, man," they'll tell you in London's Soho. So their subsequent fame has blurred the sharp, ugly lines of their rebellion even in the memories of those who found them most strange and distasteful.

What's more, our memory of some of the more brilliant young men has been touched by the aura of death, and we feel guilt that the fury of their passing was the price paid for the art they left us to enjoy unscathed: Charlie Christian, burned out by tuberculosis like a guitar consumed in a tenement fire; Fats Navarro, wrecked by the tensions and needling temptations of his orgiastic trade, a big man physically as well as musically, shrunken to nothingness; and, most notably of all, Charlie Parker, called "Bird," now deified, worshiped and studied and, like any fertility god, mangled by his admirers and imitators, who coughed up his life and died—as incredibly as the leopard which Hemingway tells us was found "dried and frozen" near the summit of Mount Kilimanjaro—in the hotel suite of a Baroness. (Nor has anyone explained what a "yardbird" was seeking at that social altitude, though we know that ideally anything is possible within a democracy, and we know quite well that upper-class Europeans were seriously interested in jazz long before Newport became hospitable.) All this is too much for memory; the dry facts are too easily lost in legend and glamour. (With jazz we are yet not in the age of history, but linger in that of folklore.) We know for certain only that the strange sounds which they and their fellows threw against the hum and buzz of vague signification that seethed in the drinking crowd at Minton's, and which, like disgruntled conspirators meeting fatefully to assemble the random parts of a bomb, they joined here and beat and blew into a new jazz style these sounds we know now to have become the clichés, the technical exercises and the standard of achievement not only for fledgling musicians all over the United States, but for Dutchmen and Swedes, Italians and Frenchmen, Germans and Belgians, and even Japanese. All these, in places which came to mind during the Minton days only as points where the war was in progress and where one might soon be sent to fight and die, are now spotted with young men who study the discs on which the revolution hatched in Minton's is preserved with all the intensity that young American painters bring to the works, say, of Kandinsky, Picasso and Klee. Surely this is an odd swing of the cultural tide. Yet Stravinsky, Webern and Berg notwithstanding, or, more recently, Boulez or Stockhausen, such young men (many of them excellent musicians in the highest European tradition) find in the music made articulate at Minton's some key to a fuller freedom of self-realization. Indeed, for many young Europeans the developments which took place here and the careers of those who brought it about have become the latest episodes in the great American epic. They collect the recordings and thrive on the legends as eagerly, perhaps, as young Americans.

Today the bartenders at Minton's will tell you how they come fresh off the ships or planes, bringing their brightly expectant and—in this Harlem atmosphere—startlingly innocent European faces, to buy drinks and stand looking about for the source of the mystery. They try to reconcile the quiet reality of the place with the events which fired, at such long range, their imaginations. They come as to a shrine—as we to the Louvre, Notre Dame or St. Peter's; as young Americans hurry to the Café Flore, the Deux Magots, the Rotonde or the Café du Dôme in Paris. For some years now they have been coming to ask, with all the solemnity of pilgrims inquiring of a sacred relic, to see the nicotine-stained amplifier which Teddy Hill provided for Charlie Christian's guitar. And this is quite proper, for every shrine should have its relic.

Perhaps Minton's has more meaning for European jazz fans than for Americans, even for those who regularly went there. Certainly it has a *different* meaning. For them it is associated with those continental cafés in which great changes, political and artistic, have been plotted; it is to modern jazz what the Café Voltaire in Zurich is to the Dadaist phase of modern literature and painting. Few of those who visited Harlem during the forties would associate it so, but there is a context of meaning in which Minton's and the musical activities which took place there can be meaningfully placed.

Jazz, for all the insistence of the legends, has been far more closely associated with cabarets and dance halls than with brothels, and it was these which provided both the employment for the musicians and an audience initiated and aware of the overtones of the music; which knew the language of riffs, the unstated meanings of the blues idiom, and the dance steps developed from, and complementary to, its rhythms. And in the beginning it was in the Negro dance hall and night club that jazz was most completely a part of a total cultural expression, and in which it was freest and most satisfying, both for the musicians and for those in whose lives it played a major role. As a night club in a Negro community, then, Minton's was part of a national pattern.

But in the old days Minton's was far more than this; it was also a rendezvous for musicians. As such, and although it was not formally organized, it goes back historically to the first New York center of Negro musicians, the Clef Club. Organized in 1910, during the start of the great migration of Negroes northward, by James Reese Europe, the director whom Irene Castle credits with having invented the fox trot, the Clef Club was set up on West 53rd Street to serve as a meeting place and booking office for Negro musicians and entertainers. Here wage scales were regulated, musical styles and techniques worked out, and entertainment was supplied for such establishments as Rector's and Delmonico's, and for such producers as Florenz Ziegfeld and Oscar Hammerstein. Later, when Harlem evolved into a Negro section, a similar function was served by the Rhythm Club, located then in the old Lafayette Theatre building on 132nd Street and Seventh Avenue. Henry Minton, a former saxophonist and officer of the Rhythm Club, became the first Negro delegate to Local 802 of the American Federation of Musicians, and was thus doubly aware of the needs, artistic as well as economic, of jazzmen. He was generous with loans, was fond of food himself and, as an old acquaintance recalled, "loved to put a pot on the range" to share with unemployed friends. Naturally when he opened Minton's Playhouse many musicians made it their own.

Henry Minton also provided, as did the Clef and Rhythm clubs, a necessity more important to jazz musicians than food: a place in which to hold their interminable jam sessions. And it is here that Minton's becomes most important to the development of modern jazz. It is here, too, that it joins up with all the countless rooms, private and public, in which jazzmen have worked out the secrets of their craft. Today jam sessions are offered as entertainment by night clubs and on radio and television, and some are quite exciting, but what is seen and heard is only one aspect of the true jam session: the "cutting session," or contest of improvisational skill and physical endurance between two or more musicians. But the jam session is far more than this, and when carried out by musicians in the privacy of small rooms (as in the mural at Minton's), or in such places as Halley Richardson's shoeshine parlor in Oklahoma City—where I first heard Lester Young jamming in a shine chair, his head thrown back, his horn even then outthrust, his feet working on the footrests, as he played with and against Lem Johnson, Ben Webster (this was 1929) and other members of the old Blue Devils Orchestra—or during the after hours in Piney Brown's old Sunset Club in Kansas City; in such places as these, with only musicians and jazzmen present, then the jam session is revealed as the jazzman's true academy.

It is here that he learns tradition, group techniques and style. For although since the twenties many jazzmen have had conservatory training and are well grounded in formal theory and instrumental technique, when we approach jazz we are entering quite a different sphere of training. Here it is more meaningful to speak not of courses of study, of grades and degrees, but of apprenticeship, ordeals, initiation ceremonies, of rebirth. For after the jazzman has learned the fundamentals of his instrument and the traditional techniques of jazz—the intonations, the mute work, manipulation of timbre, the body of traditional styles—he must then "find himself," must be reborn, must find, as it were, his soul. All this through achieving that subtle identification between his instrument and his deepest drives which will allow him to express his own unique ideas and his own unique voice. He must achieve, in short, his self-determined identity.

In this his instructors are his fellow musicians, especially the acknowledged masters, and his recognition of manhood depends upon their acceptance of his ability as having reached a standard which is all the more difficult for not having been rigidly codified. This does not depend upon his ability to simply hold a job, but upon his power to express an individuality in tone. Nor is his status ever unquestioned, for the health of jazz and the unceasing attraction which it holds for the musicians themselves lies in the ceaseless warfare for mastery and recognition—not among the general public, though commercial success is not spurned, but among their artistic peers. And even the greatest can never rest on past accomplishments, for, as with the fast guns of the Old West, there is always someone waiting in a jam session to blow him literally, not only down, but into shame and discouragement.

By making his club hospitable to jam sessions even to the point that customers who were not musicians were crowded out, Henry Minton provided a retreat, a homogeneous community where a collectivity of common experience could find continuity and meaningful expression. Thus the stage was set for the birth of bop.

In 1941 Mr. Minton handed over his management to Teddy Hill, the saxophonist and former band leader, and Hill turned the Playhouse into a musical dueling ground. Not only did he continue Minton's policies, he expanded them. It was Hill who established the Monday Celebrity Nights, the house band which included such members from his own disbanded orchestra as Kenny Clarke, Dizzy Gillespie, Thelonious Monk, sometimes Joe Guy, and later Charlie Christian and Charlie Parker, and it was Hill who allowed the musicians free rein to play whatever they liked. Perhaps no other club except Clarke Monroe's Uptown House was so permissive, and with the hospitality extended to musicians of all schools the news spread swiftly. Minton's became the focal point for musicians all over the country.

Herman Pritchard, who presided over the bar in the old days, tells us that every time they came, "Lester Young and Ben Webster used to tie up in battle like dogs in the road. They'd fight on those saxophones until they were tired out; then they'd put in long-distance calls to their mothers, both of whom lived in Kansas City, and tell them about it."

And most of the masters of jazz came either to observe or to participate and be influenced and listen to their own discoveries transformed, and the aspiring stars sought to win their approval, as the younger tenor men tried to win the esteem of Coleman Hawkins. Or they tried to vanquish them in jamming contests as Gillespie is said to have outblown his idol, Roy Eldridge. It was during this period that Eddie "Lockjaw" Davis underwent an ordeal of jeering rejection until finally he came through as an admired tenor man.

In the perspective of time we now see that what was happening at Minton's was a continuing symposium of jazz, a summation of all the styles, personal and traditional, of jazz. Here it was possible to hear its resources of technique, ideas, harmonic structure, melodic phrasing and rhythmical possibilities explored more thoroughly than was ever possible before. It was also possible to hear the first attempts toward a conscious statement of the sensibility of the younger generation of musicians as they worked out the techniques, structures and rhythmical patterns with which to express themselves. Part of this was arbitrary, a revolt of the younger against the established stylists; part of it was inevitable. For jazz had reached a crisis, and new paths were certain to be searched for and found. An increasing number of the younger men were formally trained, and the post-Depression developments in the country had made for quite a break between their experience and that of the older men. Many were even of a different physical build. Often they were quiet and of a reserve which contrasted sharply with the exuberant and outgoing lyricism of the older men, and they were intensely concerned that their identity as Negroes place no restriction upon the music they played or the manner in which they used their talent. They were concerned, they said, with art, not entertainment. Especially were they resentful of Louis Armstrong, whom (confusing the spirit of his music with his clowning) they considered an Uncle Tom.

But they too, some of them, had their own myths and misconceptions: that theirs was the only generation of Negro musicians who listened to or enjoyed the classics; that to be truly free they must act exactly the opposite of what white people might believe, rightly or wrongly, a Negro to be; that the performing artist can be completely and absolutely free of the obligations of the entertainer, and that they could play jazz with dignity only by frowning and treating the audience with aggressive contempt; and that to be in control, artistically and personally, one must be so cool as to quench one's own human fire.

Nor should we overlook the despair which must have swept Minton's before the technical mastery, the tonal authenticity, the authority and the fecundity of imagination of such men as Hawkins, Young, Goodman, Tatum, Teagarden, Ellington and Waller. Despair, after all, is ever an important force in revolutions.

They were also responding to the nonmusical pressures affecting jazz. It was a time of big bands, and the greatest prestige and economic returns were falling outside the Negro community—often to leaders whose popularity grew from the compositions and arrangements of Negroes—to white instrumentalists whose only originality lay in the enterprise with which they rushed to market with some Negro musician's hard-won style. Still there was no policy of racial discrimination at Minton's. Indeed, it was very much like those Negro cabarets of the twenties and thirties in which a megaphone was placed on the piano so that anyone with the urge could sing a blues. Nevertheless, the inside-dopesters will tell you that the "changes" or chord progressions and melodic inversions worked out by the creators of bop sprang partially from their desire to create a jazz which could not be so easily imitated and exploited by white musicians to whom the market was more open simply *because* of their whiteness. They wished to receive credit for what they created; besides, it was easier to "get rid of the trash" who crowded the bandstand with inept playing and thus make room for the real musicians, whether white or black. Nevertheless, white musicians like Tony Scott, Remo Palmieri and Al Haig who were part of the development at Minton's became so by passing a test of musicianship, sincerity and temperament. Later, it is said, the boppers became engrossed in solving the musical problems which they set themselves. Except for a few sympathetic older musicians, it was they who best knew the promise of the Minton moment, and it was they, caught like the rest in all the complex forces of American life which comes to focus in Jazz, who made the most of it. Now the tall tales told as history must feed on the results of their efforts.

chapter 26

ERIC LOTT

Double V, Double-Time:
Bebop's Politics of Style

The song and the people is the same.   — AMIRI BARAKA

Fifty years on, the story of how the crash crew made a revolution at Minton's Playhouse is so worn that we forget how disruptive bebop actually was. As Amiri Baraka remarked, the story sounds comfortably like that of the Lost Generation of Americans in Paris, all formal experimentation and narcotic junketeering (*Blues People* 198). But jazz modernism was rooted Stateside, in the toiling New York of the 1940s; indeed, it is impossible to absorb the bop attack without its social reference, as it is difficult to understand New York at that time without consulting the music. Bebop has been claimed by other, mostly unhistorical narratives rather than articulated to its own social history. White-Negro revisionists Jack Kerouac and Norman Mailer to the contrary, bebop was no screaming surge of existential abandon, its makers far from lost. And while bebop said there was a riot going on, it was hardly protest music. Nor was it simply a series of formal innovations, though, as Albert Murray wrote, the musicians' chief desire was to make the music swing harder (166). Bebop was about making disciplined imagination alive and answerable to the social change of its time. "Ko-Ko," Charlie Parker's first recorded masterpiece, suggested that jazz was a struggle which pitted mind against the perversity of circumstance, and that in this struggle blinding virtuosity was the best weapon.

Since the self-conscious advances of bebop so obviously announce themselves, many writers ignore how much those advances belong to a moment, the early forties, in which unpaid historical bills were falling due. Early in 1941, nearly ten thousand black Ford workers threw their weight behind the United Auto Workers in a strike that forced Ford to unionize; wages for blacks in some industries seemed to be on the rise. Later, in 1943, defense plants were finally desegregated under pressure from labor and civil-rights leader A. Phillip Randolph and his March on Washington movement. Black and white together routinely crowded the Track (Harlem's Savoy Ballroom) on those nights when nervous police had not temporarily closed it down. The ranks of the NAACP grew, and in 1942 the Congress of Racial Equality (CORE) was founded. In a still-segregated U.S. Army, there were eight times as many black commissioned officers as there had been in World War I, and though many in Harlem wanted little or nothing to do with what they considered someone else's war, many of those who fought did so in the name of the "Double V"—victory abroad and victory at home. Partly a result of this atmosphere, riots woke up LA, Detroit, New York, and other cities, with politicians like New York's Mayor Fiorello La Guardia denouncing such "juvenile delinquency." Push was coming to shove, and folk were willing.[1]

Amid all this turmoil, a group of young migrants from the South and Midwest was beginning to refurbish the language of riff and accent at Minton's Playhouse and at Clark Monroe's Uptown House in Harlem. The psychological shift they glossed owed largely to another round of black northward movement, a rising threshold of expectation on the part of a generation whose demands refused to be tamed. Such shifts are difficult to pinpoint, but this one came into desperate focus. On 1 August 1943, Harlem exploded—word was that a white cop had shot and killed a black soldier in a scuffle involving a black woman. This was mostly true (the soldier lived), but in the ensuing uprising Harlem's colonialist face got lifted: the youth-wants-to-know flank of the Double V went to work. The inequity of a black military man gunned down by the white Uncle he had protected overseas hit hard, and Harlem hit back, looting businesses and trashing cars to the tune of several millions. James Baldwin later said that Harlem had needed something to smash (93).[2]

The connection between such deeply intended if wasteful militancy and the new youth styles growing up around a radical new music was lost on no one at the time. This was, people said, another "zoot-suit riot," referring to the Los Angeles disturbances. The establishment press in several cities had whipped up a certain hysteria about zooted "gangsters" and "muggers"; white servicemen and some civilians began responding with mob attacks on anyone approaching the color of sharkskin. Despite official denials, these were racial attacks *tout court*. The Harlem riot was an aggressive and hugely collective response to this climate. A zoot-suited participant later declared the zootish disposition to be at odds with the desire to fight a white America's war when conditions at home were the problem: "By the time you read this I will be fighting for Uncle Sam, the bitches, and I do not like it worth a damn. I'm not a spy or a saboteur, but I don't like goin' over there fightin' for the white man—so be it." Psychologist Kenneth Clark termed the new militancy "The Zoot Effect in Personality," but his early attempt to read a subculture proved only that liberal psychologists were as defensive as the new style was dangerous.[3] To stiff-arm the alleged provocateurs—zoots were also in open defiance of the War Production Board's rationing of clothing, a visible sign of antipatriotism—the Los Angeles city council even debated declaring zoot suits illegal (Breitman).[4]

But that did not stop such styles of radical will from flourishing. Zoot-suiters grew in the mid-1940s into hipsters. Encouraged by the ostentatious usages of some bebop originators, black and white working-class bohemia made attitude and appetite signify opposition to routine inequity, and routine generally. Deep-frozen on heroin, they adopted the effrontery displayed by some musicians on the bandstand. And their jargon, itself a kind of improvisation, bucked the regulations of accepted articulateness. These were self-styled ghetto intellectuals, stifled in the kind of ambition that only the musicians were able to fulfill.[5] *Time* magazine, like most, saw it from the other side: bebop people, it said in 1948, "like to wear berets, goatees and green-tinted horn-rimmed glasses, and talk about their 'interesting new sounds,' " while their "rapid-fire, scattershot talk has about the same pace—and content—as their music" ("How Deaf"). LA station KMPC banned the music in 1946; and it is no wonder that when relative old-timer Louis Armstrong went to Paris in 1948, he was given police protection for fear of bebop devotees and their volatile habits.

All of this does merit the spin of subculture theory: zoot, lip, junk, and double-time became the stylistic answer to social contradictions (having mainly to do with generational difference and migration) experienced by the makers and followers of bop.[6] Further, we need to restore the political edge to a music that has been so absorbed into the contemporary jazz language that it seems as safe as much of the current scene—the spate of jazz reissues, the deluge of "standards" records, Bud Powell on CD—certainly an unfortunate historical irony. For in the mid-forties, Parker, Dizzy Gillespie, Powell, Thelonious Monk, and the rest were tearing it up with such speed and irreverence—sometimes so acrobatic as to feel unfinished, often world-historical—that prewar life seemed like a long, long time ago. In hindsight, there may appear to be other more radical breaks with jazz's past, but to an America fed on Bing Crosby and "Marezy Coats," bebop was the war come home. Listen to the fury as Parker roars into "Bird Gets the Worm," or to the way he and Fats Navarro suddenly transpose the head of "Move" to minor on *One Night in Birdland*, or to Monk's 1947 derangement of "April in Paris," and it is clear why many white music writers trying to preserve a sense of professional balance resorted to such denunciatory plum tones as "bad taste and ill-advised fanaticism . . . the sort of stuff that has thrown innumerable impressionable young musicians out of stride" (review of "Billie's Bounce" 15). Brilliantly outside, bebop was intimately if indirectly related to the militancy of its moment. Militancy and music were undergirded by the same social facts; the music attempted to resolve at the level of style what the militancy fought out in the streets. If bebop did not offer a call to arms, as one writer has said in another context, it at least acknowledged that the call had been made.[7] How it translated that acknowledgment into style is the subject of this essay.

New York in this period had an incalculable effect on jazz modernism's big push. Harlem was a magic place, a refuge that lent young musicians, triply alien—

migrant, Negro, occupationally suspect—the courage to conquer. Since among the major innovators only Bud Powell, Max Roach, and Thelonious Monk grew up in New York, Harlem offered a rediscovered community of things they had left behind: feasts, talk, home (Ellison, "The Golden Age" 200–201).[8] The phrase of the moment may have been "Harlem is nowhere," but for the musicians it was the logical place in which to coherently combine the various regional styles they had brought with them. Here the Kansas City 4/4 came together with popular song forms and Art Tatum's harmonic ideas, all of it grounded by the blues (skeptics are directed to "Parker's Mood"). "I think the music of today," said Parker, "is a sort of combination of the midwestern beat and the fast New York tempos," another way of saying that it incorporated formally the migratory impulse (Feather 15).

Ralph Ellison remembers turn-of-the-forties New York as a place that itself required improvisation, honing the wits of newcomers to quickness. Beyond "Harlem's brier patch" there seemed to be "no agreed-upon rules of conduct," no sense of the limits the South imposed in the "signs and symbols that marked the dividing lines of racial segregation" (Ellison, *Going to the Territory* 148–48, 152). So homegirl and wonderboy had to make it up as they went along, acquainting themselves intimately with uncertainty the way they did when it came time to stand up and blow their four-bars. Out of encounters in the streets of New York came local versions of the wisdom and agility required of all fleet-footed inventors. "Coolness helped to keep our values warm," says Ellison, "and racial hostility stoked our fires of inspiration" (167). Not even the North could abide the kinds of interracial freedom the musicians cultivated; a palpable dissidence kicks the best of the music.

The shock of relocation was "handled" by the common language that musicians developed—styles of dress, music, drugs, and speech homologous with the structures of their experience. The requisite cool of the northern city dweller was unattainable unless negotiated through style. Malcolm X reports that his transition from Michigan "country" to hip Bostonian was achieved primarily through a new zoot (39–69);[9] South Carolinian Dizzy Gillespie's windowpanes, cigarette holder, goatee, and beret signified on fancy city dress. The hip code sometimes appeared compensatory rather than avant, insecure rather than assured, but it expressed real defiance. As when Gillespie put together a big band in 1945, which later found it had been booked to tour the Jim Crow South. By the time the band got below the Mason-Dixon line, so many players had quit that it had virtually a new lineup (Feather 34). Through secrecy, exaggeration, and wit, self-images were formed, alliances made, strategies of differentiation concocted. Bop style, a kind of "fifth column fashion," was where social responsiveness became individual expression, where the pleasures of shared identity met an intolerance for racist jive (Cosgrove 85–86).

At its hippest (and meanest), such a common language became a closed hermeneutic that had the undeniable effect of alienating the riff-raff and expressing a sense of felt isolation, all the while affirming a collective purpose—even at the expense of other musicians. In preparation for Minton's, Gillespie would work out a complicated sequence of chords for the relatively simple "I Got Rhythm," then call out the tune to cut the uninitiated on the bandstand. The unhip, says bassist Milt Hinton, were "left right at the post . . . eventually they would put their horns away" (Giddins 66). On different occasions, though they knew well to the contrary, the boppers declared they *were not* in the tradition; no "respectable" classicism here. Older musicians were plausibly put off. Johnny Hodges told trumpeter Howard McGhee, "[Bird] don't play nothing," and only later got wise (Giddins 67). Drummer Davey Tough recalled his first encounter with bop: "These cats snatched up their horns and blew crazy stuff. One would stop all of a sudden and another would start for no reason at all. We never could tell when a solo was supposed to begin or end" (Stearns 224–25). Louis Armstrong never really made peace with bebop, "that modern malice" (Stearns 219); more than once Gillespie unfairly dismissed Papa Dip for tomming. Attitudes like these allowed musical youth to make their condition as outsiders meaningful, and whether they intended it to be or not, the stance was scarifying to musicians and audiences alike.

The various elements of bebop style were thus part of a new generational responsiveness to the northern city, particularly 1940s New York, a place distinguished less by its capacity to shock than by its ability to make little seem shocking.[10] What evolved in turn was an aesthetic of speed and displacement—ostentatious virtuosity dedicated to reorienting perception even as it rocked the house. Every instrument became immediately more mobile, everything *moved*. Drummers Kenny Clarke and Max Roach no longer thumped the bass drum four beats per bar, as some other drummers had done. Instead, they extended the work of such innovative swing drummers as Jo Jones and Sid Catlett, substituting for a monotonous bass beat the shimmering pulse of ride and hi-hat cymbals. Bassists like Oscar Pettiford no longer simply walked time, they provided melodic counterpoint to the soloists. Bud Powell, Duke Jordan, and other pianists discarded the full-bodied approximation of an orchestra for a series of jagged chords and hornlike, linear solos (Giddins 68; Stearns 229–36). And the cold, vibratoless edge of Parker's tone, his and Gillespie's high intervallic leaps, their penchant for shifting to double-time at a moment's notice, the breathtaking audaciousness with which they cut up their phrases, dissolved the specious equation of artistic intelligence with respectable European culture. These elements originally made up what Amiri Baraka called the "willfully harsh, *anti-assimilationist* sound of bebop," which at once reclaimed jazz from its brief co-optation by white "swing" bandleaders like the aptly named Paul Whiteman and made any future dilution that much harder (181).

In this way, bebop redefined the tradition, indeed made it possible to keep playing jazz in the face of given musical and social facts without losing self-respect. The sheer velocity of much of the music, ignited by Roach's bombs, shifted the center of gravity from grounded bass to mercurial rhythms echoed from drums to horns; base and superstructure were to a certain extent collapsed. Add the pursuit of the non sequitur to such speeds and such mobility, as in the bridge of Bird's solo on "Klaunstance" (on *The Genius of Charlie Parker*) where disconnected phrases dive at each other until the whole is "resolved" into an arpeggiated drop, and the result is some blues that gleefully critique tradition. So too does Monk's self-portrait/self-parody "Thelonious" (on *Genius of Modern Music*, Vol. 1), its one-note theme riding a lilting harmonic cycle, recalling certain vocal arrangements of Ellington's "It Don't Mean a Thing" while presaging Randy Weston's "Hi-Fly." It riffs self-consciously on tradition—Monk suddenly erupting into stride piano—and depends for its effect on a cool surface continually broken up by jarring piano, the shock of the new. Gillespie once relevantly joked that if it doesn't hurt your ears, it isn't dissonance. For me, this new attitude is captured best on a live recording of Harold Arlen's "This Time the Dream's On Me" (on *One Night in Birdland*): Bird and drummer Art Blakey trading fours, Blakey plays two triplet figures, one on bass and one on snare, one a *half-beat behind* the other. The result is an asymmetrical raucousness that seems to arrest the time as surely as it states its commitment to a caustic groove. Instances of this kind of roughhousing are numberless.

The widespread practice of appropriating the chord changes of popular tunes was another means by which a similar result could be achieved—as in Tadd Dameron's "Hot House," a reworking of Cole Porter's "What Is This Thing Called Love?" that lent itself even to Eric Dolphy's out-to-lunch sermonizing fifteen years later. Essentially an old blues impulse that was further refined in the 1930s, writing new melodies for Broadway tunes was nevertheless an intervention into the dominant popular culture of the period—in tunes such as "Hot House" a kind of ritual dismemberment. (Those like David Toop who see similar strategies in rap music correctly grasp the link between bebop and hip hop [18].)[11] Whatever its effect, this was probably not one of the distancing techniques so often ascribed to bebop, but rather a search for harmonic variety and simultaneously a pointed participation in the popular. Charlie Parker, who later flirted with what Martin Williams calls the "spurious challenge" of string formats (*Jazz Tradition* 152), once told an admirer that to understand his music one should listen to the Clovers (Giddins 104); and the course of postwar black music is arguably constituted by the twin refurbishments of bebop and R&B colliding and diverging in mutually enriching ways.[12] Part of bop's force inhered in this involvement in and struggle over the popular.

Bebop, in other words, was one of the great modernisms. Its relationship to earlier styles was one of calculated hostility. It was a soloist's music, despite the democratic ethos of jazz (in which soloists assume a momentary universality in a highly mutual context), and particularly of bop (its dependence on unison riffs, the extreme sympathy required between players to negotiate the rhythms). Its incorporation of elements of the popular (Bird was fond of quoting the "Woody Woodpecker" theme) reminds one of Joyce or Mahler. Its commitment to exploratory rigor amounted to a harshness that many took for ugliness. And its mocking defiance made a virtue of isolation. Moreover, the social position of this modernism—distanced from both the black middle class and the white consensus—gave aesthetic self-assertion political force and value.

Gary Giddins says in his biography of Bird that the chief motive for all this was not to offend but to pioneer, and that by the self-assertion of genius. I would suggest that bebop's context made the two pretty much inseparable; sociopolitical insistence was so available as both source and effect that even a self-consciously

462

tell the story

arty music could call on it effortlessly. This, together with the recording ban from August 1942 through most of 1943 that made bebop's inception seem sudden, must explain the intensity of the reaction with which the music was first greeted. The small-group format, for example, was given such prominence in part because the music demanded turns-on-a-dime and extended solo space; audiences experienced this as assault. Style wars are not known for taking any prisoners, and critics of the new music were as ruthless as the musicians. Monk's "Thelonious," said *Down Beat*, sounded like the pianist had his mind on "the stock returns or the 7th at Pimlico—anything but his piano" (review of "Thelonious" 19). The further this modernism extended the resources of African American expressive culture, the greater lengths cultural critics would go to miss the point, though (or because, as Baraka ominously suggests) they may have begun to recognize jazz's status as art.

Bebop could not in fact be heard without the alarm registering its birth; if we are to understand its radical implications, we must attend to this alarm. "It was as if," says Martin Williams, "this bop style had swept away almost everything that had gone before it, no matter how well or how badly the writers knew and understood what *had* gone before it" ("Bebop and After" 291). To many, the music read as "atonal, futuristic material, produced by the progressive modernists," to quote one of the baffled—so much a departure, as this comment indicates, that there was hardly an available language to describe it (Pease 12). It certainly did not fit into any of the "discursive categories" *Down Beat* used for its record reviews—Hot Jazz (of an earlier kind), Swing, Dance, Vocal, and Novelty—and there is an interesting bewilderment, early on, about where bebop should go. The music generally precipitated an evaluative crisis among the cognoscenti, who responded as though to a breach in the social order. (A notable exception was Leonard Feather's mid-forties work in *Esquire* and *Metronome*.) By mid-1947, polemics raged in *Down Beat* over which was the "real jazz," bebop or Dixieland (a recent reactionary reinvention), and well-known critics battered each others' sectarianism (Leonard Feather vs. Rudi Blesh, Charles Delaunay vs. Hugues Panassié, *Metronome* vs. early *Record Changer*).

Bebop's fearsomeness to many of its contemporaries is suggested not only by the vehemence of the debate, the straining quality of the polemics, but by the language of politics, so often called on to describe, dismiss, or even mock the music and its rivals. Lionel Hampton, not a musician we tend today to associate with political radicalism, said of his music in 1946: "Whenever I see any injustice or any unfair action against my own race or any other minority groups *Hey Ba Ba Rebop* stimulates the desire to destroy such prejudice and discrimination." The writer interviewing Hampton on this occasion (noted Chicago sociologist Horace Cayton, interestingly enough) responded with nervous irony to "Hampton's class struggle" and distanced himself from jazz's claim to "social significance" with a derisive "Marxian" interpretation of "Caldonia" (Cayton 8). Dave Tough, an older bebop convert, in another instance called Dixieland a "Straight-Republican-Ticket kind of music" in some public mudslinging with old-timer Eddie Condon (Gottlieb 4). As a consequence of this kind of talk, much of the forties' music press, per Frank Kofsky, figured as law and order trying to stem the furious tide.[13]

Yet in the postwar cultural formation, beboppers were a black intelligentsia—the other New York intellectuals—only dimly perceived by a myopic left. *Partisan Review*'s commitment to modernism did not extend to black music; its "Music Chronicle" columns were invariably about opera, at best Hindemith. (There was a splenetic dismissal of bop by poet Weldon Kees in its brief "Variety" section, indicative of the music's offensiveness to outsiders as well as their intellectual blindness.[14] Even Harlem Communist party intellectuals had an unsteady enthusiasm for contemporary music still in touch with black cultural roots. Given the huge undertow of protest aesthetic in which the best-intentioned of them had to wade, bebop's transgressive genius was washed aside. Just as the CP had dismissed the "Double V" campaign because Hitler, not Jim Crow was the "real enemy," and called with Mayor La Guardia for law and order after the Harlem uprising, so they distanced themselves from the rowdiness of bebop, music far beyond the reaches of the CP aesthetic (James, Breitman et al. 158, 283).[15] While the music generated a following, Beat writers like Kerouac and Ginsberg were the closest bebop came to having visible oppositional champions, a partisanship distorted by the projections of renegade romance.[16]

As it turned out, this was perhaps the only art, with the possible exception of certain painting, that proved fully equal to the moment. In their way, the bebop innovators mapped the time as intelligently as writers like C. L. R. James and George Breitman did in their political commentary.[17] James and Breitman knew the Harlem explosion was no mere hooliganism, and they defended something so seemingly irrelevant as the zoot suit when wearing one threatened to become a misdemeanor in LA. They realized style could be dangerous; and in forcing the connection between Double V and double-time, the people who made music like "Scrapple from the Apple" knew that too. This is, in the end, the importance of the cult of heroin and the eighth note, of the cocked beret and the hip code: a politics of style beyond protest, focusing the struggles of its moment in a live and irreverent art.

NOTES

Many thanks to Susan Fraiman, RJ Smith, and Peter Watrous for their suggestions on this essay.

1. For discussions of this political moment, see Anderson 290–346; Jones 232–56; Sitkoff; Cruse; Naison 193–320; Glaberman; James, Breitman, et al.; Baraka 175–207; Kofsky 56, 271; and Cosgrove.

2. Baldwin's powerful account tends unfortunately to psychologize militant energies into an unchanging ghetto mentality.

3. The participant's quote and Clark's analysis are from an article in the *Journal of Abnormal Psychology*, a publication that indicates its perspective.

4. See also Cosgrove 85–88.

5. See Newton 213–22 and Hebdige 46–49.

6. The Marxist subculture theory of the Birmingham Centre for Contemporary Cultural Studies is set forth in Hall and Jefferson and in Hebdige; see also Treichler, Nelson, and Grossberg. I rely on it primarily to think about bebop's "magical" formal solutions

to some of the social contradictions outlined here. Cosgrove's "The Zoot-Suit and Style Warfare" goes some important distance toward a reading of the subcultural dress of this period. As far as I know, little writing since Baraka's *Blues People* has taken the music's social and political meanings seriously. Three excellent works that have shaped my thinking are DeMott, "The Future Is Unwritten: Working-Class Youth Cultures in England and America"; Gilroy, *There Ain't No Black in the Union Jack*; and Carby, "It Jus Be's Dat Way Sometime."

7. I am indebted here to Charles O'Brien's argument in regard to black pop in the sixties.

8. Apart from its engrossing meditation on the meaning of Minton's, Ellison's essay can be read as a jazz counterstatement (conscious, I believe) to T. S. Eliot's idea of tradition. "In [bebop] the steady flow of memory, desire and defined experience summed up by the traditional jazz beat and blues mood seemed swept like a great river from its old, deep bed. We know better now, and recognize the old moods in the new sounds, but what we know is that which was then becoming . . . the best of it absorbed like drops of fully distilled technique, mood and emotions into the great stream of jazz" (203). Jazz has rarely been treated with this degree of moral seriousness.

9. This was suggested to me by Chibnall 60–61; see also the fine essay by Robin Kelley, "The Riddle of the Zoot." The pressures on those newcomers are typified in Miles Davis's remark that on his arrival from East St. Louis he believed everyone in New York knew more than he did. Davis's response was simply to continue to dress like a fashion plate (Carr 14; Davis 51–115).

10. I am influenced here by Franco Moretti's reading of Walter Benjamin's "On Some Motifs in Baudelaire" in *Signs Taken for Wonders* 116–17. One measure of bebop's close attention to its context is that it spoke largely to northern urban audiences. In the Southwest, Charlie Parker recalled, the music registered as a strange and meaningless noise; "in the middle west the colored audiences liked it but the whites didn't"; and "in New York *everyone* liked it" (Feather 31).

11. "Ornithology," the "national anthem of bop," was of course an appropriation of "How High the Moon." The classic recording of "Ornithology" is Charlie Parker's on *The Complete Dial Sessions*.

12. R&B gained supremacy with the expansion of capital in the sixties, contributing to the exile of many jazz musicians to Europe; jazz lamely but gamely fought back with "fusion" in the seventies, finally stabilizing itself in the currently profitable classicist mode, in whose purer forms R&B has itself been exiled. There are signs, in performers as various as Ornette Coleman, Lester Bowie, Arthur Blythe, Henry Threadgill, and younger players such as Joshua Redman, Geri Allen, and Greg Osby, that the repressed is, healthily this time, returning.

13. For the music press as social control in the sixties, see Kofsky 79–97. Leonard Feather's publisher changed the "cursed" name of *Inside Be-bop* for its second edition to *Inside Jazz*, the name it still carries. See Feather's new introduction to the book.

14. "I can only report, very possibly because of some deeply-buried strain of black reaction in me, that I have found this music uniformly thin, at once dilapidated and overblown, and exhibiting a poverty of thematic development and a richness of affectation not only, apparently, intentional, but enormously self-satisfied. . . . There has been nothing like this in the way of an overconsciousness of stylistic idiosyncrasy, I should say, since the Gothic Revival" (Kees 621–22). The second sentence is probably true and the first absolutely symptomatic.

15. Citing the *Militant*, 4 Apr. 1942 and 7 Aug. 1943. The best response to the CP aes-

thetic was Charlie Parker's. In 1952 (after he became relatively well-known) Bird was hired to play a CP benefit for embattled activist attorney and city council member Benjamin Davis. During a break, as guest Paul Robeson sang a work song called "Water Boy," Bird trotted scandalously toward the stage with a glass of water (Giddins 113–14).

16. Kerouac in 1940 did praise Lester Young in a Columbia University school paper, for which he himself deserves praise, considering the context. (What might Prez's "hum and buzz of implication" have seemed on Morningside Heights?) Later, however, the romance of the word combined with the distance between cultures resulted in a kind of updated Van-Vechtenism. See Gilford and Lee 23. Thanks to Benj DeMott for his suggestions on the Beats.

17. See particularly James, "The Revolutionary Answer to the Negro Problem in the U.S.A."

WORKS CITED

Anderson, Jervis. *This Was Harlem: A Cultural Portrait, 1900–1950.* New York: Farrar, Straus, and Giroux, 1982.

Baldwin, James. *Notes of a Native Son.* 1955. New York: Dial, 1963.

Baraka, Amiri [LeRoi Jones]. *Blues People: Negro Music in White America.* New York: Morrow, 1963.

Breitman, George. " 'Zoot Suit Riots' in Los Angeles." *Militant* 19 June 1943.

Carby, Hazel V. "It Jus Be's Dat Way Sometime: The Sexual Politics of Women's Blues." *Radical America* 20.4 (1986): 9–22.

Carr, Ian. *Miles Davis: A Biography.* New York: Morrow, 1984.

Cayton, Horace R. "Social Significance in Jazz Louses Good Stuff Up." *Down Beat* 16 Dec. 1946: 8.

Chibnall, Steve. "Whistle and Zoot: The Changing Meaning of a Suit of Clothes." *History Workshop Journal* 20 (Autumn 1985): 56–81.

Clark, Kenneth B., and James Barker. "The Zoot Effect in Personality: A Race Riot Participant." *Journal of Abnormal Psychology* 40.2 (1945): 143–48.

Cosgrove, Stuart. "The Zoot-Suit and Style Warfare." *History Workshop Journal* 18 (Autumn 1984): 77–91.

Cruse, Harold. *The Crisis of the Negro Intellectual.* New York: Morrow, 1967.

Davis, Miles, with Quincy Troupe. *Miles: The Autobiography.* New York: Simon, 1989.

DeMott, Benj. "The Future Is Unwritten: Working-Class Youth Cultures in England and America." *Critical Texts* 5.1 (1988): 42–56.

Ellison, Ralph. *Going to the Territory.* New York: Random, 1986.

———. "The Golden Age, Times Past." 1964. *Shadow and Act.* New York: Random, 1972. 198–210.

Feather, Leonard. *Inside Jazz.* (Originally *Inside Be-bop*, 1949.) New York: Da Capo, 1977.

Giddins, Gary. *Celebrating Bird: The Triumph of Charlie Parker.* New York: Morrow, 1987.

Gilford, Barry, and Lawrence Lee. *Jack's Book: An Oral Biography of Jack Kerouac.* New York: St. Martin's, 1978.

Gilroy, Paul. *There Ain't No Black in the Union Jack: The Cultural Politics of Race and Nation.* London: Hutchinson, 1987.

Glaberman, Martin. *Wartime Strikes.* Detroit: Bewicked, 1980.

Gottlieb, Bill. "Dixieland Nowhere Says Dave Tough." *Down Beat* 23 Sept. 1946: 4.

Hall, Stuart, and Tony Jefferson, eds. *Resistance Through Rituals: Youth Subcultures in Postwar Britain*. London: Hutchinson, 1976.

Hebdige, Dick. *Subculture: The Meaning of Style*. New York: Methuen, 1979.

"How Deaf Can You Get?" *Time* 17 May 1948: 74.

James, C. L. R. "The Revolutionary Answer to the Negro Problem in the U.S.A." 1948. *The Future in the Present: Selected Writings*. London: Allison and Busby, 1977. 119–27.

James, C. L. R., George Breitman, et al. *Fighting Racism in World War II*. New York: Monad, 1980.

Jones, Jacqueline. *Labor of Love, Labor of Sorrow: Black Women, Work and the Family, From Slavery to the Present*. New York: Basic, 1985.

Kees, Weldon. "Muskrat Ramble: Popular and Unpopular Music." *Partisan Review* 15.5 (1948): 621–22.

Kelley, Robin D. G. "The Riddle of the Zoot: Malcolm Little and Black Cultural Politics During WW II." *Malcolm X: In Our Own Image*. Ed. Joe Wood. New York: St. Martin's, 1992. 155–82.

Kofsky, Frank. *Black Nationalism and the Revolution in Music*. New York: Pathfinder, 1970.

Malcolm X, with Alex Haley. *The Autobiography of Malcolm X*. New York: Grove, 1966.

Moretti, Franco. *Signs Taken for Wonders: Essays in the Sociology of Literary Forms*. Trans. Susan Fischer, David Forgacs, and David Miller. London: Verso, 1983.

Murray, Albert. *Stomping the Blues*. New York: McGraw-Hill, 1976.

Naison, Mark. *Communists in Harlem During the Depression*. New York: Grove, 1983.

Newton, Francis [Eric Hobsbawm]. *The Jazz Scene*. London: MacGibbon and Kee, 1959.

O'Brien, Charles. "At Ease in Azania." *Critical Texts* 5.1 (1988): 39–41.

Pease, Sharon. "Dodo's Modern Style Is Given Pease Analysis." *Down Beat* 16 Dec. 1946: 12.

Review of Charlie Parker's "Billie's Bounce" and "Now's the Time." *Down Beat* 22 Apr. 1946: 15.

Review of Thelonious Monk's "Thelonious." *Down Beat* 25 Feb. 1948: 19.

Sitkoff, Harvard. "Racial Militancy and Interracial Violence in the Second World War." *Journal of American History* 58 (1971): 661–81.

Stearns, Marshall W. *The Story of Jazz*. New York: Oxford UP, 1956.

Toop, David. *The Rap Attack: African Jive to New York Hip-Hop*. Boston: South End, 1984.

Treichler, Paula, Cary Nelson, and Lawrence Grossberg, eds. *Cultural Studies*. New York: Routledge, 1992.

Williams, Martin. "Bebop and After: A Report." *Jazz: New Perspectives on the History of Jazz*. Ed. Nat Hentoff and Albert J. McCarthy. New York: Holt, Rinehart and Winston, 1959. 287–301.

———. *The Jazz Tradition*. New and rev. ed. New York: Oxford UP, 1983.

DISCOGRAPHY

Monk, Thelonious. "April in Paris," "Thelonious." *Thelonious Monk: Genius of Modern Music*, vol. 1. Blue Note CDP 7 81510-2 (CD).

Parker, Charlie. "Bird Gets the Worm," "Parker's Mood." *Charlie Parker Memorial*. Savoy SV-0101 (CD).

———. "Klaunstance," "Ko-Ko." *Genius of Charlie Parker*. Savoy SV-0104 (CD).

———. "Move," "This Time the Dream's On Me." *One Night in Birdland*. Columbia JG 34808 (LP).

———. "Ornithology," "Scrapple from the Apple." *The Complete Dial Sessions*. Stash 567–70 (CD).

chapter 27

HAZEL V. CARBY

It Jus Be's Dat Way Sometime: The Sexual Politics of Women's Blues*

This essay considers the sexual politics of women's blues in the 1920's. Their story is part of a larger history of the production of Afro-American culture within the North American culture industry. My research has concentrated almost exclusively on those black women intellectuals who were part of the development of an Afro-American literature culture and reflects the privileged place that we accord to writers in Afro-American Studies (Carby, 1987). Within feminist theory, the cultural production of black women writers has been analyzed in isolation from other forms of women's culture and cultural presence and has neglected to relate particular texts and issues to a larger discourse of culture and cultural politics. I want to show how the representation of black female sexuality in black women's fiction and in women's blues is clearly different. I argue that different cultural forms negotiate and resolve very different sets of social contradictions. However, before considering the particularities of black women's sexual representation, we should consider its marginality within a white-dominated feminist discourse.

In 1982, at the Barnard conference on the politics of sexuality, Hortense Spillers condemned the serious absence of consideration of black female sexuality from various public discourses including white feminist theory. She described black women as "the beached whales of the sexual universe, unvoiced, misseen, not doing, awaiting *their* verb." The sexual experiences of black women, she

*This paper was originally a presentation to the conference on "Sexuality, Politics and Power" held at Mount Holyoke College, September 1986. It was reprinted in *Radical America* 20,4 (1986): 9–24. The power of the music can only be fully understood by listening to the songs, which should be played as the essay is read.

argued, were rarely depicted by themselves in what she referred to as "empowered texts": discursive feminist texts. Spillers complained of the relative absence of African-American women from the academy and thus from the visionary company of Anglo-American women feminists and their privileged mode of feminist expression.

The collection of the papers from the Barnard conference, the *Pleasure and Danger* (1984) anthology, has become one of these empowered feminist theoretical texts and Spillers' essay continues to stand within it as an important black feminist survey of the ways in which the sexuality of black American women has been unacknowledged in the public/critical discourse of feminist thought (Spillers, 1984). Following Spillers' lead black feminists continued to critique the neglect of issues of black female sexuality within feminist theory and, indeed, I as well as others directed many of our criticisms toward the *Pleasure and Danger* anthology itself (Carby, 1986).

As black women we have provided articulate and politically incisive criticism which is there for the feminist community at large to heed or to ignore—upon that decision lies the future possibility of forging a feminist movement that is not parochial. As the black feminist and educator Anna Julia Cooper stated in 1892, a woman's movement should not be based on the narrow concerns of white middle class women under the name of "women"; neither, she argued, should a woman's movement be formed around the exclusive concerns of either the white woman or the black woman or the red woman but should be able to address the concerns of all the poor and oppressed (Cooper, 1892).

But instead of concentrating upon the domination of a white feminist theoretical discourse which marginalizes non-white women, I focus on the production of a discourse of sexuality by black women. By analyzing the sexual and cultural politics of black women who constructed themselves as sexual subjects through song, in particular the blues, I want to assert an empowered presence. First, I must situate the historical moment of the emergence of women-dominated blues and establish a theoretical framework of interpretation, and then I will consider some aspects of the representation of feminism, sexuality, and power in women's blues.

Movin' On

Before World War I the overwhelming majority of black people lived in the South, although the majority of black intellectuals who purported to represent the interests of "the race" lived in the North. At the turn of the century black intellectuals felt they understood and could give voice to the concerns of the black community as a whole. They were able to position themselves as spokespeople for the "race" because they were at a vast physical and metaphorical distance from the majority of those they represented. The mass migration of blacks to urban areas, especially to the cities of the North, forced these traditional intellectuals to question and revise their imaginary vision of "the people" and directly confront the actual displaced rural workers who were, in large numbers, becoming a black working class in front of their eyes. In turn the mass of black workers became aware of the range of possibilities for their representation. No longer were the "Talented

470

tell the story

Tenth," the practitioners of policies of racial uplift, the undisputed "leaders of the race." Intellectuals and their constituencies fragmented, black union organizers, Marcus Garvey and the Universal Negro Improvement Association, radical black activists, the Sanctified Churches, the National Association of Colored Women, the Harlem Creative Artists, all offered alternative forms of representation, and each strove to establish that the experience of their constituency was representative of the experience of the race.

Within the movement of the Harlem cultural renaissance, black women writers established a variety of alternative possibilities for the fictional representation of black female experience. Zora Neale Hurston chose to represent black people as the rural folk; the folk were represented as being both the source of Afro-American cultural and linguistic forms and the means for its continued existence. Hurston's exploration of sexual and power relations was embedded in this "folk" experience and avoided the cultural transitions and confrontations of the urban displacement. As Hurston is frequently situated as the foremother of contemporary black women writers, the tendency of feminist literary criticism has been to valorize black women as "folk" heroines at the expense of those texts which explored black female sexuality within the context of urban social relations. Put simply, a line of descent is drawn from *Their Eyes Were Watching God* to *The Color Purple*. But to establish the black "folk" as representative of the black community at large was and still is a convenient method for ignoring the specific contradictions of an urban existence in which most of us live. The culture industry, through its valorization in print and in film of *The Color Purple*, for example, can *appear* to comfortably address issues of black female sexuality within a past history and rural context while completely avoiding the crucial issues of black sexual and cultural politics that stem from an urban crisis.

"There's no Earthly Use In Bein Too-Ga-Tha If It Don't Put Some Joy In Yo Life." (Williams, 1981)

However, two other women writers of the Harlem Renaissance, Jessie Fauset and Nella Larsen, did figure an urban class confrontation in their fiction, though in distinctly different ways. Jessie Fauset became an ideologue for a new black bourgeoisie; her novels represented the manners and morals that distinguished the emergent middle class from the working class. She wanted public recognition for the existence of a black elite that was urbane, sophisticated, and civilized but her representation of this elite implicitly defined its manners against the behavior of the new black proletariat. While it must be acknowledged that Fauset did explore the limitations of a middle-class existence for women, ultimately each of her novels depicts independent women who surrender their independence to become suitable wives for the new black professional men.

Nella Larsen, on the other hand, offers us a more sophisticated dissection of the rural/urban confrontation. Larsen was extremely critical of the Harlem intellectuals who glorified the values of a black folk culture while being ashamed of and ridiculing the behavior of the new black migrant to the city. Her novel *Quicksand* (1928) contains the first explicitly sexual black heroine in black women's fiction.

Larsen explores questions of sexuality and power within both a rural and an urban landscape; in both contexts she condemns the ways in which female sexuality is confined and compromised as the object of male desire. In the city Larsen's heroine, Helga, has to recognize the ways in which her sexuality has an exchange value within capitalist social relations while in the country Helga is trapped by the consequences of woman's reproductive capacity. In the final pages of *Quicksand* Helga echoes the plight of the slave woman who could not escape to freedom and the cities of the North because she could not abandon her children and, at the same time, represents how a woman's life is drained through constant childbirth.

But Larsen also reproduces in her novel the dilemma of a black woman who tries to counter the dominant white cultural definitions of her sexuality: ideologies that define black female sexuality as primitive and exotic. However, the response of Larsen's heroine to such objectification is also the response of many black women writers: the denial of desire and the repression of sexuality. Indeed, *Quicksand* is symbolic of the tension in nineteenth and early twentieth-century black women's fiction in which black female sexuality was frequently displaced onto the terrain of the political responsibility of the black woman. The duty of the black heroine toward the black community was made coterminous with her desire as a woman, a desire which was expressed as a dedication to uplift the race. This displacement from female desire to female duty enabled the negotiation of racist constructions of black female sexuality but denied sensuality, and in this denial lies the class character of its cultural politics.

It has been a mistake of much black feminist theory to concentrate almost exclusively on the visions of black women as represented by black women writers without indicating the limitations of their middle-class response to black women's sexuality. These writers faced a very real contradiction, for they felt that they would publicly compromise themselves if they acknowledged their sexuality and sensuality within a racist sexual discourse, thus providing evidence that indeed they were primitive and exotic creatures. But because black feminist theory has concentrated upon the literate forms of black women's intellectual activity the dilemma of the place of sexuality within a literary discourse has appeared as if it were the dilemma of most black women. On the other hand, what a consideration of women's blues allows us to see is an alternative form of representation, an oral and musical women's culture that explicitly addresses the contradictions of feminism, sexuality, and power. What has been called the "Classic Blues," the women's blues of the twenties and early thirties, is a discourse that articulates a cultural and political struggle over sexual relations: a struggle that is directed against the objectification of female sexuality within a patriarchal order but which also tries to reclaim women's bodies as the sexual and sensuous subjects of women's song.

Testifyin'

Within black culture the figure of the female blues singer has been reconstructed in poetry, drama, fiction, and art and used to meditate upon conventional and unconventional sexuality. A variety of narratives, both fictional and biographical, have mythologized the woman blues singer, and these mythologies become texts about sexuality. Women blues singers frequently appear as liminal figures that play out and explore the various possibilities of a sexual existence; they are representations of women who attempt to manipulate and control their construction as sexual subjects. In Afro-American fiction and poetry, the blues singer has a strong physical and sensuous presence. Shirley Anne Williams wrote about Bessie Smith:

> the thick triangular
> nose wedged
> in the deep brown
> face nostrils
> flared on a last hummmmmmmmm.

> Bessie singing
> just behind the beat
> that sweet sweet
> voice throwing
> its light on me

> I looked in her face
> and seed the woman
> I'd become. A big
> boned face already
> lined and the first line
> in her fo'head was
> black and the next line
> was sex cept I didn't
> know to call it that
> then and the brackets
> round her mouth stood fo
> the chi'ren she teared
> from out her womb. . . .
> (WILLIAMS, 1982)

Williams has argued that the early blues singers and their songs "helped to solidify community values and heighten community morale in the late nineteenth and early twentieth centuries." The blues singer, she says, uses song to create reflection and creates an atmosphere for analysis to take place. The blues were certainly a communal expression of black experience which had developed out of the call and response patterns of work songs from the nineteenth century and have been described as a "complex interweaving of the general and the specific" and of individual and group experience. John Coltrane has described how the audience heard "we" even if the singer said "I." Of course the singers were entertainers, but the blues was not an entertainment of escape or fantasy and sometimes directly represented historical events (Williams, 1979).

Sterling Brown has testified to the physical presence and power of Ma Rainey, who would draw crowds from remote rural areas to see her "smilin' gold-toofed smiles" and to feel like participants in her performance, which articulated the conditions of their social existence. Brown in his poem "Ma Rainey" remembers the emotion of her performance of "Back Water Blues," which described the devastation of the Mississippi flood of 1927. Rainey's original performance becomes in Brown's text a vocalization of the popular memory of the flood, and Brown's text constructs itself as a part of the popular memory of the "Mother of the Blues" (Brown, 1980).

Ma Rainey never recorded "Back Water Blues," although Bessie Smith did, but local songsters would hear the blues performed in the tent shows or on record and transmit them throughout the community. Ma Rainey and Bessie Smith were among the first women blues singers to be recorded, and with Clara Smith, Ethel Waters, Alberta Hunter, Ida Cox, Rosa Henderson, Victoria Spivey, and Lucille Hegamin they dominated the blues-recording industry throughout the twenties. It has often been asserted that this recording of the blues compromised and adulterated a pure folk form of the blues, but the combination of the vaudeville, carnival, and minstrel shows and the phonograph meant that the "folk-blues" and the culture industry product were inextricably mixed in the twenties. By 1928 the blues sung by blacks were only secondarily of folk origin, and the primary source for the group transmission of the blues was by phonograph, which was then joined by the radio.

Bessie Smith, Ma Rainey, Ethel Waters, and the other women blues singers travelled in carnivals and vaudevilles which included acts with animals, acrobats, and other circus performers. Often the main carnival played principally for white audiences but would have black sideshows with black entertainers for black audiences. In this way black entertainers reached black audiences in even the remotest rural areas. The records of the women blues singers were likewise directed at a black audience through the establishment of "race records," a section of the recording industry which recorded both religious and secular black singers and black musicians and distributed these recordings through stores in black areas: they were rarely available in white neighborhoods.

When a Woman Gets the Blues . . .

This then is the framework within which I interpret the women blues singers of the twenties. To fully understand the ways in which their performance and their songs were part of a discourse of sexual relations within the black community, it is necessary to consider how the social conditions of black women were dramatically affected by migration, for migration had distinctly different meanings for black men and women. The music and song of the women blues singers embodied the social relations and contradictions of black displacement: of rural migration and the urban flux. In this sense, as singers these women were organic intellectuals; not only were they a part of the community that was the subject of their song but they were also a product of the rural-to-urban movement.

Migration for women often meant being left behind: "Bye Bye Baby" and

"Sorry I can't take you" were the common refrains of male blues. In women's blues the response is complex: regret and pain expressed as "My sweet man done gone and left me dead," or "My daddy left me standing in the door," or "The sound of the train fills my heart with misery." There was also an explicit recognition that if the journey were to be made by women it held particular dangers for them. It was not as easy for women as it was for men to hop freight trains, and if money was saved for tickets it was men who were usually sent. And yet the women who were singing the songs had made it North and recorded from the "promised land" of Chicago and New York. So, what the women blues singers were able to articulate were the possibilities of movement for the women who "have ramblin' on their minds" and who intended to "ease on down the line," for they had made it—the power of movement was theirs. The train, which had symbolized freedom and mobility for men in male blues songs became a contested symbol. The sound of the train whistle, a mournful signal of imminent desertion and future loneliness, was reclaimed as a sign that women too were on the move. In 1924, both Trixie Smith and Clara Smith recorded "Freight Train Blues." These are the words Clara Smith sang:

> I hate to hear that engine blow, boo hoo.
> I hate to hear that engine blow, boo hoo.
> Everytime I hear it blowin, I feel like ridin too.
>
> That's the freight train blues, I got box cars on my mind.
> I got the freight train blues, I got box cars on my mind.
> Gonna leave this town, cause my man is so unkind.
>
> I'm goin away just to wear you off my mind.
> I'm goin away just to wear you off my mind.
> And I may be gone for a doggone long long time.
>
> I'll ask the brakeman to let me ride the blind.
> I'll ask the brakeman to please let me ride the blind.
> The brakeman say, "Clara, you know this train ain't mine."
>
> When a woman gets the blues she goes to her room and hides.
> When a woman gets the blues she goes to her room and hides.
> When a man gets the blues he catch the freight train and rides.

The music moves from echoing the moaning, mournful sound of the train whistle to the syncopated activity of the sound of the wheels in movement as Clara Smith determines to ride. The final opposition between women hiding and men riding is counterpointed by this musical activity and the determination in Clara Smith's voice. "Freight Train Blues" and then "Chicago Bound Blues," which was recorded by Bessie Smith and Ida Cox, were very popular, so Paramount and Victor encouraged more "railroad blues." In 1925 Trixie Smith recorded "Railroad Blues," which directly responded to the line "had the blues for Chicago and I just can't be satisfied" from "Chicago Bound Blues" with "If you ride that train it'll satisfy your mind." "Railroad Blues" encapsulated the ambivalent position of the blues singer caught between the contradictory impulses of needing to migrate North and the need to be able to return, for the "Railroad Blues" were headed not for the North but for Alabama. Being able to move both North and South the women blues singer occupied a privileged space: she could speak the desires of rural women to migrate and voice the nostalgic desires of urban women for home which was both a recognition and a warning that the city was not, in fact, the "promised land."

Men's and women's blues shared the language and experience of the railroad and migration but what that meant was different for each sex. The language of the blues carries this conflict of interests and is the cultural terrain in which these differences were fought over and redefined. Women's blues were the popular cultural embodiment of the way in which the differing interests of black men and women were a struggle of power relations. The sign of the train is one example of the way in which the blues were a struggle within language itself to define the differing material conditions of black women and black men.

Baaad Sista

The differing interests of women and men in the domestic sphere were clearly articulated by Bessie Smith in "In House Blues," a popular song from the mid-twenties which she wrote herself but didn't record until 1931. Although the man gets up and leaves, the woman remains, trapped in the house like a caged animal pacing up and down. But at the same time Bessie's voice vibrates with tremendous power which implies the eruption that is to come. The woman in the house is only barely restrained from creating havoc; her capacity for violence has been exercised before and resulted in her arrest. The music, which provides an oppositional counterpoint to Bessie's voice, is a parody of the supposed weakness of women. A vibrating cornet contrasts with the words that ultimately cannot be contained and roll out the front door.

> Sitting in the house with everything on my mind.
> Sitting in the house with everything on my mind.
> Looking at the clock and can't even tell the time.
>
> Walking to my window and looking outa my door.
> Walking to my window and looking outa my door.
> Wishin that my man would come home once more.
>
> Can't eat, can't sleep, so weak I can't walk my floor.
> Can't eat, can't sleep, so weak I can't walk my floor.
> Feel like calling "murder" let the police squad get me once more.
>
> They woke me up before day with trouble on my mind.
> They woke me up before day with trouble on my mind.
> Wringing my hands and screamin, walking the floor hollerin an crying.
>
> Hey, don't let them blues in here.

Hey, don't let them blues in here.
They shakes me in my bed and sits down in my chair.

Oh, the blues has got me on the go.
They've got me on the go.
They roll around my house, in and out of my front door.

The way in which Bessie growls "so weak" contradicts the supposed weakness and helplessness of the woman in the song and grants authority to her thoughts of "murder."

The rage of women against male infidelity and desertion is evident in many of the blues. Ma Rainey threatened violence when she sang that she was "gonna catch" her man "with his britches down," in the act of infidelity, in "Black Eye Blues." Exacting revenge against mistreatment also appears as taking another lover as in "Oh Papa Blues" or taunting a lover who has been thrown out with "I won't worry when you're gone, another brown has got your water on" in "Titanic Man Blues." But Ma Rainey is perhaps best known for the rejection of a lover in "Don't Fish in My Sea" which is also a resolution to give up men altogether. She sang:

If you don't like my ocean, don't fish in my sea,
If you don't like my ocean, don't fish in my sea,
Stay out of my valley, and let my mountain be.

Ain't had no lovin' since God knows when,
Ain't had no lovin' since God knows when,
That's the reason I'm through with these no good triflin' men.

The total rejection of men as in this blues and in other songs such as "Trust No Man" stands in direct contrast to the blues that concentrate upon the bewildered, often half-crazed, and even paralyzed response of women to male violence.

Sandra Leib (1981) has described the masochism of "Sweet Rough Man," in which a man abuses a helpless and passive woman, and she argues that a distinction must be made between reactions to male violence against women in male and female authored blues. "Sweet Rough Man," though recorded by Ma Rainey, was composed by a man and is the most explicit description of sexual brutality in her repertoire. The articulation of the possibility that women could leave a condition of sexual and financial dependency, reject male violence, and end sexual exploitation was embodied in Ma Rainey's recording of "Hustlin Blues," composed jointly by a man and a woman, which narrates the story of a prostitute who ends her brutal treatment by turning in her pimp to a judge. Ma Rainey sang:

I ain't made no money, and he dared me to go home.
Judge, I told him he better leave me alone.

He followed me up and he grabbed me for a fight.
He followed me up and he grabbed me for a fight.
He said, "Girl, do you know you ain't made no money tonight."

Oh Judge, tell him I'm through.
Oh Judge, tell him I'm through.
I'm tired of this life, that's why I brought him to you.

However, Ma Rainey's strongest assertion of female sexual autonomy is a song she composed herself, "Prove It on Me Blues," which isn't technically a blues song, which she sang accompanied by a Tub Jug Washboard Band. "Prove it on Me Blues" was an assertion and an affirmation of lesbianism. Though condemned by society for her sexual preference, the singer wants the whole world to know that she chooses women rather than men. The language of "Prove It on Me Blues" engages directly in defining issues of sexual preference as a contradictory struggle of social relations. Both Ma Rainey and Bessie Smith had lesbian relationships and "Prove It on Me Blues" vacillates between the subversive hidden activity of women loving women with a public declaration of lesbianism. The words express a contempt for a society that rejected lesbians. "They say I do it, ain't nobody caught me, They sure got to prove it on me." But at the same time the song is a reclamation of lesbianism as long as the woman publicly names her sexual preference for herself in the repetition of lines about the friends who "must've been women, cause I don't like no men" (Leib, 1981).

But most of the songs that asserted a woman's sexual independence did so in relation to men, not women. One of the most joyous is a recording by Ethel Waters in 1925 called "No Man's Mamma Now." It is the celebration of a divorce that ended a marriage defined as a five-year "war." Unlike Bessie Smith, Ethel Waters didn't usually growl, although she could; rather her voice, which is called "sweet-toned," gained authority from its stylistic enunciation and the way in which she almost recited the words. As Waters (1951) said, she tried to be "refined" even when she was being her most outrageous.

You may wonder what's the reason for this crazy smile,
Say I haven't been so happy in a long while
Got a big load off my mind, here's the paper sealed and signed,
And the judge was nice and kind all through the trial.
This ends a five year war, I'm sweet Miss Was once more.

I can come when I please, I can go when I please.
I can flit, fly and flutter like the birds in the trees.
Because, I'm no man's mamma now. Hey, hey.

I can say what I like, I can do what I like.
I'm a girl who is on a matrimonial strike;
Which means, I'm no man's mamma now.

I'm screaming bail
I know how a fella feels getting out of jail
I got twin beds, I take pleasure in announcing one for sale.

Am I making it plain, I will never again,
Drag around another ball and chain.

I'm through, because I'm no man's mamma now.
I can smile, I can wink, I can go take a drink,
And I don't have to worry what my hubby will think.
Because, I'm no man's mamma now.

I can spend if I choose, I can play and sing the blues.
There's nobody messin with my ones and my twos.
Because, I'm no man's mamma now.

You know there was a time,
I used to think that men were grand.
But no more for mine,
I'm gonna label my apartment "No Man's Land."

I got rid of my cat cause the cat's name was Pat,
Won't even have a male fox in my flat,
Because, I'm no man's mamma now.

Waters' sheer exuberance is infectious. The vitality and energy of the performance celebrate the unfettered sexuality of the singer. The self-conscious and self-referential lines "I can play and sing the blues" situates the singer at the center of a subversive and liberatory activity. Many of the men who were married to blues singers disapproved of their careers, some felt threatened, others, like Edith Johnson's husband, eventually applied enough pressure to force her to stop singing. Most, like Bessie Smith, Ethel Waters, Ma Rainey, and Ida Cox, did not stop singing the blues, but their public presence, their stardom, their overwhelming popularity, and their insistence on doing what they wanted caused frequent conflict with the men in their personal lives.

Funky and Sinful Stuff

The figure of the woman blues singer has become a cultural embodiment of social and sexual conflict, from Gayl Jones' novel *Corregidora* to Alice Walker's *The Color Purple*. The women blues singers occupied a privileged space; they had broken out of the boundaries of the home and taken their sensuality and sexuality out of the private into the public sphere. For these singers were gorgeous, and their physical presence elevated them to being referred to as Goddesses, as the high priestesses of the blues, or like Bessie Smith, as the Empress of the blues. Their physical presence was a crucial aspect of their power; the visual display of spangled dresses, of furs, of gold teeth, of diamonds, of all the sumptuous and desirable aspects of their body reclaimed female sexuality from being an objectification of male desire to a representation of female desire.

Bessie Smith wrote about the social criticism that women faced if they broke social convention. "Young Woman's Blues" threads together many of the issues of power and sexuality that have been addressed so far. "Young Woman's Blues" sought possibilities, possibilities that arose from women being on the move and confidently asserting their own sexual desirability.

Woke up this morning when chickens were crowing for day.
Felt on the right side of my pillow, my man had gone away.
On his pillow he left a note, reading I'm sorry you've got my goat.
No time to marry, no time to settle down.

I'm a young woman and ain't done running around.
I'm a young woman and ain't done running around.
Some people call me a hobo, some call me a bum,
Nobody know my name, nobody knows what I've done.
I'm as good as any woman in your town,
I ain't no high yella, I'm a deep killa brown.

I ain't gonna marry, ain't gonna settle down.
I'm gonna drink good moonshine and run these browns down.
See that long lonesome road, cause you know it's got a end.
And I'm a good woman and I can get plenty men.

The women blues singers have become our cultural icons of sexual power, but what is often forgotten is that they could be great comic entertainers. In "One Hour Mama" Ida Cox used comedy to intensify an irreverent attack on male sexual prowess. The comic does not mellow the assertive voice but on the contrary undermines mythologies of phallic power and establishes a series of woman-centered heterosexual demands.

I've always heard that haste makes waste,
So, I believe in taking my time
The highest mountain can't be raced
It's something you must slowly climb.

I want a slow and easy man,
He needn't ever take the lead,
Cause I work on that long time plan
And I ain't a looking for no speed.

I'm a one hour mama, so no one minute papa
Ain't the kind of man for me.
Set your alarm clock papa, one hour that's proper
Then love me like I like to be.

I don't want no lame excuses bout my lovin being so good,
That you couldn't wait no longer, now I hope I'm understood.
I'm a one hour mama, so no one minute papa
Ain't the kind of man for me.

I can't stand no green horn lover, like a rookie goin to war,
With a load of big artillery, but don't know what its for.
He's got to bring me reference with a great long pedigree
And must prove he's got endurance, or he don't mean snap to me.

I can't stand no crowin rooster, what just likes a hit or two,
Action is the only booster of just what my man can do.
I don't want no imitation, my requirements ain't no joke,
Cause I got pure indignation for a guy what's lost his stroke.

I'm a one hour mama, so no one minute papa
Ain't the kind of man for me.
Set your alarm clock papa, one hour that's proper,
Then love me like I like to be.

I may want love for one hour, then decide to make it two.
Takes an hour 'fore I get started, maybe three before I'm through.
I'm a one hour mama, so no one minute papa,
Ain't the kind of man for me.

But this moment of optimism, of the blues as the exercise of power and control over sexuality, was short lived. The space occupied by these blues singers was opened up by race records but race records did not survive the Depression. Some of these blues women, like Ethel Waters and Hattie McDaniels, broke through the racial boundaries of Hollywood film and were inserted into a different aspect of the culture industry where they occupied not a privileged but a subordinate space and articulated not the possibilities of black female sexual power but the "Yes, Ma'ams" of the black maid. The power of the blues singer was resurrected in a different moment of black power; re-emerging in Gayl Jones' *Corregidora*; and the woman blues singer remains an important part of our 20th century black cultural reconstruction. The blues singers had assertive and demanding voices; they had no respect for sexual taboos or for breaking through the boundaries of respectability and convention, and we hear the "we" when they say "I."

REFERENCES

Brown, S. (1980). Ma Rainey. *The Collected Poems of Sterling A. Brown*. New York: Harper and Row.

Carby, H. V. (1986). On the threshold of woman's era: Lynching, empire and sexuality in black feminist theory. In H. L. Gates, Jr. (Ed.), *'Race,' Writing and Difference* (pp. 301–316). Chicago: University of Chicago Press.

Carby, H. V. (1987). *Reconstructing Womanhood: The Emergence of the Afro-American Woman Novelist*. New York: Oxford University Press.

Cooper, A. J. (1892). *A Voice from the South*. Xenia, OH: Aldine Publishing House.

Cox, I. (1980). One hour mama. *Mean Mothers*. Rosetta Records, RR 1300.

Leib, S. (1981). *Mother of the Blues: A Study of Ma Rainey*. Amherst: University of Massachusetts Press.

Rainey, G. (1974). Ma Rainey. Milestone Records, M47021.

Smith, B. (n.d.). In house blues. *The World's Greatest Blues Singer*. Columbia Records, CG 33.

Smith, B. (1972). Young woman's blues. *Nobody's Blues but Mine*. Columbia Records, CG 31093.

Smith, C. (1980). Freight train blues. *Women's Railroad Blues*. Rosetta Records, RR 1301.

Spillers, H. (1984). Interstices: A small drama of words. In C. Vance (Ed.), *Pleasure and Danger: Exploring Female Sexuality* (pp. 73–100). London: Routledge and Kegan Paul.

Waters, E. (1951). *His Eye Is on the Sparrow*. New York: Doubleday & Co., Inc.

Waters, E. (1982). No man's mama. *Big Mamas*. Rosetta Records, RR 1306.

Williams, S. A. (1979). The blues roots of contemporary Afro-American poetry. In M. S. Harper & R. B. Stepto (Eds.), *Chant of Saints* (pp. 123–135). Chicago: University of Illinois Press.

Williams, S. A. (1981). The house of desire. In E. Stetson (Ed.), *Black Sister: Poetry by Black American Women, 1746–1980*. Bloomington: Indiana University Press.

Williams, S. A. (1982). Fifteen. *Some One Sweet Angel Chile*. New York: William Morrow and Co., Inc.

tell the story

chapter 28

SCOTT DEVEAUX

Constructing the Jazz Tradition*

I don't know where jazz is going. Maybe it's going to hell. You can't make anything go anywhere. It just happens. — THELONIOUS MONK

I

To judge from textbooks aimed at the college market, something like an official history of jazz has taken hold in recent years. On these pages, for all its chaotic diversity of style and expression and for all the complexity of its social origins, jazz is presented as a coherent whole, and its history as a skillfully contrived and easily comprehended narrative. After an obligatory nod to African origins and ragtime antecedents, the music is shown to move through a succession of styles or periods, each with a conveniently distinctive label and time period: New Orleans jazz up through the 1920s, swing in the 1930s, bebop in the 1940s, cool jazz and hard bop in the 1950s, free jazz and fusion in the 1960s. Details of emphasis vary. But from textbook to textbook, there is substantive agreement on the defining features of each style, the pantheon of great innovators, and the canon of recorded masterpieces.

This official version of jazz history continues to gain ground through the burgeoning of jazz appreciation classes at universities and colleges. It is both symptom and cause of the gradual acceptance of jazz, within the academy and in the soci-

*Scott DeVeaux teaches music at the University of Virginia. He wishes to thank his colleague James Rubin for his generous advice and insight in writing this article.

ety at large, as an art music—"America's classical music," in a frequently invoked phrase.[1] Such acceptance, most advocates of jazz agree, is long overdue. If at one time jazz could be supported by the marketplace, or attributed to a nebulous (and idealized) vision of folk creativity, that time has long passed. Only by acquiring the prestige, the "cultural capital" (in Pierre Bourdieu's phrase) of an artistic tradition can the music hope to be heard, and its practitioners receive the support commensurate with their training and accomplishments. The accepted historical narrative for jazz serves this purpose. It is a pedigree, showing contemporary jazz to be not a fad or a mere popular music, subject to the whims of fashion, but an autonomous art of some substance, the culmination of a long process of maturation that has in its own way recapitulated the evolutionary progress of Western art.

The added twist is that this new American classical music openly acknowledges its debt not to Europe, but to Africa. There is a sense of triumphant reversal as the music of a formerly enslaved people is designated a "rare and valuable national American treasure" by the Congress, and beamed overseas as a weapon of the Cold War.[2] The story of jazz, therefore, has an important political dimension, one that unfolds naturally in its telling. Louis Armstrong, Duke Ellington, and John Coltrane provide powerful examples of black achievement and genius. Their exacting discipline cannot be easily marginalized, *pace* Adorno, as "mere" popular entertainment, or as the shadowy replication of European forms. The depth of tradition, reaching back in an unbroken continuum to the beginning of the century, belies attempts to portray African Americans as people without a past—hence the appeal of an unambiguous and convincing historical narrative: If the achievements that jazz represents are to be impressed on present and future generations, the story must be told, and told well.

For all its pedagogical utility, though, the conventional narrative of jazz history is a simplification that begs as many questions as it answers. For one thing, the story that moves so confidently at the outset from style to style falters as it approaches the present. From the origins of jazz to bebop there is a straight line; but after bebop, the evolutionary lineage begins to dissolve into the inconclusive coexistence of many different, and in some cases mutually hostile, styles. "At the century's halfway mark," complains one textbook, "the historical strand that linked contemporary jazz to its roots suddenly began to fray. The cohesive thread had been pulled apart in the '40s by the bebop musicians, and now every fiber was bent at a slightly different angle" (Tirro 291). Beginning with the 1950s and 1960s, the student of jazz history is confronted with a morass of terms—*cool jazz, hard bop, modal jazz, Third Stream, New Thing*—none of which convincingly represents a consensus.[3] For the most recent decades, the most that writers of textbooks can manage is to sketch out the contrasting directions pointed to by free jazz and jazz/rock fusion, implying to the impressionable student that an informed view embraces both, as it embraces all preceding styles, and that the future of jazz is bound up with a pluralism that somehow reconciles these apparently irreconcilable trends.[4] No one, apparently, has thought to ask whether the earlier "cohesive thread" of narrative might mask similarly conflicting interpretations.

At the same time that jazz educators have struggled to bring order to jazz history, a controversy over the current state and future direction of jazz has become noisily evident in the popular media. The terms of this debate pit so-called *neoclassicists*, who insist on the priority of tradition and draw their inspiration and identity from a sense of connectedness with the historical past, against both the continuous revolution of the *avant-garde* and the commercial orientation of *fusion*. At stake, if the rhetoric is taken at face value, is nothing less than the music's survival. Some have argued, for example, that the neoclassicist movement, led by youthful celebrity Wynton Marsalis, has rescued jazz from extinction. "Largely under his influence," proclaimed a *Time* author in a recent cover story,

> a jazz renaissance is flowering on what was once barren soil. Straight-ahead jazz music almost died in the 1970s as record companies embraced the electronically enhanced jazz-pop amalgam known as fusion. Now a whole generation of prodigiously talented young musicians is going back to the roots, using acoustic instruments, playing recognizable tunes and studying the styles of earlier jazzmen.   (SANCTON 66)

Other critics counter that the triumph of a retrospective aesthetic is in fact all the evidence one might need that jazz is dead; all that is left to the current generation is the custodial function of preserving and periodically reviving glorious moments from the past.[5]

The neoclassicists' nostalgia for a Golden Age located ambiguously somewhere between the swing era and 1960s hard bop resonates curiously with issues that go back to the earliest days of jazz historiography. Marsalis and his followers have been called "latter-day moldy figs" (Santoro, "Miles" 17), a term that links them to critics of the 1930s and '40s who, by insisting on the priority of New Orleans–style jazz, earned themselves the reputation as defenders of an outdated and artificially static notion of what jazz is and can be. The countercharge that either (or both) avant-garde or fusion constitutes a "wrong turn," or a "dead end," in the development of jazz represents the opposing argument, of the same vintage: Any change that fails to preserve the essence of the music is a corruption that no longer deserves to be considered jazz.[6]

The difference in tone between these assessments—the rancor of the journalistic debate, and the platitudinous certainty of the classroom—disguises the extent to which certain underlying assumptions are shared. With the possible exception of those in the fusion camp (who are more often the targets of the debate than active participants in it), no one disputes the official version of the history.[7] Its basic narrative shape and its value for a music that is routinely denied respect and institutional support are accepted virtually without question. The struggle is over *possession* of that history, and the legitimacy that it confers. More precisely, the struggle is over the act of definition that is presumed to lie at the history's core; for it is an article of faith that some central essence named *jazz* remains constant throughout all the dramatic transformations that have resulted in modern-day jazz.

That essence is ordinarily defined very vaguely; there is ample evidence from jazz folklore to suggest that musicians take a certain stubborn pride in the resistance of their art to critical exegesis. (To the question *What is jazz?* the apocryphal answer is: "If you have to ask, you'll never know.") But in the heat of debate, definition is a powerful weapon; and more often than not, such definitions define through exclusion. Much as the concept of purity is made more concrete by the threat of contamination, what jazz is *not* is far more vivid rhetorically than what it is. Thus fusion is "not jazz" because, in its pursuit of commercial success, it has embraced certain musical traits—the use of electric instruments, modern production techniques, and a rock- or funk-oriented rhythmic feeling—that violate the essential nature of jazz. The avant-garde, whatever its genetic connection to the modernism of 1940s bebop, is not jazz—or no longer jazz—because, in its pursuit of novelty, it has recklessly abandoned the basics of form and structure, even African-American principles like "swing." And the neoclassicist stance is irrelevant, and potentially harmful, to the growth of jazz because it makes a fetish of the past, failing to recognize that the essence of jazz is the process of change itself.

Defining jazz is a notoriously difficult proposition, but the task is easier if one bypasses the usual inventory of musical qualities or techniques, like improvisation or swing (since the more specific or comprehensive such a list attempts to be, the more likely it is that exceptions will overwhelm the rule). More relevant are the boundaries within which historians, critics, and musicians have consistently situated the music. One such boundary, certainly, is ethnicity. Jazz is strongly identified with African-American culture, both in the narrow sense that its particular techniques ultimately derive from black American folk traditions, and in the broader sense that it is expressive of, and uniquely rooted in, the experience of black Americans. This raises important questions at the edges—e.g., how the contributions of white musicians are to be treated and, at the other end of the spectrum, where the boundary between jazz and other African-American genres (such as blues, gospel, and R & B) ought to be drawn. But on the whole, ethnicity provides a core, a center of gravity for the narrative of jazz, and is one element that unites the several different kinds of narratives in use today.

An equally pervasive, if divisive, theme is economics—specifically, the relationship of jazz to capitalism. Here, the definition is negative: Whether conceived of as art music or folk music, jazz is consistently seen as something separate from the popular music industry. The stigmatization of "commercialism" as a disruptive or corrupting influence, and in any case as something external to the tradition, has a long history in writings on jazz. In the words of Rudi Blesh (writing in 1946),

> Commercialism [is] a cheapening and deteriorative force, a species of murder perpetrated on a wonderful music by whites and by those misguided negroes who, for one or another reason, choose to be accomplices to the dead. . . . Commercialism is a thing not only hostile, but fatal to [jazz].
>
> (11–12)

Such language was particularly popular with defenders of New Orleans–style jazz who, like Blesh, narrowly identified the music with a romanticized notion of folk culture. But the same condemnatory fervor could be heard from proponents of bebop in the 1940s:

The story of bop, like that of swing before it, like the stories of jazz and ragtime before that, has been one of constant struggle against the restrictions imposed on all progressive thought in an art that has been commercialized to the point of prostitution.   (FEATHER, *Inside* 45)

Bebop is the music of revolt: revolt against big bands, arrangers . . . Tin Pan Alley—against commercialized music in general. It reasserts the individuality of the jazz musician. . . .   (RUSSELL 202)

These attitudes survive with undiminished force in recent attacks on fusion, which imply a conception of jazz as a music independent of commercial demands that is in continuous conflict with the economic imperatives of twentieth-century America. *Agoraphobia*, fear of the marketplace, is problematic enough in artistic genres that have actually achieved, or inherited, some degree of economic autonomy. It is all the more remarkable for jazz—a music that has developed largely within the framework of modern mass market capitalism—to be construed within the inflexible dialectic of "commercial" versus "artistic," with all virtue centered in the latter. The virulence with which these opinions are expressed gives a good idea how much energy was required to formulate this position in the first place, and how difficult it is to maintain. This is not to say that there is not an exploitative aspect to the relationship between capitalist institutions and jazz musicians, especially when the effects of racial discrimination on the ability of black musicians to compete fairly are factored in. But jazz is kept separate from the marketplace only by demonizing the economic system that allows musicians to survive—and from this demon there is no escape. Wynton Marsalis may pride himself on his refusal to "sell out," but that aura of artistic purity is an indisputable component of his commercial appeal.

Issues of ethnicity and economics define jazz as an oppositional discourse: the music of an oppressed minority culture, tainted by its association with commercial entertainment in a society that reserves its greatest respect for art that is carefully removed from daily life. The escape from marginalization comes only from a self-definition that emphasizes its universality and its autonomy. The "jazz tradition" reifies the music, insisting that there is an overarching category called *jazz*, encompassing musics of divergent styles and sensibilities. These musics must be understood not as isolated expressions of particular times or places, but in an organic relationship, as branches of a tree to the trunk. The essence of jazz, in other words, lies not in any one style, or any one cultural or historical context, but in that which links all these things together into a seamless continuum. Jazz is what it is because it is a culmination of all that has come before. Without the sense of depth that only a narrative can provide, jazz would be literally rootless, indistinguishable from a variety of other "popular" genres that combine virtuosity and craftsmanship with dance rhythms. Its claim to being not only distinct, but elevated above other indigenous forms ("America's classical music"), is in large part dependent on the idea of an evolutionary progression reaching back to the beginning of the century. Again and again, present-day musicians, whether neoclassicist or avant-garde, invoke the past, keeping before the public's eye the idea that musics as diverse as those of King Oliver and the Art Ensemble of Chicago are in some fundamental sense *the same music*.[8]

Those who subscribe to an essentialist notion of jazz history (and there are few who do not) take all of this for granted. But even a glance at jazz historiography makes it clear that the idea of the "jazz tradition" is a construction of relatively recent vintage, an overarching narrative that has crowded out other possible interpretations of the complicated and variegated cultural phenomena that we cluster under the umbrella *jazz*. Nor is this simply an academic complaint: The crisis of the current jazz scene is less a function of the state of the music (jazz has, in many ways, never been better supported or appreciated) than of an anxiety arising from the inadequacy of existing historical frameworks to explain it. The remainder of this essay will show how the concept of the jazz tradition came to be, what ideas it displaced along the way (and at what cost), what contradictions it contains, and its uses for describing and influencing the music of the present and future. In conclusion, I will try to indicate ways in which the narrative of the jazz tradition might be complemented by other kinds of research.

II

In the earliest writings on jazz, historical narrative only gradually emerged from criticism. The most important full-scale study of jazz, Hugues Panassié's 1934 *Le jazz hot* (translated and widely disseminated on this side of the Atlantic as *Hot Jazz* in 1936) was primarily critical in its approach. As befits a work written in Europe, it begins with a lengthy explication of the qualities that distinguish jazz from European music: swing, improvisation, repertory, and so forth. Just as important, however, was Panassié's choosing to distinguish between "hot jazz" and other kinds of music called jazz ("sweet," "symphonic") that occupied so much attention during the jazz age. In so doing, Panassié contributed to the process by which a catch phrase of considerable vagueness, indiscriminately applied to all kinds of popular song and dance music of the 1920s, came to be appropriated (some might say reclaimed) as a term for a music the aesthetic boundaries of which could be set with some precision. And indeed, the remainder of the book is primarily concerned with Panassié's notoriously fine, often supercilious distinctions (e.g., trumpeter Red Allen's "style is feverish, occasionally intemperate, and this is hardly acceptable" [76]), separating the "authentic" from the "false."

History per se plays a decidedly subsidiary role in Panassié's scheme. And his distance from the scene (Panassié's acquaintance with jazz came solely from recordings) forced him to fall back on a dubious secondary literature, some of which is bizarre in its remove from reality; it leads him, for example, to describe "St. Louis Blues" and "Memphis Blues" as work songs passed along by banjo-strumming fathers to their children, "a national repertory which all American Negroes know and respect just as we revere our old French songs" (26). Such distortions aside, a sense of historical development is nevertheless an indispensable framework for his aesthetics. According to Panassié, it is not until 1926 that jazz "attained its stable form, . . . ceased to falter and became a definite, balanced musical form" (38). Prior to that time, the music was characterized by an upward arc from the "chaos" of the ur-styles of New Orleans through the agency of musicians like Louis Armstrong, the "greatest of all hot musicians" who "brought hot style to a peak" (27). Not until this process had been fulfilled, not only for the music as a whole but also for musicians individually (Coleman Hawkins's style was "the culmination of a progressive evolution" [101]), could criticism proper begin.

For Panassié, the history of jazz was necessarily abstract, a narrative to be deduced from the evidence of recordings and supported by shadowy speculation. In America, by contrast, that history was more concrete. Although still remote, it could be traced in the urban topography of New Orleans and Chicago, in the memory of those who listened to it, and, above all, in the direct testimony of those who created it. The impetus for historical research, exemplified by the landmark 1939 book *Jazzmen*, was essentially biographical. In the preface to *Jazzmen*, the editors, Charles Edward Smith and Frederic Ramsey, Jr., define their position as something separate from, and complementary to, the critical orientation of Panassié:

> It is the musicians, the creators of jazz, who have actually been most neglected while critical battles have been fought. . . . This book has attempted to fill the gaps left by the critics who, chiefly concerned with their appraisal of the music, have forgotten the musicians. (XII–XIII)

There is very little by way of explicit or formal argument in the highly anecdotal narrative of *Jazzmen*. But if, as Hayden White suggests, explanation in history may be conveyed through "emplotment"—the *kind* of story told (White 7–11)—then these biographical accounts reveal a great deal about the attitudes of those who wrote them. Of White's archetypal "modes" of narrative, the one most consistently and vividly represented in *Jazzmen* is the Tragic. And indeed, many of the life stories are tragic. Buddy Bolden, the charismatic, myth-enshrouded "first man of jazz," who spent the last twenty-four years of his life in a mental institution; King Oliver, reduced at the end to managing a seedy pool hall in Savannah; Bix Beiderbecke, the prototypical white jazz rebel, doomed by his association with "Negro" music and caught in a self-destructive cycle of alcohol and frustrated ambition—in *Jazzmen*, all share the experience (or the ideal) of New Orleans as a Golden Age, and fight a subsequent losing battle against the combined forces of racism, commercial exploitation, and the disdain of the cultural establishment. The shuttering of Storyville in 1917 figures as an expulsion from Paradise that sets the tragedy in motion, and the onset of the Depression is a final act that grinds our heroes under the heel of an uncaring society. "What's the use?" lamented the clarinetist Frank Teschemacher (whose own fate was to fall from a speeding car in New York City in 1932). "You knock yourself out making a great new music for people, and they treat you like some kind of plague or blight, like you were offering them leprosy instead of art" (qtd. in Mezzrow 110).

But not all stories could be configured this way. Some musicians, like Armstrong and Ellington, never suffered a decline and fall. Still others, like Benny

489

Goodman, passed through the nadir of the Depression only to reemerge triumphant, successful, and admired beyond all expectation in the breakthrough of jazz-oriented dance orchestras into the popular mainstream during the "Swing Era" of the middle and late 1930s. The proper mode for such stories would seem to be not Tragedy but Romance: "the triumph of good over evil, of virtue over vice, of light over darkness" (White 9). And indeed, this has become the dominant mode of storytelling for jazz, both for individuals and for the idiom as a whole.

Still, contemporary advocates for jazz were troubled by the transformation. On the one hand, the general enthusiasm for swing did not necessarily translate into appreciation for, or even awareness of, the jazz that stemmed from New Orleans. (Indeed, the very name *swing* emphasized its differences from the now old-fashioned *jazz* of the 1920s.) On the other hand, swing brought both a new musical language and a new economic basis for the music which threatened to make the earlier style obsolete. The former represented opportunity, a chance to proselytize on an unprecedented scale. The latter represented danger, the possibility of being seduced by commercial success into abandoning the essential qualities of the music.

Many were quick to assert that jazz and swing were essentially the same genre. Significantly, critics like Panassié had earlier embraced both small-combo jazz and the early "big bands" of Ellington and Henderson, seeing in the latter category the "hot concept" expressed through an orchestral medium (*Hot Jazz* 165). This enabled writers to strike a rhetorical stance welcoming the newcomers to the idiom and congratulating them on their good taste, while making it clear that a deeper, more mature appreciation of the music lay in an exploration of its past (and not incidentally, in the passage from popular white musicians to their more authentic black forebears). "The present interest in swing music, unfortunately, is a microscopic one," wrote Paul Eduard Miller in 1937. "Not so for the initiate: he looks upon swing music as a fad, and prefers to take a telescopic, long-range view of hot jazz" ("Roots" 5). More than anything, this line of argument strengthened historical narrative as an avenue for understanding jazz.

But constructing a suitable narrative foundered on the question of whether the music had in fact changed. One view was presented forcefully by Winthrop Sargeant in *Jazz: Hot and Hybrid.* "There was nothing new about hot jazz in 1935," he wrote in the first chapter. Its apparently novel features were "merely the result of changes in formula designed to create a public demand for dance bands, sheet music, phonograph records, or other products of the commercial music industry" (15–16). After the lengthy explication of technical features of jazz that comprises the bulk of the book, Sargeant concludes that jazz in fact lacks an historical dimension:

> One of the most striking features of jazz as compared with art music is its lack of evolutionary development. Aside from a few minor changes of fashion, its history shows no technical evolution whatever. . . . Jazz today remains essentially the same kind of music it was in 1900.   (259)

Sargeant attributes the lack of development in jazz to its roots in—indeed, virtual identity with—folk music, "the original primitive music of the American Negro." But his is a flawed view of folk culture that anachronistically characterizes the increasingly urban black community of mid-century America as a "peasant proletariat" and considers the community's cultural products to be primitive expressions incapable of further development. Folk elements, according to this view, do not change—*cannot* change. They may only be imitated and exploited by the popular music industry. Under pressure from society, however benignly intended, they may disappear altogether. Looking ahead, he notes: "It is not at all unlikely that the education of the mass of American Negroes will sound the death knell of the type of primitive jazz that the aesthetes most admire" (264).

This static, anti-developmental, anti-modernist view underlies much of the writing on jazz of the 1930s and 1940s. "You can't improve on the old boys," seconded George Avakian in a 1939 article entitled "Where Is Jazz Going?" "Jazz is jazz; it can't be modernized or streamlined" (9). The continued presence on the jazz scene of such august figures as Armstrong and Sidney Bechet; the success of jazz researchers in uncovering so much of the historical context for the origins of the music; the startling public acceptance of such authentically and previously neglected "folk" idioms as boogie-woogie; the dramatic resurrection of Bunk Johnson, providing a Romantic story of triumph over adversity to equal the superficial triumphs of the swing stars—all reinforced a view in which the thrust of jazz history was to restore and strengthen the "original" music.[9] Swing's purpose would be admirably fulfilled if, after leading the uninitiated to the "real jazz," it would simply wither away.

The most vociferous proponent of this view was Panassié, in his 1942 book *The Real Jazz*. In this volume, jazz is now specifically defined as "the spontaneous urge of a whole people" (7), a "primitive" African-American folk expression superior by virtue of its emotional directness to the tired intricacies of European art. Over this "natural, spontaneous song" (6) there is no possibility of improvement. Indeed, the very notion of progress is inherently destructive, seducing musicians from their true calling:

> These musicians who had infallibly played in a perfect manner, and had never digressed for an instant from the pure tradition of their art as long as they blindly followed their instinct, now rejected their tradition and began to reason and to "improve" their music. Of course they fell into innumerable errors. (54)

Swing was, in a sense, "more dangerous" than earlier attempts to improve jazz, such as the symphonic jazz of Paul Whiteman, "because it came much closer to the real jazz and easily misled the uninitiated" (65).

Still, metaphors of growth and evolution underlie even the most conservative stances. Panassié, for instance, was guided by a deep-rooted inclination to view art as a growing, developing organism. Small-group jazz in Chicago "evolved little by little and developed in an excellent manner" (49); Armstrong's career is divided into several "periods," "for a musician who is also a creator never ceases to evolve during his musical career" (69–70). Most telling is Panassié's evaluation of the black swing bands, already included as "hot jazz" in his 1934 book. "The growth of such orchestras as Jimmy [sic] Lunceford's, Count Basie's, and Duke Ellington's," he wrote eight years later, "is the most remarkable event in the recent history of jazz. These orchestras have contributed a great deal in maintaining jazz's vitality, and through them new blood has been infused into jazz" (235). His anti-progress stance represents not so much a disbelief in the possibility of development as a pessimistic feeling that development beyond a certain point inevitably leads to decay and decadence. Having once matured to a "balanced," "classic" state, jazz can no longer "progress." The best that one can hope is that the mature stage can be sustained and preserved for as long as possible. And this is made more difficult when black musicians "must submit to the corruption of an outrageous commercialism, as well as to the conventional musical notions of the white man and the current theories about necessary progress." The end result is that "jazz will be transformed little by little, until it becomes an entirely different kind of music" (236).

Even Rudi Blesh, who in his 1946 *Shining Trumpets* is contemptuous of the "illusion of progress" in the arts, and provides a chart to show the "deformations of Negro jazz" (to be used in identifying those "deceptive elements . . . which, borrowed from jazz, make the present-day commercial swing falsely seem another form of that music" [7]), showed himself to be a firm believer in evolution, less pessimistic in fact than Panassié about the prospects for growth and development. "The history of jazz has been a short one," Blesh writes, "a span of development and fruition remarkably compressed in time" (14); "pure jazz" emerges at "its highest point of evolution" (16). The obstacles to further development are, once again, external: misconceptions fostered by "commercial interests." Once these obstacles are removed, Blesh speculates hopefully, "can progress resume, undistorted and unvitiated, from that point?" (16).

The extent to which Blesh and Panassié already subscribed to a dynamic view of jazz history made it difficult for them to hold a position against the advocates of swing in the debates that periodically flared up in the jazz press of the 1940s. Their opponents simply accepted swing as the natural, certainly desirable, and perhaps inevitable result of development. Whereas the New Orleans purists viewed the transformation with suspicion and misgiving, others were optimistic and openly enthusiastic. "The truth happens to be that countless musicians have used the groundwork laid by the Armstrongs and Beiderbeckes and have built up from those fine foundations," argued Leonard Feather on the pages of *Esquire* in 1944. "Never before has any branch of music made such rapid progress" ("Jazz" 129). Moreover, as Feather delighted in demonstrating, the musicians themselves, more often than not, subscribed to this idea of progress, usually measured in increased technical and harmonic sophistication.[10] In any case, such optimism and enthusiasm fit the mood of the country, which was inclined to expect progress in its popular arts as in any other national exercise of ingenuity and skill. "Surely there can be an improvement over a period of twenty years," Paul Eduard Miller asserted in 1945, "and if there isn't, then the future of jazz as an art form is precariously balanced" ("Rhythm" 86).

Nothing infuriated the conservatives more than this line of argument, for it carried the obvious implication that the music of the 1920s, far from representing the idiom in its "classic," mature stage, was in fact an awkward beginning, the first phase of a dynamic evolution that inevitably rendered the earliest jazz efforts obsolete. Indeed, in the heat of argument, the idea of progress could be turned quite pointedly against the "masterpieces" of early jazz:

> The experienced and discerning jazz listener, whose ears are attuned to more advanced ideas in orchestration and improvisation, laughs at the attempts to deify the badly dated relics of the 1920s. . . . Today you can listen to each of the five trumpet players in Lionel Hampton's band, and every one of them will take a chorus which, had it been discovered on some obscure old record, would be hailed as genius by the Jelly Roll network.
>
> (FEATHER, "JAZZ" 129)

One ought not to exaggerate the significance of this sectarian dispute, however. Both sides faced the same obstacles—the indifference and ignorance of the general public, the hostility of "commercial interests" and the cultural establishment—and knew at heart that what they had in common outweighed their differences. The concept of a jazz tradition with an honorable past and a hopeful future began to emerge as a useful compromise, with the term *jazz* now covering both the original "hot jazz" of the 1920s and the swing of the 1930s. In principle, it bound together enthusiasts of different persuasions and allowed them to make a common front against outsiders. Thus, *Jazzmen* included a chapter on "Hot Jazz Today" that spoke warmly of such modernists as Art Tatum, Chick Webb, and Andy Kirk. On the other side of the fence, *Down Beat*, a periodical aimed at the modern swing musician, carried articles providing historical perspective, and persuaded many to accept and even admire earlier styles.[11] In 1944 another trade periodical, *Metronome*, canvassed ten well-known musicians to support its conclusion that there was "absolutely no dividing line between swing and jazz" (Ulanov and Feather 22–23).

III

This hard-won truce was threatened almost immediately by the rise of bebop in the mid-1940s. The birth of the new style coincided with the peak of the revival of New Orleans jazz, prompting a frequently acrimonious, occasionally hysterical war of words that did much to polarize the jazz community into opposing sides: the progressives and the "moldy figs." Bebop's success in winning the loyalty of a younger generation of musicians and the admiration of a core of jazz enthusiasts was an especially bitter pill for many conservatives. Panassié simply refused to recognize the new style. He expressed qualified admiration for the music of Charlie Parker and Dizzy Gillespie, but whatever it was, it wasn't jazz (*Real Jazz* rev. ed. 73–74). For their part, the young black musicians at the forefront of bebop often keenly resented what they perceived to be the patronizing tone of the New

Orleans camp—the idealization of "primitive" jazz; the revival of literally toothless, aging black musicians as symbols of their people's art. They saw their own music as a logical expression of modernity. "Modern life is fast and complicated, and modern music should be fast and complicated," said the arranger Gil Fuller in 1948. "We're tired of that old New Orleans beat-beat, I-got-the-blues pap" (qtd. in Boyer 28). "That old stuff was like Mother Goose rhymes," Dizzy Gillespie added. "It was all right for its time, but it was a childish time" (qtd. in Boyer 29).

If this debate seems curiously irrelevant to the modern observer, it is largely because contemporary conceptions of the term *jazz* have been shaped in bebop's image. There is a certain logic, after all, to the argument that an idiom so thoroughly transformed ought perhaps to be considered a new genre and given a new name, as bebop was. And there is no doubt that the differences between bebop and the jazz that preceded it were far from trivial. Radical changes in the rhythmic foundation, in particular the more aggressive and polyrhythmic role of the drummer, make bebop distinct, much as genres in traditional West African music are differentiated by characteristic rhythmic relationships.[12] In many other essentials, both musical and extramusical (its relationship to dance and popular song, for example, and its claims to a kind of "chamber music" autonomy), bebop was such a departure that to consider it a new type of music, deriving from jazz but separate from it, was not out of the question.

This, needless to say, is not the way the narrative of jazz history goes. An equally logical case for considering bebop as a subset of an overarching category, "jazz," can and has been built by underscoring continuity wherever possible: the influence of older musicians on younger ones (Lester Young on Charlie Parker, for example), or the essential qualities of improvisation and swing that all styles under the jazz umbrella share. Either interpretation—bebop as revolution and discontinuity, or as evolution and continuity—is possible, and the choice between them depends not on which one is right or wrong, but on the uses to which the interpretation is to be put. In emphasizing continuity over discontinuity, and the general (jazz) over the particular (bebop), the jazz community made a choice that determined how the music would henceforth be described and understood.[13]

Given the marginalized position of jazz in American society at mid-century, the choice is hardly surprising. For all the bravado of the "progressive" camp during its heyday in the late 1940s, when Dizzy Gillespie was profiled in *Life* and even Benny Goodman's swing band played bop-influenced arrangements, there was little advantage in a declaration of independence. In the long run, it proved as much in the interests of the modernists to have their music legitimated as the latest phase of a (now) long and distinguished tradition, as it was in the interests of the proponents of earlier jazz styles (whether New Orleans jazz or swing) not to be swept aside as merely antiquarian. Furthermore, it cost the modernists little to mute or even renounce their claims to progress, if that was required to make peace with their predecessors. Thus a new compromise was forged, and the term *jazz* further extended—its definition now more than ever dependent on ideas of continuous evolution and growth.

One of the earliest and most fully articulated formulations of this compromise appeared in 1948 in a series of articles by Ross Russell, owner of Dial Records, a small firm specializing in bebop. The articles (subsequently reprinted in *The Art of Jazz*) appeared in *The Record Changer*, a magazine begun as a newsletter for collectors of rare early jazz recordings. By the late 1940s, *The Record Changer* had expanded to carry feature articles, mostly about the older styles of jazz, but it became increasingly open to the discussion of new trends. Russell's approach—part polemic, part peace offering—was carefully tailored for his audience. He outlined bebop's innovations, arguing that in many respects bebop represented a decided advantage. At the same time, he defended the value of earlier jazz styles. "Those who cannot enjoy the music of [Jelly Roll] Morton and [Louis] Armstrong," he wrote in an obvious reference to bebop extremists, "are truly as poor as those who are unable to understand the no less wonderful art of Lester Young and Charlie Parker" (196). Above all, Russell appealed to the image of a tradition that linked all styles in a transcendent process of evolution: "The real nature of jazz history is organic," he insisted; it is a "living cultural form" that "constantly extends, reaffirms, and replenishes itself. . . . From Jelly Roll Morton to Max Roach, our music is a whole art extended across the time and space of twentieth-century America, and back into the roots of African culture" (195–96).

This envisioning of jazz as an organic entity that periodically revitalizes itself through the upheaval of stylistic change while retaining its essential identity resolved one of the fundamental problems in the writing of its history: the stigma of inferiority or incompleteness that the notion of progress inevitably attached to earlier styles. In Russell's model, all jazz styles are equally valid, for all are authentic manifestations of its central essence. Of course, this requires a conscious decision to overlook the obvious discontinuity in musical language—to say nothing of the social and cultural contexts for the music—in favor of a transcendent principle of continuity. That so few objected to this project shows how powerfully attractive a unitary narrative was.

One who did object was the poet and jazz critic Philip Larkin, whose reservations about the wholesale incorporation of modernist trends into jazz recall Panassié's, but whose work as a record reviewer in the 1960s required a degree of accommodation that Panassié refused to give. Larkin was circumspect about contradicting, at least in print, "the party line that presents jazz as one golden chain stretching from Buddy Bolden to Sun Ra." But in his retrospective collection of essays *All What Jazz*, he pays ironic tribute to those whose unenviable job it is to defend what he finds logically indefensible: "And so they soldier on at their impossible task, as if trying to persuade us that a cold bath is in some metaphysical sense the same as a hot bath, instead of its exact opposite ('But don't you see the evolutionary development?')" (26).

For those with no particular animus against bebop, the kind of narrative that could now be written had an encouragingly clear sense of direction and unity of purpose. "At first the history [of jazz] seems disjointed and the styles contradictory," admitted Barry Ulanov at the beginning of his 1952 survey *A History of Jazz in America*:

One marks a confounding series of shifts in place, person, and style. One finds a music dominated by Negroes in New Orleans, by white musicians in Chicago, by important but apparently unrelated figures in New York. One discovers a disastrous split in jazz inaugurated by the swing era and intensi- fied during the days of bebop and so-called progressive jazz. But then one looks and listens more closely, and order and continuity appear. . . . The his- tory of jazz is a curiously even one, chaotic at any instant, but always mov- ing ahead in what is for an art form almost a straight line.   (3–4)

But toward what goal is the "straight line" of development headed? This was not a question that historians of Ulanov's generation liked to answer—at least not directly. Having only recently renounced the temptation to equate evolution with progress (note the qualification "*so-called* progressive jazz"), they were left with the argument that the history of jazz is characterized by continuous stylistic change because it is in the nature of an art form to grow and develop. One can see in this the powerful metaphor of organicism, which suggests that the impulse to develop- ment is innate, irreversible, and (short of the demise of the organism) inevitable. Change is thus desirable in and of itself, evidence of the music's vitality. It is in this spirit that Russell cites the transformation of jazz from the New Orleans style to bebop as "the cleanest bill of health our native music could have" (188).

Most of the explanations routinely offered for the process of change in jazz derive from the metaphor of organicism. One pervasive form of argument treats the achievements of a handful of innovators as *potentials*—musical ideas that serve as the "seeds" for later development.[14] Jazz historians are fond of charts and dia- grams that amount to elaborate genealogies of style, with each new innovation flowing directly from those that precede it. On a more personal level, individual musicians are defined by a network of *influences*—the contemporaries and prede- cessors from whom they are presumed to derive a style. The most striking thing about these explanations is the assumption that the impetus for change in jazz is *internal*. Jazz evolves in certain directions because its inner logic demands it ("jazz extends, reaffirms, and replenishes *itself*"). No other explanation is necessary. While the social context for the music is rarely ignored entirely (if only for the human interest it adds to the narrative), it is generally treated as, at best, a sec- ondary cause—the cultural static of political or social upheaval that may color the process of development but is ultimately external to it.

The most ambitious attempts to organize the history of jazz through detailed musical criticism or analysis, not surprisingly, rely primarily on such internal explanations. Gunther Schuller's massive two-volume historical and analytical study of jazz through the swing era, while drawing astutely on cultural context where appropriate, is a monument to the ideal of jazz as an autonomous art. In the work of the most influential jazz critics, history is invoked as a means of framing and justifying aesthetic judgments—of establishing the boundaries within which evaluation may take place. Indeed, the more broadly those boundaries are con- ceived ("extended across the time and space of twentieth-century America"), the more inevitably historical relationships become embedded in the process of evaluation. A book like Martin Williams's *The Jazz Tradition* takes the form of a series of independent essays, each assessing the contribution of an individual artist; but these essays, arranged chronologically, form a de facto history of the music.[15] Similar collections of essays by Whitney Balliett, Gary Giddins, Francis Davis, and others delight in cross-references and the tracing of historical patterns. The "jazz tradition" in effect defines a discipline, and imparts to the critical enterprise a certain stature and dignity as well as coherence.

Nevertheless, it is curious how the concept of the jazz tradition tends to leach the social significance out of the music, leaving the impression that the history of jazz can be described satisfactorily only in aesthetic terms. In a recent review of *The Swing Era: The Development of Jazz, 1930–1945*, E. J. Hobsbawm applauds Schuller's "monumental contribution to jazz literature," but wonders how a purely stylistic framework can possibly claim to provide a complete account of "the development of jazz. . . . Mr. Schuller's book," he concludes, "is an implicit call for a social, economic, and cultural history of jazz in the New Deal years" (32). Nowhere is the disparity between the smoothness of the official narrative and the *noise* (to use Jacques Attali's term) of social disruption clearer than in the treatment of bebop. If any movement within jazz can be said to reflect and embody the political tensions of its time—the aspirations, frustrations, and subversive sensibilities of an elite group of African-American artists during a time of upheaval and rapid change—it is this musical revolution that took shape during and after the Second World War. "We were the first generation to rebel," remembers pianist Hampton Hawes, "playing bebop, trying to be different, going through a lot of changes and getting strung out in the process. *What these crazy niggers doin' playin' that crazy music?* Wild. Out of the jungle" (8).

But as Eric Lott has noted, "Bebop has been claimed by other, mostly unhistorical narratives rather than articulated to its own social history" (597). Chief among these is the narrative of stylistic change that dispenses with external referents and recasts bebop's rebelliousness in very different terms. According to this argument, the main cause of bebop is that the preceding style of jazz had reached an impasse. By the early 1940s, swing, once a vital part of the tradition, had become "threadbare" and "aging" (Russell 188); a "harmonic and melodic blind alley" incapable of further development (Feather, *Encyclopedia* 30); a formulaic popular music undergoing "death by entropy" (Shih 187); a "richly decked-out palace that was soon going to be a prison" (Hodeir 99); and a "billion-dollar rut" (Feather, *Inside* 4).

One may recognize in this something akin to what Leo Treitler has called the "crisis theory" of modern music, according to which a radically new style arises only in response to an impasse in the musical language, which has literally used itself up (124). Under normal circumstances, musicians would simply move on to the next step, extending the rhythmic, harmonic, and melodic language of jazz in the directions plainly indicated by the music itself. As the last few descriptions clearly imply, the failure for this to happen may be attributed at least in part to the malign external influence of commercialism, without which (presumably) the musicians of the swing era would not have been seduced into the unproductive pursuit of a worn-out style. Bebop thus takes on the character of revolt, not against the jazz tradition but against the circumstances that prevent jazz from following its natural course of development. Bebop comes to represent a way of breaking through this impasse, reaffirming tradition even as it rejects the ossified forms of the past. It becomes a "new branch of jazz . . . born of the desire for progress and evolution" (Feather, *Encyclopedia* 30), a "renewed musical language . . . with which the old practices could be replenished and continued" (Williams, *Jazz Tradition* 106).

But the transition from swing to bebop is more than the passage from one style to another. Bebop is the keystone in the grand historical arch, the crucial link between the early stage of jazz and modernity. Indeed, it is only with bebop that the essential nature of jazz is unmistakably revealed. There is an implicit entelechy in the progression from early jazz to bebop: the gradual shedding of utilitarian associations with dance music, popular song, and entertainment, as both musicians and public become aware of what jazz really is, or could be. With bebop, jazz finally became an *art music*. And this, in a sense, is the goal toward which the "straight line of development" in modern historical narratives, consciously or unconsciously, has always been aimed. In Hayden White's terms, it is a Romance: a triumph for black musicians and their liberal white colleagues and supporters over adverse circumstances. Bebop allowed jazz to become "what its partisans had said it should have been all along" (Williams, *Jazz Tradition* 106): an autonomous art, transcending its sometimes squalid social and economic setting, and taking its place in American culture as a creative discipline of intrinsic integrity.

Once this goal is accepted, the whole narrative for jazz history must be adjusted accordingly. For if bebop is the juncture at which jazz becomes art music, then earlier styles are once again in a precarious position—unless it can be demonstrated that in some important sense they had *always been* art music, and that this status was simply unacknowledged. Unfortunately, much that must be counted as "early jazz" can be understood as an autonomous art music only in retrospect, and with some difficulty. This strategy therefore exaggerates the tendency to make artificial distinctions between the artistic and the commercial, and assumes that the association of this nascent art with less elevated social functions was either a mistake in judgment or a burden imposed by a less enlightened time. If early jazz was intertwined with the stereotype of black man as entertainer, the jovial stage persona of Louis Armstrong can be shown to transcend and even undermine that stereotype—or the entire context of entertainment can be ignored, and the focus narrowed to Armstrong as revolutionary instrumentalist.[16] If much that went under the banner of swing is now judged as trivial, threadbare, or hopelessly commercial (not worthy, in other words, of being considered art), the best of Ellington, Basie, or Lunceford was not, and the term *swing* as a stylistic period may be reserved for them and a handful of their peers. In this way, "order and continuity appear," and the straight line of development is revealed.

The mode of historical explanation that emerged by the 1950s was increasingly conventional and academic in shape: a continuous artistic tradition encompassing several clearly differentiated "periods" or "styles," with an implied movement away from the naïveté of folk culture (more often ascribed to a putative pre-jazz phase than to jazz itself) toward the sophistication and complexity of art. For a music that had prided itself on its distinctiveness from "classical music," it is surprising how readily and unquestioningly a rough parallelism with the history of European music was accepted. But the fact that jazz could be configured so conventionally was taken by many as a reassuring sign that the tradition as a whole had attained a certain maturity and could now bear comparison with more established arts. "It is my conviction," asserts Joachim-Ernst Berendt in the introduction to *The Jazz Book*,

> that the styles of jazz are genuine, and reflect their own particular times in the same sense that classicism, baroque, romanticism, and impressionism reflect their respective periods in European concert music. . . . The evolution of jazz shows the continuity, logic, unity, and inner necessity which characterize all true art.   (4)

Of course, the "periods" in jazz in this model succeed one another not at the leisurely pace of centuries, or even generations, but roughly every ten years. (Even the swing "era" lasts only a decade.) We are far removed from the virtual identity of jazz with biography exemplified by *Jazzmen*—not surprisingly, since the music is now seen less as the idiosyncratic expression of individuals than as the outcome of abstract aesthetic forces.[17] There is a certain heedlessness, even cruelty, with which the narrative of jazz history shunts its innovators from the vanguard to stylistic obsolescence before they even reach middle age. Jazz criticism continues to wrestle with the "problem" of musicians (Armstrong, Ellington, Roy Eldridge, Earl Hines) whose performing careers far outlasted their seminal moment of importance and influence. But this vertiginous speed of change was presumably the price that had to be paid for the ground jazz had to cover in its progress from the slums of New Orleans (past the temptations of commercialism) to its newly exalted status as art music. There is a certain tone of pride with which Leonard Feather and André Hodeir independently calculate that jazz has evolved at roughly twenty times the pace of European music.[18]

What remains unspoken in this formulation is a crucial social factor: race. The progress of jazz is mapped onto the social progress of its creators—black Americans who, as Ralph Ellison noted in 1948, had been "swept from slavery to the condition of industrial man in a space of time so telescoped (a bare eighty-five years) that it is possible literally for them to step from feudalism into the vortex of industrialism simply by moving across the Mason-Dixon line" (283–84). Assimilation as full citizens in an integrated (if white-controlled) society seemed the obvious and desired outcome of this remarkable cultural journey. The equally remarkable progress of the black man's music from rural folk music to the international concert hall, a social acceptance far in advance of what could be expected in other spheres, was often taken as an encouraging sign that this outcome was possible, perhaps inevitable.

By the 1950s, then, one ready answer to the question *Where is jazz headed?* lay in the convergent paths of jazz and classical music. "The increasing indications of a wedding, or at least a flirtation, with modern classical music," wrote Leonard Feather in 1957, "mark a logical and desirable outcome of the jazzman's attempt to achieve musical maturity" (*Book of Jazz* 4). This probable outcome made the future of jazz as art music at once easier to envision and more problematic—easier to envision, because jazz had been appearing on the concert stage for several decades, and because classical music had already pervaded American society with images of what an art music should be: the frowning visages of Beethoven and Bach, a portentous mood of solemnity and dignity far removed from nightclubs and dance halls that might somehow be grafted onto jazz.[19] Classical music seemed like an exclusive club that in an egalitarian spirit might be persuaded to integrate. The discreet, gently swinging tonal structures of the Modern Jazz Quartet, performed by black men in tuxedos in concert halls for respectful audiences, provided a comforting image of what membership in this club might look like.

But the entrance fee was high. To be accepted as a kind of classical music, jazz had to be understood as a music that had outgrown its origins in a particular ethnic subculture and could now be thought of as the abstract manipulation of style and technique. Jazz was now to be measured against the "absolute" standards of greatness of the European tradition. In this comparison, the qualities of spontaneity, informality, and rhythmic excitement that had originally marked jazz as distinctive—those qualities, in other words, that marked it as African-American—now seemed to be liabilities. Jazz was a music of promise, ripe for passage from adolescence to maturity; but it still had a long way to go, and the only way to get there was to acknowledge the priority of European music.

In the 1961 movie *Paris Blues*, Paul Newman plays an expatriate jazz trombonist named Ram Bowen who works in Paris nightclubs with a small interracial group. But his success as an improviser is not enough for Bowen. His secret ambition is to be a composer, and he has been working on an orchestral piece, *Paris Blues*. (The fragments of this piece that we hear are played by the Duke Ellington orchestra—as is, indeed, all the music in the film.) He submits his score to a gray eminence of French music, M. Réné Bernard—whether composer, conductor, or impresario is never made clear—in the hopes of having it performed in concert. Finally, he is admitted to the opulent offices of the great man. Bernard is warm and generous, and admits to being an admirer of Bowen's playing. But it quickly becomes evident to Bowen that all of Bernard's compliments ("You have a genuine gift for melody") are gentle put-downs. "Your improvisations are highly personal," he tells Bowen. "They give you a stamp as a musician. But there is a great deal of difference between that and an important piece of serious music." "In other words, you're trying to tell me I'm just sort of a lightweight," Bowen replies. "I don't know what you are yet, Mr. Bowen," returns Bernard. He counsels Bowen to study composition, harmony, and counterpoint—*if* he wants to be a serious composer. Visibly dejected, Bowen leaves the office. But by the end of the movie, he decides to cancel his plans to return to America with his devoted fan and lover (Joanne Woodward) in order to "follow through with the music . . . see how far I can go." All the while, the music of Ellington plays in the background.

IV

This vision of jazz as an immature and imperfectly realized junior partner to European music did not long outlast the 1950s. Well before the appearance of *Paris Blues*, it had come under attack both from the upheavals of racial politics that made its implicit assimilationist agenda untenable and from the emergence of an avant-garde that pushed the boundaries of "modern classical music" far beyond the range of comfort.

The change in racial climate was particular dramatic, for well into the 1950s, jazz was heralded as a sphere of racial cooperation, with the 1949–50 Miles Davis *Birth of the Cool* band as its most vibrant symbol.[20] But the remainder of the decade saw a forceful reassertion of ethnicity by black musicians that paralleled, and in a few celebrated examples (e.g., Charles Mingus's "Fables of Faubus") participated in, the growing Civil Rights Movement. The music that was the result of this renewed ethnic emphasis has entered the official progression of styles as *hard bop*—an unfortunate blanket term that strains to cover the gospel-influenced popular hits of Cannonball Adderley and Horace Silver, the "experimental" music of Mingus and Monk, as well as much that could more simply be called *bop*.[21] Hard bop was vaguely defined as a musical movement, but it had a lasting effect on jazz historiography: It served to counter the notion that becoming an art music somehow required jazz to shed its "folk" (i.e., ethnic) roots. In the wake of hard bop came a new strain of historical writing, exemplified by *Blues People*, the 1963 book by LeRoi Jones (Amiri Baraka) that treated jazz as something intrinsically separate from the white "mainstream." As jazz entered the 1960s, authenticity was more than ever associated with ethnicity.

But the assertion of ethnicity in itself does not resolve the question of the nature and direction of the development of the jazz idiom. It simply suggests that whatever black Americans choose to do with their musical heritage is valid—or, more to the point, beyond the reach of white critics and historians. As always, the actual diversity of expression within the black community was masked by the tendency for any and every viewpoint within it to claim the collective history of the people as a source of legitimacy. Just as all sorts of music can flourish under the banner of ethnicity, so can all sorts of narratives about the history of jazz as black music.

The least dogmatic of these narratives is that which allows for the "fusion" of jazz with currents in popular music, especially black popular music. Fusion subverts from the outset the assumptions that *popular* and *art* are mutually exclusive categories, and that the progress from the latter to the former in jazz was irreversible. In the 1930s and early 1940s, jazz had been both artistic expression and entertainment for the black community; but by the 1950s, the earthier and less prestigious functions of the music had been passed on to rhythm and blues.[22] At the same time that musicians and critics were struggling to make a case for jazz as art music, the more commercially minded hard bop musicians strove mightily to win back audiences alienated by bebop's intellectual pretensions with hard-swinging grooves and a folksy sensibility that wore its ethnicity on its sleeve.

This transparent pseudo-populism (evident in titles such as "Dis Here" and "Watermelon Man") was easy enough to dismiss: Baraka, for example, complained in 1963 of the "hideous . . . spectacle of an urban, college-trained Negro musician pretending, perhaps in all sincerity, that he has the same field of emotional reference as his great-grandfather, the Mississippi slave" (218). But for most jazz critics, the greatest sin of the "funky" hard bop style was its accessibility, its easy and self-serving simplicity, its eagerness to please. Dalliance with popular trends seemed to betray the movement of jazz as an art music toward complexity and intricacy.[23] Only at the end of the 1960s, when Miles Davis married elements from rock and soul with avant-garde textures and harmonies (at a time when rock itself had become a kind of avant-garde counterculture), did many critics decide that perhaps a new artistic phase was under way, requiring a new stylistic category, *fusion*, to explain it.[24] But few felt entirely comfortable about the category, and even those who acknowledged fusion as a legitimate movement rarely let it stand unchallenged in the conventional progression of styles.

Fusion was inevitably counterpoised with *free jazz*, an avant-garde movement that could be traced back to the end of the 1950s. Free jazz is often associated with the black nationalist politics of the 1960s, but it hardly needed the militant rhetoric of ethnicity to be controversial. It simply carried the model of modernist experimentation (but without an explicit Eurocentric focus) to its logical, if unsettling, conclusion. If critics of the 1950s believed that jazz was in a race to catch up to classical music, their hopes were to be realized, albeit in a way they had never anticipated. By decade's end, the kind of European music jazz seemed most to resemble was not the standard repertory, or even the more accessible moderns (the Stravinsky and Hindemith admired by the beboppers), but an avant-garde bent on shattering all conventions. In 1956, Marshall Stearns could still write: "Jazz is traveling the same path as classical music—toward the stone wall of atonality—but there is still a long way to go" (229). Less than a decade later, that point of no return had been reached, and the critical reaction was predictably strident: Whatever it was, it wasn't jazz.

The crisis raised by free jazz was as inevitable as it was disquieting. Ever since bebop, the narrative of jazz history had been committed to the ideology of modernism, and the chain of continuous innovation that it entailed. Bebop itself was "steeped in the rhetoric of modernist avant-gardism" (Tucker 273); and as Ronald Radano has pointed out, the early efforts of vanguardists Ornette Coleman and Cecil Taylor were initially greeted with enthusiasm (even by critics who later excoriated them), precisely because they seemed to offer the next step on the path of development, extending the legacy of bebop in new and arguably necessary directions (Leonard Bernstein, for example, called Coleman "the greatest innovator in jazz since Charlie Parker" [qtd. in Radano 73]). The self-consciously modernist titles of Ornette Coleman albums (*The Shape of Jazz to Come, Tomorrow Is the Question, This Is Our Music*) made explicit the avant-gardists' argument that theirs was the music of the future, the "new thing." Much more quickly than the apologists for bebop, they openly claimed the whole of tradition as the source of their legitimacy.

The result was a new plot for the story of jazz. In what might be called the "Whig interpretation of jazz history," freedom—with all its rich social and political associations—became the inexorable goal:[25]

The quest for freedom . . . appears at the very beginning of jazz and reappears at every growing point in the music's history. The earliest jazz musicians asserted their independence of melody, structure, rhythm, and expression from the turn-of-the-century musics that surrounded them; Louis Armstrong symbolized the liberation of the late twenties jazz soloist; the Count Basie band offered liberation of jazz rhythm; and Parker and Gillespie offered yet more new freedoms to jazz.   (LITWEILER 13–14)

In this narrative, bebop was only one step in the process that Treitler calls "the history of twentieth-century music as striptease" (137): the progressive removal of the encumbrances of tradition. Free jazz is the logical outcome, a new idealization of jazz's essential nature revealed only when musicians throw off the accretions of convention: popular song forms, instrumentation, tonality, Western intonation systems, the explicit stating of a dance beat. And it is hard to be against freedom, especially when freedom from musical convention becomes conflated (as it inevitably did in the turbulent 1960s) with freedom from oppressive political structures.[26]

And yet freedom is a goal that can only be approached asymptotically. *Free jazz* is, in any case, an inadequate label to describe the ferment of activity within the jazz avant-garde, which has from the outset included the creation of new structures (i.e., composition) as well as free improvisation. In recent years, the one-way straitjacket of modernism has given way to a more eclectic postmodern sensibility in which "all of jazz history, up to and including the present, is grist for the mill" (F. Davis x). Even the taboo against commercialism has been broken, as avant-gardists such as Lester Bowie and Ornette Coleman have taken up (in irony and in earnest) elements from popular music. "Freedom" seems to be the freedom to escape accepted definitions of jazz—including the modernist definition of jazz-as-art-music that got jazz into the avant-garde in the first place.

Escape from modernism came from other directions as well. Critics wary of the narrative that presents the avant-garde as the legitimate jazz of the modern age began cautiously to adjust the evolutionary model, recasting concepts of innovation and development to avoid so disturbing an outcome as "total freedom." A favorite term was *mainstream*—first applied (retroactively) to swing, but quickly used to describe any body of music neither so conservative as to deny the possibility or desirability of further development, nor so radical as to send that development in uncontrollable directions.[27] Leroy Ostransky's definition in his 1977 *Understanding Jazz* captures the term's inherent vagueness: "Mainstream jazz . . . is simply the characteristic jazz of its time, moving along with the current now smoothly, now roughly, occasionally listlessly but always with direction, however imperceptible it may be at the moment" (107).

Ostransky's image is, to put it generously, open to interpretation. It accepts the necessity of continuous development as something natural—the current in the stream. And yet the music itself is curiously passive, set drifting along by this unspecified outside force. The "characteristic jazz of its time" is presumably not that of the revolutionaries, the wave makers; but it is roused by them into overcoming its essential inertia, which derives from tradition. Some forward motion is always necessary to prevent jazz from succumbing to its own weight, and for that the avant-garde is given its due. But the concept of the mainstream insists that the essence of jazz is to be found not on the cutting edge, but well back within the tradition. It follows that the keepers of the flame are in the best position to pass judgment on the music's future. ". . . Mainstream jazz . . . must inevitably be the point of departure for new styles," Ostransky continues, "and to understand the evolution of style one must stand in midstream, so to speak, and look both ways" (107).

Looking both ways is the favored stance of the neoclassicist: a careful balance between the modernist ideology of continuous innovation and an insistence on the priority of tradition. Wynton Marsalis asks, "How can something new and substantial, not eccentric and fraudulent, be developed when the meaning of what's old is not known?" (24). On this point, the neoclassicists and the avant-garde are on the same wavelength, for few would fail to invoke Ellington, Parker, or Monk as an ultimate source and inspiration. What distinguishes the neoclassicist attitude is not so much its habit of retrospection, but rather its heavy-handed attempt to regulate the music of the present through an idealized representation of the past. History is a roll call of past masters, from King Oliver to Thelonious Monk, and the responsibility of the modern musician is to create music that lives up to and extends this legacy. All else—free jazz and fusion alike—is falsity and charlatanism. Neoclassicism saves its most pointed barbs for the kind of easy pluralism that would embrace all potential definitions for jazz, and therefore all potential outcomes for the narrative of its history.[28] Only by returning to the point at which jazz began a series of wrong turns—back, in short, to the "mainstream"—can the narrative thread be reclaimed and continued.

Wynton Marsalis's remarkable visibility in the popular media as the spokesman for an entire generation of young musicians suggests that this narrow, if principled, view of jazz history may yet have increasing influence, especially where jazz is offered—by stage bands, in appreciation classes, and on PBS specials—as an art music segregated from the flux of the marketplace. Marsalis is careful to present jazz as a cultural heritage and, in a sense, a political reality, entirely separate from the European tradition. But his celebrated feat of winning Grammy awards for both jazz and classical recordings underscores the extent to which jazz has become *another kind* of classical music—one indigenous to black culture and reflecting black values, but following the same pattern of institutionalization in conservatories and repertory groups, and demanding of its musicians an empathetic response to aesthetic sensibilities of the past. Historical narrative plays a crucial role in the formation of a canon, in the elevation of great musicians as objects of veneration, and in the development of a sense of tradition that casts a long shadow over the present. The goals of the neoclassicists will have been admirably fulfilled if and when busts of Armstrong and Parker stand alongside busts of Beethoven and Bach in practice rooms and music studios across America.

The question *Where is jazz going?* is usually asked with an anxious undertone—as if, in Monk's words, "Maybe it's going to hell." And Monk's dismissive response is on target. Whether jazz will "survive" depends not on what musicians choose to do. They will continue to make music, and whether that music is called jazz is a matter of relative inconsequence. The question is rather of the uses to which the jazz tradition is to be put: whether as an alternative conservatory style for the training of young musicians; as an artistic heritage to be held up as an exemplar of American or African-American culture; or as a convenient marketing tool for recording companies and concert promoters, a kind of brand name guaranteeing quality and a degree of homogeneity.

As an educator and scholar, I inevitably find myself allied with the first two of these projects, especially the second. My courses in jazz history are designed to inculcate a feeling of pride in a racially mixed university for an African-American musical tradition that manages, against all odds, to triumph over obstacles of racism and indifference. For this, the narrative of jazz history as Romance is a powerful tool, and I have invested a good deal into making it a reality in my students' minds through all the eloquence and emotion I can muster.

And yet I am increasingly aware of this narrative's limitations, especially its tendency to impose a kind of deadening uniformity of cultural meaning on the music, and jazz history's patent inability to explain current trends in any cogent form. There is a revolution under way in jazz that lies not in any internal crisis of style, but in the debate over the looming new orthodoxy: jazz as "America's classical music." As jazz acquires degree programs, piano competitions, repertory ensembles, institutes, and archives, it inevitably becomes a different kind of music—gaining a certain solidity and political clout, but no longer participating in the ongoing formulation of meaning; no longer a *popular* music in the best sense of the word. The histories we construct for jazz also have this effect: Each new textbook dulls our sensibilities, "retells the stories as they have been told and written, . . . made neat and smooth, with all incomprehensible details vanished along with most of the wonder" (Ellison 200).

Meanwhile, music continues to change: the explosion in new technologies, the increased pace of global interaction, the continued erosion of European art music as the measure of all things. The narratives we have inherited to describe the history of jazz retain the patterns of outmoded forms of thought, especially the assumption that the progress of jazz as art necessitates increased distance from the popular. If we, as historians, critics, and educators, are to adapt to these new realities, we must be willing to construct new narratives to explain them. These alternative explanations need not displace the jazz tradition (it hardly seems fair, in any case, to deconstruct a narrative that has only recently been constructed, especially one that serves such important purposes). But the time has come for an approach that is less invested in the ideology of jazz as aesthetic object and more responsive to issues of historical particularity. Only in this way can the study of jazz break free from its self-imposed isolation, and participate with other disciplines in the exploration of meaning in American culture.

1. See, for example, Grover Sales's recent textbook *Jazz: America's Classical Music* (Englewood Cliffs: Prentice-Hall, 1984) and the address "Jazz—America's Classical Music" delivered by Billy Taylor to the Black American Music Symposium at the University of Michigan in 1985 and subsequently reprinted in *Black Perspective in Music* 14.1 (1986): 21–25.

2. The language is that of House Concurrent Resolution 57, passed by the United States Senate on December 4, 1987.

3. A sampling from recent jazz textbooks gives some of the flavor of this loss of direction. Tanner and Gerow's *A Study of Jazz* follows neatly defined chapters on "Early New Orleans Dixieland (1900–1920)," "Chicago Style Dixieland (the 1920s)," "Swing (1932–1942)," "Bop (1940–1950)," "Cool (1949–1955)," and "Funky (c. 1954–1963)," with a "period" of over forty years called the "Eclectic Era," a "potpourri of some eighty years of continuous development" (119). The "Chronology of Jazz Styles Chart" in Mark Gridley's *Jazz Styles* begins with comfortingly concise periods for "Early Jazz (1920s)," "Swing (1930s)," "Bop (1940s)," and "West Coast (1950s)," but soon degenerates into "Coexistence of Hard Bop, Free Jazz, and Modal Jazz (1960s)," "Transition to Jazz-Rock (late 1960s)," and "Coexistence of AACM, Jazz-Rock, and Modal Jazz (1970s)" (356–57). Billy Taylor's last chapter in *Piano Jazz* (after the terse chapters "Bebop" and "Cool") is entitled "Abstract Jazz, Mainstream Jazz, Modal Jazz, Electronic Jazz, Fusion" (187).

4. This strategy is followed in textbooks by James McCalla, Donald Megill and Richard Demory, and James Lincoln Collier, among others. The persistence of earlier styles of jazz is sometimes counted as yet another direction. "If we cannot predict where jazz is going . . . we can at least discern certain trends," wrote Collier in 1978, identifying three such trends: jazz-rock, free jazz, and what he called (anticipating the "neoclassicism" of the 1980s) the "neo-bop movement" (494–96).

5. See, for example, Henry Martin's recent textbook *Enjoying Jazz*. One of the basic hypotheses of the book is that contemporary jazz is facing a kind of stylistic dead end: "By the 1970s and early 1980s, jazz was unlikely to undergo any further significant evolution because it lacked the popularity necessary for continued vitality. At that time all of its previous styles became recognized as artistic vehicles for performance. Indications are, therefore, that jazz will not undergo any further significant evolution" (204). See also Kart.

6. In a 1984 interview, Wynton Marsalis complained, "I don't think the music moved along in the '70s. I think it went astray. Everybody was trying to be pop stars, and imitated people that were supposed to be imitating them. . . . What we have to do now is reclaim . . ." (Mandel 18). Martin Williams, in an article entitled "How Long Has This Been Going On?" provides this summation of the fusion movement: "Wynton Marsalis . . . and some others seem to see the whole fusion thing as a kind of commercial opportunism and artistic blind alley, maybe even a betrayal of the music, on the part of everyone involved, on the part of record companies, record producers, and the artists themselves. . . . Although it may have produced some good music, the fusion effort seems to me largely over and was even something of a mistake. (Well, look, there can be some very handsome houses on a dead-end street.)" (*Jazz in Its Time* 46–47, 56).

7. In interviews, fusion artists are typically invited, directly or indirectly, to comment on the disparity between their commercial success and the accusation by many critics that

their music falls outside the boundaries of jazz. Their answers are usually bland pronouncements about pluralism and catholicity, obviously designed to deflect controversy, that rely on *jazz* as an umbrella term which can easily accommodate current tastes. Jay Beckenstein of Spyro Gyra observes that, "if you define fusion as a previously existing jazz form that combines with outside musical influences to come up with a hybrid, you are talking about the history of jazz from day one. . . . It's our music, we love to play it, and I think time will show it's in the mainstream of the '80s" (Santoro, "Spyro" 22). Saxophonist Kenny G says that "we've gotten terrible reviews from the purist critics who don't know anything about the style of contemporary jazz we play. I live that, I'm one of the creators of it. So is [Jeff] Lorber—we're the young players who have created something new and different that's still called jazz" (Stein 181). Drummer Jack DeJohnette, a musician by no means exclusively associated with fusion, describes his music as "multi-directional, eclectic. . . . There are people who dig jazz *and* pop, and there are a lot of choices out there. Jazz runs the gamut from George Benson to Grover Washington to David Sanborn, Spyro Gyra, Weather Update, Ramsey Lewis, Wynton Marsalis, Art Blakey, Tony Williams, me—there's a lot out there" (Beuttler 17–18).

Miles Davis is undoubtedly the most frequently criticized of the fusion musicians, in no small part because his stature within the conventional narrative has made his embrace of fusion seem apostasy. A recent survey of his career by Stanley Crouch, for example, calls Davis "the most brilliant sellout in the history of jazz," and continues: "Desperate to maintain his position at the forefront of modern music, to sustain his financial position, to be admired for the hipness of his purported innovations, Davis turned butt to the beautiful in order to genuflect before the commercial" ("Play" 30). Davis's response to such criticism is understandably more caustic than the responses of most fusion musicians. In his autobiography, he turns back on his attackers the modernist themes of continuous change and innovation embedded in the conventional narrative: "A lot of old jazz musicians are lazy motherfuckers, resisting change and holding on to the old ways because they are too lazy to try something different. They listen to the critics, who tell them to stay where they are because that's what *they* like. . . . The old musicians stay where they are and become like museum pieces under glass, safe, easy to understand, playing that tired old shit over and over again. Then they run around talking about electronic instruments and electronic musical voicing fucking up the music and the tradition. Well, I'm not like that and neither was Bird or Trane or Sonny Rollins or Duke or anybody who wanted to keep on creating. Bebop was about change, about evolution. It wasn't about standing still and becoming safe" (394).

8. The Art Ensemble of Chicago makes a point of avoiding the term *jazz* as too limiting (although this deters no one from claiming them as part of a narrative of jazz). As their motto "Great Black Music—Ancient to Modern" makes clear, that is not because they are uninterested in issues of ethnicity and historical tradition, but because they wish to situate their music within an even more ambitious narrative.

9. Bunk Johnson was the most spectacular rediscovery of the New Orleans revival. Born in the nineteenth century and a contemporary of ur-jazz trumpeter Buddy Bolden, Johnson epitomized the personal connection with the shadowy origins of jazz that was still possible in the 1930s and 1940s. Research on the book *Jazzmen* led William Russell to Johnson, who was then a toothless old man driving a truck on a sugar plantation. Equipped with a new trumpet and a new set of teeth, the trumpeter embarked on a brief second career, highlighted by recordings that purported to recreate the

"prehistory" of New Orleans jazz. The story of Johnson's unlikely career (and the cycle of self-destruction that ended it, undermining in the process the note of Romantic triumph) is recounted in Turner 32–60.

10. See, for example, the chapter "New Orleans—Mainspring or Myth" in Leonard Feather's *The Book of Jazz* (30–38), in which Feather juxtaposes critical adulation of the music of Jelly Roll Morton, Johnny Dodds, and Bunk Johnson with bemused and frequently contemptuous reactions of contemporary musicians.

11. On the occasion of its tenth anniversary issue (15 July 1944), *Down Beat* boasted in an editorial that the magazine had "dug into the history of jazz and swing, and into the personal background of the so-called immortals in these fields. It made such names as Bix Beiderbecke, Fate Marable, Frank Teschemacher, and Pine-Top Smith familiar to its readers. It helped spread the interest in and acceptance of hot music" (10).

12. This would seem to be the context for understanding the controversial 1949 interview with Charlie Parker in which he was quoted as saying that "bop is something entirely separate and apart from jazz," that it "drew little from jazz [and] has no roots in it. . . . The beat in a bop band is with the music, against it, behind it. . . . [Bop] has no continuity of beat, no steady chug-chug. Jazz has, and that's why bop is more flexible" (Levin and Wilson 1).

13. *Jazz community* in this sense is meant to include not only musicians, but also critics, aficionados, industry professionals—all those who constitute the close-knit social context in which the music is produced and received. The term was popularized by the landmark sociological study of Alan P. Merriam and Raymond W. Mack, "The Jazz Community" (*Social Forces* 38 [1960], 211–22).

14. See, for example, *Modern Jazz* by Morgan and Horricks, which includes a discussion of the growth of bebop from the "logical evolutionary tree" of jazz that is ripe with organic metaphors. "In jazz every seed of evolution has been sown in the solo styles of a scattered handful of musicians, and only with the final co-ordination of their principles has the new school been wrought. . . . By 1939 the seeds were germinating" (20). These tender shoots sprang up while "swing . . . was a dying force," and had to compete against "the clinging tendrils of commercialism" (19) through the "age-old process known as the 'survival of the fittest' " (60). With the establishment of the bebop movement, "jazz was again a living music" (71).

15. The same may be said of another Martin Williams production, the anthology of recordings called *The Smithsonian Collection of Classic Jazz* (1973, rev. 1987). The selections in the anthology were chosen judiciously by Williams for their intrinsic artistic merit, but they are also arranged chronologically to form a history of style. As virtually the only comprehensive anthology of jazz recordings available, the *Smithsonian Collection* has become a staple of the classroom, and its selections the "canon" for the teaching of jazz history.

16. Gary Giddins's recent biography *Satchmo* is a brilliant attempt to rescue serious consideration of Armstrong from reductionist strategies that would isolate him from his popular context. Arguing that "a jazz aesthetics incapable of embracing Armstrong whole is unworthy of him," Giddins insists: "Armstrong was an artist who happened to be an entertainer, an entertainer who happened to be an artist—as much an original in one role as the other" (32).

17. Leonard Feather's survey of bebop, for example, pointedly refuses to follow the habit of ascribing the creation of bebop to the fortuitous contribution of a handful of musi-

cians. "There has been a tendency, in recalling the manner in which bop took shape, to focus on a few individuals, mainly Parker and Gillespie. . . . Yet over the years evidence has gradually come to light that bebop in its various manifestations, as a harmonic, melodic and rhythmic outgrowth of what had preceded it, was a logical and perhaps inevitable extension; possibly it would have happened along largely similar lines without the existence of either Parker or Gillespie" ("Bebop" 98).

18. "Beginning at the same point (popular and religious vocal music) and passing through the same stages (instrumental polyphony, accompanied melody, symphonic music, and so on)," writes Hodeir, "jazz does indeed seem to have retraced in five decades the road that European music took ten centuries to cover" (35–36). Feather observes that ". . . we find that a period extending from 590, when Gregory became Pope, until 1918, when Debussy died, produced developments in music for which a corresponding degree of development in jazz was accomplished between about 1897 and 1957—a ratio of more than 1300 years against 60, which means that jazz has been evolving more than 20 times as fast" (*Book of Jazz* 37).

19. For an overview of the process by which jazz performances were adapted to the formality of the concert hall, see my article "The Emergence of the Jazz Concert, 1935–1945."

20. Officially known as the Miles Davis Nonet, this groundbreaking group included veteran black beboppers (Max Roach, John Lewis, J. J. Johnson), white musicians normally associated with the cool school (Lee Konitz and Gerry Mulligan), and Davis's longtime white collaborator, Canadian-born arranger Gil Evans.

21. See Rosenthal for a discussion of the varieties of music included under the *hard bop* label.

22. It is interesting to note that Albert Murray's *Stomping the Blues*, which treats jazz as a music indistinguishable from the "good-time" music of the blues, deals only glancingly with development in jazz after Charlie Parker. Of Ornette Coleman, Murray says: "Some of his most enthusiastic supporters regard his innovations as representing a radical break with all tradition and others hear in them a return to the deepest roots of the blues idiom; but as of 1976 . . . Coleman compositions . . . seem to be better known and better received by concert-goers and patrons of 'new thing' nightclubs than by traditional dance-hall, honky-tonk, night-club, and holiday revelers" (228).

23. Significantly, one adjective used by critics of the 1950s to describe hard bop was *regressive*. See, for example, Martin Williams's ironically titled article "The Funky–Hard Bop Regression," which defends hard bop as a progressive form. According to Williams, in purely stylistic terms hard bop "is taking up certain pressing problems where they were left in the middle forties and is working out the solution" (*Art* 234).

24. Karl Lippegaus offers a typical summation of the birth of fusion: "In 1970, [a year after the recording was made,] when trumpeter Miles Davis brought out a double LP album under the title *Bitches' Brew*, the jazz world saw in a flash that this music marked a turning point in the history of jazz. *Bitches' Brew* became the starting point for a new phase of development. With this recording the period after Free Jazz had begun—or rather, Free Jazz had been joined by a new trend in style which was indeed fundamentally different . . ." (156).

25. The reference is to the so-called "Whig interpretation of history," the title of a 1931 book by Herbert Butterfield that criticized the teleological tendency of liberal historians to view the history of mankind as leading inexorably toward an ideal of democra-

tic freedom. "The whig historian can draw lines through certain events, some such line as that which leads to modern liberty. . . . The total result of this method is to impose a certain form upon the whole historical story, and to produce a scheme of general history which is bound to converge beautifully upon the present—all demonstrating throughout the ages the working of an obvious principle of progress . . ." (Butterfield 12).

26. As Stanley Crouch commented mordantly (in a reference to the history of the Umbria Jazz Festival in Perugia, Italy), "Music with melody, harmony, and instrumental control was considered the art of repression and the symbol of the enslavement of black people, while the opportunists of the 'avant-garde' were celebrated as the voices of freedom" (*Notes* 248).

27. The term seems to have been used first by Stanley Dance, as in a 1961 reference to "the 'swing' or 'mainstream' idiom" (13). It is clear from the context that this swing "mainstream" is defined by its position between the reactionary music of the New Orleans revival and the radical bebop movement: "By the end of 1949 the small group was securely established as the chief medium of jazz expression . . . whether playing blues, Dixieland, mainstream or modern jazz" (27).

28. Wynton Marsalis, for example, rails against "those who profess an openness to everything—an openness that in effect just shows contempt for the basic values of the music and of our society. . . . Their disdain for the specific knowledge that goes into jazz creation is their justification for saying that everything has its place. But their job should be to define that place—is it the toilet or the table?" (21).

WORKS CITED

Attali, Jacques. *Noise: The Political Economy of Music*. Trans. Brian Massumi. Minneapolis: U of Minnesota P, 1985.

Avakian, George M. "Where Is Jazz Going?" *Down Beat* Sept. 1939: 9.

Berendt, Joachim-Ernst. *The Jazz Book: From New Orleans to Rock and Free Jazz*. Trans. Dan Morgenstern and Helmut and Barbara Bredigkeit. New York: Hill, 1975.

_____, ed. *The Story of Jazz: From New Orleans to Rock Jazz*. Englewood Cliffs: Prentice, 1978.

Beuttler, Bill. "The Jack DeJohnette Interview." *Down Beat* Sept. 1987: 16–19.

Blesh, Rudi. *Shining Trumpets: A History of Jazz*. New York: Knopf, 1946.

Boyer, Richard. "Bop." *New Yorker* 3 July 1948: 26–32.

Butterfield, Herbert. *The Whig Interpretation of History*. London: Bell, 1931.

Collier, James Lincoln. *The Making of Jazz: A Comprehensive History*. Boston: Houghton, 1978.

Crouch, Stanley. *Notes of a Hanging Judge*. New York: Oxford UP, 1990.

_____. "Play the Right Thing." *New Republic* 12 Feb. 1990: 30–37.

Dance, Stanley. *Jazz Era: The Forties*. London: MacGibbon and Kee, 1961.

Davis, Francis. *In the Moment: Jazz in the 1980s*. New York: Oxford UP, 1986.

Davis, Miles, with Quincy Troupe. *Miles: The Autobiography*. New York: Simon, 1989.

DeVeaux, Scott. "The Emergence of the Jazz Concert, 1935–1945." *American Music* 7.1 (1989): 6–29.

Ellison, Ralph. *Shadow and Act*. 1964. New York: NAL, 1966.

Feather, Leonard. "Bebop, Cool Jazz, Hard Bop." Berendt, *Story* 96–114.

_____. *The Book of Jazz*. New York: Meridian, 1957.

____. *The Encyclopedia of Jazz.* Rev. ed. New York: Bonanza, 1960.

____. *Inside Be-Bop.* New York: Robbins, 1949.

____. "Jazz Is Where You Find It." *Esquire* Feb. 1944: 35, 129–30.

Giddins, Gary. *Satchmo.* New York: Doubleday, 1988.

Gridley, Mark. *Jazz Styles: History and Analysis.* 3rd ed. Englewood Cliffs: Prentice, 1988.

Hawes, Hampton, and Don Asher. *Raise Up Off Me: A Portrait of Hampton Hawes.* New York: Coward, McCann, Geoghegan, 1974.

Hobsbawm, E. J. "Some Like It Hot." *New York Review of Books* 13 Apr. 1989: 32–34.

Hodeir, André. *Jazz: Its Evolution and Essence.* Trans. David Noakes. New York: Grove, 1956.

Jones, LeRoi [Amiri Baraka]. *Blues People: Negro Music in White America.* New York: Morrow, 1963.

Kart, Larry. "Provocative Opinion: The Death of Jazz?" *Black Music Research Journal* 10.1 (1990): 76–81.

Larkin, Philip. *All What Jazz: A Record Diary 1961–1971.* Rev. ed. New York: Farrar, 1985.

Levin, Michael, and John S. Wilson. "No Bop Roots in Jazz: Parker." *Down Beat* 9 Sept. 1949: 1, 12.

Lippegaus, Karl. "Rock Jazz." Berendt, *Story* 154–71.

Litweiler, John. *The Freedom Principle: Jazz after 1958.* New York: Morrow, 1984.

Lott, Eric. "Double V, Double-Time: Bebop's Politics of Style." *Callaloo* 36 (1988): 597–605.

Mandel, Howard. "The Wynton Marsalis Interview." *Down Beat* July 1984: 16–19, 67.

Marsalis, Wynton. "What Jazz Is—and Isn't." *New York Times* 31 July 1988, Arts & Leisure: 21, 24.

Martin, Henry. *Enjoying Jazz.* New York: Schirmer, 1986.

McCalla, James. *Jazz: A Listener's Guide.* Englewood Cliffs: Prentice, 1982.

Megill, Donald D., and Richard S. Demory. *Introduction to Jazz History.* Englewood Cliffs: Prentice, 1984.

Mezzrow, Milton "Mezz," and Bernard Wolfe. *Really the Blues.* New York: Random, 1946.

Miller, Paul Eduard. "The Rhythm Section." *Esquire* Jan. 1945: 86.

____. "Roots of Hot White Jazz are Negroid." *Down Beat* Apr. 1937: 5.

Morgan, Alun, and Raymond Horricks. *Modern Jazz: A Survey of Developments since 1939.* London: Gollancz, 1956.

Murray, Albert. *Stomping the Blues.* 1976. New York: Vintage, 1982.

Ostransky, Leroy. *Understanding Jazz.* Englewood Cliffs: Prentice, 1977.

Panassié, Hugues. *Hot Jazz: The Guide to Swing Music.* Trans. Lyle and Eleanor Dowling. New York: Witmark, 1936.

____. *The Real Jazz.* Trans. Anne Sorelle Williams. Adapted for American publication by Charles Edward Smith. New York: Smith and Durrell, 1942.

____. *The Real Jazz.* Rev. ed. New York: Barnes, 1960.

Radano, Ronald M. "The Jazz Avant-Garde and the Jazz Community: Action and Reaction." *Annual Review of Jazz Studies* 3 (1985): 71–79.

Ramsey, Frederic, Jr., and Charles Edward Smith, eds. *Jazzmen.* New York: Harcourt, 1939.

Rosenthal, David H. "Hard Bop and its Critics." *Black Perspective in Music* 16.1 (1988): 21–29.

Russell, Ross. "Bebop." Williams, *Art* 187–214.

Sancton, Thomas. "Horns of Plenty." *Time* 22 Oct. 1990: 64–71.

Santoro, Gene. "Miles Davis the Enabler: Part II." *Down Beat* Nov. 1988: 16–19.

____. "The Spyro Gyra Interview." *Down Beat* Sept. 1986: 20–22.

Sargeant, Winthrop. *Jazz: Hot and Hybrid*. New and enlarged ed. New York: Dutton, 1946.

Schuller, Gunther. *Early Jazz: Its Roots and Musical Development*. New York: Oxford UP, 1968.

____. *The Swing Era: The Development of Jazz, 1930–1945*. New York: Oxford UP, 1989.

Shih, Hsio Wen. "The Spread of Jazz and the Big Bands." *Jazz: New Perspectives on the History of Jazz by Twelve of the World's Foremost Jazz Critics and Scholars*. Ed. Nat Hentoff and Albert J. McCarthy. New York: Rinehart. 1959. 171–88.

Stearns, Marshall. *The Story of Jazz*. New York: NAL, 1958.

Stein, Stephanie. "Kenny G: Songbird in Full Flight." *Down Beat* Jan. 1988: 16–18, 48.

Tanner, Paul O. W., and Maurice Gerow. *A Study of Jazz*. 5th ed. Dubuque: Brown, 1984.

Taylor, Billy. *Jazz Piano: History and Development*. Dubuque: Brown, 1982.

Tirro, Frank. *Jazz: A History*. New York: Norton, 1977.

Treitler, Leo. *Music and the Historical Imagination*. Cambridge: Harvard UP, 1989.

Tucker, Bruce. " 'Tell Tchaikovsky the News': Postmodernism, Popular Culture, and the Emergence of Rock 'n' Roll." *Black Music Research Journal* 9.2 (1989): 271–95.

Turner, Frederick. *Remembering Song: Encounters with the New Orleans Jazz Tradition*. New York: Viking, 1982.

Ulanov, Barry. *A History of Jazz in America*. New York: Viking, 1952.

Ulanov, Barry, and Leonard Feather. "Jazz Versus Swing." *Metronome* Apr. 1944: 22–23.

White, Hayden. *Metahistory: The Historical Imagination in Nineteenth-Century Europe*. Baltimore: Johns Hopkins UP, 1973.

Williams, Martin, ed. *The Art of Jazz*. New York: Oxford UP, 1959.

____. *Jazz in Its Time*. New York: Oxford UP, 1989.

____. *The Jazz Tradition*. New York: Oxford UP, 1970.

tell the story

DISCOGRAPHY

Coleman, Ornette. *The Shape of Jazz to Come*. Atlantic, SD 1317, 1959.

____. *This Is Our Music*. Atlantic, SD 1353, 1959.

____. *Tomorrow Is the Question*. Contemporary, M3596, 1959.

Davis, Miles. *Bitches' Brew*. Columbia, CS 9995/6, 1969.

Davis Nonet, Miles. *Birth of the Cool*. Capitol, T762, 1950.

Hancock Quintet, Herbie. "Watermelon Man." *Takin' Off*. Blue Note, BLP 4109, 1962.

Mingus, Charles. "Fables of Faubus." *Mingus Ah Um*. Columbia, CL 1370, 1959.

Timmons Trio, Bobby. "Dis Here." *This Here Is Bobby Timmons*. Riverside, RLP 3l77, 1960.

FILMOGRAPHY

Paris Blues. Dir. Martin Ritt. USA, 1961.

chapter 29

NATHANIEL MACKEY

Other: From Noun to Verb

I

Cultural diversity has lately become a much-discussed topic.[1] I would like to emphasize that cultural diversity *is* cultural, that it is a consequence of actions and assumptions that are socially—rather than naturally, genetically—instituted and reinforced. The inequities the recent attention to cultural diversity is meant to redress are in part the outcome of confounding the social with the genetic, so we need to make it clear that when we speak of otherness we are not positing static, intrinsic attributes or characteristics. We need instead to highlight the dynamics of agency and attribution by way of which otherness is brought about and maintained, the fact that other is something people do, more importantly a verb than an adjective or a noun. Thus, I would like to look at some instances of and ways of thinking about othering—primarily othering within artistic media, but also othering within the medium of society, touching upon relationships between the two. Artistic othering has to do with innovation, invention, and change, upon which cultural health and diversity depend and thrive. Social othering has to do with power, exclusion, and privilege, the centralizing of a norm against which otherness is measured, meted out, marginalized. My focus is the practice of the former by people subjected to the latter.

The title "Other: From Noun to Verb" is meant to recall Amiri Baraka's way of describing white appropriation of black music in Chapter 10 of *Blues People*. In that chapter he discusses the development of big-band jazz during the twenties and thirties by Fletcher Henderson, Duke Ellington, Jimmie Lunceford, and others and the imitation and commoditization of it by white musicians like Jimmy and Tommy Dorsey, Artie Shaw, Charlie Barnet, and Benny Goodman (who became known as the "King of Swing"). He calls the chapter "Swing—From Verb to Noun." Typical of the way he uses the verb/noun distinction is this remark: "But for most of America by the twenties, jazz (or *jass*, the noun, not the verb) meant the Original Dixieland Jazz Band (to the hip) and Paul Whiteman (to the square)."[2] Or this one:

> *Swing*, the verb, meant a simple reaction to the music (and as it developed in verb usage, a way of reacting to anything in life). As it was formalized, and the term and the music taken further out of context, *swing* became a noun that meant a commercial popular music in cheap imitation of a kind of Afro-American music.   (BP, 212–213)

"From verb to noun" means the erasure of black inventiveness by white appropriation. As in Lukács's notion of phantom objectivity, the "noun," white commodification, obscures or "disappears" the "verb" it rips off, black agency, black authority, black invention. Benny Goodman bought arrangements from black musicians, later hired Fletcher Henderson as his band's chief arranger and later still brought black musicians Teddy Wilson, Lionel Hampton, Charlie Christian, and Cootie Williams into his band, but for the most part black musicians were locked out of the enormous commercial success made of the music they had invented. The most popular and best paid bands were white and the well-paying studio jobs created by the emergence of radio as the preeminent medium for disseminating the music were almost completely restricted to white musicians.

"From verb to noun" means, on the aesthetic level, a less dynamic, less improvisatory, less blues-inflected music and, on the political level, a containment of black mobility, a containment of the economic and social advances that might accrue to black artistic innovation. The domain of action and the ability to act suggested by *verb* is closed off by the hypostasis, paralysis, and arrest suggested by *noun*, the confinement to a predetermined status Baraka has in mind when he writes: "There should be no cause for wonder that the trumpets of Bix Beiderbecke and Louis Armstrong were so dissimilar. The white middle-class boy from Iowa was the product of a culture which could *place* Louis Armstrong, but could never understand him" (BP, 153–154). This confinement to a predetermined status (predetermined stasis), the keeping of black people "in their place," gives rise to the countering, contestatory tendencies I'll be talking about as a movement from noun to verb.

My topic, then, is not so much otherness as othering, black linguistic and musical practices that accent variance, variability—what reggae musicians call "versioning." As Dick Hebdige notes: " 'Versioning' is at the heart not only of reggae but of *all* Afro-American and Caribbean musics: jazz, blues, rap, R&B, reggae, calypso, soca, salsa, Afro-Cuban, and so on."[3] When Baraka writes of John Coltrane's recording of Billy Eckstine's "I Want to Talk About You," he emphasizes what could be called Trane's versioning of the tune, what I would call his othering of it:

> . . . instead of the simplistic though touching note-for-note replay of the ballad's line, on this performance each note is tested, given a slight tremo-

lo or emotional vibrato (note to chord to scale reference) which makes it seem as if each one of the notes is given the possibility of "infinite" qualification . . . proving that the ballad as it was written was only the beginning of the story.[4]

Trane himself spoke of his desire to work out a kind of writing that would allow for "more plasticity, more viability, more room for improvisation in the statement of the melody itself."[5] His lengthy solos caused some listeners to accuse him of practicing in public, which, in a sense that is not at all derogatory, he was—the sense in which Wilson Harris calls one of his recent novels *The Infinite Rehearsal*.

Such othering practices implicitly react against and reflect critically upon the different sort of othering to which their practitioners, denied agency in a society by which they are designated other, have been subjected. The black speaker, writer, or musician whose practice privileges variation subjects the fixed equations that underwrite that denial (including the idea of fixity itself) to an alternative. Zora Neale Hurston writes of the gossipers and storytellers in *Their Eyes Were Watching God*:

> It was the time for sitting on porches beside the road. It was the time to hear things and talk. These sitters had been tongueless, earless, eyeless conveniences all day long. Mules and other brutes had occupied their skins. But now, the sun and the bossman were gone, so the skins felt powerful and human. They became lords of sounds and lesser things. They passed nations through their mouths.[6]

Hurston is one of the pioneer expositor-practitioners of a resistant othering found in black vernacular culture. In her essay "Characteristics of Negro Expression,"[7] published in the thirties, she writes: "What we really mean by originality is the modification of ideas. . . . So if we look at it squarely, the Negro is a very original being. While he lives and moves in the midst of a white civilization, everything that he touches is re-interpreted for his own use." Baraka's valorization of the verb recalls a similar move on her part thirty years earlier, her discussion of "verbal nouns" as one of black America's contributions to American English. She emphasizes action, dynamism, and kinetics, arguing that black vernacular culture does the same: "Frequently the Negro, even with detached words in his vocabulary—not evolved in him but transplanted on his tongue by contact—must add action to it to make it do. So we have 'chop-axe,' 'sitting-chair,' 'cook-pot' and the like because the speaker has in his mind the picture of the object in use. Action." She goes on to list a number of "verbal nouns," nouns and adjectives made to function as verbs, and "nouns from verbs," verbs masquerading as nouns. *Funeralize, I wouldn't friend with her*, and *uglying away* are among her examples of the former, *won't stand a broke* and *She won't take a listen* among those of the latter.

The privileging of the verb, the movement from noun to verb, linguistically accentuates action among a people whose ability to act is curtailed by racist constraints. I prefer to see a connection between such privileging and such curtailment than to attribute the former, as Hurston occasionally does, to black primitivity. Language is symbolic action, frequently compensatory action, addressing deprivations it helps its users overcome. The privileging of the verb, the black vernacular investment in what Hurston calls "action words," makes this all the more evident. The sort of analysis found in the passage from *Their Eyes Were Watching God* that I quoted is brought to bear on the movement from noun to verb in a piece that Hurston published in the early forties, "High John de Conquer."[8] The High John the Conqueror root that plays so prominent a role in African-American hoodoo is here personified and figured as a key to black endurance and resilience, "the secret of black song and laughter." In the title and throughout the piece Hurston elides the last syllable of *conqueror*, as is frequently done in black speech. In doing so, honoring the vernacular in more senses than one, she changes *conqueror* to *conquer*, noun to verb, practicing what she expounds upon in "Characteristics of Negro Expression."

Hurston presents High John de Conquer as an inner divergence from outward adversity, the ability of enslaved Africans to hold themselves apart from circumstance. "An inside thing to live by," she calls it. She relates High John de Conquer to a propensity for laughter, story, and song, to black liberties taken with music and language. He embodies mastery of sound and mastery through sound, "making a way out of no-way." High John de Conquer moves quickly, as mercurial as he is musical: "His footsteps sounded across the world in a low but musical rhythm as if the world he walked on was a singing-drum. . . . He had come from Africa. He came walking on the waves of sound." He embodies music, storytelling, and laughter as a kind of mobility, a fugitivity which others the slaves' condition:

> He walked on the winds and moved fast. Maybe he was in Texas when the lash fell on a slave in Alabama, but before the blood was dry on the back he was there. A faint pulsing of a drum like a goatskin stretched over a heart, that came nearer and closer, then somebody in the saddened quarters would feel like laughing and say, "Now, High John de Conquer, Old Massa couldn't get the best of *him*. . . ."

Hurston writes of the song High John de Conquer helps the slaves find: "It had no words. It was a tune that you could bend and shape in most any way you wanted to fit the words and feelings that you had."

The bending and shaping of sound, black liberties taken with music and language, caused Lucy McKim Garrison, one of the editors of *Slave Songs in the United States*, to write in 1862:

> It is difficult to express the entire character of these negro ballads by mere musical notes and signs. The odd turns made in the throat, and the curious rhythmic effect produced by single voices chiming in at different irregular intervals, seem almost as impossible to place on the score as the singing of birds or the tones of an Aeolian Harp.

Another of its editors, William Allen, likewise wrote:

> What makes it all the harder to unravel a thread of melody out of this strange network is that, like birds, they seem not infrequently to strike

sounds that cannot be precisely represented by the gamut, and abound in "slides from one note to another and turns and cadences not in articulated notes." . . . There are also apparent irregularities in the time, which it is no less difficult to express accurately.

Henry G. Spaulding wrote in 1863: "The most striking of their barbaric airs it would be impossible to write out." The compilers of the Hampton spirituals, M. F. Armstrong and Helen W. Ludlow, wrote similarly a decade later: "Tones are frequently employed which we have no musical characters to represent. . . . The tones are variable in pitch, ranging through an entire octave on different occasions, according to the inspiration of the singer."[9] One could go on and on with similar statements. Western musical notation's inability to capture the tonal and rhythmic mobility and variability such quotes remark upon confirms the fugitive spirit Hurston identifies with High John de Conquer. "It is no accident that High John de Conquer has evaded the ears of white people," she writes, punning on while poking fun at the use of accidentals by Garrison, Smith, and others to approximate the flatted or bent notes of the African American's altered scale.

Fugitive spirit has had its impact upon African-American literary practices as well. As fact, as metaphor, and as formal disposition, the alliance of writing with fugitivity recurs throughout the tradition. One recalls that in 1829 George Moses Horton hoped to buy his freedom with money made from sales of his book of poems, *Hope of Liberty*. One thinks of the role played by literacy in Frederick Douglass's escape, of Harriet Jacobs's denunciations of the Fugitive Slave Law, of the importance of the slave narratives to the anti-slavery movement. W. E. B. Du Bois referred to the essays in *The Souls of Black Folk* as "fugitive pieces," and the impact of fugitive spirit can also be found in the work of William Melvin Kelley (the mass exodus in *A Different Drummer*, the bending and reshaping of language in *Dunfords Travels Everywheres*), Ishmael Reed (Quickskill in *Flight to Canada*), Toni Morrison (the flying African in *Song of Solomon*, the "lickety-split, lickety-split" at the end of *Tar Baby*, Sethe's escape in *Beloved*), and others. Ed Roberson, for example, in a recent poem called "Taking the Print":

> See night in the sunlight's starry reflection
> off the water darkening the water
> by contrast.
> 　　　　　The dark hiding in the water
> also hid us in the river at night
> Our crossing guided by the internal sight
> on our darkness
> 　　　　　the ancient graphis
> and—from this passage of abductions and escapes—
> this newer imprimatur of the river
> cut deep in the plate.
> 　　　　　see in the river the ripples'
> picture on the surface of the wind the lifting of the
> image

has taken at the deeper face

> the starry freedom

written in the milky rivery line that pours
the brilliance of that image from a depth only black
night fleeing across this land

> has to

voice.[10]

An especially good example of the movement from noun to verb's identification or alliance with fugitive spirit is Aimé Césaire's 1955 poem "The Verb 'Marroner'/ for René Depestre, Haitian Poet."[11] Written in response to Louis Aragon and the French Communist Party's call for a return to traditional poetic meters and forms, which Depestre supported in the journal *Présence Africaine*, the poem insists upon openness, experimentation, and formal innovation:

> Comrade Depestre
> It is undoubtedly a very serious problem
> the relation between poetry and Revolution
> the content determines the form
>
> and what about keeping in mind as well the dialectical
> backlash by which the form taking its revenge
> chokes the poems like an accursed fig tree

The poem announces and enacts its poetics under the sign of a neologistic verb. Césaire invokes the history of fugitive slaves in the Caribbean, the runaway Africans known as maroons who escaped the plantations and set up societies of their own. The French noun for this phenomenon, *marronage*, is the basis for the word, the verb *marroner*, Césaire invents, an act of invention exemplifying the independence for which the poem calls. The coinage has no English equivalent. Clayton Eshleman and Annette Smith translate it "escape like slaves":

> Is it true this season that they're polishing up sonnets
> for us to do so would remind me too much of the sugary
> juice drooled over there by the distilleries on the mornes
> when slow skinny oxen make their rounds to the whine
> of mosquitoes
>
> Bah! Depestre the poem is not a mill for
> grinding sugar cane absolutely not
> and if the rhymes are flies on ponds
>
> > without rhymes
>
> > for a whole season
>
> away from ponds
>
> > under my persuasion
>
> let's laugh drink and escape like slaves

Such invention in Césaire's work, such othering of and taking of liberties with French, has been referred to as "a politics of neologism."[12] A similar practice can be found in the work of another Caribbean poet, Edward Kamau Brathwaite, who writes of Césaire: "His fabulous long poem *Cahier d'un retour au pays natal* (1939) evolved the concept of *negritude*: that there is a black Caliban Maroon world with its own aesthetics (*sycorax*), contributing to world and Third World consciousness."[13] Brathwaite's recently completed second trilogy, comprised of *Mother Poem, Sun Poem,* and *X/Self,* is characterized by a versioning of English he calls "calibanization," a creolization "that comes into conflict with the cultural imperial authority of Prospero."[14] One of the remarkable features of the work, one of the features any reader will come away from it unable to forget, is its linguistic texture—not only what is done with words but what is done to them. Brathwaite makes greater use of West Indian nation-language (the term he puts in place of "dialect" or "patois") than in the first trilogy, "The Arrivants," but what he is doing goes further than that. In his use of "standard" English as well he takes his cue from the vernacular, subjecting words to bends, breaks, deformation, reformation—othering.

Brathwaite concludes the next-to-last poem in *The Arrivants* with the lines "So on this ground,/write;/ . . . on this ground/on this broken ground."[15] Nation-language, what some would call broken English, partakes of that ground. "Calibanization" insists that in West Indian folk speech English is not so much broken as broken into, that a struggle for turf is taking place in language. "It was in language," Brathwaite has written, "that the slave was perhaps most successfully imprisoned by his master, and it was in his (mis-)use of it that he perhaps most effectively rebelled. Within the folk tradition, language was (and is) a creative act in itself."[16] This tradition of black liberties taken with language informs *Mother Poem, Sun Poem,* and *X/Self* with the weight of a history of antiimperial struggle, a weight felt in so small a thing as the word. As in the anagrammatic "derangement" Shakespeare had recourse to in fashioning *Caliban* from *cannibal,* the puns, malapropisms, odd spellings, neologisms, and strained meanings Brathwaite resorts to speak of disturbances outside as well as inside the language, social disruptions the word is thus made to register.

Changing *militia* to *malitia* is one small instance of this.[17] As in this instance, most of Brathwaite's "calibanisms" underscore senses of malice and malaise, emphasize the hurt put on the land and on the people by slavery, the plantation system, colonialism, capitalism. The words partake of that hurt. It shows in the language both as referent and as a telling misuse inflicted on English, an abuse that brings that referent more emphatically to light. *The panes of his eyes* becomes *the pains of his eyes* (SP, 6), *the games we played* becomes *the games we paid* (SP, 19), *landscape* becomes *landscrape* (SP, 55), *the future* becomes *the few-/ture* (SP, 87). *Huts* becomes *hurts* and *hillsides* turns into *hillslides:*

> but those that drone their lorries all day up the sweating
>   hill to the factory of mister massa midas
> those mindless arch
>
>   itects that cut the cane
>   that built their own hurts on the hillslide   (SP, 61)

Brathwaite avails himself of and takes part in a revolution of the word that has long been a part of Caribbean folk culture, a reinvention of English of the sort one hears in Rastafarian speech, where *oppressor* gets replaced by *downpressor*, *livicate* takes the place of *dedicate*, and so forth.

But a revolution of the word can only be a beginning. It initiates a break while remaining overshadowed by the conditions it seeks to go beyond. The shadow such conditions cast makes for a brooding humor that straddles laughter and lament, allows no easy, unequivocal foothold in either. Oppositional speech is only partly oppositional. Cramp and obstruction have to do with it as well. In Brathwaite's recent trilogy we not only get the sorts of pointed, transparent word-play I just quoted, but something more opaque and more disconcerting, not resolved as to its tone or intent. Brathwaite revels in a sometimes dizzying mix of parody and pathos, embrace complicated by a sense of the bizarre and even bordering on embarrassment here and there. His otherings accent fugitive spirit and impediment as well, the predicaments that bring fugitive spirit into being:

> but is like we still start
> where we start/in out start/in out start/in
>
> out since menelek was a bwoy & why
> is dat & what is de bess weh to seh so/so it doan sounn like
>
> brigg
> flatts nor hervokitz
>
> nor de pisan cantos nor de souf sea
> bible
>
> nor like ink. le & de anglo saxon
> chronicles
>
> &
>
> a fine
> a cyaan get nutten
>
> write
>
> a cyaan get nutten really
> rite
>
> while a stannin up here in me years & like i inside a me shadow
>
> like de man still mekkin i walk up de slope dat e slide
> in black down de whole long curve a de arch
>
> i
>
> pell
>
> ago   (X, 85–86)

Brathwaite helps impeded speech find its voice, the way Thelonious Monk makes hesitation eloquent or the way a scat singer makes inarticulacy speak. This places his work in the New World African tradition of troubled eloquence, othered eloquence, I'm here sketching. Here, that is, trouble acts as a threshold. It registers a need for a new world and a new language to go along with it, discontent with the world and the ways of speaking we already have. A revolution of the word can only be a new beginning, "beating," as Brathwaite puts it, "its genesis genesis genesis genesis/out of the stammering world" (SP, 97).

My reference to Monk, as Hurston would say, is no accident. Indeed, had Hurston written "Characteristics of Negro Expression" later, she might have included "Rhythm-a-ning" and "Jackie-ing," two Monk titles, in her list of "verbal nouns." In her section on asymmetry ("Asymmetry," she begins it by saying, "is a definite feature of Negro art") she might have quoted Chico O'Farrell's comments on the advent of bebop in the forties:

> . . . it was such a new thing, because here we were confronted for the first time with phrases that wouldn't be symmetrical in the sense that string-music phrasing was symmetrical. Here we were confronted with phrases that were asymmetrical. They would come in into any part of the phrase they felt like, and, at first, also the changes threw us off completely because it was a complete new harmonic—not new, but we'll say unusual harmonic concept that was so alien to what we had been doing. To us it was such a drastic change that I think anything that came afterwards wasn't as drastic as that particular first step from swing to bop. I think in a sense bop probably marks the real cut-off point of the old concept of swinging. I don't mean in the sense of swinging—we were still swinging—but the concept of the square structure of the music as to this new particular way of playing and writing.[18]

The bebop revolution of which Monk was a part—Ellington called it "the Marcus Garvey Extension"—was a movement, in its reaction to swing, from noun to verb. It was a revolution that influenced a great number of writers, Brathwaite included, as can be seen, among other places, in his early poem "Blues."[19] Its impact upon Baraka's work and thought can be seen not only in *Blues People* but also in the poetics, the valorization of the verb, in the 1964 essay "Hunting Is Not Those Heads on the Wall."[20] There he espouses a poetics of process, arguing: "The clearest description of now is the present participle. . . . Worship the verb, if you need something." Halfway through the essay he mentions Charlie Parker, having earlier remarked: "I speak of the *verb process*, the doing, the coming into being, the at-the-time-of. Which is why we think there is particular value in live music, contemplating the artifact as it arrives, listening to it emerge." The sense he advances that "this verb value" is an impulse to "make words surprise themselves" recalls the popular description of jazz as "the sound of surprise."

The white appropriation and commercialization of swing resulted in a music that was less improvisatory, less dependent upon the inventiveness of soloists. The increased reliance upon arrangements in the Fletcher Henderson mold led to a sameness of sound and style among the various bands. In *Blues People* Baraka quotes Hsio Wen Shih's comments regarding the anthology album *The Great Swing Bands*, a record Shih refers to as "terrifying" due to the indistinguishability of one band from another. It was against this uniformity that bebop revolted. "Benny Goodman," Howard McGhee recalls, "had been named the 'King of Swing.' . . . We figured, what the hell, we can't do no more than what's been done with it, we gotta do somethin' else. We gotta do some other kind of thing" (SB, 314). ("Some other stuff," a common expression among black musicians, would become the title of an album by Grachan Moncure III in the sixties.) Mary Lou Williams said of her first meeting with Monk in the thirties: "He told me that he was sick of hearing musicians play the same thing the same way all the time."[21] Monk himself summed up his music by saying: "How to use notes differently. That's it. Just how to use notes differently."[22] It is no accident that bebop was typically performed by small combos rather than big bands as was the case with swing. It accentuated individual expression, bringing the soloist and improvisation once more to the fore.

Baraka emphasizes nonconformity in his treatment of bebop in *Blues People*, stressing what he terms its "willfully harsh, *anti-assimilationist* sound" (BP, 181). The cultivation of a unique, individual style that black music encourages informs and inspires his attitudes toward writing. In his statement on poetics for the anthology *The New American Poetry 1945–1960* he echoes Louis Armstrong's ad-libbed line on a 1949 recording with Billie Holiday,[23] calling it "How You Sound??" The emphasis on self-expression in his work is also an emphasis on self-transformation, an othering or, as Brathwaite has it, an X-ing of the self, the self not as noun but as verb. Of the post-bop innovations of such musicians as Albert Ayler and Sun Ra, he writes: "New Black Music is this: Find the self, then kill it" (BM, 176). To kill the self is to show it to be fractured, unfixed. The dismantling of the unified subject found in recent critical theory is old news when it comes to black music. I've seen Bukka White break off singing to exhort himself: "Sing it, Bukka!" Charles Mingus's autobiography begins: "In other words, I am three."[24] A recent composition by Muhal Richard Abrams has the title "Conversation with the Three of Me." Craig Harris remarks of the polyrhythmicity of one of his pieces: "It's about cutting yourself in half."[25]

Our interest in cultural diversity—diversity within a culture as well as the diversity of cultures[26]—should lead us to be wary of hypostasis, the risk we take with nouns, a deadend that will impede change unless "other," "self," and such are "given the possibility of 'infinite' qualification." Wilson Harris, whose novel *The Infinite Rehearsal* I referred to earlier, has written of "qualitative and infinite variations of substance clothed in nouns," arguing that "nouns may reveal paradoxically when qualified, that their emphasis on reality and their inner meaning can change as they are inhabited by variable psychic projections."[27] In his new novel *The Four Banks of the River of Space* he speaks of "the instructive bite of music" on the way to suggesting that "breaking a formula of complacency" consists of "becoming a stranger to oneself."[28] As Monk's tune "Jackie-ing" tells us, even a so-called proper noun is a verb in disguise—present-participial, provisional, subject to change. John Gilmore, tenor saxophonist with Sun Ra's band for some thirty years, tells a story about the time he spent with Art Blakey's Jazz Messengers in 1965. After about a month, he says, the music was at so inventive a level that one night in Los Angeles, following one of his solos, trumpeter Lee Morgan looked over at him and asked: "Is that you, Gilmore?" Morgan then took a solo that caused Gilmore to ask the same thing of him: "Lee, is that you?"[29]

II

The "nounization" of swing furthered and partook in a commoditization of music that, in the West, as Jacques Attali points out, had been developing since the 1700s. "Until the eighteenth century," he writes in *Noise: The Political Economy of Music*, "music was of the order of the 'active'; it then entered the order of the 'exchanged.' "[30] The process was completed in the twentieth century, he argues, with the birth of the recording industry and its exploitation of black musicians: "Music did not really become a commodity until a broad market for popular music was created. Such a market did not exist when Edison invented the phonograph; it was produced by the colonization of black music by the American industrial apparatus" (N, 103). The transition from "active" to "exchanged," verb to noun, reflects the channeling of power through music it is the point of the book to insist upon:

> Listening to music is . . . realizing that its appropriation and control is a reflection of power, that it is essentially political. . . . With music is born power and its opposite: subversion. . . . Music, the quintessential mass activity, like the crowd, is simultaneously a threat and a necessary source of legitimacy; trying to channel it is a risk that every system of power must run. . . . Thus music localizes and specifies power, because it marks and regiments the rare noises that cultures, in their normalization of behavior, see fit to authorize. (N, 6, 14, 19–20)

Attali is at all points alive to the shamanic roots of music, its magicoprophetic role, no matter how obscured those roots and that role tend to be by the legal, technological, and social developments he goes to great lengths to analyze and describe.

The idea of music as a conduit of power, a channeler of violence, a regulator of society, is particularly visible—unobscured—among the Carib-speaking Kalapalo of the Upper Xingu Basin in Brazil. Ellen B. Basso, in her study *A Musical View of the Universe: Kalapalo Myth and Ritual Performances*, deals with their ideas regarding sound and what she terms "orders of animacy," a hierarchic taxonomy at the top of which the Kalapalo place entities known as "powerful beings." These beings are nonhuman, though they sometimes appear in human form, and, Basso points out, "they are preeminently and essentially musical":

> Powerful beings are different from concrete historical figures because they and their acts are "always" and everywhere. . . . This multiplicity of essence

or "hyperanimacy" is coupled on the one hand with a multiplicity of feeling and consequent unpredictability and on the other with a monstrous intensity of some feeling or trait; hence powerful beings are dangerous beings. . . . Their hyperanimacy and multiplicity of essence are perhaps what is deeply metaphorized by their association with musical invention.[31]

Music represents the highest degree or level of animacy, hyperanimacy, and in their musical performances the Kalapalo model themselves upon their images of powerful beings, aspiring to the condition of powerful beings. They seek both to endow themselves with and to domesticate hyperanimate power. Basso writes:

> . . . music (or more exactly, musical performance) is identified by the Kalapalo as having controlling force over aggressive, transformative, and wandering power; it is also a manifestation of that power. The ability of music to control and channel aggression, to limit hyperanimacy in ways that are helpful to people, has further consequences for understanding its importance within ritual contexts. This is because in such contexts of use, political life—the relations of control that some people effect over others—achieves its most concrete and elaborate expression.   (MV, 246)

I would like to highlight two features of Kalapalo thought and practice concerning music, and bring them to bear, by way of analogy, upon the minstrel show, a form of theatrical performance unique to the United States that emerged during the 1820s and reached its apex between 1850 and 1870. An appropriation of the slave's music and dance by white men who blackened their faces with burnt cork, going on stage to sing "Negro songs," perform dances derived from those of the slaves, and tell jokes based on plantation life, the minstrel show is an early instance of the cannibalization of black music to which we saw Attali refer. "Minstrelsy," Robert C. Toll observes in *Blacking Up: The Minstrel Show in Nineteenth-Century America*, "was the first example of the way American popular culture would exploit and manipulate Afro-Americans and their culture to please and benefit white Americans."[32] The first of the two aspects of Kalapalo thought and practice I would like to highlight is the fact that powerful beings are associated with darkness and with the color black, that for ritual performances the Kalapalo shaman darkens himself with pot black as a way of becoming, Basso explains, "less visibly human and appearing more like a powerful being" (MV, 248). Blacking up, the white minstrel practice of donning blackface makeup, amounts to a pseudo-shamanic performance in which the power of black musicality is complimented yet simultaneously channeled, caricatured, and contained. As is not the case for the Kalapalo shaman, for the white minstrel "less visibly human" means less than human, even as the appeal and the power of the music are being exploited.

Minstrelsy reveals the ambivalent, duplicitous relationship of nineteenth-century white Americans not only to black people but to music and language as well. The second aspect of Kalapalo thought and practice I would like to highlight relates to this, having to do with the distinctions the Kalapalo make among calls, speech, and music, and among degrees of animacy. Human beings share with entities of lesser animacy the ability to emit calls and with entities of greater animacy, powerful beings, the ability to speak and to make music, but it is speech that is regarded as quintessentially human. Speech is the form of sound by which humans are characterized and symbolized in the taxonomic order, music the form with which powerful beings are identified. Interestingly, calls as well as music are considered more truthful, more trustworthy than speech:

> . . . human beings can express truthful and empirically motivated feelings best through *itsu* [calls]. Pain of varying degrees of intensity, deep sadness, shame, joy, sexual passion, frustration with oneself, indeed, the entire range of human emotion is expressed most succinctly (and by implication as truthful feeling) this way.
>
> Human beings are distinguished from other *ago* [living things], however, by their ability to speak, and it is through language that they are most commonly symbolized and distinguished from other categories of entities. . . . But language allows people to do something very different from animals. Human beings were created by a trickster, whose name "Taugi" means "speaks deceptively about himself." . . . Hence human beings are in essence deceitful beings because of their ability to speak. Therefore, people are capable not only of truthfully expressing their feelings, but—and this is the unmarked understanding of human speech for the Kalapalo—of creating an illusory screen of words that conceals their true thoughts. (MV, 67–68)

Music, the Kalapalo believe, is more to be trusted than speech because, rather than masking the mental, powerful beings "in J. L. Austin's sense . . . are performative beings, capable of reaching the limits of awareness of meaning by constructing action through a process that is simultaneously mental and physical" (MV, 71).

Calls and music both put sound in the service of sentience. In this they differ from speech, which valorizes the sentence, the humanly constructed realm of meaning, grammaticality, predication. The minstrel show, in its recourse to music (the slave's music, moreover, in which calls, cries, and hollers played a prominent part) and in its "translation" of that music into songs of sentiment (Stephen Foster's "Old Folks at Home," "Massa's in de Cold, Cold Ground," and so forth), critiqued even as it exemplified the deceptiveness of language. The implicit critique, the recourse to music and to sentimentality, to songs that advertised themselves as innocent of ambiguity, insincerity, or circumlocution, was accompanied by an explicit critique. This took the form of the stump speech and its malapropisms, the heavy reliance upon wordplay and puns in minstrel humor and such routines as the following, called "Modern Language":

bones: How things have changed of late. A man can't depend on anything.
    A man must discount his expectations by at least 80 per cent.
midman: In other words, "never count your chickens before they are hatched."

bones: That sort of language is not up to the four hundred. You should say that this way: Never enumerate your feathered progeny before the process of incubation has been thoroughly realized.

midman: That does take the rag off the bush.

bones: Wrong again. You should not say that. You should say: That removes the dilapidated linen from off the shrubbery.[33]

While the stump speech poked fun at black people's alleged insecure hold on language, such humor as this poked fun at language itself, at language's—especially elevated language's—insecure hold on the world. Minstrelsy, under cover of blackface, was able to vent apprehensions regarding the tenuousness of language, even as it ridiculed its target of choice for a supposed lack of linguistic competence. In regard to language as in other matters, the minstrel show allowed its audience to have it both ways.

One of the reasons for minstrelsy's popularity was what Alexander Saxton terms "the flexibility of standards which flourished behind the fake facade of blackface presentation."[34] That facade made it permissible to refer to such topics as homosexuality and masturbation, which were taboo on the legitimate stage, in the press, and elsewhere. Sentimental songs and female impersonation, as did the blackface facade, allowed performers and audience alike access to a world of emotion that was otherwise held to be off-limits. Minstrelsy's wide appeal had largely to do with the illusion of escape from conventional strictures it afforded, the degree to which it spoke to a white, predominantly male imaginary. Minstrel star George Thatcher's description of his feelings after seeing his first minstrel show as a boy alerts us to the deep psychic forces at work (and also, incidentally, sheds light on the title of John Berryman's *Dream Songs*, which, dedicated to Thomas D. Rice, the "father" of blackface minstrelsy, makes use of the minstrel figure Bones): "I found myself dreaming of minstrels; I would awake with an imaginary tambourine in my hand, and rub my face with my hands to see if I was blacked up. . . . The dream of my life was to see or speak to a performer" (BU, 33).

The influence of blackface minstrelsy extended well into the present century, having an impact upon vaudeville, musical comedy, radio, movies, television, and other forms of popular culture. It tells us a great deal regarding the obstacles in the way of a genuine multiculturality or cross-culturality, a genuine, non-exploitative cultural exchange. Toll recounts that in 1877 Bret Harte and Mark Twain wrote a minstrel play based on a poem of Harte's about the "heathen chinee." On opening night Twain explained to the audience: "The Chinaman is getting to be a pretty frequent figure in the United States and is going to be a great political problem and we thought it well for you to see him on the stage before you had to deal with the problem." Toll goes on to remark that Twain's is a clear and accurate statement of one of minstrelsy's functions: "Although on the surface they just sang songs and told jokes about peculiar people, minstrels actually provided their audiences with one of the only bases that many of them had for understanding America's increasing ethnic diversity" (BU, 169). This base, however, was an impediment rather than an aid to cultural diversity, a strategy of containment through caricature designed to consolidate white privilege and power. The minstrel made use of music to channel power in the service of "orders of animacy" in which whites came out on top, to uphold unequally distributed orders of agency in which violence, albeit under control, was never out of the picture. Saxton remarks of a minstrel song: "This 'comic-banjo' piece, as it was described, appeared in a songster published in New York in 1863. Geographically and emotionally, it was only a block or two from a song such as this to the maiming and lynching of blacks on the sidewalks of New York during the draft riots of the same year" (23).

The subject of cultural diversity and the goal of a healthy cross-culturality are haunted by the specter of such appropriation as the minstrel legacy represents. We should not be surprised that not only pop-cultural but also high-cultural and avant-garde venues number among its haunts. I'm thinking, for example, of Gertrude Stein's early piece "Melanctha," described by her in "Composition as Explanation" as "a negro story." Katherine Mansfield, reviewing the book in which "Melanctha" appears, *Three Lives*, heard sentences overwhelmed by sound and sentience, much to her alarm. Moreover, she heard it as a minstrel band, a channeling of black musicality into prose:

> . . . let the reader go warily, warily with *Melanctha*. We confess we read a good page or two before we realised what was happening. Then the dreadful fact dawned. We discovered ourselves reading in *syncopated time*. Gradually we heard in the distance and then coming uncomfortably near, the sound of banjos, drums, bones, cymbals and voices. The page began to rock. To our horror we found ourselves silently singing "Was it true what Melanctha said that night to him" etc. Those who have heard the Syncopated Orchestra sing "It's me—it's me—it's me" or "I got a robe" will understand what we mean. *Melanctha* is negro music with all its maddening monotony done into prose; it is writing in real ragtime. Heaven forbid Miss Stein should become a fashion.[35]

The analogue to what Mansfield misapprehends as black-musical monotony, Stein's notorious use of repetition advances a critique of language that is not unrelated to the one we see in the minstrel show. Under cover of blackness, she issues an avant-garde caveat regarding the trustworthiness of the linguistic sign and of the discursive, ratiocinative order it promotes. The search for and the nature of "understanding" are pointedly at issue in the story, especially in the relationship between impulsive, sensation-seeking Melanctha and reflective, respectability-minded Jeff:

> "Yes I certainly do understand you when you talk so Dr. Campbell. I certainly do understand now what you mean by what you was always saying to me. I certainly do understand Dr. Campbell that you mean you don't believe it's right to love anybody." "Why sure no, yes I do Miss Melanctha, I certainly do believe strong in loving, and in being good to everybody, and trying to understand what they all need, to help them." "Oh I know all about that way of doing Dr. Campbell, but that certainly ain't the kind of

love I mean when I am talking. I mean real, strong, hot love Dr. Campbell, that makes you do anything for somebody that loves you." "I don't know much about that kind of love yet Miss Melanctha. You see it's this way with me always Miss Melanctha. I am always so busy with my thinking about my work I am doing and so I don't have time for just fooling, and then too, you see Miss Melanctha, I really certainly don't ever like to get excited, and that kind of loving hard does seem always to mean just getting all the time excited. That certainly is what I always think from what I see of them that have it bad Miss Melanctha, and that certainly would never suit a man like me. . . ."[36]

On a typical page of dialogue between the two, the word *certainly* occurs as often as twenty times. Such repetition undermines the word, underscoring the uncertainty in which the two of them are immersed. Words are treated as though, rather than sticking, as Jack Spicer put it, to the real, they were continually slipping from it. Repetition compulsively moves to make up for that slippage, accenting all the more the words' insecure grip on the world. Not unlike the Kalapalo, Jeff at one point complains that "the ordinary kind of holler" would offer "much more game," much more forthright expression (TL, 127). The story strongly suggests that the order of what the Kalapalo term *itsu* is where "understanding" most unproblematically resides:

> And now the pain came hard and harder in Jeff Campbell, he groaned, and it hurt him so, he could not bear it. And the tears came, and his heart beat, and he was hot and worn and bitter in him.
>
> Now Jeff knew very well what it was to love Melanctha. Now Jeff Campbell knew he was really understanding.   (TL, 145)

"Melanctha" recalls minstrelsy in that Stein uses one form of marginality, blackness, to mask another, to mask two others in fact—the avant-garde linguistic experimentation that we just noted (experimental writing being relegated to the fringes by middlebrow, if not outright philistine American predilections) and, albeit much less evident, lesbianism. Janice Doane and Carolyn Copeland argue that "Melanctha," as the latter puts it, "is not really a story about the ethnic reality of Negroes,"[37] that the story reworks material from the earlier novel *Q.E.D.* "Melanctha" is *Q.E.D.* done in blackface. Doane writes that "the lesbian affair of *Q.E.D.* is converted into the heterosexual affair of the 'Melanctha' story."[38] Copeland says the same at greater length:

> It will be recalled that *Q.E.D.*, written in 1903, concerned three homosexual women involved in a triangle. When one considers the trouble Theodore Dreiser had with *Sister Carrie* during that same period, it is not surprising that Gertrude Stein dropped the homosexual elements from her story before using the material again. Some very important elements of *Q.E.D.*, however, would have become problematic in a simple shift from homosexual to heterosexual in the story, and these elements must be discussed briefly.

In *Q.E.D.* Adele and Helen together undergo a full and complete series of sexual experiences, and obviously they are not married when they experience them. It is important to Adele's full realization of how completely "out of rhythm" she and Helen are that they not be married. Adele must be able to walk away from the experience with no ties such as marriage to complicate it. At the turn of this century in America the only background against which a writer could portray premarital sexual relationships without having an outraged white, middle-class public to contend with was one dealing with Negroes. It was part of the white man's view of the black man that they were sexually promiscuous. If Gertrude Stein wished to drop the homosexual elements and make them heterosexual, her choice of Negroes instead of whites allowed her to retain as much as possible of the important extramarital elements involved. And this is exactly what she did.

(24–25)

Orders of marginality contend with one another here. It is instructive that blackness is the noun-mask under whose camouflage two other forms of marginality gain an otherwise blocked order of animacy or agency, an otherwise unavailable "verb-ness." We are again at the sacrificial roots of the social order, the ritual murder of which music, Attali argues, is the simulacrum. Under cover of scapegoat blackness, the otherwise marginal cozies up to the center.[39]

I say this not to encourage turf wars among marginalized groups and/or individuals, but to raise a question. Wilson Harris writes of marginality in a way that is as promising as it is challenging. "Extremity or marginality, in my view," he writes, "lifts the medium or diverse experience to a new angle of possibility. . . . It involves us in a curiously tilted field in which spatial pre-possessions and our pre-possessions are dislodged . . . marginality is a raised contour or frontier of habit in the topography of the heart and mind."[40] I think of this tilt[41] as arising to contend with another form of tilt—that of unevenly allotted orders of agency, the unfair playing field, as it's commonly put. I think of the tilt of Edgar Pool's tenor saxophone in John Clellon Holmes's novel *The Horn*:

> Edgar Pool blew methodically, eyes beady and open, and he held his tenor saxophone almost horizontally extended from his mouth. This unusual posture gave it the look of some metallic albatross caught insecurely in his two hands, struggling to resume flight. In those early days he never brought it down to earth, but followed after its isolated passage over all manner of American cities, snaring it nightly, fastening his drooping, stony lips to its cruel beak, and tapping the song.[42]

The idiosyncratic tilt of "isolated originality," modeled on Lester Young:

> It was only one of many bands he worked those years, the tireless jumping colored bands that flourished like a backwash after the initial wave of swing. But already he was blowing strange long lines, rising out of the section, indrawn and resolute, to stand before the circling dancers, tilt the big horn roofward from his body, and play his weightless, sharply veering phras-

es over the chunking of unsubtle drums. In those days, no one heard.   (89)

I also, however, think of another tilt we see in the novel, that of a whisky bottle "tilted into the coffee as he [Pool] spiked it generously" (194) during the last night of an alcoholic binge, the last night of his life. The tilt of entropy, exhaustion, disillusionment. Hence, my question: Which tilt will it be? In order for the latter not to prevail, the discourse on cultural diversity will have to acknowledge both.

By this I mean that we need more than content analyses based on assumptions of representationality. The dislocating tilt of artistic othering, especially as practiced by African-American artists, deserves a great deal more attention than it has been given. While the regressive racial views of white writers like Stein and Ezra Pound tend to be regarded (if they're regarded at all) as secondary to their artistic innovations, black writers tend to be read racially, primarily at the content level, the noun level, as responding to racism, representing "the black experience." That black writers have been experimentally and innovatively engaged with the medium, addressing issues of form as well as issues of content, tends to be ignored. The ability to influence the course of the medium, to *move* the medium, entails an order of animacy granted only to whites when it comes to writing. The situation with regard to music is a bit better, black musicians having been acknowledged to be innovators, even though their white imitators enjoy commercial success and critical acclaim greatly disproportionate to their musical contributions. The nonrecognition of black artistic othering is symptomatic of the social othering to which black people are subjected, particularly in light of the celebration accorded artistic othering practiced by whites. This is a disparity the discussion of cultural diversity should be addressing.

Perhaps we can increase not only the quantity but also the quality of attention given to African-American art and cultural practices. Perhaps we can make it possible for the music of Henry Threadgill or David S. Ware to be as widely known as that of Wynton Marsalis, Ed Roberson's *Lucid Interval as Integral Music* or Will Alexander's *The Black Speech of the Angel* to win the sort of acclaim accorded Rita Dove's *Thomas and Beulah*, Amiri Baraka to be as well known for *The Dead Lecturer* as for *Dutchman*. If we are to do so, we must, à la Césaire, confront the neo-traditionalism that has taken hold of late with a countertradition of marronage, divergence, flight, fugitive tilt. Henry Dumas put it well in "Black Trumpeter": *"the wing praises the root by taking to the limbs."*[43]

NOTES

1. This essay was first presented as a lecture as part of "Otherness: A Symposium on Cultural Diversity" at the Detroit Institute of Arts, March 1991.
2. LeRoi Jones, *Blues People: Negro Music in White America* (New York: Morrow, 1963), p. 143. Hereafter referred to as BP.
3. Dick Hebdige, *Cut 'n' Mix: Culture, Identity and Caribbean Music* (London: Methuen, 1987), p. 12.
4. LeRoi Jones, *Black Music* (New York: Morrow, 1967), p. 66. Hereafter referred to as BM.

tell the story

5. Liner notes, *Coltrane Live at the Village Vanguard Again!* (Impulse! Records AS-9124).

6. Zora Neale Hurston, *Their Eyes Were Watching God* (Urbana: University of Illinois Press, 1978), pp. 9–10.

7. Zora Neale Hurston, *The Sanctified Church* (Berkeley: Turtle Island, 1981), pp. 49–68.

8. Ibid., pp. 69–78.

9. Garrison, Allen, Spaulding, Armstrong, and Ludlow quoted in Eileen Southern, *The Music of Black Americans: A History* 2nd Edition (New York: Norton, 1983), pp. 191–194.

10. Ed Roberson, "Taking the Print," *Hambone*, 9 (Winter 1991), p. 2.

11. Aimé Césaire, *The Collected Poetry*, trans. Clayton Eshleman and Annette Smith (Berkeley: University of California Press, 1983), pp. 368–371.

12. James Clifford, *The Predicament of Culture: Twentieth-Century Ethnography, Literature and Art* (Cambridge: Harvard University Press, 1988), pp. 175–181.

13. Edward Kamau Brathwaite, *X/Self* (Oxford: Oxford University Press, 1987), pp. 129–130. Hereafter referred to as X.

14. Edward Kamau Brathwaite, *Mother Poem* (Oxford: Oxford University Press, 1977), p. 121.

15. Edward Brathwaite, *The Arrivants: A New World Trilogy* (Oxford: Oxford University Press, 1973), pp. 265–266.

16. Edward Brathwaite, *The Development of Creole Society in Jamaica 1770–1820* (Oxford: Oxford University Press, 1971), p. 237.

17. Edward Kamau Brathwaite, *Sun Poem* (Oxford: Oxford University Press, 1982), p. 56. Hereafter referred to as SP.

18. Ira Gitler, *Swing to Bop: An Oral History of the Transition in Jazz in the 1940s* (New York: Oxford University Press, 1985), p. 153. Hereafter referred to as SB.

19. Edward Brathwaite, *Other Exiles* (London: Oxford University Press, 1975), pp. 12–16.

20. LeRoi Jones, *Home: Social Essays* (New York: Morrow, 1966), pp. 173–178.

21. Liner notes, *The Complete Blue Note Recordings of Thelonious Monk* (Mosaic Records MR4-101).

22. Liner notes, *Thelonious Monk Live at the It Club* (Columbia Records C2-38030)

23. "My Sweet Hunk O'Trash."

24. Charles Mingus, *Beneath the Underdog* (New York: Penguin, 1980), p. 7.

25. Liner notes, *Black Bone* (Soul Note Records SN 10550).

26. Artistic othering pertains to intracultural as well as intercultural dialectics. The will to change whereby African-American culture reflects critically upon the dominant white culture is intertwined with its impulse to reflect critically upon itself, the will to change whereby it redefines, reinvents, and diversifies itself. Bebop, for example, was a reaction to the datedness of the music played by black swing musicians as well as to its appropriation by white musicians. No last word, no seal of prophecy, bebop in turn became dated, subject to the changes initiated by Ornette Coleman, Cecil Taylor, Albert Ayler, and others during the late fifties and early sixties. An aspect of intracultural dialectics that we should not overlook is the role of eccentric individuals whose contributions come to be identified with the very culture that may have initially rejected them. Think of Ornette Coleman being beaten up outside a Baton Rouge dance hall in 1949 for interjecting "modern" runs into an R&B solo (A. B. Spellman, *Black Music: Four Lives* [New York: Schocken Books, 1970], p. 101). The recent ascendancy of cultural studies in academia tends to privilege collectivity and group definition over individual agency and self-expression, to see the latter as a

reflection of the former. In relating the two, however, we should remember that in matters of artistic othering individual expression both reflects and redefines the collective, realigns, refracts it. Thus it is that Lester Young was in the habit of calling his saxophone's keys his people. Bill Crow reports that when the keys on his horn got bent during a Jazz at the Philharmonic tour Young went to Flip Phillips for help. "Flip," he said, "my people won't play!" (*Jazz Anecdotes* [New York: Oxford University Press, 1990], p. 272).

27. Wilson Harris, *Explorations: A Selection of Talks and Articles 1966–1981* (Mundelstrup: Dangaroo Press, 1981), p. 139.

28. Wilson Harris, *The Four Banks of the River of Space* (London: Faber and Faber, 1990), pp. 140–141.

29. Art Sato, "Interview with John Gilmore," *Be-Bop and Beyond*, Vol. 4, No. 2 (March/April 1986), 21.

30. Jacques Attali, *Noise: The Political Economy of Music* (Minneapolis: University of Minnesota Press, 1985), p. 57. Hereafter referred to as N.

31. Ellen B. Basso, *A Musical View of the Universe: Kalapalo Myth and Ritual Performances* (Philadelphia: University of Pennsylvania Press, 1985), pp. 69–70. Hereafter referred to as MV.

32. Robert C. Toll, *Blacking Up: The Minstrel Show in Nineteenth-Century America* (New York: Oxford University Press, 1974), p. 51. Hereafter referred to as BU.

33. *Complete Minstrel Guide* (Chicago: The Dramatic Publishing Company, no date), pp. 49–50.

34. Alexander Saxton, "Blackface Minstrelsy and Jacksonian Ideology," *American Quarterly*, Vol. 27, No. 1 (March 1975), 12. Subsequent references will be cited in the text of the essay.

35. Quoted in Elizabeth Sprigge, *Gertrude Stein: Her Life and Work* (New York: Harper, 1957), pp. 124–125.

36. Gertrude Stein, *Three Lives* (New York: Viking Penguin, 1990), pp. 85–86. Hereafter referred to as TL.

37. Carolyn Copeland, *Language and Time and Gertrude Stein* (Iowa City: University of Iowa Press, 1975), p. 24. Subsequent references will be cited in the text of the essay.

38. Janice Doane, *Silence and Narrative: The Early Novels of Gertrude Stein* (Westport: Greenwood Press, 1986), p. 52.

39. For a discussion of Stein's racist view of black people and of "Melanctha" as "the signpost of modernism's discourse on the nonwhite," see Aldon Lynn Nielsen, *Reading Race: White American Poets and the Racial Discourse in the Twentieth Century* (Athens: University of Georgia Press, 1988), pp. 21–28.

40. Wilson Harris, "In the Name of Liberty," *Third Text*, II (Summer 1990), 15.

41. Hurston, in "Characteristics of Negro Expression": "After adornment the next most striking manifestation of the Negro is Angularity. Everything that he touches becomes angular."

42. John Clellon Holmes, *The Horn* (New York: Thunder's Mouth Press, 1988), p. 8. Subsequent references will be cited in the text of the essay.

43. Henry Dumas, *Play Ebony Play Ivory* (New York: Random House, 1974), p. 52.

part 6

writing the blues, writing jazz

introduction

The word *stylos* named the writer's instrument for scratching words onto the wax tablets the ancient Greeks used instead of paper. Thus the modern word *style* indicates the personal mark of the artist. The sculptor's chisel, the painter's brush, the writer's *stylos* are all used to scratch a distinctive artistic conception—a signature or scripture, if you will—onto a given work of art. Jazz music is styled to tell stories (or, to follow through on the spiritual metaphor, to tell The Story). In this sense it is profoundly literary, and one awaits full-blown studies examining the impact of literature on the art of jazz. Ellington is the obvious example here, with his Shakespearean suite *Such Sweet Thunder* (where there's a mock-tragic section on Henry V called *Hank Cinq*, i.e., "'Hank Sank") and with *Suite Thursday*, the composer's slightly ironical parallel of the novel by John Steinbeck.[1]

Are record albums (even in their miniature CD format) not little *books* of a special sort, their display-case pages originally thick paper sleeves containing a bulky record per page? (The word *album* itself denotes a kind of white paper book.) Liner notes, consisting at times of quite comprehensive booklets, stand as uniquely potent forms of writing, providing a silent verbal counterpart to the music they describe.[2] These are program notes to learn from and enjoy as one replays the music again and again; some of them are as eloquent and enduring as the music they complement. (And some of them are perfect picture books, graced with wonderful photos and, in the case of David Stone Martin's work, drawings that seem to flow right out of the music.)

Perhaps the most significant aspect of this jazz-literature correspondence is the continuing effort of writers to use what they hear in jazz to give their words a jazzlike quality. The long-standing aspiration of writers in general to capture some of the power of music in their poetry and prose is evident in the vocabulary of literary analysis, much of which is derived from music. One speaks of literature's *tone*, its *voice*, its *chorus* (in drama), its *rhythms* measured in *feet* that remind us that these poetic patterns were based on dance steps and their accompanying strings, horns, and drums.

The blues-based music of jazz has had a deep and enduring impact on literature. Blues lyrics constitute a sturdy American poetry, a body of native verbal art that has invigorated the poetry and prose of Sterling A. Brown, Langston Hughes, Jack Kerouac, Robert Hayden, Amiri Baraka, Michael Harper, Ralph Ellison, Gloria Naylor, Ntzoke Shange, Toni Morrison, Albert Murray, and Gayl Jones. These and other writers also consciously strive for jazz's full-bodied swingingness, its danciness, its range of allusion, its trickbag of quicksilver improvisational impulses. "My work has a musical *insistence*," says Amiri Baraka, echoing Gertrude Stein; it has an earthy, lively quality that one hears in the music; it is literature whose words want to dance, to worry and capture the electrifying note and line of Mingus's music or Coltrane's. Some of Baraka's best poetry works on the page but works much better in performance. His "In the Tradition" is a jazz/poetry tour de force, performed on record with tenor saxophonist David Murray.

Albert Murray has written novels that seem structured after the jazz model: musiclike vamps, choruses, riffs, breaks, and outchoruses all appear. And his writing *swings*. One senses in Murray a jazzlike will to play with form, to put a novel's sections in unexpected order, as a jazz arranger/composer would do from concert to concert, seeking the sound of surprise. Murray also creates jazz characters, some of them actual jazz players, some not, and vignettes in which "jazz stories" (such as *Frankie and Johnny*) are improvised. These are tales in which the truth of the music is asserted and celebrated. Red Ella in *Train Whistle Guitar*, for example, needs to learn the key lesson of the music: that life is a low-down dirty mess and will certainly not work out for the best in every instance. Nor, says Murray, is human experience always fair, weatherwise or otherwise. Nonetheless, just as Benny Carter or Sarah Vaughan, confronted with tricky keys and breakneck speeds (all symbolizing hostile forces of one kind or another), would strive, musically, to cope with style and verve, Red Ella needed to know how to keep on keeping on, to find a way to sing her own song in spite of trouble everywhere, to find a style—a *stylos*—to solo with, to go it alone and thereby find inside herself and her traditions the strength to combine fruitfully with others, to swing.

My first and only poem on the worksheet in the poetry class was a poem dedicated to Miles Davis, "Alone," which I've since cut to three lines; "A friend told me/he'd risen above jazz./I leave him there." It [jazz] was my bible. How would it be to solo with that great tradition of the big bands honking you on? Could one do it in a poem?
                                                                —Michael S. Harper

I think I have learned as much about writing about my people by listening to blues and jazz and spirituals as I have learned by reading novels. The understatements in the tenor saxophone of Lester Young, the crying, haunting, forever searching sounds of John Coltrane, and the softness and violence of Count Basie's big band—all have fired my imagination as much as anything in literature.
                                                                —Ernest J. Gaines

A very great American writer, Henry James, writing to a friend of his who had just lost her husband, said. "Sorrow wears and uses us but we wear and use it too, and it is blind. Whereas we, after a manner, see." And Bessie said:

> Good mornin' blues.
> Blues, how do you do?
> I'm doin' all right.
> Good mornin.'
> How are you?   —James Baldwin

wjh: Do you think of your work [as a writer] growing out of the black tradition?

ay: There are many black traditions. I would say yes, the black tradition of oral storytelling and versifying and also the black musical tradition with the many facets that entails: different musical idioms—gospel, blues, jazz, pop song and also the idea of additive rhythm and the spirit of improvisation.   —Al Young and William J. Harris

When the driver returned, he apologized for not taking me in the van with the other passengers. He wanted to know where I was from and then he said—"what language do you speak when the white people aren't around?" I said "English," and he said "No, no." What language did I speak when the white people weren't around—the second time he asked I changed my response to "American."

"Brother," he said, "when blacks are among themselves, don't they speak jazz?" I nodded, right on, brother. Send more Afro-Americans from the states; bring your record collections. The battle of the big bands begins.

—Michael S. Harper

Poetry, first of all, was, and still must be, a musical form. It is speech musicked.... Just as Blues is, on one level, a verse form, so Black poetry begins as music running into words.

—Amiri Baraka, *New Music—New Poetry* **(liner notes)**

John Lewis long ago perceived that there were many analogies between jazz and the Italian comedy .... Its improvised character attracted him instantaneously; these plays were not written down, only a bare outline of a plot was posted in the wings, and the players had to take it from there. This was not an author's theatre; it was a player's theatre, just as jazz has been in the main an instrumentalist's medium rather than a composer's. Equally important is the fact that the commedia dell'arte was popular theatre. It was put on in marketplaces and public squares. Its appeal was to the masses, and so it offered plenty of farce and slapstick. The healthy realism of the Italian comedy has a parallel in much down-to-earth jazz and blues. In one other important respect, these two art forms show similarity: the universality of their appeal. While jazz has, in a few years, experienced a worldwide diffusion, the commedia dell'arte, considering its day, spread equally fast over the European continent. In its heyday it flourished everywhere, and could be seen in towns from St. Petersburg to Seville, and from London to Naples. Thus, the comedians were just as much the wandering itinerants, always on the road, as the jazz musicians are today.

—Gary Kramer

I consciously wrote as deeply into my psyche as I could go. I didn't even want the words to "make sense." I had the theme in my mind . . . but the theme was just something against which I wanted to play endless variations. Each section had its own dynamic and pain. Going so deep into myself was like descending into Hell, I called it The System of Dante's Hell:

. . . I was tearing away from the "ready-mades" that imitating Creeley (or Olson) provided. I'd found that when you imitate people's form you take on their content as well. So I scrambled, and roamed, sometimes, blindly in my consciousness, to come up with something more essential, more rooted in my deepest experience. I thought of music, I thought myself an improvising soloist. I would go into almost a trance-like state, hacking deeper and deeper, my interior rhythms dancing me on. . . . I wrote in the jagged staccato fragments until at the end of the piece I had come to, found, my own voice, or something beginning to approximate it.

—Amiri Baraka, The Autobiography of LeRoi Jones

But Ray Charles, who is a great tragic artist, makes of a genuinely religious confession something triumphant and liberating. He tells us that he cried so loud he gave the blues to his neighbor next door.

—James Baldwin

NOTES

1. Literary scholar Theodore Hudson presented an outstanding paper on this subject at the annual international conference of the Duke Ellington Society held in Washington, D.C., in May 1987.

2. Tom Piazza's excellent anthology of liner notes, Setting the Tempo: Fifty Years of Great Jazz Liner Notes (New York: Doubleday, Anchor, 1996), is quite suggestive on the question of the liner note as a peculiarly evocative form of writing.

chapter 30

STERLING A. BROWN

The Blues as Folk Poetry

I

t.
The Blues have deservedly come into their own, and, unfortunately for the lover of folk art, into something more than their own. They are sung on Broadway in nearly unrecognizable disguises, are produced on phonograph records by the thousands, are transmitted by radio, the T.O.B.A. circuit, carnival minstrel troupes, and the returned prodigal with his songbag full. It is becoming more and more difficult to tell which songs are truly folk and which are clever approximations.

It must be said, however, that the phonograph companies seem willing to record the crudest and most naïve Blues, from most obvious folk sources. Artless cottonfield calls and levee moans are quite as likely to be found as urbanized fake folk things. Then too, the chief singers of these Blues, such as Ma Rainey, Bessie Smith, Blind Lemon Jefferson, and Cottonfield Thomas, seem to be of the folk, earthy and genuine, certainly in the main and best part of their work. Some of these singers must still sing for the jealous creators of the Blues. One likes to believe that this audience may be trusted to be severely critical of clumsy inverted rhythms, and such strained figures as this one, appearing in the "Lonesome Desert Blues," after lines speaking of the burning desert:

> My mind is lak a rowboat, out on de stormy sea.
> It's wid me right now, in de mawnin' where will it be?

Even with the flood of new Blues one finds still traces of the same folk imagery and attitude found in the earliest noted examples. One finds lines from the older spirituals. There has been such an assimilation that one might say: If these are not by the folk, they ought to be.

Therefore, although the word has become part of the popular music vernacular, and has been widened to cover songs that by no stretch of the imagination could be considered Blues, nevertheless, Blues of importance to students of folk life are still being produced, in considerable numbers and with a great degree of authenticity. One knows that when the river rises remorselessly above the high-water mark, when a loving man takes to the road and leaves the side of his good woman, when the train blows far down the track, or the steamboat heaves in sight around the bend, some singer a long ways from happiness lifts up his voice and tells the world of his trouble.

Something of an introduction to folk life might result from the mere reading of Blues titles. This list would resemble a geographical index to the South, or to the Black Belt extensions into the North, as well as a catalogue of all the melancholy afflictions that any children of Adam have suffered. A deep knowledge would result from a close study of the songs themselves. It might perhaps be recommended that this study be done with as few preconceived notions as possible. For the Blues, unlike the early "coon" songs and East Side mammy songs, do not conform to a single pattern. It would be foolhardy to say that everything is here, any more than in more sophisticated lyric poetry. But there is a great deal. Stoicism is here as well as self-pity, for instance; rich humor as well as melancholy. There are so many Blues that any preconception might be proved about Negro folk life, as well as its opposite. As documentary proof of dogma about the Negro peasant, then, the Blues are satisfactory and unsatisfactory. As documents about humanity they are invaluable.

II

It is a popular misconception that the Blues are merely songs that ease a woman's longing for her rambling man. Of course, this pattern has been set, especially by certain priestesses of the Blues cult. Nevertheless, the Blues furnish examples of other concerns. And as the lost-lover line may be dragged into a levee moan, so may an excellent bit of farm advice be found in a song about a long-lost mamma. Blues will be found ranging from flood songs to graphic descriptions of pneumonia, from complaints about Volstead to such lines as

> I got a grave-diggin' feelin' in my heart.

The diction of most of the Blues is immediately connected, as it should be, with folk life. Cottonfield parlance is in

> Makes me feel I'm on my las' go-round.

Folk parlance in general:

> Wish I was a jaybird flyin' in de air,
> Would build my nest in some of you high browns' hair.

I'm fresh from the country, yuh know I'm easy to rule.
Jes hitch me to yo' cart, girls, and drive me fo' yo' mule.

Ef I could holler lak a mountain jack,
I'd go up on de mountain an' call my baby back.

Sun gonna shine in my back door some day.

Another mule kickin' in my stall.

You been a good ole wagon, daddy, but you done broke down.

Supplementing the numerous excellent work songs we have such lines as

Cap'n, cap'n, has my pay check come?
Damn yo' pay check, get de cap'n's work done.

Cap'n, cap'n, my hands is cole.
Damn yo' hands, let de pick an' shovel roll.

Pay day, cap'n, ain't got no soap.

And the native "Cottonfield Blues," as spontaneous, as unfinished on the record, as when created in the Brazos Bottom:

542

I'm goin' downtown buy myself a plow,
Goin' downtown get me a mule.
Get up in de mo'nin', fo' o'clock,
Goin' to turn dat land in turnips.

The love for fabling, a quality of the best folklore in general and of the Negro in particular:

What makes a rooster crow every mo'nin' 'fo' day?
To let de ramblers know dat de workin' man is on his way.

Tadpole in de river hatchin' underneaf of a log.
Got too old to be a tadpole, turned to be a natchal frog.

Ef a toadfrog had wings, he'd be flyin' all aroun',
Would not have his bottom boppin' boppin' on de groun.'

I wish I was a catfish, swimmin' in de sea,
I'd have you good womens fishin' after me.

Brownskin momma make a rabbit chase a hound.

Or from city animals:

You jes lak one uh dese ole tom-cats,
Always chasin' dese alley rats.

The superstitions of the Negro folk are frequently found. There are Blues about "Black Cat's Bones," about

> Goin' to Louisiana to git myself a Mojo hand
> 'Cause dese backbitin' womens tryin' fo' to steal my man.
>
> You may tip out sweet poppa, while tippin' is grand,
> But yo' tippin' will be over when momma gits her Mojo hand.
>
> When de hog makes a bed, yuh know de storm is due.
> When a screech-owl holler, means bad luck to you.
>
> Screech-owl holler dis mawnin' right beside my front door.
> I know when he hollered trouble comin' back once more.
>
> When a black cat crosses you, bad luck, I've heard it said.
> One must have started cross me, got halfway an' fell dead.
>
> Went to de gipsy to get ma fortune tole.
> Gipsy done tole me: Damn yo' unhardlucky soul.
>
> I went to see de gipsy, he opened up my hand.
> He said: My friend, you're worried but I don't understand.
>
> I heard a hound dog bayin', an' I felt so blue.
> I dreamt he was in de graveyard, lookin' down at you.

True to folk literature there are shrewd proverbs:

> My momma tole me, my daddy tole me too:
> Everybody grins in yo' face, son, ain't no friend to you.
>
> When I had money, had friends fo' miles aroun.'
> Now ain't got no money, friends cannot be found.
>
> When you got a dollar in New York, brother, you got lots of friends,
> But when you're broke an' hungry, that's where your friendship ends.
>
> When yo' lose yo' money, baby, don't you lose yo' mind.
> You must remember all gamblers git broke sometime.
>
> You gotta reap jus' what you sow.
>
> When you love a man, he treats you lak a dog,
> But when you don't love him, he'll hop aroun' you lak a frog.

The cloudier aspects of the sunny South get their due share of lines. There are "Chain Gang Blues," "Prison House Blues," "Ball and Chain Blues." The cell is sometimes lighted up as in the "He's in de Jailhouse Now" comic variations, but is just as often darkened.

> Waitin' fo' de evenin' mail.

They gonna put you under de jail.

Settin' in de jail house, face turned to de wall,
Red-headed woman was de cause of it all.

Two mo' months fo' to do de grind.

Way down, way down dat lonesome road,
De workhouse is down dat long ole lonesome road.

Or from the "Hard Luck Blues" of Ma Rainey, who might with more reasons than her own proud sayso be called the mother of the Blues:

Mah friend committed suicide, whilst I'se away at sea.
They wanted to lock me up fo' murder in first degree.

Or from the same Ma Rainey:

When I went to de station, bad luck waitin' there too.
When dey needs mo' money, dey take out a warrant fo' you.

The sorry tricks played upon these folk by Nature do not go unsung. The St. Louis cyclone had hardly spent its rage before songs were being sung commemorating it and commiserating the sufferers. Happening to be in St. Louis in the immediate wake of the cyclone, the author believes that he was present at the genesis of many Blues. He remembers seeing in a second-story bedroom, with its front walls torn off, an old woman sitting in an old rocker, moaning and chanting, weaving from the tragedy her own Blues.

Soon after there were such phonograph records as the "St. Louis Cyclone Blues" and the "St. Louis Tornado Blues."

The wind was howlin', buildin's begin to fall.
I seen dat mean ol' twister comin' jes lak a cannon ball.

World was as black as midnight, I never heard such a noise befo.'
The people were screamin', runnin' every which a way, Lawd, help us.

The shack where we were livin' reeled and rocked but never fell.

The floods of the Mississippi Valley bring in their wake many Blues. Especially was the 1927 disaster bemoaned and besung. For authenticity of folk utterance it would be fruitful to compare the stereotyped "Muddy Water" or the "Mississippi Flood Song," a rather wet ballad:—

On the banks of the Father of Waters
. . . .
I am dreaming to-night in the moonlight
Of the friends it has taken from me.
All the world seemed so happy and gay.
The waters rose quickly above us.
And it swept my beloved ones away-ay-ay-ay.

. . . .
The wrath of the great river's might.

with the "Backwater Blues," or the "Mississippi Water Blues," or any of the lesser high-water Blues.

> It rained fo' days an' de skies was dark as night.
> Trouble taken place in de lowlands that night.

> It thundered an' lightened an' de wind begin to blow.
> Thousan's of people ain't got no place to go.

> Dey rowed a little boat about five miles 'cross de pond.
> I packed my clothes, throwed 'em in, an' dey rowed me along.

> Oh, I ain't goan move no mo.'
> My house fell down; ain't got no place to go.

> Water, water, mo' than I've ever seen.
> The water is still risin' from Memphis down to New Orleans.

> Ef it keeps on rainin', levee's bound to break,
> An' de water will come an' sweep dis town away.

The gain in vividness, in feeling, in substituting the thing seen for the bookish dressing up and sentimentalizing is an obvious one and might tell us a great deal about the Blues.

The ravages of the boll weevil have produced, besides the gem that Carl Sandburg has popularized, other Blues.

> Eigh, bo' weevil, don't bring dem blues no mo.'
> Bo' weevil here, bo' weevil everywhere I go.

> Gonna sing dis song to ease bo' weevil's travelin' mind.

> Bo' weevil got Mississippi and de women want me.

Topical allusions to other tragedies, such as the sinking of the *Titanic*, the death of Floyd Collins, railroad wrecks, can be found as well, although these belong more to folk ballads, or to sermons. The war, however, became a prolific source of Blues. Professor Howard W. Odum, in *Wings on My Feet*, and Lieutenant John J. Niles, in *Singing Soldiers*, as well as returned Negro soldiers, tell us of this. There was the "Drafting Blues":

> When Uncle Sam
> Calls out yo' man . . .
> Don't dress in black,
> 'Cause dat won't bring him back.
> Jus' say I've got dose drafted blues.

III

The longing for a far country is often encountered:

I went to the deepot, an' looked upon de boa'd.
It say: Dere's good times here, dey's better down de road.

I'm goin' up de country, baby, don't you want to go?

Did you ever wake up in de mo'nin', yo' mind rollin' two different ways—
One mind to leave yo' baby, and one mind to stay?

I'm got a mind to ramble, a mind fo' to leave dis town,
Got a mind my baby is goin' to turn me down.

Sometimes the long journey ends traditionally in the South; *à la* Jolson's mammy songs:

Dixie Flyer, come on an' let yo' driver roll,
Wouldn't stay up Nawth to save nobody's doggone soul.

If it keeps on snowin', I'll be Gulf Coast bound.

I'm goin' down South where de weather suits my clothes.

Just as often these far wanderers trek Northward.

Michigan water it tastes lak cherry wine,
But dis Nashville water it drinks lak turpentine.

I'm goin' to Chicago where I been longin' to be.

Dere's a big red headlinin' in Chicago *Defender News*,
Says my gal down South got dem Up de Country Blues.

These lovers of the open road, in their desire for the far country, turn to the train as their best friend. One young Negro author, interpreting the fascination of trains for the Negroes of the South, says: "I have often thought that the Negro farmhand would lose heart once for all, were it not for the daily encouragement he takes from the whistle of his favorite locomotives. Tied to his plow, under the red, burning sun, or aching with the loneliness of the sterile night, he can find all his desire for escape, all the courage he lacks in the face of the unknown, mingled with his inescapable hopelessness, in the deepthroated, prolonged blast of the express train, like a challenge to untravelled lands, a terrifying cry to his petty township."

This favored symbol of escape is everywhere evident in the Blues. The Blues are like a large Union Terminal. We hear of such Blues as the "Dixie Flyer," the "Santa Fe," the "Freight Train," the "Mobile Central," the "Brakeman's."

> I'm gonna leave heah dis mawnin' ef I have to ride de blind.

> T is fo' Texas, an' T's fo' Tennessee,
> And T is fo' dat train dat took you 'way from me.

> Ticket agent, ease yo' window down.

> De train I ride is sixteen coaches long.

> Did you evah ride on de Mobile Central Line?
> It's de road to ride to ease yo' troublin' mind.

From the "Freight Train Blues," a song which, as sung on the record, expresses infectiously the naïve joy in the railroad:

> Jus' as sho as de Southern makes up in de Southern yard,
> I'm gonna leave heah, baby, ef I have to ride de rods.

> I got the Railroad Blues, freight train on my min'.
> Ever' time dat train hollers, poppa gonna change his min'.

> De train's at de station, I heard de whistle blow.
> Done bought my ticket but I don't know where I'll go.

> Ticket agent said: Lady, don't sit aroun' an' cry.
> Yo' man may have been here, but he's said his las' go'-by.

> I ain't gonna tell nobody what dat Santa Fe done to me.
> It took my good man, come back an' got my used-to-be.

> All I want's my ticket, show me in my train.
> I'm gonna ride till I can't hear dem call yo' name.

> Hold dat engine, let sweet momma git on boa'd,
> 'Cause my home ain't here, it's a long ways down de road.

> Blow yo' whistle, tell 'em momma's comin' through.
> Shake it up a li'l bit, 'cause I'm feelin' awful blue.

Many of these trains are northbound: the Blues throw light on the recent migrations. Though in these Northern cities the Blues become more sophisticated and more blatantly suggestive, they still serve as registers of folk life transplanted. There are "House Rent Blues," "Black Maria Blues," "Hometown Skiffles," "Market Street Blues," "Furniture Man Blues," "State Street Blues," "Chicago Gouge Blues."

In the surly but indigenous "Snitcher's Blues":

> O mah babe, way down in Polock town
> Where de police an' de snitchers, dey tore my playhouse down.

In the classic "St. Louis Blues":

St. Louis woman, she wears a diamond ring,
Got her man tied around her by de apron string.

Ef it wasn't for de powder an' de store-bought hair,
De man I love wouldn't go nowhere.

Harlem comes in for its share, pseudo-folk but indicative:

Folks in New York City ain't like de folks down South.
Never say "Have dinner"; they live from hand to mouth.

The horses and the numbers keeps most of them alive,
All they buy is hot dogs when eatin' time arrive.

The Midwest:

I'm goin' to Kansas City, baby; honey, where they don't like you.

In "Kitchen Mechanic Blues" we have the transplanted idiom:

People talk about me, they lie on me; call me out of my name,
But dey men calls to see me jes de same.

I'm jes a workin' girl, po' workin'-girl, kitchen mechanic is what dey say,
But I'll have an honest dollar on dat rainy day.

IV

The Blues as expressions of the man-woman relationship have already received full treatment at the hands of authorities. As in frontier ballads, cowboy ballads, even many English and Scottish ballads, the plaint is generally of true love lost or turned treacherous. It seems to be the history of lyric poetry, however (and the Blues, unlike most folk poetry, are lyric), that it is generally the lover or lady in absentia who calls out poetry. This is true of the Blues. The stereotyping of the Blues into a woman's moaning for her departed man may be due to the dominant personality of some of the women singers of the Blues, such as Ma Rainey, Ida Cox, Victoria Spivey, Bessie Smith, Mamie Smith, Clara Smith, Laura Smith, and Trixie Smith. (The Smith Brothers aren't yet as popular as they might be.)

Love is not presented, however, in a single aspect. We have not only the "Sobbin'-Hearted Blues," the "Grievin'-Hearted Blues" ringing changes on the theme of "Careless Love," but also:

Ef you don't want me, baby, ain't got to carry no stall.
I can git mo' women than a passenger train can haul.

Ef you don't love me, why don't you tell me so?
I'm little an' low, can get a man anywheres I go.

Ef you don't like my peaches, don't you shake my tree.

Ef she flags my train, I'm sho gonna let her ride.

There is not only faithlessness but

I'll love my baby till the sea runs dry
And ever after on.

Gonna build me a scaffold, I'm gonna hang myself.
Cain't git the man I love, don't want nobody else.

Have you ever loved somebody—that somebody didn't love you?
But I love my good girl, no matter what she do.

There is the cynicism of

There's nineteen men livin' in my neighborhood,
Eighteen of them is dumb an' the other ain't no doggone good.

There is the fancy of

Love is like a faucet, you can turn it off or on,
But when you think you've got it, it's done turned off and gone.

In one vein there is the poetic imagery of

Love, oh, love, oh, careless love,
You fly to my head like wine.
You brought the wrong man into this life of mine.

In another:

A sealskin brown will make a preacher lay his Bible down.

The gamut can be found running from tenderness to cynicism, from tears to laughter. Love is a torment, or love is a humorous interlude. One takes his choice.

V

The images of the Blues are worthy of a separate study. At their best they are highly compressed, concrete, imaginative, original. Among the clichés, the inconsecutiveness, the false rhymes—one finds suddenly the startling figure:

My gal's got teeth lak a lighthouse on de sea.
Every time she smiles she throws a light on me.

My man's got a heart lak a rock cast in de sea.

I got de worl' in a jug, de stopper in my hand.

The gal I love is choklit to de bone.

Ef blues was whisky, I'd stay drunk all de time.

Blues ain't nothin' but a po' man's heart-disease.

There is the comic hyperbole of

I creeps up to huh window jes to hear how sweet she snores . . .

A good-lookin' woman makes a bulldog gnaw his chain.

A brownskin woman makes a cow forget her calf.

Done drunk so much whisky I staggers in my sleep.

Lemme be yo' switch engine, baby, till de main line comes.
I kin do mo' switchin', momma, than yo' main line ever done.

Big fat momma wid de meat shakin' on huh bones.
Evah time she wiggles, skinny woman los' huh home.

Settin' here wond'rin' would a match box hold my clothes.

Want to lay my head on de railroad line,
Let de train come along and pacify my mind.

You got a handful of gimme, a mouthful of much obliged.

May mean good, but he *do* so doggone po.'

There is a terseness, an inevitability of the images dealing with suffering. Irony, stoicism, and bitterness are deeply but not lingeringly expressed. There are sardonic lines like

I'm goin' to de mountain, goin' to de deep blue sea.
I know de sharks an' de fishes gonna make a fuss over me.

I got de blues but too damned mean to cry.

Yuh can read my letters but yuh sho cain't read my mind.

The tragic sense of life:

I hear my daddy callin' some other woman's name.
I know he don't mean me; I'm gonna answer jes de same.

Standin' here lookin' one thousand miles away.

I hate to see dat evenin' sun go down.

Don't yo' room seem empty when yo' gal packs up to leave?

I never loved but three men in my life:
My father an' my brother an' de man what wrecked my life.

I'm goin' to de pawnshop to hock my weddin' ring.
My man done quit me so I don't need dat thing.

Look down, look down dat lonesome road,
De hacks all dead in line.

Been down so long, Lawd, down don't worry me.

Woke up dis mawnin' 'bout de break of day.
Laid my head on de piller where my momma used to lay.

I followed my momma right down to be buryin'-groun.'
You ought to a heard me cryin' when dey let her down.

Ef you ever been down, you know jes how I feel—
Lak a broken-down engine got no drivin' wheel,
Lak a po' sojer boy lef' on de battle-fiel.'

When you think I'm laughin', laughin' jes to keep from cryin.'

The poetry of the Blues deserves close attention. Crudities, incongruities, of course, there are in abundance—annoying changes of mood from tragedy to cheap farce. There seems to be entering more recently, a sophisticated smut, not the earlier breadth of Rabelais, but the snickering of the brothel. Blues are becoming cabaret appetizers. Perhaps the American public, both Negro and white, prefers this to the simpler, more poetic phrasing of burdened folk. But at their most genuine they are accurate, imaginative transcripts of folk experience, with flashes of excellent poetry.

They show a warm-hearted folk, filled with a naïve wonder at life yet sophisticated about human relationships, imaginative here as in their fables and spirituals, living a life close to the earth. With their imagination they combine two great loves, the love of words and the love of life. Poetry results.

These Blues belong, with all their distinctive differences, to the best of folk literature. And to some lovers of poetry that is not at all a negligible best.

chapter 31

RALPH ELLISON

Richard Wright's Blues

If anybody ask you
who sing this song,
Say it was ole [Black Boy]
done been here and gone.

—SIGNATURE FORMULA USED BY BLUES SINGERS AT CONCLUSION OF SONG

As a writer, Richard Wright has outlined for himself a dual role: to discover and depict the meaning of Negro experience, and to reveal to both Negroes and whites those problems of a psychological and emotional nature which arise between them when they strive for mutual understanding.

Now, in *Black Boy*, he has used his own life to probe what qualities of will, imagination and intellect are required of a Southern Negro in order to possess the meaning of his life in the United States. Wright is an important writer, perhaps the most articulate Negro American, and what he has to say is highly perceptive. Imagine Bigger Thomas projecting his own life in lucid prose guided, say, by the insights of Marx and Freud, and you have an idea of this autobiography.

Published at a time when any sharply critical approach to Negro life has been dropped as a wartime expendable, it should do much to redefine the problem of the Negro and American democracy. Its power can be observed in the shrill manner with which some professional "friends of the Negro people" have attempted to strangle the work in a noose of newsprint.

What in the tradition of literary autobiography is it like, this work described as a "great American autobiography"? As a non-white intellectual's statement of his relationship to Western culture, *Black Boy* recalls the conflicting pattern of identification and rejection found in Nehru's *Toward Freedom*. In its use of fictional techniques, its concern with criminality (sin) and the artistic sensibility, and in its author's judgment and rejection of the narrow world of his origin, it recalls Joyce's rejection of Dublin in *A Portrait of the Artist*. And as a psychological document of life under oppressive conditions, it recalls *The House of the Dead*, Dostoevsky's profound study of the humanity of Russian criminals.

Such works were perhaps Wright's literary guides, aiding him to endow his life's incidents with communicable significance, providing him with ways of seeing, feeling and describing his environment. These influences, however, were encountered only after these first years of Wright's life were past, and were not part of the immediate folk culture into which he was born. In that culture the specific folk-art form which helped shape the writer's attitude toward his life and which embodied the impulse that contributes much to the quality and tone of his autobiography was the Negro blues.

This would bear a word of explanation. The blues is an impulse to keep the painful details and episodes of a brutal experience alive in one's aching consciousness, to finger its jagged grain, and to transcend it, not by the consolation of philosophy but by squeezing from it a near-tragic, near-comic lyricism. As a form, the blues is an autobiographical chronicle of personal catastrophe expressed lyrically. And certainly Wright's early childhood was crammed with catastrophic incidents. In a few short years his father deserted his mother, he knew intense hunger, he became a drunkard begging drinks from black stevedores in Memphis saloons; he had to flee Arkansas, where an uncle was lynched; he was forced to live with a fanatically religious grandmother in an atmosphere of constant bickering; he was lodged in an orphan asylum; he observed the suffering of his mother, who became a permanent invalid, while fighting off the blows of the poverty-stricken relatives with whom he had to live; he was cheated, beaten and kicked off jobs by white employees who disliked his eagerness to learn a trade; and to these objective circumstances must be added the subjective fact that Wright, with his sensitivity, extreme shyness and intelligence, was a problem child who rejected his family and was by them rejected.

Thus, along with the themes, equivalent descriptions of milieu and the perspectives to be found in Joyce, Nehru, Dostoevsky, George Moore and Rousseau, *Black Boy* is filled with blues-tempered echoes of railroad trains, the names of Southern towns and cities, estrangements, fights and flights, deaths and disappointments, charged with physical and spiritual hungers and pain. And like a blues sung by such an artist as Bessie Smith, its lyrical prose evokes the paradoxical, almost surreal image of a black boy singing lustily as he probes his own grievous wound.

In *Black Boy* two worlds have fused, two cultures merged, two impulses of Western man become coalesced. By discussing some of its cultural sources I hope to answer those critics who would make of the book a miracle and of its author a mystery. And while making no attempt to probe the mystery of the artist (who Hemingway says is "forged in injustice as a sword is forged"), I do hold that basically the prerequisites to the writing of *Black Boy* were, on the one hand, the microscopic degree of cultural freedom which Wright found in the South's stony injustice, and, on the other, the existence of a personality agitated to a state of almost manic restlessness. There were, of course, other factors, chiefly ideological, but these came later.

Wright speaks of his journey north as

> . . . taking a part of the South to transplant in alien soil, to see if it could grow differently, if it could drink of new and cool rains, bend in strange winds, respond to the warmth of other suns, and perhaps, to bloom. . . .

And just as Wright, the man, represents the blooming of the delinquent child of the autobiography, just so does *Black Boy* represent the flowering—cross-fertilized by pollen blown by the winds of strange cultures—of the humble blues lyric. There is, as in all acts of creation, a world of mystery in this, but there is also enough that is comprehensible for Americans to create the social atmosphere in which other black boys might freely bloom.

For certainly in the historical sense Wright is no exception. Born on a Mississippi plantation, he was subjected to all those blasting pressures which in a scant eighty years have sent the Negro people hurtling, without clearly defined trajectory, from slavery to emancipation, from log cabin to city tenement, from the white folks' fields and kitchens to factory assembly lines, and which, between two wars, have shattered the wholeness of its folk consciousness into a thousand writhing pieces.

Black Boy describes this process in the personal terms of *one* Negro childhood. Nevertheless, several critics have complained that it does not "explain" Richard Wright. Which, aside from the notion of art involved, serves to remind us that the prevailing mood of American criticism has so thoroughly excluded the Negro that it fails to recognize some of the most basic tenets of Western democratic thought when encountering them in a black skin. They forget that human life possesses an innate dignity and mankind an innate sense of nobility; that all men possess the tendency to dream and the compulsion to make their dreams reality; that the need to be ever dissatisfied and the urge ever to seek satisfaction is implicit in the human organism; and that all men are the victims and the beneficiaries of the goading, tormenting, commanding and informing activity of that imperious process known as the Mind—the Mind, as Valéry describes it, "armed with its inexhaustible questions."

Perhaps all this (in which lies the very essence of the human, and which Wright takes for granted) has been forgotten because the critics recognize neither Negro humanity nor the full extent to which the Southern community renders the fulfillment of human destiny impossible. And while it is true that *Black Boy* presents an almost unrelieved picture of a personality corrupted by brutal environment, it also presents those fresh, human responses brought to its world by the sensitive child:

There was the *wonder* I felt when I first saw a brace of mountainlike, spotted, black-and-white horses clopping down a dusty road . . . the *delight* I caught in seeing long straight rows of red and green vegetables stretching away in the sun . . . the faint, cool kiss of *sensuality* when dew came on to my cheeks . . . the vague *sense of the infinite* as I looked down upon the yellow, dreaming waters of the Mississippi . . . the echoes of *nostalgia* I heard in the crying strings of wild geese . . . the *love* I had for the mute regality of tall, moss-clad oaks . . . the hint of *cosmic cruelty* that I *felt* when I saw the curved timbers of a wooden shack that had been warped in the summer sun . . . and there was the *quiet terror* that suffused my senses when vast hazes of gold washed earthward from star-heavy skies on silent nights. . . . [italics mine]

And a bit later, his reactions to religion:

Many of the religious symbols appealed to my sensibilities and I responded to the dramatic vision of life held by the church, feeling that to live day by day with death as one's sole thought was to be so compassionately sensitive toward all life as to view all men as slowly dying, and the trembling sense of fate that welled up, sweet and melancholy, from the hymns blended with the sense of fate that I had already caught from life.

There was also the influence of his mother—so closely linked to his hysteria and sense of suffering—who (though he only implies it here) taught him, in the words of the dedication prefacing *Native Son*, "to revere the fanciful and the imaginative." There were also those white men—the one who allowed Wright to use his library privileges and the other who advised him to leave the South, and still others whose offers of friendship he was too frightened to accept.

Wright assumed that the nucleus of plastic sensibility is a human heritage: the right and the opportunity to dilate, deepen and enrich sensibility—democracy. Thus the drama of *Black Boy* lies in its depiction of what occurs when Negro sensibility attempts to fulfill itself in the undemocratic South. Here it is not the individual that is the immediate focus, as in Joyce's *Stephen Hero*, but that upon which his sensibility was nourished.

Those critics who complain that Wright has omitted the development of his own sensibility hold that the work thus fails as art. Others, because it presents too little of what they consider attractive in Negro life, charge that it distorts reality. Both groups miss a very obvious point: that whatever else the environment contained, it had as little chance of prevailing against the overwhelming weight of the child's unpleasant experiences as Beethoven's quartets would have of destroying the stench of a Nazi prison.

We come, then, to the question of art. The function, the psychology, of artistic selectivity is to eliminate from an art form all those elements of experience which contain no compelling significance. Life is as the sea, art a ship in which man conquers life's crushing formlessness, reducing it to a course, a series of swells, tides and wind currents inscribed on a chart. Though drawn from the world, "the organized significance of art," writes Malraux, "is stronger than all the multiplicity of the world; . . . that significance alone enables man to conquer chaos and to master destiny."

Wright saw his destiny—that combination of forces before which man feels powerless—in terms of a quick and casual violence inflicted upon him by both family and community. His response was likewise violent, and it has been his need to give that violence significance which has shaped his writings.

What were the ways by which other Negroes confronted their destiny?

In the South of Wright's childhood there were three general ways: they could accept the role created for them by the whites and perpetually resolve the resulting conflicts through the hope and emotional catharsis of Negro religion; they could repress their dislike of Jim Crow social relations while striving for a middle way of respectability, becoming—consciously or unconsciously—the accomplices of the whites in oppressing their brothers; or they could reject the situation, adopt a criminal attitude, and carry on an unceasing psychological scrimmage with the whites, which often flared forth into physical violence.

Wright's attitude was nearest the last. Yet in it there was an all-important qualitative difference: it represented a groping for *individual* values, in a black community whose values were what the young Negro critic Edward Bland has defined as "pre-individual." And herein lay the setting for the extreme conflict set off, both within his family and in the community, by Wright's assertion of individuality. The clash was sharpest on the psychological level, for, to quote Bland,

> In the pre-individualistic thinking of the Negro the stress is on the group. Instead of seeing in terms of the individual, the Negro sees in terms of "races," masses of peoples separated from other masses according to color. Hence, an act rarely bears intent against him as a Negro individual. He is singled out not as a person but as a specimen of an ostracized group. He knows that he never exists in his own right but only to the extent that others hope to make the race suffer vicariously through him.

This pre-individual state is induced artificially, like the regression to primitive states noted among cultured inmates of Nazi prisons. The primary technique in its enforcement is to impress the Negro child with the omniscience and omnipotence of the whites to the point that whites appear as ahuman as Jehovah, and as relentless as a Mississippi flood. Socially it is effected through an elaborate scheme of taboos supported by a ruthless physical violence, which strikes not only the offender but the entire black community. To wander from the paths of behavior laid down for the group is to become the agent of communal disaster.

In such a society the development of individuality depends upon a series of accidents, which often arise, as in Wright's case, from conditions within the Negro family. In Wright's life there was the accident that as a small child he could not distinguish between his fair-skinned grandmother and the white women of the town, thus developing skepticism as to their special status. To this was linked the accident of his having no close contacts with whites until after the child's normal formative period.

But these objective accidents not only link forward to these qualities of rebellion, criminality and intellectual questioning expressed in Wright's work today. They also link backward into the shadow of infancy where environment and consciousness are so darkly intertwined as to require the skill of a psychoanalyst to define their point of juncture. Nevertheless, at the age of four, Wright set the house afire and was beaten near to death by his frightened mother. This beating, followed soon by his father's desertion of the family, seems to be the initial psychological motivation of his quest for a new identification. While delirious from this beating, Wright was haunted "by huge wobbly white bags like the full udders of a cow, suspended from the ceiling above me [and] I was gripped by the fear that they were going to fall and drench me with some horrible liquid. . . ."

It was as though the mother's milk had turned acid, and with it the whole pattern of life that had produced the ignorance, cruelty and fear that had fused with mother love and exploded in the beating. It is significant that the bags were of the hostile color white, and the female symbol that of the cow, the most stupid (and, to the small child, the most frightening) of domestic animals. Here in dream symbolism is expressed an attitude worthy of an Orestes. And the significance of the crisis is increased by virtue of the historical fact that the lower-class Negro family is matriarchal; the child turns not to the father to compensate if he feels mother-rejection, but to the grandmother, or to an aunt—and Wright rejected both of these. Such rejection leaves the child open to psychological insecurity, distrust and all of those hostile environmental forces from which the family functions to protect it.

One of the Southern Negro family's methods of protecting the child is the severe beating—a homeopathic dose of the violence generated by black and white relationships. Such beatings as Wright's were administered for the child's own good—a good which the child resisted, thus giving family relationships an undercurrent of fear and hostility, which differs qualitatively from that found in patriarchal middle-class families, because here the severe beating is administered by the mother, leaving the child no parental sanctuary. He must ever embrace violence along with maternal tenderness, or else reject in his helpless way the mother.

The division between the Negro parents of Wright's mother's generation, whose sensibilities were often bound by their proximity to the slave experience, and their children, who historically and through the rapidity of American change stand emotionally and psychologically much farther away, is quite deep. Indeed, sometimes as deep as the cultural distance between Yeats's *Autobiographies* and a Bessie Smith blues. This is the historical background to those incidents of family strife in *Black Boy* which have caused reviewers to question Wright's judgment of Negro emotional relationships.

We have here a problem in the sociology of sensibility that is obscured by certain psychological attitudes brought to Negro life by whites. The first is the attitude which compels whites to impute to Negroes sentiments, attitudes and insights which, as a group living under certain definite social conditions, Negroes could not humanly possess. It is the identical mechanism which William Empson identifies in literature as "pastoral." It implies that since Negroes possess the richly human virtues credited to them, then their social position is advantageous and should not be bettered, and, continuing syllogistically, the white individual need feel no guilt over his participation in Negro oppression.

The second attitude leads whites to misjudge Negro passion, looking upon it as they do out of the turgidity of their own frustrated yearning for emotional warmth, their capacity for sensation having been constricted by the impersonal mechanized relationships typical of bourgeois society. The Negro is idealized into a symbol of sensation, of unhampered social and sexual relationships. And when *Black Boy* questions whites' illusion, they are thwarted much in the manner of the Occidental who, after observing the erotic character of a primitive dance, "shacks up" with a native woman, only to discover that far from possessing the hair-trigger sexual responses of a Stork Club "babe," she is relatively phlegmatic.

The point is not that American Negroes are primitives, but that as a group their social situation does not provide for the type of emotional relationships attributed to them. For how could the South, recognized as a major part of the backward third of the nation, nurture in the black, most brutalized section of its population, those forms of human relationships achievable only in the most highly developed areas of civilization?

Champions of this "Aren't-Negroes-Wonderful?" school of thinking often bring Paul Robeson and Marian Anderson forward as examples of highly developed sensibility, but actually they are only its *promise*. Both received their development from an extensive personal contact with European culture, free from the influences which shape Southern Negro personality. In the United States, Wright, who is the only Negro literary artist of equal caliber, had to wait years, and escape to another environment before discovering the moral and ideological equivalents of his childhood attitudes.

Man cannot express that which does not exist—either in the form of dreams, ideas or realities—in his environment. Neither his thoughts nor his feelings, his sensibility nor his intellect are fixed, innate qualities. They are processes which arise out of the interpenetration of human instinct with environment, through the process called experience, each changing and being changed by the other. Negroes cannot possess many of the sentiments attributed to them because the same changes in environment which, through experience, enlarge man's intellect (and thus his capacity for still greater change) also modify his feelings—which in turn increase his sensibility, i.e., his sensitivity to refinements of impression and subtleties of emotion. The extent of these changes depends upon the quality of political and cultural freedom in the environment.

Intelligence tests have measured the quick rise in intellect which takes place in Southern Negroes after moving north, but little attention has been paid to the mutations effected in their sensibilities. However, the two go hand in hand. Intellectual complexity is accompanied by emotional complexity, refinement of thought, and refinement of feeling. The movement north affects more than the Negro's wage scale; it affects his entire psychosomatic structure.

The rapidity of Negro intellectual growth in the North is due partially to objective factors present in the environment, to influences of the industrial city and to a greater political freedom. But there are also changes within the "inner world." In the North energies are released and given *intellectual* channelization— energies which in most Negroes in the South have been forced to take either a *physical* form or, as with potentially intellectual types like Wright, to be expressed as nervous tension, anxiety and hysteria. Which is nothing mysterious. The human organism responds to environmental stimuli by converting them into either physical and/or intellectual energy. And what is called hysteria is suppressed intellectual energy expressed physically.

The "physical" character of their expression makes for much of the difficulty in understanding American Negroes. Negro music and dances are frenziedly erotic, Negro religious ceremonies violently ecstatic, Negro speech strongly rhythmical and weighted with image and gesture. But there is more in this sensuousness than the unrestraint and insensitivity found in primitive cultures; nor is it simply the relatively spontaneous and undifferentiated responses of a people living in close contact with the soil. For despite Jim Crow, Negro life does not exist in a vacuum, but in the seething vortex of those tensions generated by the most highly industrialized of Western nations. The welfare of the most humble black Mississippi sharecropper is affected less by the flow of the seasons and the rhythm of natural events than by the fluctuations of the stock market, even though, as Wright states of his father, the sharecropper's memories, actions and emotions are shaped by his immediate contact with nature and the crude social relations of the South.

All of this makes the American Negro far different from the "simple" specimen for which he is taken. And the "physical" quality offered as evidence of his primitive simplicity is actually the form of his complexity. The American Negro is a Western type whose social condition creates a state which is almost the reverse of the cataleptic trance: instead of his consciousness being lucid to the reality around it while the body is rigid, here it is the body which is alert, reacting to pressures which the constricting forces of Jim Crow block off from the transforming, concept-creating activity of the brain. The "eroticism" of Negro expression springs from much the same conflict as that displayed in the violent gesturing of a man who attempts to express a complicated concept with a limited vocabulary; thwarted ideational energy is converted into unsatisfactory pantomime, and his words are burdened with meanings they cannot convey. Here lies the source of the basic ambiguity of *Native Son*, wherein in order to translate Bigger's complicated feelings into universal ideas, Wright had to force into Bigger's consciousness concepts and ideas which his intellect could not formulate. Between Wright's skill and knowledge and the potentials of Bigger's mute feelings lay a thousand years of conscious culture.

In the South the sensibilities of both blacks and whites are inhibited by the rigidly defined environment. For the Negro there is relative safety as long as the impulse toward individuality is suppressed. (Lynchings have occurred because Negroes painted their homes.) And it is the task of the Negro family to adjust the child to the Southern milieu; through it the currents, tensions and impulses generated within the human organism by the flux and flow of events are given their distribution. This also gives the group its distinctive character, which, because of Negroes' suppressed minority position, is very much in the nature of an elaborate but limited defense mechanism. Its function is dual: to protect the Negro from whirling away from the undifferentiated mass of his people into the unknown, symbolized in its most abstract form by insanity, and most concretely by lynching; and to protect him from those unknown forces *within himself* which might urge him to reach out for that social and human equality which the white South says he cannot have. Rather than throw himself against the charged wires of his prison, he annihilates the impulses within him.

The pre-individualistic black community discourages individuality out of self-defense. Having learned through experience that the whole group is punished for the actions of the single member, it has worked out efficient techniques of behavior control. For in many Southern communities everyone knows everyone else and is vulnerable to his opinions. In some communities everyone is "related," regardless of blood ties. The regard shown by the group for its members, its general communal character and its cohesion are often mentioned, for by comparison with the coldly impersonal relationships of the urban industrial community, its relationships are personal and warm.

Black Boy, however, illustrates that this personal quality, shaped by outer violence and inner fear, is ambivalent. Personal warmth is accompanied by an equally personal coldness, kindliness by cruelty, regard by malice. And these opposites are as quickly set off against the member who gestures toward individuality as a lynch mob forms at the cry of rape. Negro leaders have often been exasperated by this phenomenon, and Booker T. Washington (who demanded far less of Negro humanity than Richard Wright) described the Negro community as a basket of crabs, wherein should one attempt to climb out, the others immediately pull him back.

The member who breaks away is apt to be more impressed by its negative than by its positive character. He becomes a stranger even to his relatives and he interprets gestures of protection as blows of oppression—from which there is no hiding place, because every area of Negro life is affected. Even parental love is given a qualitative balance akin to "sadism," and the extent of beatings and psychological maimings meted out by Southern Negro parents rivals those described by the nineteenth-century Russian writers as characteristic of peasant life under the Czars. The horrible thing is that the cruelty is also an expression of concern, of love.

In discussing the inadequacies for democratic living typical of the education provided Negroes by the South, a Negro educator has coined the term *mis-education*. Within the ambit of the black family this takes the form of training the child away from curiosity and adventure, against reaching out for those activities lying beyond the borders of the black community. And when the child resists, the parent discourages him, first with the formula, "That there's for white folks. Colored can't have it," and finally with a beating.

It is not, then, the family and communal violence described by *Black Boy* that is unusual, but that Wright *recognized* and made no peace with its essential cruelty—even when, like a babe freshly emerged from the womb, he could not discern where his own personality ended and it began. Ordinarily both parent and child are protected against this cruelty, seeing it as love and finding subjective sanction for it in the spiritual authority of the Fifth Commandment, and on the secular level in the legal and extralegal structure of the Jim Crow system. The child who did not rebel, or who was unsuccessful in his rebellion, learned a masochistic submissiveness and a denial of the impulse toward Western culture when it stirred within him.

Why then have Southern whites, who claim to "know" the Negro, missed all this? Simply because they, too, are armored against the horror and the cruelty. Either they deny the Negro's humanity and feel no cause to measure his actions against civilized norms; or they protect themselves from their guilt in the Negro's condition—and from their fear that their cooks might poison them, or that their nursemaids might strangle their infant charges, or that their field hands might do them violence—by attributing to them a superhuman capacity for love, kindliness and forgiveness. Nor does this in any way contradict their stereotyped conviction that all Negroes (meaning those with whom they have no contact) are given to the most animal behavior.

It is only when the individual, whether white or black, *rejects* the pattern that he awakens to the nightmare of his life. Perhaps much of the South's regressive character springs from the fact that many, jarred by some casual crisis into wakefulness, flee hysterically into the sleep of violence or the coma of apathy again. For the penalty of wakefulness is to encounter ever more violence and horror than the sensibilities can sustain unless translated into some form of social action. Perhaps the impassioned character so noticeable among those white Southern liberals so active in the Negro's cause is due to their sense of accumulated horror; their passion, like the violence in Faulkner's novels, is evidence of a profound spiritual vomiting.

This compulsion is even more active in Wright and the increasing number of Negroes who have said an irrevocable "no" to the Southern pattern. Wright learned that it is not enough merely to reject the white South, but that he had also to reject that part of the South which lay within him. As a rebel he formulated that rejection negatively, because it was the negative face of the Negro community upon which he looked most often as a child. It is this he is contemplating when he writes:

> Whenever I thought of the essential bleakness of black life in America, I knew that Negroes had never been allowed to catch the full spirit of Western civilization, that they lived somehow in it but not of it. And when I brooded upon the cultural barrenness of black life, I wondered if clean, positive tenderness, love, honor, loyalty and the capacity to remember were native to man. I asked myself if these human qualities were not fostered, won, struggled and suffered for, preserved in ritual from one generation to another.

But far from implying that Negroes have no capacity for culture, as one critic interprets it, this is the strongest affirmation that they have. Wright is pointing out what should be obvious (especially to his Marxist critics): that Negro sensibility is socially and historically conditioned; that Western culture must be won, confronted like the animal in a Spanish bullfight, dominated by the red shawl of codified experience and brought heaving to its knees.

Wright knows perfectly well that Negro life is a by-product of Western civilization, and that in it, if only one possesses the humanity and humility to see, are to be discovered all those impulses, tendencies, life and cultural forms to be found elsewhere in Western society.

The problem arises because the special condition of Negroes in the United States, including the defensive character of Negro life itself (the "will toward organization" noted in the Western capitalist appears in the Negro as a will to camouflage, to dissimulate), so distorts these forms as to render their recognition as difficult as finding a wounded quail against the brown and yellow leaves of a Mississippi thicket; even the spilled blood blends with the background. Having himself been in the position of the quail—to expand the metaphor—Wright's wounds have told him both the question and the answer which every successful hunter must discover for himself: "Where would I hide if *I* were a wounded quail?" But perhaps that requires more sympathy with one's quarry than most hunters possess. Certainly it requires such a sensitivity to the shifting guises of humanity under pressure as to allow them to identify themselves with the human content, whatever its outer form, and even with those Southern Negroes to whom Paul Robeson's name is only a rolling sound in the fear-charged air.

Let us close with one final word about the blues: their attraction lies in this, that they at once express both the agony of life and the possibility of conquering it through sheer toughness of spirit. They fall short of tragedy only in that they provide no solution, offer no scapegoat but the self. Nowhere in America today is there social or political action based upon the solid realities of Negro life depicted in *Black Boy*; perhaps that is why, with its refusal to offer solutions, it is like the blues. Yet in it thousands of Negroes will for the first time see their destiny in public print. Freed here of fear and the threat of violence, their lives have at last been organized, scaled down to possessable proportions. And in this lies Wright's most important achievement: he has converted the American Negro impulse toward self-annihilation and "going-under-ground" into a will to confront the world, to evaluate his experience honestly and throw his findings unashamedly into the guilty conscience of America.

chapter 32

AUGUST WILSON

Preface to "Three Plays"*

W"Where to begin?" is among the first questions an artist asks himself. I have always told anyone who asks for my advice to begin anywhere, and that beginning will lead them, whether backward or forward, to the place they want to go. That the place where they arrive may be a place they have wanted to go to unknowingly or perhaps even unwillingly is the crucible in which many a work of art is fired. Romare Bearden has said art is born out of, among other things, necessity. One always knows his wants better than his needs. Each of these plays was a journey. At the end of each, out of necessity, emerged an artifact that is representative, the way a travel photo is representative, of the journey itself. It is the only record.

I have said elsewhere and will repeat here that writing a play is for me like walking down the landscape of the self, unattended, unadorned, exploring what D. H. Lawrence called "the dark forest of the soul." It is a place rife with shadows, a place of suspect quality and occasional dazzling brightness. What you encounter there are your demons which you have occasionally fed, trying, as Hansel, to make your way back home. You find false trails, roads closed for repairs, impregnable fortresses, scouts, armies of memory, and impossible cartography. It is a place where the cartographers labor night and day remarking the maps. The road is sometimes welcoming and its wide passages offer endearment with each step only to narrow to a footpath that has led you, boatless, to the edge of a vast and encompassing ocean. Occasionally, if you are willing to negotiate the perils, you arrive strong,

*This essay prefaces an edition of "Ma Rainey's Black Bottom," "Joe Turner's Come and Gone," and "Fences."

brighter of spirit, to a place that sprouts yams and bolls of cotton at your footfall.

So I will begin this preface where these plays began, in 1965, with a twenty-year-old poet wrestling with the world and his place in it, having discovered the joy and terror of remaking the world in his own image through the act of writing.

To write is to fix language, to get it down and fix it to a spot and have it have meaning and be fat with substance. It is in many ways a remaking of the self in which all of the parts have been realigned, redistributed, and reassembled into a new being of sense and harmony. You have wrought something into being, and what you have wrought is what you have learned about life, and what you have learned is always pointed toward moving the harborless parts of your being closer to home. To write is to forever circle the maps, marking it all down, the latitude and longitude of each specific bearing, giving new meaning to something very old and very sacred—life itself.

As a twenty-year-old poet faced with how little you know about life, you profess to know everything. What you know most assuredly is that you are going to live until you die. What you have, almost without knowing you have it, is a sense of immortality that allows you to approach the mine fields with the blind faith of innocence and the assurance of an indefatigable spirit that rivals St. George in his willingness to slay the dragon. *If only you could get those damn words down on paper!*

I lived in a rooming house in Pittsburgh in those early days, and as I bedded down each night with my immortal self the guns of social history and responsibility that went boom in the night and called the warriors to their stations were largely ignored. If I heard them at all they had no relation to my bearing as a poet determined to answer the question of how many angels could sit on the head of a pin, despite the fact that I was having trouble identifying the angels and the size of the pin.

Most of the truly important moments in our lives go by unnoticed. We recognize them only in retrospect after we have chosen one road or another and have seen where it has taken us. Only after we have kissed the woman for the last time unknowingly, or have left her final nakedness and been marked by the unsurety and the bruise, do these moments have any resonance.

Sometimes you are privileged to recognize these moments when they occur, and from one day to the next, life, in a single stroke of gluttony, has knocked over the lamps and rearranged the maps. One night in the fall of 1965 I put a typewritten yellow-labeled record titled "Nobody in Town Can Bake a Sweet Jellyroll Like Mine," by someone named Bessie Smith, on the turntable of my 78 rpm phonograph, and the universe stuttered and everything fell to a new place.

Although the business of poetry is to enlarge the sayable, I cannot describe or even relate what I felt. Suffice it to say it was a birth, a baptism, a resurrection, and a redemption all rolled up in one. It was the beginning of my consciousness that I was a representative of a culture and the carrier of some very valuable antecedents. With my discovery of Bessie Smith and the blues I had been given a world that contained my image, a world at once rich and varied, marked and marking, brutal and beautiful, and at crucial odds with the larger world that contained it and preyed and pressed it from every conceivable angle.

"Youth is sweet before flight, and a mighty furnace is its kiln," I have written my daughter as she approaches her twenty-first birthday and wrestles, in her becoming womanhood, with the social welter of America in the nineties. My own youth is fired in the kiln of black cultural nationalism as exemplified by Amiri Baraka in the sixties. It posited black Americans as coming from a long line of honorable people with a cultural and political history, a people of manners with a strong moral personality that had to be reclaimed by strengthening the elements of the culture that made it unique and by developing institutions for preserving and promoting it. The ideas of self-determination, self-respect, and self-defense which it espoused are still very much a part of my life as I sit down to write. I have stood them up in the world of Bessie Smith on the ground captured by the blues. Having started my beginning consciousness there it is no surprise that I would mature and my efforts at writing would come to fruition on the same ground. I saw the blues as a cultural response of a nonliterate people whose history and culture were rooted in the oral tradition. The response was to a world that was not of their making, in which the idea of themselves as a people of imminent worth that belied their recent history was continually assaulted. It was a world that did not recognize their gods, their manners, their mores. It despised their ethos and refused to even recognize humanity. In such an environment the blues was a flag bearer of self-definition, and within the scope of the larger world which lay beyond its doorstep, it carved out a life, set down rules, and urged a manner of being that corresponded to the temperament and sensibilities of its creators. It was a spiritual conduit that gave spontaneous expression to the spirit that was locked in combat and devising new strategies for engaging life and enlarging itself. It was a true and articulate literature that was in the forefront of the development of both character and consciousness.

I turned my ear, my heart, and whatever analytical tools I possessed to embrace this world. I elevated it, rightly or wrongly, to biblical status. I rooted out the ideas and attitudes expressed in the music, charted them and bent and twisted and stretched them. I tested them on the common ground of experience and evidence and gave my whole being, muscle and bone and sinew and flesh and spirit, over to the emotional reference provided by the music. I learned to read between the lines and tried to fill in the blank spaces. This was life being lived in all its timbre and horrifics, with zest and purpose and the affirmation of the self as worthy of the highest possibilities and the highest celebration. What more fertile ground could any artist want?

Though my discovery of Bessie Smith and the blues provided me with an aesthetic with which to frame my growing ideas of myself as part of something larger, it was not until I discovered the art of Romare Bearden that I was able to turn it into a narrative that would encompass all of the elements of culture and tradition, what Baldwin had so eloquently called "the field of manners and ritual of intercourse" that sustains black American life. Bearden had accomplished in painting an expression as full and varied as the blues. My discovery of his work was akin to my discovery of Bessie Smith, a moment of privilege and exaltation that comes from recognizing yourself as a vital part of a much larger world than you had imagined. "I try to explore, in terms of the life I know best, those things which are common to all cultures," Bearden had said. I took it as my credo and sought to answer Baldwin's call for a profound articulation of the black tradition that could sustain a man once he left his father's house. Armed with Bearden and the blues I began to look at myself in ways I hadn't thought of before and in which I have never ceased to think of since. I began to work with the idea that I would try to put in my work all the things I saw in his, the spirit and texture and substance and grace and elegance. But how?

Many writers anxious to see results often ignore the very thing that can produce them—craft with all its tentacles, its many facets and applications. As I was a poet and writer of short fiction, the crafting of a play was new to me. I didn't know the rules, the elements, or the tools. But, since I had been writing for fifteen years, I was not without discipline. I knew that to write and to write well one must be uncompromising and make choices based on one's heart and mind and execute them with craft. But what craft? The craft I knew was the craft of poetry and fiction. To my mind, they had to connect and intercept with the craft of playwrighting at some point and all I had to do was find that point. Fiction was a story told through character and dialogue, and a poem was a distillation of language and images designed to reveal an emotive response to phenomena that brought it into harmony with one's knowledge and experience. Why couldn't a play be both?

I thought that in order to accomplish that I had to look at black life with an anthropological eye, use language, character, and image to reveal its cultural flashpoints and in the process tell a story that further illuminated them. This is what the blues did. Why couldn't I? I was, after all, a bluesman. Never mind I couldn't play a guitar or carry a tune in a bucket. I was cut out of the same cloth and I was on the same field of manners and endeavor—to articulate the cultural response of black Americans to the world in which they found themselves. And so I began, not tentatively, but straight ahead, unswerving, unmitigating. I had, after all, nothing to lose.

An artist who stands before a blank canvas is Picasso (or Matisse, since Picasso himself said "There is no one but Matisse"), until proven otherwise. Artists have the same tools: color, line, mass, form, and their own hearts beating, their own demons, and their own necessity. When I sat down to write I realized I was sitting in the same chair as Eugene O'Neill, Tennessee Williams, Arthur Miller, Henrik Ibsen, Amiri Baraka, and Ed Bullins. I felt empowered by the chair. I was confronted by the same blank piece of paper, the same problems of art and craft—how to invest the characters with a life and history, how to invent situations that challenged the characters' beliefs, forced them into action, and prompted them to stand beside the consequences ready to reengage life on the new field of memory and observable phenomena. Feeling that sense of power, there were no rules. I was on a new adventure, with the blues and what I call the blood's memory as my only guide and companion. These plays are the result.

I could not have accomplished any of this if the black playwrights working in the sixties had not laid the groundwork. Amiri Baraka, Ed Bullins, Philip Hayes Dean, Richard Wesley, and Ron Milner are but a few of those who were particularly vocal. I have an enormous respect for their talents and work, and I place myself in that long line of the tradition of African-American letters that has nurtured us all. Also none of these plays would exist in the form they are in if it were not for Lloyd Richards and the Eugene O'Neill Theatre Center. Started by George White with characteristic vision, the Eugene O'Neill Theatre Center is the home of the National Playwrights' Conference where each summer fifteen playwrights are invited, from among the approximate fifteen hundred who submit their work, to participate. My relationship with the O'Neill began in 1980 when my good friend Rob Penny sent me the O'Neill brochure inviting submissions, on which he wrote, in his increasingly cryptic style, "Do This!" I did, and they promptly rejected five of my scripts until the summer of 1982 when I submitted *Ma Rainey's Black Bottom* and was invited by Lloyd Richards and his staff to participate in the conference. That was the first of many enjoyable summers I spent at the O'Neill working on my plays. The O'Neill's contribution to the development of my plays and my work as a playwright should not be overlooked. In each instance the O'Neill conference has been the catalyst for major rewriting and rethinking. As I am not the kind of writer who sets everything in concrete with a chisel from beginning to end, from the O'Neill to Broadway each play has enjoyed the unselfish energies of many talented theater professionals who, by their insights and provocations, have contributed to important changes in the texts. I worked with Bill Partlan as the director on both *Ma Rainey* and *Fences* and benefited from his stagings. Edith Oliver provided wise and insightful comments as my dramaturge on *Fences* and *Joe Turner*. Michael Feingold, as usual witty and brilliant, was my dramaturge on *Ma Rainey*. Amy Saltz was the director on *Joe Turner*, and her staging proved to be illuminating and resulted in more rewriting. Among the many happy events in my career was my meeting of Charles Dutton at the O'Neill in 1982. He is a rare actor of enormous talent whose intuitive sensibilities closely match my own. His inventive portrayal of Levee in *Ma Rainey* inspired me to write the roles of Harold Loomis in *Joe Turner* and Boy Willie in *The Piano Lesson* for him. I am still challenged to write a role to match his talent.

I met Lloyd Richards in the Exxon Building in New York City in 1982. The occasion was the annual luncheon given for the O'Neill playwrights. I don't think either one of us placed any undue importance on the meeting. I don't think either one of us knew what lay in store for us. When the house lights went down on the opening night performance of *Ma Rainey's Black Bottom* at the Yale Repertory Theatre on April 6, 1984, I marked it more as an accomplishment than as a point of departure for a journey through the landscape of the American theater. As it turns out it was both, and I count myself fortunate to have had Lloyd Richards as my guide, my mentor, and my provocateur. More than anyone, he can stand in loud witness to the birth and growth of these plays. From the O'Neill to Yale to Broadway, each step, in each guise, his hand has been firmly on the tiller as we charted the waters from draft to draft and brought the plays safely to shore without compromise. We were guided by the text, our own visions, and occasionally by the seat of our pants, to a port that has been worthy of the cruise. I count him as a true friend and invaluable colleague.

There is a moment in *Joe Turner's Come and Gone* at the end of the first act when the residents of the household, in an act of tribal solidarity and recognition of communal history, dance a Juba. Herald Loomis interrupts it to relate a terrifying vision of bones walking on the water. From the outset he has been a man who has suffered a spiritual dislocation and is searching for a world that contains his image. The years of bondage to Joe Turner have disrupted his life and severed his connection with his past. His vision is of bones walking on water that sink and wash up on the shore as fully fleshed humans. It is not the bones walking on the water that is the terrifying part of the vision—it is when they take on flesh and reveal themselves to be like him. "They black. Just like you and me. Ain't no difference." It is the shock of recognition that his birth has origins in the manifest act of the creator, that he is in fact akin to the gods. Somewhere in the Atlantic Ocean lie the bones of millions of Africans who died before reaching the New World. The flesh of their flesh populates the Americas from Mississippi to Montevideo. Loomis is made witness to the resurrection and restoration of these bones. He has only to reconcile this vision with his learned experiences and recognize he is one of the "bones people." At the end of the play he repudiates the idea that salvation comes from outside of himself and claims his moral personality by slashing his chest in a bloodletting rite that severs his bonds and demonstrates his willingness to bleed as an act of redemption.

I am reminded of a twenty-year-old poet in a rooming house in Pittsburgh in 1965 who came face to face with himself and did not find it wanting.

chapter 33

ALBERT MURRAY

The Function of the Heroic Image[1]

In spite of the presence of the media,[2] this will not be a media event. I hope we can get maximum participation from you before this is over, because you'll get your money's worth if you participate. If I simply come in and read you a neatly written presentation, you may be impressed but then you will say: "That was really fine; he can really put words together. What did he say?"

I don't want that. I'm going to read some notes and raise some questions, present some things, make some declarations, and I hope that you can participate as in a jam session, with me playing piano, and you'll have your various instruments that you want to represent, and I'll bang the homing chords and bring you back in line, since I have the score. That's the way we'll do this.

Normally, that would serve as my *vamp* or *improvised introduction*. Generally I begin with the vamp and then go into the third chorus, come back for the first chorus, and go into the last chorus or something like that. But tonight I did prepare a composed overture. And it goes like this:

> The following remarks or observations and declarations, if you will, are concerned with some of the fundamentals that should in my opinion always underlie any serious discussion about the imperatives of leadership. They represent elemental assumptions about the relationship of art to the quality of human consciousness. And that is really what all of my books and articles are predicated upon. They have to do with the relationship of art to the quality of human consciousness. Without a high quality of consciousness as a human being, one might as well be a snake, a dog, a tree, a rock, or a stream or a mountain or a snowfall or anything else, but not human. The

minute we deal with the quality of being human, we are dealing with the quality of human consciousness, and the highest qualities come from art. That's how we know what we are, what we want, what we want to do.

And so when it degenerates to Madison Avenue advertisement or a media event, we have a lower level of human consciousness. Art represents the *highest* level of human consciousness. That's why it lasts from epoch to epoch. It can be translated from language to language and from culture to culture, and it still has a central human core that is instructive to us and helps us to realize ourselves. As such, all my books add up to an ideational context or frame of reference that should help us to keep our definitions pragmatic. And *pragmatic* or *functional* is the word that I mean because the basic or ultimate objective of art is to provide mankind with what Kenneth Burke calls basic "equipment for living," and that comes in the form of metaphors. The adequate metaphor is the most basic equipment for living. Without an adequate metaphor, you're insane. You don't have any story, you're a ball of chaos—and chaos is the enemy.

Art provides mankind with definitions of itself, its circumstance, its situation, its condition, and also its possibilities. That is what I think stories and poems are about. It is what paintings and sculptural forms are about. It is what music is about—which after all is nothing if not a soundtrack to which we choreograph our daily activities. So let's be sure it's good music.

Now in my books I have dealt with this matter of the function of the heroic image. What you're confronted with here tonight is a working writer who will turn anything into his workshop. So I'm not interested in presenting you with a finished product—not at these prices!—but with work in progress. That's why I want you to participate, as if you were hanging out in my atelier as I work. I'll tell you what I'm doing, what I've done, and then you'll ask me about this, that, and the other, and we'll see what we come up with. And I might come up with something right here that I never came up with before. Then I'll be thankful to you. And I will be happy that I have come, whether you're happy or not!

My first book, *The Omni-Americans*, grew out of my reaction to the ever-so-popular oversimplifications of the so-called social sciences. It was an attempt to counterstate inadequate assumptions about the nature of human motives, objectives, aspirations, and incentives. I also think of the book as being about aesthetics because it deals with distorted images of human nature and conduct. Most sociological surveys are simply geared to power or the lack of it: who's on top and who's on the bottom. In the United States, it adds up to what I call a "folklore of white supremacy": I mean, the haves and the have-nots. If you don't have, then you're supposedly not human: You don't have a sense of humor. You can't enjoy a steak. You can't possibly enjoy sex or music. Not unless you have power and run the country. To me that's a misrepresentation of what civilization is, what life is, what human nature is about, what makes people happy, what makes them feel that they have realized themselves. Not the accumulation of power but something else: An accumulation of *wholeness*. An achievement of a *dynamic equilibrium* in the face of the exigencies, the ever-changing flux that we live in. That's about as near as you're going to get to happiness. And it has to be won every day. Which is why my central metaphor is the blues, as you can tell from the books that I've written. I'll tell you a little more about that as we go on.

If I accepted the generalizations, the assessments of the so-called social science surveys, I couldn't be a fiction writer. I couldn't write about myself. I couldn't write about anything except victims. And if I'm a brown-skinned writer in the United States, if I looked at the social surveys, I wouldn't even think that I was human. I'd figure I've got a long ways to go to be human. Whereas I was *always* the hero. Every time I read a story, *I* was the hero. I went to a cowboy picture, I was Tom Mix, you know? If I was reading about Ulysses, I was Ulysses. I was even Don Quixote; I was never Sancho Panza. I always was the hero. So I had to represent life as I was living it. And I had to find an intellectual discipline that was more adequate to the complexity of my experience than social science, which was simply about who was going to run this and that. You know, once you've gotten to be a banker, you don't even have to think about anything else, according to social science. If you were an elected official, you wouldn't have to worry about elections because you would be on the inside. But that had very little to do with the life that I was experiencing, the life that I was dreaming about. The one thing that I liked most about myself was that I always had such a beautiful picture of the world. It was always a fairy tale. Then I realized later on that it was a *blue-steel* fairy tale, one that had barbed wire in it and all that. But then I invented a metaphor to go with that. So as the hero of *Train Whistle Guitar* says, "I saw myself as Jack the Rabbit and my home was in the briarpatch." In other words, you're born into trouble, and trouble is why you do your thing.

So by those steps I realized I was very much concerned with the nature of heroic action, and so I had to write a book to get those distortions out of the way, and that book was *The Omni-Americans*, which counterstated the materialist, biased oversimplifications of social science in the United States—which are intrinsically racist. If there's anywhere you want to find racism in the United States, just look at any social science survey. They always categorize in terms of "races." They couldn't define "race" if their life depended on it. There's no scientist, there's no social scientist in the United States that can define what is black and what is white. Absolutely none, not in scientific terms. No such definition is possible. And yet you've had survey after survey after survey, which divides people and draws conclusions based on "racial" differences. And nobody can tell how much of this makes you white, how much of this makes you black, how much of this makes you something else. Not scientifically. It's absolutely impossible.

So I jettisoned all that stuff and went back to literature, which was *the* discipline, the human discipline to which all these other things merely provide raw materials for great minds to turn into marvelous metaphors. And it's those metaphors that we live in terms of. Oh, I know the vital statistics. *I know the facts. But I'm looking for something better.* And that something better is a story of the possibility of glory on earth. So that's what I was concerned with, see? So I figured that the main thing that I wanted to write about was heroic action. And I found that by digging into my own experience, dealing with that which is most intimate—

the idiomatic details most intimate to my everyday experiences—then I would have a chance to do what Shakespeare did, what Sophocles did, what Goethe did, what Melville did, what Hemingway did, what Thomas Mann did, what André Malraux did, what all these great ones did. It's the same thing. I wanted to be the heavyweight champion of the world. I didn't want anyone to make a richer metaphor of American experience than I was trying to make. That's the type of ambition I'm talking about.

Social science is up there like a lion in the path. You know, it says, "Black boy, sing the blues." And I say, "You don't even know what the blues are *about*. Blues is good-time music. You think it's lamentation. I know better." Just like every Baptist preacher knows better. There's no Baptist preacher that's going to tell you that the blues is not good-time music. Only problem for him is that you're having a good time *outside* the church. You might have such a good time at the Saturday night function that you don't make the Sunday morning service. But he knows what that is. So I wrote a book spelling that out.

My second book was *South to a Very Old Place*. Now this is a sort of nonfiction or documentary novel. I went south to look at things in the Old Country. I went down home to see what had been happening. And instead of coming back with a sociological report or a bunch of journalistic bullshit, I came back with a metaphor about the imperatives of heroic action. And I found that ever since the fugitive slave, the mold that I was cast in and everything that happened in my life were designed to make me and all the people that I grew up with *heroes*. Or to make us take on the responsibility for heroic action, to take on the responsibility of saviors, of Prometheus, of bringing light, of bringing fire, bringing enlightenment. It had nothing to do with being a victim. It had to do with the fact that if you were faced with a problem, the problem was a dragon and you were the hero. So you had to forge a sword and find out how to rip at the scales.

So I could always go further, I found, with fairy tales than I could with sociological concepts, which would change every ten years. When a guy needs another Ph.D. or another full professorship, he'll go revise something that somebody else did. And I found that the fiction would stay, that while the books that Henry James wrote in 1905 don't need any revision, a very large percentage of what Freud wrote in 1905 was revised by 1939. They revised it because it didn't hold up. They even had to revise a lot of Newton; they found it didn't go far enough. It did not really describe what it was supposed to be describing. But you don't have to revise Aesop's fables. Or the fables of La Fontaine. You don't have to revise Seneca. You don't have to revise Aeschylus. None of that. So I opted for that because I found that the heroic image was much more life-giving than the statistical norm, if you know what I mean. The statistical norm was a feeble attempt to create a type, and generally the survey was so unreliable that it simply represented a conclusion drawn by a person with very limited experience *and no wisdom*. Whereas to create a metaphor that's going to be enduring, there's got to be some sense of life that adds up to wisdom. And that's much more difficult than running a survey. Nowadays, computers are going to do most of the surveys. But they're not going to come up with any more than what you put in them. And so we'll still be left with

the fact that the basic equipment for living, the most reliable and the most enduring equipment for living is going to be found in the poetic or the fictional
metaphor. In aesthetic statement, not in denotative generalizations.

So my book *South to a Very Old Place* was not a sociopolitical report, although
its political import should be unmistakable. I mean, first you get life straight, and
then you discuss what the human institutions should be like. Once you've got a
conception of life, then you want to have institutions that will make that conception possible, make it possible to realize that conception. Then you'll know
what right and wrong consist of within that context because you've described
what the good life is, what you want life to be, what good people are, what good
conduct is. And when you're describing heroic action, you're describing what adequate human conduct is: that which is self-fulfilling, that which has a minimum
of conflict, that which involves living in terms of other people.

South to a Very Old Place was an attempt to process the details of my childhood
and young manhood into metaphors of heroic action. Here what counts most is
not the material facts, but the rituals that conditioned me to see life as a perpetual adventure, to see it as a picaresque story with some episodes that might be as
tightly plotted as a detective story and some that were as loosely strung together
as a farce. But always it was a story, sometimes a picaresque story, but in that
picaresque story, there could be tragic episodes, there could be comic episodes.
And there could be farcical episodes. In fact, there were always farcical episodes.
Because in *The Hero and The Blues* I really reached the point where I decided that
the form, the ultimate form, the existing literary form, that would best serve my
purpose as a contemporary writer, as a person grappling with details of contemporary world, was the straight-faced farce.

And that would be commensurate with the fact that my frame of reference was
the blues idiom, which is an idiom that has to do with improvisation, so if I could
see slapstick action for a slapdash situation, I would be in a position of a musician
in a jam session. So that once we knew what the story was supposed to be, that is,
the chordal structure and progression, then we could weave melodies and do all
kinds of things. We could do countermelodies, we could do all that, based on
whatever happened. If you intensified the rhythm or you changed it, *you could still
compose and still maintain your composure* under the various tempos, the various
stresses, and so forth. In other words, you'd be geared to the fact that life has to be
created anew everyday.

So I was already into the whole business of the blues idiom. And that includes
jazz, because to me jazz is the fully orchestrated blues statement such as you would
find in a Duke Ellington sonata—than which there's nothing better. In jazz, you'd
find the same thing you'd find in the traditional twelve-bar blues. But in jazz sometimes the players might not even state the melody of the twelve-bar blues song;
they might simply play the obligato. Well, that's the way contemporary man has
to function in order to deal with the shifting nature of his life. In other words,
entropy is the one thing you can count on. So once you see that the basic nature
of nature is entropy—that is, the tendency of all phenomena to become random
or the tendency for the void to reclaim itself—then you'll realize that the central

problem of mankind or of humanity (and thus of the artist) is *form*. Now, you've got to continue to modify that form to meet the exigencies of the changing situation. And that's what jazz music does. And that's why it's my central metaphor.

Well, I tried to deal with how that worked in *South to a Very Old Place*, and with how the heroic imperative was set up for me. It meant leadership, whether it's going to be political leadership or spiritual leadership or aesthetic leadership or whatever.

That brings me to my third book, which is *The Hero and the Blues*. In this third book, which is a theory of fiction, I spell out the things that I'm just skipping past now because this is what we do in a workshop. And it talks about the function of the storyteller. And you know what that is, I've already told you: it's to provide "basic equipment for living." Basic equipment for living, a basic pattern for you to aspire to, to raise you out of being an amoeba or something like that. I mean, equipment to prepare you to do all kinds of stuff, to make plans, to do this on top of that, plans for year *after* next, that type of thing. You've got to have a lot to have that type of foresight.

Then in this book I talked about the dynamics of heroic action. Which had to do with a central concept for my writing. The very thing that I would use to oppose the social science oversimplification of the nature of human motives is the concept of "antagonistic cooperation." How do you like that? Anybody have any idea what that means? Antagonistic cooperation. It's at the center of all stories. What is it? You know what it means? It means that you can't be a saint unless you have sin, unless there's some sin for you to avoid. You can't be a great surgeon unless you have disease that you have to operate on. Right? You can't be a good man unless there's a bad man. You can't be a great hitter unless there are great pitchers. You can't be a great champion unless you have great challengers. In other words, through the conflict. I mean, you can't have a hero without a dragon. So what does a bull do to the bullfighter? He cooperates to make the bullfighter great! That's what the devil does to the Christian, makes you a saint. Without the devil how could you be a saint? Do you understand what I mean by antagonistic cooperation? It pertains to all conflicts. If you play a homecoming game, if the opponents are not *worthy*, as they say in debates (that's about the only place we do say it these days), if your opponent is not a worthy opponent, then your victory is hollow. You follow me? All right.

So you begin any concern with heroic action, with the existence of a dragon, or of an antagonist. That's what the Greeks were talking about: protagonists and antagonists, and in the middle is the *agon*, the struggle, the conflict. Right? Can you see that the fairy tale is where it's at? Because it means just that, it means struggle. It means facing the facts of life, and that's the blues again.

The simplest blues lyrics start out facing the facts of life: "Woke up this morning./Blues all around my bed. Woke up this morning./Blues all around my bed." Now the guy doesn't jump up and cut his throat. By nine o'clock that night, he's gotten himself together, done a day's work, got in touch with a fine brown frame and is stomping at the Savoy. That's survival, you understand what I mean? That's a central metaphor. It started out with the fact that life is a low-down dirty shame.

It shouldn't happen to a dog. If you go and read Camus, that's the first thing he's going to say. He's going to say, "Well, the first question of philosophy is the question of suicide." In other words, whether or not to go on, to be or not to be, right? The blues starts you right off on that. "Woke up this morning and found out I was a damned slave. In an alien land. Now I might as well cut my throat. I'd rather cut my throat than pick cotton." Well, the other guy says, "I'll pick cotton, but there are also some honeysuckles out there, some of this out there, some molasses out there, plus a fine brown frame over on that next plantation."

So it's a matter of affirming life in the face of adversity. Because my central image of the blues—as you go from *Stomping the Blues*, my other book—is that there are invisible blue devils that beset you on all sides, and they are an embodiment of entropy. You can't destroy them, but you can push them back, *you can hold them at bay*. And as soon as you relax, they're right back.

I once wrote a thing in one of my books about how when Louis Armstrong would come to town, he could take that silver trumpet and he'd blow it and he'd freeze that blues in place like the gargoyles on Notre Dame. But after he goes, they're coming back down. That's the problem, always. But his act is a heroic act. Because he's getting rid of the dragons to an extent. But what does a hero do? In *The Hero and the Blues*, what does a hero do? I mean, if you kill the dragon, do you think you're going to retire to the golf course? If you've been through combat, you ought to have some ideas about this. When you're out in the rough looking for that ball you look over and see some other things; those might be dragon *seeds*. So the one thing you might have learned from having fought the dragon is to spot dragons when they're small. But you had better not think that they have been dispelled forever. So in this you're constantly improvising, constantly reaffirming life in the face of new adversity. And I don't see how you could have a more adequate metaphor than that. It's not a matter of meeting a statistical norm and having a fancy income, belonging to this class or that class or the other class. The intrinsic existential problem is how to be on fructifying terms with life. Life-fulfilling activity, that's the one thing that's going to get you through. And you can have *any* amount of money, but if you don't know that that's what it's all about, you're in trouble—like most people who own a lot of money. They spend most of their time dealing with money and never get around to dealing with life. And I'm for all the money I can get. (Which I won't get at Wesleyan.)

My next book, the book after *The Hero and the Blues*, is *Train Whistle Guitar*. Now this is the first installment of a trilogy about the initiation and escapades of a blues-idiom hero.[3] It is an attempt to create the literary equivalent of the blues. If I can bring the whole thing off, I would be on my way to achieving in American fiction what Duke Ellington represents for me in American contemporary music in the world at large. I shall have also achieved a strong image of my conception of the *hombre de epoca*, that is, the representative man of the period, the symbolic conduct that is most adequate to the problems of our time. That is the function of the heroic image, to give us a picture of conduct, of character and conduct, of the disposition that is commensurate with the problems that we face. So you've got to hang loose.

Constance Rourke was one of the great American women scholars and writers as far as I'm concerned. In her book *American Humor: A Study of the National Character*, she spoke of the basic objective of this thing that she was calling "humor" in her book, which was both a matter of comic humor and the other meaning of humor, which is "every man in his own humor" or he is "of the humor" to do this that or the other. *American Humor* asserts that the basic problem or the basic objective of American expression was "to provide emblems for a pioneer people who require resilience as a prime trait." To me, that just about says it. "To provide emblems," that includes all art, anything you can say—whether it's a metaphor, whether it's a sound, whether it's a sign, any thing, any artifact, anything that suggests something, any objective correlative, if you will. *To provide emblems of a pioneer people*, or let us say a frontier people, or an experimental people, or people in flux, or a nation in flux, who require resilience—in other words, the ability to snap back, to come back from defeat, not just a success story, but to come *back*. Who *require* resilience as a prime trait.

Now we're talking about basic survival technique. We're talking about what Burke called "occupational psychosis." Which is the same thing as basic survival. It means if you belong to a fishing or hunting society, all the games will be geared to chasing and capturing. Even the wedding ceremony will have to have some of that in it. Everything will be conditioned to do what you have to do to survive in that particular environment. Displaced Europeans hitting the American continent needed to know how to snap back, and they needed to know how to improvise. So the big thing is what Kouwenhoven talks about in *Made in America; or, The Arts in Modern American Civilization* as the interaction of the learned tradition and the vernacular. And that interaction, that perpetual need to create and to face new situations on the frontier, to adapt this to that, *that's* what characterizes American society. Of course, it was overtaken by materialism, and that's our big problem. But it's still a highly experimental society. And the Constitution reflects it. All the documents reflect it. All the games reflect it.

Now, if you deal specifically with the blues idiom, there's one group of Americans dealing with another—within that context. It's got to be within that American context. Otherwise it won't work. You can't get the blues in Europe. You certainly can't get it in Africa, because everything is too nailed down. No improvisation there. They'll cut your neck off if you start varying the beat. That's all, that's *classic* stuff. Like all primitive art and society, it's *classic*. It's not folk, if you understand what I mean, so it's pretty rigid. Here, everything is open a little, has to be adapted. It has to be this, it has to be that. When this particular group of Americans came over, well, they had to have resilience, even to make it. Right? Well, those who didn't make it, who didn't get past the Middle Passage, they're not my ancestors. Only the ones that made it are my ancestors. If they didn't go through the auction block, they're not my ancestors.

Because for all the things that my idiomatic ancestors have had to face, out of all the adversity that they faced, they came out with a sense of humor that's the envy of the world, a sense of beauty that's the envy of the world, a sense of movement that's unmatchable.

All those things are intrinsically human. In other words, these people came through with their *humanity* intact. No *power*, but look at all that humanity! So all I need is the *money*; I have the humanity. I know how to fit it in with anything anywhere. Once I got to the third grade and found that geography book and found out what the world was and that there were things all over the world that I could use, I was in business! Now, they have most of it over here. I was already ready for it when it came. Whether it's Korean, whether it's Indian, Japanese, Chinese, any of that, wherever it's from, I was ready. Because I already had a context. The fact that you're oriented to resilience and improvisation should make you more comprehensive, should make you ready to encompass more experience.

The opposite of that rigid situation, you know, my image of the person who gets tangled up with the rigid thing, is that person in the Charlie Chaplin movie: the guy who is in control of everything. He's the guy who wears a top hat, he's got a cane; he's kind of a caricature of J. P. Morgan back in his heyday. He walks down the street, and he's in charge. Folks are on the sidewalk, and they're looking. He's the lord of all he surveys. He doesn't see that banana peel under his foot. Steps on a banana peel and breaks his crown. On the other street, here comes a tramp, Charlie Chaplin in his raggedy-butt pants, flat shoes, toes almost out, cutaway coat that looks somewhat pretentious, a bowler hat, and with the nerve to sport a boutonniere. But instead of striding like he owns everything, he prances and dances like he's *related* to everything, like it's there for *him*. The other guy owns it, but Charlie Chaplin is *of it*: he's *of it* and *with it*. So he's dancing up, and he's obviously earning his living because someone has told him to deliver a lemon meringue pie. He's got his stick in one hand, he's swinging down the lane. And he's so busy looking, following a pretty girl, that he steps on a banana peel; but he's already hanging loose, so he just dances all over the sidewalk and finally retrieves the pie and continues prancing on down the street with his fancy walking stick.

That's an exaggerated image of what we mean by resilience, which is so connected with this whole business of improvisation. Once you get to improvisation, you're also ready for the changes, for unforeseen difficulties and so forth. And that's why I've used those things in my writing.

But when I got to my book *Stomping the Blues*, what I did was go in and sort of lay out the details underlying the metaphor. This is what blues music is, this is how you play blues music, this is how playing blues music is different from playing other music. Blues musicianship requires this, this, this, and this. Not just the ability to read the notes, but the ability to create in the presence of peers and betters, under the pressure of all tempos, with inverted chords and whatever. That's a good metaphor for me. That's a perfect metaphor for the kind of person you would like to be in life. If you could just handle everything like that, you'd be ready, because you'd be ready for the changes that are bound to come, the unforeseen changes. And that's what my central work has been about, and that's why I talk about the function of the heroic image, because the hero projects or represents a picture of conduct for us to emulate. And he's got to have in his character qualities that will enable him to confront problems with enough confidence in his technique to take on adversaries that might seem to have an advantage over him.

So you see, when I was writing in *The Omni-Americans* and somebody talked to me about "minority group," that was about the most stupid thing I ever heard. I could never think of myself as a minority group. The minority group that I belonged to was A students; they're always a minority. Good-looking guys! Sharp guys! Writers! You know, there were other minorities—like millionaires—but I didn't belong to that group. This business of *minorities* didn't make any sense, and certainly I couldn't accept it, because I was going to deal with heroic action. And nothing pains me more than to hear leaders talk about or call themselves minorities. It's saying you're *inferior*, that's all you're saying. Well, OK, who's superior? The dragon or St. George? Who's superior? The one that's bigger? Or the one that's the most nimble and the most creative? Geniuses are always in the minority. You know what I mean? How many Einsteins do you know? How many Newtons? They are always a minority. But they're talking about inferior *groups*, ethnic groups, which in the U.S. are almost always confused with *racial* groups. But you see what I've talked about tonight is the possibility of individual people. I'm talking about the hero. Everybody, at least everybody in his dreams, should be a hero. You're the princess who gets the prince. If you go through the right ritual, at first it looks like a frog, right? Frog said: "You let me come to your ball, come to your castle, sit at your table, eat out of your plate, sleep in your bed." And so the king said: "Did you promise him that?" She said: "Yes I did, daddy, I wanted my ball." "Well, you're going to have to do it." He woke up the next morning, and he was not a frog. He was a prince. He was imprisoned in a frog. So when you read that story, *you're* the princess. They don't separate heroes by groups. Whether you're Italian, or whether you're Puerto Rican, Korean, black, white, yellow, all that. *Your* aspirations are what matter. So that function of that heroic image, the first thing it does is raise our horizons of aspiration. It extends our sense of human possibility. Anybody that opts for leadership must have the ability to inspire *that* in the people that he opts to lead. If he's political, he's going to have that special quality that leaders must always have, known as charisma.

You know what charisma is? Would you like my definition of charisma? Would you really? Charisma is that human quality of inspiring people to regard you as their savior, as one who can deliver, whether them or the goods. It inspires confidence. It's *that* quality that he has: he's the one that can do it. If you want to read some more about that, look up the work of the great German sociologist Max Weber, who has a lot to say about it. I think the popularity of the term was derived from him. Probably because Talcott Parsons and those guys brought out those editions of the writings of Weber. But it has to do with that quality of authority. He's talking about various types of authority. You could designate authority so that someone who's a professor is the boss, right? Or someone has the money so he's the boss. Or he has the rank so he's the boss. That would be designated official authority. Another type of authority comes from within the personality of the person. So although someone else may be the boss, when the chips are down, you turn to *this* guy. Yeah, another guy's the boss, but so-and-so runs the office. If you want something done, see so-and-so. That's charismatic power, authority, charismatic authority. That's the way they use it. They call it charismatic authority, that type of authority that inspires faith in leadership, because it believes that this particular person holds the salvation of the group or whatever. And that's the function of the heroic image. If you and I could just be like that, then we would have it together, and things would fall into place.

And now for some questions. . . .

NOTES

1. These remarks were delivered at Wesleyan University in May 1985.
2. The talk was recorded for broadcast by National Public Radio.
3. Since this presentation, the second and third books (*The Spyglass Tree* and *The Seven League Boots*) of this have appeared.

chapter 34

BRENT EDWARDS

The Seemingly Eclipsed Window of Form: James Weldon Johnson's Prefaces

It had called her to come and gaze on a mystery. It stirred her tremendously. How? Why? It was like a flute song forgotten in another existence and remembered again. What? How? Why? This singing she heard that had nothing to do with her ears.

—ZORA NEALE HURSTON, *Their Eyes Were Watching God*

What is even more important, as we develop this business of emergent language . . . is the actual rhythm and the syllables, the very body work, in a way, of the language.

—EDWARD KAMAU BRATHWAITE, *History of the Voice*

How does literature "write" music? How do the graphic techniques of black literacy translate, or transport, the particularities of black orality onto the page? Such queries are the commonplace of African-American literary criticism, rehashed, familiar, and yet still vexing. Still, we are finding that we need to "shift the ground from underneath a criticism erected on such contraries" as orality/literacy, craft/politics, and (inarticulate) music/ (articulate) writing.[1] Perhaps, though, the task is more to allow the admittedly contrary or—in the words of Edward Kamau Brathwaite—"broken" ground of such formal conundrums to haunt what poetics we erect.[2] Starting from such a sensibility, we would read less for proof of proper translation, expecting the literary to capture the oral on the page; black poetics might instead cohere around the vicissitudes of that interface, around the fascination with edges, openness, fracture, ventilation that we encounter so often. The espousal of what eludes: what Zora Neale Hurston calls "angularity"; what

Brathwaite calls the "submarine unity"; what Richard Wright calls the "Form of Things Unknown"; what Audre Lorde calls the "open word."

We are accustomed to the assumption that black modernity, especially in the work of the so-called culture framers of the Harlem Renaissance such as W. E. B. Du Bois, Alain Locke, and James Weldon Johnson, is characterized by a politically motivated privileging of the achievement of literate culture. As Johnson famously opens his preface to *The Book of American Negro Poetry*, the "final measure" of a people's greatness is their literature and art.[3] Without reading further, we would assume that this pronouncement implies a progression and dichotomy: even if African-American literature often turns to tropes of orality, to metaphors of the "talking book," still the achievement of great writing necessitates that the oral—the so-called vernacular—be left behind. Logically, the metaphor functions, a book can "talk" only because speech and writing are radically different modes. Reading through such a lens, though, often causes us to overlook the many other, discrepant moments in the tradition that would appear to affirm a more complex project, one that troubles the seemingly clear divide between orature and scripture. To take a single instance: what do we do with the pivotal evocation of an unheard or inaccessible music in Zora Neale Hurston's 1937 novel *Their Eyes Were Watching God*, cited in the first epigraph above? Janie is stirred by a "singing . . . that had nothing to do with her ears," a music that opens or figures a certain distance in what we might call her psychic space; this music connects itself "to other vaguely felt matters that had struck her outside observation" and transforms the way she conceives her place in the world.[4] What would it mean to theorize a black poetics of transcription that would link such elusive uses of music to the more conventional or ethnographic "recordings" or referencings of music, and oral expression in general, that we have come to expect from the black literary tradition?

This essay follows the recent work of critics like Nathaniel Mackey, Harryette Mullen, and Aldon Nielsen in arguing that, in the words of the last, "African-American traditions of orality and textuality were not opposed to one another and did not exist in any simple or simplistic opposition to modernity and postmodernity. African-American poetics both birthed and fractured modernist and postmodernist poetics."[5] Whereas the work of Mackey and Nielsen generally focuses on more contemporary or "postmodernist" poetics, and Mullen's project assembles a reading of what she calls "spirit writing," or visionary texts in the tradition, my project is to extend the insights of such a reappraisal to the tenets of black "high" modernity itself. Here, I am specifically interested in the ways that James Weldon Johnson's prefaces to *The Books of American Negro Spirituals* introduce that two-volume collection by making a point not just about music, but about *transcription*, offering a remarkably complex reading of the relationship between media in black expressive culture.[6] Read in depth, Johnson's work does not allow the facile assumption that even the culture framers of the literate Renaissance conceived black creative cultures through an epistemological split between the oral and the written. His claim, what Edward Kamau Brathwaite would call the "body work" of the emergent language of black modern expression, occurs on an "elusive" edge between orality and literacy, demands to be read as the defining modern critical elaboration of the issue, with resonances throughout the tradition.

Considering such issues of transcription, we might be more tempted to turn to a passage from a work like Ralph Ellison's well-known 1945 review of Richard Wright's *Black Boy*, in which Ellison offers a compelling definition of the blues. Ellison's eloquent description, by now a touchstone of postwar African-American cultural criticism, has been cited often for definitional purposes, but there has been little if any comment about the way these two sentences, with a curious tension, disinter the bedeviling and much-evaded issue of form in black poetics. I use this passage here as a point of entry, for it can be read as one of the moments where Johnson's terms resonate. "The blues," Ellison writes,

> is an impulse to keep the painful details and episodes of a brutal experience alive in one's aching consciousness, to finger its jagged grain, and to transcend it, not by the consolation of philosophy but by squeezing from it a near-tragic, near-comic lyricism. As a form, the blues is an autobiographical chronicle of personal catastrophe expressed lyrically.[7]

The word that slips, or sticks, for me here is *lyric*, one of those common terms of poetics that has been overused to the point that it is frustratingly ambiguous. Ellison defines the blues as a kind of compulsion to record, to keep "painful details and episodes" "alive" in the individual consciousness (what this definition fails to convey in its existential emphasis, of course, is a sense of the blues as performance), and he turns to a literary term in an effort to describe this "continuous replay" effect of the blues. Or is *lyric* a literary term after all?

It is in this seldom-considered arena of poetics that James Weldon Johnson's intervention takes its full significance. In approaching *lyric*, though, it becomes necessary to step back from Ellison, so as to consider the connotations and uses of the term within the context of modern American poetics in which Johnson writes his prefaces. Etymologically, the word *lyric*, which is derived from the Greek *lyra*, or musical instrument, has a strictly defined musical connotation, referring to poems to be sung to accompaniment. But in the Renaissance, lyric poetry as *melos* (to be sung) came to be replaced by an emphasis on the lyric as *opsis* (as pictoral, a crafted structure of signs on the page), and the aspect of the word linked directly to musical performance was thereby eclipsed. By 1930, when we encounter the American modernist poet Louis Zukofsky's famous dictum that poetry is "an order of words that . . . approaches in varying degrees the wordless art of music as a kind of mathematical limit," the notion of lyric has lost all specific and generic implications and has come to be identified with poetry in general.[8]

Northrup Frye explains this development by arguing that the lyric's musical ties were always to contemporary forms: from the romantic period onwards, the lyric can no longer function as *melos* in the traditional sense because music tends to be characterized less and less by "song and pitch accent" and more by "stress accent and dance rhythm." So poetry is less musical in the traditional sense of *lyric* because poetic mimesis relies less on the tonal properties of performed language and more on the potential of written form to imply "stress" and "rhythm."[9] But Frye, in his nearly unrelenting blindness to vernacular forms, does not mention another developing meaning of the word: in the early part of this century, in the dawn of music publishing, lyric came to denote certain popular cultural forms as well: *song lyrics*, which are written to be performed, and which are generally considered to have a kind of secondary or bastard status flat on the page. So some of the performative connotations of the lyric sneak in through the back door of popular culture.

Is it possible to reconcile these competing notions of the lyric in a discussion of the literary transcription envisioned by Johnson, toward the lyrics of the spirituals or the lyrics of blues poetry? The question, it would seem, is, What does it mean to approach music? Zukofsky specifies that when he defines a poem as a "context associated with a 'musical' shape," "musical" must be placed in quotation marks "since it is not of notes as music, but of words more variable than variables, and used outside as well as within the context with communicative reference."[10] Sterling Brown, writing in the same period in an essay on themes in the blues, makes a different claim: that the blues themselves (as sung? as transcribed on the page?) *are* a lyric mode. Brown simply erases the distance between black vernacular oral and musical forms and European literary ones: "It seems to be the history of lyric poetry, however (and the Blues, unlike most folk poetry, are lyric), that it is generally the lover or lady *in absentia* who calls out poetry. This is true of the Blues."[11]

This kind of sharp divergence makes it clear that our understanding of lyric is crucial to our understanding of the poetics of transcription envisioned by Renaissance critics like Johnson and Brown. Continually, we encounter these same tangled alternate takes on the lyric when we turn our attention to the fertile period when black literary artists such as Johnson, Brown, Langston Hughes, and the Cuban poet Nicolas Guillen begin to "mine," in Johnson's words, the "genuine folk stuff" of vernacular modes of expression (the sermon, the blues, the work song, the spiritual) for formal inspiration. The first attempts in the mid-1920s at the form that has since been called the "blues poem," for instance, raise a question of critical approach similar to that in Ellison's passage: how do we read a work like Hughes's "Young Gal's Blues," which seems to play with the fuzzy area between the song lyric and the literary lyric?

> De po' house is lonely
> An' de grave is cold.
> O, de po' house is lonely,
> De graveyard grave is cold.
> But I'd rather be dead than
> To be ugly an' old.
>
> When love is gone what
> Can a young gal do?
> When love is gone, O,
> What can a young gal do?
> Keep on a-lovin' me, daddy,
> Cause I don't want to be blue.[12]

What is the conception of form in such a poetics of transcription?

As Kimberly Benston has pointed out, much African-American cultural criticism has unfortunately preempted the role of form in cultural production, either measuring works in terms of some supposedly "universal" aesthetic form or in terms of some supposedly "external" (in other words, not performed in the rhetoric or structure of the work itself) notion of blackness.[13] In employing the word *form*, I am not attempting to evoke that old treacherous form/content divide: form is abstract, timeless, anonymous; content is particular, historical, individual, and thereby where "race" appears, according to this tired binary. The opposition is false. One way out of this bind is to think of what is called content as simply the way matter is realized by form. It is not necessary to engage in phenomenological games to recognize this: in terms of writing, in referring to matter—to a *material* signifier—one refers not to ink and blotches on paper but to a consistency of the signifier (what has been called its iterability: the fact that it can be called up again, or re-cited).[14] It is this consistency, shared in oral and written languages alike, that makes communication possible. So there is no pure matter, without form (sounds or the characters of an alphabet have form, just as clay or wood has a form even before it is shaped); but form is a principle independent of matter, which can invade or alter the form of that matter—and that effect is content.[15]

Thus when we say that the lyric approaches music, the paradox is that there is a pronounced difference in the *matter* in-formed in poetry on the one hand (written language) and in music on the other (sound). The statement is possible, though, because the *form* of a poem (seen in characteristics such as stanza structure, line, spacing, punctuation, meter, rhyme, typography, orthography, and semantics) is able to suggest or mimic the *form* of a particular music. To return to Zukofsky's terms: words are used "outside the context of communicative reference" to suggest a " 'musical' shape."

Critics have read the issue of dialect in black poetry as solely an ideological one, but in fact, as Eric Sundquist has recently suggested, dialect is an issue of form as well: it is an orthographical technique by which written language represents oral language.[16] But in poetic criticism, an attention to form has been largely lacking; thus, for example, Shirley Anne Williams, in a generally excellent analysis of the Hughes poem cited above, writes of "techniques of Afro-American speech and singing that have been carried over virtually unchanged into Afro-American poetry."[17] She continues with the somewhat mystifying claim that by "transforming" elements of the "classic blues form," blues poetry "function[s] in much the same way as blues forms once functioned within the black community" (73). Even putting aside the function of blues poetry in "the black community," the problem raised here is one of determining just how such a "trans-formation" might take place and what its effects might be on a given work.

Perhaps the most ambitious theoretical effort in the field of form and black aesthetics is Stephen Henderson's "The Forms of Things Unknown," the introduction to his ground-breaking anthology *Understanding the New Black Poetry*. In a section entitled "Structure," which Henry Louis Gates, Jr., has described as at once the "most promising" and the "most disappointing" of Henderson's poetic categories,[18] Henderson attempts to come to terms with such issues, relying alternately on a version of reader-response criticism (the black reader supplements the "saturated" blues data of the poetic form by imagining the musical and performative context) and on Larry Neal's concept of the "destruction of the text" (the poem is simply a "score" to be realized) in order to argue that the difference between "singing Black songs and reading Black poems" is "merely academic."[19] However, the argument collapses into a claim more about *style* than about *form*: when Henderson suggests that "there is a Black poetic mechanism, much like the musical ones, which can transform even a Shakespearean sonnet into a jazz poem," he is writing less about composition than about realization (thus he says that the "Black poetic mechanism" is "improvisation," in a *performance* of the sonnet).

Certainly, blues poetry (and later Brown's blues ballads and Hughes's jazz poetry) should make us question the often-assumed opposition "of the poem-as-structure and the poem-as-event."[20] But the notion of the poem-as-event may refer to the semantic and structural dynamic of the poem, apart from any possible performance of it. And part of the radical force of such writing may well be that it subverts this structure/event opposition without inverting it; it keeps this tension "alive" (in the textual form itself, as I will suggest) without relegating the text to the status of a score. On the one hand, the vernacular is "more than just an enabling agent" of the literary, certainly; but on the other hand, if much black poetry is distinguished by its "resistance to the rules of genre . . . [and] its absorption of seemingly discontinuous idioms (from classical elegy to collective improvisation)," then it is possible that the specific effect of the blues poem is rooted precisely in its *not* being the "same" as the vernacular blues.[21] When we recognize the quite complex technical accomplishment of Hughes's poem (e.g., the comma after "lonely" in the repeated verse of the first stanza; the added "O" in the second stanza; or the "what/Can" shifting from its initial enjambed position to "What can" in the repetition), it seems clear that it is a reduction of the poem to relegate it to the status of a song lyric. It demands to be considered as much a formal *transcription* of a performance (again, a "recording," in Ellison's sense) as a *score* to be realized. Perhaps the power of the blues poem as a form is intimately linked to the fact that we are *not* offered a realization; the performance setting and musical backdrop are absent or unavailable.

James Weldon Johnson's prefaces explicitly attempt to theorize such issues. In the preface to the second edition of the *Book of American Negro Spirituals*, Johnson makes the rather extraordinary claim that "the recent emergence of a younger group of Negro artists, preponderantly literary, zealous to be racial, or to put it better, determined to be true to themselves, to look for their art material within rather than without, got its first impulse, I believe, from the new evaluation of the Spirituals reached by the Negro himself."[22] In what is barely concealed self-congratulation, Johnson places his own work as a collector of vernacular spirituals at the vanguard of the emerging *literary* approach to the vernacular of writers such as Langston Hughes and later Zora Neale Hurston and Sterling Brown. To come to terms with the depth of Johnson's theoretical work on the issue of transcribing vernacular form, then, it seems necessary to extend a consideration of Johnson's

"The Creative Genius of the Negro" from the *Book of American Negro Poetry* in order to take into account Johnson's equally ambitious prefaces to the *Books of American Negro Spirituals* in 1925 and 1926 and to his own 1927 collection of "seven Negro sermons in verse," *God's Trombones.*

It should be noted that the *Books of American Negro Spirituals* do not represent a significant advance in the debate around the Negro spirituals then raging among critics. As Johnson himself repeatedly notes (BANS I 14, 23, 48), his argument that the spirituals are original products of the Negro and moreover an example of an African survival is largely influenced by the ground-breaking work of Krehbiel and later Curtis-Burlin.[23] The *American Negro Spirituals* collections were celebrated, though, not only because they were published with a major press, close on the heels of the *Book of American Negro Poetry*, or because the musical arrangements by J. Rosamond Johnson and Lawrence Brown are of such high quality; their success is also rooted in the authority of Johnson's prefaces as a major intervention in the drive to document black modernity.

As in *The Autobiography of an Ex-Colored Man*, however, the ultimate aim is not sociological or musicological, despite the categorical and documentary claims Johnson makes at times. Even as the prefaces argue powerfully that "the Spirituals possess the fundamental characteristics of African music" (BANS I 19) and moreover present a continuum joining the modes of black popular expressive culture, from the spirituals, to secular music (30–31), to work songs and shouts (32–33), to dancing (BANS II 16) and the blues (20), they do not strive to prove some simple empirical connection between African and African-American music. Throughout this process of connection and differentiation, Johnson carefully employs a complex series of metaphors so as to complicate any seeming filiation into a relationship more—as he puts it—"subtle and elusive" (BANS I 29). Johnson repeatedly writes of the "body of the Spirituals," for instance (12, 15), and then extends this metaphor: "it was by sheer spiritual forces that African chants were metamorphosed into the Spirituals; that upon the fundamental throb of African rhythms were reared those reaches of melody that rise above earth and soar into the pure, ethereal blue" (21). If the spirituals are an African body, Johnson implies, then that body has somewhere, somehow undergone a miraculous transformation.

In this light, it is not without significance that Johnson opens his consideration of the origins of the spirituals with his own poem "O Black and Unknown Bards" (first published in 1908 in *The Century*), to ask about the "miracle" and "wonder" of the spirituals, to open the question of origins with a series of metaphors: "O black and unknown bards of long ago,/How came your lips to touch the sacred fire? . . ." (12) From this opening epigraph, Johnson seems to be asking about the process of such a "metamorphosis," such a beginning. And, significantly, he asks it with a poem, thereby immediately extending the province of his analysis from the "new evaluation of the Spirituals reached by the Negro himself" to the *literature* that evaluation inspired. In other words, the suggestion is that the preface strives to provide an understanding of transcription, of the "metamorphosis" from music and song into written poetry.

Nonetheless, oddly enough, Johnson's quite sophisticated and wholly unprecedented work has been read mainly as a position on so-called dialect poetry. Johnson is usually portrayed as the stilted aesthetic aristocrat who famously declared "Negro dialect" to be utterly defunct as a representational strategy, "an instrument with but two full stops, humor and pathos" (41), and who just as famously was proven wrong by the explosion of works in dialect at the end of the decade, in poetry by Hughes and Brown (both of whom were included in the 1931 expanded edition of Johnson's *Book of American Negro Poetry*) and in fiction by Hurston. This simplistic critique does not catch the real emphasis of Johnson's words: he argues quite explicitly that the younger poets are "trying to break away from, not Negro dialect itself, but the limitations on Negro dialect imposed by the fixing effects of long convention" (41). Nor does it come to terms with Johnson's active promotion of the poetry of Hughes and Claude McKay (even the 1922 edition of *The Book of American Negro Poetry* includes "Two an' Six," a selection from McKay's early Jamaican dialect poems) or his own efforts at "sermonic poetry" in *God's Trombones*. And it is often overlooked that Johnson's contribution to the *Book of American Negro Spirituals* is an ambitious *literary* project: as he notes, he is carefully composing the lyrics to the spirituals in dialect, attempting to avoid the "unintelligible," "clumsy, outlandish, so-called phonetic spelling" which had characterized too much writing in that mode (42–46). In this regard, it seems much more judicious to recognize the great complexity and influence of Johnson's creative and theoretical work on the subject. Although others, most notably W. E. B. Du Bois and Charles Chesnutt, had found inspiration in African-American vernacular forms, Johnson was the first, with the publication of "The Creation" in 1918 (later collected in *God's Trombones*), to attempt to transcribe a vernacular form—the folk sermon—into a literary work.

A concern with the transcription of African-American folk forms echoes throughout Johnson's work, from *The Autobiography of an Ex-Colored Man* to the *Book of American Negro Spirituals* and *God's Trombones*. Indeed, the extent to which black musical performance continually informs, and even frames, his approach to black modernity has not been fully recognized. In his autobiography, *Along This Way*, for example, Johnson notes that he was inspired to write his poem "The Creation," when hearing an "old-time Negro preacher." But he describes the process of "transcribing" a vernacular form into a literary work by invoking the "similarity" of *musical* composition (possibly thinking of Dvořák's 1893 "New World" Symphony?):

> I felt that this primitive stuff could be used in a way similar to that in which a composer makes use of a folk theme in writing a major composition. I believed that the characteristic qualities: imagery, color, abandon, sonorous diction, syncopated rhythms, and native idioms, could be preserved and, at the same time, the composition as a whole be enlarged beyond the circumference of mere race, and given universality. . . . My aim was to interpret what was in [the old-time Negro preacher's] mind, to express, if possible, the dream to which, despite limitations, he strove to give utterance. I chose

a loose rhythmic instead of a strict metric form, because it was the first only that could accommodate itself to the movement, the abandon, the changes of tempo, and the characteristic syncopations of the primitive material.[24]

Critical notions of orality have been consistently teleological: it is supposed that one "progresses" from orality to literacy, with the written text betraying nostalgia for or an echo of the oral. Johnson does admittedly preserve this teleological conception and its concomitant valuation of written literature as more important than oral culture, but without ignoring this prejudice, we should note the complex conception of black aesthetic form, and of transcription from one form into another, envisioned here. What interests me is the peculiar intrusion of a musical trope into Johnson's description of the compositional process. The transcription of folk material into written form is *like* the music composer's "use of a folk theme" in a symphony. In Johnson's work on poetics, there is almost never a description of a direct transmission from the oral to the written: almost always, the figure of music intercedes. Music as a metaphor seems a necessary mediating element in the process of linguistic transcription.

Johnson insists that the transcription of the spirituals in the *Book of American Negro Spirituals* is "true" to the *form* of that music: "No changes have been made in the form of songs," he claims, even when harmonizations have been "developed" (50). He describes the form as inherently cross-cultural or syncretic, supporting the argument in favor of African retentions in the spirituals but refusing to underestimate the European influence: "there was blown through or fused into the vestiges of his African music the spirit of Christianity as he knew Christianity. . . . It was by sheer spiritual forces that African chants were metamorphosed into the Spirituals" (20–21). The shape change at the origin of the spirituals is left vague here; either the Christian influence "blows" a kind of vitality into the seemingly passive primary material of the "African vestiges," or the two are "fused," or there is an unspecified "spiritual" agency that brings about a transformation. Although authorship is granted without reserve to "unknown black bards" (and this alone is an important political stance on the issue of black folk originality), the question of origins is left relatively open, as it is in the epigraph, Johnson's "O Black and Unknown Bards."

In that poem, the "wide wonder" of the spirituals is situated on two levels; it is first a somewhat ethnographic wonder ("who was he/That breathed that comforting, melodic sigh,/'Nobody knows de trouble I see'?"), but it is also what we might term a *formal* wonder, at the fact that the music is what Jay Wright would call a "distributive form" of an ungraspable "spirit,"[25] capturing the sacred:

> What merely living clod, what captive thing,
> Could up toward God through all its darkness grope,
> And find within its deadened heart to sing
> These songs of sorrow, love and faith, and hope?
>
> How did it catch that subtle undertone,
> That note in music heard not with the ears?

> How sound the elusive reed so seldom blown,
> Which stirs the soul or melts the heart to tears?

In this last stanza the personal pronoun *he* (referring to a particular originator) is abandoned for a curious *it*. Readers have generally assumed that in the phrases "merely living clod" and "captive thing" Johnson is describing the same slave "black bards" as in the first two stanzas. But the intrusion of an impersonal pronoun might point us in a different direction: the poem might be invoking the work of the musical form itself, not necessarily linked to a human agency. In a fascinating formulation, music again enters Johnson's work as a metaphor—paradoxically, as a metaphor for what is "elusive" in music! And even in this description of a wholly vernacular process, there is again an implied *transcription* at play here, as in the Ellison passage that opens this section: the "it" somehow "catches" or records (in form? in voice?) that "subtle undertone" of "soul," or the sacred, not as Henderson's empirically verifiable "saturation," but as an "elusive" presence of unheard music within the heard music of the spirituals. "He" (the "black bard") sings, and simultaneously "it" (the song form itself) metaphorically "sings," and this figure of music stands in for what is different, for the discursive "catching" of what is "elusive" (what is *not* "catchable") in the music itself.

In the text of the preface, Johnson continues this argument that what is exceptional about the spirituals is closely related to what is "elusive" about them. And for that "elusive reed," he turns to a discussion of the music. Johnson's tack is in accord with most of the writings on black vernacular forms of the period, which continually lamented black music's stubborn resistance to the European system of tonal and rhythmic notation. But Johnson, instead of complaining about the difficulty of "catching" the music properly as it is performed in vernacular traditions, takes the wholly revolutionary approach of eschewing any pretense to notational precision: "in their very nature they are not susceptible to fixation" (30). He on the contrary posits the "elusive" quality of the spirituals as exactly what must be transcribed. This pushes the transcription toward its necessary future realization in a performance; it is incomplete on the page, and the performer must "play what is not written down" (28). But a "true" transcription is possible for Johnson; it is one in which the transcriptional form somehow "catches" what it cannot represent notationally. And he says that this elusiveness of black music is based in its *rhythm*, in the form's dynamic of "swing." This masterful passage is the most often quoted part of the essay:

> The "swing" of the spirituals is an altogether subtle and elusive thing. It is subtle and elusive because it is in perfect union with the religious ecstasy that manifests itself in the swaying bodies of a whole congregation, swaying as if responding to the baton of some extremely sensitive conductor. . . . It is the more subtle and elusive because there is a still further intricacy in the rhythms. This swaying of the body marks the regular beat or, better, surge, for it is something stronger than a beat, and is more or less, not precisely, strict in time; but the Negro loves nothing better in his music than to play with the fundamental time beat. He will, as it were, take the fundamental

beat and pound it out with his left hand, almost monotonously; while with his right hand he juggles it. . . . In listening to Negroes sing their own music it is often tantalizing and even exciting to watch a minute fraction of a beat balancing for a slight instant on the bar between two measures, and, when it seems almost too late, drop back into its own proper compartment.

(28–30)

To use his own word, it is with a brilliantly "subtle" touch here that Johnson anticipates a point about the appropriation of vernacular material that Amiri Baraka would enunciate nearly thirty years later in an essay called "Swing—From Verb to Noun." Johnson places the noun *swing* in quotation marks but does not mark off the gerund or verb form of this word ("swings," or "swinging"; also "swaying"). This indicates that *swing* is a neologism (like *jazz*) emergent at the time, but it also indicates that *swing* is somehow tainted or inaccurate: it noun-ifies *swinging*, stilling the "elusive" and performative connotations of what is in its verb form a paradigmatic black cultural *action* or *process*.[26] This is not solely a racially determined appropriation, "the erasure of black inventiveness by white appropriation," as Baraka would have it; Johnson appears to mark the danger of his own transcription project in this gesture.[27] Appropriation is a threat also articulated in class—in effect, class inflected across race. Thus, for example, in Toni Morrison's *Sula*, the black congregation "sways" in mourning during Chicken Little's funeral, but Nel's oppressive and elitist mother Helene "holds sway" (thus metaphorically stopping or controlling the motion) over the community, winning "all social battles with presence and a conviction of the legitimacy of her authority."[28] One might even say that, just as the middle ground form of ragtime is crucial to his investigations of cultural passing in *The Autobiography of an Ex-Colored Man*, here in his theory of transcription Johnson is striving for a middle ground as well between the verb and noun forms of *swing*—one which he seems to want to find in the gerund *swinging*.

Johnson describes this swinging rhythm as being intimately connected to, or performed in, the black body. (He goes on to describe the difference between the spirituals and the work songs and blues as residing in the placement of the "fundamental swing" in the performing body; not surprisingly, secular music gets down further, positioning the beat in a "patting of hands and feet" as compared to the "swaying heads and bodies" of the spirituals.) He places great importance in what Zora Neale Hurston would later call the physical "mechanics" of black performance as a ground for this motion.[29] In fact, he seems to prefer the word *swaying* to *swinging* in this passage exactly because it implies a rhythm located in the body. But the performer is not the initiator of this motion, apparently: the swing is *in* the body, it "manifests" itself there, but its source is once more elusive. He can only describe it by resorting (yet again) to a musical metaphor: the congregation sways "*as if* responding to the baton of some extremely sensitive conductor."

The main struggle in the passage, its moments of hesitation and uncertainty, revolve around the issue of describing an expressly black *time* implicated in the swing of the spirituals. It is this insight that Johnson carries with him to his own composition of "The Creation"; hearing the "old-time Negro preacher" helps him to realize that the "inner secret" of black oratory is its " 'timing': that is, in the ability of the speaker to set up a series of rhythmic emotional vibrations between himself and his hearers" (AW 338). In his preface, Johnson wants to provide the consolation of a "regular" and "fundamental" beat, but his syntax stammers and betrays him: "The swaying of the body marks the regular beat or, better, surge, for it is something stronger than a beat, and is more or less, not precisely, strict in time; but . . ." In effect, though, it is this stammer that most closely approximates in literary form the bodily transfer with which swing manifests itself, as the musician "juggles" the beat, as it is "playfully bandied from hand to foot and from foot to hand" (BANS I 31). Swing is above all this physical hesitation, this continuing transfer. The rhythm is never lost, but it is never held or captured in the body either: it divides itself into "fractions," it parcels itself out, jumping from hand to foot, "pounding" and "monotonous" in one hand, "juggled" in the other, and neither "beat" nor "surge" is really acceptable as a term because the swinging never settles. It is the "play" of this hesitation that makes the swing of black rhythm elusive. And although Johnson considers the harmony of the vernacular spirituals to be quite controlled and sophisticated (unlike Hurston, who speaks of "jagged harmony"),[30] the same principle of elusive swing is at work in black melodic invention: "In addition, there are the curious turns and twists and quavers and the intentional striking of certain notes just a shade off key" (BANS I 30).

Just as this swing is manifested in the black body, it also has a metaphorical physical effect on those who would "fix" or notate it. The elusive nature of swing "constitute[s] a *handicap*" for many collectors. But, again, for Johnson, this is not a failing in black vernacular culture; in fact, a rhythmic swing linked to its manifestation in a bodily juggling or transfer is behind all American popular musical forms: "this innate characteristic of the Negro in America is the genesis and foundation of our national popular medium for musical expression" (31). In Johnson's metaphorology of the body, the accession of swing to a *national* status is the process of the rhythmic black body relentlessly invading the body of "White America." White America, he writes, has "pretty well mastered the difficulty" of getting the swing of black music because "the Negro has been beating these rhythms in its ears for three hundred years" (28). Again, there is a grammar of appropriation (and perhaps miscegenation) implicit here: white Americans "master" the difficulties of black rhythm; they "*get* the 'swing' of it" (28, emphasis added), not swinging or swaying but possessing the noun-ified form.

Returning to the passage on swing from the *Book of American Negro Spirituals*, one notices that although Johnson is convinced of the bodily nature of swing, he in fact is rather uncertain about the exact dynamic this represents. At first, swing "manifests itself" in the bodies of the *group*, the congregation, and that is its power: that it enforces an elusive group movement, a collective swaying, so unified that it seems conducted by an unseen hand. But as Johnson continues to describe black rhythm, in the second part of the passage, he comes to locate it in the *individual* black body: the beat or surge is "bandied" about a single black body, "juggled" from head to foot and back again. Johnson displays some confusion here as to whether swing is primarily founded in the demonstration of group unity or in the individual physical juggling. Does it surge through one body, or is there a common current that jumps from one body in the congregation to the next or inhabits the entire group *as though* it were a single body, all at once?

Johnson's rhetoric does not decide this question; again, as in the sentence about "beat" and "surge," we read a text that hesitates and wavers, juggling the momentum of its argument. But this should not be surprising, if we read this juggling as an attempt to register the action of swinging itself. The indecision represents a radical possibility for reconceptualizing agency because it turns (in the sense of "trope," of course; it turns a metaphor) not on the foundation of some intentional physical act, or of some communicated black "essence," but on the ground of *form itself*.[31]

When Johnson writes of the (individual/collective) black body, he is not only describing it in an ethnographic sense; he is using it as a *figure* in which to situate black musical swing. What has happened here is that the black body, rather than being locked into some individualized and essentialized notion of agency, has been wrenched out of its phenomenological focus. This is almost always read as a threat, or as an inconsistency. But in this instance, I would suggest, to quote Nathaniel Mackey, that there is a "*telling* inarticulacy" in this inconsistency: an inarticulacy that signifies.[32] When one recognizes that the body is both present (a phenomenological entity) and absent (a discursive figure), one is forced to reenvision the possible relationship between individual and community, between intentional "*activity* as a kind of mechanical process" and "*movement* as something which is rooted in some faculty of the imagination."[33] Thus, in Johnson's conception, agency is twofold: the individual is an agent-as-creator, as an active shaper of culture (the individual juggles swing through his body), and an agent-as-representative, as a part of the collective in which that elusive swaying manifests itself.

It is not by chance that such a reading is possible precisely because Johnson is figuring the musical form of swing. Only form provides the link between these two kinds of agency. Form, we should recognize, is a contradictory force in that it "designates both the principle of universalization and the principle of individuation"; thus it can be mobilized in walking the tightrope between the national and the universal. Form gives particularity to matter: for example, a cup gives form to clay. A body sways, and in that form the body is defined, it is provided with individuation. And at the same time it unifies disparate entities: paper cups, glass cups, china cups, and clay cups are all cups because of their common form. When we say that a group of people are swaying, they are unified through that common form.[34] If vernacular form is concerned with remembrance, as Ellison argues ("keep[ing] the painful details . . . alive"), then Johnson offers the stimulating possibility of seeing that task as juggled between the swaying members (limbs) of the individual body and the unified, swaying members of the congregation. We are here in much more subtle depths than "call and response."

Furthermore, in this notion of musical form being situated in a *figure* of the body, there are the birth pangs of a theory of vernacular transcription. The task is to transfer that elusive swing from the performed vernacular into some written record. But to represent swing in the semantics of a notation is to fix it, to noun-ify it, and so Johnson transfers instead the figure of an individual/collective body. To put it simply: *Vernacular musical form is transcribed through a figure of the black body*. Johnson locates swing in the body, and so he turns to a metaphorology of the body to locate that same body (and, by implication, its elusive swing) in the transcribed spirituals, and in his own text. First, we note Johnson referring to the transcribed spirituals as a body that somehow preserves its elusive swing: with a telling pun, he writes that the transcriptions are true to the vernacular form, because the "songs . . . have not been cut up or 'opera-ated' upon" (BANS I 50). Second, we note a continual series of implications that the written text itself must take on or mimic the form of a body. Not only does the preface turn to the rhetorical and syntactical stammering discussed above, but Johnson moreover moves into a brief discussion of dialect, and there he locates dialect, like swing, as an elusive bodily presence: "Nor is the generally spoken Negro dialect the fixed thing it is made to be on the printed page. It is variable and fluid. Not even in the dialect of any particular section is a given word always pronounced the same. It may vary slightly in the next breath in the mouth of the same speaker" (43).

How does Johnson apply this theory to his own lyrical transcriptions of the "old-time Negro preacher" in *God's Trombones?*[35] He writes in his autobiography, *Along This Way*, that his musical work with the spirituals inspires him to go back to the eight-year-old "The Creation" and complete the project by writing the book's six other "sermons in verse" (AW 336). Again, Johnson makes recourse to a metaphor of music in his discussions of transmission between the oral and the written. We should recall that his famous condemnation of conventional dialect depends on such a metaphor: dialect is an organ with but "two stops," humor and pathos. Here, in attempting to compose sermons in verse that would go beyond dialect, Johnson concocts another musical metaphor:

> Next to writing "The Crucifixion," my greatest difficulty was in finding a title for the book. I toyed and experimented with at least twenty tentative titles. I narrowed them down to *Listen, Lord*; *Cloven Tongues*; *Tongues of Fire*; and *Trumpets of the Lord*, or *Trumpeters of the Lord*. I liked the last two titles, but saw that "Trumpets" or "Trumpeters" would be a poetic cliché. Suddenly, I lit upon "trombone." The trombone, according to the Standard Dictionary, is: "A powerful brass instrument of the trumpet family, the only wind instrument possessing a chromatic scale enharmonically in tune, like the human voice or the violin, and hence very valuable in the orchestra." I had found it, the instrument and the word, of just the tone and timbre to represent the old-time Negro preacher's voice.   (AW 377–78)

There is no music in the sermon itself, of course. Here, Johnson is looking for a musical figure of vocalization, which by pointing the reader to black musical form will imply the performative context of the sermon and remain true to that elusive quality in the vernacular that he cannot notate.

The trombone is a remarkable choice. Johnson is evidently pleased that the trombone is an instrument that is capable of imitating the human voice: in depicting a vernacular mode that in its ecstatic cadences approaches a wordless music ("pure incoherencies," in Johnson's words [AW 377]), he turns to a musical instrument that approaches human speech. Since Johnson considers black oratory to be concerned most importantly with timing, here he again attempts to represent it using the figure of the elusive swing that characterizes black vernacular time. Now, though, he works not through rhetorical or syntactical stammering but by a semantic juggling: he finds both "the instrument and the word," because the trombone is an instrument that swings "undecided" between two forms (language and music).[36]

He goes on to note that the trombone has "traditional jazz connotations," and he may even have had in mind a performer of the period, such as Joe "Tricky Sam" Nanton, the trombonist renowned for his skill in imitating the human voice with the plunger and wah-wah mutes who played with Duke Ellington's band from the summer of 1926 until July 1946. Ellington described Nanton's contribution as bringing a different black jazz style to the orchestra:

> What [Tricky] was actually doing was playing a very highly personalized form of his West Indian heritage. When a guy comes here from the West Indies and is asked to play some jazz, he plays what *he* thinks it is, or what comes from his applying himself to the idiom. Tricky and his people were deep in the West Indian legacy and the Marcus Garvey movement. A whole strain of West Indian musicians came up who made contributions to the so-called jazz scene, and they were all virtually descended from the true African scene. It's the same now with the Muslim movement, and a lot of West Indian people are involved in it. There are many resemblances to the Marcus Garvey schemes. Bop, I once said, is the Marcus Garvey extension.[37]

Jazz as a form for Ellington recapitulates the same complex conception of subtly diasporic, individual/collective cultural agency that I noted above in Johnson's description of swing. And this take is inherently political: the notion of artistic creation as a dialogue becomes a principle not simply of individual/community collaboration but also of black diasporic collaboration, and that collaboration is always political: an "extension" of "schemes" of return. So, even in the relatively national, single-language project of *God's Trombones*, the rhetoric moves beyond the romanticized vision of the African diaspora that Edward Kamau Brathwaite has called "rhetorical Africa";[38] here, as in the preface to *The Book of American Negro Poetry*, there is a hint of a move afield.

Although Johnson attempts to catch that elusive swing in the title of *God's Trombones*, he fails to go as far as he might to this end in the poems themselves. The poems, however, are not just "translations from the vernacular into standard English."[39] While Johnson does not utilize the orthographic techniques of dialect writing, he also does not consider his compositions standard in any sense: he attempts to indicate "the tempos of the preacher . . . by the line arrangement of the poems, and a certain sort of pause that is marked by a quick intaking and an audible expulsion of the breath I have indicated by dashes. There is a decided syncopation of speech—the crowding in of many syllables or the lengthening out of a few to fill one metrical foot, the sensing of which must be left to the reader's ear" (GT 10–11). The revolutionary possibility that opens up here is that Johnson could discard the mediating figure of music: he begins to toy with the technique of transferring the swing from the vernacular, performing black body or bodies into the very formal body of the poem; in the manipulations of line, measure, and punctuation, the poem itself begins to be sketched out as a "breathing," "syncopating" body.

It is Langston Hughes, of course, who extends this possibility into a true compositional strategy. From "The Weary Blues" (the 1925 poem that Johnson himself read as the winner at the awards banquet for the *Opportunity* magazine poetry contest) into the more strict "blues poems" of *The Weary Blues* (1926) and *Fine Clothes to the Jew* (1927), Hughes perfects the deceptively simple technique of formal mimicry: his work attempts to suggest in its literary structure (stanza, line, rhyme, stress accent) the form of the vernacular (urban) blues.

George Kent, among many others, complained that Hughes's "blues poems" are impoverished compared to the performed vernacular blues, because they lack the context of the blues performance (music, audience, and above all the blues voice) and because Hughes makes no real innovation in the blues form when he uses it on the page.[40] But formal mimicry *is* the innovation. There is a problem here of two divergent mediums, two kinds of matter: the musical form of the blues, which is generally linked to the medium of sound, is here articulated in the form of a poem in written language. And how is this achieved? Not by the poem's "rhythm"; as another poet greatly influenced by African-American vernacular forms, William Carlos Williams, would later recognize, it is inaccurate to speak of "rhythm" in a poem.[41] One *can* however validly speak of "measure"; Williams makes recourse to such a term (as with Zukofsky's mathematics), because in poetry this formal mimicry relies on the quantifiable use of spacing and distance in the form of the poem to represent musical form.[42] We are not provided a musical backdrop when we read a blues poem; part of the way we recognize it is by seeing the stanza structure, the rhyme (and the words themselves, which are intimately involved in a formal dynamic: blues conventions of image or address have formal as well as semantic value). Sight is forced to infer an absent sound, in other words. And this effect sketches out a body of the poem; thus Robert Duncan refers to a "muscular correlation" of the poem, or Edward Kamau Brathwaite writes of the "body-work" of African diasporic poetry based on vernacular forms, or Monchoachi, a Martiniquan poet who writes in Creole, instructs that "it is essential to 'pass one's body' " through the form of the poem.[43] There is no intervening figure in this process. The figure of music no longer mediates between forms, as in Johnson's prefaces, but now simply describes the similarly elusive nature of both forms from the perspective of the listener/viewer or reader.

There is thus a "mood of distance"[44] in the blues poem, not only in the blues' thematic concerns with mobility and longing but also arising out of its formal mimicry. Henri Focillon, in a delicate and thoughtful book on "the life of forms" in the arts, writes that "an identical form keeps its dimensions, but changes its quality according to the material, the tools and the hand. . . . A form without support is not a form, and the support itself is form."[45] In the blues poem we encounter not a form without a support but a form that has been transferred from one support to another. And part of the special effect of the blues poem is that the effect of this transfer is legible: it leaves a trace; the form "changes its quality" when its original support is missing. One might say that in the blues poem there is an apostrophe of form: the vernacular blues form calls out to its distant prop or support.

It is a bit strange to speak of an apostrophe of form; apostrophe, one of the characteristic tropes of the lyric, is traditionally considered to be a discursive mechanism, not a formal one. The passionate address in a poem to an inanimate or mute entity ("O Nature!"), apostrophe is a trope that serves to constitute the speaker of the poem by situating his or her voice. Some have argued that the gesture of apostrophe is the paradigmatic gesture of subjectivity in the lyric.[46] The poetic address, appearing to invoke a You, actually "pre-empts the space of the you" in the end since it is directed at an object that cannot respond. This cements the lyric's status as a monologic form, a form characterized by the speaking subject's "withdrawal," a discursive subjectivity of internalization and even solipsism (c 66). In blues poetry there is a similar lyric withdrawal (one thinks of the limitless addresses to an absent lover in the blues and of Billie Holiday's "Good Morning Heartache"). So Culler's description of the discursive emphasis of the lyric is useful: "In lyrics this kind of a temporal problem is posed: something once present has been lost or attenuated; this loss can be narrated but the temporal sequence is irreversible, like time itself. Apostrophes displace this irreversible structure by removing the opposition between presence and absence from empirical time and locating it in discursive time" (c 67). In the blues poem, there is still this discursive effect but also a concomitant displacement from empirical time (the empirical time of the vernacular blues performance) into what might be termed "formal time."

When form "speaks" in this manner in the European lyric, it is usually considered to be a grave threat to discursive subjectivity; thus De Man has written of a "*piétinement* [stomping] of aimless enumeration" in Baudelaire's poem "Correspondances" where the necessity of trope undermines the lyric's quality of chanson, its "claim of being song."[47] But in a blues poem, the formal apostrophe, and its tension with the discursive apostrophe, is privileged. The blues poem *both* calls out to an "absent lover" *and* calls out to an absent music, its missing chord changes, and the two apostrophes are set in an uneasy, jagged coexistence. Since the discursive workings of the blues poem are part of its form, part of what makes the blues a lyric mode, what we encounter here is in fact a kind of stammering in the poetic form itself.

In effect, this double apostrophe in the blues poem is a radical strategic response to the version of subjectivity inscribed in the traditional lyric, which has always had treacherous implications for a black poetic practice. The lyric is not a timeless, universal form; it is marked by history—and its history couches a threat to the enunciation of black subjectivity. In Nathaniel Mackey's words, there is a "predicament of subjectivity in the lyric that we inherit within a Western tradition which has legacies of domination and conquest and moral complication that make [its] claims to subjectivity and sublimity hard to countenance."[48] The blues poem opens a new window on the problem of subjectivity by formally taking advantage of a "heterodox lyric tradition in the West": that of black vernacular forms. It becomes impossible to read the blues lyric as a discourse of individualization and internalization; one is forced to read the poem as a tension between a transcription (the musical apostrophe) and a performance (the discursive apostrophe).

The implications of this formal development are not at all limited to an African diasporic literary tradition, though. Northrup Frye offers a schematic history of developments in lyric form as it moves through four stages: classical *melos*-dominated lyric; the *opsis* of romantic lyric, announced by Wordsworth's "low mimetic" preface to the *Lyrical Ballads*; and the "ironic manifesto" of Poe's "The Poetic Principle" in 1850 (which, of course, had an incalculable impact on the French symbolists). Frye sees the "free verse" of the twentieth century as an extension of this "third period."[49] But the development of blues poetry in the 1920s inaugurates yet another period, in which the lyric is linked once more to contemporary and popular musical forms (especially blues and jazz, a principle extended in the *son* of Nicolas Guillen, the *cante jondo* of Garcia Lorca, and the calypso of Brathwaite).

The aesthetic envisioned in this *fourth* lyric form, then, is rooted in the swing of what one anonymous former slave, in describing the origin of the spirituals, called a "mixtery": "Dese spirituals am de best moanin' music in de world, case dey is de whole Bible sung out and out. Notes is good enough for you people, but us likes a mixtery."[50] This passage has been often quoted, and many have "corrected" the anthropologist's dialect transcription of *mixtery*, saying that the former slave is "really" pronouncing *mystery*. This fits into a paradigm that reads the transcription of black vernacular material as always structured around some silence, some hidden or masked original oral content, and is of a piece with the romanticized nostalgia for the oral that I discussed earlier.[51] But I prefer the idea that we are encountering (even in transcription) a provocative neologism here, which holds itself between *mystery* and *mixture*. What is being mixed, though? This could be a point about notation; the folklorist attempts to catch the "moanin' " of the spirituals, but the music's "mixtery" (a frustrating mix of notes in the tempered scale and notes "just a shade off-key") makes it impossible.[52] But there is also a point about the relationship between the oral and the written. The spirituals are a vernacular form but not a pure oral one: they are based on the texts of the Bible "sung out and out." The speaker espouses a mix of musical notes and Biblical texts and a mystery about the primacy of the music or the words. And that swing between the written and the oral is caught, and juggled, in the word *mixtery* itself. The transcription of vernacular musical forms into written linguistic forms necessarily alters our conception of literacy, but it must alter our conception of orality as well.

Wilson Harris once wrote that "the community the writer shares with the primordial dancer is, as it were, the complementary halves of a broken stage."[53] Many have noted this vision of an intimacy between the writer and the vernacular artist (notably, in terms of staged performance). But the word that has always struck me here is *broken*: an inexorable separation—what Harris would call an abyss—is inherent in this vision of community. "Broken" does not have to be a signpost of defeat, of dispossession for the literary artist, though. The task is to represent the elusive nature of that broken but intimate (shared) community.

Such a stance does not represent debilitating indecision but productive ambivalence. Indeed, Johnson's complex elaboration of what Hurston calls a "singing . . . that had nothing to do with [the] ears" may be read as an impossibly early response to Paul Gilroy's call, in *The Black Atlantic*, for a consideration of black musical expression's role in a counterculture of modernity. Gilroy says that "the power of music in developing black struggles . . . demands attention to both the formal attributes of this expressive culture and its distinctive *moral* basis. The formal qualities of this music are becoming better known, and I want to concentrate instead on the moral aspects and in particular on the disjunction between the ethical value of the music and its status as an ethnic sign."[54] But Johnson refuses such a dichotomy between form and content. Unlike Gilroy, Johnson locates the "ethical value of the music" precisely in its "formal qualities"; he reads the "subtle and elusive" swing inherent in black musical forms as providing a model for black communal production that goes beyond call and response. The ethical value of black music is that it transforms belongingness and creative originality into a quality that can never be simply owned or possessed; its roots are swung back and forth in the form itself. Form fingers that jagged grain.

NOTES

1. Kimberly Benston, "Performing Blackness: Re/Placing Afro-American Poetry," in *Afro-American Literary Study in the 1990's,* ed. Houston A. Baker, Jr. (Chicago, 1989), 167.

2. Edward Kamau Brathwaite, "Vèvè," *Islands* (1969), collected in *The Arrivants: A New World Trilogy* (London, 1973).

3. James Weldon Johnson, "The Creative Genius of the Negro," preface to *The Book of American Negro Poetry,* ed. James Weldon Johnson (1922; 2d ed., New York, 1931), 9.

4. Zora Neale Hurston, *Their Eyes Were Watching God* (1937; reprint, Urbana, 1978), 23–24.

5. Aldon Nielsen, *Black Chant: Languages of African-American Postmodernism* (New York, 1997), 34. See also Nathaniel Mackey, *Discrepant Engagement: Dissonance, Cross-Culturality, and Experimental Writing* (New York, 1993); Harryette Mullen, "African Signs and Spirit Writing," *Callaloo* 19, no. 3 (1996): 670–89.

6. This essay is a section of a larger argument about prefaces, in which I suggest that the explosion of anthologies and prefaced works on "Negro" subjects in the 1920s marked an effort to define and frame black culture, an effort that becomes central to the formulation of Western modernity in general. On the one hand, the larger argument juxtaposes works such as James Weldon Johnson's *The Autobiography of an Ex-Colored Man* and *The Book of American Negro Poetry,* Claude McKay's *Harlem Shadows,* Blaise Cendrars's *Anthologie Nègre,* and René Maran's *Batouala* to point out that such a struggle is transatlantic and that even when seemingly limited to a particular nation-

space, such prefaces consistently involve a vision of an African diaspora stretching beyond nation and language. On the other hand, the larger work considers the politics of such framing gestures and suggests that to a large degree they operate on the level of form, using the relationship between preface and text to represent and situate black expressive culture to various ends.

7. Ralph Ellison, "Richard Wright's Blues," in *Shadow and Act* (New York, 1964), 78.

8. Louis Zukofsky, "A Statement for Poetry" (1930), in *Prepositions* (Berkeley, 1981), 19.

9. Northrup Frye, *Anatomy of Criticism* (Princeton, 1957), 258–62.

10. Louis Zukofsky, "An Objective" (1930–31), in *Prepositions* (Berkeley, 1981), 16.

11. Sterling Brown, "The Blues as Folk Poetry," in *Folk-Say: A Regional Miscellany*, ed. B. A. Botkin (Norman, Okla., 1930), 335.

12. Langston Hughes, *Fine Clothes to the Jew* (New York, 1927), 83.

13. Benston, "Performing Blackness," 165.

14. See Jacques Derrida, "Signature Event Context," in *Margins of Philosophy*, trans. Alan Bass (Chicago, 1982), 307–30.

15. See Slavoj Zizek, *Tarrying with the Negative: Kant, Hegel, and the Critique of Ideology* (Durham, 1993), 135; and Henri Focillon, *The Life of Forms in Art* (1934), trans. Charles B. Hogan and George Kubler (New York, 1989), 34–35.

16. Eric Sundquist, *To Wake the Nations: Race in the Making of American Literature* (Cambridge, 1993), 309–11.

17. Sherley Anne Williams, "The Blues Roots of Contemporary Afro-American Poetry," in *Afro-American Literature: The Reconstruction of Instruction*, ed. Dexter Fisher and Robert Stepto (New York, 1979), 72.

18. Henry Louis Gates, Jr., "Literary Theory and the Black Tradition," in *Figures in Black: Words, Signs, and the "Racial" Self* (New York, 1987), 34.

19. Stephen Henderson, *Understanding the New Black Poetry: Black Speech and Black Music as Poetic References* (New York, 1973), 61. It should be noted that Henderson adopts the title of his introduction, "The Forms of Things Unknown," from Richard Wright's work on the blues. But whereas Wright is fascinated with the elusiveness of black expressive culture, Henderson attempts empirically to fix and formalize "black art"; he strives to enumerate those unknown things.

20. Benston, "Performing Blackness," 167.

21. Ibid., 183, 184.

22. James Weldon Johnson and J. Rosamond Johnson, eds., *The Books of American Negro Spirituals* (vol. I, 1925; vol. II, 1926), in a single-volume reprint (New York, 1940), 2:19. Hereafter referred to as BANS I and BANS II.

23. Henry Edward Krehbiel, *Afro-American Folksongs: A Study in Racial and National Music* (New York, 1913); Natalie Curtis-Burlin, *Hampton Series of Negro Folk-Songs*, in 4 books (New York, 1918). The other most important work on the spirituals from a musicological standpoint was published around the same time as Johnson's collection: Nicholas Ballanta-Taylor, *Saint Helena Island Spirituals* (New York, 1925). For criticism on the debates around the origins of the Negro spiritual, see D. K. Wilgus, "Appendix: The Negro-White Spiritual," *Anglo-American Folksong Scholarship Since 1898* (New Brunswick, 1959), 345–407. Wilgus considers Johnson's anthologies on 349, 351.

24. James Weldon Johnson, *Along This Way* (New York, 1933), 335–36. Hereafter referred to as AW.

25. Jay Wright, "Desire's Design, Vision's Resonance: Black Poetry's Ritual and Historical

Voice," *Callaloo* 10, no. 1 (winter 1987): 21.

26. See Leroi Jones (Amiri Baraka), "Swing—From Verb to Noun," in *Blues People* (New York, 1963), 142–65; Mackey, "Other: From Noun to Verb," in *Discrepant Engagement*, 265–86.

27. Mackey, "Other: From Noun to Verb," 266.

28. Toni Morrison, *Sula* (1973; reprint, New York, 1982), 35, 18.

29. Zora Neale Hurston, "Spirituals and Neo-Spirituals" (1934), in *The Sanctified Church* (Berkeley, 1983), 81–82.

30. Johnson, BANS I 35–36; Hurston, "Spirituals and Neo-Spirituals," 80.

31. Eric Sundquist, among others, reads such uncertainty as failure. For Sundquist, Johnson's rhetoric "unites populism and elitism," shuffling between the two. One moment, Johnson writes that "whatever new thing the *people* like is pooh-poohed; whatever is *popular* is spoken of as not worth the while. The fact is, nothing great or enduring, especially in music, has ever sprung full-fledged and unprecedented from the brain of any master; the best that he gives to the world he gathers from the hearts of the people, and runs it through the alembic of his genius" (Johnson, *Autobiography of an Ex-Colored Man* [1912; reprint, New York, 1990], 73). And then he turns the other way, emphasizing the *individual* creators of the spirituals rather than the masses, like "Ma" White and "Singing" Johnson (BANS I?? 21 ff.). Sundquist characterizes this wavering as a "residual aesthetic distrust of the folk" in Johnson; see *Hammers of Creation: Folk Culture in Modern African-American Fiction* (Athens, Ga., 1992), 24. I am suggesting that there may be another, productive potential in such ambivalence.

32. Nathaniel Mackey, "Sound and Sentiment, Sound and Symbol," in *Discrepant Engagement*, 253.

33. Wilson Harris, "Interview," *Ariel* 19 (July 1988): 48.

34. Zizek, *Tarrying with the Negative*, 135.

35. Johnson, *God's Trombones* (New York, 1927). Hereafter referred to as GT.

36. Since he is thinking in terms of musical form offering a figure of the black body, it also may be that Johnson is thinking of the trombone as an especially physical instrument. Consider jazz dancer and critic Roger Pryor Dodge's comments on trombone style in jazz: "The Negro trombone player has become a sort of dancer in the rhythmic play of his right arm. He makes this instrument live, by improvising solos as natural to a trombone as the simplest of folk tunes are to the voice. This cannot be said of the trombone in any other music save jazz" (Roger Pryor Dodge, "Harpsichords and Jazz Trumpets," *Hound and Horn* [July–Sept. 1934], collected in Dodge, *Hot Jazz and Jazz Dance* [New York, 1995], 19).

37. Duke Ellington, *Music Is My Mistress* (New York, 1973), 108–9.

38. Edward Kamau Brathwaite, "The African Presence in Caribbean Literature" (1970–73), collected in *Roots* (Ann Arbor, 1993), 211–12.

39. Henry Louis Gates, Jr., *The Signifying Monkey: A Theory of Afro-American Literary Criticism* (New York, 1988), 251.

40. George Kent, "Langston Hughes and the Afro-American Folk and Cultural Tradition," in *Langston Hughes: Black Genius*, ed. Therman B. O'Daniel (New York, 1971).

41. In Northrup Frye's words, this is a "sentimental" use of music as opposed to a "technical" use of the term (*Anatomy of Criticism*, 255–56).

42. William Carlos Williams, "On Measure—Statement for Cid Corman," in *Selected Essays* (New York, 1954), 337.

43. Robert Duncan, "Notes on Poetics Regarding Olson's *Maximus*," in *Fictive Certainties* (New York, 1985), 69; Edward Kamau Brathwaite, "History of the Voice" (1979–81), collected in *Roots* (Ann Arbor, 1993), 264; Monchoachi, "Quelle langue parle le poète?" (What language does the poet speak?), postface to *Nuit Gagée* (Wagered night) (Paris, 1992), 66.

44. Harris, "Interview," 47.

45. Focillon, *The Life of Forms in Art*, 62.

46. See, for example, Paul De Man, "Anthropomorphism and Trope in Lyric," in *The Rhetoric of Romanticism* (New York, 1984), 239–62; and Jonathan Culler, "Apostrophe," *Diacritics* 7, no. 4 (Dec. 1977): 59–69. Culler hereafter referred to as c.

47. De Man, "Anthropomorphism and Trope," 254.

48. Nathaniel Mackey, "Interview," *Talisman* 9 (fall 1992): 48.

49. Frye, *Anatomy of Criticism*, 272.

50. Jeanette Robinson Murphy, "The Survival of African Music in America" (1899), in *The Negro and His Folklore in the Nineteenth Century*, ed. Bruce Jackson (Austin, 1967), 329.

51. Sundquist, *To Wake the Nations*, 473, 531.

52. See Nathaniel Mackey, *Bedouin Hornbook* (Lexington, 1986), 39, 82.

53. Wilson Harris, "The Writer and Society," in *Tradition, the Writer and Society* (London, 1967), 52.

54. Paul Gilroy, *The Black Atlantic: Modernity and Double Consciousness* (Cambridge, Mass., 1993), 36.

chapter 35

NATHANIEL MACKEY

Sound and Sentiment, Sound and Symbol

I

Senses of music in a number of texts is what I would like to address—ways of regarding and responding to music in a few instances of writings which bear on the subject. This essay owes its title to two such texts, Steven Feld's *Sound and Sentiment: Birds, Weeping, Poetics and Song in Kaluli Expression* and Victor Zuckerkandl's *Sound and Symbol: Music and the External World*. These two contribute to the paradigm I bring to my reading of the reading of music in the literary works I address.

Steven Feld is a musician as well as an anthropologist, and he dedicates *Sound and Sentiment* to the memory of Charlie Parker, John Coltrane, and Charles Mingus. His book, as the subtitle tells us, discusses the way in which the Kaluli of Papua New Guinea conceptualize music and poetic language. These the Kaluli associate with birds and weeping. They arise from a breach in human solidarity, a violation of kinship, community, connection. *Gisalo*, the quintessential Kaluli song form (the only one of the five varieties they sing that they claim to have invented rather than borrowed from a neighboring people), provokes and crosses over into weeping—weeping that has to do with some such breach, usually death. Gisalo songs are sung at funerals and during spirit-medium seances and have the melodic contour of the cry of a kind of fruitdove, the *muni* bird.[1] This reflects and is founded in the myth regarding the origin of music, the myth of the boy who became a *muni* bird. The myth tells of a boy who goes to catch crayfish with his older sister. He catches none and repeatedly begs for those caught by his sister, who again and again refuses his request. Finally he catches a shrimp and puts it over his nose, causing it to turn a bright purple red, the color of a *muni* bird's beak. His hands turn into wings, and when he opens his mouth to speak the falsetto cry of a *muni* bird comes out. As he flies away, his sister begs him to come back and have some of the crayfish, but his cries continue and become a song, semi-wept, semi-sung: "Your crayfish you didn't give me. I have no sister. I'm hungry. . . ." For the Kaluli, then, the quintessential source of music is the orphan's ordeal—an orphan being anyone denied kinship, social sustenance, anyone who suffers, to use Orlando Patterson's phrase, "social death,"[2] the prototype for which is the boy who becomes a *muni* bird. Song is both a complaint and a consolation dialectically tied to that ordeal, where in back of "orphan" one hears echoes of "orphic," a music that turns on abandonment, absence, loss. Think of the black spiritual "Motherless Child." Music is wounded kinship's last resort.

In *Sound and Symbol*, whose title Feld alludes to and echoes, Victor Zuckerkandl offers "a musical concept of the external world," something he also calls "a critique of our concept of reality from the point of view of music." He goes to great lengths to assert that music bears witness to what is left out of that concept of reality, or, if not exactly what, to the fact that something *is* left out. The world, music reminds us, inhabits while extending beyond what meets the eye, resides in but rises above what is apprehensible to the senses. This co-inherence of immanence and transcendence the Kaluli attribute to and symbolize through birds, which for them are both the spirits of the dead and the major source of the everyday sounds they listen to as indicators of time, location, and distance in their physical environment. In Zuckerkandl's analysis, immanence and transcendence meet in what he terms "the dynamic quality of tones," the relational valence or vectorial give and take bestowed on tones by their musical context. He takes great pains to show that "no material process can be co-ordinated with it," which allows him to conclude:

> Certainly, music transcends the physical; but it does not therefore transcend tones. Music rather helps the thing "tone" to transcend its own physical constituent, to break through into a nonphysical mode of being, and there to develop in a life of unexpected fullness. Nothing but tones! As if tone were not the point where the world that our senses encounter becomes transparent to the action of nonphysical forces, where we as perceivers find ourselves eye to eye, as it were, with a purely dynamic reality—the point where the external world gives up its secret and manifests itself, immediately, *as symbol*. To be sure, tones say, signify, point to—what? Not to something lying "beyond tones." Nor would it suffice to say that tones point to other tones—as if we had first tones, and then pointing as their attribute. No—in musical tones, being, existence, is indistinguishable from, is, pointing-beyond-itself, meaning, saying.[3]

One easily sees the compatibility of this musical concept of the world, this assertion of the intrinsic symbolicity of the world, with poetry. Yeats's view that the artist "belongs to the invisible life" or Rilke's notion of poets as "bees of the invisible" sits agreeably beside Zuckerkandl's assertion that "because music exists, the tangible and visible cannot be the whole of the given world. The intangible and invisible is itself a part of this world, something we encounter, something to which we respond" (ss, 71). His analysis lends itself to more recent formulations as well. His explanation of dynamic tonal events in terms of a "field concept" is not far from Charles Olson's "composition by field," and one commentator has brought *Sound and Symbol* to bear on Jack Spicer's work.[4]

The analogy between tone-pointing and word-pointing is not lost on Zuckerkandl, who, having observed that "in musical tones, being, existence, is indistinguishable from, is, pointing-beyond-itself, meaning, saying," immediately adds: "Certainly, the being of words could be characterized the same way." He goes on to distinguish tone-pointing from word-pointing on the basis of the conventionally agreed-upon referentiality of the latter, a referentiality writers have repeatedly called into question, frequently doing so by way of "aspiring to the condition of music." "Thus poetry," Louis Zukofsky notes, "may be defined as an order of words that as movement and tone (rhythm and pitch) approaches in varying degrees the wordless art of music as a kind of mathematical limit."[5] Music encourages us to see that the symbolic is the orphic, that the symbolic realm is the realm of the orphan. Music is prod and precedent for a recognition that the linguistic realm is also the realm of the orphan, as in Octavio Paz's characterization of language as an orphan severed from the presence to which it refers and which presumably gave it birth. This recognition troubles, complicates, and contends with the unequivocal referentiality taken for granted in ordinary language:

> Each time we are served by words, we mutilate them. But the poet is not served by words. He is their servant. In serving them, he returns them to the plenitude of their nature, makes them recover their being. Thanks to poetry, language reconquers its original state. First, its plastic and sonorous values, generally disdained by thought; next, the affective values; and, finally, the expressive ones. To purify language, the poet's task, means to give it back its original nature. And here we come to one of the central themes of this reflection. The word, in itself, is a plurality of meanings.[6]

Paz is only one of many who have noted the ascendancy of musicality and multivocal meaning in poetic language. (Julia Kristeva: "The poet . . . wants to turn into a dominant element . . . wants to make language perceive what it doesn't want to say, provide it with its matter independently of the sign, and free it from denotation.")[7]

Poetic language is language owning up to being an orphan, to its tenuous kinship with the things it ostensibly refers to. This is why in the Kaluli myth the origin of music is also the origin of poetic language. The words of the song the boy who becomes a *muni* bird resorts to are different from those of ordinary speech. Song language "amplifies, multiplies, or intensifies the relationship of the word to its referent," as Feld explains:

> In song, text is not primarily a proxy for a denoted subject but self-consciously multiplies the intent of the word.

. . . Song poetry goes beyond pragmatic referential communication because it is explicitly organized by canons of reflexiveness and self-consciousness that are not found in ordinary talk.

The uniqueness of poetic language is unveiled in the story of "the boy who became a *muni* bird." Once the boy has exhausted the speech codes for begging, he must resort to another communication frame. Conversational talk, what the Kaluli call *to halaido*, "hard words," is useless once the boy has become a bird; now he resorts to talk from a bird's point of view. . . . Poetic language is bird language.[8]

It bears emphasizing that this break with conventional language is brought about by a breach of expected behavior. In saying no to her brother's request for food the older sister violates kinship etiquette.

What I wish to do is work *Sound and Sentiment* together with *Sound and Symbol* in such a way that the latter's metaphysical accent aids and is in turn abetted by the former's emphasis on the social meaning of sound. What I'm after is a range of implication that will stretch, to quote Stanley Crouch, "from the cottonfields to the cosmos." You notice again that it is black music I'm talking about, a music whose "critique of our concept of reality" is notoriously a critique of social reality, a critique of social arrangements in which, because of racism, one finds oneself deprived of community and kinship, cut off. The two modes of this critique that I will be emphasizing Robert Farris Thompson notes among the "ancient African organizing principles of song and dance":

. . . *suspended accentuation patterning* (offbeat phrasing of melodic and choreographic accents); and, at a slightly different but equally recurrent level of exposition, *songs and dances of social allusion* (music which, however danceable and "swinging," remorselessly contrasts social imperfections against implied criteria for perfect living).[9]

Still, the social isn't all of it. One needs to hear, alongside Amiri Baraka listening to Jay McNeely, that "the horn spat enraged sociologies,"[10] but not without noting a simultaneous mystic thrust. Immanence and transcendence meet, making the music social as well as cosmic, political and metaphysical as well. The composer of "Fables of Faubus" asks Fats Navarro, "What's *outside* the universe?"[11]

This meeting of transcendence and immanence I evoke, in my own work, through the figure of the phantom limb. In the letter that opens *From a Broken Bottle Traces of Perfume Still Emanate* N. begins:

You should've heard me in the dream last night. I found myself walking down a sidewalk and came upon an open manhole off to the right out of which came (or strewn around which lay) the disassembled parts of a bass clarinet. Only the funny thing was that, except for the bell of the horn, all the parts looked more like plumbing fixtures than like parts of a bass clarinet. Anyway, I picked up a particularly long piece of "pipe" and proceeded to play. I don't recall seeing anyone around, but somehow I knew the "crowd" wanted to hear "Naima." I decided I'd give it a try. In any event, I blew into heaven knows what, but instead of "Naima" what came out was Shepp's solo on his version of "Cousin Mary" on the *Four for Trane* album— only infinitely more gruffly resonant and varied and warm. (I even threw in a few licks of my own.) The last thing I remember is coming to the realization that what I was playing already existed on a record. I could hear scratches coming from somewhere in back and to the left of me. This realization turned out, of course, to be what woke me up.

> Perhaps Wilson Harris is right. There are musics which haunt us like a phantom limb. Thus the abrupt breaking off. Therefore the "of course." No more than the ache of some such would-be extension.[12]

I will say more about Wilson Harris in Section V. For now, let me simply say that the phantom limb is a felt recovery, a felt advance beyond severance and limitation that contends with and questions conventional reality, that it is a feeling for what is not there that reaches beyond as it calls into question what is. Music as phantom limb arises from a capacity for feeling that holds itself apart from numb contingency. The phantom limb haunts or critiques a condition in which feeling, consciousness itself, would seem to have been cut off. It is this condition, the non-objective character of reality, to which Michael Taussig, following Georg Lukács, applies the expression "phantom objectivity," by which he means the veil by way of which a social order renders its role in the construction of reality invisible: "A commodity-based society produces such phantom objectivity, and in so doing it obscures its roots—the relations between people. This amounts to a socially instituted paradox with bewildering manifestations, the chief of which is the denial by the society's members of the social construction of reality."[13] *Phantom*, then, is a relative, relativizing term that cuts both ways, occasioning a shift in perspective between real and unreal, an exchange of attributes between the two. So the narrator in Josef Skvorecky's *The Bass Saxophone* says of the band he is inducted into: "They were no longer a vision, a fantasy, it was rather the sticky-sweet panorama of the town square that was unreal."[14] The phantom limb reveals the illusory rule of the world it haunts.

II

Turning now to a few pieces of writing that allude to or seek to ally themselves with music, one sense I'm advancing is that they do so as a way of reaching toward an alternate reality, that music is the would-be limb whereby that reaching is done or that alerts us to the need for its being done. The first work I will look at is Jean Toomer's *Cane*. Though *Cane* is not as announcedly about music as John A. Williams's *Night Song*, Thomas Mann's *Doctor Faustus*, or any number of other works one could name, in its "quieter" way it is no less worth looking at in this regard. First of all, of course, there's the lyricism that pervades the writing, an intrinsic music that is not unrelated to a theme of wounded kinship of which we get whispers in the title. Commentators have noted the biblical echo, and Toomer himself, in notebooks and correspondence, referred to the book as *Cain* on occasion. His acknowledged indebtedness to black folk tradition may well have included a knowledge of stories in that tradition that depict Cain as the prototypical white, a mutation among an earlier people, all of whom were up to that point black: "Cain he kill his brudder Abel wid a great big club . . . and he turn white as bleech cambric in de face, and de whole race ob Cain dey bin white ebber since."[15] The backdrop of white assault that comes to the fore in "Portrait in Georgia," "Blood-Burning Moon," and "Kabnis" plays upon the fratricidal note struck by the book's title.

Indebted as it is to black folk tradition, *Cane* can't help but have to do with music. That "Deep River," "Go Down, Moses," and other songs are alluded to comes as no surprise. Toomer's catalytic stay in Georgia is well known. It was there that he first encountered the black "folk-spirit" he sought to capture in the book. Worth repeating is the emphasis he put on the music he heard:

> The setting was crude in a way, but strangely rich and beautiful. I began feeling its effects despite my state, or, perhaps, just because of it. There was a valley, the valley of "Cane," with smoke-wreaths during the day and mist at night. A family of back-country Negroes had only recently moved into a shack not too far away. They sang. And this was the first time I'd ever heard the folk-songs and spirituals. They were very rich and sad and joyous and beautiful.[16]

He insisted, though, that the spirit of that music was doomed, that "the folk-spirit was walking in to die on the modern desert," and that *Cane* was "a swan-song," "a song of an end." The elegiac weariness and weight that characterize the book come of a lament for the passing of that spirit. In this it is like the music that inspired it, as Toomer pointed out in a letter to Waldo Frank:

> . . . the Negro of the folk-song has all but passed away: the Negro of the emotional church is fading. . . . In my own . . . pieces that come nearest to the old Negro, to the spirit saturate with folk-song . . . the dominant emotion is a sadness derived from a sense of fading. . . . The folk-songs themselves are of the same order: the deepest of them, "I aint got long to stay here."[17]

So, "Song of the Son":

> Pour O pour that parting soul in song,
> O pour it in the sawdust glow of night,
> Into the velvet pine-smoke air to-night,
> And let the valley carry it along.
> And let the valley carry it along.
>
> O land and soil, red soil and sweet-gum tree,
> So scant of grass, so profligate of pines,
> Now just before an epoch's sun declines

Thy son, in time, I have returned to thee,
Thy son, I have in time returned to thee.

In time, for though the sun is setting on
A song-lit race of slaves, it has not set;
Though late, O soil, it is not too late yet
To catch thy plaintive soul, leaving, soon gone,
Leaving, to catch thy plaintive soul soon gone.

O Negro slaves, dark purple ripened plums,
Squeezed, and bursting in the pine-wood air,
Passing, before they stripped the old tree bare
One plum was saved for me, one seed becomes

An everlasting song, a singing tree,
Caroling softly souls of slavery,
What they were, and what they are to me,
Caroling softly souls of slavery.[18]

Cane is fueled by an oppositional nostalgia. A precarious vessel possessed of an eloquence coincident with loss, it wants to reach or to keep in touch with an alternate reality as that reality fades. It was Toomer's dread of the ascending urban-industrial order that opened his ears to the corrective—potentially corrective—counterpoint he heard in Georgia. In the middle section of the book, set in Northern cities, houses epitomize a reign of hard, sharp edges, rectilinear pattern, fixity, regimentation, a staid, white order: "Houses, and dorm sitting-rooms are places where white faces seclude themselves at night" (C, 73). The house embodies, again and again, suffocating structure: "Rhobert wears a house, like a monstrous diver's helmet, on his head. . . . He is sinking. His house is a dead thing that weights him down" (C, 40). Or: "Dan's eyes sting. Sinking into a soft couch, he closes them. The house contracts about him. It is a sharp-edged, massed, metallic house. Bolted" (C, 57). Compare this with Kabnis's fissured, rickety cabin in the South, through the cracks in whose walls and ceiling a ventilating music blows:

> The walls, unpainted, are seasoned a rosin yellow. And cracks between the boards are black. These cracks are the lips the night winds use for whispering. Night winds in Georgia are vagrant poets, whispering. . . . Night winds whisper in the eaves. Sing weirdly in the ceiling cracks.   (C, 81, 104)

Ventilating song is what Dan invokes against the row of houses, the reign of suffocating structure, at the beginning of "Box Seat":

> Houses are shy girls whose eyes shine reticently upon the dusk body of the street. Upon the gleaming limbs and asphalt torso of a dreaming nigger. Shake your curled wool-blossoms, nigger. Open your liver lips to lean, white spring. Stir the root-life of a withered people. Call them from their houses, and teach them to dream.

Dark swaying forms of Negroes are street songs that woo virginal houses.

(C, 56)

Thirty years before the more celebrated Beats, Toomer calls out against an airtight domesticity, a reign of "square" houses and the domestication of spirit that goes with it, his call, as theirs would be, fueled and inflected by the countering thrust of black music.

Not that the beauty of the music wasn't bought at a deadly price. Its other-worldly reach was fostered and fed by seeming to have no home in this one ("I aint got long to stay here"). What the night winds whisper is this:

> White-man's land.
> Niggers, sing.
> Burn, bear black children
> Till poor rivers bring
> Rest, and sweet glory
> In Camp Ground.   (C, 81, 85, 103)

The singing, preaching, and shouting coming from the church near Kabnis's cabin build as Layman tells of a lynching, reaching a peak as a stone crashes in through one of the windows:

> A shriek pierces the room. The bronze pieces on the mantel hum. The sister cries frantically: "Jesus, Jesus, I've found Jesus. O Lord, glory t God, one mo sinner is acomin home." At the height of this, a stone, wrapped round with paper, crashes through the window. Kabnis springs to his feet, terror-stricken. Layman is worried. Halsey picks up the stone. Takes off the wrapper, smooths it out, and reads: "You northern nigger, its time fer y t leave. Git along now."   (C, 90)

Toomer put much of himself into Kabnis, from whom we get an apprehension of music as a carrier of conflicted portent, bearer of both good and bad news. "Dear Jesus," he prays, "do not chain me to myself and set these hills and valleys, heaving with folk-songs, so close to me that I cannot reach them. There is a radiant beauty in the night that touches and . . . tortures me" (C, 83).

Cane's take on music is part and parcel of Toomer's insistence on the tragic fate of beauty, the soul's transit through an unsoulful world. This insistence begins with the very first piece in the book, the story of "Karintha carrying beauty," her soul "a growing thing ripened too soon." The writing is haunted throughout by a ghost of aborted splendor, a specter written into its much-noted lament for the condition of the women it portrays—woman as anima, problematic "parting soul." These women are frequently portrayed, not insignificantly, singing. The mark of blackness and the mark of femininity meet the mark of oppression invested in music. Toomer celebrates and incorporates song but not without looking at the grim conditions that give it birth, not without acknowledging its outcast, compensatory character. "Cotton Song," one of the poems in the book, takes the work song as its model: "Come, brother, come. Lets lift it;/Come now, hewit! roll away!" (C, 9). Like Sterling Brown's "Southern Road," Nat Adderley's "Work

Song," Sam Cooke's "Chain Gang," and Edward Kamau Brathwaite's "Folkways," all of which it anticipates, the poem excavates the music's roots in forced labor. Music here is inseparable from the stigma attached to those who make it.

This goes further in fact. Music itself is looked at askance and stigmatized in a philistine, prosaic social order: "Bolted to the endless rows of metal houses. . . . No wonder he couldn't sing to them" (C, 57). Toomer's formal innovations in *Cane* boldly ventilate the novel, a traditional support for prosaic order, by acknowledging fissures and allowing them in, bringing in verse and dramatic dialogue, putting poetry before reportage. This will to song, though, is accompanied by an awareness of song's outlaw lot that could have been a forecast of the book's commercial failure. (Only five hundred copies of the first printing were sold.) *Cane* portrays its own predicament. It shows that music or poetry, if not exactly a loser's art, is fed by an intimacy with loss and may in fact feed it. This comes out in two instances of a version of wounded kinship that recurs throughout the book, the thwarted communion of would-be lovers. Paul, Orpheus to Bona's Eurydice, turns back to deliver an exquisitely out-of-place poetic address to the doorman, then returns to find Bona gone. Likewise, the narrator holds forth poetically as he sits beside Avey in the story that takes her name, only to find that she has fallen asleep. A play of parallel estrangements emerges. His alienation from the phantom reign of prosaic power—the Capitol dome is "a gray ghost ship"—meets her detachment from and immunity to prepossessing eloquence:

> I talked, beautifully I thought, about an art that would be born, an art that would open the way for women the likes of her. I asked her to hope, and build up an inner life against the coming of that day. I recited some of my own things to her. I sang, with a strange quiver in my voice, a promise-song. And then I began to wonder why her hand had not once returned a single pressure. . . . I sat beside her through the night. I saw the dawn steal over Washington. The Capitol dome looked like a gray ghost ship drifting in from sea. Avey's face was pale, and her eyes were heavy. She did not have the gray crimson-splashed beauty of the dawn. I hated to wake her. Orphan-woman. . . .   (C, 46–47)

III

Beauty apprised of its abnormality both is and is not beauty. (Baraka on Coltrane's "Afro-Blue": "Beautiful has nothing to do with it, but it is.")[19] An agitation complicates would-be equanimity, would-be poise. "Th form thats burned int my soul," Kabnis cries, "is some twisted awful thing that crept in from a dream, a godam nightmare, an wont stay still unless I feed it. An it lives on words. Not beautiful words. God Almighty no. Misshapen, split-gut, tortured, twisted words" (C, 110). The tormenting lure of anomalous beauty and the answering dance of deformation—form imitatively "tortured, twisted"—also concern the writer I would like to move on to, William Carlos Williams. The harassed/harassing irritability that comes into the "Beautiful Thing" section of *Paterson* recalls Kabnis's

"Whats beauty anyway but ugliness if it hurts you?" (C, 83). In black music Williams heard the "defiance of authority" he declares beauty to be, a "vulgarity" that "surpasses all perfections."[20]

Williams's engagement with black music was greatly influenced by his sense of himself as cut off from the literary mainstream. At the time the two pieces I would like to look at were written, Williams had not yet been admitted into the canon, as can be seen in the omission of his work from the *Modern Library Anthology of American Poetry* in 1945, at whose editor, Conrad Aiken, he accordingly takes a shot in *Man Orchid*, the second of the two pieces I'll discuss. His quarrel with T. S. Eliot's dominance and influence doesn't need pointing out, except that it also comes up in *Man Orchid*. Seeing himself as a victimized poet, Williams celebrated the music of a victimized people. In a gesture that has since been overdone ("the white negro," "the student as nigger," analogies between "women and blacks"), he saw parallels between their lot and his own. This can also be seen, though in a slightly more subtle way, in the first of the two pieces I would like to turn to, "Ol' Bunk's Band."

Both pieces grew out of Williams's going to hear New Orleans trumpeter Bunk Johnson in New York in 1945. A revival of interest in Johnson's music was then going on, and Williams caught him during a three-and-a-half-month gig at the Stuyvesant Casino on the lower East Side. He soon after wrote "Ol' Bunk's Band," a poem whose repeated insistence "These are men!" diverges from the dominant culture's denial of human stature to black people. He goes against the grain of accepted grammar in such things as the conscious "vulgarity" of the triple negative "and/not never/need no more," emulating a disregard for convention he heard in the music. The poem in full:

> These are men! the gaunt, unfore-
>   sold, the vocal,
> blatant, Stand up, stand up! the
>   slap of a bass-string.
> Pick, ping! The horn, the
>   hollow horn
> long drawn out, a hound deep
>   tone—
> Choking, choking! while the
>   treble reed
> races—alone, ripples, screams
>   slow to fast—
> to second to first! These are men!
>
> Drum, drum, drum, drum, drum,
>   drum, drum! the
> ancient cry, escaping crapulence
>   eats through
> transcendent—torn, tears, term
>   town, tense,

turns and back off whole, leaps
    up, stomps down,
rips through! These are men
    beneath
whose force the melody limps—
    to
proclaim, proclaims—Run and
    lie down,
in slow measures, to rest and
    not never
need no more! These are men!
    Men![21]

The "hound deep/tone," reminding us that Johnson played in a band known as the Yelping Hound Band in 1930, also conjures a sense of underdog status that brings the orphaned or outcast poet into solidarity with an outcast people. The repeated assertion "These are men!" plays against an implied but unstated "treated like dogs."

Threaded into this implicit counterpoint are the lines "These are men/beneath/whose force the melody limps," where *limps* reflects critically upon a crippling social order. The musicians do to the melody what's done to them, the social handicap on which this limping reports having been translated and, in that sense, transcended, triumphed over. Williams anticipates Baraka's more explicit reading of black music as revenge, sublimated murder. Looking at *Paterson*, which hadn't been under way long when "Ol' Bunk's Band" was written, one finds the same complex of figures: dogs, lameness, limping. In the preface to Book One the image conveyed is that of a pariah, out of step with the pack:

Sniffing the trees,
just another dog
among a lot of dogs. What
else is there? And to do?
The rest have run out—
after the rabbits.
Only the lame stands—on
three legs. . . .   (P, 11)

This leads eventually to the quote from John Addington Symonds's *Studies of the Greek Poets* that ends Book One, a passage in which Symonds comments on Hipponax's choliambi, "lame or limping iambics":

. . . Hipponax ended his iambics with a spondee or a trochee instead of an iambus, doing thus the utmost violence to the rhythmical structure. . . . The choliambi are in poetry what the dwarf or cripple is in human nature. Here again, by their acceptance of this halting meter, the Greeks displayed their acute aesthetic sense of propriety, recognizing the harmony which subsists between crabbed verses and the distorted subjects with which they dealt—

the vices and perversions of humanity—as well as their agreement with the snarling spirit of the satirist. Deformed verse was suited to deformed morality.   (P, 53)

That Williams heard a similar gesture in the syncopated rhythms of black music is obvious by Book Five, where, after quoting a passage about Bessie Smith from Mezz Mezzrow's *Really the Blues*, he makes his well-known equation of "satiric" with "satyric":

<blockquote>
a satyric play!
All plays
were satyric when they were most devout.
Ribald as a Satyr!
</blockquote>

<blockquote>
Satyrs dance!
all the deformities take wing.   (P, 258)
</blockquote>

This would also be a way of talking about the "variable foot," less an aid to scansion than a trope—the travestied, fractured foot.

Williams here stumbles upon, without naming and, most likely, without knowing, the Fon-Yoruba orisha of the crossroads, the lame dancer Legba. Legba walks with a limp because his legs are of unequal lengths, one of them anchored in the world of humans and the other in that of the gods. His roles are numerous, the common denominator being that he acts as an intermediary, a mediator, much like Hermes, of whom Hipponax was a follower. (Norman O. Brown: "Hipponax, significantly enough, found Hermes the most congenial god; he is in fact the only personality in Greek literature of whom it may be said that he walked with Hermes all the days of his life.")[22] Like Hermes's winged feet, Legba's limp— "deformities take wing"—bridges high and low. Legba presides over gateways, intersections, thresholds, wherever different realms or regions come into contact. His limp a play of difference, he is the master linguist and has much to do with signification, divination, and translation. His limp the offbeat or eccentric accent, the "suspended accentuation" of which Thompson writes, he is the master musician and dancer, declared first among the orishas because only he could simultaneously play a gong, a bell, a drum, and a flute while dancing. The master of polyrhythmicity and heterogeneity, he suffers not from deformity but multiformity, a "defective" capacity in a homogeneous order given over to uniform rule. Legba's limp is an emblem of heterogeneous wholeness, the image and outcome of a peculiar remediation. *Lame* or *limping*, that is, like *phantom*, cuts with a relativizing edge to unveil impairment's power, as though the syncopated accent were an unsuspected blessing offering anomalous, unpredictable support. Impairment taken to higher ground, remediated, translates damage and disarray into a dance. Legba's limp, compensating the difference in leg lengths, functions like a phantom limb. Robert Pelton writes that Legba "transforms . . . absence into transparent presence,"[23] deficit leg into invisible supplement.

Legba's authority over mix and transition made him especially relevant to the experience of transplantation brought about by the slave trade. The need to accommodate geographical and cultural difference placed a high premium on his mediatory skills. He is thus the most tenaciously retained of the orishas among New World Africans, the first to be invoked in *vodoun* ceremonies, be they in Haiti, Cuba, Brazil, or elsewhere. There is little wonder why Williams's work, concerned as it is with the New World as a ground for syncretistic innovation, would be paid a visit by the African bridge between old and new. What he heard in Bunk Johnson's music was a rhythmic digestion of dislocation, the African genius for enigmatic melding or mending, a mystery of resilient survival no image puts more succinctly than that of Legba's limping dance.

Legba has made more straightforward appearances in certain works written since Williams's time, showing up, for example, as Papa LaBas (the name he goes by in New Orleans) in Ishmael Reed's novels. Or as Lebert Joseph in Paule Marshall's *Praisesong for the Widow*, a novel whose third section is introduced by a line from the Haitian invocation to Legba and in which one comes upon such passages as: "Out of his stooped and winnowed body had come the illusion of height, femininity and power. Even his foreshortened left leg had appeared to straighten itself out and grow longer as he danced."[24] One of his most telling appearances in the literature of this country, though, is one in which, as in Williams's work, he enters unannounced. In Ralph Ellison's *Invisible Man* one finds adumbrations of Legba that, bearing as they do on the concerns addressed here, deserve more than passing mention.

Invisible Man, like *Cane*, is a work that draws on black folk resources. While collecting folklore in Harlem in 1939 for the Federal Writers' Project, Ellison was told a tale that had to do with a black man in South Carolina who, because he could make himself invisible at will, was able to harass and give white people hell with impunity.[25] This would seem to have contributed to the relativizing thrust of the novel's title and its long meditation on the two-way cut of invisibility. On the other side of invisibility as exclusion, social death, we find it as revenge, millenarian reversal. The prominence of Louis Armstrong in the novel's prologue brings to mind Zuckerkandl's discussion of the case music makes for the invisible, as invisibility is here both social and metaphysical. The ability to "see around corners" defies the reign of strict rectilinear structure lamented in *Cane* by going outside ordinary time and space constraints. Louis's horn, apocalyptic, alters time (and, with it, space):

> Invisibility, let me explain, gives one a slightly different sense of time, you're never quite on the beat. Sometimes you're ahead and sometimes behind. Instead of the swift and imperceptible flowing of time, you are aware of its nodes, those points where time stands still or from which it leaps ahead. And you slip into the breaks and look around. That's what you hear vaguely in Louis' music.[26]

This different sense of time one recognizes as Legba's limp. It leads to and is echoed by a later adumbration of Legba, one in which Ellison hints at a similarly "offbeat" sense of history, one that diverges from the Brotherhood's doctrine of history as monolithic advance. Early on, Jack describes the old evicted couple as "already dead, defunct," people whom "history has passed . . . by," "dead limbs that must be pruned away" (IM, 284). Later "dead limbs" plays contrapuntally upon Tarp's contestatory limp, a limp that, as he explains, has social rather than physiological roots. It was caused by nineteen years on a chain gang:

> You notice this limp I got? . . . Well, I wasn't always lame, and I'm not really now 'cause the doctors can't find anything wrong with that leg. They say it's sound as a piece of steel. What I mean is I got this limp from dragging a chain. . . . Nobody knows that about me, they just think I got rheumatism. But it was that chain and after nineteen years I haven't been able to stop dragging my leg.   (IM, 377–378)

Phantom limb, phantom limp. Tarp goes on, in a gesture recalling the protective root Sandy gives Frederick Douglass in the latter's *Narrative*, to give Invisible Man the broken link from the leg chain he dragged for nineteen years. Phantom limb, phantom limp, phantom link: "I think it's got a heap of signifying wrapped in it and it might help you remember what we're really fighting against" (IM, 379). This it does, serving to concentrate a memory of injustice and traumatic survival, a remembered wound resorted to as a weapon of self-defense. During his final confrontation with the Brotherhood, Invisible Man wears it like a set of brass knuckles: "My hand was in my pockets now, Brother Tarp's leg chain around my knuckles" (IM, 462).

IV

"The trouble has been," Charles Olson writes, "that a man stays so astonished he can triumph over his own incoherence, he settles for that, crows over it, and goes at a day again happy he at least makes a little sense."[27] Ellison says much the same thing toward the end of *Invisible Man* when he cautions that "the mind that has conceived a plan of living must never lose sight of the chaos against which that pattern was conceived" (IM, 567). This goes for both societies and individuals, he points out. Legba's limp, like Tarp's leg chain, is a reminder of dues paid, damage done, of the limbs that have been "pruned away." It is a reminder of the Pyrrhic features every triumph over chaos or incoherence turns out to possess. The specter of illusory victory and its corollary, the riddle of deceptive disability or enabling defeat, sit prominently among the mysteries to which it witnesses. "No defeat is made up entirely of defeat," Williams writes (P, 96).

In *Man Orchid*, the second piece that grew out of Williams's going to hear Johnson's band, the stutter plays a significant role. What better qualification of what can only be a partial victory over incoherence? What limping, staggering, and stumbling are to walking, stuttering and stammering are to speech. "*To stammer* and *to stumble*, original *stumelen*, are twin words," Theodore Thass-Thienemann points out. "The use of the one and the same phonemic pattern for denoting these two different meanings is found in other languages too. Stammering and stuttering are perceived as speech *im-pedi-ments*."[28] The stutter enters *Man Orchid* largely because of Bucklin Moon, the author of a novel called

The Darker Brother. Moon was at the Stuyvesant Casino on the night of 23 November 1945, the second time Williams went to hear Johnson's band. He ended up joining Williams and his friends at their table, among whom was Fred Miller, editor of the thirties proletarian magazine *Blast* and one of the co-authors of *Man Orchid*. Because of his novel and his knowledge of black music, Moon was incorrectly taken by them to be black, though Miller asked Williams in a letter two days later: "Would you ever think that Bucklin Moon was a Negro, if you passed him—as a stranger—in the street? He looks whiter than a lot of whites."[29] Moon evidently spoke with a stutter whenever he became nervous and unsure of himself, which was the case that night at the Stuyvesant Casino. Miller goes on to offer this as a further peculiarity: "A stuttering or stammering Negro is a pretty rare bird indeed: your darker brother is articulate enough, when he isn't too frightened to talk." Like Legba's limp, Moon's stutter would come to symbolize a meeting of worlds, a problematic, insecure mix of black and white.

At the Stuyvesant Williams suggested that he and Miller publish an interracial literary magazine. Miller was enthusiastic at the time but soon lost interest. He suggested within a couple of weeks, however, that he and Williams collaborate on an improvisatory novel that was to be written as though they were musicians trading fours: "You write chap. I, send it to me, I do the 2d Chap., send mess back to you, you do 3—and so on." Williams liked the idea and *Man Orchid* was launched. They spent the next year working on it, off and on, bringing in a third collaborator, Lydia Carlin, in March. The work was never completed, and what there is of it, forty pages, remained unpublished until 1973. It is going too far to call it a novel and outright ludicrous to call it, as Paul Mariani does, "Williams's black novel," but the piece is interesting for a number of reasons, not the least of them being its anticipation of the bop-inspired attempts at collaborative, improvisatory writing that became popular among the Beats a decade later.[30]

Wray Douglas, *Man Orchid*'s black-white protagonist, is based in part on Bucklin Moon and intended to embody America's yet-to-be-resolved identity. As Williams writes: "To resolve such a person would be to create a new world" (MO, 77). But other than his presumed black-white mix and his stutter not much of Moon went into the figure. Wray Douglas is clearly his creators' alter ego, the narrated "he" and the narrator's "I" in most cases the same. Want of resolution and the stubborn problematics of heterogeneity are what *Man Orchid* most effectively expresses, the latter symptomized by the solipsistic quality of the work and the former a would-be flight from the resolute self (false resolution) that the solipsism indulges even as it eschews. Two white writers sit down to create a black protagonist whose model is another white writer. The ironies and contradictions need not be belabored.

The stutter thus becomes the most appropriate, self-reflexive feature of an articulation that would appear to be blocked in advance. Williams's and Miller's prose in *Man Orchid* both stutters and refers to stuttering. Here, for example, is how Williams begins Chapter I:

Is it perchance a crime—a time, a chore, a bore, a job? He wasn't a musician—but he wished he had been born a musician instead of a writer. Musicians do not stutter. But he ate music music wrinkled his belly—if you can wrinkle an inflated football. Anyhow it felt like that so that's what he wrote (without changing a word—that was his creed and always after midnight, you couldn't be earlier in the morning than that). All good writing is written in the morning.

Is *what* perchance a crime? (One) (or rather two) He ate and drank beer. That is, he ate, he also drank beer. A crime to be so full, so—so (the thing the philosophers hate) poly. So p-p-poly. Polypoid. Huh?   (MO, 77)

Thinking, perhaps, of the use of singing in the treatment of stuttering, Williams identifies writing with the latter while looking longingly at music as the embodiment of a heterogeneous wholeness to which his writing will aspire, an unimpeded, unproblematic wholeness beyond its reach. Miller's contribution to *Man Orchid* is likewise touched by a sense of writing's inferiority to music. Early on, referring to Bessie Smith's singing, he asks: "What were the little words chasing each other like black bits of burnt leaves across the pages he held—[compared] to that vast voice?" (MO, 79). Two pages later he answers:

More printed words like black bits of burnt leaves. They had the right keyhole, those guys, but the wrong key. The only words that could blast like Bunk's horn or smash like John Henry's hammer were the poet's, the maker's, personal, ripped out of his guts: And no stuttering allowed.

(MO, 81)

Throughout *Man Orchid*, however, the writer's emulation of the musician causes rather than cures the stutter. Imitating the spontaneity of improvisatory music, Williams and Miller approach the typewriter as a musical keyboard on which they extemporize "without changing a word." Wrong "notes" are left as they are rather than erased, though the right ones do eventually get "played" in most cases. This results in a repetitiveness and a halting, staccato gesture reminiscent of a stutterer's effort to get out what he wants to say. Thus Williams: "American poetry was on its way to great distinction—when the blight of Eliot's popular verse fell pon— upon the gasping universities—who hadN8t hadn8T hadn't tasted Thames water for nearly a hundred years" (MO, 82). By disrupting the fluency and coherence available to them Williams and Miller attempt to get in touch with what that coherence excludes, "the chaos against which that pattern was conceived." This friendly relationship with incoherence, however, constitutes a gesture toward but not an attainment of the otherness to which it aspires, an otherness to which access can only be analogically gotten. *Man Orchid*, to make the obvious point, is a piece of writing, not a piece of music. Nor, as I have already noted, is the color line crossed. The stutter is a two-way witness that on one hand symbolizes a need to go beyond the confines of an exclusionary order, while on the other confessing to its at best only limited success at doing so. The impediments to the passage it seeks are acknowledged if not annulled, attested to by exactly the gesture that would overcome them if it could.

One measure of *Man Orchid*'s flawed embrace of otherness is the prominence in it of Williams's all too familiar feud with Eliot, a feud into which he pulls Bunk Johnson. Johnson's music is put forth as an example of an authentic American idiom, "the autochthonous strain" (MO, 85) whose dilution or displacement by "sweet music" paralleled and anticipated that of a genuine "American poetry [which] was on its way to great distinction" by *The Waste Land*:

> Eliot would not have been such a success if he hadn't hit a soft spot. They were scared and rushed in where he hit like water into the side of a ship. It was ready for it a long time. Isn't a weak spot always ready to give way? That was the secret of his success. Great man Eliot. They were aching for him, Aiken for him. He hit the jackpot with his popular shot.
>
> But long before that, twenty years earlier ol' Bunk Johnson was all washed up. Sweet music was coming in and jazz was through. But I mean THROUGH! And when I say through, I mean through, Go ahead, quit. See if I care. Take your band and go frig a kite. Go on back to the rice swamps. See if I care. Sell your ol'd horn. See if I care. Nobody wants that kind of music any more: this is a waste land for you, Buddy, this is a waste land! I said Waste Land and when I sez Waste land I mean waste *land*.
>
> . . . Thus American poetry, which disappeared about that time you might say, followed the same course New Orleans music had taken when sweet music displaced it about in 1906 or so.   (MO, 83–84)

Fraternity with Johnson is less the issue than sibling rivalry with Eliot, a literary quarrel in which Johnson has no voice but the one Williams gives him. What it says is simple: "Black music is on Williams's side." (The Barbadian poet Edward Kamau Brathwaite provides interesting counterpoint, picturing Eliot and black music as allies when he notes the influence of Eliot's recorded readings in the Caribbean: "In that dry deadpan delivery, the riddims of St. Louis . . . were stark and clear for those of us who at the same time were listening to the dislocations of Bird, Dizzy and Klook. And it is interesting that on the whole, the Establishment couldn't stand Eliot's voice—far less jazz!")[31]

The possibility that otherness was being appropriated rather than engaged was recognized by Miller, and for him it became an obstacle to going on. When he began to voice his misgivings Williams brought in Lydia Carlin, who not only added sexual otherness to the project but a new form of ethnic otherness as well, in that, though she herself was English, one of the two chapters she contributed was about a Polish couple, the Czajas. Her two chapters are much more conventional, much less improvisatory than Williams's and Miller's and tend to stand apart from rather than interact with theirs. Her taking part in the project did nothing to solve the problem, and as late as Chapter 7 Miller is asking:

> Now returning to this novel, Man Orchid. Why the orchid?—to begin with. There's the old, tiresome and at bottom snobbish literary assumption that the Negro in America is an exotic bloom. Negro equals jungle. Despite the fact that he has been here longer than the second, third, even ninth

generation Eurp European—Negro equals jungle. Then why doesn't the ofay bank president of German descent equal Black Forest? The Rutherford doctor of Welsh descent equal the cromlechs? or Welsh rarebit?   (MO, III)

As bad if not worse is the fact that the choice of that particular orchid because of its phallic appearance plays upon a stereotypic black male sexuality. The distance from this to Norman Mailer's "Jazz is orgasm" is not very great, which is only one of a handful of ways in which *The White Negro* bears upon this predecessor text.

Miller, though he could agonize as in the passage just quoted, was no more free than Williams was of stereotypic equations. To him Johnson and his music represent a black essence that is unself-conscious and nonreflective: "Only the Bunks're satisfied to be Bunks, he told himself enviously. Their brain don't question their art. Nor their left hand their RIGHT. Their right to be Bunk, themself" (MO, 79). The vitiation of "black" non-reflective being by "white" intellectuality is largely the point of his evocation of Wray Douglas and the trumpeter Cholly Oldham. The latter he describes as having "too much brain for a musician." Oldham stutters when he plays and wants to be a painter:

There was between Cholly and Bunk—what? a difference of thirty, thirty-five years in age, no more. But the difference otherwise! Hamlet son of Till Eulenspiegel. Showing you what the dry rot of intellectuality could do to the orchid in one generation. Progress (!) Up from Slavery. That night-colored Hamlet, he wants to paint pictures now.   (MO, 82)

Black is nonreflective, white cerebral. So entrenched are such polarizations as to make the notion of a black intellectual oxymoronic. In May, Miller wrote to Williams that it had been a mistake to model their protagonist on Bucklin Moon: "I don't know enough about him and his special type, the colored intellectual (although I've been acquainted with and've liked lots of ordinary Negro folk, laborers, musicians et al)" (MO, 73). Small wonder he questioned the idea of an interracial magazine by writing to Williams:

Is there sufficient Negro writing talent—of the kind we wd. have no doubts about, AS talent, on hand to balance the white talent? I don't believe any more than you that publishing second-rate work with first-rate intentions would serve any cause but that of bad writing.   (MO, 68)

To what extent was being looked upon as black—as, even worse, that "rare bird," a black intellectual—the cause of Moon's nervousness that night at the Stuyvesant? Could a sense of distance in Williams's and Miller's manner have caused him to stutter? Miller's wife recalls in a letter to Paul Mariani:

Moon began with easy speech and there was talk at first of the interracial magazine but Moon soon took to stammering. To me Williams was always a warm congenial person, but he would become the coldly analytical surgeon at times and the effect it had on those around him at such a time was quite devastating.   (MO, 67)

That "coldly analytical" scrutiny would seem to have been disconcerting, making Williams and Miller the agents of the disarray about which they would then go on to write—as good an example as any of "phantom objectivity," the social construction of Moon's "mulatto" self-consciousness.

What I find most interesting about *Man Orchid* is that it inadvertently underscores a feature that was then coming into greater prominence in black improvised music. With the advent of bebop, with which neither Williams, Miller, nor Carlin seem to have been much engaged, black musicians began to assume a more explicit sense of themselves as artists, conscious creators, thinkers. Dizzy Gillespie would don a beret and a goatee, as would, among others, Yusef Lateef, who would record an album called *Jazz for the Thinker*. Anthony Braxton's pipe, wire-rim glasses, cardigan sweater, and diagrammatic titles are among the present-day descendants of such gestures. The aural equivalent of this more explicit reflexivity would come at times to resemble a stutter, conveying senses of apprehension and self-conscious duress by way of dislocated phrasings in which virtuosity mimes its opposite. Thelonious Monk's mock-awkward hesitancies evoke an experience of impediment or impairment, as do Sonny Rollins's even more stutterlike teasings of a tune, a quality Paul Blackburn imitates in "Listening to Sonny Rollins at the Five Spot":

> There will be many other nights like
> me standing here with someone, some
> one
> someone
> some-one
> some
> some
> some
> some
> some
> one
> there will be other songs
> a-nother fall, another—spring, but
> there will never be a-noth, noth
> anoth
> noth
> anoth-er
> noth-er
> noth-er
>   Other lips that I may kiss,
> but they won't thrill me like
>   thrill me like
>   like yours
> used to
>   dream a million dreams

> but how can they come
> when there
>   never be
> a-noth—[32]

Though Williams and Miller insist that Bunk Johnson doesn't stammer, the limp he inflicts on the melody is ancestral to the stutter of Monk, Rollins, and others.

As among the Kaluli, for whom music and poetry are "specifically marked for reflection," the black musician's stutter is an introspective gesture that arises from and reflects critically upon an experience of isolation or exclusion, the orphan's or the outsider's ordeal, the "rare bird's" ordeal. Like Tarp's leg chain, it symbolizes a refusal to forget damage done, a critique and a partial rejection of an available but biased coherence. Part of the genius of black music is the room it allows for a telling "inarticulacy," a feature consistent with its critique of a predatory coherence, a cannibalistic "plan of living," and the articulacy that upholds it. *Man Orchid*, where it comes closest to the spirit of black music, does so by way of a similar frustration with and questioning of given articulacies, permissible ways of making sense. In Chapter 6 Williams attempts to make racial distinctions meaningless, the result of which is part gibberish, part scat, part wisdom of the idiots ("the most foolishest thing you can say . . . has the most meaning"). His inability to make sense implicitly indicts a white-dominated social order and the discourse of racial difference by which it explains or makes sense of itself:

> Not that black is white. I do not pretend that. Nor white black. That there
> is not the least difference is apparent to the mind at a glance. Thus, to the
> mind, the eye is forever deceived. And philosophers imagine they can have
> opinions about art? God are they dumb, meaning stupid, meaning philoso-
> phers, meaning schools, meaning—learning. The limits of learning are the
> same as an egg to the yolk. The shell. Knowledge to a learned man is pre-
> cisely the sane—that's good: sane for same—the same as the egg to the hen.
> No possibility of interchange. Reason, the shell.
>
>   No matter how I try to rearrange the parts, to show them interchange-
> able, the result is always the same. White is white and black is the United
> States Senate. No mixing. Even if it was all black it would be the same:
> white. How could it be different?   (MO, 100–101)

The very effort to talk down the difference underscores the tenacity of the racial polarization *Man Orchid*'s liberal mission seeks, to some degree, to overcome—a tenacity that is attested to, as we have seen, in other ways as well, not the least of them being the authors' preconceptions.

V

The play of sense and nonsense in Wilson Harris's *The Angel at the Gate* is more immediately one of sensation and non-sensation, a complex mingling of endowments and deprivations, anesthetic and synesthetic intuitions. One reads, for example, late in the novel:

621

Mary recalled how deaf she had been to the voice of the blackbird that morning on her way to Angel Inn and yet it returned to her now in the depths of the mirror that stood beside her. Half-reflected voice, shaded sound, silent echo. Was this the source of musical composition? Did music issue from reflections that converted themselves into silent, echoing bodies in a mirror? Did the marriage of *reflection* and *sound* arise from deaf appearance within silent muse (or was it deaf muse in silent appearance) from which a stream of unheard music rippled into consciousness?[33]

In dialogue with and relevant to such a passage is a discussion in Harris's *The Womb of Space* that touches upon Legba as "numinous shadow." Harris writes of "metaphoric imagery that intricately conveys music as the shadow of vanished but visualised presences": "Shadow or shade is alive with voices so real, yet strangely beyond material hearing, that they are peculiarly *visualised* or 'seen' in the intricate passages of a poem. *Visualised presence* acquires therefore a *shadow and a voice* that belongs to the mind's ear and eye."[34] Music described in terms pertaining to sight is consistent with inklings of synesthetic identity that run through *The Angel at the Gate*. It is also part and parcel of Harris's long preoccupation, from work to work, with an uncapturable, ineffable wholeness, a heterogeneous inclusiveness evoked in terms of non-availability ("silent echo," "unheard music") and by polysemous fullness and fluency ("a stream . . . rippled").

The Angel at the Gate's anesthetic-synesthetic evocations recapitulate, in microcosm, the translation between media—aural and visual, music and writing—it claims to be. The intermedia impulse owns up to as it attempts to advance beyond the limits of a particular medium and is a version of what Harris elsewhere calls "a confession of weakness."[35] The novel acknowledges that its particular strength can only be partial and seeks to "echo" if not enlist the also partial strength of another art form. Wholeness admitted to be beyond reach, the best to be attained is a concomitance of partial weaknesses, partial strengths, a conjunction of partial endowments. This conjunction is facilitated by Legba, upon whom *The Womb of Space* touches as a "numinous frailty" and a "transitional chord." In *Da Silva da Silva's Cultivated Wilderness*, an earlier novel that likewise leans upon an extraliterary medium, the painter da Silva's advertisement for a model is answered by one Legba Cuffey, whose arrival infuses paint with sound: "The front door bell pealed it seemed in the middle of his painting as he brooded on past and future. The sound of a catch grown sharp as a child's cry he thought in a line of stroked paint."[36] In this case painting, like music in *The Angel at the Gate*, is an alternate artistic arm with which the novel extends or attempts to extend its reach. "So the arts," Williams writes in *Man Orchid*, "take part for each other" (MO, 85).

Music figures prominently at the end of Harris's first novel, *Palace of the Peacock*, where Legba's limp, the incongruity between heaven and earth, is marked by the refractive obliquity and bend of a passage from one medium to another. The annunciation of paradise takes the form of a music that issues through the lips of Carroll, the black namesake singer whose father is unknown but whose mother "knew and understood . . . [that his] name involved . . . the music of her undying sacrifice to make and save the world."[37] The narrator notes a discrepancy between the sound Carroll's lips appear to be making and the sound he hears: "Carroll was whistling. A solemn and beautiful cry—unlike a whistle I reflected—deeper and mature. Nevertheless his lips were framed to whistle and I could only explain the difference by assuming the sound from his lips was changed when it struck the window and issued into the world" (PP, 147). The deflection from apparent sound reveals not only the insufficiency of the visual image but that of any image, visual, acoustic, or otherwise. Heaven is wholeness, meaning that any image that takes up the task of evoking it can only fail. Legba's limp is the obliquity of a religious aspiration that admits its failure to measure up to heaven, the bend legs make in prayer. As in the *Paradiso*, where Dante laments the poem's inability to do heaven justice by calling it lame, the narrator's evocation of Carroll's music is marked by a hesitant, faltering gesture that whenever it asserts immediately qualifies itself. It mimes the music's crippling, self-correcting attempts to register as well as redeem defects. The music repeatedly breaks and mends itself—mends itself as a phantom limb mends an amputation:

> It was an organ cry almost and yet quite different I reflected again. It seemed to break and mend itself always—tremulous, forlorn, distant, triumphant, the echo of sound so pure and outlined in space it broke again into a mass of music. It was the cry of the peacock and yet I reflected far different. I stared at the whistling lips and wondered if the change was in me or in them. I had never witnessed and heard such sad and such glorious music.
>
> (PP, 147)

This is the ongoingness of an attempt that fails but is repeatedly undertaken to insist that what it fails to capture nonetheless exists. Legba's limp is the obliquity of a utopian aspiration, the bend legs make preparing to spring.

Inability to capture wholeness notwithstanding, *Palace of the Peacock* initiates Harris's divergence from the novel's realist-mimetic tradition. The accent that falls upon the insufficiency of the visual image is consistent with the novel's earlier suggestions of an anesthetic-synesthetic enablement that displaces the privileged eye:[38] "I dreamt I awoke with one dead seeing eye and one living closed eye" (PP, 13–14). And again: "I had been blinded by the sun, and saw inwardly in the haze of my blind eye a watching muse and phantom whose breath was on my lips" (PP, 16). That accent encapsulates Harris's quarrel with the cinematic pretense and the ocular conceit of the realist novel, a documentary stasis against which he poses an anesthetic-synesthetic obliquity and rush. This obliquity (seeing and/or hearing around corners, in Ellison's terms) is called "an angled intercourse with history" in *The Angel at the Gate* (AG, 113), the medium for which is the Angel Inn mirror, described at points as "spiritual" and "supernatural." Mary Stella is said to perceive the world "from a meaningfully distorted angle in the mirror" (AG, 113), a pointed subversion of the mirror's conventional association with mimesis. Angularity cuts with a relativizing edge: "How unreal, yet real, one was when one saw oneself with one's own eyes from angles in a mirror so curiously unfamiliar that one's eyes became a stranger's eyes. As at the hairdresser when she invites one to inspect the back of one's head" (AG, 21).

Late in the novel Mary Stella's "automatic codes" are said to have "propelled her pencil across the page of a mirror" (AG, 122)—clear enough indication that the novel sees itself in the Angel Inn mirror, that reflection and refraction are there the same. Angled perception is a particular way of writing—writing bent or inflected by music. *The Angel at the Gate* is said to be based on Mary Stella's automatic writings and on notes taken by her therapist Joseph Marsden during conversations with her, some of which were conducted while she was under hypnosis. In the note that introduces the novel mention is made of "the musical compositions by which Mary it seems was haunted from early childhood," as well as of "a series of underlying rhythms in the automatic narratives" (AG, 7). Like the boy who became a *muni* bird, Mary Stella, an orphan from the age of seven, resorts to music in the face of broken familial ties—those with her parents in the past and in the present her troubled marriage with Sebastian, for whom she's "the same woman broken into wife and sister" (AG, 13). Louis Armstrong's rendition of "Mack the Knife," the song her mother frequently sang during her early childhood, animates a host of recollections and associations:

> . . . the music returned once again coming this time from an old gramophone her mother possessed. It was "Mack the Knife" sung and played by Louis Armstrong. The absurdity and tall story lyric, oceanic city, were sustained by Armstrong's height of trumpet and by his instrumental voice, hoarse and meditative in contrast to the trumpet he played, ecstatic cradle, ecstatic childhood, ecstatic coffin, ecstatic grieving surf or sea.
>
> . . . Stella was shivering. The fascination of the song for her mother was something that she grew up with. Mack was also the name that her father bore. Mack was her mother's god. And her mother's name? *Guess*, Stella whispered to Sebastian in the darkened studio. Jenny! It was a random hit, bull's eye. It struck home. Jenny heard. She was weeping. It came with the faintest whisper of the sea, the faintest whisper of a flute, in the studio. Mack's women were the Sukey Tawdreys, the sweet Lucy Browns, of the world. Between the ages of four and seven Stella thought that the postman was her father. Until she realized that he was but the middleman between her real father and Jenny her mother. He brought the letters from foreign ports with foreign stamps over which Jenny wept. On her seventh birthday the last letter arrived. Her father was dead, his ship sunk. It was a lie. It drove her mother into an asylum where she contemplated Mack clinging for dear life to sarcophagus-globe even as she vanished into the arms of god, bride of god.
>
> Stella was taken into care by a Social Welfare Body and placed in an orphanage in East Anglia.   (AG, 44–45)

Mary Stella's automatic narratives, prompted by her thirst for connection and "her longing to change the world" (AG, 46), instigate patterns of asymmetric equation into which characters named Sukey Tawdrey, Mother Diver, Lucy Brown, and so forth enter. The song, it seems, populates a world, an alternate world. Her music-prompted hand and its inscription of far-flung relations obey intimations of unacknowledged wholeness against a backdrop of social and psychic division. "To be whole," we are told at the end, "was to endure . . . the traffic of many souls" (AG, 156).

The novel's concern with heterogeneous wholeness invokes Legba repeatedly—though, significantly, not by that name. As if to more greatly emphasize Legba's association with multiplicity, Harris merges him with his trickster counterpart among the Ashanti, the spider Anancy, tales of whose exploits are a prominent part of Caribbean folklore. An asymmetric equation that relates deficit leg to surplus legs, lack to multiplicity, brings "a metaphysic of curative doubt" (AG, 78) to bear upon appearances. Apparent deficiency and apparent endowment are two sides of an insufficient image. When Sebastian discovers Mary Stella's attempt at suicide "his legs multiplied" (AG, 14), but later "there was no visible bandage around his ankle but he seemed nevertheless as lame as Anancy" (AG, 33). Other such intimations occur: Marsden described as a cane on which "something, some invisible presence, did lean" (AG, 29), Sebastian asking of the jockey who exposed himself to Mary Stella, "Did he, for instance, possess a walking stick?" (AG, 50), and Jackson, Mary Stella's "authentic messenger" (AG, 125), falling from a ladder and breaking his leg. The most sustained appearance occurs when Mary Stella happens upon the black youth Anancy in Marsden's study. The "funny title" of a book has brought him there:

> . . . He turned his eyes to the desk. "The door was open and I saw the funny title of that book." He pointed to the desk.
>
> "Sir Thomas More's *Utopia*," said Mary, smiling against her fear and finding her tongue at last. "I put it there myself this week." His eyes were upon hers now. "I put it . . ." she began again, then stopped. "I brought you here," she thought silently. "*Utopia was the bait I used.*" The thought came of its own volition. It seemed irrational, yet true. There was a ticking silence between them, a deeper pull than she could gauge, a deeper call than she knew, that had sounded long, long ago, even before the time when her father's great-great-grandmother had been hooked by an Englishman to bear him children of mixed blood.   (AG, 26–27)

Mary Stella's pursuit of heterogeneous relations carries her out as well as in. She discovers an eighteenth-century black ancestor on her father's side. That discovery, along with her perusal, in Marsden's library, of seventeenth- and eighteenth-century parish accounts of money spent to expel children and pregnant women, several of them black, arouses her desire for a utopian inclusiveness, the "longing to change the world" that "baits" Anancy. The world's failure to comply with that desire leads her to distance herself from it, to practice a kind of cosmic displacement. Her schizophrenia involves an aspect of astral projection, as she cultivates the "capacity to burn elsewhere" (AG, 85) suggested by her middle name: "Ah yes, said Stella, I am a mask Mary wears, a way of coping with truth. We are each other's little deaths, little births. We cling to sarcophagus-globe and to universal cradle" (AG, 44).

Displacement and relativizing distance account for the resonances and agitations at work in the text, an animated incompleteness whose components tend toward as well as recede from one another, support as well as destabilize one another. The pull between Mary Stella and Anancy is said to arise from "a compulsion or infectious Cupid's arrow . . . related to the target of unfinished being" (AG, 26). Some such pull, together with its other side, aversion, advances the accent on relationality that pervades the novel and has much to do with Harris's distinctive style. The sought-after sense of dispersed identity makes for staggered equational upsets and elisions in which words, concepts, and images, like the characters, are related through a mix of contrast and contagion. The musicality of Harris's writing resides in its cadences, imaginal concatenations, and poetic assurance, but also in something else. *The Angel at the Gate* offers a musical conception of the world whose emphasis on animate incompleteness, "unfinished being," recalls Zuckerkandl's analysis of tonal motion:

> A series of tones is heard as motion not because the successive tones are of different pitches but because they have different dynamic qualities. The dynamic quality of a tone, we said, is a statement of its incompleteness, its will to completion. To hear a tone as dynamic quality, as a direction, a pointing, means hearing at the same time beyond it, beyond it in the direction of its will, and going toward the expected next tone. Listening to music, then, we are not first in one tone, then in the next and so forth. We are, rather, always *between* the tones, *on the way* from tone to tone; our hearing does not remain with the tone, it reaches through it and beyond it . . . pure betweenness, pure passing over.   (ss, 136–137)

A mixed, middle ground that privileges betweenness would seem to be the realm in which Harris works. He alludes to himself as a "no-man's land writer" at one point (AG, 23) and later has Jackson say, "I must learn to paint or sculpt what lies stranded between earth and heaven" (AG, 124). An "attunement to a gulf or divide between sky and earth" (AG, 123) probes an estrangement and a stranded play in which limbs have to do with limbo, liminality, lift:

> The women were dressed in white. They carried covered trays of food and other materials on their head. There was a statuesque deliberation to each movement they made, a hard-edged beauty akin to young Lucy's that seemed to bind their limbs into the soil even as it lifted them very subtly an inch or two into space.
> That lift was so nebulous, so uncertain, it may not have occurred at all. Yet it was there; it gave a gentle wave or groundswell to the static root or the vertical dance of each processional body.   (AG, 122)

What remains to be said is that to take that lift a bit further is to view the outsider's lot as cosmic, stellar. Social estrangement is gnostic estrangement and the step from Satchmo's "height of trumpet" to Sun Ra's "intergalactic music" is neither a long nor an illogical one. In this respect, the film *Brother from Another Planet* is worth—in what will serve as a closing note—mentioning briefly. That it shares with *The Angel at the Gate* a theme of cosmic dislocation is obvious enough. That the Brother's limp is the limp of a misfit—the shoes he finds and puts on don't suit his feet—is also easy to see. An intermedia thread is also present and bears on this discussion, especially the allusions to Dante (the Rasta guide named Virgil) and *Invisible Man* (the Brother's detachable eye), where it would seem the film were admitting a need to reach beyond its limits. What stronger suggestion of anesthetic-synesthetic displacement could one want than when the Brother places his eye in the drug dealer's hand? Or than the fact that the movie ends on a seen but unsounded musical note as the Brother gets aboard an "A" train?

NOTES

1. Examples of *gisalo* and other varieties of Kaluli song can be heard on the album *The Kaluli of Papua Niugini: Weeping and Song* (Musicaphon BM 30 SL 2702).

2. Orlando Patterson, *Slavery and Social Death: A Comparative Study* (Cambridge: Harvard University Press, 1982).

3. Victor Zuckerkandl, *Sound and Symbol: Music and the External World* (Princeton: Bollingen Foundation/Princeton University Press, 1956), p. 371. Hereafter referred to as SS.

4. Stephanie A. Judy, " 'The Grand Concord of What': Preliminary Thoughts on Musical Composition and Poetry," *Boundary 2*, VI, I (Fall 1977), 267–85.

5. Louis Zukofsky, *Prepositions* (Berkeley: University of California Press, 1981), p. 19.

6. Octavio Paz, *The Bow and the Lyre* (New York: McGraw-Hill, 1973), p. 37.

7. Julia Kristeva, *Desire in Language: A Semiotic Approach to Literature and Art* (New York: Columbia University Press, 1980), p. 31.

8. Steven Feld, *Sound and Sentiment: Birds, Weeping, Poetics and Song in Kaluli Expression* (Philadelphia: University of Pennsylvania Press, 1982), p. 34.

9. Robert Farris Thompson, *Flash of the Spirit: African and Afro-American Art and Philosophy* (New York: Vintage Books, 1984), p. xiii.

10. LeRoi Jones, *Tales* (New York: Grove Press, 1967), p. 77.

11. Charles Mingus, *Beneath the Underdog* (New York: Penguin Books, 1980), p. 262.

12. Nathaniel Mackey, *Bedouin Hornbook* (Charlottesville: Callaloo Fiction Series/University Press of Virginia, 1986), p. 1.

13. Michael Taussig, *The Devil and Commodity Fetishism in South America* (Chapel Hill: University of North Carolina Press, 1980), p. 4.

14. Josef Skvorecky, *The Bass Saxophone* (London: Picador, 1980), p. 109.

15. Quoted by Lawrence W. Levine in *Black Culture and Black Consciousness: Afro-American Folk Thought from Slavery to Freedom* (New York: Oxford University Press, 1977), p. 85.

16. Jean Toomer, *The Wayward and the Seeking* (Washington, D.C.: Howard University Press, 1980), p. 123.

17. Quoted by Charles W. Scruggs in "The Mark of Cain and the Redemption of Art," *American Literature*, 44 (1972), 290–291.

18. Jean Toomer, *Cane* (New York: Liveright, 1975), p. 12. Hereafter referred to as C.

19. LeRoi Jones, *Black Music* (New York: Morrow, 1967), p. 66.

20. William Carlos Williams, *Paterson* (New York: New Directions, 1963), pp. 144–145. Hereafter referred to as P.

21. William Carlos Williams, *Selected Poems* (New York: New Directions, 1969), p. 115.

22. Norman O. Brown, *Hermes the Thief: The Evolution of a Myth* (New York: Vintage Books, 1969), p. 82.

23. Robert D. Pelton, *The Trickster in West Africa: A Study of Mythic Irony and Sacred Delight* (Berkeley: University of California Press), p. 80.

24. Paule Marshall, *Praisesong for the Widow* (New York: Dutton, 1984), p. 243.

25. Levine, pp. 405–406.

26. Ralph Ellison, *Invisible Man* (New York: Vintage Books, 1972), p. 8. Hereafter referred to as IM.

27. Charles Olson, *Human Universe and Other Essays* (New York: Grove Press, 1967), p. 3.

28. Theodore Thass-Thienemann, *The Subconscious Language* (New York: Washington Square Press, 1967), p. 96 n.

29. Quoted by Paul L. Mariani in "Williams's Black Novel," *The Massachusetts Review*, XIV, I (Winter 1973), 68. This article is part of "A Williams Garland: Petals from the Falls, 1945–1950," edited by Mariani, which includes *Man Orchid*, 77–117. Subsequent citations of Mariani's article and of *Man Orchid* are incorporated into the text, referred to as MO.

30. See, for example, "This is what it's called" by Albert Saijo, Lew Welch, and Jack Kerouac in *The Beat Scene*, ed. Elias Wilentz (New York: Corinth, 1960), pp. 163–170.

31. Edward Kamau Brathwaite, *History of the Voice: The Development of Nation Language in Anglophone Caribbean Poetry* (London and Port of Spain: New Beacon, 1984), p. 31.

32. Paul Blackburn, *The Collected Poems* (New York: Persea Press, 1985), p. 316.

33. Wilson Harris, *The Angel at the Gate* (London: Faber and Faber, 1982), p. 109. Hereafter referred to as AG.

34. Wilson Harris, *The Womb of Space: The Cross-Cultural Imagination* (Westport: Greenwood Press, 1983), pp. 130–131.

35. Wilson Harris, *Explorations: A Selection of Talks and Articles 1966–1981* (Mundelstrup: Dangaroo Press, 1981), pp. 43–48.

36. Wilson Harris, *Da Silva da Silva's Cultivated Wilderness and Genesis of the Clowns* (London: Faber and Faber, 1977), pp. 8–9.

37. Wilson Harris, *Palace of the Peacock* (London: Faber and Faber, 1960), p. 83. Hereafter referred to as PP.

38. "The eye and its 'gaze' . . . has had a lockhold on Western thought," notes, as have others, Paul Stoller in "Sound in Songhay Cultural Experience," *American Ethnologist*, 11, 3 (1984), 559–570.

writing the blues, writing jazz

sources

OF ESSAYS, INTERVIEWS, AND ARTICLES

Baraka, Amiri. "Jazz and the White Critic." *Black Music*. New York: Morrow, 1960.

Brown, Sterling A. "The Blues as Folk Poetry." In *Folk-Say: A Regional Miscellany*, ed. B. A. Botkin. Norman: University of Oklahoma Press, 1930. 324–39.

Carby, Hazel V. "It Jus Be's Dat Way Sometime: The Sexual Politics of Women's Blues." *Radical America* 20, no. 4 (1986): 9–22.

Crouch, Stanley. "Blues to Be Constitutional." In *The All-American Skin Game; or, The Decoy of Race: The Long and the Short of It, 1990–1994*. New York: Pantheon, 1995. 5–20.

Dance, Stanley. *The World of Duke Ellington*. New York: Scribner's, 1970. 2–22.

DeCarava, Sherry Turner. "Celebration." In *Roy DeCarava, Photographs*, ed. James Alinder. Carmel, Calif.: Friends of Photography, 1981. 7–20.

DeVeaux, Scott. "Constructing the Jazz Tradition: Jazz Historiography." *Black American Literature Forum* 25, no. 3 (fall 1991): 525–60.

Douglas Ann. "Skyscrapers, Airplanes, and Airmindedness: 'The Necessary Angel.'" In *Terrible Honesty: Mongrel Manhattan in the 1920s*. New York: Farrar, Straus, and Giroux, 1995. 434–61.

Dyson, Michael Eric. "Be Like Mike? Michael Jordan and the Pedagogy of Desire." *Reflecting Black: African-American Cultural Criticism*. Minneapolis: University of Minnesota, 1993. 64–77.

Early, Gerald. "Pulp and Circumstance: The Story of Jazz in High Places." In *The Culture of Bruising*. New York: Ecco, 1994. 163–205.

Edwards, Brent. "The Seemingly Eclipsed Window of Form: James Weldon Johnson's Prefaces," unpublished paper.

Ellison, Ralph. "The Golden Age, Time Past" and "Richard Wright's Blues." *Shadow and Act*. 1st ed. New York: Vintage, 1972. 199–212, 77–94.

Evans, Bill. "Improvisation in Jazz." Liner notes for Miles Davis, *Kind of Blue*. Columbia **lp cl**1355.

Golson, Benny, and Jim Merod. "Forward Motion: An Interview with Benny Golson." *boundary* 2 (summer 1995): 53–93.

Hurston, Zora Neale. "Characteristics of Negro Expression." *The Sanctified Church*. Berkeley, Calif.: Turtle Island, 1981. 49–68.

Jafa, Arthur. "Black Visual Intonation." *Black Popular Culture*, ed. Gina Dent. Seattle: Bay, 1992. 249–54.

Jefferson, Margo. " 'Noise' Taps a Historic Route to Joy." *New York Times*, November 26, 1995, 4, 27.

Kouwenhoven, John A. "What's 'American' about America." *The Beer Can by the Highway*. Baltimore: Johns Hopkins University Press, 1961; reprint 1988. 37–73.

Levine, Lawrence W. "Jazz and American Culture." *The Unpredictable Past: Explorations in American Cultural History*. New York: Oxford University Press, 1993. 172–88.

Lott, Eric. "Double V, Double-Time: Bebop's Politics of Style." In *Jazz Among the Discourses*, ed. Krin Gabbard. Durham: Duke University Press, 1995. 243–55.

Mackey, Nathaniel. "Other: From Noun to Verb." In *Discrepant Engagement: Dissonance, Cross-Culturality, and Experimental Writing*. New York: Cambridge, 1994. 265–85. Originally published in *Representations* 39 (summer 92): 51–70.

———. "Sound and Sentiment, Sound and Symbol." In *Discrepant Engagement: Dissonance, Cross-Culturality, and Experimental Writing*. New York: Cambridge University Press, 1994. 231–259. Originally published in *Callaloo* 10, no. 1 (winter 1987): 29–54.

Malone, Jacqui. "Jazz Music in Motion: Dancers and Big Bands." In *Steppin' on the Blues: The Visible Rhythms of African American Dance*. Urbana and Chicago: University of Illinois Press. 91–110.

Marsalis, Wynton, and Robert G. O'Meally. "Duke Ellington: 'Music Like a Big Hot Pot of Good Gumbo.' " Interview, April 9, 1992.

Merriam, Alan P., and Fradley H. Garner. "Jazz—The Word." *Ethnomusicology* 12, no. 3 (September 1968): 373–96. With translations by Brent Edwards.

Murray, Albert. "Improvisation and the Creative Process." *Stirrings of Culture*, ed. Robert J. Sardello and Gail Thomas. Dallas: Dallas Institute Publications, 1986. 191–93.

———. "The Function of the Heroic Image." Lecture, Wesleyan University, May 17, 1985.

Powell, Richard J. "Art History and Black Memory: Toward a 'Blues Aesthetic.' " In *History and Memory in African-American Culture*, ed. Geneviève Fabre and Robert O'Meally. New York: Oxford University Press, 1994. 228–43.

Snead, James A. "Repetition as a Figure of Black Culture." In *Black Literature and Literary Theory*, ed. Henry Louis Gates, Jr. New York: Methuen, 1984. 59–79.

Thompson, Robert Farris. "African Art and Motion." In *African Art in Motion*. Washington, D.C.: National Gallery of Art; Los Angeles: University of California Press, 1974. 1–45.

Tomkins, Calvin. "Profiles: Putting Something Over Something Else." *The New Yorker*, November 28, 1977, 53–77.

Troupe, Quincy, and Ben Riley. "Remembering Thelonious Monk: When the Music Was Happening Then He'd Get Up and Do His Little Dance." Interview, April 9, 1990.

sources

Ulanov, Barry. "The Ellington Programme." In *This Is Jazz*, ed. Ken Williamson. London: Newnes, 1960. 131–45.

Wilson, August. Preface. *Three Plays*. Pittsburgh: University of Pittsburgh Press, 1991. vii–xiv.

Wilson, Olly. "Black Music as an Art Form." *Black Music Research Journal* (1983): 1–22.

OF QUOTATIONS

Baldwin, James. "The Uses of the Blues." *Playboy* (January 1964): 241.

Baraka, Amiri. *The Autobiography of LeRoi Jones*. New York: Freundlich, 1984. 47, 50, 51, 55–56, 58, 61, 68, 92, 159, 166, 176, 236–37, 260, 312, 314–15.

———. *Black Music*. Westport, Conn.: Greenwood, 1980. 32–33, 40, 114, 160, 188, 199, 203–4, 209.

Bearden, Romare. Conversation with Robert G. O'Meally, April 1980.

———. 1994 *Calendar*. New York: Harry N. Abrams, 1993. January.

Bronstein, Hugh. "Farrakhan's Nation Breaks Brothers Who Bend." *Daily News*, Dec. 8, 1993, B1.

Brown, Frank London. *Trumbull Park*. Chicago: Regnery, 1959. 415–16.

Crouch, Stanley. "Bull Feeney Plays the Blues." In *Always in Pursuit*. New York: Pantheon, 1998.

Dance, Stanley. *The World of Duke Ellington*. New York: Scribner's, 1970. 2.

Ellington, Duke. Interview in *Esquire*, November 1973. In *Esquire's World of Jazz* (New York: Esquire, 1975). 148.

Ellison, Ralph. *Going to the Territory*. New York: Random House, 1986. 301–2.

———. *Shadow and Act*. 1st ed. New York: Vintage, 1972. 234, 244.

Fax, Elton C. *Seventeen Black Artists*. New York: Dodd, Mead, 1971. 184–85.

Gaines, Ernest J. "Miss Jane and I." *Callaloo* 1, no. 3 (May 1978): 33.

Gottschild, Brenda Dixon. *Digging the Africanist Presence in American Performance*. Westport, Conn.: Greenwood, 1996. 60.

Grosvenor, Verta Mae. Quoted in John F. Szwed, *Space Is the Place: The Lives and Times of Sun Ra*. New York: Pantheon, 1996. 231.

Harper, Michael S. "Don't They Speak Jazz?" *Melas* 10 (spring 1983): 6.

Hentoff, Nat. "An Afternoon with Miles Davis." *Jazz Review* 1, no. 2 (December 1958): 10.

Hodeir, Andre. *Jazz: Its Evolution and Essence*. New York: Grove, 1956. 198.

Howard University Gallery of Art, College of Fine Arts. *Catalog for Tenth Annual Art Faculty Exhibition*. 1980. Alfred J. Smith, Jr., section.

Jones, Gayl. *Corregidora*. New York: Random House, 1975. 45, 56, 59, 96, 146–47.

Kelder, Diane, and Stuart Davis. *Stuart Davis*. New York: Praeger, 1971. 12, 21–22, 92, 104, 130–31.

Kramer, Gary. "The Comedy." Liner notes for *The Comedy*, by the Modern Jazz Quartet. Atlantic 1390, 1962.

Landau, Ellen G. *Jackson Pollock*. New York: Abrams, 1989. 163–66, 168, 174, 182–83, 196.

McPherson, James A. *Elbow Room*. Boston: Little, Brown, 1977. 4.

Murray, Albert. *Hero and the Blues*. Columbia: University of Missouri Press, 1973. 107.

Pemberton, Gayle. *The Hottest Water in Chicago*. Boston: Faber and Faber, 1992. 223.

Robinson, Sugar Ray, with Dave Anderson. *Sugar Ray*. New York: Viking, 1970. 75.

Schwartzman, Myron. *Romare Bearden: His Life and Art*. 107, 288.

Taylor, Arthur. *Notes and Tones*. Liège, Belgium: Arthur Taylor, 1977. 9, 43, 53–54, 55, 61, 86, 96, 106, 131–32, 133, 165, 185, 187, 262, 263, 277, 289.

Walker, Barry. *Jackson Pollock: Defining the Heroic*. Houston: The Museum of Fine Arts, 1996. 10.

Wideman, John Edgar. *Sent for You Yesterday*. New York: Avon Books, 1983. 68, 161, 189.

Wilder, Joe, and Jim Merod. "Interview." *Boundary 2* (summer 1995): 144.

Williams, Martin. *The Jazz Tradition*. New York: Oxford, 1983.

Young, Al, and William J. Harris. "I Write the Blues: An Interview with Al Young." *Greenfield Review* (summer/fall 1982): 16–17.

632

index

Abrams, Muhal Richard, 522

Abstract expressionism, 231, 232, 236–37

Adams, Henry, 436

Adams, Pepper, 38

Adderley, Cannonball, 59, 501

Adderley, Nat, 609

Adler, Phillipe, 440

Africa: and African-American culture, 83–84, 89, 113, 183, 184, 586, 588; American artists and, 169, 230, 238, 239, 521, 614; ancestorism in, 360–62; art in, 87–88, 230, 311–65, 341; coolness in, 362–65; culture of, 67, 303, 356; dance in, vi, 275, 312–14, 317–31, 336–41, 343–45, 350, 352, 356, 365, 494; diaspora from, 598n6; influence of, 208; moderation in, 352, 354, 356, 361; music of, v–vi, 330, 331–32, 334, 343, 494; and origins of jazz, 118, 274, 293, 389, 417, 434, 483, 484; and origins of term "jazz," 7, 15, 16–20, 27; sculpture of, 317, 323–24, 327, 332, 338, 341, 343, 345, 358–59, 361–62, 363; textile patterns in, 320–21, 350–51; views of, 65–66, 576

African-American culture: aesthetic of, 89, 182–94; and Africa, 83–84, 89, 113, 183, 184, 586, 588; and anthologies, 598n6; asymmetry in, 301–2, 521; dance in, 209; in DeCarava's photographs, 262; and European culture, 78n8, 531n26; exploitation of, 524; expression in, 298–310, 515, 516; family in, 556–57, 559–60; in film, 264–68; heroes in, 303, 372; and imitation, 304–5; intellectuals in, 469–71; and jazz, 3–4, 158, 164, 530; jazz in, 118–19, 138; Jooks (pleasure houses) in, 306–9; literature in, 72–74, 188, 580–601; music in, 70–72, 80n25, 82–100, 151, 158, 159, 304–5, 414, 425, 500, 505, 541, 586, 605, 607–9, 611–13, 621; originality in, 304, 515; percussion in, 113, 177; repetition in, 62–81; and spirituals, 89, 160, 166–67, 415; and spontaneity, 374–75, 500; and sports, 372–79; views of, 552–62, 565, 566; whites' attitudes toward, 418–19, 530, 557–59

African Americans: associations of, 411,

413, 438, 471; churches of, 72, 186; duality of, 88–89; history of, 484; and jazz, 3–4; language of, 309–10, 414, 537–38, 584, 587, 593, 594–95; migration of, 226, 239, 547, 558–59; and photography, 180–81; and skyscrapers, 209; stereotypes of, 162, 395

Afro-American (periodical), 227

Afro-American Folksongs (Krehbiel), 414

"Afro-Blue" (Coltrane), 610

Afro-Bossa (album), 143

Aiken, Conrad, 611

Ailey, Alvin, ix

Alexander, Will, 530

"Alexander's Ragtime Band" (Berlin), 425

Ali, Muhammad, vii, 374

Alix, Mae, 291

"All Coons Look Alike to Me" (Hogan), 415

Allen, Frederick Lewis, 212

Allen, Geri, x, 465n12

Allen, Red, 488

Allen, Sam, 233

Allen, William, 516–17

All What Jazz (Larkin), 495

"Along Came Betty" (Golson), 52

Along This Way (Johnson), 587, 593

Alston, Charles, 228–29, 230, 237

Ambersoll, Jamie, 55

Americana (Cortor), 191

American culture: and African-American culture, 78n8, 426; and black music, 83, 88–100, 591; characteristics of, 123–36, 155–56, 160, 449; cynicism in, 157; and Europe, 422, 433, 435, 440–41, 442, 445, 500–501; gridiron town plan in, 124, 126, 136; hybrid identity of, 208–9, 222–23, 236; and jazz, vi–vii, viii, x, 117–19, 124, 145, 400, 406, 409, 410, 412, 431–45, 505; outlaw in, 155, 156–57; and popular culture, 426, 432, 524–26; process and, 133–36; views of, 208–9, 576. *See also* Europe: culture of

American Federation of Musicians, 437, 453

American Humor: A Study of the National Character (Rourke), 130, 576

The American Scene (James), 124

American Thesaurus of Slang (Berrey), 21

Ammons, Gene, 38

Amos, Emma, 237

"Amos 'n' Andy," 408

An Anthology of Verse by American Negroes (White and Jackson), 413

Anatomy of a Murder (album), 147

Anderson, Marian, 558

Anderson, William ("Cat"), 149, 287

The Angel at the Gate (Harris), 621–27

Anthologie Nègre (Cendrars), 598n6

anti-jazz, 141

antiphony. *See* call-and-response

Apollo Theater (Harlem), 232, 279, 284–85, 449

"The Appeal of Primitive Jazz" (Kingsley), 407, 410

"April in Paris," 44, 459

Apthorp, William, 435

Arabic language, 17–18, 19–20, 27

Aragon, Louis, 518

architecture, 86, 249; dancing about, v; of Jazz Age, 196–213, 219–20

Arendt, Hannah, 234

Arlen, Harold, 462

Armory Show, 179

Armstrong, Louis, vii, x, 3, 139, 423, 444, 491; and America, 118–19; and Bearden, 224, 242; and bebop, 461, 495, 498, 522; biography of, 508n16; career of, 489, 491–92, 499; and dance, 274, 284, 291; and free jazz, 503; importance of, 142, 396, 484, 489; and improvisation, 121, 128; in literature, 614, 624, 627; and neo-classicism, 504; in New York, 211; and strings, 401; and swing, 287; views of, 288, 575; white musicians and, 439, 514; world tours of, 442, 459; and young people, 56, 439, 455

Armstrong, M. F., 517

Arnold, Matthew, 405, 407, 434

The Arrivants (poems: Brathwaite), 519

Arseth, Art, 24

art: Abstract-Expressionist, 231, 232, 236–37; African, 230, 311–65, 341; African-American, 418–19; asymmetry in, 301–2; definitions of, 85–88, 111–12; embellishment of, 300–301; and jazz, viii, 4, 130, 146, 175–81, 236–37, 428, 443, 463, 464, 484, 498–505; and national culture, 117; oriental, 235, 238, 269; and personalities, 149–50; political content of, 183; purpose of, 146; and race, 419–22, 426; and social problems, 164; suspending the beat in, 327, 329–31; theories of, 85; unity of, v–vii; views of, 555–56, 569–70, 576

Art and the Social Order (Gotschalk), 86

Art Deco, 36, 185, 208, 209, 211, 218, 219

Art Ensemble of Chicago, 507n8

"Art of the American Negro" (exhibit), 240

Art Students League, 228, 229

Ashe, Arthur, 374

Ashton, Dore, 183, 190, 191

Aspects of Negro Life (paintings; Douglas), 186, 187, 195n20

Astaire, Fred, 384

As the World Turns (film), 210

Atkins, Cholly, 279, 284, 293, 384

"A-Train" (Billy Strayhorn), 35

Attali, Jacques, 497, 523, 524, 529

Attoe, Wayne, 198

Austin, Cecil, 21, 23

Austin, J. L., 525

Austin High (group), 404

Autobiographies (Yeats), 557

The Autobiography of an Ex-Colored Man (Johnson), xiin12, 420, 586, 587, 598n6

The Autobiography of LeRoi Jones (Baraka), 121, 392

Autumn Rhythm (painting; Pollock), 277

Avakian, George, 491

avant-garde, in jazz, 485, 486, 487, 502, 503, 504

aviation, 213–19, 221–22

Awful Sad, 168

Ayler, Albert, 522, 531n26

b

Bach, Johann Sebastian, 150, 402, 403, 500, 504

"Back in Your Own Backyard," ix

"Back Water Blues," 474

Bacon, Francis, 68

Bailey, Bill, 281

Baker, Chet, 403

Baker, Harold, 169, 170, 171

Baker, Houston, x

Baker, Josephine, 279, 396

Balanchine, George, 275

Baldwin, James, 232, 391, 458, 537, 539, 565, 566

Ball, John, 17

ballads, 58–59

Balliett, Whitney, 281, 497

ballin' the jack (dance), 415

Bang, Billy, 402

Bannarn, Henry, 228, 229

Baraka, Amiri, viii, x, xi, 118, 137–42, 457, 530; on African-Americans, 89, 502; and bebop, 461, 463, 521, 522; on Coltrane, 610; and jazz, 536, 538–39; on music, 5, 392, 590, 605, 612; on styles, 193; on white jazz musicians, 513–14, 515; Wilson on, 565, 566

Barnard conference (1982), 469, 470

Barnet, Charlie, 284, 513

Barron, Kenny, 53

Barthelme, George, 441

Barzun, Jacques, 442

Basie, Count, x, 35, 60, 118, 289, 450; and dancers, 279, 284, 288, 292; education of, 421; on Ellington, 291; and film, 177; and free jazz, 503; Gaines on, 537; and swing, 423, 492, 498; and visual arts, 188; and Whiteman, 410

Basin Street Blues, 450

Basso, Ellen B., 523–24

The Bass Saxophone (Skvorecky), 606

Bates, Ad, 229

Bates, Peg Leg, 284

Batouala (Maran), 598n6

Baudelaire, Charles, 596

Baziotes, William, 231, 232

Bearden, Bessye J., 227

Bearden, Howard, 227

Bearden, Nanette Rohan, 234–35

Bearden, Romare, viii, 194n3, 224–42, 285; and black art, 183–84, 190–92; on blues, 391; on dance, 275; and jazz, 176, 178, 183–84, 190; Wilson on, 563, 565–66

Beats, 273, 464

Beatty, Talley, 384

bebop, ix, 390, 424, 457–64; and black intellectuality, 620; and Ellington, 143, 521; and Garvey, 594; Golson on, 36; and hip hop, 462; and jazz, 27, 127, 406, 483–84, 493–94, 497–98, 502–3, 508n14, 521–22; and Minton's Playhouse, 454, 455, 457; and Monk, 109, 140, 459, 463, 521, 522; as music of revolt, 487, 494, 497, 498; origins of, 450, 451, 508n17; and Parker, 401, 461, 462, 465n10, 493, 495, 508nn12&17; and Pollock, 180; and swing, 140, 497, 508n14, 510n27, 521, 531n26; and white culture, 531n26; and zoot suits, 458–59, 460, 464

Bechet, Sidney, 211, 233, 440, 491

Beckenstein, Jay, 506n7

Beckett, Samuel, 58

Beer Can by the Highway (Kouwenhoven), 211

Beethoven, Ludwig von, 74, 129, 145, 150, 152, 443, 500, 504

Beiderbecke, Bix, 211, 419, 423, 424, 492, 508n11; and Armstrong, 514; and black music, 138, 489; tragedy of, 404, 489; in Whiteman band, 418

Bell, Clive, 85

Bellson, Louis, ix, 281

Beloved (Morrison), 517

Bender, Harold H., 13, 17, 18

Benjamin, Joe, 256

Benson, George, 506n7

Benston, Kimberly, 584

Benton, Thomas Hart, 230

Berendt, Joachim-Ernst, 499

Berger, David, 145, 148

Bergson, Henri, 202

Berlin, Irving, 407, 424–27, 441

Bernays, Edward, 215

Bernhardt, Sarah, 205, 218

Bernstein, Leonard, 56, 502

Berrey, Lester V., 21

Berry, Chuck, 401

Berry, John, 37

Berryman, John, 526

Bethune, Mary, 227

Beverly Hills Cop (film), 156

A Bibliographical Check List of American Negro Poetry (Schomburg), 414

big apple (dance), 286

Bigard, Barney, 168, 170

big bands, 57, 59, 60; music of, 144, 278–94, 455, 487, 490, 513

"Big Boy Leaves Home" (Wright), 188

Billie's Bounce (Parker), 141, 459

Billy the Kid, 155

Bingham, Vincent, 382

Bird. *See* Parker, Charlie

Bird, Charles S., 363

Bird, Larry, 266, 267

"Bird Gets the Worm," 459

Birth of the Cool band, 501

Bishop, Walter, Jr., 103

Bitches' Brew (Davis album), 509n24

Black, Brown, and Beige, 166–67, 168

Black, Dave, 281

"Black and Blue" (musical), 381

Black and Tan Fantasy, 168

Black Beauty, 168, 169

Black Bottom (dance), 306–7, 308

Black Boy (play; Tully and Dazey), 210

Black Boy (Wright), 552–62, 582

Blackburn, Paul, 620

Blackburn, Robert, 178

The Black Eagle (Julian), 216

"Black Eye Blues" (Ma Rainey), 477

Blacking Up: The Minstrel Show in Nineteenth-Century America (Toll), 524

Blackman, Teddie, 285

Black Manhattan (Johnson), 417

Black Music in our Culture (de Lerma), 83

Black Nationalism, 565. *See also* African Americans

blackness, 118, 119, 121, 413, 426. *See also* African Americans

The Black Perspective in Music (magazine), 84

Black Renaissance, x, 413. *See also* African Americans; Harlem Renaissance

blacks. *See* African Americans

The Black Speech of the Angel (Alexander), 530

"Black Trumpeter" (Dumas), 530

Blake, Ron, 47, 48, 56

Blakey, Art, 40, 45, 178, 281, 462, 506n7, 523

Blanchard, Terrence, 56

Bland, Edward, 556

Blanton, Jimmy, 143, 170, 402

Blesh, Rudi, 28n2, 463, 486, 492

"The Block" (painting; Bearden), 240

Blücher, Heinrich, 234

Blue Belles of Harlem (Ellington album), 167

Blue Boy (Saar), 189

Blue Harlem (Ellington album), 168

"Blue Monk," 105–6

Blue Note (Philadelphia), 44

blues, 13, 142, 159, 392, 474; and African music, 586; and Constitution, 158–59; and Ellington, 145, 147, 168; Ellison on, 553–54, 562, 582; and folk tradition, 89, 474; images in, 549–51; improvisation in, 112; and jazz, 4, 5, 117, 119, 121, 122, 140, 290, 306, 405, 439, 444, 460; in literature, 536; Murray on, 509n22, 571–77; origins of, 28n2, 152, 160, 167, 306, 391; percussion in, 113; as poetry, 540–51, 583–84; railroad, 475, 546–47; and religion, 196; repetition in, 73; St. Louis, 302, 422; superstition in, 543; swing in, 590; and visual arts, 184, 188, 190–94; and white critics, 137, 138, 139, 141; white singers of, 308; Wilson on, 564, 565, 566; and women, 160–61, 383, 396, 469, 472–75

Blues (Niles and Handy), 414

"Blues" (poem; Brathwaite), 521

Blues People (Baraka), 501, 514, 521, 522

blues poetry, 583–85, 596–97

Blythe, Arthur, 465n12

Boas, Franz, 209

"Body and Soul," 40, 58

"Body and Soul" (essay; Crouch), 163

Bogart, Humphrey, 156

Bohannan, Laura, 336, 337, 359

Bojangles. *See* Robinson, Bill

Bok, Edward, 418

Bolden, Buddy, 489, 495, 507n9

boogie-woogie, 491

The Book of American Negro Poetry, 413, 581, 586, 587, 594, 598n6

The Book of American Negro Spirituals, 581, 585, 586, 587, 588, 591

Borden, Mary, 199

Bordwell, David, 265

Borglum, Gutzon, 199

Bostic, Earl, 56

Bourdieu, Pierre, 484

Bowie, Lester, 465n12, 503

Boyer, Anise, 280

Bragdon, Claude, 199

"Bragging in Brass," 144

Brancusi, Constantin, 232

Brando, Marlon, 156

Braque, Georges, 232

Brathwaite, Edward Kamau, 519–22, 580, 581, 594, 595, 597, 610, 618

Bratton, Johnny, 276

Braxton, Anthony, 620

"break." *See under* improvisation

break dancing, 384

Breitman, George, 464

Brer Rabbit tales, 118

Brice, Fanny, 396

The Bridge (Crane), 213

Briggs, Bunny, 284, 291

Brigham, Carl C., 412

"Bring in da Noise, Bring in da Funk" (musical), 381, 382–84

Bronstein, Hugh, 121

Brooks, Peter, 210

Brooks, Van Wyck, 434

Brother from Another Planet (film), 626

Brown, Buster, 284, 291, 383

Brown, Clifford, 178

Brown, Frank London, 122

Brown, James, 71, 293

Brown, Jim (football player), 276

Brown, King Rastus, 281

Brown, Lawrence, 148, 149, 150, 170, 586

Brown, Norman O., 613

Brown, Piney, 453

Brown, Sterling A., ix, 540–51; and blues, 536, 583, 585; and dialect, 414, 587; on

Ma Rainey, 473–74; works by, 188, 609

Brown, Tom, band of, 24–25

Brown, Wesley, 267

The Brown American (magazine), 410

Brubeck, Dave, 128

Bryant, Ray, 34, 35–36, 37, 48

Bubbles, John, 274, 281, 283, 384

Buchanan, Charles, 229, 286, 287

Buck and Bubbles (dance team), 291

Bullins, Ed, 566

bunny hug (dance), 286

Burke, Kenneth, vi, x, 570, 576

Burleigh, Harry T., 415, 416, 420

Burns, Tommy, 210

Bushell, Garvin, 278, 279

Byas, Don, 33, 34, 40, 56, 121

Byrney, Charles, vi

Caesar, Shirley, 393, 394

Cage, John, 444

Cagney, James, 156

Cahier d'un retour au pays natal (poem; Césaire), 519

cakewalk (dance), 275, 415

"Caldonia," 463

call-and-response, 3; in dance, 281–82, 334, 357–60; Marsalis on, 290; in music, 84, 95–97, 357–60, 592, 598; and repetition, 70; in visual arts, 176; and work songs, 94, 473

Calloway, Cab, vii, 279, 280, 284, 288, 291

Campbell, E. Simms, 227

Camus, Albert, 575

"Canal Street Blues," 439

Cane (Toomer), 73, 606–10, 614

Carby, Hazel V., viii, x, 265, 390, 469–81

Carey, Addison, 285

Caribbean music, 44

Carlin, Lydia, 616, 618, 620

Carmichael, Hoagy, 439

Carnegie Hall concerts: Benny Goodman, 411, 422–23, 424, 425; Billie Holiday, 427; Duke Ellington, 166, 170; James Reese Europe (1912), 417; tribute to Fats Waller (1942), 426

Carney, Harry, 60, 148, 149, 170

Carolina Moon (Monk album), 102

Carolina Shout (painting; Bearden), 191, 192

Caroling Dusk (Cullen), 413

Carpenter, John Alden, 441

Carter, Benny, 46–47, 536

Carter, Betty, 178

Carter, Ron, 56

Castle, Irene, 418, 453

Castle, Vernon, 418

"Catfish Sam'mich," 175

Catlett, Sid, ix, 281, 283, 461

Cato, Minta, 227, 233

Cavanaugh, Inez, 233

Cayton, Horace, 463

Cendrars, Blaise, 598n6

Césaire, Aimé, 518, 519, 530

Cézanne, Paul, 241

"Chain Gang" (Cooke), 610

Challis, Bill, 410

Chamberlain, Clarence, 216

Chan, Jackie, 385

Chanel, Coco, 223

Chaney, Lon, 383

Chanin Building (New York), 202, 207

Chaplin, Charlie, 134, 156, 382, 577

Chapman, Jack, 16, 19, 23, 218

"Characteristics of Negro Expression" (essay; Hurston), 515, 516, 521

Charles, Ray, 539

Charleston (dance), 279, 286, 291, 307, 382, 384

Charleston Bearcats (band), 285

"Cherokee," 155

Chesnutt, Charles, 587

Chicago, 197–98, 211, 219; clubs in, 14, 24–25, 291; origins of term "jazz" in, 24–25

"Chicago Bound Blues," 475

Chicago Defender (newspaper), 227, 437

Chicago Tribune Building, 209, 211

Chocolateers (dance group), 280

Chocolate Kiddies, 278

Chopin, Frédéric, 168, 443

chops, 117–18

chorus lines, 278, 279, 285

Christian, Charlie, 450, 451, 452, 454, 514

Chrysler Building (New York), 197, 198,

index

200, 202, 207, 209, 218, 219

Chuck and Chuckles (dance team), 280

Cinque Gallery (New York), 241

Circus Club (St. Louis), 42

Civil Rights Movement, 239–40, 458, 501

Clarinet Lament, 167

Clark, Kenneth (psychologist), 458

Clarke, Kenny, 281, 443, 450, 454, 461

classical jazz, 401–2, 500, 502, 504

classical music, 74–75, 402, 484, 487, 500, 502, 504, 505, 509n18; Monk on, 104–5

Clef Club (New York), 417, 420, 453

Clovers (group), 462

Coeuroy, André, 10, 21, 23

Cohan, George M., 214, 425

Cole, Bob, 414

Cole, Cozy, 281

Cole, Nat King, 291

Coleman, Ornette, 56, 142, 401, 465n12, 509n22; as avant-gardist, 502, 503; and bebop, 531n26; and white critics, 139, 140

Coleridge-Taylor, Samuel, 415, 416, 420

Coles, Honi, 273, 279, 280, 283, 284, 285, 384

Coles, Johnny, 38, 42

collage, 190, 237–39

Collins, Floyd, 545

color, vi, 146, 167

The Colored American Magazine, 414

The Color Purple (Walker), 471, 479

Coltrane, John, vii, x, 55; Baraka on, 610; on blues, 473; and Ellington, 143; experimentation of, 375; Feld on, 602; and film, 177; Gaines on, 537; Golson on, 32, 34–35, 37, 38–39, 48, 56, 57; Jafa on, 264, 267; and literature, 536; and Monk, 102; political importance of, 484; and rhythm, 71; Riley on, 109; and Rollins, 43; and Sanders, 58; and versioning, 514–15; and white critics, 139, 140, 142

comic strips, 124, 132, 133, 210

The Coming Victory of Democracy (Mann), 161, 163

commedia dell'arte, 538

commercialism, vii, 486, 487, 492, 493,

497, 499, 503, 521

The Commonwealth of Art (Sachs), vi

The Complete Dial Sessions (Parker album), 465n11

"Composition as Explanation" (Stein), 396

Concerto (Rodrigo), 403

Concerto in F (Gershwin), 400

Condon, Eddie, 404, 426, 439, 463

Congress of Racial Equality (CORE), 458

Connie's Inn (Harlem), 229

Connor, A. J., 90

The Conquest of America (Todorov), 161

Constitution, U.S., 129, 154, 157, 158–59, 165

"Conversation With the Three of Me" (Abrams), 522

Cook, Charles (Cookie), 384

Cook, Will Marion, 416, 419–20, 423

Cook and Brown (dance team), 280

Cooke, Sam, 610

cool jazz, 483, 484

Cooper, Anna Julia, 470

Cooper, Ralph, 284

Copasetics (tap dancers' club), 282

Copeland, Carolyn, 528

Corbett, Harvey Wiley, 212

Corn, Joseph J., 215

Corregidora (Gayl Jones), 479, 481

Cortés, Hernando, 161–62, 165

Cortissoz, Royal, 211

Cortor, Eldzier, 191, 193

Cosby, Bill, 376

Cotton Club (Harlem), 169, 170, 210, 229, 288

Cotton Club Review, 280

"Country Preacher," 175

country western music, 57

Courbet, Jean, 234

Cox, Baby, 168

Cox, Ida, 474, 475, 479, 480, 548

The Craftsman (magazine), 417

Crane, Hart, 213

Crawford, Alonzo, 265

Crawford, Jimmy, 283, 288

"The Creation" (Johnson), 587, 591, 593

creole language, 16, 17, 18, 19, 20, 22, 519

Creole Love Call, 168

Crichlow, Ernest, 229, 238, 241

The Crisis (magazine), 437

critics, 163, 463, 496, 499, 502, 503; of
    jazz, 406, 435–38, 441, 442; Negro,
    137, 138, 437–38; white, 137–42, 437,
    501

Crosby, Bing, 459

Crosby, Caresse, 231

Crosby, Harry, 196, 213, 214

Crouch, Stanley, viii, x, 144, 181, 605; on
    avant-garde, 510n26; on Constitution,
    154–65; on Davis, 506n7; on Monk,
    176

Crowley, Daniel, 317

Crucifixion (painting; Douglas), 185–86,
    188

Crump, Freddy, 292

Cullen, Countee, 413, 420, 421

Cullen, Frederick A., 420

Culler, Jonathan, 596

Cuney-Hare, Maud, 90, 437, 441

Curtis-Burlin, Natalie, 586

Czech Musicians' Union, 440

Dabney, Ford, 418, 423

Dadaism, 76

Daily News Building (New York), 206,
    211

Dameron, Tadd, 41–42, 462

Damrosch, Frank, 438

Damrosch, Walter, 400

dance: acrobatic, 280–81; adagio, 280;
    African, vi, 275, 312–14, 317–31,
    336–41, 343–45, 350, 352, 356,
    363–65, 494; African-American, 209;
    and Armstrong, 274, 284, 291; ballet,
    275, 280, 352; ballroom, 280; and
    Basie, 279, 284, 288, 292; Bearden on,
    275; in black church, 72; in black cul-
    ture, 79n17; buck, 283; buck and wing,
    415; call-and-response in, 281–82, 334,
    357–60; comedy, 280; contests for, 285,
    288, 289, 291; in DeCarava pho-
    tographs, 252–53, 256, 258; eccentric,
    280, 284; Ellington on, 278, 284, 287,
    288, 289, 291; fear of, 418; flash, 280,
    281; and freedom, 122, 284; and

Gillespie, 282, 284, 291–92; improvisa-
    tion in, 281, 283–84, 286; jazz, 273,
    274, 275, 281, 293–94, 384; and jazz,
    viii–ix, 59, 144, 273, 274, 278–94, 290,
    292, 452; in literature, 536; in minstrel
    shows, 130; modern, 209, 221, 274;
    Monk's, 106; and music, vi, 90, 273–74,
    276, 287; Negro vs. white, 302; and
    percussion, 81n42, 281, 292, 336–38,
    343, 345, 363–64; players for, 144; pop-
    ularizing, 418–19; and repetition, 68;
    and rhythm, 144, 160, 273; and social
    reality, 605; and sports, 274, 276; stop-
    time, 415; as storytelling, 275, 281; and
    Stravinsky, 75; vernacular, 290–94,
    381, 436. *See also* break dancing; tap
    dancing; *particular dances*

Dance, Stanley, 5, 284, 510n27

dance halls, 279, 285–86, 287, 452. *See
    also* Savoy Ballroom

dancers: and angularity, 301; and Basie,
    279, 284, 288, 292; Ellington on, 281;
    and jazz musicians, 274, 278–94, 291;
    and music, 274, 276; and singers, 291,
    293; Young on, 287

Dans les nuages (In the Clouds;
    Bernhardt), 205

Dante Alighieri, 623, 627

The Darker Brother (Moon), 616

"Darkies' Delights" (Johnson and
    Johnson), 414

Darwin, Charles, 198

Da Silva da Silva's Cultivated Wilderness
    (Harris), 622

Dauer, Alfons, 323

Davis, Benjamin, 465n15

Davis, Charlie, 279, 285

Davis, Eddie (Lockjaw), 454–55

Davis, Francis, 497

Davis, Meyer, 26

Davis, Miles, vii, 4, 5, 54, 156, 403,
    509n20; and African-American tradi-
    tion, 94–95; as boxer, 274; and fusion,
    502, 506n7, 509n24; Golson on, 33, 38,
    52; Harper on, 537; imitators of, 37;
    improvisation of, 97–99, 269–70; Jafa
    on, 264; and Marsalis, 144; on New
    York, 465n9; and racism, 501; and

rhythm, 178; Riley on, 109; on *Sketches of Spain*, 443; and visual arts, 176

Davis, Richard, 402

Davis, Stuart, viii, 176, 178–79, 224, 229

A Day at the Races (film), 288

"Daybreak Express," 144, 145

"The Day of Atonement" (story; Raphaelson), 405

d'Azevedo, Warren, 343

Dazey, Frank, 210

The Dead Lecturer (Baraka), 530

Dean, James, 156

Dean, Philip Hayes, 566

DeCarava, Roy, xi, 176–77, 180–81, 243–63; and jazz, 256

DeCarava, Sherry Turner, 243–63

"Deep River," 607

de Falla, Manuel, 443

de Franco, Buddy, 55

Degas, Edgar, 151

DeJohnette, Jack, 506n7

de Kooning, Willem, 232, 235

Delacroix, Eugène, 224, 234, 235, 238

Delaunay, Charles, 463

de Lerma, Dominique-René, 83

De Man, Paul, 596

democracy: and black culture, 552, 554, 555; and blues, 154–58, 161; and improvisation, 162; and jazz, 117–19, 145, 161, 164–65, 400–401

Democratic Vistas (Whitman), 135

Dent, Gina, 119

Depression, Great, 186, 188, 203, 211, 287, 489, 490; Bearden in, 227, 228, 229

Descartes, René, 68

Desmond, Paul, 142, 403

Deveaux, Scott, 483–505

Dewey, John, 85, 134, 135

Dickinson, Marie, 217

Dictionary of American Slang (Weseen), 21

A Different Drummer (Kelley), 517

"Diminuendo and Crescendo in Blue," 144, 167

The Disappearing City (Wright), 200

Divine, Father, 217

Dixieland, 127, 180, 398, 401, 463

Dixieland Jazz Band, 14, 138; Original,

23–24, 28n3, 404, 409, 514

"Dixie to Broadway" (Negro show), 307

Dixon, Aland, 280

Dixon, William, 440

Doane, Janice, 528

Doctor Faustus (Mann), 606

Dodds, Baby, 23, 24, 288, 389, 439

Dodds, Johnny, 439, 508n10

Dodge, Roger Pryor, 141, 600n36

Dolphy, Eric, 462

Donne, John, 351

Don Quixote (Cervantes), 75

"Don't Fish in My Sea" (Ma Rainey), 477

Dorham, Kenny, 443

Dorsey, Jimmy, 513

Dorsey, Tommy, 513

Dostoevsky, Fyodor, 553

Douglas, Aaron, 176, 184–88, 190, 191–92, 228; politics of, 186–87, 195n20

Douglas, Ann, 176, 196–223

Douglas, Larry, 234

Douglas, Wray, 619

Douglass, Calvin, 237

Douglass, Frederick, 517, 615

Dove, Rita, 530

Down Beat magazine, 15, 26, 141, 463, 493, 508n11

Downes, Olin, 397

drama, 298–99, 305

Dream Songs (Berryman), 526

Dreiser, Theodore, 528

the Drifters (group), 401

Driskell, David C., 188

Drop Me Off at Harlem, 168

A Drum Is a Woman, 167, 169

drumming. *See* percussion

Dubček, Alexander, 157

Dubin, Al, 207

Du Bois, W. E. B., 6, 89, 229, 413, 415, 517, 581, 587

Dudley, Bessie, 293

Duhamel, Georges, 441

Dumas, Henry, 118, 530

Duncan, Isadora, 221

Duncan, Robert, 595

Duncanson, Robert S., 240

Dunfords Travels Everywheres (Kelley), 517

Duquesnay, Ann, 382, 383
Durham, Eddie, 292
"Dust My Broom," 188
Dust Tracks on a Road (Hurston), 419
The Dutchman (Baraka), 118, 530
Dutton, Charles, 567
DuVall, Marcia, 241
Dvořák, Antonín, 435
Dyson, Michael Eric, 372–79

eagle rock (dance), 415
Eaglin, Snooks, 139
Earhart, Amelia, 214, 222
Earle, Jack, 207, 221
Early, Gerald, 393–430
East St. Louis Toodle-Oo, 168
Ebony and Topaz (Johnson), 414
Echoes of Harlem, 167, 168, 169
Eckstine, Billy, 234, 279, 284, 514
Ecole des Beaux Arts (Paris), 211
Edison, Thomas, 156, 523
Edwards, Brent, vii, 580–601
Egypta (dance; St. Denis), 209
Eiffel Tower, 198
Eisenhauer, Peggy, 383
Ekstrom, Arne, 224, 237–38
Eldridge, Roy, 233, 451, 454, 499
Elgar, Edward, 409
Eliot, T. S., x, 76, 132, 133, 407–8, 611,
    617–18
Ellington, Duke, vii, viii, x, 166–71, 455;
    and Africa, 166, 169; background of,
    418; and Bearden, 224, 227; and bebop,
    143, 521; and big-band jazz, 513; and
    blues, 145, 147; career of, 489, 499; as
    colorist, 146, 167; compositions of,
    425; and dance, 278, 280, 281, 284,
    287, 288, 289, 291; on Garvey, 594;
    and Hood, 212; importance of, 142,
    484; influence of, 504; on jazz, 5, 443,
    444; and literature, 535; Marsalis on,
    143–53; Murray on, 573, 575; and
    Nance, 402; as New Orleans musician,
    150; on New Yorkers, 207; orchestra of,
    59–60, 147–50, 423, 490, 492, 500;
    performances of, 152, 166; as pianist,
    150; rhythm of, 143; and Savoy
    Ballroom, 288, 289; and Strayhorn,

282, 289; and swing, 498; *Swing* maga-
    zine series of, 166–67; symphonic jazz
    and, 421–22; and trains, 152; and visu-
    alization, 175, 176, 178, 188; vocal
    arrangements of, 462; on Whiteman,
    410
Ellison, Ralph, vii, ix, x, xi, 122, 390,
    448–56, 623; and Bearden, 236; on
    bebop, 465n8; and black culture, 78n8,
    499, 614, 615; and blues, 536; and
    James Weldon Johnson, 589, 592; on
    jam sessions, 282–83, 453; on jazz, 4, 5,
    120, 175, 287, 290; on New York, 460;
    on Savoy Ballroom, 290; use of repeti-
    tion by, 72; on Wright, 552–62, 582
Emerson, Ralph Waldo, 128, 133–34
Empire State Building (New York), 176,
    198, 199, 200, 202, 219
Empson, William, 557–58
*Encyclopédie de la musique et dictionnaire du
    conservatoire* (Lavignac), 9
Engelbrecht, Barbara, 286
Engels, Friedrich, 223
England, 63, 199–200, 215
English language, 299–300, 309–10,
    515–16, 519
the Enlightenment, 68
Ernst, Hugh C., 402
Eshleman, Clayton, 518
Esquire (magazine), 463, 492
ethnicity, 51, 52, 486, 487, 501, 502. *See
    also* African Americans
Etting, Ruth, 396
Etude (magazine), 7
Eugene O'Neill Theatre Center, 567
Europe, 199–200, 215, 576; art in, 241;
    and Bearden, 228, 235, 237, 238, 239;
    culture of, 63–70, 74–77, 78n8, 85–87,
    182, 183, 208, 561–62; and jazz, 90,
    452; music of, 74–75, 104–5, 402, 484,
    487, 500, 502, 504, 505, 509n18. *See
    also* American culture
Europe, James Reese, 11, 23, 411, 416–20,
    423, 453
Evans, Bill, 269–70
Evans, Gil, 391, 443, 509n20
Evans, Oliver, 135
Evans-Pritchard, E. E., 357

"Every Day," 122

"The Evolution of Afro-American Artists: 1800–1950" (exhibit), 240

"Fables of Faubus," 501

Farmer, Henry George, 17

Farrakhan, Louis, 157

Fascism, 64, 78n7, 216

Faulkner, William, 76, 390, 561

Fauset, Jessie, 471

Feather, Leonard, 463, 492, 493, 499, 500

Federal Writers' Project, 614

Feingold, Michael, 567

Feld, Steven, 602–3, 604

Feldman, Mark, 32

"Fences" (play; Wilson), 563, 567

Ferguson, Perry, 237

Ferriss, Hugh, 197, 199, 202, 207, 220

Fetchit, Stepin, 382

Fieve, Ronald, 201

"Fifty Year and Other Poems" (Johnson), 414

film: on aviation, 215; and Bearden, 191, 238; and black culture, 264–68; and jazz, 177, 181; and repetition, 74, 76

Finck, Henry T., 15, 16

Fine Clothes to the Jew (Hughes), 595

The First Book of Negro Spirituals (Johnson and Johnson), 414

Fisher, Jules, 383

Fisk Jubilee Singers, 309

Fitzgerald, Ella, 118, 274, 291–92

Fitzgerald, F. Scott, x, 407, 408, 412; and airmindedness, 197, 201, 210, 213, 218, 219

Fitzgerald, Zelda, 197

Five Spot (New York club), 102, 103

Flanner, Janet, 213

Flight to Canada (Reed), 73, 517

Floyd, Samuel, 90

"Flying Home," 118

Focillon, Henri, 596

folk music, 435, 444, 474, 486, 491, 499, 501

folk tradition, 302–4; black, 188–90, 607–8, 614; of black music, 89, 91–94, 99, 585–88; blues as poetry of, 540–51; Caribbean, 625; and jazz, 499, 501; in literature, 553; and origins of term "jazz," 8, 15

"Folkways" (Brathwaite), 610

Ford, Abiyi, 265

Ford, Ford Madox, 206

Ford, Henry, 156, 218, 302, 303–4

Ford, John, 181

Forest, Jimmy, 41

For His Mother's Sake (film), 210

Forrest, Leon, 73

Foster, Frank, 60

Foster, Pops, 287

Foster, Stephen, 434, 525

The Four Banks of the River of Space (Harris), 522

Four Bobs (vaudeville act), 284

Four Negro Poets (Locke), 413

Frank, Waldo, 607

Frankie and Johnny, 536

Franklin, Aretha, 177, 267, 396

free jazz, ix, 72, 483, 502–3, 503, 504, 506n4

The Free-Lane Pallbearers (Reed), 73

Freeman, Bud, 404, 439

"Freight Train Blues," 475

French language, 16, 18–20, 27–28, 63–64

Freud, Sigmund, 85–86, 203–5, 223, 572; on plurality of lives, 208–9; on repetition, 66, 70, 76, 78n11

From a Broken Bottle Traces of Perfume Still Emanate (Mackey), 605–6

Fry, Roger, 85

Frye, Northrup, 582, 597

Fuller, Gil, 494

funk, 140

fusion, 465n12, 483–87, 501, 502, 504, 506nn6&7, 509n24

Futurists, 215, 219

G, Kenny, 506n7

Gaines, Ernest J., 537

Gaines, Reg E., 382, 383

Gales, Larry, 105, 107

Gammon, Reginald, 237

García Lorca, Federico, 229, 231, 597

Garner, Errol, 277, 401

Garner, Fradley H., 7–28

Garrison, Lucy McKim, 516, 517

Garvey, Marcus, 217, 411, 413, 471, 521, 594

Gates, Henry Louis, Jr., ix, x, 584

Gatewood, Willard B., Jr., 431

Genius of Charlie Parker (album), 461

Genius of Modern Music (album), 462

"The Geomonic Band" (jazz workshop), 180

George Washington Carver Art School (Harlem), 244

Gerima, Haile, 265

German language, 64

Gershwin, George, 308, 398, 400, 403, 409, 424, 426

GhettOriginal Productions, 384

Gibson, Althea, 374

Giddins, Gary, 462, 497, 508n16

Gilbert, Cass, 198, 201, 202

Gilbert, Gama, 423

Gillespie, Dizzy, vii, 61, 443, 459, 462; and bebop, 460–61, 493, 508n17; and dance, 282, 284, 291–92; and free jazz, 503; Golson on, 34, 36, 37, 38, 39, 48; as intellectual, 620; at Minton's Playhouse, 450, 454, 460; and Pollock, 180; profile in *Life*, 494; Riley on, 108, 109; on unity in jazz, 120; and white critics, 141; world tours of, 442

Gilliam, Sam, 194n3

Gilmore, John, 523

Gilroy, Paul, 598

Ginsberg, Alan, 464

Giroux, Henry, 377

Glover, Savion, 381, 382, 383

God Bless, 289

"Go Down, Moses," 607

God's Trombones (Johnson), 185, 414, 586, 587, 593, 594

Goffin, Robert, 10, 11, 16, 21, 23, 25

Going to the Territory (Ellison), 120

Goldberger, Paul, 208

Goldkette, Jean, 404

Goldwater, Robert, 324

The Golliwog Revue, 284

Golson, Benny, 32–61, 53–55, 57–58

Gonsalves, Paul, 60, 148, 171, 176

Goodman, Benny, 128, 149; and bebop, 494; and black culture, 237, 439, 514;

Carnegie Hall concert (1938), 411, 422–23, 424, 425; and classical music, 403, 443–44; and Great Depression, 489–90; as King of Swing, 426, 514, 522; at Minton's Playhouse, 450, 455; at Savoy Ballroom, 289; and Whiteman, 422, 423, 424; world tours of, 442

"Good Morning Blues," 118

"Good Morning Heartache," 596

Gordon, Dexter, 33, 39, 40, 58, 59

Gorham, Joseph K., 20, 21, 22

Göring, Hermann, 216

gospel music, 89, 90–91. *See also* spirituals

Gotschalk, D. W., 86

Gottlieb, Adolph, 231

Gottschild, Brenda Dixon, 275

Graham, Charles, 448

Graham, Martha, 209, 221

Grant, Madison, 412

Grant, Percy Stickney, 437

Grappelli, Stephane, 402

Gray, Harold, 133

The Great Audience (Seldes), 208, 222

The Great Gatsby (Fitzgerald), 197, 210, 400, 407, 408, 409, 411

The Great Swing Bands (album), 522

Green, B. W., 21

Green, Chuck, 383

Greene, Carroll, 240

Greer, Sonny, 143, 167

Grofe, Ferdie, 22, 398, 410

Grosvenor, Verta Mae, 276

Grosz, George, 228, 229

Groundhog (tap dancer), 281

Guillen, Nicolas, 583, 597

Gurdjieff, Georges Ivanovitch, 202

Guy, Joe, 454

gypsies, 235–36

Gysen, Fritz, v, vii

h

Hadlock, Richard, 138

Haig, Al, 456

Hall, Adelaide, 168

Hall, Stuart, 264

Hall, Tubby, 291

Hamilton, Jimmy, 149, 150, 170

Hammerstein, Oscar, 453

Hammond, John, 229

Hammons, David, 194n3

Hampton, Lionel, 118, 282, 291, 309, 423, 463, 514

Handy, W. C., 28n2, 188, 414, 422

hard bop, 483, 484, 485, 501–2, 509n23

Hardenbergh, Henry Janeway, 197

Hardwicke, Toby, 170

Hargrove, Roy, 48, 56

Harlem, 217, 417; artists in, 228, 232, 244, 471; Bearden in, 224, 226, 227–31; in blues, 548; and Ellington, 168, 169, 171; and European culture, 444, 452; Minton's Playhouse in, 449–56, 460; Renaissance Ballroom in, 274; riots in, 458, 464; sports in, 274; Uptown House in, 454, 458; whites and, 440. *See also* Savoy Ballroom

Harlem Air-Shaft (Ellington), 168

The Harlem Express (revue), 279

Harlem Flat Blues (Ellington), 168

The Harlem Footwarmers (Ellington band), 169

"Harlem on My Mind" (exhibit; Metropolitan Museum of Art), 240

Harlem Renaissance, xiin12, 209, 413, 419, 420, 471, 581

Harlem Renaissance (basketball team), 274

Harlem River Quiver (Ellington), 168

Harlem Shadows (Claude McKay), 598n6

Harlem Speaks (Ellington), 168

harmony, 146, 147, 436

Harmony in Harlem (Ellington), 168

Harper, Leonard, 280, 285

Harper, Michael S., ix–x, 536, 537–38

Harper, Peggy, 324

Harrell, Ed, 431

Harris, Craig, 522

Harris, Joel Chandler, 415

Harris, William J., 6, 537

Harris, Wilson, 515, 522, 529, 597–98, 606, 621–27

Harrison, Hubert H., 411, 426

Hart, James D., 10, 12, 13, 19, 25

Harte, Bret, 526

Harvest Moon Ball (dance competition), 289

Hausa language, 17

Hawes, Bess Lomax, 352

Hawes, Hampton, 497

Hawkins, Coleman, 278, 489; Golson on, 33, 36, 38, 40, 43, 56; at Minton's Playhouse, 450, 454, 455

Hawkins, Erskine, 284

Hawthorne, Nathaniel, 434

Hayakawa, S. I., 27

Hayden, Robert, 536

Hayes, Roland, 305

Hayes, Vertis, 229

Haynes, Don C., 141

Haynes, Roy, 105, 256

Hayton, Lennie, 410

Hearn, Lafcadio, 16, 17

Hebdige, Dick, 514

Hegamin, Lucille, 474

Hegel, Georg Wilhelm Friedrich, 64–70, 74, 75, 78n15, 327

Heidegger, Martin, 78n11

Held, John, Jr., 210

Hélion, Jean, 232

Hellzapoppin' (film), 288

Helms, Jesse, 157

Hemingway, Ernest, 120, 212, 213, 451, 554, 572

Henderson, Eddie, 33

Henderson, Fletcher, 188, 210, 284, 285, 421, 424, 490; and white musicians, 513, 514, 521

Henderson, Harry, 225, 240

Henderson, Joe, 33

Henderson, Richard, 364

Henderson, Rosa, 474

Henderson, Stephen, 584–85, 589

Henderson, W. J., 442

Hendrix, Jimi, 157

Hentoff, Nat, 6, 287

Herbert, Victor, 409

Herder, Johann Gottfried von, 64

"Heritage" (poem; Cullen), 413

Herman, Woody, 284

Hernandez, Riccardo, 383

The Hero and the Blues (Murray), 161, 573, 574, 575

Hey Ba Ba Rebop, 463

Hickman, Art, 22, 398

"Hi-Fly" (Weston), 462

Higginson, Thomas Wentworth, 435

Highbrow/Lowbrow (Levine), 431

highbrow/lowbrow distinction, 436–38, 443

"High John de Conquer" (Hurston), 516, 517

Hill, Dulé, 382

Hill, Teddy, 280, 449, 452, 454

Hindemith, Paul, 464, 502

Hine, Lewis, 200

Hines, Earl ("Fatha"), viii, 428n2, 499; at Apollo Theater, 279; and Bearden, 224–25, 242; and dancing, 280, 284, 291; Davis on, 176; influences on, 443; and Whiteman, 441

Hines, Felrath, 237

Hines, Gregory, 384

hip-hop (dance), 385

Hipponax, 612–13

history, ix, 78n15; African-American, 381–82, 413; cyclical views of, 67–69; of jazz, 384, 390, 483–505; and race, 384

A History of Jazz in America (Ulanov), 495–96

History of the Voice (Brathwaite), 580

Hitler, Adolph, 214, 216, 222, 464

Hobsbawm, Eric, 441, 497

Hobson, Wilder, 15, 19

Hodeir, André, 6, 128, 499

Hodges, Johnny, 148–50, 170, 390, 461; Golson on, 33, 35, 38, 60

Hofstadter, Richard, 129

Hogan, Ernest, 415

Holder, Geoffrey, 291

Holder, Roland, 283

Holiday, Billie, vii, ix, 6, 118, 427–28, 522, 596; and Bearden, 224; death of, 404

Holland, Josiah, 21

Hollingsworth, Al, 237

Hollyday, Christopher, 403

Holmes, John Clellon, 529–30

Holty, Carl, 231, 232

honky tonk, 19

"Honky Tonk Train," 175

Hood, Raymond, 200, 206, 207, 209, 211–13, 218, 220

Hoofer's Club (New York), 283

Hooker, Dynamite, 280

Hooks, Bell, 265

Hope of Liberty (Horton), 517

Hopkins, Claude, 279, 284

Hopkins, Lightning, 139, 324

Hopper, Edward, 200

Horne, Lena, 450

The Horn (Holmes), 529–30

Horton, George Moses, 517

Hot Chocolate (musical short), 288

"Hot House," 462

Hot House Flowers (Marsalis album), 401, 425

hot jazz, 425, 463, 490, 492, 493

Hot Jazz (Panassié), 488

The Hot Mikado, 288

Houdini, Harry, 205–6, 208, 218, 220

The House of the Dead (Dostoevsky), 553

Howard, Darnell, 23

Howl (poem; Ginsburg), 117

Hubbard, Freddie, 50

Huckleberry Finn (Twain), 132, 133

Hudson, Theodore, 539n1

Hughes, Langston, ix, 192, 229, 414, 536; and DeCarava, 245, 262; poetry of, 301–2, 305, 420–21, 583, 585, 587, 595

Hughes, Robert, 199

humor, 117, 130, 146, 280, 293, 480, 576

Humphrey, Doris, 229

Hunt, Richard, 194n3

Hunter, Alberta, 474

"Hunting Is Not Those Heads on the Wall" (essay; Baraka), 521

Hurst, Fannie, 395

Hurston, Zora Neale, 209, 212, 265; on African-Americans, 298–310, 515–17, 521; on black aesthetic, 188–90; and Johnson, 580, 581, 585, 598; on spirituals, 590, 591; use of dialect by, 587; on white influence, 419; on women, 471

Husserl, Edmund, 78n11

"Hustlin' Blues," 477–78

Ibsen, Henrik, 208, 566

I Ching (Book of Changes), 80n22
"I Got Rhythm," 460–61
"I'm Coming Virginia," 419
"I'm Gonna Sit Right Down and Write
    Myself a Letter," 426
improvisation, 6; in black music, 80n25;
    in blues poetry, 585; and the break,
    111–13; of Catlett, 283; of Coltrane,
    515; and creative process, 111–13; in
    dance, 281, 283–84, 286; of Davis,
    97–99, 269–70; and DeCarava, 246;
    and democracy, 162; Golson on, 47, 48,
    50; in jazz, 5, 121, 128, 162, 163, 441,
    453, 486, 494; in minstrel shows, 130;
    Murray on, 161, 277, 569, 573, 577; of
    Parker, 155; and repetition, 70–71; and
    seeing jazz, 180, 181; in sports, 374–75;
    in storytelling, 537; in writing, 616–21
I'm Slappin' Seventh Avenue, 168
India, vi
Indian Suite (MacDowell), 435
individualism: in American culture, 124,
    125, 155; in black culture, 556–57,
    559–60; in DeCarava's photographs,
    262; of jazz musicians, 117–18, 120,
    146, 147–49, 159, 161–63, 283, 439,
    443; in minstrel shows, 130; Murray on,
    578; in spirituals, 592–93; and unity,
    117, 120, 125, 128
The Infinite Rehearsal (Harris), 515, 522
Ingalls, Clyde, 207
"In House Blues" (Bessie Smith), 476–77
International style (architecture), 211
In the Realm of the Senses (film; Oshima),
    266
"In the Tradition" (Baraka), 536
Invisible Man (Ellison), 72, 175, 614, 615,
    627
"I Remember Clifford" (Golson), 53
Is America Safe for Democracy?
    (MacDougal), 412
Italy, 215
"It Don't Mean a Thing If It Ain't Got
    That Swing," 143, 148, 426–27, 462
"It's Monk's Time" (Monk album), 103
It Was a Sad Night in Harlem, 168
Ives, Charles, 434

"I Want to Talk About You" (Eckstine),
    514–15

Jackson, Bo, 378
Jackson, Bullmoose, 41, 42
Jackson, Janet, 383
Jackson, Jesse, 194n3
Jackson, Mahalia, 383
Jackson, Quentin, 171
Jacobs, Harriet, 517
Jacobson, Bud, 23
Jacquet, Illinois, 292
Jafa, Arthur, 264–68
James, C. L. R., 464
James, Harry, 411
James, Henry, 124, 434, 537, 572
James, William, 136, 196, 198, 200–202,
    206–9, 211; and Freud, 203–5
"Jam on the Groove" (revue), 384–85
jam sessions, 282–83, 453–54
Japanese art, 269
Jarrett, Keith, 401, 403
Jasbo Brown stories, 8–11, 13, 16
jazz: definitions of, viii, 3–4, 128, 486;
    euphemisms for, 25–27; forms of, 3, 5;
    as freedom music, 117–19, 122, 163,
    439, 440; history of, 384, 390, 483–505;
    interdisciplinary views of, v–xi; main-
    stream, 503–4; as New Thing, 484,
    502; orchestration of, 398; origins of,
    118, 130, 152, 155, 274, 293, 389, 432,
    483, 484; origins of word, 7–28,
    416–17; as primitive music, 407–8, 491,
    494; as revolt, 440, 451; as Romance,
    490, 505; in school curriculum, 60–61;
    soul in, 118, 152, 164; and strings, 401,
    402; structure of, 127–30, 146; terms
    in, 484; timing in, 111–13, 129,
    130–31; types of, 127, 463; visualiza-
    tion of, 175–81; and wholeness, 163;
    world stature of, 442. *See also particular
    artists and types*
Jazz (Whiteman), 397, 403–4
Jazz: Hot and Hybrid (Sargeant), 490
Jazz: Its Evolution and Essence (Hodeir), 128
Jazz and the White Americans (Leonard),
    410

jazz bands: and dancing acts, 279, 280, 281, 293; and media, 279, 514; saxophone in, 423–24, 437, 454; vs. symphony orchestras, 441; white, 404. *See also individual bands*

The Jazz Book (Berendt), 499

Jazz E Sazz Band, 24

Jazz for the Thinker (Lateef album), 620

"Jazz for Young People" (lecture; Wynton Marsalis), 143

Jazzmen (ed. Smith and Ramsey), 24, 489, 493, 499

Jazzmen (Russell), 507n9

jazz poetry, 420, 421, 585

The Jazz Revolution: Twenties America and the Meaning of Jazz (Ogren), 403

jazz-rock, 506n4

The Jazz Singer (play and film; Raphaelson), 405, 408

Jazz Study Group (Columbia University), xi–xii

The Jazz Tradition (Williams), 163, 497

Jefferson, Blind Lemon, 540

Jefferson, Margo, 381–85

"Jelly's Last Jam" (musical), 381

Jenkins, Freddy ("Little Posey"), 170, 242, 291

Jews, 155, 405, 422, 424, 425, 595

"Jig Walk" (dance), 278–79

jitterbug jive (dance), 286

Joachim of Floris, 68

"Joe Turner's Come and Gone" (play; Wilson), 563, 567, 568

Johnson, Bunk, 141, 491, 507n9, 508n10, 611–12, 614–19, 621

Johnson, Charles S., 414

Johnson, Edith, 479

Johnson, Frank, 90

Johnson, Guy B., 14, 21, 414

Johnson, Jack, 73, 209–10, 220

Johnson, James P., 242, 422, 443

Johnson, James Weldon, x, xii n12, 185, 229, 413–20, 580–601

Johnson, J. J., 509n20

Johnson, J. Rosamond, 414–15, 586

Johnson, Lem, 453

Johnson, Magic, 266

Johnson, Myra, 284

Johnson, Robert, 113, 188

Johnston, Joshua, 240

Jolson, Al, 155, 157, 405, 408, 546

Jones, A. M., 316, 320, 331, 340, 365

Jones, Bessie, 352

Jones, Bill T., ix

Jones, Elvin, 56, 71

Jones, Gayl, 120, 277, 392, 479, 481, 536

Jones, Jimmy, 256

Jones, Jo, ix, 281, 389, 461

Jones, LeRoi. *See* Baraka, Amiri

Jones, Philly Joe, 42, 106, 281, 282

Jones, Richard M., 23

Jooks (pleasure houses), 306–9

Joplin, Scott, 28n2

Jordan, Clifford, 33

Jordan, Duke, 54, 461

Jordan, Louis, 56

Jordan, Michael, ix, 266, 267, 372–79

The Journal of Negro History, 413

Joyce, James, 76, 118, 462, 553, 555

Jubilee Singers, 435

Judge, Louis, 38–39

Julian, Essie, 217

Julian, Hubert Fauntleroy, 215–19, 222

The Jungle Band (Ellington band), 169

Jungle Blues, 169

Jungle Jamboree, 169

Jungle Nights in Harlem, 168, 169

K

Kahanga, Sukari, 315

Kalapalo (Brazil), music of, 523–25

Kaluli people, 602–3, 604, 605, 621

Kaper, Bronislau, 95

"Katie Left Memphis," 91–94

Kaye, Sammy, 142

Kees, Weldon, 464

Keil, Charles, 312, 336

Kelder, Diane, 179

Kelley, William Melvin, 517

Kendall, Elizabeth, 202, 221

Kent, George, 595

Kenton, Stan, 27

Kenyatta, Jomo, 312

Kerlin, Robert T., 413

Kern, Jerome, 424

Kerouac, Jack, ix, 457, 464, 536

Kersand, Billy, 293

Kierkegaard, Soren, 74, 426
"Kind of Blue," 175
Kind of Blue (Davis album), 269–70
King, Martin Luther, Jr., 155, 156, 266
The Kingdom of Swing (Goodman), 411
Kingsley, Walter, 7, 11, 15–17, 19, 25, 407, 410, 416
Kirk, Andy, 284, 421, 493
Kirkpatrick, Douglas, 375
Klugh, Earl, 401
Kofsky, Frank, 463
"Koko" (Parker), 144, 154, 166, 457
Konitz, Lee, 509n20
Koolhaas, Rem, 198–99, 202, 203, 212
Kool Moe Dee, 375
Kootz, Samuel, 231, 232
Kouwenhoven, John A., viii, 123–36, 211, 576
Kramer, Gary, 538
Krasner, Lee, 180
Krehbiel, Henry Edward, 414, 586
Krell, William H., 28n2
Krenek, Ernst, 441
Kristeva, Julia, 604
Kronos Quartet, 402
Krupa, Gene, 289, 439
Krutch, 203

Lacan, Jacques, 70
"Lady Be Good," 118
Lady Sings the Blues (Holiday), 427
Ladzekpo, S. Kobla, 332
La Guardia, Fiorello, 458, 464
Lambert, Constant, 170–71, 443
Landau, Ellen G., 180, 277
Lang, Fritz, 383
Langewiesche, Wolfgang, 126
language, 63–64, 72, 77; of African-Americans, 309–10, 414, 537–38, 584, 587, 593, 594–95; jazz as universal, 442. *See also particular languages*
Lanier, Sidney, 435–36
Lapham, Dorothy, 207
Larkin, Philip, 495
Larsen, Nellie, 471–72
Lateef, Yusef, 620
"Laura," 58
Laurence, Baby, 281, 282, 283, 284, 291, 384

Lawd Today (Wright), 401
Lawrence, D. H., 133, 209, 563
Lawrence, Jacob, 228, 229, 230, 237
"Lay Away Your Troubles" (Johnson and Johnson), 414
Lazarillo de Tormes, 75
Leadbelly, 113
Leaves of Grass (Whitman), 124, 125, 132–33
Le Corbusier, 127
Lee, Canada, 227
Lee, Spike, 156, 378
Legba (African spirit), 613–14, 615, 616, 622, 623, 625
LeGon, Jeni, 284
Leib, Sandra, 477
Leibnitz, 64
Leonard, Neil, 409
Leonard, Sugar Ray, ix
Leroy and Edith (vaudeville act), 284
Let My Children Hear Music (Mingus), 390
Levine, Lawrence W., 431
Levinson, André, 441
Lewis, John, 52, 56, 403, 444, 509n20, 538
Lewis, Norman, 176, 229, 237, 241
Lewis, Ramsey, 506n7
Lewis, Ted, 27
Lewisohn, Sam, 232
Liberian Suite, 167, 169
Life magazine, 494
"Lift Every Voice and Sing" (Johnson and Johnson), 414
Lincoln, Abby, 176
Lincoln, Abraham, 155, 156, 401
Lindbergh, Anne Morrow, 221
Lindbergh, Charles, 213–14, 215, 218, 221
Lindsay, Vachel, ix, 212
"Lindy: A Love Song" (Johnson and Johnson), 414
Lindy Hop (dance), 275, 284, 286–89, 292, 382, 384
liner notes, 535, 539n2
"Listening to Sonny Rollins at the Five Spot" (Blackburn), 620

Literary Digest (magazine), 22, 438
literature, ix–x, 535–39; and black
    anthologies, 413–14, 415; blues singers
    in, 473; criticism of black, 580–601;
    European, 75–77; Murray on, 571–72;
    and music, 602–28. *See also particular
    authors*
Little Orphan Annie (comic strip), 133
Little Richard, 266
Live at the Bal Masque (Ellington album),
    144
Liveright, Horace, 210
Livery Stable Blues, 23, 409
Locke, Alain, 183, 413, 414, 439, 581
Locke, Eddie, 281
Lomax, Alan, 316
London, Jack, 210, 220
"Lonesome Desert Blues," 540
Long, Johnny Lee, 284
"Long Track Blues" (Brown), 188
Lopez, Vincent, 13, 25–26, 404, 422, 423
Lorber, Jeff, 506n7
Lord, Audre, 581
Lord, Francisco, 229
Lott, Eric, 457–81, 497
Louis, Joe, 374
Loussier, Jacques, 403
Lucas, John, 27
Lucid Interval as Integral Music
    (Roberson), 530
Ludlow, Helen W., 517
Ludwig, William, 23
Lukács, Georg, 514, 606
"Lullaby of Birdland," 118
Lunceford, Jimmy, 42, 391, 498, 513; and
    dancers, 279, 280, 284, 292, 492
Lynch, Johnny, 39
lyrics, 175, 596–97

Mablin, Harold, 283
McDaniels, Hattie, 481
MacDougall, William, 412
MacDowell, Edward, 435
McGhee, Howard, 461, 522
McKay, Claude, 228, 229, 230, 232, 587,
    598n6
Mackey, Nathaniel, 513–30, 581, 592,
    597, 602–28

"Mack the Knife," 624
McLuhan, Marshall, 200, 221, 412
McPartland, Jimmy, 404, 439
McPherson, James A., 275
Made in America (Kouwenhoven), 576
Madison Square Garden, 198
Madonna, 156, 383
A Magician among the Spirits (Houdini),
    205
Mailer, Norman, 395, 457, 619
Majors, William, 237
Malcolm X, 156, 266, 460
Malone, Jacqui, 273, 278–94
Malraux, André, 112, 556, 572
Mance, Junior, 103
Manhattan. *See* New York City
Manhattan Company Bank (New York),
    198
Manhattan School of Music, 148
Mann, Thomas, 161, 163, 164, 572, 606
Manning, Frankie, 288, 289
Manone, Wingy, 129
Man Orchid (Williams), 611, 615–21, 622
Mansfield, Katherine, 527
Marable, Fate, 24, 508n11
"Ma Rainey" (poem; Brown), 474
"Ma Rainey's Black Bottom" (play;
    Wilson), 563, 567
Maran, René, 598n6
marching bands, 90, 273
"Marezy Coats," 459
Mariani, Paul, 616, 619–20
The Marianne Moore Reader, 206
Marinetti, Filippo Tommaso, 215
Mark, Zane, 383
Markham, Pigmeat, 284
Marsalis, Wynton, 290, 401, 487, 506n7;
    and Bearden, 176; on Ellington,
    143–53, 291; on fusion, 506n6; and
    jazz, 403, 425, 510n28; neo-classicism
    of, 485, 504
Marshall, Paule, 614
Martin, David Stone, 535
Marx, Karl, 223
Mason, Daniel Gregory, 437
"Massa's in de Cold, Cold Ground"
    (Foster), 525
Massey, Cal, 37

index

Mathews, Mitford M., 21
Mathis, Johnny, 401
Matisse, Henri, 176, 179, 233, 566
matriarchy, 202–8
Mayhew, Richard, 237
Mbiti, John S., 360
McGraw-Hill Building (New York), 211
McNeely, Jay, 605
McRae, Carmen, vi
Mein Kampf (Hitler), 216
"Melanctha" (story; Stein), 527–28
melody, 70, 71, 93–94, 146, 147, 436;
    Golson on, 51–52, 59
"Memphis Blues," 488
Menashe, Sam, 233
Mencken, H. L., 21, 406, 437
Mensah, Nana Ntiamoah, 350, 351
Menzel, Brigitte, 329
Mercer, Kobena, 194n4
Merod, Jim, 32–61, 391
Merriam, Alan P., 7–28, 357
Merritt, Jymie, 40, 42
Metronome magazine, 284, 463, 493
The Metropolis of Tomorrow (Ferriss), 197,
    199, 202, 207
Metropolitan Life Insurance Company
    Building (New York), 198
Mexican muralists, 230, 245
Mezzrow, Milton ("Mezz"), 439, 444, 613
Micheaux, Oscar, 216, 265
A Midsummer Night's Dream
    (Shakespeare), 171
Miles Davis Nonet (group), 509n20
Miley, Bubber, 167, 168, 169–70
military music, 90
Millender, Lucky, 41
Miller, Arthur, 566
Miller, Earl, 237
Miller, Fred, 616–21
Miller, Lois, 284
Miller, Mulgrew, 33
Miller, Norma, 288
Miller, Paul Eduard, 490, 492
Miller brothers, 284
Millinder, Lucky, 284
Mills, Florence, 169
Millstein, Gilbert, 427
Milner, Ron, 566

Milwaukee (Wisconsin), 24
mind-cure ethos, 221
Mingus, Charles, ix, 150, 175, 282, 402,
    522; and Civil Rights Movement, 501;
    Feld on, 602; and literature, 536; and
    storytelling, 390
minstrel shows, 156; and blues, 474; and
    European music, 90, 435; and Gertrude
    Stein, 527–28; and origins of jazz, 130,
    155, 409; and origins of term "jazz," 7,
    15–16, 27, 28; and popular culture,
    408, 524–28
Minton, Henry, 449, 453, 454
Minton's Playhouse (Harlem), 449–56,
    460
Mitchell, Margaret, 395
"Moanin'," 175
Model-T Ford, 127
modernism, 178, 182
Modern Jazz Quartet, 403, 444, 500
*Modern Library Anthology of American
    Poetry*, 611
Moke and Poke (dance team), 280
Monchoachi (poet), 595
Moncure, Grachan, III, 522
Mondrian, Piet, 176, 224, 238, 241
"Money Jungle," 175
Monk, Nellie, 110
Monk, Thelonious, v, xi, 102–10, 139,
    425, 462; and bebop, 109, 140, 459,
    463, 521, 522; and dance, 292; and
    film, 177; on future of jazz, 483, 505;
    Golson on, 44–45, 51, 52; and hard
    bop, 501; influence of, 504; at Minton's
    Playhouse, 450, 454; and New York,
    460; and seeing jazz, 176; and stutter-
    ing, 620, 621
Monroe, Clarke, 454, 458
Montgomery, Wes, 401
The Mooche, 168
"Mood Indigo," 146, 148, 168
Moon, Bucklin, 615–16, 619
"Moon over Cuba," 145
Moore, Danny, 224
Moore, George, 553
Moore, Marianne, 206
Moore, Tom, 217
Morgan, Lee, 40, 523

Mori, Placido, 211

Morrison, Toni, x, 73, 517, 536, 590

Morton, Jelly Roll, x, 211, 224, 403, 425, 495, 508n10

Mossdorf, Heinrich, 209

Moten, Bennie, 288, 421

"Motherless Child," 603

Mother Poem, Sun Poem, and X/Self (poems; Brathwaite), 519

Motherwell, Robert, 231

"Move," 459

Moynahan, James H. S., 13, 14, 15

Mozart, Wolfgang Amadeus, 139

Mullen, Harryette, 581

Mulligan, Gerry, 509n20

"Multicolored Blue," 175

Mumbo Jumbo (Reed), xiin12, 67, 73–74

Murphy, Eddie, 156

Murphy, Rose (Chi Chi), 383

Murphy, Spud, 35

Murray, Albert, x, 284; on American culture, 236; and Bearden, 183, 190, 232, 234, 239–42; on bebop, 457; on Coleman, 509n22; on Ellington, 146, 151, 291; on the heroic image, 121, 569–79; on improvisation, 111–13, 161, 277; and jazz, 292–93, 536, 573–74; on Savoy Ballroom, 290

Murray, David, 536

music: composition of, 52–53; terms in, 72, 596–97; versioning in, 514. *See also particular types*

Musical Courier, 25–26

Musical Leader, 26

A Musical View of the Universe: Kalapalo Myth and Ritual Performances (Basso), 523–24

musicians, jazz: and chorus line, 285; and classical tradition, 440–44; criticism of, 438; and dancers, 274, 278–94; as dancers, 274, 291–92, 293; demand for, 416–17; guitarists, 401; individualism of, 117–18, 120, 146, 147–49, 159, 161–63, 283, 439, 443, 487; influence of older, 494; influences on, 443, 496; pianists, 150, 401, 461; as primitives, 407; and racism, 107, 487, 489; and singers, 161, 278, 280; symbolism of,

159; white, 138, 456, 486, 489, 490, 496, 513, 514, 530. *See also individual artists*

Music in American Life (Barzun), 442

The Music of Black Americans (Southern), 90

Music Trade Review, 8, 9, 15

Mussolini, Benito, 216

n

Namuth, Hans, 277

Nance, Ray ("Floorshow"), 148, 149, 151, 170, 291, 402

Nanton, Joe "Tricky Sam," 149, 168, 169, 170, 594

The Narrative of the Life of an American Slave, 117

Nasmith, Hans, 266

Nast, Frederick, 435

National Association for the Advancement of Colored People (NAACP), 184, 414, 458

National Association of Jazz Educators, 60

National Playwrights' Conference, 567

Native American culture, 66, 184, 208, 209; and origins of term "jazz," 19, 27

Native Son (Wright), 555, 559

Navarro, Fats, 451, 459, 605

Naylor, Gloria, ix, 536

Neal, Larry, 311, 585

The Necessary Angel (Stevens), 218

"The Negro-Art Hokum" (article; Schuyler), 421

"The Negro Artist and the Racial Mountain" (article; Hughes), 421

Negroes. *See African Americans*

Negro Poets and Their Poems (Kerlin), 413

The Negro Speaks of Rivers (poem; Hughes), 262

Negro Workaday Songs (Odum and Johnson), 414

Negro World (newspaper), 411

Nehru, Jawaharlal, 553

Nelson, Stanley R., 12, 13, 16, 23, 25

neo-bop movement, 506n4

neo-classicism, 485, 486, 487, 504

Newell, George, 16

Newman, Paul, 500

The New Negro (Locke), 414

New Negro Movement, 186

New Orleans, 420, 431, 499; origins of term "jazz" in, 16, 23–24, 25, 27–28, 416–17; style of jazz in, 150–51, 483, 485, 486, 489, 490, 493–94, 496

New Orleans band, 150

New Orleans Rhythm Kings, 404

"New Orleans Suite," 150

New Orleans Times-Picayune, 436

New World A-Comin', 167

New World Symphony (Dvořák), 435

New York City, 176; aviation in, 215, 217; Bearden in, 234–42; jazz scene in, 55, 211; origins of term "jazz" in, 23, 24; skyline of, 124, 125–27, 132; skyscrapers in, 197–213, 219–20

New York Syncopated Orchestra, 419

New York Times, 397, 423, 427, 437, 442

The Next Development in Man (Whyte), 135–36

Nicholas brothers, 384

Nielsen, Aldon, 581

Nietzsche, Friedrich Wilhelm, 62, 66, 79n15

"A Night in Tunisia," 44

Night Shadows (painting; Hopper), 200

Night Song (Williams), 606

"Night Train," 41

Niles, Abbe, 414

Niles, John J., 545

Nixon, Richard, 159

Nketia, Kwabena, 312, 316

Noailles, Anne, Comtesse de, 213

"Nobody in Town Can Bake a Sweet Jellyroll Like Mine," 564

Noise: The Political Economy of Music (Attali), 523

"No Man's Mamma Now," 478

Noone, Jimmie, 439

Norman, Fred, 234

Norton, Harold, 280

The Notorious Elinor Lee (play; Micheaux), 216, 219

Now's the Time (Parker), 141

Nugent, John Peer, 217

Nugent, Pete, 389

The Nutcracker Suite, 151

Oakley, Helen, 411

O'Connor, Sandra Day, 156

Odum, Howard W., 414, 545

O'Farrell, Chico, 521

Of the Blues (series of paintings; Bearden), 191, 224–25

Ogren, Cathy, 403, 407

O'Higgins, Myron, 232

"Ol' Bunk's Band," 611–12

"Old Folks at Home" (Foster), 525

Oldham, Cholly, 619

Old King Dooji (Ellington), 166

Old Wine, New Bottle (Evans recording), 391

Oliver, Edith, 567

Oliver, Joe, 439

Oliver, King, 169, 423, 488, 489, 504

Olson, Charles, 604, 615

O'Meally, Robert G., 143–53

The Omni-Americans (Murray), 570, 571, 578

"One Hour Mama," 480

O'Neill, Eugene, 142, 566

One Night in Birdland (album), 459, 462

"One O'Clock Jump," 118

"On Green Dolphin Street," 94–99

onomatopoeia, 20, 184

"On the Sunny Side of the Street," 35

On the Trail of Negro Folksongs (Scarborough), 414

opera, 57

Opportunity (magazine), 397, 420

Ordinance of 1785, 126

oriental culture, 67–68, 269

orientalism, 209, 221

"Ornithology," 465n11

Ortega y Gasset, José, 163

Osby, Greg, 465n12

Osgood, Henry Osborne, 11, 12, 13, 16, 20, 22, 23, 438

Oshima, Nagisa, 266

Ostransky, Leroy, 503, 504

Othello (Shakespeare), 171

The Outlook (magazine), 21, 434

Ozu, Yasujiro, 265

Pacific Standard Time (Evans recording), 391

Page, Homer, 245

Paik, Nam Jun, 266
Palace of the Peacock (Harris), 622, 623
Palais Royal (New York club), 399
Palmieri, Remo, 456
Panassié, Hugues, 441, 463, 488, 490,
 491–92, 493, 495
Pantaleoni, Hewitt, 332
Paris (France), 231–34
Paris Blues (film), 500, 501
Parker, Charlie (Bird), vii, 118, 282, 459;
 on acceptance of jazz, 443; and ballads,
 58–59; and Baraka, 521; and bebop,
 461, 462, 465n10, 493, 495,
 508nn12&17; and Coltrane, 39–40; on
 contemporary music, 460; and CP aesthetic, 465n15; death of, 154, 404, 427,
 451; Feld on, 602; and free jazz, 503;
 Golson on, 33, 34–35, 36, 37, 38, 41,
 50, 54; imitators of, 43; and improvisation, 155, 162; influence of, 504; as
 innovator, 502; at Minton's Playhouse,
 450, 454; and Pollock, 180; recordings
 of, 401, 457, 461; and rhythm, 178; and
 seeing jazz, 176, 178; and white critics,
 140–41, 142
"Parker's Mood," 118, 460
Parsons, Talcott, 578
Partisan Review, 464
Partlan, Bill, 567
Pascal, Blaise, 77n5
The Passing of the Great Race (Grant), 412
"The Passion of Christ" (series; Bearden),
 231
Paterson (Williams), 610, 612
Patterson, Frank, 19
Patterson, Orlando, 603
Patti, Black, 396, 415
Paz, Octavio, 604
peabody (dance), 286
Peck, Gregory, 156
peckin (dance), 280
Pelton, Robert, 613
Pemberton, Gayle, 275
Pennington, Ann, 308
Penny, Rob, 567
percussion, 128, 276, 283, 383, 450;
 African, 113, 323; and bebop, 461, 494;
 in black music, 84; and dance, 81n42,

273, 281, 289, 292, 336–38, 343, 345,
 363–64; and sports, 276; and trains,
 152
The Perfume Suite, 167
Perper, Mark, 245
Perry, Bruce, 266
Perry, Karen, 383
Persip, Charlie, 35
Peterson, Oscar, 401
Peter the Apostle, 303
"The 'Pet Negro' System" (article;
 Hurston), 419
Pettiford, Oscar, 234, 461
Peyton, Dave, 437
"Phantoms" (Barron), 53
Philadelphia (Pennsylvania), 55
Phillips, Flip, 531n26
photography, 180–81, 201–2, 243–63
photomontages, 237–38
The Piano Lesson (play; Wilson), 567
Picasso, Pablo, 232, 566
Pierce, Nat, 292
Pittsburgh (Pennsylvania), 225–27
Plato, 85, 311, 338
the Platters, 401
play, concept of, 111–12
Pleasure and Danger (Barnard conference;
 anthology), 470
A Pluralistic Universe (James), 208
poetry: African-American, 413, 414, 584,
 587, 594, 598n6; anthologies of, 522,
 611; blues, 583–85, 596–97; blues as,
 540–51, 583–84; of Hughes, 301–2,
 305, 420–21, 583, 585, 587, 595; jazz,
 420, 421, 485; and jazz, 536; lyric,
 582–83; and music, 580–601, 603–6,
 610; rhythm in, 595
Poiret, Paul, 222
Pollock, Jackson, 176, 179, 180, 232, 235,
 277
Pomare, Eleo, ix
"Pomp and Circumstance" (Elgar), 409
Ponty, Jean-Luc, 402
popular music, 395–98, 400, 418–19, 422,
 425, 426, 505, 523
Porter, Cole, 462
Portia Faces Life (soap opera), 133
A Portrait of the Artist (Joyce), 553

index

postmodernism, 182

Potter, Tommy, 54

Poulenc, Francis, 290

Pound, Ezra, 530

Powell, Bud, 177, 459, 460, 461

Powell, Richard J., 182–94

Powell, William, 217

Praisesong for the Widow (Marshall), 614

Présence Africaine (magazine), 518

"Pretty Woman," 175

Prez. *See* Young, Lester

Price, Richard, 334

Primitive Art (Boas), 209

Prince (singer), 156

Pritchard, Herman, 454

progressive jazz, 127, 496

"Prove It on Me Blues" (Ma Rainey), 478

Pryor, Richard, 375

Public Enemy (group), 156

Pudd'nhead Wilson (Twain), 130–31

Putnam, George, 222

Pythagoras, 67

q

Q.E.D. (Stein), 528–29

Quicksand (Larsen), 471–72

Quirt, Walter, 229

r

racism, 394–95, 505, 605; and black musicians, 107, 428, 487, 489; Crow Jim,
139; theorists of, 412–13, 416, 424

Radano, Ronald, 502

Radiator Building, American (New York),
200, 202, 207, 209, 210, 211, 220

radio, 200, 279

Radio City Revels (film), 288

ragtime, ix, 28n2, 90, 414–15, 417, 420;
ban on, 437; and Berlin, 425–26; and
jazz, 13, 22, 403, 483

Rahda (dance; St. Denis), 209

"railroad onomatopoeia," 113. *See also*
trains

"Railroad Blues," 475–76

Rainey, Gertrude (Ma), 473–74, 540, 544,
548; Brown on, 473–74; and dance,
293; as Mother of the Blues, 396, 474,
479; rejection of men by, 477–78

Ramsey, Frederic, Jr., 489

Randolph, A. Phillip, 458

Raphaelson, Samson, 405–6, 420

rap music, 57, 117, 157, 430n, 462

Razaf, Andy, 227, 229

Razz's Band, 416, 417

R&B. *See* rhythm-and-blues (R&B)

RCA Victor Building (New York), 200

Read, Allen Walker, 21

Read, Margaret, 312

Really the Blues (Mezzrow), 613

Record Changer (magazine), 141, 463, 495

Rector, Eddie, 281, 285

Rector and Cooper (dance team), 291

Redman, Don, 283, 284, 409, 421

Redman, Joshua, x, 465n12

Redway, Jacques Wardlaw, 18

Reed, Ishmael, xiin12, 67, 73–74, 517,
614

Reed, Leonard, 283

Reeves, J. Gordon, 200

reggae, 514

Reichardt, Johannn, vi

Reinhardt, Django, 402

Reiss, Winold, 184

religion: African-American, 72, 186, 559;
and jazz, 6, 196, 420; and Wright, 555,
556

religious music, 88, 90–91. *See also* gospel
music; spirituals

Reminiscing in Tempo, 167

Rent Party Blues, 168

repetition, in black culture, 62–81

Repetition (Kierkegaard), 74

The Republic (Plato), 85

Return to Laughter (Bohannan), 336, 337

revues, 278–80, 284–85

Rhapsody in Blue (Gershwin), 398, 400,
403, 409

rhumboogie (dance), 286

Rhyne, Ten, 364

rhythm, 302, 436; in black music, 84;
dance, 144, 160, 273; of Davis, 98–99;
in DeCarava's photographs, 256,
261–62; of Ellington, 146; in European
music, 74–75; Golson on, 51; in humor,
130; in literature, 536; and momentum,
129, 132; of Monk, 106–7; in poetry,
132–33, 595; poly, 128; in religious
music, 6, 72, 589–93; as repetition,

70–71; Roach on, 178, 276; in story-telling, 537; in work songs, 93, 160

rhythm-and-blues (R&B), vii, 117, 119, 465n12

Rhythm Club, 453

Rice, Thomas D., 526

Rich, Buddy, ix, 281

Richards, Lloyd, 567

Richardson, Halley, 453

Richardson, Jazzlips, 284

Richmond, Dannie, 282

Rickenbacker, Eddie, 196

Riggs, Marlon, 264, 265

Riley, Ben, 102–10, 292

Rilke, Rainer Maria, 603

Rimbaud, Arthur, 155

The Rising Tide of Color Against White World Supremacy (Stoddard), 411–12, 426

Ritchie, Donald, 265

Roach, Max, viii, 105, 402, 460, 495; and bebop, 461; and classical music, 443; and dancers, 281; and Davis, 509n20; on entertainment tax, 293; on rhythm, 276; on seeing jazz, 175, 178; and Young, 389, 390

Robbins, Jerome, 384

Roberson, Ed, 517–18, 530

Robertson (architect), 207

Robeson, Essie, 210

Robeson, Paul, 210, 465n15, 558, 562

Robinson, Bill ("Bojangles"), 274, 281, 283, 309, 383; at Apollo Theater, 284, 285; and Astaire, 384; asymmetry of, 302; and Ellington, 169

Robinson, Clarence, 280, 285

Robinson, Edgar G., 156

Robinson, Jackie, ix, 228, 374

Robinson, Sugar Ray, 274, 276

"Rock-a-Bye Basie," 35

Rockefeller, John D., 302, 303–4

Rockefeller Center, 126, 211, 212

rock music, 156, 160, 401, 408, 502

Rodney, Red, 55

Rodrigo, Joaquin, 403, 443

Rogers, Denise, 224

Rogers, J. A., 9, 207, 397

Rogers, Will, 382

Rolling Stones (group), 157

Rollins, Sonny, 109, 140, 440, 620, 621; Golson on, 32–33, 42–44, 45–46, 56, 57, 59

Romare Bearden, 1970–1980 (exhibition catalogue), 183

Room No. 6 (Cortor), 193

Roosevelt, Eleanor, 222, 227

Roosevelt, Franklin D., 216, 222

Root, John Wellborn, 197–98

Roots of The Blues (New World Records), 91

Roppolo, Leon, 404

Roseland Ballroom (New York), 279

Rosenkrantz, Timme, 233

Rouch, Jean, 312, 332

"'Round Midnight," 52

'Round the World (African-American theater circuit), 279–80, 285

Rourke, Constance, 118, 130, 222–23, 576

Rouse, Charlie, 107

Rousseau, Jean-Jacques, 413, 553

Rowles, Jimmy, 48

Rudolph, Wilma, 374

Runyon, Damon, 214

Rushing, Jimmy, 274, 287, 290

Russell, Ross, 495, 496

Russell, William, 507n9

Ruth, Babe, 210

Ryder, Edward, 121

S

Saar, Alison, 189

Sachs, Curt, vi

Le Sacre du printemps (Stravinsky), 75, 81n41

Said, Edward, 117

St. Augustine of Hippo, 68, 78n15

St. Denis, Ruth, 208, 209, 221, 385

"St. Louis Blues," 188, 422, 488

"St. Louis Cyclone Blues," 544

Salter, Nigger Mike, 425

Saltz, Amy, 567

Sampson, Edgar, 424–25

Sanborn, David, 506n7

Sandburg, Carl, 545

Sanders, Pharoah, 58, 59

Sandow, Gregory, 157

San Francisco (California), 22, 23, 28, 55

Santayana, George, 124

Sargeant, Winthrop, 128, 129, 490–91
Sartre, Jean-Paul, 136
Savage, Augusta, 228, 229
Savage, Jack, 215
Savoy Ballroom (Harlem), 279, 285–90, 458; dancing at, 229, 285, 287–89
saxophone, 48–49, 60, 188; alto, 33, 34, 38; tenor, 32–35, 38–39, 42–43, 57, 58
Saxophone Colossus (Rollins recording), 43
Saxton, Alexander, 526, 527
Scarborough, Dorothy, 414
scat singing, 178
Schaeffner, André, 10, 21, 23
Schelling, 127
Schindler, John, 238
Schmitz, Robert, 312
Schneider, Louis, 9
Schomburg, Arthur A., 413, 414
Schrier, Dan Moses, 383
Schuller, Gunther, 56, 320, 410, 420, 496
Schuyler, George S., 421
Schwartzman, Myron, 178
Schwerke, Irving, 10, 18
Scott, Hazel, 5
Scott, Tony, 450, 456
"Scrapple from the Apple," 464
Screen (magazine), 265
sculpture: African, 317, 323–24, 327, 332, 338, 341, 343, 345, 358–59, 361–62, 363; African-American, 275, 301
"Seabreeze" (Bearden), 234
The Second Book of Negro Spirituals (Johnson and Johnson), 414
Segovia, Andrés, 61
Seifert, Charles Christopher, 230
Selassie, Haile, 215, 217
Seldes, Gilbert, 208–9, 222, 223, 398, 438
Senghor, Léopold, 70
Sennett, Richard, 433
The Seven League Boots (Murray), 579n3
The Seven Lively Arts (Seldes), 398, 438
Severance, H. Craig, 198
Sex (play), 308
sexuality: black female, 469–81; and origins of term "jazz," 20–21, 24, 25–26, 28
"Shades of Dameron" (Golson), 42
Shadow and Act (Ellison), 122
Shakespeare, William, 76–77, 149, 151, 170, 171, 304, 444, 519
Shange, Ntzoke, 536
Shaw, Artie, 513
Shaw, George Bernard, 208
Shawn, Ted, 221, 385
Shearing, George, 450
Shelton, Chris, 241
Shepheards Calendar (Spenser), 68
Shih, Hsiao Wen, 522
shimmy (dance), 286
Shim Sham Shimmy (dance), 292
Shining Trumpets (Blesh), 492
The Shock of the New (Hughes), 199
Shreve, Richmond, 198
Sieber, Roy, 329, 331
Silver, Horace, 501
Silverman, Sime, 209
Simpson, Merton, 237
Sims, Sandman, 285
Sinatra, Frank, 6, 450
Singing Soldiers (Niles), 545
Sissle, Noble, 429n5
Sister Carrie (Dreiser), 528
Sketches of Spain (Evans), 443
Skvorecky, Josef, 606
The Skyscraper (Goldberger), 208
skyscrapers, 124, 126–27, 145, 146, 196–213, 219–20; and jazz, 206–7, 209, 211–12
"Slaughter on 10th Avenue," 385
slavery: and jazz, 164, 275, 382, 391, 404, 417; and language, 519, 525–26; narratives of, 517, 518
Slave Songs in the United States, 516
Sloan, John, 245
Sloan (architect), 207
Slyde, Jimmy, 383
small-group jazz, 144, 402, 491
Smith, Alfred J., 176
Smith, Annette, 518
Smith, Bessie, vii, 540, 548, 553, 557, 613, 617; as blues singer, 161, 383, 473–80; as dancer, 293; importance of, 142, 396; as lesbian, 478; Wilson on, 564, 565
Smith, Captain John, 123
Smith, Charles Edward, 19, 24, 489
Smith, Clara, 474, 475, 548
Smith, Clay, 20, 22, 23, 26

Smith, Harry, 292
Smith, Laura, 548
Smith, Mamie, 278, 548
Smith, Pete, 33
Smith, Pine-Top, 508n11
Smith, Seba, 130
Smith, Stuff, 402
Smith, Sydney, 434
Smith, Trixie, 383, 475, 548
Smith, Willie ("The Lion"), 34, 169
The Smithsonian Collection of Classic Jazz, 144, 508n15
Snake Hip Dance, 169
snakehips (dance), 286, 292, 302
Snake Hips (dancer), 302, 309
Snead, James A., 62–81
Snowden, Shorty, 286, 288
soap operas, 124, 132, 133
social realism, 183, 230
Song of Solomon (Morrison), 73, 517
"Song of the Son," 607–8
Song of the Towers (painting; Douglas), 186–88
soul music, 89
The Souls of Black Folk (Du Bois), 89, 517
Sound and Sentiment: Birds, Weeping, Poetics and Song in Kaluli Expression (Feld), 602–3, 605
Sound and Symbol: Music and the External World (Zuckerkandl), 602, 603, 604, 605
Sousa, John Philip, 15, 118, 435
Southern, Eileen, 90
"Southern Road" (Brown), 609
South to a Very Old Place (Murray), 572, 573, 574
Spaeth, Sigmund, 439
Spanier, Muggsy, 439
Spanish language, 19, 27
Spaulding, Henry G., 517
Spellman, A. B., 141
Spencer, Edith, 291
Spencer, Herbert, 198
Spender, Harold, 441
Spenser, Edmund, 68
Sphere (group), 109
Spicer, Jack, 528, 604
Spillers, Hortense, 469–70

Spiral Group, 237
"The Spirit of the Banjo" (Johnson and Johnson), 414
spiritualism, 201–2, 205–6, 207
spirituals, 117, 305, 309, 420, 517, 541; and African-American culture, 89, 160, 166–67, 415; beginning of, 152; and blues poetry, 583, 585–86; Ellison on, 122; Johnson on, 588–93; and swing, 590–94
Spivey, Victoria, 474, 548
sports, ix, 228, 266–67; black participation in, 373–74; culture of, 372–79, 426; and dance, 274, 276; and music, 276, 277; sneaker in, 377, 378. *See also* Jordan, Michael
Sports Illustrated, 245
The Spyglass Tree (Murray), 579n3
Spyro Gyra (group), 506n7
Srp, Karel, 440
"Stablemates" (Golson), 52
"Stack-Up" (musical), 384
Stallings, Mary, 59
Stannard, Douglas, 15, 19, 21, 23, 25
"Stars Fell on Alabama," 59
Stearns, Marshall, 27, 440, 502
Steichen, Edward, 245
Steig, Bill, 229
Stein, Gertrude, 206, 396, 527–29, 530, 536
Steinbeck, John, 535
Stephen Hero (Joyce), 553
Steppin' on the Blues: The Visible Rhythms of African-American Dance (Malone), 273
Stepto, Robert, 4
Stern, William, 412
Sterne, Laurence, 75
Stevens, Wallace, 201, 202, 203, 219, 220
Stewart, Rex, 146, 148, 169, 170
Stewart, Sammy, 229
Still, William Grant, 409, 422
Stitt, Sonny, 43–44
Stoddard, Lothrop, 411, 412, 413, 426
Stokowski, Leopold, 438
"Stolen Sweets," 175
stomp (dance), 286
Stomping the Blues (Murray), 575, 577

Stoppard, Tom, 76–77
Storm, Jack, 284
storytelling, 117, 389–90, 391, 427, 535–36, 537, 542
Stowe, Harriet Beecher, 395
Stowell, Peter, 181
Stravinsky, Igor, 75, 290, 444, 452, 502
Strayhorn, Billy, 35, 170, 282, 289
stride, ix, 48, 426, 443, 462
Strindberg, August, 208
Studies in Classic American Literature (Lawrence), 209
Studies of the Greek Poets (Symonds), 612
A Study of American Intelligence (Brigham), 412
Stump and Stumpy (dance team), 280
Such Sweet Thunder (Ellington), 167, 444, 535
Suite Thursday (Ellington), 535
Sula (Morrison), 590
Sullivan, Joe, 439
Sullivan, Louis, 127, 198, 207
Sundquist, Eric, 584, 600n31
Sun Ra, 495, 522, 523, 627
Sunset Club (Kansas City), 453
Swanson, Carl, 17
Sweatman, Wilbur, 24
The Sweet Flypaper of Life (Hughes and DeCarava), 245
"Sweet Rough Man," 477
Swift, Jonathan, 63, 64
swing, ix, 6, 26–27, 36, 118, 287, 390; in Africa, 319–21, 330, 365; and bebop, 140, 497, 508n14, 510n27, 521, 531n26; and Ellington, 143, 498; era of, 176, 485, 490, 496, 497, 499, 521; and Goodman, 422, 423, 425, 513–14, 514; and jazz, 127, 425, 483, 486, 491, 492, 493, 494, 498; in spirituals, 590–94; and Whiteman, 461
The Swing Era: The Development of Jazz, 1930–1945 (Schuller), 497
"Swing—From Verb to Noun" (Baraka), 590
Swingin' the Blues, 289
"Swing It! And Even in a Temple of Music" (*New York Times*), 423, 424
Swing magazine, 166

Swing Time (film), 385
Symonds, John Addington, 612
symphonic jazz, 402, 404–7, 417, 418, 420–25
syncopation, 52, 128, 273, 286, 382, 403, 417; vs. African off-beat phrasing, 330, 331
syncopep, 26
Synge, John Millington, 208
Szwed, John, 337

Tabmen, George, 313, 315
"Taking the Print" (poem; Roberson), 517–18
Tamony, Peter, 18, 21, 22, 23
Tangle Eye (singer), 91
tango (dance), 415
Tanner, Henry Ossawa, 240
"The Tap Dance Kid" (musical), 381
tap dancing, viii, 106, 273, 279–85, 293, 381, 383
Tar Baby (Morrison), 517
Tarkovsky, Andrei, 266
Tate, Greg, x
Tate, Jimmy, 382
"Tattooed Bride," 147
Tatum, Art, 450, 455, 460, 493
Taussig, Michael, 606
Taylor, Arthur, 120, 121, 276, 277
Taylor, Cecil, 140, 180, 444, 502, 531n26
Tchaikovsky, Pyotr Ilich, 171, 402
Teagarden, Jack, 455
television, 200
Temp Club, 418
Temple, Shirley, 383
The Ten Blackberries (Ellington band), 169
"Ten Hierographic Paintings" (series; Bearden), 231
Terman, Lewis, 412
Terrell, Mary Church, 429n3
Terry, Clark, 170, 171
Teschemacher, Frank, 404, 439, 489, 508n11
Textilien Aus Westafrika (Menzel), 329
Thass-Thienemann, Theodore, 615
Thatcher, George, 526
Their Eyes Were Watching God (Hurston),

471, 515, 516, 580, 581
"Thelonious," 462
Theosophy, 202
"There Goes My Baby," 401
There Is a Tree More Ancient than Eden (Forrest), 73
"This Time the Dream's on Me," 462
Thomas, Cottonfield, 540
Thomas and Beulah (Dove), 530
Thompson, Bob, 176
Thompson, Kristin, 265
Thompson, Lucky, 40
Thompson, Robert Farris, ix, 188, 274, 311–65, 605, 613
Thomson, Virgil, 442
Thoreau, Henry David, 198
Threadgill, Henry, 465n12, 530
Three Lives (Stein), 527
Tiananmen Square incident, 157
Time magazine, 459, 485
timing: in industry, 134–35; in jazz, 129, 130–31; in sports, 276. *See also* rhythm
Timmons, Bobby, 40, 103
Tin Pan Alley, 160, 425, 444, 487
Tires, William, 416
"Titanic Man Blues" (Ma Rainey), 477
Tiv Dance: A First Assessment (Keil), 312–13
Tizol, Juan, 170
Todorov, Tzvetan, 161–62
Toll, Robert C., 524, 526
Tolstoy, Leo, 85
Tomkins, Calvin, 224–42
A Tone Parallel to Harlem, 167, 168
Toomer, Jean, 73, 202, 606–10
Toop, David, 462
Tough, Dave, 404, 439, 461, 463
Toward Freedom (Nehru), 553
Tower Building (New York), 197
Towerson, 361
Tracy, Steven, 176
trains, 113, 152, 392, 553; in blues, 475, 546 47; tunes about, 35, 41, 175, 475, 536, 571, 575
Train Whistle Guitar (Murray), 536, 571, 575
"Transblusency," 175
Travesties (Stoppard), 76–77

Treitler, Leo, 497, 503
"Trinkle-tinkle" (Monk), 51
Tristram Shandy (Sterne), 75
Trotter, James Monroe, 90
Troupe, Quincy, 102–10
Trumbull Park (Brown), 122
"Trust No Man," 477
Tub Jug Washboard Band, 478
Tucker, Sophie, 396
Tully, Jim, 210
Turkey in the Straw, 435
turkey trot (dance), 286, 415
Turner, Frederick Jackson, 128, 433
Turtle Island String Quartet, 402
Twain, Mark, 124, 125, 130–32, 133, 435, 526
Tweed, Boss, 159
2 Live Crew (group), 157
Tyner, McCoy, 401

U

Ulanov, Barry, 166–71, 495–96
Ulysses (Joyce), 76
Uncle Remus stories, 415
Uncle Tom's Cabin (Stowe), 395
Understanding Jazz (Ostransky), 503
Understanding the New Black Poetry, 584
Up in Errol's Room, 277
Uptown Downbeat, 168
Uptown String Quartet, 402
urban culture: DeCarava and, 245, 247, 252–53

V

Vaché, Warren, 401
Valentino, Rudolph, 304
Valéry, Paul, 241, 554
the "vamp," 112, 569
Van Alen, William, 198, 207, 220
van Gogh, Vincent, vi, 241, 245
Van Vechten, Carl, 229
The Varieties of Religious Experience (James), 208
Variety, 209
vaudeville, 155, 252, 279, 385, 474; and origins of term "jazz," 14, 15–16, 27
Vaughan, Sarah, 118, 291, 536
Veblen, Thorstein, 134
Venuti, Joe, 402
"The Verb 'Marroner'/for René Depestre,

Haitian Poet" (poem; Césaire), 518

Vermeer, Jan, 224

Vernon, Grenville, 11, 25

Vico, Giambattista, 79n15

Vietnam War, 55

Vinson, Eddie, 34, 38–39

Vizetelly, Frank H., 16, 17, 18, 19

Vlach, John, 283

vodoun, 614

Vogel, Susan, 323

"Voyage" (Barron), 53

Vreeland, F. P., 19

W

Wagner, Richard, 75

Walker, Alice, 395, 471, 479

Walker, Joe, 291

Walker and Williams, 415

A Walk in Paradise Gardens (Bearden),
191

Waller, Fats, 3, 284, 422, 426, 443; and
Bearden, 224, 227, 242; at Minton's
Playhouse, 450, 455

Ward, 334

Ware, David S., 530

Ware, Wilbur, 102

Warren, Earle, 289

Warren, Harry, 207

Washington, Booker T., 560

Washington, Dinah, 401

Washington, Freida, 288

Washington, Grover, 506n7

Washington, James, 6

Washington, Ned, 95

The Wasteland (Eliot), 618

Waterman, Richard Alan, 316, 330–31,
336, 357

"Watermelon Man," 502

Waters, Daryl, 383

Waters, Ethel, 210, 396, 474, 478–79, 481

Watkins, Doug, 402

We (Charles Lindbergh), 218, 222

The Weary Blues (Hughes), 420, 595

Weather Update (group), 506n7

Webb, Chick, 284, 288, 289–90, 493

Webb, Margot, 280

Weber, Eva, 209

Weber, Max, 578

Webster, Ben, 33, 40, 48, 60, 169, 170,

453; at Minton's Playhouse, 450, 454

Wecliffe, John, 23–24

Weidman, Charles, 229

We Insist! (Abby Lincoln album), 176

Weisz, Ehrich. *See* Houdini, Harry

Wells, Dicky, 285, 287, 289

Weseen, Maurice H., 21

"We Shall Overcome," 157

Wesley, Richard, 566

West, Cornel, 119, 264

West, Mae, 308

Weston, Randy, 292, 462

"West Side Story" (musical), 384

Wettling, George, 439

"What Is This Thing Called Love," 462

When Africa Awakes (Harrison), 411

White, Bukka, 522

White, Charles, 244

White, George, 567

White, Gonzelle, 292

White, Hayden, 489, 498

White, Herbert, 288

White, Lucien H., 438

White, Michael, 402

White, Richard Grant, 434–35

White, Stanford, 229

White Collection (of African art), 314,
317, 330

Whiteman, Paul, 396, 424, 429n6, 461;
Aeolian Hall concert (1924), 397–402,
404, 408, 409, 411, 416, 417, 425; and
black music, 304; and black musicians,
409, 418, 441; and British upper class,
399, 400; and Goodman, 422, 423,
424; on jazz, 402–3, 404, 405, 417; as
King of Jazz, 426; music of, 404, 410,
491; and music scores, 401–2, 418, 423;
on origins of term "jazz," 10, 15, 20, 27

The White Negro, 619

Whitey's Lindy Hoppers, 288, 289

Whitman, Walt, 124, 132–33, 135, 198,
428

Whitney, Eli, 156

Whyte, Lancelot Law, 135–36

Wideman, John, x, 179, 391, 392

Wiedemann, Erik, 440

Wilder, Baakari, 382, 383

Wilder, Joe, 55, 391

Wilkes, Albert, 391
Williams, Bert, 169, 419
Williams, Cootie, 148, 149, 150, 151,
    170, 514
Williams, Fess, 285
Williams, Joe, 122
Williams, John A., 606
Williams, Martin, 120, 144, 163, 462,
    463, 497
Williams, Mary Lou, 522
Williams, Mississippi Joe, 139
Williams, Shirley Anne, 473, 584
Williams, Ted, 277
Williams, Tennessee, 142, 566
Williams, Tony, 506n7
Williams, William Carlos, 538, 595,
    610–21, 622
"Will the Circle Be Unbroken" (Dumas),
    118
The Will to Power (Nietzsche), 62
Wilson, August, 563–68
Wilson, Derby, 281
Wilson, Edmund, 220, 441
Wilson, Olly, 82–100
Wilson, Shadow, 102
Wilson, Teddy, 423, 514
Wilson, Woodrow, 305
Winfield, Raymond, 283
The Winged Gospel (Corn), 215
Wings on My Feet (Odum), 545
Wise, Rabbi Stephen, 437
Wolfe, George C., 381, 383
"Woman in a Harlem Courtyard"
    (Bearden), 239
The Woman Warrior, 117
The Womb of Space (Harris), 622
women, 160–61, 383, 396; black, 469–81;
    and matriarchy, 202–8
Woode, Jimmy, 143
Wooding, Sam, 278
Woodman, Britt, 171
Woodruff, Hale, 237
Woods, James, 22
Woods, Phil, 54
Woodson, Carter G., 413

Woodward, Joanne, 500
Woodyard, Sam, 143, 150
Woolcott, Alexander, 425
Woolf, Virginia, 76
Woolworth Building (New York), 198,
    201, 202, 220
Wordsworth, William, 597
"Work Song" (Adderley), 609–10
work songs, 89, 91–94, 160, 166, 473,
    488, 590; blues as, 541–42
Works Progress Administration (W.P.A.),
    228
Worktime (Rollins recording), 43
The World of Ellington, 278
World War I, 214–15
Wright, Frank Lloyd, 198, 200
Wright, Jay, 588
Wright, Richard, ix, 118, 188, 401, 581,
    599n19; and Bearden, 232; Ellison on,
    552–62, 582
Wright, Specks, 38
Wright brothers, 156, 214

Yamekraw (*Negro Rhapsody*), 422
"Yankee Doodle Dandy," 118
Yeargans, James, 237
Yeats, William Butler, 76, 557, 603
Young, Al, 6, 537
Young, Lester ("Prez"), 178, 287, 453,
    495, 529, 531n26; and American cul-
    ture, 118; death of, 404; Gaines on,
    537; Golson on, 33, 40–41; influence
    of, 494; Kerouac on, 465n16; at
    Minton's Playhouse, 450, 454, 455; and
    Roach, 389
"Young Gal's Blues" (poem; Hughes),
    583–84
"Young Woman's Blues," 479–80

Zen, 6
Ziegfeld, Florenz, 418, 453
zoot suits, 458–59, 460, 464
Zuckerkandl, Victor, 602, 603, 604, 614
Zukofsky, Louis, 582, 583, 584, 604

index

credits
(continued from p. iv)

Columbia University Press gratefully acknowledges permission to reprint from the following:

Murray, Albert, "Improvisation and the Creative Process." This paper was delivered at the conference sponsored by the Dallas Institute of Humanities and Culture, Dallas, Texas in 1983 entitled "What Makes a City: The Economics of Taste."

Kouwenhoven, John A. *The Beer Can By the Highway.* Pages 37–73. © 1988. The Johns Hopkins University Press.

Text of pages 11–20 from *Black Music* by LeRoi Jones. Copyright 1967 by LeRoi Jones. By permission of William Morrow & Co., Inc.

Marsalis, Wynton and Robert G. O'Meally. "Music Is Like a Big Hot Pot of Good Gumbo." Used with the permission of Wynton Marsalis Enterprises.

Pages 5–20 from *The All-American Skin Game* by Stanley Crouch. Copyright © 1995 by Stanley Crouch. Reprinted by permission of Pantheon Books, a division of Random House, Inc.

Ulanov, Barry. "The Ellington Programme" from Williamson, Ken, ed., *This is Jazz.* Used with the permission of Barry Ulanov.

"Art History and Black Memory: Toward a 'Blues Aesthetic' " from *History and Memory in African-American Culture,* edited by Robert G. O'Meally & G. Fabre. Copyright © 1994 by Genevieve Fabre and Robert O'Meally. Used by permission of Oxford University Press, Inc.

"Skyscrapers, Airplanes, and Airmindedness: 'The Necessary Angel' " and *Bibliographical Essay* from Terrible Honesty: Mongrel Manhattan in the 1920s by Ann Douglas. Copyright © 1995 by Ann Douglas. Reprinted by permission of Farrar, Straus & Giroux, Inc.

"Putting Something Else Over Something Else" by Calvin Tompkins. Reprinted by permission; © 1977 *The New Yorker* Magazine, Inc. All right reserved.

"Preface" from *Three Plays*, by August Wilson, © 1991 by University of Pittsburgh Press. Reprinted by permission of the University of Pittsburgh Press.

Murray, Albert. "The Function of the Heroic Image." Used with the permission of Albert Murray.

Edwards, Brent. "The Seemingly Eclipsed Window of Form: James Weldon Johnson's Prefaces" is used with the permission of Brent Edwards.

Mackey, Nathaniel. "Sound and Sentiment, Sound and Symbol" from *Discrepant Engagement*, pages 265–285. Reprinted with the permission of Cambridge University Press.